WHO WAS LINDA LOVELACE?

A SEX-CRAZED NYMPHOMANIC?

OR A

TRAGIC VICTIM OF RAPE AND ABUSE?

"Deep Throat, strange as it may seem, changed America's sexual attitudes more than anything since the first Kinsey Report in 1948. It altered the lives of everyone associated with it. It super-charged the feminist movement. It gave the Mafia its most lucrative business since Prohibition. And it changed the nation's views on obscenity forever."

—Journalist **Joe Bob Briggs**

"Somebody told me that the two best-known names of 1973 were Henry Kissinger and Linda Lovelace. We each made notable breakthroughs: The distinguished Mr. Kissinger helped open the doors to Red China and Russia. I opened my throat for all the world to enjoy…I've learned to do things with my mouth and my vagina that few women anywhere can ever hope to achieve."

—**Linda Lovelace**

"Norman Mailer and I had a competitive relationship. Frankly, he wanted to be Hemingway but never made it. He always had to top one of my stories. One night at a party in Brooklyn, he told me that he came home, woke up his wife, and bragged to her that he had just fucked a black drag queen. He also told me that one night he hired Linda Lovelace, who brought him to three climaxes without removing his penis from her throat. Oh, that Norman."

—Author **Gore Vidal**

"My initiation into prostitution was a gang rape by five men, arranged by Chuck Traynor. It was the turning point in my life. He threatened to shoot me with the pistol if I didn't go through with it. I had never experienced anal sex before, and it ripped me apart. They treated me like an inflatable plastic doll, picking me up and moving me here and there. They spread my legs this way and that, shoving their things at me and into me. They were playing musical chairs with parts of my body. I had never been so frightened, disgraced, and humiliated in my life. I felt like garbage."

—**Linda Lovelace**

"The biggest status symbol this year is to have your cock sucked by Linda Lovelace. You guys had better book a date with her, or else you'll no longer be the Kings of Cool."

—**Sammy Davis, Jr.**, to fellow Rat Packers at the
Sands Hotel in Las Vegas in February, 1973

"Sammy Davis,Jr. was subject to bouts of debauchery and dissipation that nearly wrecked his life and threatened to compromise his career. For instance, he spent periods of his life hanging out with the denizens of the hard-core porn industry and with practitioners of Satanism. He even suggested marriage to Linda Lovelace when she was at the height of her career, cruising Hollywood and Las Vegas as a sex toy for the very rich and famous."

—**Gerald Early**, from *The Sammy Davis, Jr. Reader*

"I have met stars who were my idols when I was little—Elvis Presley, Warren Beatty, Hugh Hefner, Elizabeth Taylor, Ann-Margret, and Frank Sinatra—and I've been keeping a diary."

—**Linda Lovelace**

"Steve McQueen's seduction of Linda Boreman marked a turning point in her life. Upon the sensational release of Deep Throat, she became the reigning Queen of Porn. Not only that, she became the 'party favor' [her words] to movie stars, sports figures, one U.S. senator, and one vice president of the United States. In all, she estimated that she performed fellatio on more than fifty household names who range from Frank Sinatra to Joe DiMaggio, from Elvis Presley to Desi Arnaz, from Marlon Brando to Johnny Carson."

—Columnist **James Bacon** at a stag roast
for Ed McMahon in Palm Springs, 1978

"The reason I attended a showing of Deep Throat in Los Angeles was because I suspected that Desi had had a fling with her. Frankly, I wanted to see the girl's technique. I didn't want to lose Gary Morton the way I'd lost Desi. After I saw the movie, I knew I could never top her. You see, I have this gag reflex."
—**Lucille Ball** to Ethel Merman

"I went to see Deep Throat at a movie theater on Duval Street in Key West. I don't know what all the excitement is about. I can swallow bigger cocks than that."
—**Truman Capote** to Tennessee Williams

"I was the Queen of Porn and John C. Holmes was the King of Porn and known for his 13½ inch penis. A private film collector offered me $5,000 on a bet, claiming that he knew for sure I couldn't swallow the whole thing. He paid Holmes $1,000 and I won the $5,000. Yes, indeed, I did it! Down to the last inch. That was a private film. Porn collectors should try to find a copy of Exotic French Fantasies if they want to see John and me together."
—**Linda Lovelace**

"Linda Lovelace has the air of fresh carnality, the air of thoroughly debauched innocence, the sense of a woman exploring the limits of sexual expression and feeling. Linda Lovelace is the girl next door grown up into a shameless woman."
—**Kenneth Turan** and **Stephen F. Zito** in their book, *Sinema*

"Linda kept staying at my house, and I was having sex with the three or four other girls living with me. We had a giant waterbed, and Linda just sort of became one of the girls on the giant waterbed. She now says that the orgies went on there were actually setups for hooker deals, and that she hated that. She said I'd beat her up if she didn't do it, but that was bullshit. Everybody just got stoned and partied."
—**Chuck Traynor** in *The Other Hollywood*

"Giving more head, she became frantic—her tongue and lips were everywhere. Then I felt the muscles in the back of her throat opening up. Her head lowered over me. Suddenly, I could feel my cock go right into her throat. I couldn't believe she ate the whole thing. My cock and balls and half my pubic bush were all engulfed in that cavernous, deep throat of hers."

—**Harry Reems**, co-star of *Deep Throat*

"Throughout most of the 1970s, I was used as a sex toy in New York, Las Vegas, Palm Springs, and Hollywood. I was treated like a cheap whore. Once I'd satisfied a client, I was shown the door. Dozens of celebrities—mostly men, but also Katharine Hepburn—wanted to date me. For the most part, they requested only one thing. My specialty."

—**Linda Lovelace** in a speech before feminists in Denver, 1984

"Imagine: A major adult star like Linda Lovelace in a bestiality movie. It was very graphic. Linda is indeed having sex with the dog in nearly every position one can imagine in a porn flick. Bestiality is illegal in most states now, so one must take care to view it. It was made in a time when things were more liberal."

—**Csmineatlast's** online review of *Dogfucker*

"In a memoir, I wrote about a famous movie star and his son who did all sorts of perverted things at the same time with me. My publisher wouldn't let me reveal their names. But I can tell you who they were. Paul Newman and his son, Scott. Okay, Newman does a lot for charity, and I give him credit for that, but he's not so squeaky clean. He can get down and dirty. I've gone to bed with enough Hollywood stars to know that their image is one thing, reality the other."

—**Linda Lovelace**

"All of us do that kind of stuff—but not all of us want to be on camera."

—**Shirley MacLaine**, after viewing *Deep Throat*

"If you're having a male sexual experience, after you have your orgasm, your next impulse is not to bend down and look over and watch someone's scrotum pounding against someone's shaved beaver or whatever."
—**Jack Nicholson** during an interview with
Screw magazine regarding his viewing of *Deep Throat*

"By the time I got around to sampling the specialty of Linda Lovelace, her throat was too loose. I turned the bitch over and fucked her in the ass. She was real tight."
—Gangster **Mickey Cohen** to Liz Renay

"Linda Lovelace said she was forced into sex. Like hell she was. She couldn't get enough of me. She wore me out, and I'm what is known as a sex maniac."
—Actor **Forrest Tucker** to John Wayne at a health club in Los Angeles

"My husband, Chuck Traynor, beat me physically. I literally became a prisoner. I was not allowed out of his sight, not even to use the bathroom, where he watched me through a hole in the door. He slept on top of me at night; he listened to my phone calls with a .45 automatic eight pointed at me."
—**Linda Lovelace**

"This is the woman who never took responsibility for her own choices, but instead blamed everything that happened to her in her life on porn."
—Adult film actress **Gloria Leonard**

"Teddy Kennedy rented Linda Lovelace's deep throat for one night. She was taken to this house in Palm Springs. I heard about it, but I didn't personally arrange it. Sammy Davis did the honors."
—**Chuck Traynor**

"Does Dick Nixon look like a man who has ever gone down on a woman? If he had, or if he could, I bet the country would be different."

—Linda Lovelace

"In her book, Ordeal, *Linda left out a number of incidents involving Hugh Hefner and his Playboy Mansion in Los Angeles, even though they were news-worthy incidents about sex and celebrities."*

—Gloria Steinem

[Note: We at Blood Moon do not share Linda's restraint. Her heavily censored allegations are published for the first time in this book]

"Good riddance to trash. She was a good cocksucker. She was a piece of shit. Her book, Ordeal, was a lying piece of crap. She was a hooker, a scumbag, a lying trollop. I'm glad Chuck Traynor taught her to suck cock. I dropped several ejaculations down her throat. I want to do a final load, so that when she goes to hell, my sperm will go with her."

—Al Goldstein, in his epitaph to Linda Lovelace in 2002

"It was really hard and kind of terrifying playing Linda Lovelace. The director gave me some liberties, but I had to play someone who existed in history, someone who had quite an established reputation for something very extreme. I don't have to say what that specialty is, since millions of people saw her do it."

—Amanda Seyfried, star of the biopic *Lovelace*

"The movie, Lovelace, stars Amanda Seyfried as Linda Lovelace. It also stars Hollywood favorite James Franco as a young Hugh Hefner, who also seduced Lovelace. Sarah Jessica Parker plays the feminist Gloria Steinem. Demi Moore had to drop out of the role during her split with Ashton Kutchner and his cheating heart. Lindsay Lohan was to play Lovelace, but was fired after her repeated bouts in court."

—Advance publicity associated with *Lovelace* (the movie)

INSIDE
LINDA LOVELACE'S
DEEP THROAT

Degradation, Porno Chic, and the Rise of Feminism

"There are guilty pleasures. Then there is the master of guilty pleasures, Darwin Porter. There is nothing like reading him for passing the hours. He is the Nietzsche of Naughtiness, the Goethe of Gossip, the Proust of Pop Culture. Porter knows all the nasty buzz anyone has ever heard whispered in dark bars, dim alleys, and confessional booths. And lovingly, precisely, and in as straightforward a manner as an oncoming train, his prose whacks you between the eyes with the greatest gossip since Kenneth Anger. Some would say better than Anger."

—Alan W. Petrucelli
The Entertainment Report
Stage and Screen Examiner
Examiner.com

OTHER BOOKS BY DARWIN PORTER

BIOGRAPHIES
Elizabeth Taylor, There is Nothing Like a Dame
Marilyn at Rainbow's End: Sex, Lies, Murder, and the Great Cover-up
J. Edgar Hoover & Clyde Tolson--
Investigating the Sexual Secrets of America's Most Famous Men and Women
Frank Sinatra, The Boudoir Singer. All the Gossip Unfit to Print
The Kennedys, All the Gossip Unfit to Print
Humphrey Bogart, the Making of a Legend
Howard Hughes: Hell's Angel
Steve McQueen, King of Cool, Tales of a Lurid Life
Paul Newman, The Man Behind the Baby Blues
Merv Griffin, A Life in the Closet
Brando Unzipped
The Secret Life of Humphrey Bogart
Katharine the Great: Hepburn, Secrets of a Lifetime Revealed
Jacko, His Rise and Fall, The Social and Sexual History of Michael Jackson
and, co-authored with Roy Moseley
Damn You, Scarlett O'Hara, The Private Lives of Vivien Leigh & and Laurence Olivier

COMING SOON:
Those Glamorous Gabors, Bombshells from Budapest
Pink Triangle: The Feuds and Private Lives of Tennessee Williams, Gore Vidal, Truman Capote, and Famous Members of their Entourages

FILM CRITICISM
50 Years of Queer Cinema--500 of the Best GLBTQ Films Ever Made (2010)
Blood Moon's Guide to Recent Gay & Lesbian Film
Volumes One (2006) and Two (2007)
Best Gay and Lesbian Films- The Glitter Awards, 2005

NON-FICTION
Hollywood Babylon-It's Back!
Hollywood Babylon Strikes Again!

NOVELS
Butterflies in Heat, Marika
Venus (a roman à clef based on the life of Anaïs Nin)
Razzle-Dazzle, Midnight in Savannah
Rhinestone Country, Blood Moon, Hollywood's Silent Closet

TRAVEL GUIDES
Many editions and many variations of *The Frommer Guides* to
Europe, the Caribbean, California, Georgia and the Carolinas,
New England, Bermuda, and The Bahamas

INSIDE
LINDA LOVELACE'S
DEEP THROAT

Degradation, Porno Chic, and the Rise of Feminism

Darwin Porter

INSIDE LINDA LOVELACE'S DEEP THROAT

DEGRADATION, PORNO CHIC, AND THE RISE OF FEMINISM

by Darwin Porter

Copyright ©2013, Blood Moon Productions, Ltd.
ALL RIGHTS RESERVED
www.BloodMoonProductions.com

Manufactured in the United States of America

ISBN 978-1-936003-33-4

Production design by Danforth Prince, with
Special thanks to Photofest in New York City
Cover designs by Richard Leeds (Bigwigdesign.com)
Videography and Publicity Trailers by Piotr Kajstura

Distributed in North America and Australia
through National Book Network (www.NBNbooks.com)
and in the UK through Turnaround (www.turnaround-uk.com)

1 2 3 4 5 6 7 8 9 10

COITUS INTERRUPTUS:
LINDA LOVELACE EXPOSED
HOW A PUBLISHING DREAM OF THE LATE 1980S
DEVELOPED STREP THROAT

(A message from this book's publisher)

The degradations, celebrity liaisons, court trials, and legal anguish of Linda Lovelace have never been given a detailed accounting, in spite of the publication of her quartet of ghost-written "memoirs": *Inside Linda Lovelace* (Pinnacle Books, 1973); *The Intimate Diary of Linda Lovelace* (Pinnacle Books, 1974); *Ordeal* (Bell Publishing Company, 1980), and *Out of Bondage* (Lyle Stuart, 1986). Although each of these blunt and earthy memoirs purported to be full and candid assessments of the tragic star's career, they described only the tail of the elephant, not the beast itself.

Had circumstances been different way back in 1988, a more complete and unbiased "book of record," or something reasonably equivalent, might have been marketed with klieg lights and fanfare. There was, in fact, a burning ambition among some people back then to produce a block-busting and uncensored overview of the remarkable life of an unlikely woman who, because of her starring role in history's most famous porn film, became a cultural icon of the 20th century.

Then something went terribly wrong...

LINDA BOREMAN LOVELACE MARCHIANO
AT LAST, 40 YEARS AFTER THE RELEASE OF HER INFAMOUS
MOVIE, HER STORY CAN BE TOLD

In the late 1980s, the concept for a potentially best-selling memoir unfolded within the high-pressure Manhattan office of what was at the time one of the hottest literary agencies in the world, Jay Garon-Brooke Associates. Jay Garon, the company's abrasive and occasionally brilliant president, was the most sought-after literary agent in America for authors with celebrity sagas to peddle. Garon's previous triumphs had included the development and packaging of

Hedy Lamarr's graphically controversial *Ecstasy*, and scandalous overviews of such stars as Bette Davis. Garon, who was a close personal friend of both Darwin Porter (author of this book) and the most feared and hated lawyer in America (Roy Cohn), would go on to launch the career of the best-selling novelist John Grisham.

Sixteen years after the release, in 1972, of *Deep Throat*, Garon proposed a tell-all autobiography of Linda Lovelace, which would not only list the names of the movie stars she'd seduced, but would give intimate, graphic details of their performances in bed. The very successful *Here Comes Harry Reems*, written by the actor who had co-starred with Linda in Deep Throat—released by Pinnacle Books in 1975—was cited as a good omen for the potential success of the Lovelace project.

By now a world-famous figure in her own right, Linda was bursting with revelations harvested from years as a celebrity whose sexual specialty was widely discussed, widely visible, and available for hire. Even the name of the low-budget porn movie she'd starred in had transcended the standards of modesty, having been adopted by the mainstream media as the code name for an (otherwise anonymous) key witness during Richard Nixon's Watergate scandal.

Sammy Davis, Jr., had even been credited with suggesting to his fellow Rat Packers, including Frank Sinatra, that "you're not cool until you've sampled Linda's specialty."

During the development phase of the Lovelace project, the first question addressed by Garon's team was, "Would Linda's story be believed?" Both Lyle Stuart, publisher of her previous memoir, and Garon himself had already subjected her to lie detector tests, which she had successfully passed.

Based on a subjective quirk, Linda refused to be interviewed by Garon's male research team. She preferred instead to deliver her ideas to Reba-Anne Howard, who had briefly trained as a psychologist in Austin, Texas, and who had some vague previous connection to Linda. Present at many of the editorial meetings, with access to the project's notes and ongoing discussions, was Garon's client and frequent dining companion, Darwin Porter, author of this book.

At this point in the project's development, no one had designated who would actually author the as-yet-unwritten book. Garon had asked one of his most successful clients, author James Leo Herlihy, if he would work with Linda on the project. Previously, Herlihy had enjoyed a hit with an ultimately famous book he had written, one that centered on male prostitution, *Midnight Cowboy*. It was later adapted into a film, the first X-rated movie ever to win an Oscar as Best Picture of the Year in 1969. Herlihy, after interviewing Linda and after reading the Lovelace material, rejected Garon's offer, citing her as "too sleazy for me."

Even without a designated author, a sales proposal was bashed together for what promised to be Lovelace's most comprehensive and controversial memoir, tentatively entitled *Linda Lovelace Exposed*.

Garon's team distributed the proposal throughout New York's publishing community. It received positive and potentially lucrative responses from more than thirty publishers. For a brief moment, the concept of *Linda Lovelace Exposed* showed a frenzied promise of being something that major publishing houses would want to promote.

Then something went terribly wrong: Lyle Stuart's publishing group, attacked for statements she had made in the Lovelace memoir he had printed in 1986 (*Out of Bondage*), was hit with two crippling libel suits.

When news of these lawsuits became public, the Garon/Lovelace book project died overnight. "Despite its potential for enormous sales, the fear of additional lawsuits almost guaranteed that no publisher would ever touch it," Garon claimed.

Fascinated by the project and by Linda's scandalous and almost heartbreaking story, Darwin Porter paid Ms. Howard for her research and acquired the rights to the still-unfocused project for authorship at some undetermined future date.

Porter was partly motivated by a sense of political outrage. He had been horrified when *Deep Throat*'s co-star, Harry Reems, the only actor ever prosecuted by the government for obscenity on film, was threatened with a jail term because of his role in the movie. Porter became a key player in raising money among celebrities for the actor's defense.

Deep Throat, both the movie and its legend, never died. More than 40 years after its inaugural release, it's still for sale or rent in at least 170 countries. Now, with the renewal of interest in Linda Lovelace and with her configuration as the subject of an upcoming A-list movie, Blood Moon has decided that the time has come to release her complete story without any of the censorship or legal dangers imposed in the past. Her revelations from the late 1980s, enhanced by numerous eyewitnesses to her life and legend, can now be unleashed upon the public.

As of this writing, only three movie stars who enjoyed intimate contact with Linda are still alive—and although the full details of their association with her are not laid out within this book, they know who they are.

Danforth Prince
President and Founder,
Blood Moon Productions

THE LEGACY OF *DEEP THROAT*

"There is a disconnect between the freedom of expression that *Deep Throat* promised and what actually transpired. Now we have total liberation of sexual things, but we also have the Patriot Act. We never made the connection between sexual speech and political speech. Sex today has nothing to do with revolution anymore. It's about capitalism and protecting little profit centers."

—Novelist **Erica Jong**

"I was in Toronto recently, and the city is like being in middle America. And you've got very hot, young 18- to 20-year old girls with tongue studs, and they are simply publicly advertising that they are interested in and capable of giving you really good oral sex if you're interested. And that's not even designed to be shocking. We owe it all to Linda Lovelace."

—**Brian Grazer**, producer of *Apollo 13* and
How the Grinch Stole Christmas

Her style was sometimes crude. But as a witness to subcultures and lifestyles imagined and whispered about by millions of consumers, yet directly experienced by only a few, her saga has merit and dignity.

Therefore, because of what her story tells us about the bizarre social and sexual dramas of the greatest nation on earth, we dedicate this book to

LINDA LOVELACE

LINDA BOREMAN LOVELACE MARCHIANO
GONE BUT NOT FORGOTTEN. REST IN PEACE
(1949-2002)

CONTENTS

PROLOGUE
The Price of Fame

On a fading Monday afternoon in 1988, in Durango, Colorado, a rather drab-looking housewife, known locally only as "Mrs. Marchiano," shopped for bargains on an extremely limited budget. At a very modest home, she had a husband, a son, and a daughter to feed. She wore a military jacket, blue jeans, and a plain cotton blouse. Her tangled hair screamed for a beauty parlor, a luxury far beyond her means.

It was winter and the town got dark in the late afternoon. She claimed that friendly, ebullient Durango, surrounded by the San Juan Mountains, was set in "God's country."

Founded in 1880, it was perched 6,512 feet above sea level and was nestled in the Animas River Valley. Already there was heavy snow, and the surrounding mountains seemed an eerie blue on this foggy early evening.

From the store, she carried three bags of groceries, one of which was filled with tinned goods which had either been dented or else had missing labels. "My husband and my kids eat anything," she had told the clerk at the check-out counter. "Whenever we open one of these mystery cans, we're glad to eat whatever's inside."

Planning to close the store early, the manager had wished her a good night. "We're shutting down early. You're our last customer. Big storm coming tonight. You'll be glad you stocked up."

She walked across the slippery parking lot that contained only one van parked about forty yards from her own battered Ford.

She set her grocery bags down on the snow near the trunk of her car and breathed the fresh air.

She loved being called "Mrs. Marchiano." But she didn't know how long she could go on living in the community before her true identity was revealed to locals. She was known as a hard-working housewife struggling to keep her family fed, housed, and clothed. But to millions of fans around the world, she was the notorious Linda Lovelace, star of the most successful porn flick of all time, *Deep Throat.*

As she lifted the lid to the trunk of her car, she felt the approach of two men who had emerged from that lone van.

She wasn't really afraid, as she turned and looked at them. They appeared to be athletes from Fort Lewis College, perhaps football players. One of the young men was tall, slender, and rather good looking. The shorter, beefier one reminded her of a bouncer she'd known when she'd worked at a seedy bar in Miami.

The taller of the two men helped her place her groceries inside the trunk of her car and then slammed the lid shut. He stood close to her, lifting the collar on his red-and-black checkered parka. "You're Linda Lovelace, aren't you?"

The mention of her own name sent a bolt of anxiety through her. She'd been discovered. That always meant she'd have to leave this town like she'd left so many others. Women didn't want to live in the same town as Linda Lovelace, and men, once they learned who she was, often pursued her with indecent propositions.

"My name is Linda," she said, growing nervous. "But not Lovelace. I've never heard of her."

"You're telling me you've never seen or heard of *Deep Throat?* " the short stocky guy asked.

"I don't go to movies," she said, "except to see Susan Hayward—she's my favorite—or else Clint Eastwood. I also watch Elvis Presley movies on TV."

"Cut the bullshit!" the more handsome of the two said. "We know you're Linda Lovelace. The word is out. We want you to go with us for a little ride to meet some of our buddies from the college. All of us are turned on to be living in the same town as Linda Lovelace, the world's greatest cocksucker."

The bigger man grabbed her arm, but she jerked it back. "I'll scream."

"Who'll hear you?" the good-looking one asked. "This place is deserted."

The other, shorter, man said, "I've got a gun, but I don't want to use it."

The tall man took her by the arm. "The ride will be a pleasure trip. If you cooperate, we won't hurt you. If you put up a fight, you'll regret it. We can get really rough when a gal doesn't put out."

"Let's face it," the beefy one said. "It's not like you're sucking cock for the first time."

For an entire decade of her life, she'd lived under the threat of a gun. Since they seemed determined to take her prisoner, meekly, she gave in to them.

"Johnny will ride in the back with you," the tall man said. "I'll drive."

Shoved into the rear of the van, she became apprehensive as the shorter man crawled in with her. "I'll have to blindfold you and tie your hands behind your back," he told her. "We don't want you to know where we're taking you."

"And just where is that?" she asked. "This is kidnapping!"

"No, it's not," he said. "You're going to meet the most sought-out guys in Durango. Most of the local gals would love to be in your shoes right now."

The van was already out of the parking lot and onto the open road.

"Step on it, Phil," Johnny called up to the front. "We don't have all night, and the boys are waiting."

"You'll like our buddies," Phil said. "They're great guys. We've been planning for days to get it on with Linda Lovelace. All of us have seen *Deep Throat* seven times."

Only the other day, Linda had slipped into one of Durango's back-alley stores where the owner sold porno tapes and magazines. She was horrified to see nearly a dozen copies of *Deep Throat* displayed up front and for rent.

Still blindfolded, she rode with the two college men for about forty minutes on the open highway until they came to a stop somewhere outside of town.

Both men helped her out of the van, because Johnny still had her hands tied. She was guided along a slippery, snow-covered pathway. "Step up!" Phil ordered her.

She stumbled as she mounted the steps and was told to lower her head. Once inside the room, Phil told her, "We are going to take off your blindfold. If you aren't real friendly to us, Johnny here might have to cut up your face."

Phil ripped off the blindfold. After she adjusted her eyes, she saw that she was in a trailer. In its combined living room and kitchen, in addition to Phil and Johnny, she spotted about a half-dozen other college-aged athletes, sitting tightly next to one another in the cramped space. As they swilled beer, they looked her over.

"Guys," Phil said, "meet Linda Lovelace." A roar of approval went up from the young men, all except for one who sat in the corner.

"My god, the bitch doesn't look as young as she did in that movie," he protested.

"But she's had even more experience and is better at cocksucking than ever," Phil said.

"Well," said the man in the corner, "I guess I'll just close my eyes and imagine my mother is giving me a blow-job."

"Since I rounded her up," Phil said, "I, along with Johnny here, will go first. Let's get this show on the road."

Another of the young men yelled, "Stretch her some for me!"

Phil shoved Linda forward, and she stumbled past the young men toward the rear of the trailer. She was sobbing, but no one seemed to care.

***

Once alone with her in the small cramped bedroom of the trailer, Phil unbuttoned his shirt and unzipped his jeans, pulling down his jockey shorts. Ordering her to get down on her knees, he held up an uncut penis that looked rather large. "Suck it!" he ordered.

With his hand pressing against the back of her neck, he moved her head forward until her lips touched the tip of his cock. As she'd done so many times before, she ran her tongue back and forth along the length of it. His response was immediate, as his penis uncoiled. She sucked on it until it became ramrod straight and hard.

As she worked on him, he had little trouble advancing toward his climax. He was not one to hold back. As he started to shoot, he began to cry. She'd rarely known a man to cry like a child at climax. But she'd long ago learned that no man was the same as his predecessors. When she attempted to spit out his semen, his hand clamped down on her mouth. "Swallow it."

She knew that Johnny would be next, and she dreaded it. He'd already roughed her up in the back of the van, so she more or less knew what to expect from him. Phil had hardly zipped up before an overeager Johnny was in the room. She was still on her knees, and he stood in front of her, pulling down a dirty pair of jeans. His penis was just as short and stubby as he was, and also had an incredibly awkward curve. It was just as crooked as Phil's cock had been straight.

She'd had sex with worse specimens, certainly with men old enough to be Johnny's grandfather, so she began to work on him.

After about fifteen minutes, she'd broken into a sweat, but he seemed nowhere near climax. Then one of his friends called in from the front of the trailer, "Hurry up, Johnny, I don't have all night. I've got a hot date."

Under pressure and with a kind of desperation, he began to masturbate rapidly into her mouth, finally spurting his seed.

Perhaps embarrassed to her being privy to his sexual failure, he pushed her back. She fell over onto the floor, but uprighted herself quickly, getting back onto her knees again.

Phil and Johnny were quickly replaced by two boys who looked like brothers. Both of them, perhaps seventeen and eighteen, had red hair and freckles. Each of them evoked all-American boys. Fathers might have trusted them to date their daughters.

Hardly looking like oral rapists, each of them stood before her, unzipping their jeans and removing their cocks. Their penises were almost identical. Her suspicion was confirmed when the older boy ordered her, "Do my little brother first."

The older boy became excited watching his younger brother get fellated. With his hand, he moved his younger brother aside and inserted himself into her mouth. She was directed to go back and forth, servicing one, then the other.

4

Both of them had nice, well-shaped cocks, each average in size. The brothers signaled to each other when they were about to reach their climax. Throughout her ordeal, each of the brothers had been rather gentle with her, eager to get off, but not anxious enough to cause her any particular pain.

A large, broad-shouldered young man suddenly stood at the door. "She's all yours, Gene," the older of the brothers said.

Gene must have been the captain of the football team, as he had more of a commanding presence than the other men. As he stripped down, he revealed a body that was powerfully muscular, hairy, manly, and well endowed. His muscles were firm and solid, and his biceps were beefy. He obviously worked out in a gym. His chest was hairy, his rippled stomach the only smooth place on his body. He reached into the slip of his blue shorts and removed a very large penis. Intuitively, she just knew he would be large. "It's been a hell of a long time since a bitch has taken care of me," he told her.

His thighs and calves were also massive. His penis bent to the left, and was long and thick as it slid into her mouth. It wasn't the largest cock she'd ever known, but it was among the biggest.

His thighs locked her head into position. It felt like a fist going into her mouth. Without warning, he shoved his cock deep into her throat, and she knew he was in for the duration. He held her head firmly in place, and she struggled to accommodate him. Only at the last second did he remove his penis and allow her to gasp for air before assaulting her again.

He allowed her head to retreat only a bit before pressing down on her again. He repeated the actions for about ten minutes, as she struggled to satisfy him. Picking up speed, she managed to relax her jaw muscles which at first had felt like they were going to snap. Finally, his penis contracted, expanded, and contracted again. Then he shot deep into the back of her throat.

Her throat felt raw after he pulled out. Then he told her, "That was terrific, baby. I want to meet up with you every afternoon. I know where you live. I'll come around when your old man isn't home."

"No, don't do that!" she pleaded.

As he zipped up, he said, "You're Linda Lovelace. I know what you want. Of all the boys here, I'm the only real man. I'll see you around, sweet stuff. You've got other holes for me to fill."

The next athlete was only about five feet nine, a pale white boy with a mean look about him. He had a shaved head and wore one gold earring. His face was covered with a black stubble of beard, and he had bloodshot eyes as if recovering from a hangover. "Okay, bitch, have I got a treat for you," he told her as he unzipped. She'd heard men brag like that before, so she knew not to expect very much. "If you don't satisfy me, I'll knock the hell out of you."

Not undressing, he only unzipped his jeans and pulled out an unimpressive penis. "You're going to take it all," he said, which almost made her want to laugh at his own evaluation of his manhood.

He grabbed her by her hair and jerked her face toward him before he slapped her. The violence toward her caused him to harden. He took only five minutes before exploding into her mouth. When he pulled out, he looked down at her with contempt. "I've had better," he sneered, zipping up.

The next boy who entered the cramped back backroom looked no more than sixteen, not even old enough for college. Under masses of curly blonde hair, he had thick, sensual lips and warm, blue eyes. She knew at once that he wouldn't be rough on her. He removed his shirt, jeans, underwear, and shoes, retaining only his white athletic socks. He wanted to stand completely nude in front of her.

His was the cock of a young boy still developing. She worked on him with more passion than she'd shown with her other rapists. He was a gentle, hesitant lover until he approached his climax, when he became a bit wild, crying out and pressing his pelvis tightly against her face.

He took a long time removing himself from her mouth, as if he wanted to deposit his last drop. Then he put back on his clothes and looked down at her with a certain affection. He bent over and kissed her lips. "I've never done this with a woman before," he said. "Thank you, ma'am."

Another young man, looking no more than eighteen, came into the room. Without saying a word, he too removed his clothes. By the time he pulled down his jockey shorts, he was already erect. Except for Gene, he was the most endowed so far. "I've had blow-jobs before," he told her. "I don't want one now." He grabbed her and ordered her to lie down on the bed, face down. "I've heard about this, but can't find a gal who'll let me do it to her. But whores like you have to submit to it." Then he slapped her buttocks four times really hard.

Without preparation, he rammed his large, fat penis into her. She cried out. "Shut up, bitch, and take it!" he mumbled to her. He drove into her, causing great pain. Once inside, he twisted and turned like a screwdriver, causing her more agony. She'd never liked this form of sex, and he showed no restraint. She was moaning, and at one point she began to cry. He paid no attention to her pain, and five minutes later, began to moan himself, but his moans were very different from hers. After a few more twists of his penis inside her, he exploded, lowering himself onto her body and biting real hard into her neck. As soon as he climaxed, he withdrew at once, leaving her gasping.

A final rapist remained. He appeared to be the oldest of her attackers, although no more than twenty. Except for Johnny, he was the ugliest of the young men, his ruddy face badly pockmarked.

Seeing that she'd been used from the rear, he turned her over onto her back. "First some deep throating," he ordered.

Actually, he had nothing to reach the back of her throat with, as his was the smallest penis of all her attackers. She worked furiously on him, because she wanted for him to get off. Finishing him off would mean her freedom, or so she hoped. She prayed that they had no more games for her.

But he never produced an erection inside her mouth. Finally, in disgust, he pulled out and attempted to mount her. Again, he could not produce an erection. "Damn you!" he said to her, as he rose off her body. "I told the guys, I can't get off fucking grannies. But don't you mention what happened in here, or I'll rip your guts out."

Within minutes of the departure of her last attacker, Johnny returned with the blindfold and a cord to retie her hands behind her. "I'm taking you back to your car," he said. "Your good time is over. I hope it was fun for you getting a chance to have all these young studs work you over. Any gal would have loved that and begged for more."

She said nothing as he blindfolded her again. Then he walked her up toward the front of the trailer. She suspected that most of the other men had already left.

As he guided her along the pathway back to the van, the way her feet dragged against the snowdrifts informed her that the snow had fallen heavily. She recognized Phil's voice as he ordered her to "get in and keep your mouth shut." He seemed to laugh at his own order. "Imagine Linda Lovelace keeping her mouth shut. That'll be the day."

No one spoke during the ride in the van back to her car in the snowy parking lot. Then someone ripped the blindfold from her eyes. Other than her own battered Ford, there was no other car, nor anyone to be seen in the whole vast parking lot. "You tell anybody about this, and you'll find yourself in a ditch one night with your tits cut off!" Johnny said.

Opening the back door of the van from the inside, he pushed her out into the snow. She fell down crying and stayed there for nearly five minutes, long after the van had pulled away. Pushing herself up, she washed her face in the newly fallen snow and dried herself with her woolen scarf.

She still had time to get home with her groceries and cook dinner for her family, but only after she scrubbed her body and cleansed her throat with antiseptic. She wanted to wipe away any semblance of her attackers, as she'd done so many times when she was in her twenties.

Back home again, neither her husband nor her children paid much attention to her when she came in through the front door carrying groceries. She noticed that no one got up to help her, as they were engrossed in a Western on TV.

After showering and putting on a housecoat, she stood in front of a wood-burning stove frying shoulder pork chops, the cheapest cut.

She wanted to run away, not only from her husband but from her children. But she had no money and no place to run to.

7

What had gone so wrong in her life? What had led her to this point of desperation? She wanted only to find a loving husband and to raise wonderful children with him. Yet she found herself viewed virtually everywhere in the world, from Los Angeles to London, from Brazil to Australia, as a cocksucking whore.

How could her life have taken such a bizarre turn?

top photo **Linda Boreman** (aka Linda Lovelace) vs.
lower photo: a fantasy version of the celebrity with the porn industry's deepest throat

CHAPTER ONE
"MISS HOLY HOLY" BECOMES UNHOLY

Born in the Bronx in New York City on January 10, 1949, Linda Boreman was the daughter of a traffic cop whose ancestors had come from England. She remembered him as a kind, gentle man, but one who could not openly display affection for either his wife or daughter. Her mother was a short, dark-complexioned Italian woman who was a devout Catholic. She believed in strict discipline and often beat Linda with a belt for even a perceived infraction.

Linda did not grow up in the Bronx because her family moved to Westchester County, north of New York City, before she entered grade school.

Even in grade school, when Linda attended St. John the Baptist in Yonkers, New York, her mother warned her about boys. To her mother, sex was a dirty business, a kind of filth that men and boys forced on women and girls.

Her mother claimed that sex was very painful too, something a woman had to endure so that she could have a child. "Men claim they enjoy it, but there's nothing pleasurable about it," her mother said. "It's also degrading, a vile act that reduces a woman to the status of a barnyard animal."

Her mother rarely allowed her to participate in any activities, although she did let her visit the Lyme family because she knew the mother, Jane Lyme, from church. Jane always attended services with her husband, Bill, their six-year-old son, Tom, and their eleven-year old daughter, Hilda.

After school let out for the day, Linda often visited the Lyme household.

"It seemed that Jane was always baking cookies in the afternoon for her family," Linda said. "Bill came home every afternoon at four. He hugged and kissed Jane, and I had never seen such intimacy between a man and a woman. I'd never seen my father even hug my mother. Bill reminded me of Fred MacMurray, who was appearing in a TV series at the time, *My Three Sons.*"

One summer, with some reluctance, her mother agreed to let Linda join Bill, Hilda, and Tom on a camping trip in the Catskills when Jane went to visit her ailing mother in Trenton, New Jersey.

It was Linda's first trip away from home, and she was thrilled at being freed from the rigid control her mother imposed on her.

That afternoon, she joined the Lyme family in a communal swim in a small, cold lake near their campsite.

At night a hot dog dinner was cooked over an open fire.

Bill had erected a large tent for all of them to sleep under. A bed was made

Baby Linda
(both photos, above)
A nondescript childhood

Linda's first sexual experience was with a family friend, a secret child molester, in a tent.

for Tom in a corner of the tent, and Bill slept between his daughter, Hilda, and Linda on sleeping mats.

She would later describe that night as "my first sexual experience." At around two o'clock that moonlit morning, she was awakened when she felt Bill's large hand on her knee. Slowly, very slowly, that hand of his began to travel north, moving along her leg.

As she later recorded in a memoir, "His big daddy hand eased between my thighs and grabbed my aching pussy and squeezed it." She loved the sensation. She eventually fell asleep with his hand between her legs.

When Bill first felt her body, Linda said, "I was just beginning to gather a few pussy feathers and hadn't even dreamed of boobs."

For the rest of the camping trip, Linda followed Bill around all day. She wished her own father could be like him. When Tom and Hilda went for a swim, Bill took her for a walk in the woods. At one point, he lifted her up and kissed her, inserting his tongue into her mouth. She clung to him.

When he had to urinate, he didn't go into the bushes or behind a tree, but unzipped and pulled out his penis directly in front of her. She had never seen a nude man before, and she was thrilled at the sight of a male penis. "I had no basis of comparison, but he was exceptionally large, unlike the boy with whom I had my second sexual experience. That one had a penis that

10

looked like one's little finger."

Bill did not invite her to play with his penis, but he kept it out long enough for her to observe it at length.

She welcomed the oncoming night. When he began to fondle her again, she reached over and felt his penis. "At first, I was horrified. It had risen and enlarged. I couldn't believe how big he was. We spent a good part of the night feeling each other. Hilda was right near us, but she slept soundly."

Linda was horribly disappointed when the camping trip came to an end, and Bill drove them back to their homes in Westchester County.

"Up to that time, I'd never had such an enjoyable experience in my life," she said.

Bill never had a chance to be alone with her again. She cried the day the family moved to Atlanta, where Bill's office had transferred him.

Linda found it hard to make friends when she entered Maria Regina High School in Hartsdale, New York, just north of Yonkers. Bill had been an exception for her. She found boys her own age intimidating. As she'd gotten older and started to develop, her mother had stepped up her warnings about what happens to girls who let boys get too close to them.

At Maria Regina, a fellow classmate, Ryan Sandler, claimed in 1973 that Linda grew to her full height of five feet, eight inches. "We called her 'Miss Holy Holy' because she was such a prude."

"She was the last girl in school I ever thought would deep throat any guy," Sandler said. "I came on to her a few times, but was rewarded with a slap in the face. The guys in the locker room mocked her, claiming she wore a chastity belt. We thought she was going to enter a convent after graduation."

There was some truth in that. During her formative years, Linda admitted to spending half of her time masturbating, or thinking about it, and the rest of her day contemplating what life would be like as a nun.

For the most part, she had little to confess to her priest, as she spent most of her nights at home in bed playing with her tomcat, which she had nicknamed "Hitler" for some reason.

At school, she followed Catholic dogma, even

"Miss Holy Holy"
Two views of **Linda Boreman** at her graduation from Maria Regina High School

11

a mandate from the Pope, banning Catholic schoolgirls from wearing patent leather shoes because it was believed that a girl's crotch could be viewed in the high gloss of the shoes. Linda would later recall this as "religious brainwashing" when she turned from the teaching of her native-born religion.

In 1965, when she was sixteen, her father decided to investigate life in Florida, with the intention of perhaps buying a condo there now that he was off the police force. He selected Fort Lauderdale and rented a dingy apartment in the center of that city. Linda was enrolled in Carol City High School for her junior year.

In need of a friend, she bonded with Christine Lemon, mainly because she was shunned by her female classmates, although highly sought after by the boys in her school. Christine was extremely well-developed and "didn't mind displaying my Marilyn Monroe boobs." As she paraded around naked in the locker room getting ready for physical education classes. Linda recalled there was so much red hair between Christina's legs "she looked like she could model for *Playboy.*"

One afternoon, Christine invited Linda over for what Michael Jackson in years to come would call "a sleepover."

In her bedroom, Christine confessed that her secret dream involved becoming an actress. She'd collected a theatrical wardrobe and stripped down repeatedly as a preface to modeling various outfits for Linda, from her mother's black *négligée* to red bikini panties.

In a memoir, Linda, who referred to herself as skinny with small breasts, admitted that she was turned on by Christine's "red pussy hair and red-nippled boobs."

Before Linda went to bed with Christine that night, she claimed that they danced naked around the room. Christine pretended she was Paul Newman. Linda later said that she'd like to replay the same scene, but with the real Paul Newman—"and those baby blues of his." Unknown to her, that dream would eventually come true.

In bed with Christine later, Linda had her first experience with lesbian sex—and it would not be her last. "I locked her luscious body between my legs, and she kept rubbing her pussy against mine," Linda confessed in a memoir.

But the next day at school, Christine didn't speak to her and had nothing else to do with her. "I felt great about the experience," Linda said, "but Christine must have had a lot of guilt and embarrassment. After all, we'd had a lot of wine that night."

Linda was invited to several house parties where necking was the chief attraction. "I would let a boy kiss me, but go no further. That really pissed them off. I became known as a prick teaser."

Finally, she met a young man, Burt Clifton, who would not take no for an answer. He began by inducing Linda to have three beers. She'd only had wine before, with Christine.

Burt was a senior in high school in Hollywood, Florida. He made Linda forget about her 11pm curfew as he lured her into one of the back bedrooms of a house where they'd been invited to a party. The double bed there was already in use by a couple. But almost from the moment the newcomers entered the room, the two competing couples decided to ignore each other.

Slowly, Burt removed Linda's clothes and stripped down himself. "He sure wasn't endowed like Bill Lyme. I realized for the first time that all men aren't the same. You practically needed a magnifying glass to find what Burt had. He got me on the bed and rubbed his little Boy Scout cock against my clitoris, which up until then had seen action only from my finger."

Not really knowing any other experience, she just assumed that her action with Burt was what sex was all about. Her affair with him lasted for about six weeks. Even so, she found herself walking through the hallways of her school feeling like one of those fictional heroines such as Lady Chatterly or Fanny Hill.

Amazingly, in all those weeks, Burt never really took my cherry," Linda recalled.

During her final weeks in Florida, she made one friend, Betsy Quinn, who was very popular with the boys. She told Linda that the only reason she became her friend was that none of the other girls would have anything to do with her.

"I was still a girl of the Eisenhower 50s, although Betsy was firmly planted in the sexual revolution of the 60s," Linda said.

At the end of the school year, Mr. Boreman decided that Florida was not for him. He missed his native New York. He moved his family back to Yonkers, where they lived in a modest, furnished apartment, paying a rent of sixty dollars a month.

Linda still had one year of high school to go, and re-enrolled in Maria Regina.

As a student, she was only mediocre, earning a C average. She could not grasp certain subjects, particularly mathematics and history. All the European monarchs became one big blur for her.

During her final year, as she turned seventeen, she kept waiting for Mr. Right. "He never came. I worked off my excess energy playing basketball."

Upon graduation, Linda was told by her father that he liked Florida after all, and planned to retire there. She worked briefly in a boutique with a lesbian manager, but soon was ready to go south herself.

When her father purchased a two-bedroom condo for them in Fort Lauderdale, she drove down U.S. Highway 1 with her parents.

From the beginning, she planned to move out of their condo into her own apartment as soon as she could find the right job. "I wanted to entertain potential boyfriends without my mother hounding me day and night."

She felt that a new life awaited her in Florida, and she was anxious to begin living it.

***

Her father was much kinder to her than her mother. Although living on a very limited income, he promised her that he might get a job as a security guard at a private airline, where he could earn enough extra money to send her to college. That never happened.

After graduation, Linda found work as a waitress, four blocks from her house, in a small diner. It served a complete meal for sixty-five cents, plus drinks.

A lot of the patrons made passes at her, and even asked her out on dates, but she never accepted these invitations. "During high school, some of the girls had dropped out of school when they became pregnant. I didn't want that to happen to me."

During one brief interlude in her life, Linda fantasized about becoming a "biker chick" like the model depicted above. But, alas, the dream turned into a nightmare when she became pregnant by a motorcycle-riding Marlon Brando wannabe who was already married.

At the diner, Guy Stahl, a high school dropout who'd migrated to Florida from Albany, New York, was a short order cook. He befriended her, and on a few occasions slipped three or four steaks out the back door of the restaurant for her to take home to her parents.

When he invited her for a Sunday drive to see Miami Beach, she accepted. Although she'd lived north of this fabled area, she'd never ventured south before.

She remembered the drive as being totally innocent. He drove up and down the beach strip, as she took in all the hotels. With their clothes on, he took her for a walk along the beach and out onto a pier. For lunch, they had some burgers and a milkshake at a local stand. The climax of the evening was a movie on Lincoln Road.

When Stahl drove her back home, it was about 11:30pm. Her mother was waiting up for her. She accused her of having sex with her co-worker and imposed an 11pm curfew on her if she went out on any future dates.

14

Stahl and Linda dated on at least seven more occasions, always with a kiss at the door before eleven o'clock in the evening.

"He was a good and decent man, but we really weren't into each other that much," Linda said. "We gradually drifted apart, although for as long as I knew him he kept slipping me those steaks."

She dated some other men who came into the diner until she found out they were either married or cheating on their girlfriends. Years later, her Svengali and "master," Chuck Traynor, claimed that in Fort Lauderdale, Linda was known as "a hot-to-trot, sleep-around kid." There appears no basis for this charge, not as long as Linda lived with her strict parents. Her mother supervised her dates, demanding that they come into the house where she would ask to see their driver's licenses to find out if any of the men had any traffic violations. She also asked them how much money they had in the bank. "After facing mother's inquisition, most guys didn't ask me out any more."

Linda's first real romance was with a biker, Bob Raith, whom she'd met at the diner. He was tall and handsome, with thick "dirty blonde" hair and clear blue eyes. Long, lean, and muscular, he moved with a certain grace. "I remembered how sunburned his face was from all that bike riding in the hot sun," she said. "When he smiled at me, he showed strong white teeth. A stubble of beard appeared like golden flecks against his brown skin."

"The other waitresses were also after him," Linda said. "He wore tight blue jeans that left little to the imagination and a white T-shirt that showed off his build," she said. "At least two of the waitresses were much prettier than me, but Bob seemed to go for me. He always played Hank Williams tunes on the jukebox. He was a big fan of country music, and invited me to go with him to Miami one night to hear the Tennessee Possums."

On their first date, Raith taught her to square dance. Before that evening, she'd never danced with any man, but she was a quick learner. After the Possums performed, he drove her over to the beach at Crandon Park.

Before that, he'd told her he couldn't invite her to his apartment because he lived way out in Hialeah with two other guys. He also claimed that he was a construction worker on a housing development in South Miami.

Linda later said she knew what he was going to do to her, and she genuinely liked him and didn't plan to resist. "He was gentle with me," she later recalled. "There was no forced entry. He kissed me all over my body and nibbled a lot at my breasts. He buried his face in my neck as his fingers worked below. He had me moaning softly. When he entered me, I felt pain at first, but it gradually went away."

"I wrapped my legs around him, as he plunged deeper," she recalled. "I was on fire. If only all my future love-making had been like this. It was definitely not a preview of things to come."

Linda and Raith dated for the next year and a half. "Always the same," she said. "Country music, perhaps dinner in a Mexican canteen. A Susan Hayward movie. That boy sure loved his tacos."

She never went to his apartment in Hialeah because he told her that his roommates always had other men in to play gin rummy. "I knew things couldn't go on like that forever with us," Linda said. "I hinted at marriage, but he always changed the subject. He said his job was seasonal and in the past, he'd been out of work for long periods of time and had a hard time paying his share of the rent. I suggested we might save up. I told him that with all the tips I'd made at the restaurant, I had saved up five-hundred dollars."

And then, in her words, "the shit hit the fan." She discovered that she was pregnant.

She was terrified and called the only girlfriend she had, Betsy Quinn, who had gone to high school with her. Unlike Linda, Betsy claimed she'd slept with at least ten men, usually much older than herself. "I'm not a whore," she said, "but I am not opposed to taking a gift here or there." During the day, Betsy worked in Miami as a sales clerk at Burdines Department Store.

That afternoon, Betsy and Linda met at a hamburger joint on Miami's lower Flagler Street. "I'm going to have Bob's kid. I know it's his because there's never been anyone else."

"Okay," Betsy said. "I never wanted to tell you this, because you're Catholic. I know you religious fanatics are dead set against abortion. But one of my guys knocked me up and arranged for me to sail over on a boat from Key West to Havana. In this Cuban hospital, I got an abortion. How much money have you got in the bank?"

"The last time I counted, about seven hundred and fifty dollars," Linda said. "One drunk the other night left me a hundred dollar bill, and I've worked three private parties serving drinks and food for fifty dollars a night, real good pay."

"That's more than enough," Betsy said.

"But I can't kill my baby," Linda said. "I could never do that."

"Okay, then, why don't you tell all this to Bob and get him to marry you?"

"I've got a date with him tonight," Linda said. "I'll hit him between the eyes with the news. Sometimes it seems it's the gal who has to propose to the boy. Which reminds me: When are you getting hitched with one of the men you date?"

"When I turn thirty-five or maybe when I'm pushing forty," Betsy said. "I'm known as a type of gal who likes to play the field. There are a lot of guys running around Florida in tight bathing trunks, and I want to enjoy as many of them as I can while I've still got it."

That night over a dinner of Raith's favorite tacos, she told him she was pregnant, but only after he was in a relaxed state induced by four cold Mexican beers. He looked stunned and showed even more disappointment when she asked him—begged him, really—if he would marry her. "My baby boy needs a father," she said. "I just know it'll be a boy."

"Look, babe, I feared something like this might happen, because we've been getting too carried away," he said. "I've never told you this. I don't have an apartment in Hialeah with some guys. I live in a small house in South Miami with a good woman, my wife, I love her very much and I have three really cute blonde-haired kids—two boys and a girl. So, as you see, I'm not in any position to get married, and I certainly don't want to father some bastard child. Besides, how do I know it's my kid?"

As she'd later recall, his words stunned her, like pouring acid onto her face. "My face was actually burning. If there's one moment in life when a gal has to grow up, that was it for me. I fled the canteen. He didn't go after me, either. That was the last I ever saw of my first love, the man who took my virginity in more ways than one."

***

When Linda returned in tears to the Boreman condo, she found her mother still awake. She didn't have to tell her what had gone wrong. Her mother guessed it. "The little harlot I raised is pregnant, isn't she?"

"I didn't mean for it to happen," Linda said.

"No gal means for it to happen unless she's trying to trap a man," her mother said. "Did you trap him?"

"He's married…I didn't know."

"Then you're dumber than you look," her mother said. "You can't stay here. I'll be disgraced. You'll have to go away somewhere."

"I don't have any place to go," Linda said. "My friend Betsy said I should go to Cuba and have my baby aborted."

"That's a sin! If you do something like that, I might kill you myself, or else send you to jail. You're a wicked little whore. I'm sorry I ever gave birth to the likes of you. Now go to bed."

The next evening, Linda met with Betsy again and told her what her mother had said.

"Frankly, I'd tell your mother to go fuck herself and get down to Key West and hop onto that private boat."

"I can't…I just can't."

"I've got another idea," Betsy said. "I've got an uncle, a mechanic, who lives outside New York City. He's married with three kids. They're real nice people and might take you in until you have your baby. You could help with the housework and cooking, because his wife is sickly all the time. I'll call them tonight."

"Oh, Betsy, that would be wonderful if you could."

Within three days, Linda was on a Greyhound bus heading for New York, where Betsy's uncle, Ralph Quinn, met her at the bus terminal on 42nd Street in Manhattan and drove her to his place in the country. There, Linda met his wife, a pale, blonde-haired woman named Shelley. She also was introduced to the children.

For the next five months, she lived in the Quinn home and on three different occasions, visited the local hospital. Back at the Quinn's house, she told her hosts, "Mother and baby are doing fine."

Linda's 1969 car crash on the Taconic Parkway, in a way similar to the woman in the photograph above, dislocated her eye from its socket, broke her jaw, many of her teeth, and four of her ribs, and lacerated her spleen.

In a macabre replay, an equivalent car crash in Colorado killed her in 2002.

Ralph was at work when her pains came. In the family car, a very old Chevrolet, Shelley drove her to the hospital where her baby was born. She'd been right. It was a baby boy, weighing in at ten pounds. It had been a difficult delivery. She named the child Billy Boreman.

Within two weeks, Linda and her newly born baby were back living with the Quinns. The baby cried a lot, and Ralph complained that the infant kept the family up all night. Every night, he suggested that she write to her mother and ask to return to Fort Lauderdale.

When Linda had sufficiently recovered, she resumed her household duties with the Quinn family even though she knew that both Ralph and Shelley wanted her to leave. Having an infant in the household didn't please either of them.

Shelley was totally house bound, and never wanted to go out. She agreed to look after Linda's baby if she'd run the family errands during the day, including the shopping.

Before he departed for work one morning in his pickup truck, Ralph asked her to drive down to a local farm and pick up several bushels of produce, especially big fat beefsteak tomatoes. He had this fetish about homemade catsup, and he wanted Linda and Shelley to can bottles of it for the winter in ten different flavors.

He had a book of recipes which he gave to Linda for instruction. He was also going to buy a stalk of bananas at a wholesale market, because he also wanted them to cook and can several bottles of banana catsup. Before that, she never knew such a condiment even existed.

Driving along the Taconic Parkway after visiting the farm, Linda noticed that a storm was brewing. It was late in the afternoon and getting dark as the first of the heavy rain began pouring down.

She was just coming out of second gear when she spotted a large Chrysler speeding over a hill.

It appeared to be going more than eighty-five miles an hour along the slippery highway. All of a sudden, the driver lost control of his vehicle and veered dangerously into her lane at high speed. It was a dead-on crash.

She wore no safety belt, and the impact of the crash sent her face smashing into the windshield. She passed out and didn't wake up until hours later in a hospital.

Groggy and drugged, she found herself attended by a kindly older doctor, Bruce Ferguson, who, along with two other doctors, had performed emergency surgery on her.

"You're lucky to be alive," he told her. "The driver of that other car, a man in his seventies, was killed instantly."

In her condition, she could hardly comprehend his report on her condition. It seemed that her left eye had become dislocated from its socket and had to be surgically placed back into position. He warned her that her vision might be impaired for several days.

Not only that, but her jaw had been broken, and the steering wheel of her car had lacerated her spleen and broken four of her ribs.

More surgery was needed, including extensive dental work. Her lower front teeth had been knocked down into her chin, and had pierced the skin there. Not only that, but blood was leaking through her intestines.

She had a hard time remembering the days and weeks ahead, as she drifted in and out of surgery and consciousness. A doctor seemed to hover over her, as she underwent one procedure after another. Dr. Ferguson told her that there would always be a very large scar on her body.

Shelley came to visit her only two times during her stay in the hospital. Linda thanked her profusely for looking after her infant boy. When she inquired about her son, Shelley was rather vague, always saying, "He's doing just fine— no trouble at all."

Linda even asked Shelley to bring the boy to the hospital on her next visit, but she refused. "I'm not that good a driver," Shelley said. "There's no way in hell I'm going to drive with a little baby in the car, not after what happened to you."

Linda was still very weak and could only walk with a cane when Dr. Ferguson told her that she was going to be released the following morning. He warned her that she would need weeks of recuperation and should not even attempt to do any work or strenuous activity for at least three months. She was also advised to report for regular medical check-ups.

Ralph Quinn had promised to drive to the hospital and pick her up, but when she was released at eleven o'clock he hadn't shown up. She made repeated phone calls to Shelley, who seemed annoyed at her. "Ralph is on his way," she snapped. "Maybe he had a flat tire. STOP CALLING!"

Finally, a very sullen Ralph arrived to take her away. He carried her lone suitcase to his pickup. Linda thanked Dr. Ferguson and hobbled out of the hospital, having some difficulty getting into the front seat with Ralph.

After twenty minutes on the road, she sensed something terribly wrong. Ralph hadn't said anything, and he was taking the wrong route, driving along the southbound Parkway, heading toward New York City.

"My wife has packed your things, and they're in the trunk," he told her. "I'm taking you to the Greyhound bus station in Manhattan. I've talked with your mother. She knows you'll be a while recuperating, and she thinks it best for you to go back to Fort Lauderdale."

"My baby!" she screeched, fearing at first that her boy had died. "Where is he?"

Very firmly, he told her that he'd called her mother, who had come north and taken the infant back with her to Florida. "We're in no position to look after the kid, and you can't expect Shelley to be its mother. My wife is sickly. She has a hard enough time looking after our own brats."

After hearing this news, Linda burst into tears.

Ralph assured her that Mrs. Boreman had everything under control. "The last time I talked to her, the baby was doing great. Your mother is a good, strong woman. She'll be there for you and your son."

After their arrival in New York City's Times Square area, Ralph left her on the street in front of the Port Authority Bus Terminal. Before she got out, he gave her a hundred dollars and a one-way bus ticket to Fort Lauderdale.

She told him good-bye and thanked him for his generosity. "Please give my love to Shelley."

Staring only at the pavement in front of him, Ralph, in his mud-spattered old pickup truck, merged into the traffic without looking back at her or saying a final word.

During that long bus ride back to Fort Lauderdale, Linda cried a lot, but muffled it so she would not attract unwanted attention from her fellow passengers. She sat near the rear of the bus, where there were fewer passengers, so she'd have more privacy.

As the Greyhound was rolling southward through Virginia, she began to feel that Ralph had lied to her about her baby. Something about his demeanor suggested that he was not telling her the full truth.

The road to Florida stretched endlessly before her, and she was counting the hours until she could hold her son in her arms again. "Oh, please God," she said to herself, "let him be safe. Protect him from all harm. He's all I have in the world that belongs to me."

***

At the Greyhound bus station in Fort Lauderdale, there was no one to meet her, so she took a taxi to her parents' condo. When she got there, she pounded on the door, since she no longer had a key.

It took a few minutes before her mother opened the door a crack, looking out at her skeptically. "So my prodigal daughter has returned, no doubt to disgrace her parents once again."

"Oh mother, please stand back and let me in," Linda said. "I want to see my baby boy."

Leaving her suitcases outside, she rushed into the apartment on wobbly legs. "Where is he? In your room?"

Sit down, Linda," her mother ordered. "I have some bad news for you."

"IS MY BABY OK?"

"He's doing well, but he had to have an expensive operation—in fact, he's going to need several expensive operations."

"But why?" Her voice reflected her desperation. "What's the matter with him?"

"His leg was growing in deformed," her mother said. It was like one leg was turning to face the other. That would put him in a wheelchair for life. Elizabeth Taylor had the same thing happen to her daughter, Maria Taylor Burton, that she'd adopted in Germany. It cost Miss Taylor a fortune to get her Maria to walk again. We have no such fortune to spend on your Billy Boreman. Neither do you."

"But what is going to happen to him?" Linda asked. "Where is he? I want to see him."

"All in good time, my dear. While you were in the hospital, I brought Billy to Florida after rescuing him from that horrible family where you were staying. Poor Billy, after a series of operations will have to spend two years in a cast."

"What did you do with him?"

"We turned him over to a Catholic charity hospital in Miami," she said.

"The sisters there will take care of him. Charity contributions will pay for his operations. He'll get the best of care. When he can walk again and play like a normal boy, he'll be turned over to you again."

"I've got to see him." Linda came over to her mother and grabbed her. "You can't keep me away from my son!"

"I can and I will," she said. "Even your weak-minded father, who always gives in to you, doesn't know how to get to your son. I've done what is best for the boy and, ultimately, best for you. Besides, what kid would want to grow and learn that his mother is a cheap whore. By the time he's turned over to you, hopefully you'll have a good and respectable job, or else will settle down with a fine young man who's Catholic and a family man."

Linda hobbled toward her bedroom where she collapsed, sobbing. In her heart, she knew her mother was right. The Boremans could not afford those operations, and she wanted her boy to grow up and be able to lead a normal life.

She looked at the same tired white walls she'd known since she was sixteen.

"I'm free, white, and twenty-one," she said to herself. "Well, at least white and twenty-one."

After she recovered from all her own operations, she would maintain one goal: She wanted to find a good man to marry her. "Perhaps when Billy can walk again, my new husband will adopt him and make him his own, just like he was his own kid."

***

After that, Linda spent long weeks recuperating at her parents' condo in Fort Lauderdale. Most afternoons, she lounged at the rear of the condo complex beside the communal swimming pool. She'd renewed her friendship with Betsy Quinn, whom she'd known in high school. Before she had to report to work in the evening, Betsy often drove by and spent time with Linda.

Betsy told Linda that she was working in a topless bar in North Miami Beach.

"I could never do that," Linda said. "Besides, with all the scars on my body, I look like the Bride of Frankenstein."

In spite of the crisscross of scars on her body, Linda still wore her white bikini. Sometimes, male occupants of the condo, when their wives weren't around, would hit on both Linda and Betsy. Linda spurned such offers, although Betsy flirted back. On three different occasions, Betsy accepted the men's offers and spent time with each of them in their condos before their wives returned.

"Mostly, I can't be bothered," Betsy said. "I have more men than Marilyn had lovers."

On one hot afternoon as she dozed beside the pool, Linda became aware of a shadow blocking her from the sun. She opened her eyes to see Betsy standing over her with a handsome young man with dirty blonde hair. Instinctively, she reached to cover her exposed body with a beach towel.

"Linda, this is Chuck Traynor, my boss at the Las Vegas Inn," Betsy said.

Linda remembered that she and Chuck spent at least two minutes sizing each other up. She later asserted that she found him an attractive man, standing six feet, two inches and wearing motorcycle goggles, a white T-shirt, and tight blue jeans. What impressed her even more was Chuck's brand new Jaguar XKE parked in the condo's driveway. It was burgundy-colored, with black leather upholstery.

She offered each of them a beer, returning quickly to her condo's kitchen, where she slipped into her bedroom and put on a cotton dress. Back at the pool, she handed each of them a beer.

"What, no beer for yourself?" Chuck asked.

She explained to him that, "My liver got screwed up in that auto accident. My doctor said no booze for two whole years."

"In that case, why not a smoke?" Chuck asked. He reached into his denim shirt pocket and produced a marijuana cigarette. After lighting it, he sucked the smoke deep into his lungs and handed it to her. After taking two drags, she passed it on to Betsy. All three of them finished off the joint.

"My mother caught me smoking pot once when I was in high school," Linda said. "She beat me and threatened to call the police and have me arrested until my father stopped her."

Since no one was at the pool but them, Betsy pulled off her top. "Chuck here is looking for models to pose in bathing suits for fashion magazines."

"Then don't look my way," Linda said. "I've got these scars on my body from a car accident. The last thing I plan to do is model a bathing suit."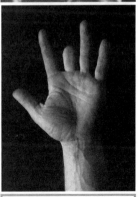

"I also shoot fashion models," Chuck told her. "You're thin and would look great modeling clothes."

After he finished his beer, Chuck told her that he and Betsy had to drive to North Miami Beach to open his bar, and he invited her to go along. Eager to escape from the condo complex, where she'd spent the last few weeks, she accepted.

With the wind in her hair, she enjoyed the south-

Chuck Traynor

bound ride. When Chuck produced another joint for them en route, she noticed that one of his fingers was missing. "I do quite a bit of skin-diving. One time, underwater, I encountered this snapping turtle. Presto! No more finger!"

On the way south, Chuck did most of the talking. His favorite subject was himself. He spoke of his service in the U.S. Marines, where he was a top marksman.

When Chuck Traynor won a marksmanship contest in the Marine Corps, his prize was a date with **Natalie Wood** (above).

Was she as excited by the prospect as she appears in this photograph?

Dubious endings from wholesome beginnings: Chuck Traynor asserted that the money he raised to buy his bar originated during his stint as a crop duster in Florida's orange groves.

"Tell her about that prize you won," Betsy said. She had positioned herself in the car's back seat.

"I don't like to brag," he said, "but I won the marksmanship award for the entire Marine Corps. The honor was appreciated, and the prize was a date with Natalie Wood."

"Natalie Wood!" Linda exclaimed. She was very impressed. "If I could ever be a movie star, I'd want to appear in the very same pictures she makes."

"She was something else," Traynor said. "I thought she was just doing her bit for the U.S. Marines, and that she'd be very reserved—polite but formal, if you know what I mean. Hell, five minutes into the date, on the way to the restaurant, she was all over me. I practically lost control of the car. She got so aroused, she suggested we skip the restaurant and go to her house."

"He got to fuck her, too," Betsy chimed in from the back seat.

"She told me I had a much bigger cock than Warren Beatty or Robert Wagner, and three times the size of Elvis Presley," Chuck said. "That really goaded me on."

"I mean, Chuck was screwing from the A-list." Betsy said. "And let's face it: Natalie also had James Dean, Frank Sinatra, and Steve McQueen. I read the movie magazines. She practically stole Nicky Hilton from Elizabeth Taylor."

After Chuck was discharged from the Marines, he moved to South Florida, where he was hired as a crop-dusting pilot for Minute Maid Orange Juice. "I had saved up $2,000 and with it, I bought the Las Vegas Inn. It's a beer bar on

123rd Street in North Miami Beach. It mostly attracts bikers, construction workers, and hotel janitors. I hired four topless dancers, but my customers demanded that they go bottomless. I obliged, but it's illegal. I'm always afraid the cops will raid me."

"About the last thing I will ever do is dance topless," Linda said. "Unlike Betsy here, I'm flat-chested, as I'm sure you've already noticed. As for total nudity, there's no way in hell I'd appear stark naked in front of a group of horny men. Not for all the money in the world."

"Never say never," Chuck said as he pulled his Jaguar into the gravel-covered parking lot of his tacky bar.

***

Across from a police station, a bad location for such a business as the Las Vegas Inn, Chuck's bar was an ugly, flat-roofed, cement block construction that was painted in tones of slime green.

Linda was even less impressed when she wandered into the dimly lit bar, with its Day-Glo decorations. In the rear was a pool table and in one corner, a jukebox.

Chuck excused himself to take a leak in a nearby toilet. While he was out of earshot, Linda asked Betsy, "Are you and Chuck having a thing?"

"No, I've even slept over once or twice in his bedroom with another gal, and he didn't even come on to me."

"Then you're a free agent doing what comes naturally?" Linda asked.

"Not quite," Betsy said. "You might as well know. My parents just left Miami one day and didn't want to take me with them. I was dumped at my uncle's house in Homestead. I was twelve years old. Today, he's fifty-two. Almost from the first night, he started seducing me, and he's still going at it."

"Isn't that incest?" Linda asked.

"Call it what you will," Betsy said. "All I know is that my uncle is the only man in the world who's been good to me."

"My mother constantly accuses my father of sleeping with me," Linda said. "There are big fights over that. But, I swear, he's never had sex with me, although he did pull the sheet off of my naked body one afternoon when mother was out of the house. He told me he wanted to examine the scars on my body after all those operations. He ran his fingers across the scars, and then said, 'Too bad,' and left the room."

"At least he didn't screw you," Betsy said.

"If he had, I would not have resisted," Linda confessed. "The point, though, is that he didn't. I'm sure it's crossed his mind, though. Perhaps that's what mother senses."

25

While Chuck and a lone Cuban bartender were setting up for the evening, the door opened and in walked "Elvis Presley." On closer inspection, it wasn't Elvis, but an impersonator.

In a pink shirt, white boots, and black jeans, the man, who appeared to be in his late 30s, came over to the bar and embraced Chuck warmly.

Then he walked over to meet Linda. Betsy introduced her to Ronald Roberts, who wasn't an Elvis impersonator at all, but a fan who worshipped at his shrine and imitated him in dress.

Roberts was the same height as Chuck, his best friend, and he had piercing blue eyes which he immediately focused on Linda. He showed off a lot of muscle in a tight T-shirt. He was employed during the day in the maintenance department at the University of Miami.

Linda quickly learned that Ronald was married, but that his wife had caught him cheating with other women and had kicked him out of their house.

"I'm going to be one poor boy when that divorce comes through," he told Betsy and Linda. "I'll be living with Chuck for a few weeks until I get on my feet again."

The Cuban brought him a cold beer, setting down a Coca-Cola for Linda. Betsy claimed she couldn't have anything, as she was performing that night.

"You look better than Elvis himself," Linda said. "The King has put on too many pounds."

"I keep in shape," he said, winking at her.

Betsy excused herself to go to one of the dingy rooms in the rear. When she'd gone, Ronald said, "You don't want to sit in this dump all night. Why not ride down the beach with me and eat at Joe's Stone Crab House. Best food on the Beach."

"Let's do it," she said. "I'm starving, and I love seafood."

After telling Chuck goodbye, Ronald later treated Linda to the best meal she'd ever had in Florida. After dinner, he took her to one of the hotels that em-

Linda's boyfriend
Impersonated **Elvis:**

ployed a small band. He danced with her, holding her tenderly. She was glad to be having a social life again.

When he drove her home that night, he kissed her and arranged a date with her for the following evening. "If you don't mind, we'll go out with Chuck and his girlfriend, Ginger."

"Don't mind?" Linda said. "I'd love it!"

The next day, she couldn't wait for the evening to come. Ronald picked her up at exactly six o'clock, her mother spying on them from behind the curtains of her living room.

As Linda had admitted in a phone call to Betsy the following day, "I really go for that Ronald. I want to get him on the rebound after his wife divorces him. Is there any bad stuff on him?"

"I always found him a sweet guy if you don't mind listening to Elvis all day and night," Betsy said. "That's his big hang-up."

When Ronald picked her up that night, he was wearing a baby blue jump suit evocative of Elvis in one of his Las Vegas acts.

On the way south from Fort Lauderdale, Linda tried to see beyond the Elvis drag to the man beneath it. Ronald was an attractive man with long black hair. Ascetic eyelids appeared to be half-closed over his brown eyes. They were nearly black, giving him an air of mystery. His flesh was smooth and tanned.

Stopping off at the Las Vegas Inn, Ronald picked up Chuck and his girl-friend, Ginger Hoisen. Linda was a bit shocked when Ginger got into the car with her and freely admitted, "I've just turned fifteen, so I have to date Chuck without my parents finding out."

"Good thinking," Linda said.

Chuck paid for all of their dinners at a steakhouse before they went to see Steve McQueen appearing in *The Reivers.*

Later, Ronald dropped off Chuck and Ginger at the bar before taking Linda home.

This double dating went on for some time before Ronald became more amorous. Finally, he got around to inviting her to Chuck's house in Miami.

She knew what was going to happen and was perfectly prepared to go along with the seduction. As she would later tell Betsy, Ronald had a magnificent physique even though he was pushing forty. His narrow hips tapered to an ex-quisitely defined chest, with large nipples. When his jeans came down, his navel looked like a perfectly formed Litton button tucked into a round alcove in a hairless abdomen. Then a fleshy pole was revealed—thick and wide, with a pinkish cap.

He turned out to be a skilled lover while locking onto her lips in a moist kiss. In and out he went, each stroke bringing her more satisfaction. As she'd tell Betsy, "I could really go for this man."

Although Chuck on occasion eyed her seductively, most of his concen-trated attention was on Ginger.

After his initial seduction of Linda, Ronald took her to Chuck's home for sex every night before driving her back to Fort Lauderdale. She told Betsy, "I'm hopelessly in love with him."

The only bizarre note was revealed one night at Chuck's house when he opted one day to remain at home and not head off to the Vegas Inn for work. After a drink with him, Ronald took Linda upstairs for sex. About an hour later, he went with her into the bathroom for a shower. She always washed thoroughly after one of their encounters before going home to face her mother.

"Then the strangest thing happened," Linda told Betsy. "In the middle of our shower, Ronald and I were kissing when the curtain was pulled back. It was Chuck standing there jaybird naked. I was too startled to say anything, and Ronald didn't seem in the least surprised. Chuck stepped into the shower with us. Since Ronald didn't protest, I didn't either. Chuck soaped our backs and that was it. When he'd done that, he rinsed himself off and went back to his own bedroom. On the way home, Ronald didn't say anything about it, treating it like it was an everyday happening."

One Sunday night, Ronald didn't show up for their date at the scheduled hour of six o'clock. Frantically, ninety minutes later, Linda called Chuck at his bar. "What happened to Ronald? An accident? I hope he's not hurt?"

"I've got some bad news for you, and I'm so very sorry," Chuck said. "The other night when he came into the bar after dropping you off, his wife was waiting here for him. She's agreed to take him back. All is forgiven and they're starting over again."

"Thanks, Chuck," she said, putting down the phone.

Her romance with Ronald had been too good, too perfect. A two-minute phone call, or one that was even shorter, was all that was needed to throw a woman's life into total chaos.

She felt a sharp pain in her side, and, for a moment, wished she'd died in that car accident in New York.

***

For a month, Linda led the lonely life. Even Betsy didn't come by anymore, because she'd gone north with one of her johns and might be away for a long time. At least that's what she claimed when she'd called to say goodbye.

One afternoon, as Linda was lying beside her condo's pool in her white bikini, a shadow suddenly blocked her exposure to the sun. She looked up to see Chuck standing over her.

"How are you doing, baby?" he asked her. "Long time, no see. I've missed you."

"How's Ginger?" Linda asked.

"Ginger is no more. Her daddy found out about us. He's threatening to go to the cops."

"For your sake, I hope not."

"How about driving down the beach for some dinner?" he asked. "We'll stop by later to see how business is doing at the bar."

"That sounds great," she said. "It's been a while since I've been invited anywhere. Have you heard from Ronald?"

"He's still shacked up with his wife," Chuck said. "He comes into the bar every so often and asks about you. I think he'd like to get it on with you on the side."

"That idea doesn't excite me," she said. She went upstairs and within twenty minutes was dressed and ready to go riding with him in his Jaguar.

[As she'd remember later, Chuck, during the first weeks she started dating him, was a real gentleman. "He lit my cigarettes, paid for my dinner, bought me an occasional dress, and even opened car doors for me," she said.]

When they arrived on the outskirts of Miami Beach, Chuck cut across the causeway and headed for Coral Gables where he parked in front of Worth Devore's apartment. He explained to her that Devore was an airplane pilot who supplied him with pot. Inside Worth's apartment, Linda found that it was filled with artifacts from such African countries as Senegal and Nigeria.

While the three of them shared a joint, Chuck made his pitch. "Why don't you come and live with me?" he asked her in front of Worth. "Leave your parents behind. As for clothes, I'll buy you new ones."

"Chuck's a great guy," Devore said. "With him, you'll have an exciting life. He told me how domineering your mother is."

"But I can't just up and leave," she protested. "They'll have the police searching for me."

"They won't look for you guys here," Worth said. "Why not spend the night with me?"

It took the two men only half an hour to convince her to stay. In the meantime, Worth called out for pizza delivery.

Before midnight, and feeling high, she retired to Worth's guest bedroom with Chuck. She hadn't really thought about this as a sexual arrangement, but she quickly got the idea that she was Ginger's replacement.

As she'd later recall, "For the first time, I was taking a stand against my parents, and Chuck was there holding me, stroking my hair, and loving me."

When he pulled off his clothes for bed, he stood nude before her. She'd already seen him naked that time in the shower. However, she kept on her bra and panties as she jumped into the bed with him. "Am I getting a vir-

Strangers in the Night

29

gin?" he asked. "Not from what Ronald told me."

When Chuck moved on top of her, she let him kiss her. But when he tried to seduce her, he could not obtain an erection.

Years after the publication of her 1973 memoir, *Inside Linda Lovelace,* she claimed that the account of what appeared in that memoir about his sexual performance that night had been ghost written by Chuck himself:

"I automatically pushed him back when his big cock started pushing into me. Actually, I didn't want to run away. The fat rocklike muscle tore into me like a battering ram, and I nearly fainted from the shock. It hurt. The explosive pain shot from my groin over every inch of my body. I came in seconds and the rockets were all on time. That night, from midnight until six in the morning, we fucked and I came at least ten glorious times. It was a very good night. The best of my entire life."

That account, at least, was Chuck's fantasy. "It didn't really happen," Linda claimed.

In 1974, Linda published a very different memoir, *The Intimate Diary of Linda Lovelace,* in which she presented a completely different version of what happened the first night Chuck took her to bed. In this revised version, she claimed that he failed to produce an erection and that he asked her to "suck me off."

She said she found such an act disgusting and told him, "I could never do that to a man."

She maintained that in spite of the hot sex described in Chuck's fantasy version, neither of them had a climax. She claimed that the attempts to have sex with Chuck failed miserably for them both. "He was frustrated and unsatisfied, and so was I," she later said.

Their attempt at sex together had been loveless and without passion. In its aftermath, she fully expected that he'd drive her back to her parents' condo in the morning, dump her, and replace her with some other woman who could give him what he wanted.

But amazingly, he kept her in his life.

***

The next morning, Linda called her father at work, where he was employed as a security guard for a small airline.

"Where have you been?" he asked. "Your mother is hysterical. She was up all night."

"I'm with Chuck," she said. "You remember him. I won't be staying with you guys anymore."

"But what about your things?" he asked.

"Give them away," she said. "Chuck is going to buy everything new for me."

"But I was going to save up enough money to send you to college and buy you a used car," he protested.

"It's too late for that now," she told him. "I've got to go. Good-bye."

***

After breakfast that morning, Chuck took her down to a shopping mall south of Coral Gables and purchased a new, sexier wardrobe for her, including some provocative lingerie that she would never have dared wear before.

She didn't really plan to be a kept woman, so she told him she should try to find a job somewhere. She'd had previous experience as a waitress.

"You can help me run the Las Vegas Inn," he promised her. "You'll make good money there. The guys, especially when they're drunk, are big tippers."

That same day, he moved her into his own small house which had two bedrooms upstairs. Downstairs there were two more bedrooms, where three or four different girls slept on a large waterbed. After dark, they danced bottomless at the Las Vegas Inn.

Linda didn't have to worry about cooking. Although he occasionally preferred a lavish dinner, Chuck was a fast-food junkie. It was waffles for breakfast and hamburgers with fries for the rest of the day, with an occasional bucket of fried chicken. At least she didn't have to cook for him.

At the bar, she didn't have to learn about special drinks. The patrons liked their liquor straight—"No Shirley Temples here," he told her—or else they drank wine. When the wine ran low, she drove over to buy more of it in big gallon jugs from the Seven-Eleven, which Chuck would then sell by the glass at inflated prices.

He took her to a lot of movies. They went to one theater in North Miami that showed double features, with a program that changed three times a week. "We saw every film released," she said. "Chuck told me I was pretty enough to be a movie star."

"Are you out of your mind?" she asked him. "There's no way I'll ever star in a movie. Who do you think I am? Elizabeth Taylor?"

"No, she's much too voluptuous for your image. You're more the Audrey Hepburn type."

As she moved deeper and deeper into Chuck's sordid world, Hollywood stardom seemed the most elusive ghost to chase.

Chuck told the girls at the bar, "I'm having to teach Linda the fine art of sex.

31

She's got a lot to learn and a long way to go before she's turned into a world class prostitute. Would you believe that when I first picked her up, she'd never sucked a cock? I know that's hard for you *putas* to believe. Each of you never met a cock you haven't sucked."

Gradually, he coached her to perform fellatio on him, claiming he could not achieve an erection unless she did that. The first time, she merely inserted the tip of his penis into her mouth and masturbated him. But she yanked her face away when he ejaculated. That made him angry and he slapped her for the first time, the first of many slaps to come.

In the days ahead, she finally relented and agreed to swallow his offering. When at first she'd attempted to pull away at the last minute, he'd held her head in place and refused to remove his penis from her mouth until she'd completely sucked him dry. Forcing her into sex turned him on—in fact, he began to like that more than when she meekly submitted.

Although they slept together in the same bed together every night, he did not make another attempt to penetrate her. He preferred to go down on her for almost an hour at a time. She later claimed that she felt that was a "dirty, filthy act, and oh, so vulgar." But he insisted and she invariably gave in to him, although she repeatedly showered and scrubbed herself afterward, out of fear of smelling bad.

She claimed that the first three times she was able to swallow his semen, she felt sick and wanted to throw up. But then, "after a few weeks, I began to enjoy this sticky, salty stuff. In time, it became my favorite high-protein food."

She also began to look forward to his performing oral sex on her. She admitted in a memoir that after one of their cunnilingus sessions, "I came so heavily I really thought I was peeing in his face. I was insane and wanted to scream at the top of my lungs."

She began to know the girls who lived downstairs in Chuck's two bedrooms. There was a small swimming pool out back, and after the bar closed down, the girls would often strip down, pull off Chuck's clothes, and have a swim party.

Gradually, the girls lured Linda into the pool, although she insisted on wearing a suit. In time, though, with enough pot smoking, she took off all her clothes, too, and swam nude with Chuck and his prostitutes.

"It took me a while, but I finally overcame my shyness," Linda recalled. "I envied the other girls, though, because they had Jane Russell breasts and I did not."

Four girls worked the bar at night. She never knew their last names and even suspected that their first names were pseudonyms. They were known as Marilyn, Veronica, Lana, and Rita, obviously in honor of movie stars. As far as was possible for them, the working girls dressed, talked, and made themselves up to resemble Marilyn Monroe, Veronica Lake, Lana Turner, and Rita Hayworth.

As she'd later admit, "I saw some pretty revolting acts. There was a little stage in the rear of the bar. The girls even masturbated themselves in front of the guys, who later stuffed dollar bills into their wet vaginas. The men felt them up in the most disgusting ways, mauling their breasts and even inserting their fingers up their asses or into their vaginas. I found it sickening. I never planned to join them, although I ultimately did."

Marilyn had grown up in a Cuban-American family in Miami. When she was eight years old, her father had forced her into oral sex. When his wife left him, he lived with his daughter in a house where he brought in men who worked with him during the day in a garage. By the time she was twelve, she was already a professional.

Veronica came from Jacksonville, Florida. She lived with her mother until she died when Veronica was thirteen. She never knew who her father was. She was taken in by a guardian who was in his fifties. He introduced her to anal intercourse, which he greatly enjoyed, although she screamed out in pain. Even-

Sex and Celebrity Obsession
Chuck Traynor's bar hired lookalike strippers impersonating *(clockwise from left)*
Lana Turner, Rita Hayworth, Veronica Lake, and **Marilyn Monroe**

tually, she ran away from him and ended up living on the streets of Miami, where she became a prostitute. She was later taken in by a black pimp who demanded she service five or six "of my brothers" a night.

Lana was a beautiful, blonde-haired, very light-skinned girl, the daughter of German expatriates. After a childhood in Puerto Rico, she had moved to Miami with her parents. One day, when she was thirteen, a group of boys from her school threw her into the back seat of a car and drove with her to a remote garage. All six of them raped her and afterwards, threw her out onto the street. Her father blamed her for "enticing" the boys and kicked her out of the house, despite her mother's protests. She eventually went to work with an older woman

in her fifties, helping her with housework. Lana told Linda she'd been introduced to lesbian sex by her patron.

Finally, strawberry blonde Rita grew up in Brunswick, Georgia, where she had two older brothers. When she was nine years old, her sixteen-year-old brother seduced her and later forced her into having intercourse with her fourteen-year-old brother. Sometimes, the brothers brought in friends from school to seduce Rita, charging them three dollars each. Eventually, she was pimped to older johns until she fled from home, taking the Greyhound bus to Miami, where she went to work for Chuck when he ran a whorehouse.

Linda was shocked at this latter revelation. She'd never known that Chuck had operated a house of prostitution. When she asked him about it, he admitted it. "I had an apartment in North Miami and I usually had three to five girls working for me. But I got arrested and had to shut the place down. I never had to go to jail because I got the right lawyer."

"Chuck, I learn more about you every day," Linda said. "I sleep with you every night, but I don't really know you."

"Oh, if you only knew the half of it," he said.

Linda was delighted when Traynor said that her erotic image evoked **Audrey Hepburn,** depicted in the photos above as a prostitute in *Breakfast at Tiffany's*

***

At the Las Vegas Inn, where rival clubs were being established nearby, customers were demanding sexual displays that were increasingly raw.

Chuck feared he'd lose most of his business. "The girls will have to do a lot more than they are doing now," he told Linda.

The following morning, she heard a loud noise coming from his kitchen. He had always been an early riser and had left her bed that morning at 6am to cook breakfast for himself.

Rising quickly from the bed, she ran to the kitchen. Chuck was lying on the floor, thrashing around and gasping for breath. She assumed he was having a heart attack. "Get a doctor," he gasped.

She immediately called an ambulance.

That afternoon at the hospital, Chuck's doctor, Harve Fernsten, told her, "Your husband is a serious diabetic. He's had a seizure."

She'd never known that Chuck was a diabetic because he'd never mentioned it and because he often drank a lot—a destructive habit which might have contributed to his seizure.

For two days, he remained in the hospital, which gave him time to dream of big plans to increase his bar business and to keep him from going under financially.

He shared his hopes with her: "I'm going to buy some cheap sofas for the rear of the bar, where I have all this empty space. The sofas can surround the little stage we have back there. I may have to hire some extra girls to come in for the midnight shows. I'm going to stage some exhibitions."

"What are you talking about?"

"You'll see for yourself," he said. "We got three rooms in the back, four if we get rid of the shelves in that storage closet. I'm going to put in army cots. Each room will also have a washstand and some towels."

"You think the girls at our house will do shit like that?" Linda asked. "I know I won't."

"We'll see about that," he said ominously. "My guys no longer want to settle for groping pussies, breasts, or plugging assholes with their greased fingers. They want blow-jobs or screws from one of my bitches."

"I doubt if the girls will go for that," she said.

"I'll start with Marilyn and Veronica," he said. "They're the most compliant. I haven't told you this, but they're druggies. I keep them supplied. They'll do my bidding. When my gals aren't putting on a show, they can serve liquor to the patrons."

Linda later admitted that at the time, she didn't really know what Chuck was talking about, but that within two weeks, she'd find out. "It was beyond my wildest fantasy that I would ever become one of Chuck's performers myself."

***

35

One afternoon, Marilyn and Linda went shopping together at a mall in South Miami. Chuck had given Linda $250 to spend on a sexy new wardrobe to wear for her work at the bar. He wanted Marilyn to pick out the garments for her.

Of all the women who lived in Chuck's house, Marilyn was Linda's favorite, but that day, she got into several arguments with her over her choice of outfits. Linda kept protesting, "Oh, I couldn't be seen in that!"

It was about eight o'clock when Marilyn dropped Linda off at Chuck's house before her scheduled shift at his bar in North Miami Beach.

She was surprised to find Chuck in the kitchen talking to a muscular giant of a man who was shirtless and clad in a pair of blue jeans.

"Linda, this is El Toro, or 'The Bull,' as he was known in Havana," Chuck said.

"What's your real name?" she asked.

In accented English, he said, "Juan Garcia. Good to meet you, Linda."

"El Toro is going to be staying in our guest room for a while," Chuck said.

An hour later, over pizza out by the pool, Linda learned a lot more about El Toro. In 1958, when he was only eighteen years old, this Afro-Cubano performer was one of fourteen "Supermen" working as performers in sex shows in Havana.

"What kind of show was that?" she asked.

"All of us men were hired because of the size of our cocks," El Toro explained. "To be a Superman we had to have a foot-long cock with a circumference of at least seven inches. In front of mostly Gringo audiences, we came out and screwed a lineup of girls, sometimes as many as six at a time."

"Some show!" she said.

"But when Castro took over Cuba, he closed down all the sex shows and all the bordellos. I came to Miami and have been working as a bartender in a Cuban bar. But through Chuck, I'll be getting back into show business."

Chuck explained to her that Veronica had already agreed to perform as part of an exhibition with El Toro scheduled for that upcoming Saturday night. "I'm going to pitch the idea to Marilyn too. And I'll have to work on Rita and Lana a bit after that."

top photo: **El Toro**
lower photo: What El Toro did to his sex partners on stage

36

Linda was flabbergasted, yet tantalized in some strange way.

"I don't want to wear El Toro out before the show, but I'm moving Lana and Rita into the living room for a few days. I'm going to let El Toro here sleep with Marilyn and Veronica in the downstairs bedroom, sort of break them in before they have to do it in front of sixty guys."

"This I've got to see," Linda said.

"You're part of the show," he said. "I want you to go around at the end of the show in your sexiest outfit and collect tips from the men. A ten-dollar bill from each of them is suggested. You've been at the bar long enough to see where the men put some of those tips."

"I can't do that," she said.

He grabbed her arm and swung her around. "Listen, bitch, you don't defy me, got that?"

He'd never been that violent with her before, other than an occasional slap. For the first time, she clearly feared him. Years later, she wondered why she didn't escape from his trap that night. She had had to admit that he had some hold over her.

One part of her mind told her to run away, the other part compelling her to stay. Secretly, she longed for the excitement of forbidden pleasures, although she would spend her later years denying that.

That night, even though sleeping upstairs with Chuck, she heard a lot of giggling and even a scream or two coming from the guest room downstairs, where El Toro had retreated with Marilyn and Veronica. By now, Marilyn had already told Chuck she'd be thrilled to perform with El Toro.

The sounds of the Afro-Cubano making love to two of Chuck's girls seemed to goad Chuck into a sexual fury. "He attacked me like a savage," Linda later told Marilyn. "Last night he didn't have any trouble getting an erection."

Over a late breakfast, Chuck, in front of Linda, told both Marilyn and Veronica that each of them should scream when penetrated by El Toro on stage. "It will make the guys watching get more excited."

Linda wondered if Chuck were just speaking for himself.

That afternoon, Linda spent an hour with El Toro out by Chuck's pool He was asleep upstairs, and three of the girls were asleep in the downstairs bedroom. Rita had gone on what she called an "afternoon date" with a john at the Roney Plaza Hotel on Miami Beach.

By the time she'd served El Toro his third *cerveza,* she warned him, "Better not drink too much. I understand you men have trouble getting it hard if you've had too much to drink."

"No problem for me in that department," he said.

She went back into Chuck's house and from his stash, raided two already-rolled marijuana cigarettes.

The two of them enjoyed sitting outside, smoking pot, as El Toro told her fascinating stories of pre-Castro Havana.

He constantly bragged about having known Steve McQueen when he'd first worked at the *Havana Nocturne* Night Club when he was a very young boy.

El Toro shocked her when he told her that McQueen, back in the early 1950s, had been a sex performer at the club. "He was very good looking, blonde and blue-eyed, and all the girls who worked for the madam, Olga Tamayo, wanted to do Steve for free."

He did three shows a night at the Shanghai Theater in the *Barrio Chino*," El Toro said. "That place could hold as many as eight hundred people. There were several acts. It was good that Steve was real young. He had to shoot off at three different shows a night."

"What did he do?" she asked.

"The act opened with a beautiful woman sitting at a café table," El Toro said. "Steve came out dressed as a waiter. She asks him for silverware, which he takes out of his waiter's jacket. She wants salt and pepper, which he also removes from his jacket. Then the bitch asks for coffee. Steve leaves the stage and comes back with a cup of coffee. The puta then asks for sugar. He reaches into his pocket and produces a pack of sugar. She then says to him, 'You forgot the cream.' He unbuttons his pants and takes out his cock, and she goes down on him. At one point, he takes his cock out of her mouth, so the audience will know that he's hard and that he's not faking it. Then he jerks off into her coffee. Then she drinks all of the coffee and the crowd goes wild. The skit was called '*La crema en el cafe de ella (The Cream in Her Coffee).*' It was a big

HOT NIGHTS ON THE PORN CIRCUIT IN HAVANA

Spectators who came to see McQueen as a (then unknown) sex performer included: **Cary Grant** *(upper left photo)*; **Frank Sinatra** *(lower left)*; and FBI Director **J. Edgar Hoover** *(photo above, right)*

photo above:
Steve McQueen

hit."

"Well, McQueen went on to bigger things, didn't he?"

"He's a great guy," El Toro said. "We still keep in touch. Actually, I want to go and work for him in Los Angeles. He'll be on Miami Beach in two weeks. Maybe I'll bring him over to the bar to watch me perform."

"I'd love to meet him."

"I'll do that," he said. "I bet he'd go for you."

At this point, a nude Chuck came out onto the patio. Spotting them together, he said, "Mr. Bull, you'd better get some sleep. It's gonna be a long night tonight."

***

At midnight that Saturday night, as previously announced, the doors to the crowded bar were locked, and Chuck announced that a "private party"—which would cost each patron a "membership fee" of ten dollars—was about to begin. Linda was among those who herded the customers to the rear as they jockeyed for positions on the club's newly installed sofas. For their view of the stage, some of the patrons had to stand in positions behind the sofas.

Wearing spike heels, a pair of scarlet-colored hot pants, and a pink halter top, Linda tended bar. Many patrons slipped dollar bills up the legs of her hot pants or else into her flimsy bra. She didn't like being touched that way, but she was grateful for the money. In the dimly lit bar, she hoped that her scars were not too obvious.

Chuck cut the house lights and pulled back a curtain, exposing a small stage area. The room went black until a spotlight was turned on a few seconds later. It illuminated a double bed in which Marilyn and Veronica laid nude and horizontal, making love to each other. Then men shouted their approval, as they seemed to like watching women performing lesbian love acts.

After five minutes of foreplay, El Toro appeared from the rear, clad only in a Tarzan-style loincloth and carrying a spear.

He looked down at the girls before he ripped off his loincloth. Both Veronica and Marilyn screamed, but made no move to run away.

Several whistles were heard when the audience saw El Toro's genitals. Above a large pair of testicles, he had a penis that was nearly nine inches long when flaccid.

He crawled onto the bed with the girls and began to fondle them. With her blonde, white goddess body, Marilyn contrasted artfully with the dark, heavily muscled body of El Toro. The harsh black hair of his mustache encircled the pink rosettes of her hardening nipples before he bit into them.

A blonde all over, Veronica crouched, her face at the level of El Toro's

39

groin. She took his soft cock between her full lips and moved with her lips up and down, rhythmically. Linda stared in amazement. This was her first introduction to a public display of deep throating.

After working on El Toro for a few minutes, Veronica raised her head, exposing his hard penis to the audience, who gasped at the size of it. She performed like a dynamo, licking his testicles with her tongue before polishing his penis, which she eventually managed to swallow whole, even though it took her a few attempts to get it down. She rose up frequently for air. The audience was mesmerized.

In the meantime, Marilyn had risen up and squatted on El Toro's face. His tongue darted out to explore her blonde, cavernous hole.

When that particular part of the act ended, the room went silent. El Toro positioned the two girls side by side on the bed before plunging into Veronica with no preparation or foreplay. She screamed as Chuck had instructed her. In the darkened room, Linda noticed that many of the patrons had unzipped their pants and were masturbating.

El Toro would spend one minute on top of Veronica, another minute mounting Marilyn. This went on for about ten minutes, the girls screaming and protesting that El Toro was splitting them apart. Their cries of protest only seemed to goad him into swifter action.

He was inside Marilyn when his orgasm approached. During the final thirty seconds before he climaxed, he dismounted, spewing his semen over the nude, supine bodies of both women. As the audience cheered wildly, Chuck drew the stage's curtain shut and switched off the spotlight.

Then Linda turned on the house lights and returned to the bar to fill drink orders. The men were animated, talking of nothing but the show they had just witnessed.

Before the night ended, Chuck reported to her that he'd taken in the most cash of any night since he'd opened the business. Back at Chuck's house, she counted out her own money, realizing that she had accumulated eighty-five dollars in tips, her best night yet.

***

At the Las Vegas Inn, El Toro continued with performances of his show during the coming weeks. After the third night, he finally persuaded Lana and Rita to join the act, which meant he seduced four girls at a time, in full, exhibitionistic view of the leering men in the bar. Linda continued to look on in fascination at the act.

El Toro continued to talk about the impending arrival of Steve McQueen. He still planned to lobby to become his bodyguard, and he promised Linda that he'd invite McQueen to the bar to see one of his midnight shows.

El Toro asserted that McQueen was very anxious to see the show, claiming he hadn't seen entertainment like that since he'd left Havana years ago.

El Toro requested three nights off in the immediate aftermath of McQueen's arrival, as he and his movie star friend wanted to ride motorcycles down the length of the Florida Keys and stay together at a small lodge on Big Pine Key, just north of Key West.

"Before Castro, movie stars flocked to Havana," El Toro said. "Frank Sinatra once attended Steve's show. Cary Grant was in Havana one night, and he had boys sent to his hotel suite. Even the Director of the FBI, J. Edgar Hoover, showed up. But Steve is not like most movie stars. He likes ordinary guys— mechanics, bikers, even poets. His friends don't necessarily have money, and he likes to be treated like everybody else. He doesn't go in so much for hookers, but likes plain, simple gals like you."

"I guess I should take that as a compliment," Linda said.

"He likes to talk endlessly about cars, bikes, or girls," El Toro said. "One of his favorite topics is car injuries. He's got a mania for speed and danger. While he's in Florida, he plans to rent a boat and sail over to Nassau, too. If he likes you, maybe he'll invite you to go with us."

McQueen was hardly her favorite movie star—she was a devoted Clint Eastwood fan—but before his arrival in Florida, she read everything she could about him, ignoring any stories covering his marriage to Neile Adams.

One newspaper report referred to McQueen as "a shy rapist." She'd never heard such a term before. Another magazine article claimed he was "a latter day Bogie with a hint of old-fashioned Jean Gabin." She knew who Bogart was, but she'd never before heard of Jean Gabin.

Rich, famous, and a Cover Boy/Movie Star: **Steve McQueen**

In one article, he said that in his car racing he was "not courting death, but courting being alive."

He sounded like her kind of man, although she knew half the female population of Florida would probably be pursuing him as well.

At least the arrival of McQueen gave her something to dream about. As regards her affair with Chuck, she later admitted, "the sex was bad. He screwed me about once a month, maybe once every six weeks. When I lived with him, my closest

41

companion was a vibrator."

Chuck wanted to be included in any activities that involved McQueen, but El Toro said he couldn't be a member of the party. Instead of flying into a jealous rage, Chuck seemed unexpectedly resigned to it. "He wanted any connection with a famous star," Linda said. "At least he'd have bragging rights, telling his friends that he was pimping his gal out to Steve McQueen."

Chuck had hoped that Linda would ingratiate herself with McQueen, but she feared that as part of the process, she might make Chuck jealous. She had been instructed to be very clear with McQueen about Chuck's ability to supply an almost constant stream of women to him—"redheads, blondes, brunettes, whatever…even bald ones if he got off on that."

El Toro arranged the logistics with both Linda and Chuck on the night of McQueen's scheduled arrival at the Las Vegas Inn. Linda was to lock the door to the bar and meet McQueen in the parking lot. El Toro informed her that McQueen would arrive in one of his customized cars, a 1967 Porsche 9112S.

She was to stand in the parking lot and usher him into the bar only after the room had gone dark. Then, just before the curtain descended and before the lights went back on, she was going to escape with him in the Porsche.

The plan called for El Toro to hook up with them later in a villa Steve had rented on Key Biscayne.

On the day she was to meet McQueen, Linda experienced such excitement it was difficult for her to contain it.

By nightfall, she was almost shaking. Her fear matched her excitement. The show had been live for two minutes before a Porsche pulled into the parking lot.

The young man stepping out of the car didn't look like the Steve McQueen she'd seen in the movies. He wore a plain red shirt, khaki pants, a light jacket, sunglasses, and had on a cap that looked like those worn by Nazi soldiers during World War II. Also, he had a beard.

Wearing a tight-fitting blouse, a wide-brimmed straw hat, and a mini-skirt, she walked over to his car, as he slid out from behind the wheel.

"Hi ya, gorgeous," he said. "You must be Linda."

"And you're Steve McQueen," she said, "or should I say 'Redbeard?'"

"I am, or else I've got on the wrong underwear."

CHAPTER TWO
SEX—Hot and for Sale

Steve McQueen marked a crossroads in the life of Linda Lovelace. He was the first male movie star who seduced her. He would not be the last.

Chuck Traynor was always telling her how dumb she was, so she was very tongue-tied around McQueen. It didn't seem to matter. He was far more interested smoking pot, generously sharing his joints with her. When he finished one, he lit another.

He also offered her a drink, which she refused, and then said, "We've got to wait for El Toro. Good show, tonight, don't you think?"

"It's amazing," she said. "I've never seen anything like him."

"At first when I met him, I had a case of penis envy, but I got over it," he said. "What's the point of envying other men? I've been compared unfavorably to Marlon Brando, the late James Dean, and Paul Newman."

"I think you're better than all those guys," she said.

"You're such an adorable liar." He looked her up and down carefully. "You look like a girl I used to date. I liked her very much until I found out she was really a whore."

"I'm sorry it didn't work out for you," she said.

"I should have been more forgiving of her," he said. "After all, when I was a teenage boy, I was a whore myself."

She giggled nervously. "You're putting me on. Let's face it: There's no way a man can be a whore. They're not built the right way for that."

"You've got a lot to learn," he said. "I like that. Around Hollywood, I just meet girls who have fucked and sucked off a thousand guys—and I'm being kind."

While waiting for El Toro, it became obvious that McQueen was an inveterate pot smoker. Dressed in faded jeans with a hole revealing his right knee, he tossed his jacket aside. He seemed to have an endless supply of Old Milwaukee beer he'd stashed in the car with him.

There was something about him that frightened her, as he seemed like a time bomb that might go off at any minute. One moment, he seemed to ooze boyish, blue-eyed charm, but he was quick to flash anger, exposing a certain menace in his face, as when he heard the incessant ringing of his phone. He even denounced the décor of his rented villa, referring to it as "Jewish Renaissance."

At times, he looked at her, as if wondering why she was in his villa. "I've got only two physical lusts," he told her. "Sex and competitive racing, but I'm not sure in which order they come."

Back from the kitchen with another beer, he ripped off his shirt, revealing a taut physique. He went over to a wall which seemed to be filled with electronic equipment. He manipulated some buttons before the music of the Beatles came on. "They're my favorite," he said. "I knew all the Beatles, mostly John and Ringo. One night in London, John begged me to let him suck my cock. Even though I'm crazy about their music, I'm actually tone deaf. What's your taste in music?"

"Elvis, Elvis, and more Elvis," she said. She kept turning down offers of beer, but whenever he lit up a joint, she shared it with him.

"You probably know stuff about me," he said. "At least the bullshit they publish about me. But I'm really not sure who you are."

"A girl in search of myself," she said. "I live with this guy, Chuck Traynor. He defines me every day, telling me what I'm going to do. I'm not very independent. I hope that's not a turn-off for you."

"Not at all," he said. "I don't like cocky, bossy women. In fact, my attitude

Two views of **Steve McQueen** from around 1965
(right photo): Kissing **Natalie Wood**.
Linda: "I used to imagine I was her."

44

toward women has been called 'as tight as a hog's ass in fly season.'"

She laughed at that. "Chuck believes that women were put on this earth to serve men."

"He sounds like my kind of guy," McQueen said. "They say that during my fuck-flings, I treat women badly. Do you believe that about me?"

"I don't at all," she said. "Since we hooked up together, you've been very nice to me."

"I love anything on wheels and with tits," he said. "I drive a car fast and perhaps in the heat of passion with a chick, I get carried away. I don't like a woman running my life. When I go to bed with a chick, I don't want to be tricked into getting her pregnant. I always use a condom." He smiled at her. Actually, it was more of a smirk. "Some chick claimed I even have a condom over my heart."

"Maybe someday you'll meet the right girl," she said.

"Maybe I already have," he said. "I have this theory. A man can meet Miss Right several times in his life. I'm always changing. My needs in 1970 might not need fulfilling in 1980, or even in 1974. I smoke too much, drink too much, race cars too much, and fuck too much. But I have a secret for bouncing back in the morning."

"Please share it with me."

"It's all in my breakfast drink," he said. "I make breakfast in a blender. Here are my secret ingredients, but don't tell anyone. Take yesterday's stale coffee and blend it with eight fresh eggs and a pint of yogurt that has mold on the top."

"That sounds awful," she said.

"If you're still here in the morning, I'll make breakfast for you," he promised. "You'll love the drink. It will give you energy all day."

Suddenly, he stood up. In front of her, he unbuttoned his jeans, stepping out of them after he'd removed his shoes. He kept on a pair of white jockey shorts with yellow piss stains on their front. He looked down at her."Why don't you take off some of your clothes?"

"I think I will," she said. "It's a little stuffy in here in spite of the air conditioning. But I've got to warn you. I was in a car accident. I have this big scar."

"Hey, that's great!" he said. "I don't mean about the accident. But I like a chick who's been scarred by life. Of course, I'm not as kinky as my late friend, Jimmy Dean. He actually preferred one-legged women with stumps!"

Somewhat reluctantly, she removed her light clothing, retaining her bra and panties.

He studied her scar with a certain fascination. "Do you mind if I run my fingers over it?"

Although she was embarrassed, she agreed. Very carefully, he traced the line of her scar along her body. "I became fascinated by looking at scars in the locker rooms of America when I showered with my fellow racers. Sometimes, they'd misinterpret my intentions when I wanted to take my finger and trace the scars on their bodies. It's not a come-on. I much prefer feeling a woman's scars, but a lot of women, unlike men, don't have scars, especially big ones like you do. I want to know everything about how you crashed your car. Don't leave out any detail. I'm not faint of heart."

In vivid detail, she related the story of her car accident in New York State, with all its blood and gore. He slipped off his jockey shorts and started to masturbate. When she'd more or less finished her story, he reached over and unfastened her bra. "Suck me off until El Toro gets here. I noticed you don't have the biggest tits in the world. Well, I don't have the biggest dick, so that sorta evens things out."

Placing his hand on the back of her neck, he lowered her head over his crotch. She began to suck on him, and he seemed to be enjoying it, moaning and urging her on.

After five minutes of that, she heard a car arriving in the driveway. El Toro came into the living room and caught her performing fellatio on McQueen. He took no special notice of them. "I'll join you guys in a minute," he said. "I've got to take a leak and get myself a beer."

"El Toro used to be a great buddy of mine," McQueen told her. "I want you to take care of him tonight."

Her body tensed. "I'm not one of those whores from the Las Vegas Inn. Any one of them could handle a tree trunk up there. But I haven't had a lot of experience."

"Don't worry about it," he said. "We'll go easy on you."

For the first time that evening, her body tensed. She was afraid of what was coming up. El Toro emerged from the kitchen totally nude, his penis dangling halfway down his leg.

All three of them sat on the sofa, smoking pot. McQueen and El Toro did most of the talking, mainly about Havana. She slowly began to relax.

Shortly before 1:30am, McQueen stood up and reached for Linda's hand. "Let's all go to the bedroom," he said.

"Great idea, man," El Toro said. "I'll get some more beer."

McQueen led her into the

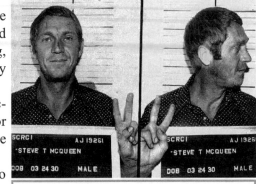

Steve McQueen, bad boy and iconic hero, after his 1972 arrest in Anchorage, Alaska

bedroom. Gently easing her onto the bed, he pulled down her panties, and she rose up to make it easier for him. He lay down beside her and began to kiss her gently at first, increasing the pressure and finally inserting his tongue. At that point, El Toro entered the bedroom. He placed his beer on the dresser. Fully erect, he was an awesome sight. She was frightened.

"I've got this little hangup," McQueen said to her in a low voice. "I like my buddy, or buddies as the case may be, to go first. I'm that rare guy who gets off on sloppy seconds."

She started to protest, but within the minute El Toro was on her other side, fondling her body and squeezing her breasts. She went from one man's mouth to the other.

Although he'd treated her politely at the club, El Toro was growing increasingly aggressive when aroused. McQueen stared intently as he watched the Cuban move his heavy body on top of hers. He placed the massive head of his penis against her vagina and attempted to penetrate her. "Relax, bitch," he said. "I thought you whores could take anything."

"I'm not a whore," she protested.

"Well, you will be before this night is over," he said. "Take the salami!" With that, he threw all his weight onto her frail body, ignoring her screams. Deeper and deeper he plunged. She felt she was giving birth to a baby. Mercifully, she blacked out.

When she regained consciousness, she felt sore. McQueen was on top of her. If anything, his penetration felt soothing after that attack from El Toro.

She wrapped her arms around McQueen and kissed him. She knew she could fall in love with him and regretted it was going to be only a one-night stand.

After he'd climaxed and threw his used condom on the floor, he fell asleep in her arms. She lay awake for about an hour, listening to the sound of his heavy breathing.

At around 4AM, he woke up and pulled himself out of bed. "Listen," he said, looking down at her. "Put your clothes back on, I'll call a taxi to take you home. It should cost no more than twenty dollars."

After using the bathroom, she followed him into the living room to rescue the rest of her outfit. He reached into the pocket of his jeans and removed his wallet. It looked stuffed with bills. He took out a twenty.

Fully dressed, she stood before him, her feelings crushed at the way she was being dismissed. "I guess I won't get to sample that yogurt and egg drink for breakfast."

"You got that right," he said. "I've got these two hot bitches arriving here at ten o'clock, and I've got to get some more sleep. You can't imagine how many demands are made on this dick of mine."

"Well, thank you for the cab fare," she said. "I didn't have any money on me."

"She headed toward the door, and he opened it for her. "Why don't you wait outside until the cab comes. It won't be long."

"Thank you, Mr. McQueen," she said politely. "It was great meeting you. I'll look forward to seeing your next picture."

"Yeah," he said. "It was great." As she stood on the stoop, he closed his front door and flipped on the porch light.

She was tearing up as the taxi pulled into the driveway fifteen minutes later. The evening hadn't lived up to her fantasy.

***

At Chuck's house, she walked up the sidewalk to the door with great trepidation. She found him wandering around in his underwear in the kitchen. He glared at her with hostility. "Okay," he said. "How much?"

"What do you mean?"

"What do you mean, what do I mean?" he asked. "How much did the big time movie star lay on you? At least five-hundred dollars, I bet."

"He was cheap," she said. "He just gave me twenty dollars for cab fare."

"You're a fucking liar!" he said, moving toward her as she backed away. Then he reached out and slapped her so hard she fell on the floor. "Don't hold out on me."

She screamed, "It's the truth."

His foot stomped on her belly, taking her breath away. "El Toro moved out tonight. He's going to work for McQueen. I've lost my big attraction."

She tried to rise from the floor, but he kicked her back down. "You're gonna pay for this. Tonight I'm going to have you on the bill, and you're going to do every god damn thing I tell you to."

"I'm not a sex performer," she said, as she lay whimpering on the floor.

"You're going to become one." He looked down at her and spat on her. "Or else I'll kill you."

***

At the Las Vegas Inn at midnight, patrons were disappointed that the star attraction, El Toro, would no longer be performing, but Chuck promised his most faithful barflies that they could an-

Beer, tequila, and a chaser

ticipate a hot show that night anyway. Linda still had not been told what she was to do.

At midnight, from the outside, the bar looked like it had closed for the night, although the dozens of cars crammed into its parking lot would surely have alerted the police that there was some kind of illegal activity inside. Obviously, Chuck was paying off the police.

Inside the bar, the jukebox in the corner could be heard, but not at high volume. About thirty men had remained for the show Chuck had promised. He'd already collected their ten-dollar "cover charges."

Linda was brought backstage by Chuck and told to take off all her clothes. She protested, but he slapped her face and demanded that she remove her clothes. Terrified that she'd be asked to perform, she continued insisting, "I'm no dancer."

After the audience was comfortably seated, at midnight, the show began.

From behind the curtain Linda had a clear view of Veronica, on stage and illuminated with a spotlight. She gyrated for about ten minutes, masturbating herself and fondling her ample breasts. At the end of her act, she walked around the stage as men stuffed dollar bills into her vagina. When no more money could be stuffed inside her, she removed the bills and made room for more contributions. As she told the laughing, jeering men, "I'm not opposed to a few gratuities around here."

Rita followed with an equivalent act. She was more sensual than Veronica, and was obviously more of a crowd pleaser, getting more dollar bills stuffed into her vagina.

Backstage, Linda turned to Chuck. "I won't do that. It's disgusting."

"You'll do it, bitch," he warned her under his breath, "or *not* live to regret it."

The third act, Marilyn, had the largest breasts of any of the performers. Her routine was slightly different. She descended from the stage onto the concrete floor and moved from man to man, allowing them to fondle or even lick her breasts. It appeared that several of the men had removed their penises and were masturbating as she made her rounds. Backstage, Marilyn encountered Linda and told her that some ten and twenty-dollar bills had been included with the singles stuffed into her vagina.

Linda sensed that Chuck had to have some sort of grand finale that went beyond merely the erotic dancing featured so far during the course of that evening.

For Lana's set, Chuck himself took the stage. "This next act calls for volunteers." The spotlight then focused on a plywood partition into which five holes had been sawed out, each positioned at the level of a man's crotch, and each big enough for him to comfortably insert his genitals but conceal his face and the rest of his body from the audience. "I'm sure you men have used glory holes before when you haven't had a woman nearby! You've been drunk and horny, and maybe from time to time you've considered sticking your dick into one of these for some queer to suck you dry!" Some of the men cheered and applauded.

"Well, tonight, I want five volunteers to stick it through the glory hole." He motioned for Rita to come out onto the stage. She was stark naked. Lasciviously, her lips parted and her tongue darted out.

Chuck continued his role as a circus barker. "So take your positions, gentlemen, behind the magic screen, where your identity will be protected and where the lips of 'luscious Rita' will bring you pleasures you cannot imagine."

Then the spotlight was switched off as Chuck maneuvered five volunteers into position behind the plywood screen.

When the stage was illuminated again, five penises and five scrotums had been inserted, for a full view by the audience, into the five glory holes. Linda was shocked yet transfixed. One by one, Rita moved from one penis to another, none of which appeared very appetizing to Linda.

Rita fellated each of the bar patrons to climax, each eruption of which was met with either cheers or catcalls from the audience. At the end of the act, as

New ways, onstage, to make dessert memorable

each man adjusted his pants, Rita moved through the room, collecting her tips.

"You're next," Chuck told Linda.

"But what do you want me to do?" she asked.

"I've got a cot on stage," he said. "All you have to do is go and lie down on that bed."

"I'm not going to be gang-raped," she exclaimed. "I'll scream. I'll run out the door."

"Listen, bitch, no one is going to have sex with you," he said. "Just lie down on that bed."

When the lights went off, Chuck led her onto the stage and, in the darkness, placed her on the cot. He carried a paper bag with him. He reached inside it for one of the cans.

When the spotlight came on, he was holding a can of whipped cream. "Tonight, gentlemen, we're presenting Linda from the bar. She has eagerly agreed to be your dessert for the evening. Come on up, men, and help yourself."

After that introduction, he turned to her as she lay supine on the cot, took one of the cans of whipped cream and discharged its contents across her body. It was cold, and she shivered. "Come on

50

up, men, and help yourself."

She shut her eyes, conjuring what she imagined would happen next.

Then, virtually every man in the bar lined up for the feast. It seemed that every part of her body, including her toes, got licked. Whenever an area of her body became too bare, Chuck sprayed it with fresh cream. Before the night ended, he'd gone through three cans of it.

Backstage, Linda told Marilyn, "I've never been so degraded in my life. Technically, I wasn't raped. But I was raped."

"Oh, honey, if that is the worst shit you'll ever face, you're one lucky gal. You can't imagine what johns will demand of you."

"But I'm not a whore!" Linda protested.

"And Richard Nixon is not president of the United States. Honey, if you don't like the vibes here, you can make thirty-five dollars a week standing on your feet all day, working as a sales gal at Woolworth's."

"But Chuck has threatened to kill me if I leave him," she said.

"In that case, you'd better stick around and get used to being 'the Whipped Cream Girl of North Miami Beach,'" Marilyn said. "The guys really went for that dessert tonight. I'll probably have to star in that act myself one day. What are you going to do now?"

"Chuck is taking me back to the house," Linda said. "I'm going to scrub myself raw. I feel like every nasty man's tongue along the Beach has tasted me tonight."

"Maybe they didn't want you at all," Marilyn said. "Maybe they just love whipped cream."

In one of her memoirs, Linda, in spite of her protestations, wrote that "all those gourmet tongues" found her body most satisfying.

***

In the autumn of 1969, South Florida had been warned about the approach of a tropical storm for three days. Finally, it struck Greater Miami, seriously damaging the flimsy roof of the Las Vegas Inn and soaking the bar inside. Fortunately, Chuck had already bought insurance against that eventuality. In all, he was to collect $15,000 in damages.

During the period that the bar was closed for repairs, he announced to Linda that they were going to fly to Banner Elk in the Blue Ridge Mountains of western North Carolina for a vacation. During his time in the Marine Corps, he'd befriended Sam Phillips, who lived in North Wilkesboro, west of Winston-Salem. He'd offered Chuck and Linda the use of a mountain cabin, where he could do some fishing, and she could amuse herself as best she could.

From Miami, they flew together to Winston-Salem, where he rented a car and headed west. He stopped over in North Wilkesboro, where he bought her a sixty-five cent lunch at Jimmy's Grill, which was run by a Greek. After their meal, he walked with her up the street to the Liberty Theater, a seedy movie house that had enjoyed its heyday in the 1930s and during World War II.

In his theater, Chuck's friend, Phillips, was featuring a personal appearance of "whip-tossing Lash La Rue," along with two of his most popular films, *Law of the Lash* and *Return of the Lash,* both of which had been released in 1947.

As a girl, Linda had seen some of Lash's movies featured at Saturday matinees during her childhood. When she'd first seen him, she thought he was Humphrey Bogart appearing in a western. But, as it turned out, La Rue only looked like Bogie, without that star's talent.

During the late 1950s, with the decline in popularity of westerns such as La Rue made, the "King of the Bullwhip" earned his living appearing at carnivals and in movie theaters in remote American towns, including such obscure backwaters as North Wilkesboro.

Since the decline of his career, she'd read about him in the papers, including an account of a 1956 arrest in Memphis for receiving stolen property and a 1958 scandal when he overdosed on sleeping pills in a suicide attempt. In 1964, all his whips, guns, saddles, western outfits, and movie memorabilia had been stolen. His last arrest had occurred in Tampa, where he was discovered with only thirty-five cents in his pocket, on a charge of vagrancy.

Inside the Liberty Theater, Linda was introduced to its manager. Phillips stood 6 feet, 4 inches, and looked like he weighed at least three hundred pounds, maybe a lot more. Even so, he exuded a powerful masculinity with his muscles, gruff voice, and swagger.

He turned to Linda. "So, Chuck, this is your latest nude dancer. We're not allowed to book acts like that in Wilkes County, except at private smokers."

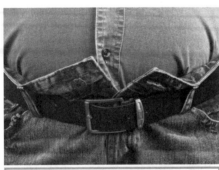

Linda had heard that in the case of Sam Phillips, it was what lay below the belt that mattered.

She said nothing, as Chuck whispered something in Phillips ear. "Why don't you two stay in town and have supper at my apartment? I'm shacked up with this yaller gal who's a good cook, if you like corn bread, turnip greens, and ribs. Lash will be sharing the cabin with you guys. His show is at eight o'clock. Why don't you hang out here and drive up the mountain with him tonight after his act. He's a bit destitute these days, and doesn't have a car."

"A big movie star like him broke?" Linda asked.

"I know," Phillips said. "He's gone through about twelve wives. That's a lot of alimony. Hell, Lash La Rue comic books sold at least twelve million copies. The money is all gone. Alimony to every bitch in the country is ball breaking."

"Sure, we'll stay over and drive Lash up the mountain," Chuck said.

"He's in my apartment right now," Phillips said. "I live over the theater. Lash has been staying with me. I'm giving him only a hundred dollars for each personal appearance. Tonight is his last."

Phillips came over to Linda and took her by the arm. "How about a little kiss, girlie?"

She jerked her arm from him. "No thank you."

Phillips turned to Chuck with a smirk. "It looks like we've got to break in this filly."

"Give him what he wants, bitch!" Chuck said to her with such fury that she was afraid he'd attack her. She held up her face to Phillips. As she'd later recall, "He didn't want a kiss. He sucked my face."

As she was leaving his office, Phillips called after Chuck. "Maybe Linda will dance for us sometime during your vacation. Not on my stage, of course, but in private, for me."

She hurried out the door and up the steps leading to the owner's apartment.

La Rue would be the second movie star she was to meet.

Unlike Steve McQueen, La Rue was a genuine American cowboy icon, once worshipped by thousands of young boys throughout the country. As she approached the door to Phillips' apartment, with Chuck trailing her, she heard the sound of a guitar.

***

Referred to as "Bogie with a whip," **Alfred (Lash) La Rue** was not a westerner at all, having grown up on the streets of Chicago. He enjoyed popularity at Saturday matinees across the country from 1947 to 1956. Later, he became a born-again evangelist in Florida, "whipping" drunks and derelicts into shape for the Lord.

In his jockey shorts, Lash La Rue sat in an armchair in the living room playing the guitar. After introductions, Chuck said, "I didn't know you were one of those singing cowboys like Gene Autry."

"I'm not, at least not in the movies," La Rue said. "Whenever I go back to my native New Orleans, I join in jam sessions at the Dew Drop Inn. The blacks there really dig my music."

Chuck extended an invitation for La Rue to appear at his bar in North Miami Beach. "We'll call it 'Lash La Rue Night.' You can play the guitar and we'll show one of your movies."

"I think I'll take you up on that offer," he said. "I've got copies of *King of the Bullwhip* from 1950 and *Black Lash* from 1952. I can also do tricks with my bullwhip."

Over a greasy Southern dinner cooked by Phillips' "yaller gal," Chuck forced Linda to agree to appear on the stage with La Rue as part of his 8pm show that night. She was to stand perfectly still, holding an unopened Coca Cola bottle near her face. With his bullwhip, La Rue would then pop the top off the green glass bottle with his 18-foot-long bullwhip.

"I've brought down a lot of bad guys with that whip during my heyday."

La Rue was only a shadow of his former self and looked much older than his fifty years. Linda felt rather sorry for him when the former "Cheyenne Kid" confessed, "After I got kicked out of Hollywood, I went low, mighty low, and I've been trying to find a solution in liquor. But, so far, 'Bogie with a Bull-whip,' as they call me, sees no solution to my troubles."

During the time they planned to briefly live together in Banner Elk, Chuck made it clear that Linda might offer the fading cowboy star some comfort. "I just assumed she was your girl," La Rue said.

"She is, but I believe in sharing when I come across a great guy like you, a big time movie star," Chuck said.

"Not so big time," La Rue said. "But I've been offered a star part in a new western called *Hard on the Trail*. It may mean a comeback for me."

"We wish you all the luck," Linda said.

That night at the jam-packed theater, Linda became very nervous on stage when she was forced to hold up that coke bottle. She just hoped La Rue hadn't become rusty in his whip-tossing skills. A miss of only a few inches might take a chunk out of her face, sending it flying as a bloody mass into the air.

As the moment approached, Linda found herself shaking. From the wings, Chuck hissed at her, "For god's sake, stand still."

Forcing herself to remain stationary, she heard a loud crack of the bull-whip. La Rue had uncapped the bottle, the carbonated drink fizzing over its top. "Drink the damn thing," Chuck yelled at her, although his voice was almost drowned out by the loud applause.

That night marked her first debut in front of a mixed audience, mostly families with young boys in tow. She bowed and exited as the curtain was drawn. Backstage, La Rue grabbed her and kissed her. She nearly swooned as the cowboy, dressed entirely in black, held her tightly. "You did great, kid."

She looked over at Chuck, who seemed to beam with pride that another movie star wanted his woman.

A few hours later, Chuck, La Rue, and Linda were drinking and smoking pot in a log cabin on the outskirts of Banner Elk. Both La Rue and Chuck stripped down to their jockey shorts, and Chuck removed all of Linda's clothing except for her bra and panties.

As the evening wore on, and as Chuck seemed to relish directing and controlling the party, she knew what was coming. And despite his deteriorating physical condition, the fading cowboy star was still attractive to her.

Chuck finally ushered La Rue and Linda into the cabin's master bedroom. His invitation was "Let's take off our clothes and get comfortable. It's your call." As he said that, he looked over at La Rue.

"I prefer to take a woman dog style," he said, "although only one of my dozen or so wives really liked it that way."

As if directing a porn movie, Chuck lay down on his back on the bed, motioning for Linda to fellate him. As she did, La Rue entered her vagina from the rear.

A skilled seducer, the cowboy had obviously had a lot of women in his day, and not just from among his coven of wives.

Japanese depiction of a "snake geisha" with a contortionist throat, from the Edo period (1650-1868).

As she was fellating Chuck, Linda gagged several times, especially when he tried to forcibly invade the back of her throat with his penis. She still found the taste and smell off-putting.

After about ten minutes, Chuck finally climaxed in her mouth, forcing her to swallow his semen. She choked, which displeased him immensely.

On the other hand, La Rue seemingly enjoyed his intimacies with Linda, and even complimented her before he wandered nude out the door and into the spare bedroom, where he fell into a drunken sleep.

Linda's soon-to-be-world-famous throat was broken in at something akin to this innocent-looking cabin in North Carolina's Blue Ridge Mountains.

La Rue rose early to go fishing with Phillips. Linda and Chuck remained behind, and he spoke harshly to her over their late breakfast. "You're a fucking lousy cocksucker, and I'm thinking of dumping you if you don't improve your technique.'

"I can't help it if I gag," she protested.

"I think I can do something about this," he told her. "You look like a bitch who might be very susceptible to post-hypnotic suggestion."

"Just what are you talking about?" she asked.

"When I was a pilot in Honduras, I met this ninety-year-old crone, a native woman, who taught me the ancient secrets of hypnotism. Not only that, but when I was in the service in Japan, I met this geisha girl who could take almost anything down her throat. I want to take what I've learned and break you in. If I don't, a man might poke his dick down your throat and fuck up your larynx or whatever."

Intrigued, she allowed him to hypnotize her, wanting to believe that it might work.

He insisted that she had to trust him completely, and she promised that she would. As he guided her through the paces of what he knew about hypnotism, she entered into a hypnotic trance.

When she came out of it, he predicted that in the future she'd be able to open her throat muscles to any male organ presented to her.

He began by inserting two fingers into her throat. To her amazement, she was able to tolerate that without her usual gag reflex.

"Don't ever try to swallow with a large object in your throat," he told her. "Open up your throat and learn to allow a man's dick to go to as deep a level as you can. Once your muscles are opened and relaxed, length is no longer a problem."

Since La Rue wasn't due back until dinner, Chuck spent the entire day coaching her into relaxing her throat. Once it was penetrated, he instructed her to back off at occasional intervals as a means of controlling her breathing before plunging down deep on the man once again.

She even discovered the best position for deep throating. She lay down on her back on their bed, with her head dangling over the edge of the mattress. Chuck knelt on the floor

After his brush with Hollywood stardom, and during his stint as a born-again evangelist, **Lash La Rue** was arrested after attempting to trade his Bible to two teenage boys in exchange for some marijuana.

beside her and inserted his penis. To her surprise, he went deeper and deeper, soon reaching the very back of her throat. For the first time, the head of his cock passed beyond the barrier of her restricting throat muscles.

She continued fellating him, opening her throat completely to him. Her newly discovered expertise brought him to orgasm. When he exploded down the back of her throat, she didn't even taste his semen.

Rising from the bed, she was pleased with her accomplishment. For the first time ever, he complimented her on her sexual performance instead of complaining about it.

"We'll have to work on this every day until it becomes second nature to you," he said.

When Phillips dropped La Rue off at the cabin that afternoon, Linda stayed in her room. She didn't like the way the movie theater owner looked at her. As the men were drinking, Chuck must have told about putting her under a hypnotic spell which opened her throat to his penetration. Through her closed door, she heard the frequent sound of laughter.

Later, the "yaller gal" came over to cook dinner, and Phillips had to go back to his theater. About an hour after he'd gone, Chuck came into the room. "Lash is all stripped down and ready for you in the next room," he said. "I told him all about your lessons in deep throating. He wants you to practice on him."

She agreed to do that. Before, she might have put up some kind of protest. But now, she felt under some kind of spell, as if her own ability to make decisions had been taken from her.

When she knocked on La Rue's bedroom door, he told her to enter. In the light of a bedside lamp, he lay fully nude on top of his quilt, fondling himself into a semi-erection. "I want you to do what I hear you do so well," he said.

In spite of his descent into middle age, his body was in reasonably good shape. Without a kiss or foreplay, he guided her head to his groin. Within a minute, she had his penis erect to anywhere from six to six and a half inches. Unlike with Chuck, she could easily swallow him whole. He moaned as he seemed to express the pent-up needs of deprived sexuality. Thanks to her newly relaxed muscles, he was hardly a challenge for her. His stomach heaved and relaxed, then heaved again, writhing with pleasure.

She loved the feeling of his cock gliding in and out of her mouth. She was giving him pleasure, but also taking pleasure in what she was doing.

She now had La Rue writhing in delirious anticipation of his oncoming orgasm. Up and down she went on his penis, as her fingers toyed with his testicles. Then he erupted into her mouth, load after load. She tasted it. Instead of her former revulsion, she found his semen had a sweet, honey flavor. She worked on him until the last drop, and he virtually had to force her head off him.

For a long time, she lay in position, kissing, feeling, rubbing, touching, and enjoying his groin.

"That was good," he said. "Real good. I'll be hanging out here for three more days. I want you to take care of me every day."

"Your wish, my command," she said.

She spent so much time with La Rue during his final days in the cabin that Chuck became jealous. He wanted to demand about five hundred dollars from La Rue, but Phillips told Chuck that he'd had to give La Rue money to get to the location where *Hard on the Trail* was to be filmed.

Before he left, La Rue summoned Linda into his bedroom and kissed her goodbye. The kiss was long and passionate, and she felt it would be so easy to fall for him.

"If I had some money, like in the old days, I'd ask you to run off with me and leave Chuck behind," he said. "I don't like the way he treats you." On hearing that, she clung to him.

Her own vacation with Chuck came to an end a few days later. His bar in North Miami Beach was scheduled to re-open, and it was urgent that he return.

Before flying back to Florida, Chuck and Linda stopped off at the Liberty Theater to return the key to the cabin. Phillips was thanked profusely, and Chuck volunteered to return the hospitality when Phillips planned a visit to Miami in a few months. He and Florida-based friends of his wanted to rent a boat and go fishing in The Keys.

Phillips came over to Linda for one of his sloppy kisses. "Me and you, gal, didn't get to hook up on this trip. I guess Lash kept you very busy. But in Miami, we'll make up for lost time." Then he issued a warning that she didn't fully understand at the time. "Get a lot of practice before I come down," he said. "You'll need it."

Years later, in her memoirs, Linda claimed that she became "one of the supreme cocksuckers of all time. What I may lack in beauty, I make up for in ways men never forget. Deep throating became my doctorate study in sex."

When Linda viewed Chuck Traynor's gun collection, she asked him if he was planning to commit a murder.

He was facing serious jail time after retrieving bundles of marijuana dropped onto a field near Homestead, Florida, from a small airplane originating in Bimini, in The Bahamas.

Caught red-handed, Chuck invented an unlikely defense and, with his lawyer, convinced a Florida judge and jury that it was true.

***

Back in Florida, the outlook appeared gloomy. Rita, Veronica, Lana, and Marilyn had moved out of Chuck's house with no forwarding address. Obviously, during the bar's temporary closure, they'd gone on to better jobs.

With Linda's help, Chuck reopened the bar. Opening night drew only five customers, who didn't remain for very long. Far more alluring strip clubs with plusher surroundings and more exotic acts were only a short drive away. "Zorita" and her snake act was a current fad at one competing club.

"The money's running out," Chuck warned her. "I've got to get back into prostitution. You could be the madam."

"That's not for me," Linda said. "I couldn't do a job like that."

"You'll do it all right and learn to love it," he said to her, jerking her arm. "The deal is, you do what I say."

The next morning, he ordered her to clean up the rooms downstairs, which had been so recently vacated by their four showgirls. While cleaning out a dresser, she discovered two marriage licenses. Chuck had told her that he'd never been married, but obviously he had. She wondered if she was this Bluebeard's third wife—or maybe his tenth for all she knew. She decided not to confront him with this evidence, fearing a beating for snooping into his private affairs.

In that same dresser, she also discovered that her husband had a police record. He'd once been jailed for eight months on a serious assault-and-battery charge. In a brutal dispute within his former apartment, he'd beaten one young woman nearly to death over some alleged offense never made clear. She shuddered with the fear that something like that might happen to her.

Even more serious, she learned that he was facing current charges for smuggling marijuana into South Florida. That case was still pending.

From what she read hidden in that drawer, Chuck had picked up 400 pounds of marijuana in a vacant field. The bundles of pot were wrapped around containers of cocaine, speed, LSD, and hash and had been dropped from an airplane originating on the island of Bimini in The Bahamas. The drop landed about eight miles from Homestead, which had been Chuck's hometown. Through some distant relative, he still had access to a house there, where he was to have stored the stash for later dispersal to drug dealers.

Chuck and another man, Bryan Bedford, had been arrested with the haul, but a third accomplice had gotten away. In an article that appeared in *The Miami Herald,* the third man was referred to as "Mister X."

Their financial situation grew tighter as Chuck struggled to find some money-making scheme. His Jaguar disappeared, and was replaced by a broken

59

down old Volkswagen.

His days of taking her to fancy restaurants on Miami Beach were over. He found an old Holiday Inn that advertised a lavish buffet for $2.95, and most evenings, he drove her there for dinner. He told her to eat all she could hold because he would no longer be treating her to breakfast and lunch.

When she'd cleaned his rooms downstairs, she climbed the stairs. She found him in the living room playing with his guns, which included a .45 caliber Walther pistol. He had a semi-automatic machine gun and an eight-shot automatic, both of which he claimed had once belonged to a policeman friend of his.

"Are you planning on committing mass murder?" she asked.

"Shut up, bitch," he yelled at her. "I'm going back into selling whores to guys, and when you're in the prostitution business, you need to be armed. Me and you will go on living upstairs, but the rooms down below will be occupied from time to time."

He ordered her to go into the bathroom and take off all her clothes. "I'll be in in a minute," he said.

"You want to take a shower with me?" she asked.

"That will come later," he said, getting up from his chair. "I went to the drugstore today and bought some stuff. Tonight, I'm going to shave your pussy."

Although at first she resisted, Linda became a sex performer at Chuck Traynor's Las Vegas Inn on North Miami Beach.

To her surprise, the straight patrons liked to watch women engaging in lesbian sex. "It was a turn-on for them—and also for me—although my reputation was never that of a card-carrying lezzie."

***

Over the course of three nights in a row, Chuck had left Linda at home alone. He threatened her with violence if she even walked out the front door. On the fourth night, he brought home a woman named Barbara, introducing her as "Babs." Linda suspected that Babs (or Barbara) was not her real name. As she got to know her, she learned that her real name was Sheilah Dunne.

Born into a family of eight in Columbia, South Carolina, she had been reared in poverty. Her father had worked as a farmhand, but when Linda turned eight years old, he died in a tractor accident.

"When bad news rains, it pours," she said. "Within a few months, my mama found out she was eaten up with cancer. She soon died. My older brothers left home, but the younger ones, like myself, were sent off to orphanages."

At the orphanage, she was repeatedly raped by an attendant. He charged some of the male members of the orphanage staff five dollars each to have sex with her.

She remained at the orphanage until she was about thirteen. Then her pimp concocted a plan wherein he would remove her from the orphanage without alerting other members of the staff.

Late one night, he slipped her into his old Ford. He drove all night until he reached Atlanta, where he moved her into a $35-a-month apartment infested with cockroaches.

"The bastard rented me out and lived off my earnings until I was fifteen," she told Linda. "One night when he was drunk, I emptied all the cash out of his wallet, took the Greyhound bus to Miami, and earned a living picking up tricks in Bayfront Park."

As Chuck's plans for Babs and Linda became more obvious, he wanted them to perform "girl-on-girl action" for the customers at his bar. "Men really like to watch all this lezzie stuff," he told Linda.

Once again, he hypnotized Linda, telling her during the deepest period of her trance that when she woke up, she would have an overwhelming desire to have sex with Babs.

Influenced by the posthypnotic suggestion, Linda admitted in a memoir that she was sexually attracted to Babs. "We took each other's clothes off, played with each other's boobs, and compared pussies.

Lash La Rue Does Porno!

Adults xxx only

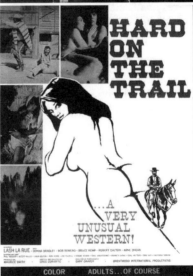

HARD ON THE TRAIL

...A VERY UNUSUAL WESTERN!

COLOR   ADULTS...OF COURSE

Lash La Rue, the Lonesome Cowboy, was shocked at the "premiere" of his latest film, *Hard on the Trail*.

During its filming, its director had made it clear that La Rue would be portrayed as a villain. What he didn't tell him was that his footage was later reconfigured into an X-rated movie. Fully clothed and unsuspecting, the former matinee idol discovered that his "legit scenes" had been interspersed with porno loops, including the depiction of an orgy.

Horrified, he faced unwanted headlines: FORMER COWBOY STAR DOES PORNO.

61

Mine was shaved, and hers was like a bush of red copper. I took the game very seriously, but, to be honest, I don't think I was hypnotized at all."

To beef up his sagging bar business, Chuck staged an ongoing series of what he called "Lezzie acts" at his inn. "Barbara ate me and it was the greatest," Linda wrote in her confessions, "but I was really looking forward to my trip on her."

That night, Linda was designated by a collective vote from the bar patrons as the winner in a "cunnilingus competition," picking up one-hundred dollars worth of prize money which was immediately relinquished to Chuck. As Linda recorded in her memoirs, "I discovered for sure that I dug pretty girls."

For five nights in a row, Chuck staged encore performances of the "pussy-eating contest," featuring girl-on-girl acts between Linda and Barbara on the stage of the Las Vegas Inn. For each of the first four nights, the patrons—with prizes awarded based on the intensity of their applause—defined Linda as the winner. Then Chuck intervened and instructed Linda to hold back and let Barbara win on the following night.

The winner of each night's contest, in theory at least, received a prize of one-hundred dollars. But whereas Chuck kept all four of Linda's hundred-dollar prizes, he split even with Barbara. "I made off with fifty bucks," Barbara told Linda.

"That's fifty more than I got," Linda complained.

Late one night after the show, Lash La Rue walked into the Las Vegas Inn. Most of the patrons had already gone home for the night. Lash immediately

The bisexual aviator, Howard Hughes, also operated as a film producer, directing the heavily censored 1940s movie, *The Outlaw,* starring big-busted Jane Russell. What the public didn't know at the time was that Hughes also produced porno films, privately, and for his own amusement.

In the mid-1940s, when **Guy Madison** (*above,left*) and **Marilyn Monroe** (*right*) were each impoverished actors struggling to break into movies, they agreed to co-starring roles in one of Hughes' private X-rated films.

In the late 1960s, brief (pirated) scenes from this film were screened at the Las Vegas Inn on North Miami Beach. But a precedent was set, at least for Linda, about how a performance or two in porn could be configured as a successful entree into show-biz.

spotted Chuck and went over to shake his hand. "I've decided to take you up on your offer."

After Linda greeted the cowboy star with a kiss, and introduced him to Barbara, Chuck invited him to come and stay with him since he had no money and no place to live.

As Chuck and La Rue talked for a good part of the night, Linda stayed with them, although Barbara eventually drifted off to bed.

Before the evening broke up, Chuck had come up with an idea. "Since you sing and guitar pick better than Roy Rogers or Gene Autry, let's stage a 'Lash La Rue Week' at the Vegas Inn After your guitar playing, we'll run your latest film. You've still got a lot of fans who remember you from all those westerns. My favorite was when you played all those different roles in that TV show, *Judge Roy Bean,* back in the 50s."

La Rue went for the idea. "In the film I just made, I'm no longer the good guy, but the villain. I've got a copy of the film with me, and you can show it. I haven't seen the whole thing myself. I didn't have a projector."

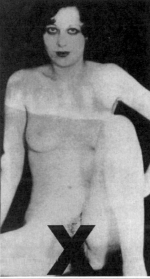

An hour later, Chuck agreed that it was bedtime, inviting La Rue to join Barbara in the bedroom downstairs.

"If you don't mind, I'd like to visit with you and Linda, doing what we did up in the mountains."

Linda was thrilled that he'd chosen her over Barbara. "Come on, kid," La Rue said to Linda. "As you remember, I like it doggie style." He motioned to Chuck. "Come and join us. It'll be more fun."

To lure patrons into the Las Vegas Inn, Linda and Chuck Traynor screened rented versions of porno loops featuring performances by then-struggling actors who later became stars.

The most notorious of these featured X-rated performances derived from **Joan Crawford**, who falsely denied in her memoirs that she ever appeared in any blue movie.

Here, Miss Crawford is seen in all her pornographic glory in *The Casting Couch* (circa 1924).

On stage the following night, La Rue "played hell out of his guitar" [Chuck's words]. The star was a success with the bar's patrons, especially when he sang such Western favorites as "Back in the Saddle

Again" and "Don't Fence Me In."

After La Rue's gig, Chuck announced that patrons should stick around for the world premiere of La Rue's latest movie, *Hard on the Trail,* which had not yet been released.

As soon as the movie began, Linda sensed that La Rue was upset. Without his being aware of it, the director, Greg Corarito, had provisionally changed the title to the more suggestive *Hard Trail.* In it, La Rue played a villainous outlaw named Slade, who was always dressed in La Rue's trademark color, black.

Although La Rue was fully clothed during each of his scenes, a series of pornographic orgy scenes had been inserted into the context of the film, including a torrid bath scene between the director, Corarito, and the female star, Julie Conners, cast as a farm girl named Sue. Before the end of the film, La Rue stormed out of the bar.

Later, at Chuck's house, Linda found him deep into the process of getting very drunk. "I'm ruined," he said. "The last fans I have will lose all respect for me. I'm completely disgraced. I'm going to pray to God every night to forgive me for my sins."

"Honey," Linda said. "Those weren't your sins up there on the screen."

When Chuck arrived back home, La Rue told him he couldn't let him show *Hard Trail* anymore. Chuck became "seriously pissed off" at Lash, but he always gave in to movie stars and agreed to a policy of not screening the film again.

In those days, the acquisition of porn films was difficult for fans and aficionados. The sex scenes in *Hard Trail* had been so enthusiastically received by the bar patrons that the next morning, Chuck drove with Linda to a retail outlet in South Miami Beach. Osten-

Before Linda ever saw *Rocky,* starring **Sylvester Stallone**, she witnessed his naked charms in a porno flick, *Italian Stallion,* in which he starred during his lean-and-hungry days before he rose to stardom.

After he became famous, she tried in vain to contact him in Hollywood to offer the services of her throat, but failed to ever reach him by either phone or letter.

sibly, it was what was known as a "dirty book store." In one of its back rooms, porno films could be rented.

The owner, Clarke E. Clark, from Clearwater, Florida, referred to his inventory as "stag films." Fraternity men from the campus of the nearby University of Miami rented them for private viewings and parties.

Although he never explained to Linda how he knew Clark, the dealer invited Linda and Chuck into the back room. She tagged along, although Chuck warned her "to keep your god damn mouth shut."

"I got some hot stuff that will pull the suckers in," Clark told Chuck. "It's not your typical stag film—some hooker getting screwed by some guy still wearing his black socks. These films feature movie stars before they became famous. I've got the porno films Joan Crawford made in the 1920s. A loop with Marilyn Monroe and Guy Madison, shot around 1946. A hot homosexual loop with Chuck Connors."

Before the afternoon ended, Chuck had rented the entire batch.

Whereas La Rue still agreed to sing onstage with his guitar, the film loops that would be shown in tandem with his act featured young movie stars.

The film that showcased the pornographic allure of the then-unknown Chuck Connors featured the six-foot, five-inch movie star sodominzing a young man with what looked like a ten-inch weapon. "That guy in the film is one lucky bottom," Barbara remarked when she saw it.

During her flapper era, Joan Crawford had starred in blue (i.e., pornographic) movies whose titles included *What the Butler Saw, The Plumber, The Casting Couch, Coming Home,* and *She Shows Him How.* In a loop entitled *Bosom Buddies,* Crawford appears in a topless lesbian romp, which was also featured in the bar's film selection.

In a brief loop, which was obviously not a complete film, a pornographic clip was shown of Marilyn Monroe and that heartthrob of the 1940s, Guy Madison. Because of Monroe's posthumous fame, she got the loudest applause.

Another of the films Chuck eventually screened in his bar included a "celebrity porno" film which featured an actor, Sylvester Stallone, who eventually evolved into a major star. He had studied drama at the University of Miami. During his lean days, he was one of the main attractions in a porno movie later entitled *The Italian Stallion.*

When he became famous as the star of *Rocky,* blackmailers tried to extort money from him, but he refused to pay them off. Therefore, beginning around 1970, *The Italian Stallion* was promoted as a porno venue starring Sly Stallone (aka Rocky Balboa) and marketed around the world.

Years later, after Linda became a star herself because of the fame and notoriety of *Deep Throat,* she made several attempts to get in touch with Stallone, hoping for a rendezvous. But her calls were never returned, her letters never answered.

On the way home in his Volkswagen, Chuck looked upset. "By the end of the week, the guys will have tired of Lash. I'll have to ask him to move on. They will even have tired of the Monroe clip and Crawford as well. And the loop with Connors is more for the gay crowd."

"What are you going to do for an encore?" she asked. "Go back to Clark and ask for a new batch of films. You can't promise celebrity-based porn forever. The supply will eventually run out."

"I know that," he said. And after a long silence, he continued. "I'm going to produce my own stag films," he told her as he pulled into his driveway. "And you're going to be a star. I've even come up with a new name for you. Boreman is too close to boring. From now on, you're gonna be known as Linda Lovelace."

[Later, linda would contradict her mentor, asserting that she started using the moniker "Lovelace" much later in her career.]

***

At long last, Chuck got around to confessing to Linda that he was facing a jail term for receiving 400 pounds of marijuana dropped off by a private plane originating in Bimini. She did not let him know that she was already aware of his involvement in the affair because of documents and letters she'd discovered in his house.

He planned to consult with three attorneys, hoping for the best deal. When he'd lived in the Homestead area, he'd grown up with Billy Campbell, a lawyer who handled a lot of drug-smuggling cases. Chuck invited Linda to go with him to the attorney's office to keep an appointment he'd made the day before.

Campbell's office was in a clapboard-sided structure that had already survived devastating hurricanes. During World War II it had been used as a recruiting station for the Homestead Air Force base. Campbell and Traynor had once played football together, but Campbell had not aged well, having gone bald. He was also quite flabby.

He looked Linda up and down. "Chuck, I see you're still in the same business."

She was insulted. The lawyer obviously considered her a prostitute.

Up until that day in Campbell's office in Homestead, Linda had never been introduced to the legal system. In time, she would encounter a lifetime of trouble with the law.

Her session with Campbell taught her a lot. It was obvious that Chuck was guilty, so all the attention focused on how he could beat the rap.

It was Chuck who came up with a plausible fantasy narrative, at least one that Campbell thought might be believable.

Chuck claimed that he and his friends were organizing a sky-diving club in South Dade County, and that they were scouring the barren fields around Homestead to find an unpopulated target area where members might safely parachute down from an airplane.

"In other words, you were not on site to pick up a bale of pot, but checking out a suitable drop zone," Campbell said. "That's not the worst excuse I've ever heard. It beats the defense in my last case. A 37-year-old man, a former boxer in Miami, was caught raping his fourteen-year-old cousin. He claimed in court that she was actually raping him, forcing him to have sex with her in spite of his protests."

"To make my story believable," Chuck said, "I'll round up three or four guys who will testify that they were charter members of the sky-diving club. They'll say that because I was the one with the pilot's license, I had to scout out the landing site for their next jump."

"That's great," Campbell said, "but what about getting caught with those tons of marijuana?"

"I can testify that while we were scouting for a suitable jump site, we spotted a private plane as it dropped the pot. Because kids play in that area. I decided, as a community service, that the best thing would involve me retrieving the pot and hauling it to the authorities. Better that than letting some stupid teenagers discover it."

"That's bullshit, of course," Campbell said. "But it's so looney that some court might believe it."

Campbell looked Linda over one final time. "So is this your latest *puta*? Let's face it: There's no point in arguing taste. Before you go into court, you'd better marry it. My clients always look better with sympathetic wives crying crocodile tears behind them."

Linda claimed that she "just knew" that the question of Campbell's fee would come up. The two men agreed, without consulting her, that Campbell would be paid from Linda's $40,000 insurance settlement, which was due to arrive in a few weeks, derived from her car accident on the Taconic Parkway.

"As a result of that confab in Homestead, I ended up paying for Chuck's legal defense, which completely wiped out the nest egg I'd been dreaming about. That nest egg had meant freedom for me."

In the days ahead, Chuck rounded up three friendly witnesses, promising two of them that they'd be invited to "wild sexual adventures beyond your imagination" in exchange for their testimony. One of them, Bob Phillips, was a fireman who agreed to testify about the sky-diving club. Ironically, this was the same Bob Phillips who later had a small role in *Deep Throat.*

Before the trial, Campbell placed an urgent call to Chuck, telling him "Your

Linda gal knows too much, and the district attorney has the power to haul her in to testify against you. Before the trial, you've got to marry her—and that's that!"

***

In bed that night, Chuck announced to Linda that they'd be heading out the following morning at 4am for the Georgia border.

"I don't want to go to Georgia," she protested.

"Like I give a rat's fart about what you want," he said. "We're going to Georgia. I've got friends up there who can arrange things. We're getting married, bitch."

"Forget that! Ever since I was a little girl, I've dreamed of getting married to a loving husband. A rose-covered cottage, family, children."

"Dreams are made to be dreamed, so what? Pack your bag for an early morning departure." He moved menacingly toward her, grabbing her by the throat and squeezing so hard she choked. "Don't you ever say no to me. Never ever again. Got that, you fucking whore?"

Releasing her throat from his grip, he began slapping her as she gasped for air. His blows were so hard she fell onto the floor, where he began to kick her. As she'd relate in a memoir, "This time I had the feeling that he wasn't going to stop in time, that he was going to go all the way and kill me."

Battered and bruised, she set out along U.S. 1 leading north to Georgia in the pre-dawn hours. At one point, she asked if they could stop for breakfast, and he told her he had only twenty dollars in his pocket.

"How in hell are we supposed to get to Georgia and get married on twenty dollars?" she asked.

"I've got it handled," he assured her. "When dawn comes, I'll put my money-making scheme to work."

With the arrival of the morning's bright Florida sunshine, he ordered her to take off her blouse and expose her breasts. At first she refused, at least until he belted her.

His scheme soon became evident to her. He would drive alongside a large truck. The driver could look down from his position in his cab for a clear view of Linda's breasts. Chuck would then pull ahead of the truck if he felt he'd encountered an interested client. He'd activate his right-turn signal as they approached either a truck stop or a rest area.

Once he pulled off at the exit, Chuck was almost certain that the trucker would follow. An experienced pimp, Chuck rented out Linda for blow-jobs within the driver's cab of the truck, asking twenty dollars, but often settling for ten.

Before they reached the Florida/Georgia state line, she'd performed fellatio on five different truckers. Sometimes, she gave two truckers a blow-job in the same van.

Before nightfall came, she learned Chuck's scheme for getting free gasoline. He cased the stations carefully before pulling in. Earlier in the day, he'd ordered her to remove her panties. As they pulled up to the pump, he'd instructed her to yank up her dress so that her unshaven vagina would be exposed to the attendant.

Before stopping at the gas station, Chuck would insert "Red Hots," small pill-sized cinnamon candies, into her vagina to make her squirm.

In every case but one, he negotiated a deal whereby Linda would give the attendant a blow-job in the gas station's toilet in exchange for free gas. The one attendant who turned them down was denounced by Chuck as "a queer."

Because darkness was setting in, he pulled into a seedy roadside motel that displayed a sign advertising rooms for six dollars a night. At that price, she didn't expect much. In what she would later describe as "the ugliest motel room in my life, a mixture of oranges and browns," she spent an awful night. For dinner, he ordered an anchovy pizza sent to their room, knowing how much she detested "those hairy little fishes."

He told her that even though she'd mastered the art of deep throating, he had to continue with her sex education. He said that in the future, a lot of men would request analingus.

"What in hell is that?" she asked.

"I can see I'll need to hypnotize you again to break you into the joys of analingus. Some men I know prefer to perform it only on pre-teen boys, but other men will only want to perform it on you, and they'll expect you to reciprocate."

"I don't know what the hell you're

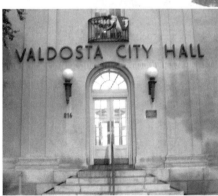

Linda's unromantic wedding
(How to "underwhelm" a bride)

69

talking about," she said. "I assume you're talking about screwing me in the ass. That ain't gonna happen, big guy."

"That's a lesson for another day," he said, before beginning the process of hypnotizing her again. When she came out of her trance, both of them were lying nude on a bed with creaky springs. He ordered her to stick a darting tongue into his asshole. She later claimed that analingus was one of the most "disgusting" sexual acts she was ever required to perform.

But like a willing pupil, and perhaps influenced by the power of his post-hypnotic suggestion, she attacked his anus with her tongue. Never before had she seen him driven so wild by a sexual act. During the days and weeks ahead, she began to think she'd discovered his "hot spot."

A few weeks after her marriage to Chuck, she suggested to him that he might like to hire some young man to insert more than his tongue into his asshole. For that remark, he belted her in the face, seriously bloodying her nose.

**

In the years to come, Linda claimed she could not even remember the date of her marriage, although it must have occurred around mid-September of 1969. "I didn't plan to be celebrating any anniversaries with Chuck," she said.

He drove into the town of Valdosta in southwest Georgia. Before heading for the Valdosta City Hall, he stopped into a novelty store and bought her a "puzzle ring" crafted from twelve pieces of plastic, each a different shape and color. Although she couldn't remember the date of her wedding, she recalled the price of the ring: $2.12.

At City Hall, an attendant ushered them into an ominous looking, high-ceilinged room where in previous years black men and boys had been sentenced to death on charges of murder, but not white men and boys.

The Justice of the Peace was a dead ringer for the reactionary senator from North Carolina, Jesse Helms. The Justice "obviously regarded me and Chuck as white trash," Linda later recalled.

Chuck had some contact in City Hall who had arranged the paperwork, which included the issuance of a marriage license. The ceremony itself took just a few minutes, and not once did the Justice of the Peace look either of them in the eye. The highlight of the ceremony, if it could be called that, was when Chuck dropped the plastic wedding ring. It separated into a dozen crooked pieces. The justice himself tried to reassemble it, but the puzzle ring proved too baffling for him. Linda rescued it, hurriedly reassembling it before Chuck slipped it on her finger. Then they made a hasty getaway from the courthouse.

"What about your friend?" she asked. "The one who made all the arrangements, including getting us the license."

"Would you shut your big trap?" he said. "I promised him a hundred dollars for his trouble, but I'm skipping out. C'mon. We have to drive back to Florida."

Linda later recalled her honeymoon night at that same seedy $6-a-night motel where she'd been indoctrinated into the techniques of analingus. Before their wedding supper, Chuck placed a call to his redneck mother in North Carolina.

After informing her of the marriage, he put Linda on the phone to speak to her new mother-in-law.

"Bless your heart, honey," the older woman said. "I know that my son will make you a wonderful, loving husband, and you two will have a big family. I want lots of grandchildren."

"I was very lucky," Linda told her mother-in-law, "to marry a fine man like Chuck. He was regarded as a real catch and all the girls were after him."

"Well, you won him, sugar, and I want you to take good care of my boy and mind him, you hear?"

"I hear," Linda said. "I'll always honor and obey him."

"I want you all to come and see us," the mother-in-law said.

"As soon as we can, we'll be up in those hills."

Linda didn't tell Chuck's mother than en route to Banner Elk in North Carolina, Chuck had driven within thirty miles of her home and had not stopped in to see her.

Linda declined Chuck's suggestion that she call her own mother. She did think that night about her son, Billy Boreman, and wondered if she should try to reclaim him now that she was married.

She rejected the idea, fearing that if he had easy access to him, Chuck would feature the boy in child porn. All he seemed to talk about were the pornographic loops he planned to film after his return to Miami.

Their dinner that night consisted of two greasy cheeseburgers at a diner near their motel. The short order cook wore an apron that looked like it had been fresh and clean in 1940. Throughout the time he fried their burgers, he kept scratching himself as if he had crabs.

She wanted a slice of apple pie for dessert, but Chuck refused her, claiming, "What in hell are you trying to do? Get fat?"

During future revelations about her marriage, she had almost nothing to say about her wedding night in that seedy motel dive. "He wanted me to do unspeakable things to him…and I did."

***

Once he'd crossed the state line and re-entered Florida during their long drive back to Miami, he told her that he'd sold his bar, the Las Vegas Inn. "It was losing money, and I owed back taxes. I didn't sell it, exactly. I practically gave it away. But I'm picking up the money today from Billy Campbell's office and signing some papers. By next week, I'll be launched as a film producer, although I'm also going to have to relaunch my old business."

"You mean prostitution?" she asked.

"Call it whatever you like. I refer to myself as 'a businessman who provides pleasure.'"

Before the trial, Chuck needed extra cash immediately. He was under a lot of pressure, and he was about to lose his house because he was so far behind in its mortgage payments. Now that he no longer had access to his bar, he needed the house as a centerpiece for his prostitution ring.

Chuck had a distant relative who operated a construction company in southern Dade County. After driving south from Miami to see him, Chuck was offered a three-week job installing sheetrock.

"He took the work, but feared that I might escape from his clutches if left at his house all day by myself," Linda said. "But Chuck always had a solution for everything."

The construction boss operated out of a shabby, wood-framed bunkhouse. About half of it was devoted to office space with telephones, filing cabinets, and desks. The other part consisted of some open shower stalls and, in yet another room, an Army style cot and some bunk beds.

Chuck's boss agreed to keep Linda confined to these barracks during the day while he worked. He promised to pick her up at five o'clock. But the boss was given Chuck's permission, at any time during the day, to have sex with Linda.

He also suggested that some fellow members of his construction gang might also want to take her into the back room, too.

Locker Room Linda *(top photo)*
Working as a sex groupie on a Florida construction site

After looking Linda over, the boss agreed to the proposition, and even gave

Chuck a raise of fifty extra dollars per week.

"My so-called honeymoon was spent as a sex slave doing the bidding of any guy who walked into the room," Linda later claimed. "For the first three days, the boss couldn't get enough of me. I don't think his wife had put out in months. During the time Chuck worked for this creep, I had to submit to at least ten guys, two of them black. They came to me stark naked, still drying themselves off from the showers in the next room."

She also said that no one harmed her, referring to them as regular guys—"no kinky stuff. They just wanted a blow job in some cases, or else sex in the missionary position."

One young man she really liked, and she wished she could have run away with him. "He told me his name was Hank. The other guys were married, but Hank wasn't. He had just turned nineteen."

She later remembered calling him "The Cowboy," because he wore cowboy boots with a wide leather belt, a plaid Pendleton shirt, and a red-and-black bandanna he'd tied into a knot around his neck. Originally from Oklahoma, Hank was very appealing to her. Unlike the other construction workers, he stood about five feet, eight inches tall. "He was a skinny guy, but very strong."

When he came in to have sex with her, he kept his bath towel tightly wrapped around his lean body. He seemed very reluctant to drop it. "There were other guys who wanted me that afternoon, and I knew that with Hank, I had to be the aggressor."

She pulled the towel from him. At first, he reached to cover his exposed genitals. She later described his body as that of an immature boy. He had tight muscles under smooth, hairless skin, but his penis was rather small. "I felt he didn't really want to come in to see me, but had more or less been goaded to do so because of the older men," she said.

Since she liked him best of all, she moved in on the young man, feeling his body and fondling his genitals. Soon, he produced an erection which she fellated. "I don't know if he'd ever seduced a girl before me," she said, "but he shot off within three minutes. He seemed to love it, and something about him made me want to see him again. He was so different from Chuck. I asked him to come back tomorrow, but I never saw him again. When he left, he was so embarrassed that it touched me in some sort of way. Those other guys on the crew didn't miss whatever chance they had with me."

After his first week working with the construction crew, Chuck drove her to a nearby Holiday Inn, the establishment which featured the $2.95 buffet he frequently ordered for her. She was very hungry that night, having had no breakfast or lunch. But instead of taking her into the restaurant for dinner, he told her to follow him to the rear of the property, where they climbed steps to the building's second floor. At the green-painted entrance to room 509, he knocked on the door, but received no answer. Then she noticed someone part the draperies of the window that opened onto the motel's balconied walkway. In a few moments, the door was opened. A man whispered something to Chuck, who turned to Linda and instructed her to wait outside. Chuck went inside the room, and was gone for about five minutes. When he returned, he was putting some bills into his wallet.

"Okay, it's safe to go in now," he said.

Inside, the room was relatively dark, as the Venetian blinds were closed and the draperies drawn. It was sparsely furnished with only twin beds separated by a nightstand on which a small lamp was illuminated. There was only one chair in the room, and it was placed in front of a writing desk on which a number of briefcases rested.

To her astonishment, there were five men in the bedroom. She estimated their ages as anywhere from thirty-five to sixty-five. Each of them was dressed in a business suit, each with a white shirt and necktie.

"Hi, guys, this is Linda," Chuck said. "She's a nymphomaniac. Never can get enough."

She had never been presented in such a way, and she felt her face burning in embarrassment.

None of the men spoke to her, but each of them was looking at her so intently she felt she was being undressed. Finally, an older man, who was overweight, began to loosen his tie.

When Chuck pulled up at a Holiday Inn, Linda thought he'd be treating her to the $2.95 all-you-can-eat buffet.

There, she confronted a feast that included a lot more than food.

In her memoir, *Ordeal*, Linda gave a rather detailed description of what she claimed was her initiation into prostitution. Actually, it wasn't her initiation. Her trip to Georgia to get married had been filled with instances of prostitution. Even before she encountered these five men at a Holiday Inn, she was already engaged in prostitution at the construction site where Chuck worked.

In the motel room, Chuck took her by the wrist and led her to the bathroom, where he shut the door. "Here's the deal: You're going to let every guy in that room fuck you in any hole they so desire."

"Like hell I am!"

He slapped her so hard she almost fell down on the tile floor. "I've already collected the money from these guys, and you're going to deliver. I told you I was re-launching myself into the prostitution business."

"In other words, you've become a pimp," she said.

"Cut the shit and strip off all your clothes."

"I'm not going to do it," she said, defiantly.

Then he slapped her again, really hard. "Get out of those clothes. I've got a gun and you know I'm mean enough to use it."

"Those guys in the other room are witnesses who'd send you to the electric chair," she said.

"So you think. What do they care about a nickel-and-dime hooker like you? They're married men with reputations to protect back in their hometowns."

Finally, after looking into his eyes, she came to believe that he would really kill her. Very reluctantly, she removed all of her clothes, including her bra and panties. She later claimed she'd never felt as vulnerable before.

"Here's your choice: Fuck those guys or end up one dead chick," he warned.

She was trembling and tearing up. When he saw that, he slapped her again. "These boys don't want to fuck some crying little waif unless she's a 13-year-old virgin. Wipe your eyes, bitch."

She later claimed that when he walked through the door into the bedroom, "It was the turning point in my life." In later years, she made the claim that if she had this moment in her life to live over again, "I would have taken the bullet."

In the bedroom, two of the men, each completely naked, were lying on each of the two twin beds. The other three had each stripped down to his underwear. In *Ordeal,* she described one of the men as a bank president, another as his chief executive, and the final trio as the owners of small businesses. But actu-

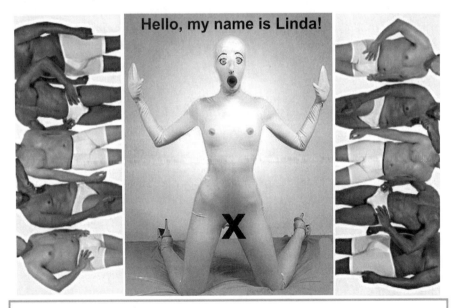

Hello, my name is Linda!

"They treated me like an inflatable plastic doll, picking me up and moving me here and there."

75

ally, she had no way of knowing what their professions were, other than assumptions she made based on their suits, neckties, and demeanors. Chances are that all of them were salesmen from out of town, perhaps attending a conference that week in Miami. How Chuck made his contact with them is not known.

A middle-aged man in his forties with a reasonably good body summoned her over to his bed and started playing with her breasts. "You've got us a young one, and that's what I like," he called out to Chuck. "If I want an old lady, I've got one at home." He took her hand and placed it on his penis. "Jerk me hard," he ordered her. After a minute or so of this, he pulled her down onto the bed. "Kiss it, bitch, and put some feeling into it."

Then an older guy in his sixties complained to Chuck loudly enough for Linda to hear. "You promised us a hot-to-trot nymph. This battle-scarred gal looks like she's not into it."

Showing off her new techniques, Linda fellated the man on the bed. Obviously, she impressed all but the oldest of the men in the room with her expertise.

After the man on the bed had had enough of her tongue and throat, he pulled her up on top of him and entered her vagina with no preparation. She yelled out, but that seemed to excite him. She'd later claim, "A man always feels he's more of a man if he's causing a woman pain as she struggles to accommodate him."

Then another man, stripped to his underwear, came toward her. Having seen her bobbing up and down above the man below her, he was drawn to her buttocks. From a standing position, he laid himself down on top of her, turning her into the middle section of a sandwich. Then she felt him fingering her anus. "No," she said, rising up from the man below her. "I've never had it that way before."

She heard the men in the room laugh in disbelief.

He greased his finger to insert inside her. It hurt and she unsuccessfully struggled to get away. Then he laid his body's full weight on her, and, as he did, penetrated her rectally. She screamed in pain.

"I fuck rough, kid," he whispered in her ear. Searing, wracking, splitting pain ricocheted through her backside as his hard prick probed deeper. "Don't fight it," he whispered to her. "It'll just hurt more if you do."

"Please stop!" she pleaded.

"Are you kidding?" he said. "I've paid for this, baby. Now tell me about how this ass-splitting dong is tearing into you."

It was five, maybe ten minutes later—she wasn't sure—of hell.

Her greatest relief came when both men, after their respective explosions—pulled out of her ass and mouth and headed off to the bathroom.

When she looked up through blurred vision from her supine position on one of the beds, she realized that she was still surrounded by the other three naked men.

As she'd later write, "They treated me like an inflatable plastic doll, picking me up and moving me here and there. They spread my legs this way and that, shoving their things at me and into me. They were playing musical chairs with parts of my body. I had never felt so frightened, disgraced, and humiliated in my life. I felt like garbage."

Finally, when each of the men seemed to have exhausted themselves, Chuck stood over her, contemptuously. "What a fucking mess you are. Get your ass into that shower."

She scrubbed herself until she almost bled. Try as she might, she felt she couldn't wash the "dirt and filth off myself." When she came back into the bedroom, the men were gone.

Chuck had collected $180, having charged each of the men $40. But because the older man had complained that Linda didn't show enough enthusiasm, Chuck had refunded him twenty dollars.

When she was fully dressed, Chuck grabbed her and twisted her arm. "Before I rent you out again, I've got to break you into anal sex. Some men get their jollies through the rear door, and you've got a lot to learn. Now I'll feed you, although you don't deserve me spending my hard-earned bucks on you, bitch."

***

To operate as a fully functioning prostitute, according to the Gospel of Chuck Traynor, a hooker has to be able to be entered through either the front or the rear. While waiting for his upcoming trial, he concentrated on Linda's anus, which, before the Holiday Inn orgy, she'd referred to as "no man's land." Before her rape in the motel, she'd known only a rare enema syringe back there.

Once again, Chuck used hypnotism. She underwent a series of sessions with him until, after and perhaps because of post-hypnotic suggestion, she became convinced that sodomy was something pleasurable.

He entered her a few times, but most of her training came through the use of tubular vibrators coated with K-Y. The vibrators allowed her to relax her anal muscles. As the days passed, he used increasingly large vibrators on her until she began to accept objects ten to twelve inches in length, without pain, but only with a slight discomfort.

[In the months ahead, she claimed that she developed such pleasure in being sodomized that she could have "bombastic orgasms," with no clitorial stimulation whatsoever. In *Deep Throat,* of course, the plot revolved around her having a clitoris in her throat. Of course, that was fantasy. With hyperbole, she wrote, "I developed a clit of its own in my ass." By 1973, when she published her first memoir, she made an astounding claim: "I can entertain the world's

77

largest cock in my ass and it doesn't hurt a bit.]

Chuck warned her that "vaginal control would be the next lesson learned." In the meantime, her deep-throating techniques had improved until she could "take a pair of average-sized cocks in my mouth and do justice to both," as she confessed in her 1973 memoir, *Inside Linda Lovelace.*

Eventually, she became so adept at satisfying two men at the same time that she pursued a side business that involved couplings between homosexuals and straight men. Chuck developed a lucrative business when he discovered that many young gay men at the University of Miami maintained crushes on straight men with little chance of ever maneuvering them into bed.

However, some gay men learned that they could lure the object of their affection into "erect penis contact" by having both of them simultaneously insert their dicks into the mouth and throat of Linda Lovelace. Of course, the homosexual man would have preferred bringing his love object to climax himself, but settled instead for using Linda as a kind of surrogate.

Linda later reported that some homosexual men told her that they were eventually able to lure straight men into receiving blow-jobs from them directly by first turning them on to the oral pleasure that she provided.

***

Linda dreaded the visit of Sam Phillips, the heavyset owner of that movie house in North Carolina, who descended on them during his winter vacation.

During their first dinner together, Chuck had bragged so profusely about Linda's newly acquired sexual techniques that Phillips hired her as the "party favor," with the understanding that she'd be sailing aboard a yacht he had rented in Miami for a trip to the Florida Keys.

Chuck, too, was invited along, and there was some talk on board about filming some porno "loops" of Linda engaged in various sex acts.

In preparation for her boat trip, Chuck bought three new outfits for her. For her initial meeting with their fellow passengers, he dressed her in a pair of scarlet-colored hot pants, a sunflower yellow top, and a pair of red stiletto high heels.

"If I'm going to be a whore, I might as well look the part," she said.

"Shut up!" he yelled at her. "We've got bills to pay, and you need to earn your keep. We're not running a charity here for wayward girls."

On board, Chuck disappeared below deck after shaking the hands of the five fishermen introduced to him by the boat's sixth passenger, Sam Phillips. Standing alone before them, Linda was overcome with an acute sense of embarrassment. "I felt like a piece of meat being evaluated." Presumably, each of the men had wives somewhere. Only first names were given—Larry (the handsomest and youngest of the men), Bob, Steve, Wayne, and Rick.

Phillips took her below, where he installed her in the yacht's master bedroom, which she was to occupy with him jointly. She was also introduced to a teenaged boy identified only as "Juan," who was in charge of cleaning and cooking for the men. Phillips had not hired a captain, as each of the men on board was said to be a skilled boatman.

Later, she stood on deck watching the skyline of Miami fade into the distance as she sailed south in the bright sunshine to Key Largo.

During the rest of the day, she was not molested by any of the men. Actually, no one paid any attention to her. They were intent on drinking and fishing. Larry seemed the nicest of the passengers, and he sometimes smiled at her, but said nothing.

Chuck kept busy during the day working with some equipment in the dining galley. She looked in on him and saw that he was checking a movie camera. She knew that at some time during the trip, he would announce that it was "showtime," as she later recalled. She dreaded what she'd have to do on film.

Whenever Phillips passed near her, he pinched her buttocks and called her "girlie," a term she hated.

The men did catch some fish on their first day out, and Juan cleaned filets for their lunch, which he prepared on deck over an open grill.

Larry sat next to her as she was eating her lunch. Standing ten feet away, Chuck glared at them.

"It's nice of Chuck to lend us his wife for this trip," Larry said to her. "I'm so jealous of my wife that I would go crazy out of my mind to imagine her with another man. Yet to show what a hypocrite I am, I sometimes go out with other women, especially when I fly to New York for conferences with my head office."

"I've learned that men have needs that can't always be satisfied at home," she told him. Looking over at Chuck, she said, "Sometimes a woman, too, has needs that a husband can't always fill."

"I hope that's not true in my

MEN WHO ARE "ON VACATION FROM THEIR WIVES" AND INTERESTED IN FISH:

Linda goes to work in the Florida Keys

case," Larry responded. "Maybe she's fibbing to me, but my wife tells me I'm all the man she could ever want, desire, hope for, or dream about."

"You know, talking to you, I can actually believe," Linda said, "that your wife is telling the truth about you. I think a man who looks like you and is built like you could have any girl he wants."

"Thanks a lot," he said, flashing a smile at her. "I take that as a real compliment. I hope that on this trip I can live up to such advance billing."

"I think you will," she said, patting his hand. "You'll more than live up to your praise, even exceed it."

"You're a woman after my heart," he told her.

Then Chuck came over to Linda and ordered her below. "Sam's in his cabin and wants you to come downstairs." Chuck was obviously jealous of Larry, and this was evident to Linda, but in his role as the trip's pimp and party-maker, he had to mask how upset he was.

Even though she'd already been seduced by El Toro and would later make a film with John C. Holmes, she later asserted that "Sam Phillips was the sexual challenge of my life."

It soon became obvious to her that as his penis began to rise, it was the thickest she'd ever seen or would ever see again, extending almost fourteen inches in length and seemingly measuring some seven inches in circumference. As she'd later tell a fellow prostitute, Barbara, "Comparing it to a milk bottle would be no exaggeration. Phillips was a freak of nature."

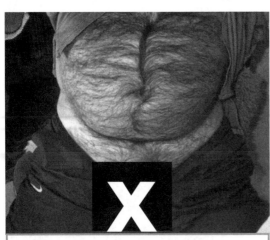

Sam Phillips may not have had a body to compete with a Greek statue, but when he took off his trunks, he revealed what he boasted was "the biggest dick in the Blue Ridge Mountains."

Never again would Linda face such a daunting challenge.

When she entered his cabin, Phillips was standing completely nude, looking out a porthole. She gasped at the sight of him. Never again would she be so awed by a penis. Flaccid, it hung down the side of his leg, measuring at least nine inches. She feared what it would become when erect. Like El Toro, Phillips, if he lost weight, could have appeared on stage in one of those Superman shows staged in pre-Castro Havana.

"Girlie, I've warned you that I have something for you," he said, leering at her. "Now get your ass over here and prove to me that you can take a real deep-dicking up that skilled throat of yours."

Although she wanted to flee, she knew there was no place to run aboard this boat. She'd have to go through with this ordeal.

As she held up his penis, his pre-cum had already begun to ooze. She ran her tongue over its head, swallowing its liquid, and then began concentrating on its huge head, running her tongue over its slit time and time again.

Removing her mouth, she changed her position, placing her head off to the side of the mattress. She later felt that if she could even get its head, which was his dick's widest and heaviest part, into her mouth, she'd be able to manage. Straining, gagging, licking, and pushing, she finally managed.

He was breathing heavily at this point as he began his journey toward the back of her throat.

Her jaws opened wide as he gave one final push, the head of his penis entering the gateway to her throat. Her jaws felt like they were about to become dislocated.

Phillips gasped with pleasure, obviously having inserted himself deeper into a mouth and throat than ever before. As if to confirm that, he exclaimed, "It's a miracle!"

She had to inhale quickly before he filled her throat again. The pain in her jaws was almost unbearable, and she was getting dizzy, but she carried on.

He clamped his hands onto her head, making it more difficult for her. Then he ripped into her throat with great force, and for a moment she feared she was going to faint.

She tasted blood in her mouth. Then, clamping her head even harder, he released a cry of joy. There was no movement as he exploded into her throat. Finally, just as she approached a point near suffocation, he released her.

"Before the trip ends, I want to get Chuck to film you doing that to me," he said. "Now get the fuck out. I want some sleep."

As she later told Barbara, "I was proud of myself. I had swallowed a milk bottle and a quart of semen."

***

After her ordeal with Phillips, the other men, except for Larry, were what she called "Average Joes, average in the cock department, average in looks." Bob, Steve, Wayne, and Rick were each men in their forties, and each had developed a middle-aged paunch of varying shapes and sizes.

Since Chick had bragged profusely about her deep throat skills, each client wanted her to individually demonstrate her specialty. After her near-suffocation with Phillips, fellating these fishermen "was no more difficult than eating a marshmallow."

She recalled Wayne after her sexual encounter with him. At least that was how she had been introduced to him. But she noted afterward that his buddies called him "Rev." Was he really a minister? She wondered. Tall and slender, and relatively thin except for the bulge in his stomach, he had intimidating steel-gray eyes. After she blew him, he had fornicated with her. As he did, he kept his eyes piercingly open, almost glaring down into hers, as if warning her that she was being sentenced to hell and damnation.

Rick had agreed "to submit to a blow-job," but told her he was secretly a homosexual. He agreed to close his eyes and fantasize about a football jock he'd known at the University. "Let's get this over with," he told her. "I'm not into it. I'm just doing it so the other guys won't find out I'm secretly gay. Frankly, I'd rather be locked in this room with Larry. You'll get him later. What a lucky whore you are."

Steve was a relatively handsome man, at least he probably had been good looking when he was much younger. He told her he was in his fifties and worked as an attorney. He said that ten years ago, his wife had been in a car accident, and that she was confined to a wheelchair. "That's why I have to get sex outside the house," he said, as if he needed to defend what he was doing. He preferred not to take off his clothing, but merely unzipped and presented an unimpressive penis, which she had a hard time bringing to life. After she'd worked on it for a few minutes, he pulled away from her. "I can't come today," he said, "but you tried. It felt good. I'm having a hard time rekindling my youthful passion." Then he zipped up and left the cabin.

Bob was the least attractive of the men on board. He said he wanted "the works," meaning both fellatio and vaginal intercourse. "When I'm with a whore, I always get my money's worth."

He also told her that he had an odd request. "To get hard, I have to have a woman suck my toes first. I took a shower this morning, so my feet are clean."

She obliged, performing a toe-sucking act, something she'd never done before.

But it worked. He achieved an erection. After fellating him for a while, he rolled over and inserted himself in her vagina. As he did, he told her, "My wife just hates to get fucked, and that's why I insist on it every night."

Of all the men on board, she found him the most creepy, and was happy to see him dismount. "You're okay, kid," he said, "but I've had better."

The best for last: Larry finally came into the cabin. She was still lying on the bed. He lay beside her and reached down and gave her a passionate, long, deep kiss. She was really turned on by him.

Except for Phillips and his freak appendage, Larry was the best hung of all the fishermen, some eight and a half inches, and very thick. He was definitely an artist in bed.

After stripping down, he revealed a rock-hard body. He began by cupping her breasts and fingering her nipples before showering her neck, shoulders, and chest with a heavy rain of kisses. His tongue sloshed across her collarbone before sliding down the cleft between her breasts, where he licked her like a lovesick puppy. He soon had her writhing with pleasure.

When he raised himself up, she kissed his face, her tongue whirling around his ears. Her hands reached below to fondle his heavy-hanging testicles. He raised himself up with a mushrooming erection and planted himself deep into her mouth.

Her throat opened to allow her lips to encircle the base of his cock. After a few intense minutes of this, she pulled back, beginning a backward journey toward the purplish blood-engorged cap. Once there, her tongue darted into its slit, licking around the base of the large head before plunging all the way down the shaft again.

"Oh, Linda," he said. "My Linda, suck that! It feels so good! That's a girl. Take it all."

She didn't need that instruction, as she swallowed him whole. Suddenly, he pulled away and abruptly inserted his cock into her vagina.

The torpedo zeroed in on her tremulous target, and she found herself thinking, "If only Chuck could make love like this man." On top of her, he pumped furiously. She raised her legs up into the air and wrapped them around his lean waist, as he penetrated deeply.

Here was the lover she'd been seeking all her life. Her fingers glided over his muscular body as he kissed her passionately, inserting his tongue like a serpent slithering through the dark.

She felt his thigh muscles tighten like iron. Suddenly, he raised himself to his knees, pulling out. Her vagina was quivering uncontrollably. "Baby, baby, baby," he said, as he entered her again with more force than ever. For a moment, she thought he would split her in half before he erupted, gasping for breath.

When he'd finished, he lay on top of her, as if wanting it to last. She ran her hands over his back and nibbled at his neck.

Like a brilliant display of fireworks on the Fourth of July, the moment was passing too quickly. Larry was the man of her dreams. But he was also married, and if that was the right word in her case, she was married, too. She wanted Larry as her lover. She'd never had

As a prostitute, Linda learned a valuable lesson during her encounter with Larry on the orgy boat.

As she'd later advise, "Never fall in love with one of your johns."

such satisfaction before.

"Oh, please, give me your phone number," she pleaded with him. "I've got to see you again. You're the world's greatest lover."

"And you're my hot mama."

"I don't even know your last name," she said.

"It's Larry Boone, and I can't wait to hook up with you again."

"It'll be our secret," she said. "Chuck must not find out, and your wife will never know."

"I'm going to pull out now," he said.

Her muscles tightened, as if wanting to hold onto him. She realized that both of their bodies were drenched in sweat.

"The door's locked," he said. "Let's shower together."

Under the shower's cleansing stream, he held her as he soaped her down. At one point, she fell to her knees under the running water and fellated him again.

The shower must have lasted twenty minutes. She suddenly heard a loud pounding on the cabin's door.

"Is everything all right in there?" Chuck called.

"Be right out," Larry yelled back. "I had to shower."

She dried him off, massaging his well-developed chest and kissing his nipples. After getting dressed, she also kissed his soft, sweet lips.

She knew after the boat docked, and after Chuck got her home, she'd have to endure a severe beating. But to her, it had been worth it.

Larry slipped her a phone number that would reach him at work. "Don't make me wait too long," he said. Then, as he embraced her, he promised that their farewell would not mean goodbye.

CHAPTER THREE
Shadows in Sunny Florida

At long last, the delayed trial of Chuck Traynor, caught by the police with 400 pounds of marijuana, was heard before a judge and jury in Dade County. Chuck seemed confident that a court would believe his highly improbably alibi.

Although she dared not reveal her true thoughts, Linda welcomed the trial. She viewed it as her liberation. With Chuck in jail, her release from him, or so she believed, would follow.

Later, she had few memories of the actual trial. "I wasn't really listening," she claimed. "All I was thinking about was my freedom. Chuck and some of his pals had rehearsed their story about how they were looking for a field for their sky-diving club to land on."

Like actors memorizing a movie script, Chuck and his cronies had learned their lines, each delivering false testimony about how they were hauling the bale of marijuana to a local police station as a means of preventing local children, who played in the area, from finding it. According to Linda, "I'd heard these lies so long that I almost came to believe them myself."

On the stand, wearing a cheap three-piece brown suit, a stiffly starched white shirt and a Hallowe'en orange tie, "He was damn convincing in his testimony," Linda said. "The faces of the jury were blank, giving no indication of how they would cast their vote. Throughout the week-long trial, Chuck seemed to glow with self-confidence and a belief that he would be vindicated."

When the verdict was read, Linda let out a gasp. Chuck was found "not guilty," and all charges against him were dismissed.

In her autobiography, *Ordeal,* Linda made a strange confession. "As we were leaving the courtroom, I reached out and took a handful of Exhibit A— some marijuana—and stuck it in Chuck's jacket pocket. I know how irrational I was, but I was half hoping they'd search him on the way out of the courtroom, find the stuff, and try him all over again."

Not aware of her motive, that night at his house, he thanked her for making off with some of the stash. On his third smoke, he bragged about what a great debater he'd been in high school and how, in the courtroom, he'd made the District Attorney "look like a monkey's asshole."

With the trial behind him and with bills mounting, Chuck moved rapidly ahead with what he hoped would be money-making schemes. To Linda's dismay, all of them involved her.

He had finally managed to acquire the equipment he needed to begin filming 8mm porno loops. Chuck told her that he would function as cameraman, lighting director, producer, writer, and paymaster. And whereas it was understood that whatever services she provided would be without pay, other actors, both male and female, could be procured for fifty dollars a day. "The most expensive film he planned to shoot would cost $500, but he hoped to bring in some for around $200," Linda said.

He still faced the challenge of finding a laboratory which would process and develop the film, and then he'd have to contact a distributor which sold pornographic films (illegally). Chuck claimed that in all, for a total cost of $1,000, he'd be able to produce an 8mm porno film with Linda as its star.

He planned to shoot it with a 16mm camera using half the width of the film. The 16mm porno flick would then be split by a lab processor and made into finished 8mm finished reels.

Linda's first porno loop demonstrated her deep-throating techniques even more graphically than *Deep Throat.*

It was made of and for Sam Phillips. Phillips had offered to pay Chuck for a private film of Linda deep-throating him, strictly for his own private library, as she'd done aboard the fishing boat. The film that was eventually made from this, entitled *The Cum Shot,* was the first-ever porn movie featuring Linda Lovelace. Sam never envisioned it for commercial release, although surely it would have been a hit. It is not known if a copy of it exists today. Phillips may have destroyed it.

After that, Phillips spent yet another weekend with Chuck and Linda and decided he wanted yet another film. "I want to do a film called *The Deep Dicker,* featuring me."

When Chuck told Linda about this next assignment, she was filled with anxiety. "My god," she protested. "Sam's cock is so big it'll go in the front and come out my asshole."

"You'll take it, bitch, and make sure that on camera, your face shows that you're loving every inch."

The loop was eventually shot. It took Linda only a few minutes to get a full erection from Phillips. Then, with no attempt to go easy on her, he brought his heavy cock straight down and aimed it at his target. As he thrust forward, she screamed in pain.

Chuck interrupted the filming. "I told you to take it!" Then he turned to Phillips. "I know how to make her open up." He unbuckled his belt, pulled it off, and began to beat her with the leather. It felt like a knife slashing across her skin. There came another slash, and then two more in rapid succession.

She begged for mercy, promising him she'd try harder next time.

During Phillip's second assault on her, the pain was enormous, but at least he was going in more slowly. He pressed harder, but still couldn't go much deeper. In desperation, she reached down and placed her fingers around his fat assault weapon, determined to take all of him inside her. He continued his agonizing assault.

Fearing she'd be ripped open, she raised her pelvis, pushing it against his cock. She was being engulfed by it as he pushed harder and further into her. Somehow, her vagina loosened a bit. More, more, and more. He finally plunged in all the way. This time, he was screaming, but with joy. "No one, no one has ever taken all of it," he shouted.

He began to move in and out of her. His driving increased in savagery, but she ceased to respond. The pounding was becoming unbearable, but she was escaping somewhere to a far and distant place. He was in ecstasy, but her body seemed to have gone numb.

Mercifully, she blacked out.

***

A few days after Phillips' return to North Carolina, Chuck screened *The Rape of a Virgin,* the 8mm loop Linda had recently filmed. Barbara, who sat in on the "premiere" of Linda's loop, had returned from one of her mysterious trips with a Miami businessman, and was ready to begin working for Chuck again.

After viewing it, Chuck informed Linda that she'd successfully mastered deep throating, analingus, and sodomy. Now he wanted "to work on your vagina so you'll be able to take anything."

She agreed, although accurately claiming, "If I live to be ninety-nine, chances are I'll never encounter a guy built like Sam Phillips, a damn freak of nature."

Nonetheless, Chuck announced his plan to work with her on the muscles of her vagina, and told Barbara that he might have to enlist her help.

Once again, he used post-hypnotic suggestion. Barbara was also of great help, telling Linda that when she'd worked as a performer in stag shows, she was taught how to pick up fifty-cent coins from tabletops with her vagina.

Chuck started Linda's vaginal exercises with a tubular, battery-operated vibrator. Both Barbara and Chuck coached her in the repeated contraction and relaxation of the muscles of her vagina. "You know you're getting it when you can stand up and hold the vibrator in place without touching it with your hands," Barbara said. "You've really got to get acquainted with your pubococcygeus muscle."

"Before I heard that, I didn't know I had such a muscle," Linda recalled. "I never learned to pronounce it."

Barbara also encouraged Linda, when she was urinating, to stop the flow in the middle of her pee. "That's a really good exercise, kid."

In a memoir, Linda warned readers to use caution in following her exercises. "When you learn to take large objects, devote equal time to taking the smaller ones, too. Otherwise, you'll end up with a box that's big enough for a size ten shoe."

Barbara told her that a really good whore is one who can take (and exert vaginal pressure on) a penis the size of a little finger, as well as on one as large as a bull's.

During practice sessions, both Chuck and Barbara took turns inserting first two fingers, then three, four, and ultimately their entire fist inside Linda's vagina, up to their wrists. Linda eventually became adept at getting vaginally "fist-fucked." She'd never heard of such a sexual practice before, although it was destined to come into increasing vogue, both vaginally and rectally, during the 1970s and 80s.

When Chuck felt that Linda had learned her lessons, as he put it, he declared that she was ready to appear in yet another loop. Its title would be *The Foot.*

At the University of Miami, Chuck, through some means, had met Ryan Bosworth, a locally prominent football player who wore a size thirteen shoe. Chuck had promised him "all the pussy he could handle" in exchange for the involvement and appearance of his feet, but not his face, in this porno loop.

Both Barbara and Linda were impressed with this six-foot, four-inch athlete, whom Barbara compared to a Viking god. "Honey, I'd do him for free."

Chuck, Bosworth, Linda, and Barbara discussed the script beside the swimming pool of Chuck's house in Miami. Bosworth had stripped down to his jockey shorts, and Linda and Barbara each wore bikinis. Bosworth looked no more than twenty, and his body contrasted with Chuck's less than Greek physique. The athlete's shirt bulged with muscles and his legs would have challenged those of a Roman gladiator. Hair curled through the open neck of his shirt. Both women focused on the husky bulge in his crotch. Bosworth seemed to bask in the attention, flashing an understanding grin at both Linda and Barbara.

For the opening sequence of the film, Chuck framed a shot of Bosworth's feet on a bed, sticking out from beneath a sheet. The camera zoomed in on his left foot.

His legs and feet were then filmed getting out of bed and heading for the shower. At that point, Bosworth dropped his underwear. His thick, uncut penis was revealed to the cameraman and the other actors, but within the camera's frame, however, all that was recorded was the sight of his underwear falling down around his ankles before being tossed aside.

Later, the camera recorded frames of Boswell's feet being meticulously dried with a towel and a pair of pants being drawn upward within, once again, a camera frame that included only a view of his legs below the knees. Then his feet were filmed as socks and then shoes were donned. Outside, in the sunlight and open air, his feet and lower legs were filmed walking purposefully along a sidewalk.

The scene then shifts to a view of Boswell's feet as they approach someone's front door. The actor knocks and the camera records his legs and feet being admitted inside, where, without ever showing the actor's face, he places a hundred-dollar bill into a woman's hand, with the clear implication that she is a prostitute.

The next scene was filmed in Chuck's bedroom, where a view only of Bosworth's feet was filmed as he removes his shoes and socks.

A fully nude Linda, revealing both her body and her face, then appears within the frame. (At no point in the loop was Boswell's face shown.) His pants fall below his knees, and a view of his feet, walking toward Linda on the bed, is shown.

Gently, one of Boswell's feet caresses Linda's breast, sliding down vertically across her stomach until it reaches her shaven vagina. He orders her to turn over. His big toe slowly rubs against and then penetrates her anus.

After a minute or so of that, he orders her to turn over and lie on her back once again. Only his feet are depicted. Linda laps his toes with her tongue, cleaning the crevices between them.

One by one she fellates all ten of them, sucking and devouring. After she finishes, his left foot, beginning with his big toe, begins a penetration of her vagina. Soon, she has absorbed each of his five toes, and then his large foot is gradually inserted and pressed into her vagina. At this point, he begins to gently pump her, using long, heavy strokes. This continues for

Fetish:
"An object of irrational reverence or obsessive devotion."

Merriam-Webster (m-w.com)

a while until suddenly, his foot is withdrawn just before "semen" is splashed across her stomach.

Barbara herself had concocted the "semen" with a mixture of evaporated milk and egg whites, which she poured into a condiments dispenser and squirted out onto Linda at the crucial moment.

Near the end of the sequence, Bosworth's feet were filmed as their owner pulls on his pants and then puts on first his socks and then his shoes and walks across the bedroom floor, down the hall, and out the door.

After all the footage had been shot, Chuck called Linda aside. "You take care of him, and I mean really good. I don't have to tell Barbara what to do. But in your case, you've got to be directed, because you're a total idiot."

As the sun faded, Bosworth, Linda, and Barbara stripped down for a nude romp together. That gave him a chance to feel their breasts and vaginas. Barbara was very aggressive, doing some feeling of her own between the football star's legs. Unknown to Bosworth, Chuck was observing their activities through a peephole.

Bosworth, as it turned out, was a star not only on the football field, but in the boudoir as well. As Barbara recalled, "If only all my clients were like him instead of the puny runts or fatties I usually get. Most of my clients are men who can't attract a girl on their own, but have to pay for sex."

After his first climax, Bosworth rested in bed with a cigarette and a cold beer which Linda had provided. He told the women that he'd been broken into sex by a fat Cuban female cook his family had employed, as well as by a gay cowboy who worked on their cattle ranch.

"Ryan certainly knew how to keep two horny women overheated at the same time," Linda recalled. "And he did have a fetish or two, if it could be called that. He said his sexual fantasy, which he'd never had fulfilled, was to have two women in bed at the same time, one licking his anus with her tongue and the other sucking his foreskin."

Barbara volunteered for the rear attack as Linda nibbled and then devoured his dick. Soon, Bosworth was squirming with pleasure.

At the end of their time together, Bosworth kissed both Linda and Barbara goodbye, and thanked Chuck at the door.

After he'd gone, Barbara headed for the shower. As she started to go upstairs, Linda was grabbed by Chuck. He slapped her several times before knocking her down and kicking her in the stomach.

"I saw it all," he shouted at her.

"But you told me to take care of him," she yelled back.

"You're nothing but a god damn whore!" he said, spitting on her as she lay helpless on the floor. Impulsively, he unzipped his pants. Taking out his penis, he urinated on her, a first for her. But it would not be the last.

***

Chuck told her to stay in the house all day as he went out to find a distributor for *The Foot*. He knew there were a lot of foot fetish freaks in the country, and he'd made two or three appointments with distributors who could tap into this underground niche market.

It was a Saturday, and Linda put through a phone call to Larry, whom she hadn't seen since the fishing expedition, even though she'd thought about him every day. His voice sounded eager after he picked up the receiver. He told her that he had access to a house in Coconut Grove during a period when two of his friends, with their adopted son, visited relatives in New York. After she told him she had the day free, he gave her the address and asked her to be there at 12:30pm if she could.

The house was one of those old Spanish style structures with a red tile roof built in South Florida during the heyday of the Roaring Twenties. She had to ring the doorbell three times before it was answered. Looking out, Larry saw who it was and opened the door. A towel in hand, he had just emerged dripping wet from his bath.

He held her tightly and passionately kissed her. "I'm getting your clothes wet," he said. "Take them off. She pulled off all her garments, letting them drop onto the pink-tiled floor.

Taking her hand, he led her to the bathroom in the rear. Loud music was playing in the living room. He directed her into the most spectacular bathroom she'd ever seen. Like the floor tiles in the vestibule, everything was pink. Two scented candles gave off their fragrance. Before her was a large sunken pink marble tub, with a ledge lined with exotic oils, bath salts, and perfumes. Not just the fixtures, but all the towels, walls, and vanity cabinets were pink. Even the big mirrors had a rose-colored tint. "This man and his wife really get off on pink," she said.

"Actually, it's not a Mr. and Mrs., but a Mr. and Mr.," he said. "They're two guys. Sometimes when I come over, they like me to get into the tub with them so they can scrub me down."

She wanted to ask more questions, but was distracted as he led her into a bubble bath. With the scented candles glowing, the music in the background, and the perfumed fragrances emanating from the water, she felt she'd entered paradise.

There was a gleam in his eyes, and when he smiled at her with a boyish grin, she felt she could love him forever. He kissed her for a long time before he began to sponge her breasts with his long fingers. She returned the favor. Like a sea serpent, his blood-engorged cock rose from the water.

His hands slid across her skin. He even fingered her scar, but didn't seem turned off by it. He didn't ask her how she'd gotten it. She took her hand and moved it across the slippery surface of his chest. She could not believe he was thirty-five years old. Many twenty-year-old men didn't have picture-perfect bodies like Larry's.

As he squeezed her breasts, she secretly wished they were larger, perhaps like the size of an average cantaloupe. Under his touch, the red buds of her nipples blossomed and hardened. He rubbed soap through her cleavage.

As he did that, she stroked and placated what she jokingly defined to him as "a sea monster." When she teased the sensitive globes underneath, he wriggled with pleasure.

He soaped her shaved vagina before impaling her on his throbbing cock. For five minutes they bobbed back and forth like corks in the water, the bathwaters swirling and splashing around them. Deeper and deeper he lunged. She kissed him with more passion than she had any other man. With each thrust, she seemed to fall more in love with him.

He drove his tongue down her throat as he exploded inside her. It was like hot molten lava. She screamed as spasm upon spasm overcame her. She thrilled to his low moans, knowing she'd satisfied him.

Later, they stood under a shower together. With her eyes half closed, he dried her and carried her into the master bedroom, which was also entirely decorated in pink. Between pink sheets, she fell asleep in his arms. His body smelled of the flowery scent of bath oil and perfumes.

When she finally woke up, he was awake, staring dreamily into her eyes. They were loving, in direct contrast to the blazing hostility she encountered whenever she made eye contact with Chuck.

Larry took his hand and gently placed it on the nape of her neck. That signal was all too familiar to her. She knew what he wanted, and she was eager to oblige. She threw back the sheet for the debut of what she increasingly defined as her "specialty."

He was already erect and throbbing with anticipation. She began by kissing and licking his dick, descending to tantalize both of those dangling orbs. After placing his hand on the nape of her neck, he guided her to his anus, which she sucked voraciously, as his moans increased in their intensity. Then she returned to her main target with more vigor than ever.

A thought flashed through her mind. She knew that this illicit relationship could not continue forever without a complete rearrangement of each of their lives. He had a wife and family, and she was both married to and menaced by Chuck.

But for a brief moment, all such thoughts faded. She was determined to give him such a thrill that he'd always come back for more. Her cheeks were sucked in and out before she opened her throat to him. He plunged as far as he could go before shouting out in ecstasy.

He was hers.

***

Chuck never knew that Linda had left his house for a rendezvous with Larry. In fact, when he returned to his house that night, he was in a relatively good mood, as he'd found a distributor for his movies. Three men had viewed *The Foot,* and they had told him, "There's a real market for this kind of stuff."

That night, he grew increasingly obsessed with his next loop. "I think he was beginning to think of himself as another Hugh Hefner," Linda said.

After breakfast the next morning, Chuck announced to Linda and Barbara that he wanted to film some girl-on-girl action. "Straight men really go for that," he said.

Since Barbara and Linda were already attracted to each other, that proved no challenge for either of them.

Stripping down for Chuck's camera, Barbara, as could be predicted, emerged as the aggressor in their love-making scenes. "Her tongue seemed as long as a penis," Linda recalled, "and she must have had cannibal blood in her the way she chewed me alive. But I loved it. We forgot all about Chuck and his damn camera and let ourselves go."

Barbara had starred in both straight and lesbian porn before, and was a real professional. "I certainly had not mastered cunnilingus as well as Barbara had, but I found her an exciting diversion," Linda said. "I was more the fellatio artist."

"We fondled each other's breasts as we French kissed, and we ended the loop in a wild sixty-nine," Linda said.

After the shoot, Barbara and Linda took a bath together. Under the "rain forest shower," Barbara confessed that when she was sixteen years old, and living in Manhattan's East Village, she'd worked in a lesbian bordello, a large apartment with three bedrooms.

When Linda kissed Barbara goodnight, she came back into Chuck's bedroom, where she saw him lying nude on top of the bedcovers. He was fondling himself. Seeing her, he called out, "Suck it, bitch!"

She dutifully responded, always obeying his orders, although she'd rather be cuddling with Barbara downstairs.

After he'd climaxed in her mouth, he informed her that during the days ahead, there would be other girls living in the rooms downstairs. "I'll be getting a lot of requests from johns. You and Barbara can't fill all my orders for whores."

In her memoirs, Linda recalled the fake names associated with these young women: "Sunshine," "Moonshine," "Chicklet," "Debbie," and as associated with a later arrival, "Melody."

Each of the women had a specialty, and the more beautiful ones were very particular about the type of clients they would serve. Linda did not have that option.

Auburn-haired Debbie was the most particular. The twenty-two year old hooker evoked the actress Arlene Dahl as she looked in the 1950s. Debbie had very clearly informed Chuck that she would go to bed only with men under thirty-five who were also good looking. That certainly limited her options, since most of Chuck's clients did not fall into that category. But since she had a sugar daddy on the side, money was not a vital component of her negotiations.

Moonshine, age 18, was very different. She imposed no requirements. As Linda described her, "There was nothing she wouldn't do, except she'd work only at night. No day jobs. Perhaps that was why she was nicknamed Moonshine."

The teenager did not live downstairs at Chuck's house, because she had a john, an architect, who paid her rent. Another man, a mechanic, paid her phone bill, and yet another, a salesman, provided her with gas and electricity. She'd come to work for Chuck because she needed extra money for her car payments and for clothing. Unlike so many of his women, Moonshine was not a tough, brazen whore, but carried an air of innocence in spite of the tricks she turned.

Chuck believed that whenever possible, his stable of *putas* should look like movie stars, and he ordered them to apply their makeup and arrange their hair to emulate individual stars. To him, Moonshine evoked Mitzi Gaynor, a singer-dancer popular in the 1950s whose sexual allure was relatively discreet and un-

Actresses who inspired a generation of porn-industry lookalikes:

(left to right) **Arlene Dahl**, **Mitzi Gaynor**, and **Debbie Reynolds**

derstated. Fox had wanted to replace Betty Grable with Gaynor. She'd starred in one of Chuck's favorite movies, *South Pacific.*

Chicklet, who tried to look as close to Debbie Reynolds as possible, was the sweetest-looking girl in Chuck's whorish coven. "I think her role model was Tammy, that hit movie with Miss Reynolds," Linda said. "She preferred older men, such as businessmen, lawyers, or doctors, preferably in the forty-to fifty-five age range."

Chicklet was the smallest girl Chuck ever hired, standing no more than five feet tall. She claimed she had just turned twenty. She proved to be very popular with johns who preferred sex with thirteen or fourteen-year-old girls. In preparation for her sessions with tricks, Chicklet was dressed like a schoolgirl, complete with pigtails. She was rehearsed by Chuck, who ordered her to pretend to be a virgin, and to scream when penetrated.

Chuck's list of clients expanded weekly. "If he was an eighty-year-old man on crutches, or a 305-pound mama's boy, or a customer asking whether we supplied whips, then Chuck would turn to me: 'This one's for you, Linda.'"

One night, Chuck drove both Linda and Chicklet to the filthy and disorganized home of an obese photographer in South Miami. He lived in squalor. Chuck introduced them, and told her that the man wanted to take photographs of them.

He brought out a mammoth dildo with two heads. Perhaps because of the angle at which it was inserted, Linda found the penetration painful. Tears were coming down Chicklet's cheeks, but she bravely held herself together. From ten feet away, Chuck glared at them while they were being photographed.

At the end of the session, the photographer ordered them into the bathroom, where he gave each of them an enema.

There was more humiliation for Linda when Chuck drove both of them back home. His sadistic impulses seemed to have been ignited.   "I found a new way to get turned on by you," he said. "All your other shit bores me. Tonight, I'm going to give it to you even if you scream. I'm turned on by fist fucking."

Mitzi Gaynor in *South Pacific*

***

"Perhaps to punish me for unknown sins, Chuck continued to see that I got the weirdos," Linda said. "Take Herbie, for instance. I didn't know his real name. All I knew was that he sold women's lingerie. Maybe he wore it himself. He had the most bizarre request. He wanted to piss in my pussy. Can you believe this crap? People are sick."

[Amazingly, in spite of her original revulsion, Linda in time gravitated to this curious form of sexual expression. In her shameless memoir, *Inside Linda Lovelace,* she wrote: "There can sometimes be a problem for a man keeping a hard-on while peeing, but it's been done to me many times. The sensation is terrific for a woman. The stream of pee feels great as it washes your insides."]

About a week later, the situation was reversed. Chuck took her to the home of a client, known only as Peter, who wanted her to urinate in his mouth. He lived in a garden apartment in the southwest section of Miami. A tall, skinny man, he seemed hostile from the very beginning of their meeting. A day before the appointment, Chuck had insisted that she drink nothing but apple juice as a means of sweetening the smell and taste of her urine.

Peter took her into his bedroom and ordered her to strip. When he told her to "sit on my face," she assumed that he was going to perform cunnilngus on her. But after she mounted into position, he yelled at her, "Now piss, bitch!"

Try as she might, she just could not do it. She tried, but something in her caused her to tighten her muscles.

Finally, after several unsuccessful minutes, he pushed her off the bed. "There's a Mason jar in my bathroom," he said. "Go in there and pee in it and bring it back."

In the privacy of his bathroom, she had no trouble peeing into the jar. Then she carried the jar into the bedroom, where he took it from her and downed it like it was lager.

After he'd swallowed the last drop, he ordered her to get dressed. "I never want to see her again," he told Chuck, who had been waiting on site . Then he and Chuck got into an argument over the fee, and Chuck finally agreed to cut it in half. On the way home, he yelled at her for failing to deliver what a client wanted.

She knew a beating was inevitable.

***

She'd later claim in the years ahead that running off from time to time to meet secretly with Larry probably saved her sanity. "Here was a man I thought truly loved me," she'd recall. "He made sex beautiful. Everybody else in my life made it something cheap and vulgar. I almost cried every time I had to leave Larry. I just couldn't stand leaving him, knowing that he was

BIOLOGICAL SAMPLES: DO NOT DRINK

going back to the bed of another woman who loved him and had even given him children."

Some of her assignments were relatively easy, but not many. An example of one, which she defined years later as "easy," involved an episode at a resort hotel on Miami Beach. There, she was ushered upstairs to an elegant suite overlooking the ocean. For $150 a session, an aging movie director, in his late 70s, requested that she strip down and take a bubble bath in a large tub. He, too, took off his clothes and he fondled himself as she bathed, although he never produced an erection. He sat on a stool directing her bath.

After her bath, in the living room and still nude, he talked to her for about an hour. She claimed that she never knew his identity, "although he must have been very famous at one time. He name-dropped quite a bit."

He told her that he'd won three Oscars for Best Director, and had been nominated a dozen times for Academy Awards. "I was married to a famous movie star in the 1930s," he said. "I was friends with Greer Garson and Fredric March. I used to bang Bette Davis. Audrey Hepburn and Gary Cooper are also my friends. Monty Clift once gave me a blow-job."

[When Linda in New York was negotiating the aborted, never-published *Linda Lovelace Exposed* with the literary agent, Jay Garon, she told him this story. Garon, a film buff and historian, knew immediately who it was. "That description could only fit one man: William Wyler. He was married to Margaret Sullavan, Henry Fonda's first wife. He also won Oscars for *Mrs. Miniver* (1942), *The Best Years of Our Lives* (1946), and *Ben-Hur* (1959)."

Garon continued, "He would have known Garson and March from those films. And he also directed Bette Davis in *The Letter (1940)* and *The Little Foxes* (1941). Later, he helmed Audrey Hepburn in *Roman Holiday* (1953) and Gary Cooper in *Friendly Persuasion* (1956). As for that blow-job, Wyler had directed (the homosexual and very promiscuous) Monty Clift in *The Heiress (1949)."*

After hearing all this, Linda did not seem impressed. "Movie stars, I know," she said. "Maybe he could get it up for Bette Davis but I couldn't even get a rise out of him."]

***

One morning, Chuck expressed yet another money-making scheme involving Linda and his girls. He went to the marina where Linda had first met Larry on that fishing boat trip arranged by Sam Phillips.

Chuck offered to cut the marina manager in on the profits if he'd suggest to various groups of men, usually fishermen, that he could arrange for one, two, or even three girls for day trips or overnight jaunts to The Bahamas. "Unless your men want to spend all day fishing," Chuck added. The manager opted to pass this proposal on to selected, pre-screened clients.

The following week, Chuck received a call from the marina.

Six baseball players, each a team member of the New York Yankees, had finished their spring training in St. Petersburg and were planning a week's vacation before heading back north. For their holiday, they planned to sail from Miami to Bimini on a rented yacht.

Linda knew nothing about baseball, but she figured that all players in the game would be nice, decent guys. The only associate of the New York Yankees she'd ever heard of was Joe DiMaggio, and that was because he'd once been married to Marilyn Monroe.

Before Linda met the athletes at the marina, she was somewhat leery of sailing away to Bimini with them. But they seemed wholesome enough, and she was reassured that no harm would come to her. Actually, she would have dated any of them, as all of the players were well built, and two of them were actually handsome in a clean-cut American way.

Each of the players wore bathing trunks, not skimpy bikinis, and none of them looked like a sadist, but the idea of being cooped up with them on a boat for a full week made her uncomfortable. She had begged Chuck to let another of his girls sail alongside her, but he refused. "All of them are busy, and these Yankees are a bit cheap," he told her. "They said they could afford only one girl, and I told them that you and your specialty were more than adequate for all of them."

The first few hours of the cruise aboard the yacht passed without incident. She sunbathed in a bikini. After lunch, the tallest of the players, Dick Hoddeson, came over and took her hand. "Let's go below, Linda."

In the cabin, there were no formalities. He told her, "I'm horny, baby." He pulled off his clothes and lay down on the bed. "You can have me below the neck only. I reserve my kissing for my gal in Queens, New York City."

"That's fine with me," she said. "I have a boyfriend myself, so I understand about the kissing part."

Top photo: Film director **William Wyler**
Bottom: **Bette Davis**, as directed by Wyler, in *The Little Foxes*

"I want your specialty," he said. "I've heard a lot about it. My girlfriend gives blow-jobs, but really lousy ones."

Determined to show him a good time, she went to work as he rose to a rather thick seven and a half inches. She sucked and licked, opening her throat to him. Again and again he moaned, and his back arched. His muscles convulsed, and he gripped her shoulders. She could almost feel the veins pulsing in his penis. Then, he erupted.

"And how!" she'd later tell Barbara. "He was a volcano. He must have been away from that gal in Queens for a long time. Unlike any other man I've ever known, he seemed to manufacture cream by the quart."

After the resumption of his normal breathing, he rose from the bed and got dressed. He patted her on the head and said, "Thank you."

As she'd later tell some of Chuck's in-house prostitutes, "Each of the baseball players was different, but all the same somehow. It was a lot of sucking. The fucking was in the old-fashioned way. My ass was safe on that boat. All the guys had sort of average equipment, nothing special, and basically they just wanted some relief after finishing spring training."

Later she'd claim, "Sex with those guys was really mild compared to the stuff that Chuck had planned for my future."

Before she left the marina, Jerry Michaud, one of the shorter players, came up to her, "Thanks, Linda," he said. "You sure know how to suck cock. Your throat's a suction pump. I've got to tell Joe about this. He's coming down next week on a vacation."

"Could he have meant Joe DiMaggio, THE Joe DiMaggio, Mr. Marilyn Monroe himself?" she wondered. She knew, of course, that the Yankee great had long ago retired from baseball, but on occasion, he appeared at the spring training camp maintained by the Yankees. She hadn't seen a picture of him since the 1950s, and she figured he must be old at this point. Even so, she looked forward to hooking up with him.

Chuck drove her back to his house, "I've had no complaints," he told her. "Each of the guys gave me a hundred-dollar bill."

As was usual, Linda got nothing except a twenty dollar tip slipped to her by Dick Hoddeson.

During the weeks ahead, it would not be unusual for her to service up to five or even a half-dozen men in a single evening. In her confessional, *Inside Linda Lovelace,* she recalled seducing six men, one after the other, in the same room together. The Yankees had been more modest, using her services one man at a time. But she noticed that in her interaction with male groupings, many men who hired the same prostitute in the same room at the same time tried to maneuver her individual bouts with them into a communal scene.

In her memoirs, she described one such orgy, which she compared to a daisy chain. On that occasion, two girls had been hired to service six men. "I'm getting fucked dog fashion," she wrote, "while I'm blowing one guy. He's eating the next girl, and so on."

During many of these orgies, she noticed how the johns often surreptitiously fulfilled their homosexual fantasies. "The better looking or younger young men participating would often end up by getting fellated by one of the so-called straight guys. Here they were, next to a handsome stud with an erection, and they often took advantage of it."

"Long before I starred in *Deep Throat,* I'd lost all modesty," Linda recalled years later. "Although it didn't happen with the Yankees, balling a guy in front of his buddies was par for the course. I had no embarrassment in doing that. If my johns wanted to see me with another gal, I was game for that, too. Chuck had won the battle. He'd turned me into a bona fide, card-carrying whore—that was for sure. Worse things were in store for me…If only I had known."

***

Always desperate for a quick dollar, Chuck was willing to immerse himself in any subdivision of the sleaze industry. The competition was growing among directors hustling "conventional" 8mm porno loops—especially with films depicting straight couples having sex. Such loops, by then, were being made in virtually every state in the union, usually for private viewing.

Chuck determined that many private collectors, especially those who harbored fetishes, would be willing to pay a lot more money for porno loops featuring less conventional forms of sexual expression. These included many that were illegal, including pedophilia and bestiality, the latter having been defined as illegal in only some states at the time.

Linda became aware of Chuck's latest plot for a movie when he arrived back at his house with two young boys in tow. She was introduced to the two brothers, one named Ramon, who looked no more than thirteen, and his younger brother, Diego, who was as young as ten. After treating them to take-out hamburgers and milkshakes, he invited them to jump into his pool out back, telling them that they didn't need to wear swimming trunks because his prop-

erty was fenced in. Linda was dumbfounded as to why he'd brought these boys home. "Are you adopting them, or what?" she asked.

"Not at all," he said. "I want you to appear in a loop with them."

100

"You've got to be *kid*ding."

"I've been told by a dealer that I can make up to $5,000 by producing a loop with these boys." He explained that they were light-skinned Afro-Cubans whose father had abandoned them. Their mother, originally from Cuba, worked as a prostitute. The boys had been recruited by a black pimp who rented young, light-skinned boys to older homosexuals who used them for anal intercourse or fellatio. The boys told Chuck that they'd never had experience with a live woman before, so Linda would be the first.

Showing her ignorance, she expressed disbelief. "I didn't know boys could even have sex until they reached the age of fourteen, maybe sixteen."

"You are one stupid girl," he said. "Hell, when I was five years old, I was jerking off. Have you never heard about child sexuality? In ancient times, children were sold as sex slaves. In some parts of the world, that's still going on, especially in Africa and the Middle East."

"This sounds like something that could land all of us in jail," she said.

"I know what I'm doing," he said. "You don't know this, but a loop featuring underaged boys can bring in ten times as much money as one with a regular whore like you."

"I'm not a whore," she protested.

"Call it by some other name, then," he said. "Their pimp rents these boys out for lots of jobs, including exhibitions at gay smokers when they're set up for sex, brotherly love style, with each other. Sometimes they're rented out to older creeps who want to spank them."

"Just how do I fit into all this?" she asked.

"Later tonight, after I set up the camera, I want you to strip and lie down on the bed. I'll have the boys pull off their clothes and get into bed with you. Let nature take its course. And then I want you to perform your specialty on them."

"What if I told you I won't do it?" she asked.

"Oh, I think you will," he said, "or else you'll be waterboarded."

"What in the hell is that?"

"You wouldn't want to know, but if I'm forced to do it to you, it's an experience you'll remember to your dying day."

"I believe you really would pull some shit like that on me," she said.

"You know I would," he said, rising from the table. "Now put on some make-up and make yourself camera ready. Your

101

sexual horizons are about to be expanded."

[Years later, as Linda was interviewed extensively about her life, she was usually very outspoken. As her autobiographies revealed, she was very blunt, even when it came to writing about her experiences making porno movies with a dog. But on the subject of her secretly taped loop with Diego and Ramon, she was much more reticent. This was perhaps a reflection of the sensitive nature of the subject, with recognition that what she did was illegal and might have subjected both her and Chuck to time in jail.

She did admit, however, that she performed fellatio on both of the young brothers. She found Ramon especially well developed for boy his age. He also engaged in vaginal intercourse with her, confirming to her later that he'd never had sex before with a woman.

Chuck zeroed in on scenes where both brothers explored her genital area as part of a voyage of discovery, since each of their previous clients had been men. Copies of this controversial loop are said to exist today, although even ownership of such a film is illegal.

Although reluctant to articulate a blow-by-blow description of her experience making the loop with the two underaged brothers, Linda showed her relative indifference to the issue in a memoir. She wrote, "It makes no difference to me personally if adults make it with kids, boys with boys, grandpas with granddaughters or whatever."]

***

During the weeks ahead, even though Chuck had discovered a lucrative fetish market for his more controversial 8mm loops, he was still "hawking my whores," as he put it.

One night, he told Linda that she could expect a visitor at around midnight. He refused to give her any additional details about this stranger arriving on their doorstep. But she envisioned what was in store for her when he borrowed leather gear from the hookers downstairs. He dressed her up in black leather boots, a leather halter, and a gladiator-inspired kilt composed of vertical leather straps. He also provided her with a spiked wooden paddle, a multi-strand leather flogger, and—despite her protestations—instructions on what to do with them. "Tonight, you're gonna make your film debut as a dominatrix."

She wasn't sure what that meant, so he had to explain it to her.

Apprehensive and nervous, she was shaking when the client arrived. He looked harmless enough, a traveling salesman, in his forties, from New Jersey. It was clearly understood that his face would never appear in the film. When he stripped down, he revealed a body almost as hairy as an ape's, with a sagging belly—a style unappetizing to her. Chuck had already stripped her down for the camera.

Since the loop did not have its own sound track, Chuck barked orders at her as he recorded his footage. As she later recalled to Barbara, "My heart wasn't in it. I don't get off spanking or whipping people, even if they beg for it."

As Linda told Barbara, "This New Jersey creep wanted a rather severe beating. He kept urging me to go 'harder and harder,' the same orders Chuck was barking out at me. Every few minutes, the guy would call a halt and ask to see a mirror Chuck had provided. He held it up to his ass, and seemed pleased with the results, defining the color of his asscheeks as 'lobster red. But I want you to make them purple,' he told me. I beat him some more and some more after that. He had me put clothespins on his nipples and balls, and he wanted me to pull on them, causing him agonizing pain, which he enjoyed. Throughout the whole damn thing, he addressed me as 'Mistress.'"

In her autobiography, *Out of Bondage,* Linda recalled a far more painful experience during the creation of one of Chuck's 8mm loops.

In this S&M fantasy, she was forced to star in a brief porno film with an older dominatrix identified as "Michelle." As described in Linda's memoirs, "Dressed all in black, she wore a dress whose collar virtually covered her throat like some 1930s school marm."

Linda was ordered to strip before the woman, who appeared to be in her fifties. Trembling, Linda didn't like the sadistic way the woman appraised her body. She seemed fascinated by the scar on Linda's body and asked if she'd gotten those cuts at the hands of another sadist. She was disappointed to learn that the scar was the result of a car accident.

Chuck had told Linda that this was to be her first "bondage" film. Again, Linda wasn't exactly sure what that meant. But she got the idea when Chuck tied her to the bed. She was positioned on her stomach, her buttocks exposed to the sadist.

"Linda, darling," Michelle said in a soothing voice. "Please know this is going to hurt you more than it hurts me. But you've been a naughty girl, and you must be punished. I know what you did with those two innocent little boys. They're pupils in my school."

By this time, Linda realized that Michelle was inventing her own plot. She was creating a scenario that focused on Diego and Ramon as pupils in some mythical elementary school run by her.

Michelle had brought her own props, including a high-powered hair dryer. The session began with her turning on that hair dryer and aiming it at Linda, especially at her buttocks. She set the dryer to its highest setting and pressed it against Linda's anus, causing her to squirm in pain. Removing it, Michelle then inserted the dryer between her legs.

As Linda reared up in pain, she opened the way for the dryer to be pressed into her vagina. At this point, she screamed. Finally, after a few agonizing moments, Michelle removed the hairdryer.

"Linda, my darling," she said in her most soothing voice. "That was just foreplay, the opening act, so to speak."

With a stiff riding crop, Michelle began to beat Linda's back, buttocks, and thighs. Her upper body throbbed, and she felt her stomach knotting as she erupted in sweat. Racking pain, interspersed with a persistent, agonizing ache, shot through her body. Then she realized that parts of her body had grown numb. Her throat was so dry she couldn't swallow.

For her final instrument of torture, Michelle produced a fourteen-inch long black leather-sheathed dildo. "I'm going to use this on you until you beg for mercy," she threatened. She kept her word.

Without preparation, Michelle rammed the dildo up into Linda's rectum. The pain was the greatest she'd ever known.

"What in hell are you screaming about?" Michelle hissed at her. "I was told your ass can take four cocks at once!"

"Without relenting, she plunged and retracted and plunged the dildo in and  out of Linda. "I felt like I was being torn apart," she recalled. "I never had a second of relief from the unrelenting pain."

Suddenly, Michelle ripped the dildo out of her. "You like that, don't you, bitch?"

"No, no, please," Linda begged. "You're killing me!"

That seemed to goad Michelle into an even more ferocious attack, as she rammed the dildo into Linda even harder than before.

Searing, wracking, splitting pain ripped through Linda's guts. "Kill me!" she shouted at Michelle. "Go ahead. Get it over with!"

Linda didn't know how long Michelle worked. Mercifully, she passed out from the assault.

When she woke up, she was still in the same bed, but was no longer tied up. In great pain, she rose weakly, trying to sit up. To her horror, she saw that the sheets were red with her blood.

My Michelle

Forcing herself to stand vertically, she put on a robe and hobbled along the hallway to the stairway, where she called downstairs. Only Barbara was in the house. Linda didn't know where Chuck had gone.

Rushing upstairs to her aid, Barbara examined her wounds. "Honey, some-body did a number on you, and Chuck allowed it, that bastard. I've got to get you to a doctor."

Within ten minutes, Linda was in Barbara's car, driving to a private clinic where one of her johns was a doctor who would examine her.

Everything that happened next seemed like a blur for Linda. She required rectal stitches.

Once back at the house, Chuck still hadn't come home. Barbara changed her sheets and gave her some sleeping pills—enough to knock her out for a long time.

When Linda awoke late the next morning, she still ached. Managing her toilet as best she could, she slipped on a robe and went out by the pool, where Chuck was sunbathing in the nude.

She launched into an attack: "I had to have stitches. That cunt tried to kill me."

He seemed indifferent. "Listen, honey, all that means is that only one hole of yours is not in working order at this time. There's nothing wrong with either your pussy or your throat. I can still rent those out: Michelle had a real grand time and paid very well for that dildo rape of you. She'll be a good client of ours in the future."

***

Chuck had kept Linda so busy that she'd had little time to slip away to see Larry. To an increasing degree, she had come to view her intimate moments with him as her main reason for living. In his arms, she felt truly free of Chuck and the kinky, often painful, assignations he was constantly arranging for her.

During her time with Larry, she never wanted to mention, or hear about, his wife and children. If anything, he continued to be devoted to them from what she gathered. She loved him, but at times she feared being merely a diversion for him. He did cry out expressions of his love for her, but it only occurred during moments of extreme passion, where a lover is likely to say anything.

Years later, she was vague in relaying details about her intimate moments with Larry. Too close an examination seemed, in her view, like an invasion of her privacy, since so much of her sex life was on view to any stranger who opted to screen some of Chuck's 8mm loops.

Linda did admit that she went "all the way with Larry. I did things to him that no woman, especially his wife, would ever do to him. He loved it and wanted more. I held back nothing. He got the works. Through me, he discovered erotic zones on his body that he didn't know existed. A lot of people would call some of the things we did low down and dirty, but I called it love."

As she'd long suspected, her love affair with Larry did not last forever. "Nothing good in life ever does," she later said. The end of their relationship resulted from learning more about him than she ever wanted to know.

One afternoon, she reached Larry by phone, and he said that his male friends had returned from their trip and moved back into their home. Then he told her that they were organizing a boating trip to Bimini, and that his two friends wanted to make an arrangement for her to accompany them. "We could spend some time at sea together," he promised her, "and get someone else to pay for it."

"I don't understand," she said. "You told me your friends are gay. Why would they want me to go along?"

"I'll explain later," he said. "I can't talk now. The guy at the marina will call you with details about departure time. It'll be early Sunday morning."

That Sunday morning at 5am, Chuck drove her to the marina. Larry was already aboard the vessel and below deck, as he wanted to avoid a personal encounter with Chuck.

The marina's manager, Dusty Gunther, introduced Chuck to the gay couple who had rented the yacht for the sail to Bimini.

In his forties, Michael Crehan, who seemed to be in charge, resembled the actor, Treat Williams, whom she'd seen on TV. Crehan stood about six feet tall, and had a trim physique. He was reasonably handsome, with a deep tan.

His partner, David Sands, was the less attractive member of the pair, and stood about five feet nine. He, too, had a good physique. Both men looked like they spent a lot of time in the sun and at the gym. Sands seemed energetic and anxious to please, but it was obvious that Crehan was the boss.

When the two men were in the manager's office, Chuck told Linda, "To me, these guys are two fags. They even wear matching pink shorts for god's sake. You're going to have an easy trip with them. Neither of them looks like he knows how to handle a woman. But who knows? Perhaps they're bisexuals."

As Chuck on the pier faded into the distance, she felt like a free woman getting rid of him. Along with other hookers who shared their house, she privately referred to Chuck as "Satan."

She'd thought many times of escaping from him, in spite of the hold he seemed to have on her, but he constantly reminded her that wherever she went, he would hunt her down and kill her. She truly believed that he would.

Once aboard, Crehan and Sands stayed on deck to talk to the captain. Eagerly, Linda went below, where she found Larry in the galley. He embraced her warmly and kissed her passionately. "I've missed you, my little darling," he told her. "No one takes care of me like my baby."

"Oh, Larry," she said. "I love you so much. I want you right now."

"And I want you, honey," he said, whispering into her ear before tonguing it. "Let's knock off a quick one before lunch with our hosts."

Love-making with Larry was as wonderful and as satisfying to her as it always was, maybe better. Their sessions always began the same way. "It didn't take me long to make that fat, lazy banana turn into a leering cobra."

Greedily devouring his ramrod, she made slurping noises as her cheeks sucked in and out and her throat opened to him. Galvanized by their lovemaking, she kissed, cradled, caressed. He responded with equal fervor.

When Crehan knocked on their cabin and called them to lunch, both of them had exhausted all desire. She felt awkward about greeting their hosts and wondered if anything would be expected of her for their financing of this paid vacation with her lover. She was grateful, but hoped it was an act of generosity based on their friendship with Larry.

She had wanted to ask Larry why his two best friends were gay, but thought better of it. In her world, gay men hung out together, separately from straights. She'd never seen these two different worlds meet in a close-knit friendship. It made her wonder if something was going on that she had not yet detected.

At lunch, Linda met a sullen young man who looked no more than nineteen. To her, he evoked a shadow version of the late James Dean. He had a pack of Lucky Strikes rolled up in the sleeve of his white T-shirt. His hair was disheveled and bleached by the sun. When Linda offered her hand, he did not bother to shake it, but picked up a bottle of beer instead.

It turned out that Sands was the cook of the family, and he had prepared fresh Bahamian lobster for them. After all these months with "fast food Chuck," she'd forgotten what home cooking tasted like, even if home was a temporary rented yacht. For desserts, he'd made chocolate éclairs. Three bottles of champagne were consumed.

Before the end of the luncheon, Linda had learned that the young man's name was Tim Slater, and that Crehan and Sands had picked him up in a parking lot at some mall and taken him home.

By two o'clock, she'd finally learned what his role was within this seagoing drama. Slater appeared to be straight, if that were the right word for it. When Larry stayed on deck after the three other men went below deck, he explained the arrangement to her.

"To lure Slater into their nest, the boys had to promise him a woman," he told her. "You're the gal."

"You mean, you want me to go below deck and into the cabin with the three of them?" You would really want

Resemblances that Linda Remembered:

"Trim and reasonably handsome, and deeply tanned, he (Michael Crehan) looked like **Treat Williams**"

107

me to do that?" She was stunned, although she didn't know why. Larry was well aware that when she was not with him, she was seducing other men and making porno loops. She felt cheap.

"The guys are across the hall from us, babe," he said. "I'm going back to our cabin and get some sleep. See you later. Good luck."

Tears welled in her eyes. The captain, a Cuban skipper in his fifties, came over to her. "I'm taking a break at five o'clock. I want you to come to my sleeping quarters then. It's pretty cramped in there, but we can maneuver. Crehan told me I could have you then."

What Linda said about her client Tim Slater:

"He evoked a shadow version of **James Dean**"

She didn't answer him or say anything. As she went below, her dreams about Larry were becoming nightmares. He didn't love her. It was all too obvious. Barbara had told her that the best way to get out of a trap alive was to be a trouper, and that's what she was prepared to be.

To an interviewer years later, she claimed that she had blocked out her memories of most of the rest of that trip to Bimini. She did, however, remember entering the cabin with Crehan, Sands, and Slater.

"Most of what I was hired for was to arouse Slater so Sands and Crehan could enjoy him," she said. "He was something special, a real stud, and I knew why these two gay guys had gone ape-shit over him."

Dinner was configured ashore on Bimini after about an hour in a place called "The End of the World" bar.

Even her hope of spending a night alone with Larry was dashed. He confessed that he had to routinely sleep with Sands and Crehan, referring to them as "my benefactors. I can't really live on my salary and raise a family. The boys subsidize my lifestyle. But neither one of them can give blow-jobs as good as you."

An hour later, Slater entered her cabin. "Larry's sleeping with those two queers tonight, and I got you."

She dreaded his attack on her. Far from being worn out, he seemed to be able to continue all night.

Who you're likely to meet at the End of the World:

Linda's hangout in **Bimini, The Bahamas**

She knew in advance that her homecoming, where she'd have to report to Chuck, would be dismal. But her life took a distinct turn for the worse about thirty minutes before the yacht returned to its home port in Miami, when Larry told her he wanted to talk to her in private. She fully believed that he might apologize for the ordeal he'd subjected her to, but his conversation was about something much more wrenching.

"All good things come to an end," he said. She thought he was referring to the yacht trip to Bimini. "I didn't mean for this to happen, but I've fallen in love with a girl in her twenties, Sally Beemham. She works in my office. A real good looker. I'm visiting her about three nights a week in her apartment."

Linda looked at him, as if not comprehending what he was telling her. "You mean, you don't love me anymore?"

"That's right," he said. "Shit happens. Sally's father is a big shot business-man in Newark, New Jersey. I'll probably get a divorce, marry Sally, and go work for his firm. I wouldn't have to struggle any more to make a living. I'd have everything I wanted. Her old man is loaded, and if I get bored in Newark, New York City is just a short hop away."

"Do you really love this girl, or are you just hustling her?" she asked, not concealing the anger in her voice.

"Since when does a whore have the right to put down a hustler?" he asked. "All of us play the same wicked games. And I see your boy Chuck waiting on the pier." He looked into her eyes. She found no feeling there, only an empti-ness. "I'm going below. Thanks for everything. See you around, kid."

As she disembarked from the yacht, she was determined not to cry. She knew she must not let Chuck see her crying.

"How was your trip?" Chuck asked, coming over to her. He'd already col-lected his fee from the marina manager.

"Rather boring," she said. "You were right. Two fags. The guys never touched me. I don't know why they booked me. Easiest money I ever earned. Let's get the hell out of here."

***

So many days had passed that Linda had come to believe that the New York Yankees never delivered a personal recommendation of her to Joe DiMaggio. She'd read in *The Miami Herald* that the former Yankee slugger was in town and staying at the Roney Plaza on Miami Beach.

But a few days later at around noon, Chuck received the call she'd been waiting for. The man who'd once been married to Marilyn Monroe wanted to see her for dinner that night at his hotel, beginning at eight o'clock.

The invitation brought a state of near hysteria to Linda, who immediately turned to Barbara for advice about what to wear.

Barbara suggested that she should try to look like Lauren Bacall in *How to Marry a Millionaire (1953)*, when she'd co-starred opposite Betty Grable and Monroe herself. Barbara owned an olive green suit with pink accessories that were tasteful and chic. "It'll make you look like the vice president of a cosmetics company," Barbara said. "You'd embarrass DiMaggio if you showed up looking like a dime-a-dance whore."

Even Chuck approved of her new look. "Joe can have any woman he wants," he said. "I'm amazed he even called for you. Those baseball players must have really given you some recommendation. It's sure not your looks. It must have been your cocksucking talent. A lot of gals—most gals, really—can't do that like you do it."

Over dinner, she found DiMaggio rather shy, treating her with respect—like a lady. He was vaguely annoyed at the fellow diners who kept approaching his table and asking for autographs, but he concealed his impatience with his famous smile.

She had wanted to ask questions about Monroe, but she didn't dare, having been warned by Chuck that "Joe doesn't like to talk about her. Even though she's dead, he's still carrying a torch for her. At least that's what one of those Yankee players told me."

DiMaggio ordered fish but wasn't pleased with the catch of the day. "I know about two things—fish and baseball. My father, Zio Pepe, was a fisherman. He moved his family from Sicily to San Francisco. He was very disappointed in me when I didn't follow the family trade."

"And deny the world the greatest baseball player of all time?" she said.

"You don't have to flatter me, but I appreciate it."

In his hotel suite, he invited her to "go into the bathroom and powder your nose, if you wish. There's a silk robe in there. When you finish, I'll be in my bedroom."

When she entered the bedroom, he was lying nude on the bedspread. There was no kissing, no fondling, no foreplay. He wanted her to begin performing her specialty almost immediately. From an unpromising beginning, his uncut penis rose up like a stallion.

She tentatively took it in her mouth, and soon it throbbed with a vitality of its own. She savored the taste and odor. He smelled so clean.

"Take it!" he commanded.

She liked to be ordered by him, and she gobbled hungrily, opening her throat to him, taking it all. Her nose was soon buried in his fragrant, curly crotch. She came up time and again for air. He didn't want a quick climax, but signaled her to make it last. She relaxed her pressure from time to time before having him moaning again. She fingered his testicles. Then he called out to her, "Here it comes."

He was sweet-tasting and delivered a feverish load before his body sank back onto the bed, completely exhausted. He was an older man at this point in his life, and the throes of a violent climax called for a recovery period. She kept him in her mouth until he deflated. He placed a hand, which had hit many home runs, onto the back of her neck, signaling it was enough.

"Thanks," he said softly. "That was good. Better even than Marilyn."

That was the first time tonight that he'd mentioned her name.

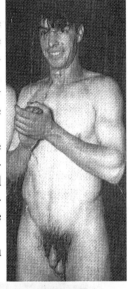

As part of her final goodbye, he kissed her on the cheek. "You really know how to do that. Wow! A home run. About ten times better than that Marilyn imperson-ator I picked up in the club down the beach, the Kit-Cat. You might have thought that if a drag queen knew how to do anything, it would involve sucking cock. This one did more choking than sucking—so unlike you."

Not wanting to return to Chuck right away, she walked along the beach. It was a cool night and a north-ern wind was blowing through the palms. She had wanted so much more, but DiMaggio hadn't been inter-ested. "As my gals can tell you, I'm good for only one big blast a night, and then I'm through."

"You might come only once a night, but when you do, it goes on and on. What a man!"

"I'll take that as a compliment," he said, shutting the door to his suite behind her.

The next morning, she didn't feel so bad about it when he sent her three dozen red roses.

Barbara cornered Linda and asked her, "So what is the Slugger like in bed?"

"Let me put it this way. That guy can always swing his bat in my direc-tion."

She told Barbara that she was hoping he'd call again for a repeat

Two views of baseball superstar
Joe DiMaggio

In the shower, and with his wife at the time,
Marilyn Monroe

performance, but she never heard from him. "If I'd been Marilyn, I would never have divorced that one. Joe's a real nice guy."

"How much did you get?" Barbara asked.

"I got nothing," she said. "Chuck was hoping to get five hundred, but he settled for two. I heard from one of the baseball players that Joe is a bit of a tightwad with women. But he can blow in my ear any time, and I'd follow him anywhere."

***

Linda had hated the last three marina bookings Chuck had arranged, mostly with businessmen from the Middle West vacationing without their wives in South Florida. One afternoon in 1970, Chuck seemed particularly overjoyed at Linda's latest booking from the marina.

"We hit the bigtime!" Chuck announced. "We didn't do so well with DiMaggio, but with the latest deal, we'll be in gravy. Bebe Rebozo and George Smathers are sailing to Bimini on a private yacht, and they need some company—in this case, you and Barbara."

"Never heard of them," Linda said. "Sports or movies?"

"Neither," he said. "Rebozo happens to be the best friend of Richard Nixon, and Smathers was a longtime Florida senator who used to be JFK's best friend. There's a rumor afloat that Smathers once fucked Jackie, who wanted to get even with her husband for chasing after all those bimbos."

Linda was apprehensive about meeting two such important and politically connected men. She had absolutely no knowledge of politics, and she feared she'd say something stupid. She knew that Richard Nixon was president of the United States, and that was about the extent of her knowledge. She wasn't sure who was a Democrat and who was a Republican.

In preparation for the following Sunday morning, Chuck had instructed both Barbara and Linda to dress in conservative business suits, hoping that they might be taken for secretaries if seen boarding the Smathers/Rebozo yacht.

But despite the care they'd taken during their preparations, Linda, with Barbara, felt awkward as they stepped aboard Rebozo's yacht. She sensed that during this jaunt with Smathers and Rebozo, there would be no group scenes. The men seemed too formal for that.

She felt embarrassed during her evaluation by Rebozo. He and Smathers seemed to share some kind of signaling language, and used it to define which man would pair off with which woman.

She preferred the tall and handsome former senator, but Rebozo had been told about Linda's special talent by Chuck, so he chose her.

Whenever Nixon came to Key Biscayne, Rebozo and the President sailed alone. This preference was in distinct contrast to when Smathers used to entertain President Kennedy during boating parties in the late 1950s and early 1960s. During those events, Smathers had become known in press circles for inviting women aboard "to pleasure" the Chief Executive.

Journalist Roger Mudd, a television network representative in JFK's press pool, aboard their own boat, tried to follow the presidential yacht whenever Smathers and Kennedy were entertaining on board. Mudd later wrote: "Together or singly, Smathers and President Kennedy were wolves on the prowl, always able to find or attract gorgeous prey. It was a joke, our pretending to be covering the president, bobbing around the ocean, squinting through binoculars to find out who was coming and going but always having our view blocked by a Secret Service boat just as another long-legged Palm Beach beauty climbed aboard."

At the time Rebozo came into Linda's life, the self-made Florida millionaire was spending more time with Nixon than the President did with his wife, Pat. He was also rumored to be Nixon's "bagman," picking up covert payments such as those from aviator Howard Hughes and ultimately giving the President access to the funds.

Although Rebozo had once been voted "the most beautiful boy in Tampa," he had lost his youthful appeal. But Smathers still lived up to his press reputation as "Gorgeous George," named after the celebrated professional wrestler (George Wagner; 1915-1963) who appeared in professional wrestling matches using that moniker.

Whereas the recently retired Democratic Senator Smathers, who had represented Florida in Washington from 1951 to 1969, exuded charm, Rebozo was

Presidential Protocol, with babes, on the high seas:

President Kennedy with Democratic Florida Senator (1951-69), **"Gorgeous George" Smathers**

More Presidential protocol (without babes):
Richard Nixon *(right)* with the man the press defined as "The President's First Friend," Florida businessman **Bebe Rebozo** *(left)*.

more withdrawn.

Although she hadn't been familiar with his name, Linda recognized Smathers from his appearances on TV. He was also a friend of Jackie Kennedy and had been a groomsman at her wedding to the president.

As the rented yacht sailed toward Bimini, the quartet rested on deck in bathing suits. Rebozo had very little to say, but Smathers entertained Linda and Barbara with stories about Washington. He liked to talk about himself, whereas Rebozo was secretive.

According to Smathers, had JFK lived, he would have replaced Lyndon Johnson on the 1964 presidential ticket. "As vice-president, I would have been the heir apparent to become the Democratic nominee for President in 1968 unless Bobby Kennedy got in my way."

Smathers also told them that after dropping out of politics, he'd divorced his first wife, the heiress Rosemary Townley. The former senator also impressed them when he told them that he'd sold his home on Key Biscayne to Nixon who had turned it into "The Winter White House."

After a lobster lunch, Smathers preferred to stay on deck after Rebozo went below to read through papers in his briefcase.

The more Smathers drank, the more scandalous his stories became. "I was also a close friend of Lyndon's," he told Linda and Barbara. "Any time Lyndon could, he'd parade around bare ass naked, even in the Oval Office. One time, he came out of the bathroom without a stitch on when the Japanese ambassador was in the room. I'm sure that 'lil ol' Jap envoy got a case of penis envy. I nicknamed Lyndon's penis 'Jumbo.'"

"I'm about two inches short of Lyndon, but I've got far more than most men," he said. "I often wear boxer shorts when I address women's groups in Florida. I hang better on the right than the left, and I instruct my tailor to make my pants tight in the crotch. I want the ladies to have something to look at when I make one of my typical stump speeches. Would you believe that at crowded cocktail parties, many women reach out with their delicate hands and feel the package?"

When it was time to go below, Linda envied Barbara when she disappeared with Smathers into his private cabin. Looking on wistfully as Smathers shut his cabin door and locked it, she finally knocked on Rebozo's door. "Come on in," he called.

Fun in the Sun	Roger Mudd:
George Smathers *(left figure)* with **JFK** *(right)*	"Smathers and JFK were wolves on the prowl."

"It's open."

She was startled to find him lying nude on top of the bedspread. "I'm ready, able, and willing for you to go to work on me."

With no other preliminaries than that, she moved over to the bed and removed her halter, leaving on the bottom of her bathing suit.

"I usually come pretty quick," he said.

"Fine with me," she told him. With her right hand, she guided his penis into her mouth. The muscles in his legs tightened around either side of her head. He got an erection almost immediately, measuring about seven inches. From a wide base, it narrowed to a tapered head, a bit unappetizing, but she worked hard to give him pleasure. With her left hand, she teased his testicles.

"Take it all, girl," he said, pushing her head down and holding her there in a strong grip. His eruption was quick, almost violent.

Without saying anything, he got up immediately and went into the bathroom. "I'll be out in a minute," he called to her. "Then you can come in and wash up."

Without meaning to, and knowing how out of line she was, she said, "When the President comes down, and if he'd like some of the same action, I want you to know I'm here and available."

Standing with a wet washcloth at the door to the bathroom, he laughed at her invitation. "You've got to be kidding. His name may be Dick but you're not going to get access to his dick."

She felt humiliated and excused herself to go back on deck.

The next morning after breakfast, Rebozo whispered something to her when they were alone. "You're good at what you do. But what happened yesterday will hold me for the rest of the trip, so you can just relax and have a vacation."

As she headed below, he called her back. "I'll tell George about your specialty...maybe he or his two sons might be interested."

Later that day, Linda and Barbara gossiped as they sunned themselves on deck while Smathers and Rebozo played a game of cards below.

"Gorgeous George is a man and a half," Barbara told her, "and I'll say no more."

When the yacht returned to its berth in Miami, Rebozo formally shook Linda's hand as he headed down the gangplank to discuss money with Chuck, who was waiting on the pier.

Smathers told her he was delighted to have met her. "I have two sons," he said, "John and Bruce Smathers. Both boys were born in the early 1940s. I think they'd

Bebe Rebozo

115

love to book you as a mascot on one of their fishing trips. Bebe told me about your specialty. Perhaps I'll present you as a Christmas present to my boys. They deserve some fun in life."

Like so many promises made to Linda, the senator never called again. Nor did either of his sons.

*****

[Unlike Senator Smathers, Bebe Rebozo would make a final appearance in Linda's life three months after the release of 1972's Deep Throat, *when she and Chuck Traynor returned to Miami.*

During a telephone call to Chuck, Rebozo requested that Linda visit his home in Key Biscayne where President Nixon was a frequent visitor. When Nixon wasn't in residence with him there, Rebozo was famous in the Miami area for the wild gay parties he hosted every Saturday night.

When Linda was informed of Rebozo's request, she assumed that it was for another sexual liaison similar to the one she'd had with him aboard his yacht.

Arriving exactly on time at Rebozo's home, she was ushered onto his pool terrace by a young Chinese man in a white jacket.

Shirtless, but wearing a pair of white shorts, Rebozo was lying on a chaise longue. *Sitting under an umbrella at a table beside him was a man in his fifties, dressed in a business suit. Rebozo introduced her to Leonard Liss, announcing that he was an attorney. At first, Linda was seized with a sense of panic, fearing she was facing some legal problem associated with* Deep Throat.

After drinks were served and some friendly chit-chat had ended, Rebozo looked very serious, almost outraged. "You are, of course, familiar with Al Goldstein and his Screw *magazine?" he asked.*

"I am," she said. "Everybody I know knows about Screw.*"*

Liss reached over and handed her the latest edition of Screw. *In a photo montage, Goldstein had published a fake picture of President Nixon looking down her throat. The caption read: "Capital gossips say Linda Lovelace, here showing her esophagus to the Chief of State, may replace H.R. (Bob) Haldeman under Nixon's desk."*

"It's all a joke," she said. "I've become the laughing stock of the country. I should get royalties from the jokes Johnny Carson and Bob Hope make about me on TV."

"There's more to that caption than meets the eye," Rebozo said. "Goldstein obviously knows that Haldeman is a bisexual. If he doesn't, J. Edgar Hoover knows that. Haldeman often sucks off the more handsome and virile members of Nixon's Secret Service. What Goldstein is suggesting is that Haldeman sometimes crawls under Nixon's desk in the Oval Office and gives him

blow jobs."

"I can't imagine anyone, male or female, ever giving Nixon a blow job. And I'm sure Dick's dick has never touched Pat's lips."

"Don't be vulgar," Rebozo warned her. "Dick is my friend and the finest man in this country."

"There's more," Liss said. "Here's another issue, pure libel. Goldstein has called Screw 'The newspaper of record for the Nixon administration.' Not only that, he also wrote, 'If you took a coconut and sliced it open, poured out the milk, scooped out the meat, and then shoveled in steaming shit, you would have a re-creation of the brain of Richard Milhous Nixon.'"

"I heard on TV the other night that another president, Harry S Truman, said that in politics, if you can't stand the heat, get out of the kitchen," Linda said.

"That's different," Liss said. "Truman, that asshole, was talking about political debates over issues. Goldstein is attacking Nixon on a personal level of the most vulgar sort, and therefore is vulnerable for libel."

"How do I fit into all this?" she asked.

"Bebe and I are seriously considering recommending to the President that he sue Goldstein for libel, which would effectively put that underfinanced publication out of business," Liss said. "In a separate lawsuit, we also suggest that you, too, file charges against Goldstein."

"I'd have to talk that over with my manager, Chuck Traynor. I can't make a decision like that for myself."

"I understand," Liss said. "Right now, I have an important luncheon engagement and must go. Delighted to have met you, Ms. Lovelace. I haven't seen your film. I'm a John Wayne fan myself, but I wish you luck in your future projects." He shook Rebozo's hand. "I hope to hear from you soon, Bebe, about Ms. Lovelace's decision."

After the attorney had gone, Linda turned to Rebozo. "Even though I'm now a movie star, I'm still a working gal. Always good for some private entertainment."

"I figured that," he said, "but I didn't want to bring that up when Liss was with us."

"Which do you prefer?" she asked. "Out here by the pool or in your bedroom?"

"It'll be different this time," he said. "My new lover, Guido, is living with me. When Dick flies down from Washington on Air Force One, I have to move Guido to a hotel."

"Don't tell me you're gay," she said. "I'm surprised. "You certainly weren't gay when we took that boat trip with Smathers."

"I'm not gay," he said. "You of all people should know the meaning of bi-

117

sexual."

"I do," she said. "I swing both ways myself."

"Guido is anxious to meet you," he said. "He's a student in Florence, but for the moment, at least, he's on vacation. He wants us to have a three-way, and I promised him I would. He's working on his English. By the way, I showed him your film the other night. He's very impressed with you. Guido also has a lot to impress you with as well."

"I can't wait," she said, almost meaning it.

Rising from the chaise longue *he was occupying, he said, "I've got to make a call. Why don't you go to the door at the end of the hall? Knock softly. Guido's waiting. You guys can get started, and I'll be in to join you soon."*

Following his instructions, she walked down the corridor where Nixon had trod. After her knock on the door, a heavily accented Italian voice asked her to enter.

As she came into the darkened room, she was greeted with "one of the most glorious sights of my life," as she'd later describe the scene to Barbara. "He was an Italian version of that fabulous-looking French movie star, Alain Delon."

"Did you guys get it on?" Barbara asked.

"That is hardly the word for it," Linda said. "When Rebozo came in, he helped me work on Guido. We sent that boy into heavenly delights. As a performer, I should have won an Oscar. Rebozo even took us to dinner afterward. It was midnight before I got home."

At Rebozo's favorite restaurant, Key Biscayne's English Pub, he placed food orders for both Guido and Linda without consulting with them first. They consumed martinis until their food arrived—chopped steak medium rare with Caesar salad, and key lime pie for dessert. Rebozo told her this was Nixon's favorite order at this pub.

At the end of the meal, paid for by Rebozo, he placed a fifty-dollar bill on the table as a tip. Both cash-poor Linda and even poorer Guido were impressed.

Noting that, Rebozo said, "Not bad for a little Tampa-born kid, one of nine children of an underpaid cigar maker from Cuba. When I was a teenager, I earned my living killing and plucking chickens."

"You've come a long way, baby," Linda said, having learned at dinner that night that Bebe in Spanish translated as "baby."

What Linda Remembered:
"Rebozo's lover, Guido, looked like
(the French movie star)
Alain Delon" *(photo above)*

That night, Rebozo and Guido were sexually exhausted, as was Linda. He invited them for champagne in his living room, where he played Broadway show tunes for them. "Dick and I can sit here for hours listening to our favorites like Ethel Merman and Carol Channing. Judy Garland might have been a favorite of ours, but she was fucked by Kennedy. Dick feels he was also fucked by Kennedy in a different way, so Judy is persona non grata *in my record collection."*

When Linda finally arrived home, Chuck was furious with her for staying away for so long. But when she presented him with ten one-hundred dollar bills, he was delighted and all smiles. "Just for that, I'll throw you a fuck tonight. You deserve it."

Physically worn out from Guido, that was the last thing she wanted. She really would have preferred to be left alone and allowed to sleep.

Later, she told him about her possible lawsuit against Al Goldstein and Screw *magazine, including the Nixon link. She didn't know what his reaction would be.*

"I'm all for that," he said. "It will be the lead story on all three networks. It'll make you even more famous than you already are."

During the weeks to come, Rebozo may have proposed such a lawsuit to Nixon, but the wily politician rejected the idea, perhaps denouncing it as ridiculous.

She never heard from Rebozo again. But in 1974, in the wake of Nixon's resignation, she had her own comments to make about the disgraced president. In The Intimate Diary of Linda Lovelace, *she wrote:*

"Does Nixon look like a man who has ever gone down on a woman? If he had, or if he could have, I bet the country would have been different. It would be nice if he'd announced on television, 'Hey, everybody. Dig this. Next Tuesday is sex day. I am going to stay home all day, and no business is going to get done. Your president will be getting his rocks off."]

***

One night, Chuck showed up at his house with a teenage girl known only as "Sunshine."

Jealous at first, Linda checked her out skeptically. "Well, we've already employed Moonshine," she said. "Why not Sunshine?" She asked the girl, "Just how old are you?"

"Just turned seventeen," Sunshine said.

Linda didn't believe her. Later, she found out that Sunshine was only fourteen years old. Linda confronted Chuck. "Jailbait is dangerous," she said, as if he didn't already know that.

119

Her jealousy of Sunshine quickly faded. The teenager had immense appeal and charm and quickly won Linda's friendship.

In previous cases, Chuck had groomed his prostitutes to look like specific movie stars. But it was obvious that as things applied to Sunshine, he was planning something different.

"You could be my older sister," Sunshine said.

That was already obvious to Linda. Sunshine looked like no movie star she'd ever seen. Her skin tones, her hair, her height, her bone structure, even her breasts, were practically a perfect match with Linda's features.

Sunshine announced that she would be available only part time, as she had a steady boyfriend, who was twenty-eight years old and worked in the advertising department of *The Miami Herald.*

That night, Chuck ordered a large pizza for them to share. Around the kitchen table, they consumed that pie and drank beer. Chuck said that because Sunshine and Linda looked like sisters, he'd conceived the idea of booking them as a "joint gig. Some men would really get off fucking two sisters, especially one as young as Sunshine. What I suggest is that you, Linda, perform your specialty on the guys, and that Sunshine join in for the actual penetration. There's nothing a forty-year-old man likes better than young, tight pussy."

"I know a lot of guys who like to see two gals getting it on," Sunshine said. "I really like Linda a lot, and we could perform sex acts together to turn on men. I go both ways. How about you, Linda?"

"I've been known to do that," she said.

"When I send you gals out on your first gig, I want both of you to dress like you're real young—perhaps with the suggestion that Linda is in her senior year in high school and that you, Sunshine, are still in junior high school. In the meantime, why don't you gals adjourn to my bedroom, where I'll show both of you what a real man is like."

In *Inside Linda Lovelace,* she gave few details about Sunshine, the jobs they were sent to, and the clients they serviced. But in that memoir, Linda stated that on the first night together with Sunshine in Chuck's bed, she engaged in a sixty-nine with Sunshine while "Chuck fucked me dog fashion. After Chuck came, I took my turn on Sunshine and had a double delight. Not only did I get to savor her own sweet juices, but the *entrée* was topped off with all of Chuck's precious come. Hate to waste that good stuff."

On the dawn of her filming of *Deep Throat,* Linda and Sunshine indulged in a series of bizarre sexual encounters, since they were catering to what Chuck called "the kink market, one that was peopled with weirdos, panty sniffers, incest freaks, child molesters, voyeurs, vampires, Peeping Toms, potheads, poon stalkers, cooze lickers, sadists, masochists, and lezzies."

For her age, Sunshine seemed far more sophisticated than Linda in navigating her way through the twilight world in which they traveled together over the coming weeks.

For their first sex booking of what Linda called "the dynamic duo," Chuck drove them along Alhambra Drive, a leafy street in Coral Gables, until they came to a very large Spanish-style house. He told them he'd be back at eleven o'clock to pick them up.

Ushered inside by a maid in a uniform with a white apron, they were led onto a terrace where they met their hosts, Mike Hardy and his young son, Joel. Whereas Mike appeared to be in his late thirties, Joel was no more than thirteen or fourteen. Mike seemed very prosperous, and at some point, Linda and Barbara learned that he was a successful electronics engineer. Joel was still in Junior High school.

Linda was surprised when they were invited to join father and son at a well-prepared dinner, where Linda ate far more than she should have, requesting second helpings. Joel merely picked at his food.

By the time dessert arrived, the social niceties were dispensed with, and Mike told them why they were here. He'd been married and divorced twice, and Joel was a by-product of his first marriage. "I want Joel to be straight. I have nothing against gays, but I know it'll be a lot easier for him to be straight in life. Trouble is, Joel is in love with me. I've been having sex with him every night because I'm afraid that if he goes out for partners, he might get involved in some scandal or even arrested."

"So," Sunshine said, "our job is to turn him on to women?"

"But I don't want them!" Joel protested.

"You've got to, or I'll give you a beating," Mike said.

"Okay, I'll take the beating from you if you strip naked when you're beating me," Joel said.

At that point, Linda realized Joel was hopelessly, irrefutably homosexual, and that anything she and/or Sunshine did would probably not help in transferring his gender preference onto women.

"I'll only have sex with them if you're in bed with us at the same time," Joel said to his father.

"I'll agree to that."

Once the deal was finalized, Linda joined father and son and Sunshine in bed. Linda immediately began fellating Mike, who rose to the occasion.

Sunshine, however, was having much more difficulty with Joel. It didn't help matters when Joel told her, "Women smell bad down there. My father always has a wonderful aroma, even when he's been with me on a two-day fishing trip and hasn't had a real bath."

Mike removed his penis from Linda's mouth. "Ok, son. Now get on top of Sunshine, and I'll lie on top of you and fuck you. We'll see what happens then."

121

Joel readily agreed to become the center of the sandwich. "Father knew best," Linda later recalled to Chuck.

Sunshine asserted to Linda that when Mike penetrated Joel, he got an immediate erection.

"He wasn't really that turned on by me," Sunshine said. "He concentrated on enjoying his father's dick—not me."

"I felt like the unwanted guest at the party," Linda said. "There was no need for me, really."

"Joel never got off," Sunshine said. "When Linda and I left the bedroom, we looked back. Mike was going down on his son. Then the maid showed us to the door."

Later, during the report she delivered to Chuck about how the evening had transpired, she said, "I think they'll be happy together. At least they're keeping their loving in the family."

"Oh, shit!" Chuck responded. "You guys screwed up this booking. That means they won't be calling me again. They would have been great customers. They paid me two hundred dollars for you two worthless bitches."

***

Lonely and desperate for friendship, Linda bestowed her affection on "my little sister and lookalike," Sunshine herself. Out by the pool sharing some weed, or making chocolate milkshakes together in the kitchen, the two women bonded.

Sunshine told her that her older lover, Fred Lowe of *The Miami Herald,* was good to her, but that she wasn't in love with him. "When the right man comes along, I'll settle down and become a housewife and raise five kids—two boys and three girls."

She also confided intimate secrets to Linda about her boyfriend after Linda noticed teeth marks and bruises on her neck. "Did you make it with a tiger at the zoo?" she asked Sunshine.

"Fred has his good points, but he's not very well endowed—not at all, and he has trouble getting off. The only way he can pop a nut is by biting me, sometimes hard. That excites him."

"It sounds like my so-called husband—read that, pimp—and your ad salesman are not the kind of men we plan to settle down with for life."

"If I don't settle down as a housewife, I might end up with a woman, maybe with a woman like you. You're very nice to me, Linda."

"I don't know if I could live with a woman," Linda said, "even one as sweet as you. I've been trained to receive a deep penetration in all three holes, and that's my ultimate turn-on. To me, lesbian sex is just the icing on the cake, not

122

the cake itself. A woman strapping on a dildo for me isn't quite the same. I like to be invaded by something alive."

That day after a take-out lunch, courtesy of Chuck, Linda learned more about Sunshine. Born in San Francisco, her real name was Joy Haller. "I became a whore in junior high. I started going out with older child molesters for ten dollars a throw. That went on for about ten months before my stupid parents found out. They didn't give a shit about me anyway. My mama reminded me every day that she should have had me aborted. When they found out I was selling it, they sent me to this foster home to live with two frightening assholes, both Born Again Christians. I tried to play by their rules and suffered their nightly beatings for three months. Then I ran away."

"I found refuge at this hippie camp outside San Francisco. Every night I slept with a different dude, each with long hair. They shot me up with all sorts of junk. People were always sticking needles in my arm. I smoked hash every day. I didn't know anything about drugs. I just took them. Finally, I hooked up with this older guru who said he'd show me 'the way to enlightenment.' I found out what his way was. He drove me across the country, renting me out to older guys at truck stops. Once we got to Florida, he dumped me. I screwed a lot of guys before meeting Fred, who likes them young."

"You never got pregnant?" Linda asked.

"No," she answered. "A doctor in San Francisco told me I have an inverted uterus. It's weirdly positioned. I can't drop a kid."

At that point, Chuck came out onto their patio in his jockey shorts. "You are two lucky *putas,*" he said. "Guess what I'm going to do for both of you today? I'm going to make movie stars of you. I've roughed out a film scenario for you gals. I'm entitling it *Two Sisters.*"

Without objection, Sunshine rushed inside to make herself camera ready. Chuck detained Linda. "There's a real market for this young stuff. Lolita lovers will go crazy for it."

"You don't believe Sunshine is seventeen, do you?" Linda asked.

"She's probably thirteen or maybe just fourteen," he said. "But what the hell? I could make even more money on this loop if she were twelve, even ten. I met this filmmaker guy who had a best-seller with a nine-year-old twat servicing two older men."

In the bedroom, Chuck ordered Sunshine and Linda to strip. Their first scenes together would involve Sunshine lying on her back, masturbating herself. After a few minutes of this, her "older sister," as played by Linda, would enter the bedroom and catch Sunshine in the act of pleasuring herself.

"Play the whole thing like you're a very perverted fourteen-year-old," Chuck ordered.

Linda helped with the camera work as Sunshine got to work.

Since there was no sound track, Chuck shouted his instruction to Sunshine. "Play with your clit." "Fondle your tits!" "Stick your finger up your cunt!" and "For god's sake, look excited. I'm paying you fifty bucks for this clip!"

After the sequence with Sunshine, Chuck turned to Linda. "It's showtime for you, kid. Get on the bed with Sunshine and start with some *kisserinos.*"

Sunshine became the aggressor in the kissing scene with Linda—long and passionate tongue contacts. When Chuck had had enough of that, he ordered them to "get into your positions for the sixty-nine shots." Again, Sunshine took the lead as if she'd been making porn for a decade. Linda was uncomfortable being filmed with her face buried against Sunshine's vagina, but she bravely carried on. "What if my mom and dad saw me like this?" she asked herself, before dismissing the possibility. Her parents didn't watch lesbian porno loops.

Like all things, the loop eventually ended after each of the performers brought her partner to a shattering climax. As Linda later recalled, "It was real. There was nothing fake about it. Whoever buys this damn loop will get their money's worth."

A few nights before, Chuck had replenished his stash of marijuana. Linda was used to being attacked by Chuck for whatever she did, but she felt relaxed around him for the first time after he praised both of their efforts in *Two Sisters*.

Sharing one of many marijuana cigarettes with Chuck and Sunshine, Linda felt at peace with the world, even though she knew they couldn't go on forever living as they did.

Before midnight, Sunshine drove off in her Volkswagen so that she could meet her boyfriend, Fred Lowe, after he got off from his night shift at *The Herald*.

She and Chuck retired to bed after 2am. As she'd later remember, "He did that odd thing: He actually had regular sex with me, I mean man-and-woman in missionary position. What had come over him?"

Exhausted by the day's events, she fell into a deep sleep. She was rudely and terrifyingly awakened two hours later. Two flashlights were piercing through the gloom of their darkened bedroom. One shone directly into her eyes, the other into Chuck's.

Then a deep, authoritative voice announced, "You're under arrest!"

The ultimate underaged sex fantasy: **Sue Lyons** interprets LOLITA.

124

CHAPTER FOUR
Servicing the Kink Market
For a Place in the Sun

There wasn't much about Chuck Traynor that impressed Linda. But he had an uncanny ability to extricate himself from a jam. Without a warrant, three young police officers had broken into his house to arrest Linda and him.

Within twenty minutes, Linda and Chuck learned of the potential charges against them. Ramon, that Afro-Cuban teenager who had made a child porn video with them, had been arrested. He had been caught breaking into a deli at two o'clock on the morning of the previous day. Under intense questioning, he'd confessed that he and his brother, Diego, had made a porn film for Chuck—"with some woman."

Ramon had led the police to Chuck's house. The inexperienced officers, without a search warrant, had broken into the building as Chuck and Linda were asleep. Perhaps the police feared that if they waited, Chuck might conceal the incriminating tapes elsewhere.

Chuck insisted that Linda remain in the bedroom while he negotiated with the two officers out back beside the pool.

She knew that he was trying to talk himself out of this latest charge. She reminded herself of how he had successfully avoided conviction on that marijuana charge. Even so, she'd feared she'd be arrested along with Chuck, as she was just as guilty as he was.

Police corruption in Dade County was a decades-old tradition, and Chuck knew a lot about how it worked. A few hours after they'd broken in, the police left his house without placing him under arrest. At no point had Linda ever left the bedroom.

When Chuck returned to their room, it was around 4:30am. "They're gone."

"What happened?" she asked.

"Get back in bed, bitch, he said. "I need some sleep. We made a deal, that's all."

125

"What kind of deal?" she asked.

"That's for me to know and you to find out…maybe tomorrow."

Seemingly without guilt or fear of repercussions, he turned his back to her and fell into a coma-like sleep. For her, however, there would be no sleep, as she plotted how she might run away, leaving Florida altogether and returning to New York, where she felt safer.

That morning over breakfast, he was non-committal. All he told her was that "shit happens."

By the following Sunday afternoon, his unvoiced plan began to take shape. He ordered her to get into his Volkswagen, where he drove her to a dreary little house in South Miami. It looked desolate. Painted a yellow faded by the sun, it had only one lonely shrub in its front yard, and a bush dying of thirst.

Before he ordered her from the car, he told her, "Those cops who broke in on us are single guys who share payments of the rent on this dump. They're not going to press charges if we cooperate. In exchange for our going free, you've got to be good to them. You're one lucky broad. They're nice looking and young. One of them, Greg, the ringleader, could make it in porno himself."

"What am I to do?" she asked.

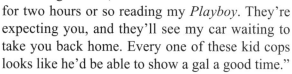

"Just walk up to the door and ring the bell," he instructed. "I'll sit out here for two hours or so reading my *Playboy*. They're expecting you, and they'll see my car waiting to take you back home. Every one of these kid cops looks like he'd be able to show a gal a good time."

As mentioned by Chuck, the policeman named Greg opened the door for Linda and invited her in. He looked like a poster boy representing Hitler's claim of Aryan racial superiority. In his bulging jockey shorts, he looked "too pornographic" to pose as an underwear model. Under dirty blonde hair, he stood about six feet two and had at least a fifty-inch chest with sixteen-inch biceps. A pattern of chestnut hair began in the center of his chest, narrowing to a thin line as it headed toward his navel.

She didn't know what to expect, but because they were police officers, she didn't anticipate any physical harm from them. Greg went into his kitchen and opened the refrigerator, taking out a Budweiser.

He offered a can to her, but she refused. "From what we heard from this Ramon kid, you know how to take care of little boys. How about taking care of some big boys?"

"That's what I'm here for," she said.

From a back bedroom emerged two other officers, each wearing his underwear and each looking as if he had just emerged from a long sleep. Greg introduced them only as Joe and Howard. In contrast to Greg, Joe and Howard were ordinary-looking young men.

Of the three, Howard was the least well built, with the beginning of a small paunch. His red hair was starting to recede. Yet he was not unattractive, and had kissable lips and a sexy smile. He was a bit shorter than the rest, and had an almost hairless body.

Joe, the stockiest of the group, had broad shoulders and a barrel chest, with thick arms and legs. His body was covered with hair that was almost invisible except when it caught the deflected rays of the bright sunlight flooding the room. His sandy blonde hair looked almost platinum in the bright glare.

The talk in the living room was about sports, a subject of which she knew absolutely nothing. It was Greg who finally got up to announce, "Let's get this party started." He directed all of them to the back bedroom.

"Will it be all three at once, or one at a time?" she asked Greg.

"My buddies and I like to share a woman," he answered. "Let's face it: A woman has three holes, and we like to make a gal happy by filling all of them at once."

She braced herself for the ordeal she knew was coming. She'd welcome sex with Greg, but she'd have preferred him alone. Her wish would not be granted.

Greg stripped off his jockey shorts and lay flat on his back, as his penis began to grow erect. "Ride Jumbo," he said. She mounted him guiding his helmet-shaped cockhead into her vagina.

Howard arranged himself to the right of Greg's head, inviting her to fellate him. Mounting her back, Joe slowly began to insert himself into her anus. "I'm going to re-arrange your guts, baby," he warned her.

He didn't do anything of the sort. She felt she could take three penises the size of Joe's. She also wasn't that impressed with Howard.

Greg was clearly the powerhouse of the trio, and she was attracted to him. As she rose above him, she noticed his head 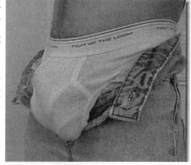 shifting from one side to the other, obviously in ecstasy. Howard, crowding in to the right of Greg's head, was an unwanted distraction. She welcomed the invasion of her body from Greg, but resented the other two, wanting them to climax and leave her alone to enjoy Greg.

But it didn't work out that way. The three

officers no doubt had gone through scenes like this before. All three of the men succeeded at timing their climaxes at the same time. For a moment, she felt she was drowning in a sea of semen.

Without any other formalities, Howard and Greg got out of bed and headed for the bathroom and a shower. "Joe was the pervert of the lot," she'd later confess to Chuck. "After pulling out of my ass, he demanded that I lick him clean. Fortunately, I was pretty clean myself. Otherwise, I would have upchucked."

Thoroughly tongue-washed, Joe left the bed to answer an urgently ringing phone. She escaped to the bathroom where she washed at the sink. Through the plastic shower curtain, she saw Howard fellating Greg under the running water of the shower.

Fifteen minutes later, she put on her red cotton dress and came into the living room. Howard, Joe, and Greg were each drinking Budweiser and watching a football game on TV.

"You're good, girlie," Greg called to her. "We'll phone Chuck to arrange for your next visit. He's promised that next time, he'll bring over your littler sister, Sunshine."

"That's okay with me," Linda said, "but I don't know if she can handle you."

"There's always you, then, Mama," Greg said. "I hope you don't mind if we invite two or three of our buddies. We owe them a favor."

"The more the merrier," she said, smiling a smile she didn't feel.

"I bet you'll have a sore ass tomorrow," Joe said. "Thanks!"

"Yeah, thanks," Howard said, returning to the TV.

"Until next time," Greg said. "It's the butler's day off, so show yourself out."

"Will do," she said, weakly, turning her back on the officers and heading out the door.

In the fading sunshine of a Florida Sunday, she shivered a bit, even though it wasn't cold. Behind the wheel of his Volkswagen, Chuck looked impatient.

As she'd later record in her diary, "I truly felt like a working whore being given her next assignment. If Greg lived there alone and without those other two jerks, and if he wanted a wife, I could really go for him."

She also told her diary that she had not completely abandoned her dream of becoming a housewife with two children. "It could still happen," she wrote.

But with the sordid encounter of the afternoon, her dream seemed more remote than ever.

"Get in, bitch," Chuck called to her from his Volkswagen. "I don't have all day."

***

128

Chuck was only too aware that there were far more hookers in Greater Miami than requests for their services. For him to survive, and pay his mounting bills, he had to cater to what he called "The Kink Market." That led to an increasingly degrading set of sexual encounters for Linda, and to a lesser degree, for Sunshine, too.

How Chuck promoted his big sister/little sister act always remained a mystery to Linda. She knew he couldn't advertise, so Chuck had to hawk his services through some sort of underground grapevine.

At any rate, that word of mouth system led to an encounter Linda and Sunshine had with two German brothers, Erich and Hans von Berchtoldsburg. Only one year apart in age, they were often mistaken for identical twins. Their parents asserted that they had originally derived from Austria, although by some accounts, they might have been Prussians from North Germany, near Berlin.

During the nearly three years their parents lived in an old mansion in Coral Gables, they flourished briefly in society. They'd been known for their charm and old-world graciousness, until rumors destroyed their social standing. They abruptly fled from the Greater Miami area.

There emerged a report that the family patriarch, Carl von Berchtoldsburg had been a Nazi officer, perhaps a minor one. Even as late as 1970, a quarter of a century after the end of World War II, such a taint was powerful enough to turn a family into outcasts.

Boys from the local high school painted a Swastika on Erich's locker. In reaction to that, his father enrolled both of his boys in a private school.

Despite their father's rumored Nazi associations, both boys were extremely popular with impressionable young girls. With their blonde hair, trim physiques, and athletic prowess, they each resembled a Teutonic version of Tab Hunter, The sixteen-year-old Hans and the seventeen-year-old Erich were each champion swimmers.

Chuck drove Linda and Sunshine to the Von Berchtoldsburg home, which was surrounded by gardens, and flanked with a swimming pool and a garage house. An aging emerald-green Mercedes was parked outside the garage. To Linda, the address evoked the house occupied by the fading silent screen actress Norma Desmond (as portrayed by Gloria Swanson) in the 1950 movie *Sunset Blvd.* It was a spooky old place, and both the house and grounds looked as if they needed maintenance.

But instead of delivering them to the main house, Sunshine and Linda were instructed to ring the doorbell of the garage house. It appeared that an apartment had been constructed over the garage.

Chuck had told Linda and Sunshine that he'd return for them at six o'clock that afternoon. It was only 2:30pm, so Linda suspected that she was in for a long session with the boys.

Erich came down the steps and opened the door, introducing himself and leading them up the stairs to the apartment. "I'm sorry I can't take you into the main house," he said in English that had only a slight German accent. "Father insists that Hans and I entertain here."

As Linda was ushered into the apartment, she said, "This is some place. All this gilt furniture. Amazing."

He introduced both of the women to his younger brother, Hans, who looked amazingly similar to Erich. It would have been impossible to tell which one of them was older. Both of them had long, straight, blonde hair.

At first, conversation among the four of them was awkward. Erich offered them beer, and Sunshine had a mugful, although Linda turned it down because of her liver problems.

The silence was broken when Erich stood up from the sofa. "I play the violin. Would you like to hear me?"

Top photo: Über-diva **Gloria Swanson**, in *Sunset Blvd.*, playing the crazed occupant of a house *(lower photo)* that reminded Linda of the site of one of her gigs: **the Von Berchtoldsberg mansion**.

Both Sunshine and Linda said they'd be delighted. Erich gave a short concert for their benefit. Linda found the music smooth enough, but she couldn't tell good violin playing from bad. She was still an Elvis fan.

After he placed the violin on top of a piano, Erich looked over at Hans with a mischievous grin. "Let's play a little game," he said to Linda and Sunshine. "Let's strip Hans naked."

The boy put up some protests, but Erich started to take off his younger brother's clothes. Feeling that she had to, Linda joined in, signaling Sunshine to take off his boots.

Hans giggled and squirmed, but they quickly stripped him bare. He had a somewhat small, uncut penis. Erich turned to Linda. "Mr. Traynor told me about your specialty. Make Hans hard."

As instructed, Linda bent over the boy and swallowed his penis and testicles in one gulp. He shot up quickly. "Suck him!" Erich shouted at her.

He put his face so close to the action at one point that he was only two inches from Hans' penis. He seemed to so entranced with it that she suspected that Erich wanted to replace her.

As she'd later record in her diary, Erich stripped down and Linda got a rise out of him. Their cocks were almost identical. When Erich escorted them into the bedroom, Hans got on top of Sunshine, and Erich topped Linda.

As she'd later describe to Chuck, "These brothers didn't seem interested in us at all, but in watching each other. At one point, they passionately kissed each other. Both of them had a climax at the same time and kissed each other as they did."

The brothers occupied the bathroom first to clean up and then invited Linda and Sunshine to use the facilities. Fully dressed, Linda and Sunshine came back into the room. Soft classical music was playing, and the two brothers sat close to each other on the sofa.

Sunshine wanted to leave. In the bathroom, she'd whispered to Linda, "These brothers are two sickos. It's obvious they want to make it with each other."

Sunshine suggested that they leave, but Erich reminded her that "we still have another hour of your time."

As the quartet chatted pleasantly, Erich informed her of "our darkest secret. Hans and I have made a vow never to have sex with any woman unless the other was also in the bed at the same time. Most of the time, we have sex with only one woman, but we thought it a thrill to have sex with two sisters. Actually, our fantasy involves having sex with two girl twins."

By now, Linda was feeling slightly provocative. "Why don't you have sex with each other? A lot of brothers do, you know."

Anger flashed across Erich's face. "That's perverted. But then I forget. You're nothing but a cheap whore."

"Our father has taught us to hate homosexuals," he said. "Hitler was right. They are the scourge of the earth and should have been exterminated."

"I'm sorry," Linda said. "I didn't mean to cause trouble."

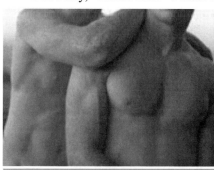

Erich and Hans

Erich stood up, ushering them toward the door. "Our interview with you girls is over. In your filthy business, Mr. Traynor has failed to teach you some manners. Please leave at once. Walk to the gate. I don't want you on our property any more."

Hans was even more emphatic. "Get out!"

On the way to the gate, where they hoped Chuck was waiting, Linda said to

Sunshine, "I sure hit a sensitive nerve. They're in love with each other, but can't admit it. Let's face it" They kept their erections by kissing each other."

"They called our jam session an interview," Sunshine said. "I never heard it called that before."

"The boys looked spic and span," Linda said. "But they needed to skin those little dicks back and wash down there. Chuck told me it's called head-cheese. Not my favorite food. I guess a whore has to get used to it."

***

Whenever an underground customer in South Dade County was on the lookout for an unusual sex gig, Chuck seemed ready and willing to fulfill it, using Linda as his bait. That led to one of her most bizarre sexual experiences, something she'd never heard of nor would ever repeat again.

Driving along U.S. Highway #1 at eight o'clock one night, Chuck informed her that they were heading in the direction of a mansion on Key Largo, where she was to be featured as part of the entertainment at an otherwise all-male sex auction.

"What the hell?" she asked. "Didn't that end with the Arab slave markets in Biblical times?"

"The history of sexual slavery doesn't interest me," he said. "Twelve studs have been recruited from the Homestead Air Force base. These boys have agreed to appear nude on the stage to be auctioned off to the highest bidder. The buyers in most cases are older, very rich businessmen who will have driven all the way from Palm Beach or Boca Raton. If a stud can hold out, he might be auctioned off as many as three times in a single evening."

"How do I fit into all this?" she asked, her apprehension growing.

"It's an easy job for you. After the stud strips and the buyers get a good look at his body, your job is to deep throat him. From past experience, bidding is highest when the young man is displayed erect. Surely, with your suction pump, you can give a guy a hard-on. At no point is he to come in your mouth. That precious stuff is saved for the buyers. They're paying enough for it."

"I've been asked to do worse things," she said, "although I've always found it embarrassing to perform in front of an audience."

"Don't worry about it," he said. "All the buyers are gay. They don't give a fuck what you look like."

In the mansion on Key Largo, a Cuban houseboy ushered Linda and Chuck into the private suite of Barry Cobb, who was dressed like a Wall Street broker in a pin-striped suit. "Chuck has told me about your specialty," he said to Linda. "Most of the guys I'm auctioning tonight are basically straight, and they'll enjoy your throat. But don't let them get too carried away."

"Chuck has already warned me about that," she said.

"Show time is at ten o'clock," Cobb said. "I'm conducting the auction myself. In the meantime, why don't you guys rest in my den?"

As Linda and Chuck started to leave, he called to her, "We didn't agree on wardrobe. You can wear a G-string if you wish, but I want you to be topless."

"That I can do," she assured him.

Chuck told her that some of the estimated thirty customers had already arrived and were being shown porno loops in a small theater Cobb had built. "This house contains ten bedrooms, and all of those beds will be actively in use until dawn."

"So the films feature cumming, not coming attractions?" she quipped.

"What in hell are you doing?" Chuck asked. "Rehearsing for standup comedy?"

The men from the air base unhurriedly entered into the den. Each had removed his shirt, but had kept on his pants. She talked to one of them, a tall blonde named Charlie. Between swigs on a can of beer, he told her why he was here. "I've got a wife and two kids and another on the way. I need the bread. Airmen like to get their cocks sucked and queers like to suck us. So it's a fair exchange, especially if big bucks are involved. Before I drive back to Homestead, I'll probably pocket three hundred bucks—not bad for a night's work." He wiped beer foam off a faint stubble of beer. "What are they paying you?"

"My pimp. See him over there?" She pointed to Chuck talking to two young men. "He pockets all the money."

"You're not bad looking," he said. "If you live in Homestead or South Miami, perhaps you'll give me your phone number. Maybe we can get together some night. My wife is in her advanced pregnancy. Need I say more? I've got a pretty big one."

"Then you'll really go over tonight," she said.

"All the guys Cobb hired have big ones, or else we wouldn't be here tonight."

As Chuck signaled for her to come over, Linda said, "Well, I'll be getting better acquainted with you in front of thirty or so guys."

Well scrubbed and well built, with some servicemen a bit bashful, the young men were paraded out shirtless and introduced one by one to the enthusiastic buyers.

For their second introduction, each man had removed his pants and appeared in tight, almost see-through briefs supplied by Cobb. Each of the studs received rippling waves of applause.

Finally, as an introduction to the third act, Linda was paraded out on stage and ordered to sit down on a cot placed there. When she arrived at her spot onstage, wearing nothing but a black G-string, she received no applause at all.

Each of the other performers was instructed to drop his briefs and come out on stage completely nude. The first airman was Charlie, her favorite. His penis was rather long, uncut, and thick. He faced the audience, but was then ordered by Cobb to turn around so that viewers could encompass a view of his rear.

After that, he walked over to Linda, who stuck out her tongue. He came up close to her, and she reached for his penis. As she began to fellate him, he rose quickly.

After no more than a minute of that, Cobb seemed satisfied that Charlie was at full staff. He took Charlie by the shoulders and pulled him away from Linda, although he seemed reluctant to leave.

Facing the audience, standing side by side with Charlie, Cobb held up his left hand. "He's available for a price. Eight and a half ruddy inches, as you can plainly see. He's also married. But tonight, his baby maker can belong to you. Let the bidding begin."

The process of selling Charlie was repeated eleven more times with each of his fellow airmen. Between two of the "sets," as Cobb called them, he whispered to Linda, "For reasons I don't completely understand, cock fanciers pay more for a stud if he emerges from a woman's mouth or cunny."

Before dawn, most of the airmen were sold two or three times, often for what Linda considered outrageous prices.

By six o'clock, she fellated an exhausted Charlie for a final time. Like some sexual athlete, he was sold yet again, although the price was lower than during previous biddings since he was no longer fresh.

Linda's gig? Fluffing up the contestants in a Key Largo "slave auction"

Later, backstage, she encountered Charlie again. He was battered beyond recognition. He'd been the star attraction of the night, sold into sexual bondage a record five times. "I need three days to recover. They drained me dry."

Before they left the mansion in Key Largo, a wilted Cobb called Linda and Chuck into his suite. "Good job!" he said to Linda, as he counted out ten one-hundred dollar bills for Chuck. He looked Linda over carefully. "You really seemed to enjoy your work. I envied you getting to work those boys over. I'd do the job myself, but a woman brings more money." Then he turned to Chuck. "I want to use her again. I've never seen a woman's throat in action like that. I auditioned all the boys before I hired them and two or three challenged even a sword swallower like me. Me, who has swallowed half the male organs on the planet."

Chuck assured Cobb that Linda would be primed and ready for the next event.

"Perhaps next time we'll have the guys fuck her on stage and then pull them off her while they're still hard," Cobb said. "That might lead these perverts to bid even higher."

Driving up U.S. 1, heading north, she fell asleep twice from exhaustion. She sort of day-dreamed about Charlie. He had been her favorite. Her problem involved escaping from Chuck and slipping away to see him. There were other problems as well. He was married, about to become the father of a third child. To earn extra money he sold his cock to prick connoisseurs.

As she'd later confide to her diary, "The man of my dreams is only to be dreamed."

***

Although Sunshine wasn't always available because of her involvement with her boyfriend, she and Linda became *confidantes*. As Linda expressed in a memoir, "Sunshine and I titty-timed all over the place, and had a ball doing it."

Once on a rainy day, wearing nothing but their raincoats, Sunshine drove Linda to the University of Miami. "If old men in the park can flash young girls, why can't we reverse the situation?" Linda asked.

When they spotted three young men leaving the engineering school, they opened their coats and flashed their naked torsos at them. The men yelled catcalls after them as they raced away to avoid heckling and perhaps rape. "We spent an afternoon doing that. It was a hell of a lot of fun, and I bet we gave a lot of the male students hard-ons."

Also in a memoir, Linda confessed that Sunshine was the first woman to put her foot in her vagina, although Linda had already made that porno loop (*The Foot*) with a man. With Sunshine, Linda learned to enjoy a double dildo, referring to the experience as "fabulous." They preferred a device measuring a foot and a half long, with heads measuring three and a half inches at each end.

"Chuck had a lot of sex parties in those days—yes, guests had to pay—and Sunshine and I were the life of the party with that double dildo. The guests cheered us on. By that time, I was a true exhibitionist."

She also claimed, in a memoir, "Sunshine and I would come again and again simultaneously. Another way we used it was to put one end in my cunt and the other end in my ass. Then we'd hold a vibrator against it to drive me insane."

Linda's close friendship with Sunshine did not survive its initial intensity. They drifted apart as Sunshine spent more time with her adman lover and less time doing sexual gigs for Chuck.

To replace Sunshine, Chuck linked up with a very different kind of prostitute. A woman identified in Linda's memoirs as "Melody" came into their lives. Perhaps for legal reasons, Linda even disguised Melody's physical attributes, defining her as "cute," and asserting that she evoked a high school cheerleader. Her real name was Lori Grahame.

Nothing could be farther from the truth. If anything, Melody evoked Jane Fonda as she looked in the early 1970s. Instead of whorish drag, she wore well-tailored, pin-striped women's business suits. Her auburn hair was closely cropped, and she had a beautiful face with sea-green eyes and cheeks so chiseled they looked sculpted. She stood five feet, seven inches tall and had a trim 36-26-36 figure.

Her most alluring feature was her breathy voice. Everything she said sounded like a sultry invitation to sex. For a while, she'd worked in radio in Chicago, announcing the weather report "Chicago 34. New York City 42; Boston 41; Cleveland 36; Phoenix 62; Miami 69."

Broadcasters predicted a bright future for Grahame in radio, and she was increasingly known as "The Voice." However, she succumbed to a $185-a-day heroin addiction, which wrecked her advancement and led to her being fired.

Lori ("Melody") Grahame, who would play such an important role in Linda's (temporary) escape from Chuck, evoked **Jane Fonda** (*photo above*) as she looked in the early 1970s.

Born in Toronto, Grahame was a lesbian who had drifted south to live in Illinois. After she was fired from radio, she lived for eight months with a rich lesbian designer in Chicago until she was dumped.

She quickly found another love nest in the luxurious orbit of a Frenchwoman, Gabrielle Capellan, who was said to have inherited a vast fortune from her marriage to a German baron with a fondness for beautiful boys, ages six to ten.

Melody had lived with Madame Capellan in her mansion in Boca Raton for eight months. The couple parted amicably, and the "baroness" gave Grahame ten thousand dollars, which she quickly managed to spend on her heroin habit.

Once the money was gone, she drifted into prostitution within the Greater Miami area, having sex with men, although privately she found

136

them distasteful.

Melody quickly filled a void in Linda's life created by the departure of Sunshine. In spite of her drug habit, Melody looked much younger than her thirty-five years. There were shadows around her eyes, but the discoloring appeared to be the result of artfully applied make-up.

In between gigs, Linda spent hours talking with Grahame, whom she found very educated, having finished college in her native Toronto.

Her theories about sex intrigued Linda. Grahame had wrapped herself around Robert Sherwood's theory that women have a "triple clit"—that is, a brain clit, a heart clit, and an actual vaginal clit. Grahame told Linda that a good, satisfying relationship with a partner demanded stimulation (and satisfaction) of all three.

[Years later, when Linda became an ardent feminist and anti-pornography crusader, she credited Grahame with "turning my head in the right direction."]

It was Grahame who gave Linda a copy of Germaine Greer's *The Female Eunuch,* which had become an international best-seller in 1970.

Linda became fascinated by the teachings of this self-styled "anarchist communist" from Australia. She was fascinated to read such Greer slogans as "There can be no liberation for women, no matter how highly educated, as long as we are required to cram our breasts in bras constructed like mini-Vesuviuses into stitched white cantilevered cones which bear no resemblance to the female anatomy."

Partly because of her master/slave relationship with Chuck, Linda resonated deeply with Greer's observations about male oppression. Her opinions delighted Linda, who had never heard a woman speak with a voice like Greer's. The author claimed that the word "cunt" was one of the few remaining words in the English language that had the genuine power to shock.

Germaine had been the editor of an underground magazine called *Suck,* in which she'd published a full-page photograph of herself—"Stripped to the buff, looking at the lens through my thighs." She also suggested that straight women knit "cock socks, a snug

Top photo: The brilliant and confrontational Australia-born feminist, **Germaine Greer,** whose best-seller was defined as "a scholarly plea for personal freedom."

When Chuck Traynor caught Linda reading it, he slugged her.

corner for a chilly prick."

Linda confided to Grahame that the Greer slogan that meant the most to her was the one that described how much men actually hate women, and how women even hated themselves. "I can understand that," Linda said. "She's talking about me."

Page after page of Greer's ideologies intrigued Linda, especially Greer's radical assertion that women should "accept their own bodies, taste their own menstrual blood, and give up both celibacy and monogamy."

One night when Chuck came home after making one of his sleazy deals, he caught Linda reading *The Female Eunuch,* which was in the news at the time and exploding into controversies on television. He grabbed the book from her hands and ripped out its pages. "You dirty bitch," he yelled.

She described the incident later to Grahame. "I told him I bought it in a drugstore. He gave me the beating of my life." Then she showed Grahame the bruises he had inflicted upon her.

"Both of us have to figure out some way to escape," Grahame said. "I've got to kick this heroin habit before I do anything. If we can work it right, maybe we'll run away together."

"I want out and I want my freedom," Linda said. "But I don't understand myself. One side of me wants to run away and be my own woman. But another side of me wants to be dominated by a master. I'm one sick girl."

"Welcome to the real world," Grahame said. "I'm sick, too. The trick is learning to survive."

***

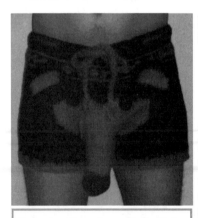

Germaine Greer is credited with inspiration for the knitting craze wherein **"cock socks"** or "knitted prophylactics" became a crafting craze among knitters.

For information about this particular model for consumers who care about the dicks in their lives, click on Etsy.com

Chuck was so furious at Linda for even reading about women's liberation that he assigned her the most repulsive gigs. As she cited in her memoir, *Ordeal,* all the most degenerate assignments went to her. If a man wanted to tie up a woman and urinate on her, it was Linda who was sent to do his bidding. If a john wanted to give a woman an enema, or get one from her, it was Linda who Chuck designated to go on-site to service the request.

Once, she was assigned to perform fellatio on a man who weighed more than four-hundred pounds. As she'd tell Grahame, "He told me that because of his belly's overhang, he hadn't seen his penis since he was a teenage boy. I almost couldn't find it either. It was the tiniest I've ever seen, almost like a matchstick. It was all I could do to find it amid all that blubber, and all that I could do to keep from vomiting."

The fat man paid $150 a session, which Chuck, who took all the money, claimed was "a tidy profit."

Grahame consoled Linda as much as she could, but often, she was of almost no help. She would perspire, her whole body shaking nervously, as she desperately sought to get paid for a sexual encounter so she could buy more heroin. Linda felt sorry for her when she saw her in such a ravished condition, and prayed she'd never become a drug addict herself.

During one long talk about drugs with Linda, Grahame explained that sticking needles into herself was masochistic but also a "very, very sexual thing. When I first started shooting dope, I would climax."

One weekly assignment particularly disgusted Linda. For this gig, Grahame usually accompanied her, along with four other hookers Chuck lined up.

The client, a former industrialist who had accumulated a vast fortune, was confined to a wheelchair. He wanted four young women to strip nude in front of him and then make passionate lesbian love to each other.

Grahame was assigned the task of holding the elderly man upright, whereas Linda was commissioned with the most difficult task: "My job was to kneel in front of him and suck him off," she wrote.

Sometimes, as Grahame drove her back to Chuck, Linda would burst into tears, feeling both ashamed and sickened at what she had to do.

Not all assignments were repulsive. Grahame tried to work Linda in on some less daunting gigs, as when they visited "Leo," who sold a line of bargain women's clothing, including gowns and lingerie whose designs copied, to some degree, whatever was fashionable that season with Victoria's Secret.

Leo would allow Grahame and Linda to select whatever sexy clothing they wanted, knowing they would get to take the garments away with them after the session.

"He never touched us," Linda later said, "but ordered us to remove our clothing and make love to each other on the carpet. He masturbated looking at us. But there was a problem. During those sessions, Lori was putting too much passion into our love-making. A person can tell about those things. I feared she was falling in love with me. I was desperate to maintain our friendship. I wanted her as a friend, not as a lover."

One of the most bizarre clients Linda became involved with on a weekly basis was a mortician she referred to as "Jason" (not his real name). In her memoirs, *Ordeal,* she revealed only a very limited preview of the extent of her involvement with him.

Although he paid $45 a session, she found him weird, suspecting that he might be a necrophile, a sexual perversion whose very existence had been revealed to her by Chuck. But once she got to know Jason, she found him not a threat. Actually, this father of three, who was a middle-aged deacon in his church, seemed completely harmless, at least at first.

Instead of asserting a *John vs. Prostitute* context to their relationship, he preferred to define her as a romantic lover, calling her "dear one" or "my darling Linda." For the first three weeks, he didn't even touch her, warning her that it was wrong to kiss on the first date, or even the second, or third.

During their fourth session, he told her that since they were "romantic lovers," they could indulge in some harmless necking. He held her in his arms and kissed her rather gently on the lips.

Before the end of the next three weeks, he was fondling her breasts, but there was never any penetration. After they'd been "dating" for two months, he suggested that they meet in his apartment, which was located upstairs from a mortuary.

In the beginning of that date, she'd viewed it as one of the most romantic she'd ever had. He even had champagne for her, along with fresh crab and shrimp he'd ordered from a fish restaurant. There was also blueberry pie.

She almost never drank, but this time, she broke her own rules and had three glasses of champagne. By eleven o'clock, she was feeling drowsy and asked if he would drive her back to Chuck's house.

"But, my dear, the evening is just beginning," he protested.

She became dizzy and the room blurred. The furniture seemed to be dancing. Then she passed out.

She revived with the arrival of dawn. Slowly, ever so slowly, she tried to recall the events of the previous night. Her last memory was of them sitting together in his living room.

As she gradually regained consciousness, she was suddenly paralyzed with fear. To her horror, she realized that she was nude, lying in a coffin lined with pink satin.

She raised herself up as a stench assaulted her nostrils. Taking in her surroundings, she realized that there were a pair of corpses laid out in what appeared to be an embalming room. She shrieked in horror and rose up from the coffin, wondering if perhaps she was indeed rising from the dead.

Her groin ached, and she feared she'd been assaulted, but didn't know if it were by Jason's penis or because of a dildo he'd used to rape her while she'd been in a coma—perhaps a combination of both.

She looked around for something to cover her nudity and found a large towel. She picked it up and wrapped it around her body, even though it was stained with blood.

As she was rushing toward the rear door, she came face to face with Jason. "Leaving so soon without breakfast?" he asked.

"I'm not hungry," she said. "What happened last night? What did you do to me? Where are my clothes?"

"So many questions from my true love," he said. "You can get dressed in the back room."

She rushed in there and found her clothing draped carefully across a chair. Putting on her dress and stepping into her shoes, she was terrified. Did he have any more twisted fun planned for her?

As she headed toward the door, he appeared again, but made no attempt to block her escape.

"My lonely weeks are over," he said to her. "You and I are now one. You were perfectly still last night, just as if you were dead. It was wonderful."

That was her last encounter with Jason. She feared he might be some "super-freak" who would eventually corner her alone again and kill her for his sexual satisfaction. "For the rest of my life, I want to avoid necrophiles and vampires."

***

At one point in a memoir, Linda claimed that during one of her bookings arranged through Chuck, she had to take on fifteen guys. But she gave no details of that amazing sexual rendezvous. Initially, she did, but her editor cut the revelations from *Inside Linda Lovelace*. Along with Grahame, Linda was driven to a mansion in Miami that had originally functioned as a private home, but now belonged to a fraternity based at the University of Miami. Chuck told Linda and Grahame that whereas many members of the fraternity lived either off-campus or in dormitories, fifteen of them lived in the house, and that these "brothers" had organized a "gang hang" with the two of them.

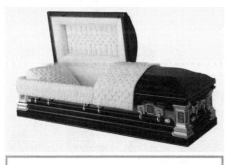

As a means for Chuck to pay his mounting bills and legal fees, he had to cater to what he called **"The Kink Market."** That led to an increasingly degrading (and sometimes terrifying) series of sexual encounters for Linda.

"Linda, I told them about your specialty," Chuck told her, bluntly. He also claimed that the fraternity men wanted the orgy filmed so that they could show it at their next smoker, and presumably as a souvenir many years later.

Within the fraternity house, the brothers were waiting. They ranged in age from eighteen to twenty. As for their looks, they varied from extremely handsome to ugly and raunchy. She knew that the evening would involve a lot of sheer, grunting labor, and that she'd have to take on all of them.

The president of the fraternity, Woody Cameron, asked the most questions. "What is it like to be a whore?" he wanted to know.

"It's a lot of fun," she lied, cheerfully. "I love sex and I love men. Every night I get my fill."

He reached for her hand, placing it between his legs. "See what your talk is doing to me? You're lucky tonight. I bet some times you get a lot of over-the-hill old guys. But here's the good news: Everyone tonight is young and hot."

Within the hour, Chuck had arranged the setup for the filming of the orgy about to take place. He'd even devised a title for the loop, *Fraternal Line-up.*

Grahame had been rehearsed in what she was to do, but Linda had not. "I'll wing it," she said.

Each of the young men in the line-up was to enjoy Linda's special deep-throating before they could then take their turns having sex with her in the missionary position.

As she'd later recall, "I sucked and sucked until my throat was sore, but I bravely carried on. Big cocks, little cocks, and everything in between."

The line-up was a misnomer. The frisky studs circled around the bed, jostling and displaying themselves, waiting for their turn inside Linda's mouth. So far, Grahame's role wasn't yet clear to Linda. She'd been instructed to lie nude on the bed, masturbating herself.

As the first young man impaled Linda and reached his climax, Grahame, as instructed by Chuck, swung into action. She went down on Linda, sucking out the juices that had so recently been deposited in her vagina. The fraternity brothers went wild with this added attraction. At least, according to what Linda later said, "They felt that their sperm wasn't being wasted."

"I was pinned down, pummeled, completely in the power of these frat kids," Linda said. "My throat ached, and my tongue felt furry, as jism after jism was shot into me. But Lori was there to

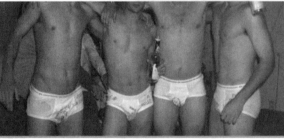

Frat House

142

suck it out of me. I looked forward to her more than I did those relentlessly horny men."

At the end of the marathon sex session, some of the guys wanted to go for another round, but Chuck said that would cost a lot more. No one wanted to part with any more money.

A bruised and battered Linda was put into the car alongside Grahame. Chuck had collected a hundred dollar bill from each of the men.

Grahame was awarded with three-hundred dollars for the night, which would buy her 36 hours worth of heroin. Linda got nothing. When she asked him for a hundred dollars to buy some much needed supplies from the drugstore, Linda was rewarded with a slap.

"You don't know how lucky you are," he said. "Imagine all the love-starved gals who'd like fifteen hot young guys to take them on in one evening. You should be licking my ass in gratitude for setting you up for that orgy. I could tell that you loved every minute of it, like the true whore you are."

That night, Chuck slept downstairs, breaking in two new girls whom Linda hadn't met.

Grahame bedded down with Linda, and both of them were exhausted. "I know what's in my future," Linda told her. "Chuck is going to use me, exploit me, and then give me the boot when I'm no longer useful. To reproach him would be about as useful as a third testicle."

"Don't worry about it," Grahame responded. "Your chance to run away might be coming sooner than later. I'm trying to pull off our best gig yet."

"Tell me about it," she said eagerly.

"I'm too tired," Grahame said. "Tomorrow, tomorrow."

***

The next day, Linda learned that Grahame had made contact with her former lover in Boca Raton, a French woman known as the "Baroness" Gabrielle Capellan. Actually, Grahame wanted to get back into the good graces of the aging woman. Emerging from the renewal of their dialogue came an offer of a sex gig.

A special party was about to be staged at the Baroness's Boca Raton mansion. Two of the scheduled performers had dropped out at the last minute. During the search for replacements, Gabrielle remembered that Grahame had studied dance in Toronto for six years before moving on to Chicago.

The Baroness requested that Grahame and "some other young woman" arrive a day before the event for rehearsals. The dance routine choreographed for Grahame and a partner would pay $5,000 for the one-night event and its day-before rehearsals.

When Chuck heard about their upcoming gig for Saturday, he was delighted. This was the most money he'd ever received for an engagement. But he was very disappointed that no men would be allowed onto the estate. Not even a servant. He was also told that a limousine would be sent to drive Linda and Grahame to Boca Raton, and that his services would not be needed.

Grahame said she expected that at least $1,500 of her fee would be paid in advance, and Chuck reluctantly agreed to her demand.

When the limousine arrived that Friday morning at 10am to retrieve the performers, Chuck didn't kiss Linda goodbye. All he said to her was, "Be a good girl and bring home the bacon."

In all her life, Linda had never ridden in a limousine, and it was thrilling for her to be transported to Boca Raton in such style. The German-accented chauffeur was rather snobbish, and Linda felt he was treating them like gutter trash, but she wasn't going to let him dampen her good spirits.

Inside the "Baroness's" palatial home, Linda was shown to her own luxuriously furnished room with a view of the ocean. When she asked for Grahame, she was informed that she was in rehearsals. Linda wondered why she wasn't also summoned.

Later, a butler knocked on her door to take her order for lunch. She was told she could have anything she wanted, even lobster, caviar, and champagne if she chose. She ordered a steak with fries instead, and devoured lunch on her own private sea-view terrace.

Grahame came by her suite at six o'clock for drinks. She'd had a shot of heroin and her nerves were calm. "I'm going to perform this dance as Salomé."

"I hope I don't have to dance," Linda said.

"You don't." Grahame told her. "You just have to come on stage naked wearing a slave collar. It's like a dog collar. All you have to do is stand there and take my veils as I shed them one by one. We'll both end up naked to take our bows."

"I can't believe it'll be that easy for me."

"It won't," Grahame said. "After we've taken our bows, the women in the audience will want to see us make wild, passionate love on a bed that will be on the stage."

"I guess we can do that."

"Honey, for five-thousand dollars, I'd go down on a buffalo."

Linda and Grahame dined alone that night, and this time, Linda ordered lobster. Eight of the rich lady friends of the Baroness had arrived, and their hostess was busy entertaining them. Some had flown in on a private plane from Southampton on Long Island.

The night would have been beautiful for Linda had not Grahame confessed "my undying love for you."

"Oh, Lori," Linda said, "I can make love to you, but I can't be in love with you. I just can't. It's not in me."

"You may change your mind before the weekend is over," Grahame said, showing almost no disappointment. "If the plan I'm working on for your escape comes through, you'll be so grateful to me for freeing you from Chuck that you'll eventually fall for me—and I'm sure of that."

***

Five hours before the show, Linda was taken into a small theater which held no more than thirty guests. A former community theater director, Thelma Murray, went through a final rehearsal with Grahame. Other than standing on-stage nude wearing a slave collar, Linda felt she had very little to do, "except appear naked."

As showtime drew near, Linda met six female strippers backstage, Normally associated with a club catering to men in West Palm Beach, each had been hired for their role in this special gig. Their act would precede Grahame's dance. The women told Linda that their schedule called for them to wrap up this "gig for the dykes" and get back to Lulu's Club for a midnight performance in West Palm Beach.

When Murray fitted a spiked leather collar around Linda's neck and ordered her to strip, she felt naked and vulnerable, waiting backstage to go on.

Finally, Grahame stood beside her. "Wish me luck," she said. "I've had my shot and I'm in control."

The stage was decorated like a Hindu temple, as incense wafted across the little theater. Linda had seen the guests, each of them female, as they'd filed in following a cocktail party. It had been a masquerade, and all the guests were dressed like Amazons.

"They seemed to be sniffing the perfumed air like hound dogs on the scent of a foxy lady," Linda later recalled.

The *faux* temple had been positioned beneath a rotunda that had been decorated with flowers around a lavishly draped bed beneath a garlanded canopy. The curtain opened to reveal a four-armed dancing Shiva *(Siva Nataraja)* from India, which was encircled with depictions of flames. The statue could be seen crushing with its bronze feet a sculpted replica of a ferocious-looking dwarf .

A hushed tremor fell over the audience as the sound of some mysterious music from India filled the theater. A very masculine-looking woman appeared at the edge of the stage dressed in a modern man's business suit with a wooden male doll perched on her shoulder.

She had a deep voice. "All of you shall die," she addressed the audience. "The beautiful dancer you're about to see will also die. So will her handmaiden slave. Since life on this Earth is so short, we must live it to the fullest, defying society and its laws if necessary. Better to have lived and experienced the intensity of unlimited passion than to drag about in your bodily decay filled only with regrets at what might have been. Indulge yourself. Take what you want from life. Don't be restrained."

Then she departed from the stage as Murray signaled Grahame and Linda to make their entrance. The lights dimmed. When they came on again, Grahame was seen mysteriously in silhouette behind a sheer curtain, leading a nude Linda by a gold chain. The curtain parted to see Grahame in her costume of seven veils, evoking the legend of Salomé dancing in the court at Jerusalem before Herod. A golden collar had been fastened around her neck, along with ten long strands of dangling pearls.

With her long thighs and supple torso, Grahame dominated the stage with her dance. The veils seemed to move gracefully with her body movements, a rainbow of colors ranging from scarlet to turquoise.

The audience seemed to anticipate with pleasure the finale, as Grahame began to remove one veil after another. Linda stood by to rescue each veil in her arms as they came off this love goddess. When the final veil dropped, the women applauded loudly.

Grahame then took Linda's hand, leading her to the lavishly adorned bed.

Before the onlookers, Grahame as Salomé ordered her sex slave to go down on her. As Linda attacked Grahame's vagina, as she had been ordered to do, "Salomé" moaned and groaned, exaggerating her pleasure and sexual passion. Grahame held back for at least fifteen minutes, since the audience seemed to be enthralled by the performance of Linda and her lips. At her climax, Grahame screamed. The clapping and cheers from the audience were thunderous.

Then the stage went black as Linda and Grahame rushed back to their dressing room before the lights went back on in the theater. They

Linda and Melody were not the first erotic dancers to interpret the Biblical character of Salomé, the siren whose grisly request to King Herod led to the beheading of John the Baptist.

Silent Screen star **Nazimova** *(photo above)* had set a cinematic tone for the role in her *avant garde* but commercially unsuccessful film (*Salomé*) in 1923.

146

had been instructed to remain out of sight after their act, and not to stick around for bows and curtain calls.

Suddenly, the door to their dressing room was thrown open and in barged the woman in the man's business suit, still with the male doll perched on her shoulder. "Good evening, I'm Joe Carstairs, the sponsor of tonight's entertainment. The little guy here is Lord Tod Wadley." She motioned toward the doll on her shoulder, a foot-tall replica of an impish-looking man dressed in a black tuxedo. "He goes with me everywhere except when I'm speed boat racing. I'm afraid he'd fall overboard."

"I'm very impressed with you, Miss Grahame," Carstairs said. "I've heard wonderful things about you from our mutual friend who owns this house."

"Thank you, Miss Carstairs," Grahame said.

"Please, don't *Miss* me, whatever you say. Call me Joe. I want you to come back with me to my suite in the west wing."

"I'd be honored," Grahame said.

"As for you, Lovelace, regrettably there's more work for you. Some of the Amazons in the audience have requested that you return to that bed on stage. Please go out there and lie down nude. That will allow them to get up close and personal with your body. You don't object to that, do you? Trust me, receiving the soothing love of a woman is far preferable to the jabbing pain of a male phallus."

"I'm glad to be of service," Linda said, not really meaning it.

Carstairs turned once again to Grahame. "As for you, my lovely, I have two ambitions for you: To make you my latest girlfriend, and to cure you of your wretched heroin addiction."

***

It was a long, two-hour ordeal on that bed on stage. Linda later claimed she could hardly recall the details of that gang-rape by women. "I thought it would never end," she later said.

But she did record in her memoirs that after that experience, she felt she could write an entire book "on pussy eating, although half the male readers still wouldn't catch on."

In her first autobiography, she even published tips on how to become an expert practitioner of cunnilingus, including details about how to "suck, lick, and blow inside the vagina, providing that the tongue should be constant against the clitoris."

***

Two views of her era's most liberated lesbian, **Marion Barbara ("Joe") Carstairs**, heiress to a branch of the Standard Oil fortune, and temporary protector, on her private Bahamian island, of both Linda and Melody.

Her fetish doll, **"Lord Wadley"** is visible in the upper photo.

The events associated with Linda's escape from the clutches of Chuck Traynor evolved so fast they left her dazed. She was awakened at 5am Sunday morning by Grahame, who told her to get packed. "I've got the five-thousand dollars" she said, "and we're going to hold onto all of it. Fuck Chuck Traynor. Not only that, but Joe Carstairs is going to fly us to her private island in The Bahamas, a place called Whale Cay."

"My god," Linda said. "This is so sudden. It's okay for me to come along?"

"Joe is very rich," Grahame said. "I've become her new girl friend, and you can live on her island in luxury until you decide what you're going to do with your life."

Having grabbed the opportunity for Linda, Grahame directed her to get ready for a 6:30am flight in a private airplane. Linda wanted to ask many questions, but there was no time. Leaving Florida represented an impulsive choice, and the terms of her life on Whale Cay had not been spelled out in any detail. Nonetheless, she agreed to run away with Grahame under the protection of Carstairs.

It would take several weeks for her to learn who this mysterious woman was, but gradually, she pieced together a profile of one of that era's most famous lesbians. In the 1920s, she'd held the world record as the fastest female speedboat racer.

A crossdresser who smoked cheroots, Marion Barbara ("Joe") Carstairs had inherited a fortune from her parents, heirs to a branch of the Standard Oil fortune. She once said, "I collect fast cars, fast boats, and fast female lovers."

A close friend of the Duke and Duchess of Windsor, Carstairs was infamously associated with previous lovers who included Tallulah Bankhead, Marlene Dietrich, Greta Garbo, Katharine Hepburn, and heiress Libby Holman, a once-famous torch singer who was notoriously suspected of murdering two of her rich husbands.

Carstairs had even had a famous affair with Dolly Wilde, Oscar Wilde's niece and a fellow ambulance driver, during World War I.

Whale Cay, which was technically classified as a member of the Berry Islands archipelago within The Bahamas, had been purchased by Carstairs for $40,000. She'd constructed a Great House for herself and her celebrated guests there, and also a lighthouse, a school, a church, and cannery. She'd also acquired the small adjoining islands of Bird Cay, Devil's Cay, and half of Hoffman's Cay.

Linda quickly realized that Whale Cay operated as Carstairs' personal kingdom, where she ruled virtually unchallenged as a feudal autocrat. The island was the site of a tiny village, a small museum, and a 200-member "army" of local Bahamians, whom she kept busy maintaining the roads. Also on site was a squadron of maids, cooks, and gardeners. She liked to race up and down the length (nine miles) and width (four miles) of her island in any of her many sports cars and motorcycles.

In all, she ruled without challenge over 750 Bahamians, each living at her beck and call. Author Diana McLellan described her as "a combination medieval monarch and witch doctor." In spite of her many sexual adventures, she insisted on punishing local men who committed adultery. Her usual punishment involved banishment from Whale Cay, but on at least one occasion, she had horsewhipped a Bahamian man.

Linda had left everything she owned at Chuck's house, and she had no clothes except those she'd brought with her. But Carstairs told Grahame and Linda that she would fly them to Nassau to restock their wardrobes.

From Fort Lauderdale, Carstairs imported a live-in registered nurse who had special training in the treatment of drug addictions.

For two weeks, Grahame disappeared, with the nurse, into the premises of one of Whale Cay's remote cottages. Natives reported hearing screams coming from the cottage. Linda shuddered to think of the horrible withdrawals her friend was enduring.

Carstairs had little time to spend with Linda, and showed absolutely no romantic interest in her. Linda didn't mind. She was too busy experiencing the good life for the first time ever. Sometimes, she thought of

An Empress with a sense of Macho Chic

Carstairs at home and in control on Whale Cay.

her son, Billy, but only rarely.

Linda's health gradually improved, and often, she explored the island's rocky, scrub-covered terrain on her own. It had white sandy beaches and coral reefs with shoals of fish, such as grouper, and extensive colonies of conch. Dangerous barracudas and sharks lurked off its coast.

Linda's favorite of the island's beaches was Gavylta Beach, which Carstairs had deeded to Marlene Dietrich. On a rocky bluff adjacent to its sands, Carstairs had even built a cottage for Dietrich and her friends, far from prying eyes.

Each day brought something new to do—poker games (Linda learned how to play), boxing matches among the beefier members of the Bahamian workers, and endless films, including homemade movies. Sometimes Carstairs organized hunting expeditions to neighboring islands to shoot wild goats, which the locals would barbecue at native feasts with junkanoo music.

On occasion, Carstairs would invite Linda to ride along behind her on a loud red motorcycle along the island's reasonably good roads. Linda referred to her as a "speed demon." Whenever the locals heard the sound of her motorcycle or her sports car, they ran for shelter.

Once, she invited five of her house guests for a Bahamian picnic on one of her beaches. When she spotted a dangerous snake in the bushes, she took her knife and hurled it at the snake, injuring it and then swiftly beheading the reptile.

Sometimes, Linda joined other guests in a boat trip to the large nearby island of Andros, where Carstairs owned a large tract of land which she cultivated, growing bananas, potatoes, strawberries, and cantaloupes. Fish was served at every meal, and Linda learned to adore "sweet, sexy, conch."

Marlene Dietrich
on stage in 1972

Carstairs always seemed to have about a dozen guests in residence. One night over dinner, she announced that she was planning to sell Whale Cay and "retire as its queen," with the intention of retreating to a mansion in Miami. She announced that as a finale to her reign, she would organize a gala week of festivities wherein she promised to invite "many of my more celebrated friends before they get too wobbly to make it here."

Linda just hoped that she'd be around to meet these world famous figures, whoever they were.

Over dinner, Carstairs often amused her guests with stories about the wild and rollicking days of Whale Cay, which flourished during America's experiment with Prohibition. Rum

150

parties, hosted by Harold Christie, the most affluent and visible real estate developer in the West Indies, became the stuff of legend. Whale Cay flourished as a holiday resort, offering entertainment labeled as "whatever the heart desires."

To the island, she'd invited the Duke and Duchess of Windsor when the Duke, who had briefly ruled England as Edward VIII, was shuttled off, after his abdication of his throne, to an obscure post as governor of The Bahamas during World War II. Noël Coward popped in for a visit, as did Tallulah Bankhead. A very butch lesbian, the heiress Louisa Carpenter du Pont Jenney, was a sometimes visitor too.

Carstairs told Linda that "girlfriends just fall into my lap, like your friend Lori. One time, I palmed off one of my girls, Phyllis Gates, onto Rock Hudson. Eventually, he was ordered by his agent, Henry Willson, to marry her as a means of concealing his homosexuality."

One hot afternoon, Carstairs showed Linda an assemblage of 8" by 10" photographs of her former girlfriends, 102 in all, some of them famous but most of them obscure. "I'm adding that darling Lori to my collection—maybe you, too, one day. We'll see."

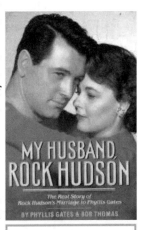

*   *   *

Finally, after two and a half weeks of leisure, Linda was allowed to see Grahame. A nurse granted her entrance into the cottage where Grahame was staying with a "tough dyke of a nurse who got her training from the Bitch of Buchenwald" [Grahame's assessment].

Linda was shocked at Grahame's appearance. Her bloodshot eyes were sunken, and she'd lost about fifteen pounds. She grabbed Linda and embraced her. "I've come through," she said. "It was living hell, but I'm off the stuff. No more needles going into me.

Linda sat with her and talked for an hour. "I'm so happy to see you entering the world again."

"Not only that," Grahame said, "but Joe is throwing this big gala and inviting some of her famous friends. I'm going to get my strength back and I'm going to dance for the former King of England. Ain't that grand?"

In 1955, in an ill-conceived plot designed to conceal his homosexuality, **Rock Hudson** married one of Joe Carstairs' lesbian ex-girlfriends, **Phyllis Gates**, who later blackmailed him.

Later, as a means of capitalizing on her "investment," she co-authored the (whitewashed and heavily censored) book whose cover is depicted above.

For years afterward, Joe Carstairs took credit for having introduced them.

Linda thought it was, but she also felt jealous. Somehow, she didn't fit in with what she called "a swanky crowd. I'm just a two-bit whore," she told Grahame.

"Your day will come," Grahame assured her.

***

During the next three weeks, Grahame was busy every day rehearsing for her part in Carstairs' upcoming black tie extravaganza with her A-list guests.

Linda didn't seem to fit into any role and came to think of herself as a professional guest, ever grateful for the help she was getting from Carstairs, who asked nothing in return.

The Queen of Whale Cay kept herself busy making preparations for her upcoming week-long celebration. She did not have enough bedrooms, certainly not enough luxurious ones, to accommodate her guests, so many of them would have to sleep aboard their yachts.

Linda was asked if she'd give up her bedroom for the event and sleep in a warehouse, where cots had been installed. Of course, she readily agreed to that. Her room would be relinquished to Rock Hudson, who was arriving with his lover of the moment, the actor, Sal Mineo.

Linda had no idea how Hudson had become friends with Carstairs, although she was aware that Carstairs had arranged to maneuver one of her former girlfriends, Phyllis Gates, into a sham marriage with Hudson as a cover for his homosexuality. Of course, the marriage ended in disaster, and Hudson never went down the matrimonial road again.

Linda confided to Grahame, "I'm sorry that Rock and Sal are gay. I'd sure like to deep throat both of them."

"I've heard many stories about those two," Grahame said with a smirk. "Between the two of them, they have nineteen and a half inches, but I won't tell you how those inches are assigned."

Linda sat in on Grahame's dance rehearsals. She was to interpret three dance routines originally performed by Mata Hari. Linda had never heard of Mata Hari (1876-1917), the Dutch-born exotic dancer, courtesan, and accused spy who had been executed by a firing squad in France on charges of pro-German espionage during World War I. Greta Garbo had popularized the legend of Mata Hari in a pre-code American movie filmed in 1931.

For Grahame's dances, Carstairs, through her many contacts, had rented one of the costumes designed for Garbo at a cost of $2,000, a large sum for a garment back then. Weighing fifty pounds, the gown had been designed by the famous Gilbert Adrian, who had been inspired by Paul Poiret's costume creations for the 1909 Ballets Russes.

The costume was rented and would have to be shipped back to MGM in Hollywood when the party was over. Two other costumes Garbo wore in the film were either not available or had been destroyed, so Carstairs, at great expense, had paid to have them replicated based on Adrian's original sketches.

One hot afternoon, Carstairs went down to her pier to receive a "priceless artifact" [her words]. She planned to unveil the mysterious object as the climax of the theatrical presentation scheduled for the final night of her week-long gala. She was extremely secretive about the exhibit, and arranged for it to be locked away within her private suite of rooms.

A talented and flamboyantly gay choreographer, Ted Hook, was flown in from New York to coach Grahame in the performance her dances. All of them seemed too artsy and stylized for Linda, who quickly grew bored watching them, and usually drifted away from rehearsals to the beach. Her personal taste in dancers included Ann Miller, the famous tap dancer from the age of Hollywood musicals, and Gene Kelly, famous for his roles at MGM. Her all-time favorite dance musical was *Singin' in the Rain,* which had starred Kelly with Debbie Reynolds.

"Mata Hari's" mystical dancing with eerie music didn't impress Linda at all. She told Grahame, "It's just an excuse for you to get naked. I noticed at the end of each of your numbers, you're wearing only jeweled ornaments on your arms and head—nothing else. It's all hanging out."

"That's how Mata Hari danced," Grahame said. "I read that the Parisians went wild for her because she became almost naked at the end of each of her

HOW LINDA PARTICIPATED IN A LATTER-DAY RE-EROTICIZATION
OF THE MATA HARI LEGEND:

Left photo: **Greta Garbo** impersonating her in 1931 and *(right)* the exotic dancer and convicted pro-German spy, **Mata Hari** herself.

dances—all except for a bra. She had small breasts and didn't want to reveal them to the audience. That has never been my problem, so I plan to show my tits during every dance, in all their glory."

"I'm not proud of my tits either," Linda said. "I wish they were so much bigger. I'd like them to look like Marilyn Monroe's when she posed for that nude calendar."

"Maybe one day you'll save up enough money to visit a plastic surgeon in Miami," Grahame said. "But I don't think even plastic surgery will ever get rid of that scar."

"That's right," Linda said. "I'm marked for life. But Chuck said my other talents will make up for that imperfection."

"Marlene Dietrich is arriving tomorrow, or so Joe claims," Grahame revealed. "One night, Joe told me that Marlene is not proud of her breasts either, but she relies on her other attributes as a *femme fatale*. Men talk about her other attractions, and never mention her breasts."

"Perhaps both of us can use her as a role model," Linda said. "I'm very anxious to meet her. Is she a complete dyke, or does she do men, too?"

"Marlene is said to have sex without gender."

"That's what I want written on my tombstone," Linda said. "Here lies Linda Lovelace. She had sex without gender."

***

At least two hundred Bahamians turned out to witness the arrival of Marlene Dietrich on the island. She had been flown in from Miami in Carstairs' private plane. When she arrived, she was wildly cheered by the locals, who presumably had never seen any of her exotic movies, such as *Blonde Venus* (1932) or *Destry Rides Again* (1939).

In advance of the diva's arrival, Linda had discussed her with some of the natives, who had been told that "a blonde sex goddess" from Hollywood was about to land on their tiny island. She quickly discovered that there was some confusion about who Dietrich really was.

It seemed that the Bahamians were expecting Marilyn Monroe, whose nude calendar hung in the men's toilets at several petrol stations on nearby Andros Island. Monroe's *Gentlemen Prefer Blondes* had played at a movie house on Andros, emerging as one of that island's all time most popular films.

It is not known if Dietrich disappointed the locals who saw her in the flesh. Perhaps they didn't expect a heavily made-up grandmother, born in Berlin at the turn of the 20th Century. In lieu of low-cut *décolletage* and flowing veils, as her fans might have hoped for, she was attired in a severely tailored and rather subdued women's business suit. Nonetheless, she was greeted with wild applause and junkanoo music.

At the time of Dietrich's arrival on Whale Cay in 1970, she had not made a film since the 1964 release of *Paris When It Sizzles.* Audrey Hepburn and William Holden had been the stars of that movie, with Dietrich making only a guest appearance.

Dietrich and Carstairs had met in Hollywood during the 1930s. Later, the "Blonde Venus" remembered the heiress as having "Jack Dempsey shoulders, a tattooed body, and a blonde crewcut." Their romance blossomed, even as the lesbian Carstairs and the bisexual Dietrich continued to date others.

Carstairs at one point was so besotted with Dietrich that she offered her all of Whale Cay, which Dietrich declined. Carstairs then agreed to build a luxurious home for Dietrich, a building that fronted a private white sandy beach, which she would will to her for transfer of title after Carstairs' death. "You will be a princess on a lovely tropical island, with natives at your command," Carstairs told Dietrich as an enticement. The star turned that offer down.

As Carstairs' biographer, Kate Summerscale, put it, "Marlene was the mysterious star; Joe the androgynous boy to Marlene's ambiguous nymph. They were intrigued and excited by each other."

But as the years went by, Carstairs and Dietrich became disenchanted with each other. At one point, Carstairs widely denounced her former friend. She was quoted as saying, "Marlene Dietrich is a wicked old woman, a bitch, not a good person. She is a very stupid woman. No mind, nothing up there. I don't think she could act, either."

Later, she softened her position, "In spite of Marlene's faults, in some part of my heart, I still love her."

Dietrich's reunion with Carstairs on the occasion of the island's final gala was mostly motivated by sentiment, rather than by romantic passion. Dietrich fully realized, as did all the other guests at the event, that the Queen of Whale Cay would soon be "dethroned," because of the island's impending sale.

"With Marlene back in her cottage, it's nostalgia time for both of us," Carstairs told Linda. "We chose to remember the good times, not the bad times."

During her first night on Whale Cay, Dietrich dined alone with Carstairs, not making a public appearance until the following day.

At dinner the following evening, however, Dietrich appeared in a gown that was the color of the pinkish heart of a Bahamian conch. She wore a diamond necklace and earrings and what Linda suspected was a wig.

Before dinner, as a means of entertaining guests, Dietrich brought along an LP phonograph record. The guests expected that perhaps it would focus on her renditions of some of her famous songs, but the sounds emanating from the disc consisted entirely of applause generated at her various concerts in London, Munich, Tel Aviv, Paris, and Copenhagen.

"One ovation lasted for fifty minutes," she told the dinner guests. "Finally, I had to tell the audience, 'Please, go home, I'm tired.'"

There was much talk about Dietrich performing three songs as part of Carstairs' entertainment agenda at the upcoming gala. Although initially reluctant, Dietrich agreed to sing "Lili Marlene" in German; and "I Wish You Love" and "Where Have All the Flowers Gone?" in English.

Linda observed that evening's interchanges, recording her impressions later in her diary. Eventually, the impending sale of Whale Cay brought tinges of nostalgia into the dialogue. Dietrich launched into a discussion of her own mortality. "I will eventually have to make a choice," she said. "I can disappear from view completely, and maintain myself as a myth and legend, or else I can play matronly, way-past-her-prime Ethel Barrymore parts."

She also spoke about love. "In time, the young men wander off to find fresh young flowers, and we older stars are reduced to being surrounded by a pack of adoring gay males who still worship us. Judy Garland understood that better than anyone."

"Incidentally, the last time I talked to Judy, she told me she wanted to die. Therefore, I don't weep for her. Since she wanted to die, I was glad for her. If you want to die, go die. But don't be a bore about it."

After dinner, Linda found herself alone in the library with Dietrich for about fifteen minutes. She complimented the star on her great beauty.

"I used to evoke sex on the screen," Dietrich said. "Now, *Time* magazine has said I evoke the illusion of sex."

Linda wasn't sure if Dietrich knew anything about her, but soon ascertained that Carstairs had already informed the star about her life as a prostitute and sex performer.

"You aren't like any prostitute I've ever known, especially in Berlin. Your freckle-faced appeal is very American."

"I don't like to think of myself as a prostitute," Linda said.

"I never minded being called that," Dietrich said. "I played a prostitute in many of my films, beginning with *Der Blaue Engel*. I've also prostituted myself many times to Hollywood moguls. I have this theory: If you're going to be a prosti-

INHABITING THE PERSONA OF A HOOKER, THE OLD-FASHIONED WAY

Dietrich to Lovelace: "I never minded being called a prostitute. I played a prostitute in many of my films, I've also prostituted myself many times to Hollywood moguls "

Photo above: **Marlene Dietrich** in *Der Blaue Engel (The Blue Angel*; 1930)

tute, then you should be paid very well for it."

"I'm afraid I haven't followed your advice," Linda said.

"That is unfortunate, my dear," Dietrich said. "Perhaps you should consider another career...or perhaps not. Joe tells me you have this remarkable specialty, this thing you do with your throat."

"I'm not one to brag, but it's true."

"If I still had use for such an endeavor, I might ask you to give me lessons. I've always preferred to perform fellatio on my lovers, but men always want to put their things in. That's all they want."

"It becomes very mechanical with me because there's no love," Linda said. "I've gotten more true love from women. Men always seem willing to use and discard you."

"I know the feeling," Dietrich said. "But it's impossible for one woman to live with another woman."

"Perhaps not to live with a woman, but at least to spend a night. Would you like me to visit your cottage?"

"You flatter me, my dear," Dietrich said, "but the fires of autumn burn on a very low flame."

***

The next morning, when Linda appeared for breakfast, she found that only Joe Carstairs was sitting at the table, accompanied by Lord Wadley. After Linda sat down, Carstairs launched into a complaint about her wooden doll.

"He's become a real playboy," she said. "A rogue, in fact. He's taken to drinking a quart of my most expensive brandy every day. He stays up until four o'clock in the morning playing poker with his cronies. Incidentally, he cheats. Not only that, but he smokes these dreadful Cuban cigars."

At first, Linda thought she might be joking, but she seemed completely serious. So, the stories were true. Carstairs had come to think that Lord Wadley was a living, breathing, human figure.

She continued with her litany of complaints: "A lot of people don't know this, but Lord Wadley was a great friend of Jack Kennedy's. I introduced them. Like JFK, Lord Wadley is sexually voracious. He's been married twice before. In all, he's probably had five-hundred girlfriends, which dwarfs my one-hundred and twenty conquests. Two months before Jack was assassinated in Dallas, Lord Wadley had a dreadful blow-up with the president, who caught this little fucker sleeping with Jackie. I'm sure if Lord Wadley had pressed the issue, Jackie would have run away with him, abandoning her husband and her two kids."

Linda listened politely and indulged her hostess, who was most generous and had yet to ask a favor of her.

By the time her final cup of coffee had been served, Carstairs had shifted her attention from Lord Wadley to the imminent arrival of her latest two guests, Rock Hudson, who was dating the younger Sal Mineo, who would be flying in with him. The two actors had met on the set of *Giant,* which they had filmed with Elizabeth Taylor and James Dean in 1956.

"I'll be busy for the rest of the day," Carstairs said, "so keep yourself amused. I've known Rock for years. We once had the same wife, Phyllis Gates. For their arrival at around five o'clock today on my private plane, I'm planning the most spectacular reception for them in the history of The Bahamas. If only Cecil B. DeMille was here to direct it."

A Fetishistic Obsession
TWO VIEWS OF
LORD WADLEY

Top photo: With Carstairs in the 1930s, and
(bottom) a solo act in the 70s.

As Linda finished her final cup of coffee, she wondered what Carstairs had meant. What kind of reception could she be planning? She decided to hang out at the beach for most of the day, but definitely planned to be at the island's landing strip to witness the arrival of these two Hollywood heartthrobs.

Right before the landing of Carstairs' plane, Grahame joined Linda during her walk to the island's landing strip. Both were eager to meet the stars, especially Hudson. "I think Rock is a dreamboat," Grahame told Linda. "I'll give you Mineo."

"Forget it!" Linda said. "They have each other. What do they need us for?"

"You've got a point there."

As they neared the landing strip, they were stunned to see about twenty of the beefier members of Whale Cay's male population gathered into a threatening-looking gang. They were dressed like cannibals from the set of one of those Tarzan films starring Johnny Weissmuller.

"I must say, when Joe plans a welcoming party, she goes all out," Grahame said. "Hell, these guys even have spears."

"They look hostile," Linda said. "Not exactly my fantasy of a happy welcoming party."

"Don't be a racist, darling," Grahame cautioned.

As the small craft taxied along the runway,

Carstairs had not appeared to welcome them. Neither had any member of her personal staff.

Linda and Grahame stared in amazement as Hudson and Mineo got off the plane, looking around suspiciously. The Bahamian natives crowded up against them, brandishing their spears as the two actors stepped onto the tarmac.

"What in hell is this?" Mineo shouted.

"The local reception committee, I guess," Hudson said.

Within a minute, the native blacks had overpowered both of the newly arrived Hollywood actors, lifting them into the air. Hudson and Mineo kicked, screamed, and fought back, but the sheer brute force of these "jungle men" overpowered them.

Linda and Grahame looked on—first with amusement, then with horror. What had been defined as a happy and convivial house party was turning hostile. Something was seriously wrong.

"I was told that a lost African tribe operates from an unexplored part of Andros Island, deep in the mangrove swamps," Grahame told Linda. "Do you think these guys are from that tribe?"

"Carstairs told me she was planning a fantastic reception for these guys," Linda said.

"So that's it," Grahame said. "She's known for playing practical jokes on her guests. This must be one of those jokes."

At a site in a clearing about two hundred yards away, the natives ripped off every thread of Hudson's and Mineo's clothing, including their underwear. Each of them fought against their attackers, but each was overwhelmed.

Linda spotted a pair of timbers jutting vertically upward from the scrubland. Hudson yelled to Mineo, "What the fuck! These guys are cannibals!"

Two views of Tarzan (as interpreted by **Johnny Weissmuller**), tied up and in bondage— an inspiration for Carstairs before her "Welcome to Whale Cay" party.

Mineo screamed for help, but no one came to their aid.

The men were tied nude to the stakes as the natives danced around what Linda quickly ascertained was a funeral pyre. Emerging from the fracas was the sound of beating drums. The sounds of their heavy drumbeats echoed halfway across the island.

Hudson and Mineo were yelling at fever pitch as the natives set fire to the dried brush at the foot of each stake. The men struggled to free themselves from the ropes that held them in bondage.

Suddenly, from the bushes, emerged Carstairs herself. "Put out the fire!" she shouted imperiously at the natives.

Linda and Grahame learned later that Carstairs had outfitted herself as the legendary 19th century Jamaican adventuress, a woman associated with notorious implications as a sorceress, Annie Palmer, whose exploits had been intricately detailed in a best-selling historical novel, first published in 1929, *The White Witch of Rose Hall,* by Herbert G. de Lisser. It was based on the life of a female land- and slave-owner in Jamaica, who rode around her plantation flourishing a heavy riding whip to beat unruly slaves. She took the beefier and better-endowed men as lovers until they displeased her. As Jamaican folk tales instruct, before bedding another of her studs, she killed his predecessor by publicly flogging him to death. Eventually, according to the legends, she met a tragic and violent death in the wake of a slave uprising.

Imperiously, Carstairs stood before Hudson and Mineo, who looked on in amazement and disbelief. "WELCOME TO WHALE CAY!" she shouted at them. "Glad to see you again, Rock! As for you, Sal, happy to see you, too!"

Suddenly, the butler from the Great House emerged with freshly laundered sheets, which Hudson and Mineo used to wrap around their bodies to conceal their nudity.

"God damn you, Joe, you scared me to death," an angry Hudson confronted her.

"I nearly shit my pants," Mineo said. "That is, if I were wearing any pants."

"Please forgive me," Carstairs said. "I'll make it up to you. I had to do something to relieve my boredom. Hell must be a place of utter boredom, which is the worst torment a soul can endure."

Annie Palmer, the Anglo-Irish White Witch of early 19th century Rose Hall, Jamaica.

A purported nymphomaniac, sadist, sorceress, and serial killer, she was the inspiration for the dress code of Joe Carstairs during costume parties on Whale Cay.

***

That evening at dinner, Linda was delighted to be seated at table with Hudson and Mineo. Carstairs had assigned all the "singles" (including herself, Hudson, Mineo, and Dietrich) to a separate, somewhat more risqué, table on the terrace, while married couples sat more sedately inside. Grahame and Linda were included with the singles. In all her life, Linda had never dined in such august company, and she owed it all to Grahame.

At times, she was jealous of Grahame, who was better looking, better dressed, better educated, and more talented than she was. She knew she couldn't directly compete with her friend, but was grateful not only for saving her from the clutches of Chuck, but bringing her to this idyllic island paradise.

Linda was aware that her welcome on Whale Cay was associated with a time limit, and that she'd soon have to move on. When the time was right, she intended to ask Carstairs if she might get her some work in New York. Linda imagined that she'd willingly function as a domestic servant at one of the Southampton estates of Carstairs' rich friends.

At table, Hudson and Mineo had seemingly fully recovered from Carstairs' roguish prank of that afternoon, and apparently, they had forgiven her. There seemed to be no tension between them and Carstairs when she arrived at table in a pants suit, with Lord Wadley plopped on her shoulders.

"I know you'd never give us such a scare," Hudson said. "But I wouldn't put it past Lord Wadley to have plotted the whole thing."

"Actually, the blame is entirely mine," Carstairs said. "Lord Wadley here was too drunk on rum to have plotted anything. I've got to cure myself of pulling these practical jokes. I've been staging them for years. One night, when I had a house full of guests, I rounded up a group of construction workers employed on the island and dressed them in those same costumes."

"At around 2am, accompanied by the sound of drum beats, they surrounded the Great House, waking up my guests. Frantically, I told them the natives were rioting. I surrounded myself with four men from my hired security force, We broke windows and started firing from inside the house at the natives outside. They fired back, but the guns of everyone on both sides had been loaded with blanks. 'They're going to kill us!' I shouted at my guests. 'Pansies first; women last.'"

"Joe, if I didn't love you so much, I would turn you over my knee and give you the spanking of your life," Hudson warned her.

Thirty minutes later, after Carstairs wandered off to tend to her other guests, Dietrich became more animated. She seemed very attracted to Grahame, who wore a simple black gown that showcased her Jane Russell cleavage.

Dietrich had been drinking in her cottage, but held her liquor well. She was in a teasing mood. "I understand that if not for Joe's intervention, we'd be eating you two guys for dinner tonight. I make *vonderful* sauces. I vonder what sauces would be best for each of you."

"Tabasco for me," Mineo said. "I'm hot stuff, but any old barbecue sauce would taste good with Rock."

"I've actually met people who have eaten human flesh," Dietrich said.

"You've been on an African safari?" Linda asked.

"No, my dear, I've met prisoners from Nazi concentration camps. To keep from starving, they devoured uncooked human flesh whenever one of their fellow inmates died."

There was a sudden silence at the table. Grahame tried to change the subject. "Tonight, it's going to be barbecued goat caught in the wild, along with fresh grouper hooked right offshore."

"For my after dinner treat," Marlene said, "I should give Rock the key to my cottage—that is, if Sal hasn't completely exhausted him. After all, I read that your list of seductions have included Tallulah Bankhead, Joan Crawford, and Elizabeth Taylor. Surely, I'm more alluring than any of those hags."

"Indeed you are," Hudson responded. "But please give me a raincheck. Just when you least expect it, I'll arrive knocking on your door after midnight one of these days."

Dietrich seemed in an impish mood as she looked first at Grahame, then at Linda, before finally focusing on Mineo. "Would you believe that a thirteen-year-old Sal Mineo and I once competed for the same man?"

"That I can't believe," Linda said.

"It was on Broadway when I was appearing with Yul Brynner in *The King and I*," Mineo chimed in. "It all started one night in his dressing room when he was showing me how to apply body makeup."

"I also took up with Yul," Dietrich said, "after Michael Wilding dumped me

Lovers:
Sal Mineo *(left)* and **Rock Hudson** *(above)*

for that whore, Elizabeth Taylor. I even lined by bedroom walls with mirrors to get a better look at Yul. His son, also named Rock, claimed that I was the 'most determined, passionate, and possessive lover Yul had ever known.' His son also said I swept into his life 'like Venus rising from a sea of Broadway babies.'"

"Yul gave both of us our walking papers after our flings," Mineo said.

"Yes, and I was delighted to learn that the son of a bitch moved on and ended up with a broken heart," Dietrich said. "He fell madly in love with Frank Sinatra, but the love wasn't returned. Frank let him down easy, though, by inviting Yul to spend weekends at his Palm Springs house but in separate beds."

Linda would later recall, "I was in my glory listening to this 'Inside Hollywood' gossip from movie stars. I wanted to be a movie star myself. Of course, I knew I'd never make it big like Crawford or Dietrich. I had to aim lower, like Diane Baker. I saw her play the older sister in *The Diary of Anne Frank.* Maybe I could be a Betsy Blair, the gal who married Gene Kelly. I saw her play that dowdy schoolteacher romanced by Ernest Borgnine in *Marty.*"

"Once, I shared my dreams of stardom with Chuck," Linda had earlier confessed to Grahame. "He laughed at me. He said my best hope might involve a walk-on in a B movie playing a maid. He also claimed that I might be cast in some gangster picture as a victim whose hoodlum boyfriend cut her body with a switchblade—hence, my scar."

"We'd both be lucky if we never crossed paths with Chuck Traynor as long as we live," Grahame told her.

***

For the final night of the gala, some fifty A-list guests had arrived by yacht to enjoy the festivities and to attend what Carstairs had defined as "a cultural presentation."

She was angered that the Duke and Duchess of Windsor had canceled at the last minute, pleading ill health. "They could attend a party of Richard Nixon's but not mine," she complained.

Linda was greatly disappointed that she would not get to meet the former King of England and one-time Emperor of India.

[An inveterate smoker, the Duke died on May 28, 1972, after six months of acute pain from throat cancer.]

Linda was upset that she was not asked to participate in the presentation. Instead, Carstairs had assigned her a role as Grahame's wardrobe mistress, helping her in and out of her Mata Hari costumes. Linda didn't even get to see the show, other than what she could glimpse from the wings.

It began on a comical note. Sal Mineo and Rock Hudson appeared fully dressed in business suits and in white shirts and ties. In good fun, they performed a striptease, beginning with the removal of their ties. One by one, each piece of their clothing was removed until, with a sense of casual comedy and good-natured show-biz, they exhibited themselves in flimsy briefs. As more and more of their well-sculpted bodies were revealed, the audience responded with increasingly wild applause.

The musical highlight of the evening was the glittering appearance of Marlene Dietrich in a gold lamé gown. She sang three songs from her repertoire of hits, including a rendition of her signature, "Lili Marlene" that brought tears to some eyes. Her standing ovation seemed to thunder on and on.

Grahame later complained to Linda, "How in hell does anyone follow a presentation by Marlene Dietrich?"

After an interlude, the finale was presented, with Lori Grahame performing three dances of Mata Hari. She looked more like Greta Garbo in her interpretation of her movie role of *Mata Hari* than the Dutch/German spy herself. The choreography was avant garde and intensely stylized, drawing only polite responses from the audience.

When most members of the generally very wealthy audience assessed that the evening as over, Carstairs made a dramatic appearance to announce one final surprise. She strode onto the stage wearing a neatly tailored woman's suit, a low-cut blouse, and a tricorn hat, a replica of the outfit that Mata Hari had worn to her execution before a French firing squad on October 15, 1917.

"Good evening, ladies and gentlemen," Carstairs announced loudly. "I've had to move mountains to rent this valuable final exhibit, which is on temporary loan to me by a private collector."

At that point, two members of her Bahamian staff wheeled out a glass cabinet resembling, to some degree, an exhibition case in a museum. It was covered with a red satin sheet.

"Tonight's presentation of this rare and valuable talisman is my final tribute to Mata Hari," Carstairs announced. "After I unveil it, I wish for all of you to line up in an orderly fashion here, onstage, to gaze at the mysteries it represents." Then she signaled the Bahamians to remove its satin covering. "Ladies and gentlemen, I give you the embalmed head of the erotic legend, Mata Hari."

Waves of shock rippled through the audience. One by one, eager curiosity seekers came to stare into the glass casing that surrounded the withered, meticulously embalmed head of a once-beautiful woman.

Linda herself deserted her post backstage and joined the lineup. When her turn came to gaze at the sunken face of the macabre-looking head, she gasped in horror.

***

The morning after, Linda still could not believe that she'd seen an actual body part from the legendary Mata Hari.

Carstairs had told Grahame, Linda, and others that the embalmed head had been surgically removed after her execution by a firing squad.

After embalming, it was donated to the Museum of Anatomy in Paris, which placed it in storage, at least until 1954. During the process of moving artifacts from that museum to a new location, the head disappeared. Amazingly, its theft was not discovered until 2000, when archivists were compiling an inventory of the museum's possessions.

Today, the head is believed to rest in the private collection of a billionaire in Connecticut.

***

After all the guests had either sailed or flown away for the final time from Whale Cay, Carstairs invited Linda and Grahame to fly with her in her private plane for a brief shopping excursion in Miami. Her inventories of supplies had been depleted by her having entertained so many guests at her gala.

During this trip, she promised to buy some new clothes for Linda and for Grahame, each of whom had fled from their previous lives in South Florida, each of them abandoning their wardrobes.

In Miami, since she was a guest of Carstairs, not an employee, Linda was modest in her choice of a wardrobe, avoiding anything expensive and searching for bargains. She opted for only a small selection of semi-tropical clothing, none of it suitable for cold climates.

As part of the agenda associated with their trip, Carstairs arranged for a limousine to drive them to Boca Raton for a visit with her friend at the mansion where Grahame and Linda had entertained.

Linda asked not to be included in the excursion to Boca Raton because she wanted "to see a friend." Consequently, without even telling Grahame where she was going, she agreed to meet them at the airport at 8am the following morning for their return flight to Whale Cay.

The day before their flight from Whale Cay, she had called Sunshine and asked if she could visit her at her home in South Miami. Without wanting to admit it, Linda was eager to learn what had happened to Chuck Traynor. For the most part, she wanted to know if he planned to hunt her down for deserting him, or if he were plotting some sort of retribution.

She had abandoned her previous life so quickly that she was anxious for news about what had happened since her departure. As painful as it was to admit, even to herself, she wanted to know whether Chuck had found another sex slave to replace her. After all, he was still, technically, her legal husband.

After a taxi ride from the airport, at the entrance to Sunshine's modest home, her friend let her in, but seemed nervous and filled with anxiety. It was not a friendly welcome. It was obvious to Linda that their once warm relationship had soured.

Sunshine offered her a seat in the living room and brought her some coffee. Sunshine sat across from her, looking very tense. "If you want an update on Chuck and what's been going on, you've come to the wrong gal. I no longer work for Chuck. I'm out of the business. My boyfriend, that adman on *The Herald,* and I are talking about getting married. He wants two or three kids, and so do I."

"Why are you so fucking nervous?" Linda asked.

"I hate to tell you this, but I've turned my back on my old life," Sunshine said. "I don't want to see anyone from that time. I want to go respectable."

"I applaud you for that," Linda said. "I know you and your boyfriend will make it. I envy you. But you were around when I left Chuck. Can't you at least tell me what happened?"

"Just what do you want to know?" Sunshine asked.

"How did Chuck handle it when he found out I'd fled his prison? Give me some idea of what the son of a bitch is planning to do. Is he going to go after me?"

"Why not ask me yourself?" Chuck asked. Apparently, he'd been standing just inside the open bedroom door and had heard every word.

Linda screamed at the sight of her tormenter. She glared at Sunshine. "You double-crossed me, you little bitch!"

As Chuck crossed the living room, moving menacingly toward her, Linda jumped up and tried to make it to the front door. He tripped her and sent her tumbling to the floor.

"I've got a gun, you cunt," he barked at her. "Get up. I'm taking you on a very long ride."

From his jacket, he removed a revolver and aimed it at her head. Sobbing, she pulled herself up from the floor. She looked back at Sunshine. "I'll never forgive you for this."

"He made me do it," Sunshine said as she ran toward the bedroom.

Chuck called to her. "Thanks for the hospitality and the fuck. I had a lot of fun working with you. Good luck with those kids."

Then he shoved Linda out the door. "See our Volkswagen? Get in it! I sold the house. I'm taking you all the way to Juárez, where you'll go over big on stage. There are some well hung donkeys waiting to get it on with you."

CHAPTER FIVE
On the Road to Hell

As Chuck's car headed north from Miami along U.S. 1 during that autumn of 1971, he told Linda, "Guys like me always need to hook up with some whore we can use as a meal ticket. Why I chose an unattractive bitch like you, a real scarbelly, I'll never know. But you're my wife, and you owe it to me to earn a living for us. Ideally, on this trip, I'll have you in a production line with three guys plugging all three of your holes at once."

"You're kidnapping me?"

"A husband can't kidnap his own wife, you dumb cunt."

"Just where are you taking me?"

"Aspen."

"Where in hell is that?"

"It's in Colorado," he said, "a real high-class ski resort attracting celebrities. Maybe you'll get to fuck Ryan O'Neal or Warren Beatty. I notice that you carry around one of those little publicity shots of Beatty in your wallet."

Although it seemed inconceivable at the time, Warren Beatty would one day proposition her.

"A friend of mine has opened a bar in Aspen," he said. "He needs go-go dancers for the winter who'll turn into hookers after midnight."

"How thrilling," she said, sarcastically.

"Don't give me lip, bitch." He reached across the seat and slapped her, hard. "Listen, and listen good. I sold my house, but I owed all the money in bad debts. I didn't get much for it after the mortgage was paid off. As we go across country, I'm going to rent you out. We'll need money for gas, food, and motels."

"I don't want to go anywhere with you," she protested. "Please let me out of this car."

"I'll do so only on one condition: That you let me put a bullet into your head before dumping you beside the road. Now shut your face. You'll do what I tell you. Accept every date I set up for you. God, how I wish you were a replica of Marilyn Monroe. Then I could make some real money."

"Since she's been dead for eight years, even Marilyn probably doesn't look so hot these days."

In one of her memoirs, Linda tried to explain how she felt as a prisoner in the Volkswagen with Chuck. "I wasn't a person anymore, I was a robot, a vegetable, a wind-up toy, a fucking–and-sucking doll." She knew if she didn't do what he commanded, he'd beat her severely, or maybe do something even worse.

Once again, he planned to rely on horny truck drivers for much-needed cash. Every day, he was going to drive as far as he could before dinner. Then he'd pull into a truck stop and seek guys willing to buy Linda's services.

South of the Georgia border, he located a truck stop that had a dirty spoon café and advertised rooms renting for only $8 a night, its blinking neon sign flashing throughout the night. "Truckers every now and then have to stop to shower and shit," he told her, "and to get laid. That's where you come in, of course."

Before going inside the café, he warned her, "I've got enough to buy you a hamburger—and that's it. No coke."

At a table covered in Formica, he ordered the blue plate special of pork with fries and vegetables. She got her rather thin burger and chewed slowly to make it last.

She felt awkward being the only woman in the joint. The truckers kept staring at her. After eating, Chuck paid the check and booked a room for them in the rear. The manager warned, "There are no private baths. Our showers are communal. No place for a woman."

When Chuck opened the door of a dreary, musty room out back, she noticed a small bed and a rusty sink with a little mirror that had been placed there in 1940. "You can take a whore's bath in the sink while I go to the bar and try to dig up some business."

As she washed herself, she heard raucous laughter coming from the shower room next door. The walls were paper thin. One drunker trucker yelled, "Guys, Bill just bent over to get a bar of soap. Plug him!"

Exhausted, she fell asleep on the uncomfortable bed. At around 11pm, Chuck pounded on the door and walked in immediately with two burly truckers. "Linda, baby, this is Roger here," he said, noting the heavier trucker. "He's with his friend, Joe. They've come to have a little fun with you."

"Hi, guys!" she said weakly.

What happened during the next hour would be repeated endlessly across the country as they continued their westward journey. The older trucker, Joe, was in his forties and had a bushy mustache. The younger guy, Roger, was under thirty and was the better-looking of the two men.

Heading for the door, Chuck said, "She's all yours, boys, at least until midnight."

Not wanting to waste any time, both men stripped before her. She also took off her dress and underwear. Totally nude, she lay on the bed as the truckers descended on her.

She was amused at the large butterfly Joe had tattooed on his left butt cheek. Completely at ease in their nudity, each man had a somewhat average cock. They both went to work right away on her, Roger invading her mouth and Joe pounding into her vagina. Before midnight, both men had sampled all three of her holes.

Before leaving, each of them left a twenty dollar bill, which Chuck collected when he came back into the room.

"Those guys really wanted me to earn my dough," she told him. "What a workout."

"Lucky gal," he said. "If I were queer, I'd fuck that Roger myself."

By 1am, the shower room had emptied, and most of the other residents had fallen asleep, since each of them had to hit the road at around 4am. Chuck guarded the door to the shower room, and she stepped inside the smelly place. She soaped herself and washed her hair, wanting to wipe away the smell of Joe and Roger.

She knew that worse nights would be in store for her before this road trip ended.

Before she went to sleep, Chuck told her, "Truckers make fine clients, but beginning tomorrow, we've got to make twice what we made tonight. What do you expect? That I can live off air?" Then he rolled over and fell into a deep, snoring sleep.

She dreaded what the following day would bring.

***

At breakfast the next morning, Chuck ordered scrambled eggs, bacon, toast, and potato pancakes. He gave her his toast and allowed her to have a cup of coffee.

As they drove across the Georgia border and headed west, he revealed his latest money-making scheme to her.

They would hit very small towns, where he said, "Most of the men see little action

169

since they're probably married and everybody knows everybody else's business. We're going to seek out some stores, perhaps on Main Street—maybe a men's clothing store or else a place staffed only by men. When there are no customers, I want you to walk in and make them an offer. Tell them you'll give them a blow job for twenty dollars each. If you meet sales resistance, lower your price to ten dollars each."

In some small town in southern Georgia she'd never heard of, and could not remember the name of, Chuck found a clothing store. Through the windows, he spotted an older male customer being fitted for a suit from off the rack. After he left, there were two salesmen left, as she related in her memoirs, *Ordeal.*

Chuck then ordered her to go into the store and proposition the salesmen. She was mortified at having to do something that blatant, but she was too afraid to defy him.

On the way into the store, she invented a scheme to double-cross him. She remembered what a hard time her father had in finding a shirt in his right size. Instead of propositioning the salesman, she decided to impersonate a shopper, asking for a size she knew would probably not be in stock. She requested one with a fifteen-inch neck and a forty-six inch sleeve.

"That's impossible," one of the salesmen said. "What the hell? Is your old man an orangutan with measurements like that?"

Through the window, Chuck spied on the salesmen as each rejected her. He could tell by their expressions and the movement of their heads.

Outside, Chuck was furious. Before she could tell him that her offers had been rejected, he said, "Those fucking hillbillies probably never saw a real live cunt before." Back in the car, he blamed her for not exposing the salesmen to her specialty.

Before the day ended, he stopped into two other towns and waited until there were no customers in a small shop with only one or two salesmen. She pulled the same routine, proud of herself for requesting something that she knew the store would not have in stock.

He began to panic over their dwindling funds. At one gas station where he had to fill up the Volkswagen, he engaged in a serious talk with the station manager. At first, she thought he was trying to sell her to the gas jockey.

Back in the car, he revealed what his next move was. Since it was growing darker, he said he'd learned of a place where they could spend the night.

"It's a truck stop diner and sleazy motel for niggers," he told her. "As you know, black guys really dig white chicks. If I can't sell you to white men, I'll peddle your ass to the darkies."

She sank deep into her seat in fear, but still she said nothing.

Linda had spent many a night in sleazy places, but none was as bad as the Hoot Owl Lodge. The matriarch who checked them in reminded Linda of an elderly version of Pearl Bailey. "This is a hotel for Negroes," she said.

"We know," Chuck said. "You don't allow whites?"

"We're integrated here," the old woman said. "Okay, sign in." As if aware of his scheme, she said, "Whatever turns you on, baby."

Their bedroom looked like a prison cell made of concrete blocks, with a cement floor. "Before I went to bed at night, my grandmother used to say, 'Don't let the bedbugs bite,' Chuck said. "That sounds like an apt warning for this hell hole."

Once again, she regretted that there was no private bathroom. She and Chuck would have to use a communal toilet and shower room. She could hear some truckers showering before dinner. They'd rented rooms for the night after driving big rigs all day.

"I've got an idea," Chuck said. "I read during the war, when Marlene Dietrich was entertaining our troops, she used to strip down and shower with the nude GIs. If Dietrich could pull off a stunt like that, so can you."

She protested vigorously, telling him she wouldn't do it. But he slapped her into submission. "Now strip and grab that dirty towel. We're both going into the shower room with the nigger bucks."

With trepidation, she entered the shower room where six nude black men were soaping themselves. Chuck trailed her.

The men stared at her in amazement. They'd been talking and laughing, but fell silent when she entered. As instructed by Chuck, she stopped under one of the shower heads and began to lather her body with her own bar of soap, paying particular attention to her breasts and vagina. Chuck opted for a shower head in one of the room's far corners.

The men quickly entered into the spirit of the scene. They assumed "this white chick" was turned on by black men, so they began to soap their genitals. Linda tried to block out what was happening around her, and didn't really look at the men, but continued soaping herself, erotically.

After she'd finished, she rinsed off and rushed from the shower room, but could not help but notice that two of the men were showing big erections.

Chuck stayed behind to negotiate a deal with the truckers. Of the six, only one bowed out.

Drying herself in the bedroom, she knew what was coming next. Chuck returned to their room, covering himself with a towel. Five of the truckers came in after him. Two of them didn't bother to cover themselves with a towel.

"Guys, this is Linda," Chuck announced. "She digs black dick."

"Hi, baby," the tallest and biggest of the truckers said. "My name is Corey. I want the special that your main man here bragged about. But I've got to warn you, bitch—I come in buckets."

He was huge and forceful as he plunged into her throat. It was as if he were deliberately trying to be rough enough to harm her. "Suck that big thing," he ordered her. He stayed deep in her throat until she felt dizzy from lack of air. Then he attacked her again with his humongous whopper, and she demonstrated her skills in front of the other truckers, hoping that her performance would please Chuck as well as Corey.

Her throat opened again and again. When he started yelling, she prepared herself for a flood. Unlike many of her previous clients, Corey lived up to his self-proclaimed billing. She didn't have to be told to "swallow every drop."

After she fellated two other men, the fourth made a different demand: "I can get any white queer between here and New Orleans to give me a blow job. I want some white pussy and I want it now." Before mounting her, he warned her, "I like to make 'em squeal, baby."

By the time the fifth trucker had straddled her face on the bed and ordered, "Suck it, white bitch," she was exhausted. Fearing a beating from Chuck, she opened her throat for yet another time, working hard to bring the overweight trucker to a roaring climax.

Her night wasn't over. After Chuck collected ten dollars from each of the men, he announced that he was heading to the bar and intended to remain there until it closed at midnight. He turned to the men. "Big, strong guys like you surely aren't satisfied yet! I'm leaving Linda with you until I get back. Do what you want with her. A word of advice: To really turn her on, she likes it rough."

With that pronouncement, he headed out of the room, leaving her to the mercy of the five beefy truckers.

Years later, when asked to recall her ordeal that night, she burst into tears. "I can't...I just can't. There are some things a woman in my circumstances has to blot out of her mind."

***

Another night, another truck stop, except that this time, rooms were rented only to white men. Between eight o'clock at night and four in the morning, she managed to service eight men, some of whom gave Chuck twenty dollars, others paying only ten.

In the car, from there all the way to Alabama, she sat in stone silence. They stopped for a quick coke at the Buena Vista Café, where the sound of old Hank Williams records filled the air. Most of the male patrons were drinking Budweiser. She was grateful that Chuck wanted to press on for the night. There would be no tricks to hustle.

Back in the car, silence prevailed as the long, boring highway stretched ahead of them. The blazing sun had died, but left behind an orange-yellow light. The fields looked brown. In the houses off the highway, TV sets had been turned on. In this part of the country, that was the only entertainment available. She and Chuck offered a different type of amusement.

These smug little households—steeped in family values—would condemn her. Her only comfort on this bleak night involved the belief that her secrets would never be exposed to the world.

As Chuck neared the Georgia/Alabama border, he gave in to Linda's pleas to stop for a hamburger. Inside the café, there was a stray trucker or two; a family of four with complaining children, and two military men based in Mississippi, to judge from their accents.

At the far end of the counter, two men in work shirts and jeans—one in his forties, another perhaps in his late teens, finished off their hot plate specials. "I'll meet you outside, Dad," the younger one said.

His chunky, masculine-looking father headed for the single toilet in the rear. Impulsively, Chuck got up and followed him into the john.

Chuck remained away from their table for nearly fifteen minutes. She wondered what was going on. Surely, Chuck was not having gay sex with that man…not Chuck!

The middle-aged man emerged first and looked Linda over with a very suggestive gaze. Then he went outside and joined his son.

At the counter, Chuck quickly paid the bill. "Let's scram," he said. "I've fixed you up with a father-son combo. You'll love it."

Then, he grabbed her arm. Outside, he introduced her to the men. "This is Mike," Chuck said, "and Jeff here is his son."

"Hi, ya, woman," Mike said. "Let's walk over to our truck. We were going to try to make it to Mobile tonight, but we've been going all day through the Panhandle and need some rest. Care to join me and my boy in our rig's sleeping compartment?"

"We've got a nice bed in there," Jeff said, "Cuts down on motel bills."

Chuck signaled to her that he'd already made the payment arrangements. "Sure, guys, I'll inspect your quarters," she said.

Rather awkwardly, Jeff maneuvered her into the compartment as Mike followed. It was such a small area, she didn't feel there was room enough for three.

"It's hot as hell in here," Mike said. "Let's strip down and get comfortable."

Reluctantly, she removed her cotton dress, panties, and bra. "Help the kid," Mike ordered. "He's had only two gals before you, and he's bashful."

The teenager's face grew redder and redder. Wanting to get this seduction behind her, she lowered herself to her knees and unbuttoned his shirt and waistband, lifting his penis upward and out of his jeans. She wasn't surprised to be greeted with his erection. She took hold of him and sucked him into her mouth, as Mike looked on, fascinated.

Then Mike removed his clothes, too, and moved to a position in front of her and stood beside his son. She knew at once what he wanted. She took the head of both penises inside her mouth and began to work on them as a unified pair. For fifteen minutes, they seemed to enjoy the closeness of each other. It was as if they were having sex with each other.

She noticed that Mike had taken his hand and was feeling his son's butt, as the kid moaned with pleasure. Suddenly, Jeff lurched forward. She suspected that Mike had inserted his finger into his son's butt. "Tight hole, kid," Mike said.

During the next few minutes, she managed to bring both men to climax at the same time in her mouth and throat. Each was still recovering his breath as she quickly dressed. She had a hard time finding one of her shoes in the cramped quarters of the sleeping enclosure. Stepping out of the cab, she climbed down, filling her lungs with the exhaust-polluted air from the nearby highway. She suspected that Mike and Jeff wouldn't be needing her again, as they seemingly had found each other.

"Get in the car," Chuck said. "I've already collected the dough."

"I figured you had," she said. "Can I go in and wash up?"

"Fuck that!" he said. "Get in. I want to cross into Alabama before it gets too dark. We'll be in New Orleans tomorrow, if all goes well...Just in time for Mardi Gras."

***

The Mardi Gras Hotel in New Orleans had seen better days. A few grimy chandeliers, frayed carpeting, and a magnificent grand staircase suggested that it had once known a more upscale clientele. But it was deep in decay. All of the original furnishings were gone, sold off long ago at auction.

At Mardi Gras time in New Orleans, all the hotels and boarding houses, including motels on the outskirts, had been fully booked, in some cases, a year in advance.

On the edge of the French Quarter, Chuck, without a reservation, entered the lobby of the seediest hotel he could find. Indeed, it would be torn down a few years later.

In the dimly lit lobby, which smelled of marijuana, she sensed that the guests fell into any of four distinct categories—hookers, pimps, drug addicts, and alcoholics—each client trying to rip off the others.

When Chuck asked for a room, not expecting to find one available, he was surprised when the desk clerk said he had something on the fifth floor. Unshaven, he looked like he'd started drinking early that morning. "It's available because the cops just left. They hauled off the guy who'd been renting it."

174

"We'll take it," Chuck said. "Sight unseen."

"Okay, but I'm warning you," the clerk said. "It's really small. There's no maid service during Mardi Gras. And I don't know what shape the guy left the room in."

As there was no elevator, and no bellhop service, Linda and Chuck hauled their possessions up to the fifth floor. Their room was at the end of the hall, past a smelly communal toilet. When he opened the door, she was dismayed, since this rabbit hole, as she called it, contained only a three-quarter bed shoved against peeling wallpaper. There was no window, also no toilet, no sink, and no ventilation. Perhaps it had once been a maid's pantry. The only place for their three suitcases was under the creaky bedsprings.

The small amount of floor space was littered with crumpled beer cans, an empty bourbon bottle, and the remains of a pizza that had molded.

An hour later found them walking along raucous, overcrowded Bourbon Street, which was filled with pickpockets. In the French Quarter, he grabbed her arm, pushing her into a sleazy bar named The Mississippi River Bottom, where he ordered a rum and coke, giving her half the coke. The word "bottom" in the club's name was apt. Six bottomless dancers were on the bill that night.

Excusing himself, Chuck went toward the back of the bar to confer with the manager. Within ten minutes, he'd returned, ordering her to come back to the manager's office. Once there, she met R.J. Osterhoudt, who immediately ordered her to strip down completely. "I don't have all night, girlie," he barked at her.

Embarrassed, she pulled off all her clothes, including her bra and panties, in front of this beefy club owner. "I've seen better," he said. "But Chuck here tells me that when the hour grows later, and anything goes, you'll entertain stag parties in the back room and that you can handle a fourteen-inch dildo."

She looked in fright at Chuck, who signaled her to agree. "My other strippers won't do shit like that. I can rent one of my private rooms for twenty-five dollars a head—perhaps crowding in a dozen or so horny guys. I understand you can suck off all of them before the end of your act. Agreed?"

"I guess so," she said.

"Okay, go in the back room and introduce yourself to Maude," he said. "She'll give you a costume. Your first show begins at 2am, and we'll keep staging them until at least 10am, since it's Mardi Gras."

Years later, Linda would relate how every night became the same throughout five complete 24-hour cycles. She claimed that her time in New Orleans had become a blur to her.

"It was just a sea of men," she tried to recall between tears. "At one point, I felt like a wound-up toy. I related to no client. Nor did they seem to relate to me. I was their plastic doll. To make matters worse, Chuck brought some of the

175

patrons back to our hotel. They came upstairs one by one. He gave each of them twenty minutes with me. If they stayed longer, he knocked on the door, warning them their time was up."

[Under intensive interviewing in the late 1980s, a researcher asked Linda how many men she'd had sexual relationships with in New Orleans. She seemed stumped by the question. There were three shows a night for five nights, attracting at least fourteen men per show. "I can't figure it out."

Her researcher suggested at least forty men per day. Five nights entertaining forty men would come to around two hundred men.

At this point, Linda burst into tears again. "Don't write that down. No...no, it couldn't be! I was given drugs during this period by Chuck. I was out of my mind. I didn't know what I was doing."

She couldn't go on with her story. "Oh, please," she said. "Please. I'm not a bad girl. Really, I'm not. I went to a Catholic school."

During that stage in Linda's latter-day narrative, there would be gaps in her story, especially since it involved days and periods when she was either too busy or too stoned to make notations in her diary. She'd blotted out her more traumatic experiences.

***

After leaving New Orleans, Chuck, with her in tow, headed north, telling her he was going to Little Rock, Arkansas. His face was locked in a steely determination, suggesting he had a grudge to settle there. The night before, he'd been checking his guns, making her wonder if he planned to kill someone in Little Rock because of some perceived outrage years before.

En route to Little Rock, he told her that he'd talked to his friend in Aspen, who had told him that he had no need for her go-go services until the ski season began in December.

"After Little Rock, I plan to head south and west again," he told her. "Our goal is Ciudad Juárez in Mexico."

In her book, *Ordeal,* Linda related her shock and distaste about what Chuck planned to have her do once they reached Juárez. Along the way, he informed her that it was better for her if she liked donkeys. "In Juárez, I'm getting you a booking fucking donkeys on stage."

At first, she couldn't believe him. But he'd been there before and knew how hard it was for local club owners to persuade American girls to appear naked in an arena, otherwise used for cockfights, where men could witness a donkey fucking them.

"The spectators take bets as to how many inches from a donkey a woman can take," he told her. "You'd be a natural for that. They don't use the expression 'donkey dick' for nothing."

He claimed that the last woman he'd hauled to Juárez for the donkey shows had made "three-thousand dollars for him. The crowd cheers when the chicks come out, just like at a prizefight. And then they strap the chick up on this contraption and then they bring out their trained donkey. They lead the animal right into the fucking cunt."

She could not believe such a sexual coupling was possible, but the more he talked, the more he convinced her it was. She was terrified at the thought.

"Of course, sometimes the gal gets ripped up a bit," he said.

"A woman could die getting fucked by a donkey," she protested.

"Don't worry," he said. "They have a doctor on site. Sometimes a chick will start hemorrhaging, but a local *medico* will come to her aid."

Linda prayed she'd never have to go with him to Juárez. In fact, the more he talked, the more she decided she'd make a break for it. Without him, she could hitch rides to New York in trucks. By now, she knew how to work the system.

With Chuck at the wheel, the road stretched endlessly before them as she plotted various schemes. Suddenly, he yelled in panic. The drunken driver of an oncoming station wagon seemed out of control. Seeing him barreling toward their car, she braced herself for a collision. Then the station wagon rammed into their Volkswagen, which turned over, landing in a ditch. Without a seat belt, she was thrown into the back. Although she was severely bruised, she miraculously escaped without any broken bones.

She later thanked God for "sabotaging" that Juárez project. When the police arrived, Chuck was told that his car was damaged beyond repair. The drunk who'd rammed them had been in a stolen car and had fled the scene of the damage he had caused. Having abandoned the ruined station wagon, he was nowhere in sight, and the police believed he'd hitched a ride south, even though he was drunk.

The police drove them to a trucker's motel on the outskirts of Little Rock. After hamburgers in the adjoining café, Chuck told her that without a car, he couldn't go on to Mexico. While waiting for that gig in Aspen to open for her, he announced, "Tomorrow, we're going to hook up with some truckers who are heading for New York or New Jersey. There are a lot of sex jobs there, and we'll find some work for you."

"Why not stay here in Little Rock for a while on what little money we have?" she asked. "Maybe I could earn a few bucks. I don't want to get on the road again. I need some rest after that ordeal in New Orleans."

"We're leaving early in the morning, probably around 4am, and we're going to New York. It has some special sex jobs that most hookers won't do. But I'm sure you won't object."

Fearing what he had in mind, she turned over in bed, but sleep would not come.

Chuck never revealed why he'd wanted to come to Little Rock. Just before the accident, he had made a phone call. After a few minutes, he slammed down the receiver. "The bastard's dead," he said, almost to himself.

Four o'clock seemed to come especially early the next morning.

***

By renting out Linda's body to truckers, Chuck negotiated a circuitous passage to New York City. Once there, they realized that their rapidly diminishing reserve of cash meant that they couldn't live in Manhattan.

In Jersey City, just across the Hudson River from Manhattan, they found a shabby, two-room apartment for rent. They had to post $130 up front, which included the first month's rent and a security deposit. That left them with just $50.

Saving just enough money for rice and beans, Chuck invested the cash in copies of most of the underground sex tabloids that were flourishing in the wake of the "sexual revolution" of the late 60s.

Many of the ads were coded ("SEEK GREEK SLAVE;" "FRENCH LESSONS GIVEN"), but Chuck knew what the advertisers wanted, even if Linda didn't. Many of the ads were solicitations for S&M.

Her first bookings were not in response to personal ads, but as a staff member at clubs featuring topless dancers. There were especially plentiful in and around Manhattan's West 42nd Street. Appearing in a flimsy G-string, she went bottomless in any act she was booked into after 2am.

After only three nights of this, Chuck knew that these gigs weren't going to work. Linda had learned none of the tricks of a battle-hardened professional sex worker. She evoked a hapless go-go dancer stranded in a milieu that was focusing on hard-core sex. One club manager even accused her of trying to put his audience to sleep.

Chuck set out like the most

Chuck's promise to Linda:
"Things will be better in Juárez!"

aggressive agent—or "bodyseller," as he put it—in a city with more flesh peddlers than Los Angeles. He began to meet eight millimeter directors, lining up future deals for Linda. "Within a week or two, Chuck managed to meet every prominent pervert in New York," Linda wrote in her memoir, *Ordeal.*

He even arranged for an audience with Xaviera Hollander, who at the time was the most famous and notorious madam in New York City. Within a few months, Xaviera would see the publication of her best-seller, *The Happy Hooker,* describing her early childhood as an intern, with her mother, in a Japanese internment camp during World War II and her subsequent exploits in the sex industry.

The uniformed doorman at Hollander's East Side apartment had Linda and Chuck wait endlessly in the building's elegant lobby. Finally, Linda, trailed by Chuck, was ushered in to see the infamous Dutch/Thai-Vietnamese/Indonesian madam. Linda was not impressed, writing, "She was fat. Her hair was dirty, all caked with grease. She had piled the make-up on a face that needed more than make-up."

Hollander interrupted their meeting to pick up the phone. During the dialogue that ensued, she discussed the details of her upcoming book, *The Happy Hooker,* published in 1971, which would eventually sell fifteen million copies worldwide.

When Hollander went into another room to tend to some other urgent business, Church urged her "to get it on" with the madam, who was known to have had sex with women. "I'm sure she's also got a dildo around here. Show her what you can do with a fourteen-inch dildo. Go down on her."

"But I just can't start licking her!" Linda protested.

When the madam came back in, she began an attack on the clothes worn by both Linda and Chuck, who were each attired in boots, blue jeans, and U.S. army jackets. "I get no calls for hippie chicks."

"A lot of my clients are movie stars, judges, top lawyers, perhaps an astronaut who flew to the moon," Hollander said. "They want chic-looking girls they can take to nightclubs and fancy restaurants. Not exactly Grace Kelly, but not some floozie streetwalker either." Then she turned directly to Chuck. "Your gal is far too skinny. No tits. Besides, I have enough brunettes. Redheads are suddenly in demand, however."

"Linda can be a redhead," Chuck chimed in,.

When he realized that the job interview was hopelessly failing, Chuck made one last-ditch appeal. "Linda can do all the kinky stuff. She's an expert at that. You must get a lot of calls from freaks and sicko pervs."

"The answer is no," Hollander said firmly. "Now please leave. I have important clients arriving tonight from the Coast."

***

Linda's next interview was with a Stockholm-born madam who called herself "Milka." It too, bombed. The retired hooker interviewed both Chuck and Linda alongside her partner, a man who introduced himself only as "Martin."

This time, Chuck pleaded with Milka to let Linda demonstrate her deep-throat technique on Martin. He disappeared with her to the privacy of a bedroom with a canopy-topped love nest, where she removed her bra. Martin pulled down his pants.

Linda was grateful that Chuck wasn't able to hear her. While fellating Martin, she burst into tears, which immediately deflated his erection.

"You're being forced by your pimp to do this?" he asked. "You're not into it." Perhaps knowing she'd get a beating for not performing, he covered for her. Ten minutes later, Martin proclaimed to Milka, "The gal's terrific. What a cocksucker!"

But he sent some private signal to Milka, who then looked Linda over skeptically. "If we need you, we'll call you. Now, you must leave."

On the way back to their dingy life in Jersey City, Chuck looked at Linda in disgust. "I can't even peddle your ass as a hooker. I didn't want to have to do this to you, but there's one market where your lack of physical beauty is not that important. In prostitution, it's called 'The Last Resort.'"

***

The weeks preceding Linda's filming of *Deep Throat* are like a missing link in the tortured context of her life. In the late 1980s, she'd tell researchers, "I've blacked out that period in my life. I can't remember a single incident. Chuck was peddling me on the perv market. It was disgusting. I experienced the most degrading, the most humiliating experiences a woman can go through. No human should endure what I did. Wherever I go today, people ask me why I didn't run away. I'm embarrassed that I don't have an answer for that. I did run away in time, of course, but I stayed too long at that party. I'm ashamed of myself for doing that."

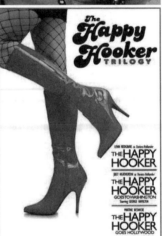

Sex industry entrepreneur, author, and columnist **Xaviera Hollander** in 2004

180

Linda faced extensive questioning from agent Jay Garon's chief researcher, the psychologist, Reba-Anne Howard. Gradually, Linda was lured into re-creating some of the details of this bizarre chapter of her life, although the ghastly experiences were often recalled through tears.

She admitted that she'd lied about blacking out that "awful period of my life. Those times I went through still bring on nightmares. I didn't want to talk about them because I didn't think readers would actually believe me, but I know that people who work the sex industry—and there are thousands of them—will believe me. It's amazing how many Americans do really sick things to get off, to satisfy their desires. The average member of the public, at least in the Bible Belt, views homosexuality as the ultimate taboo. Believe me, that is not true. The majority of gay men and lesbians lead fairly ordinary lives. But there is a lunatic fringe of people in America in both the gay and straight world who are just plain sick. In some of those cases, and with extreme pervs, Chuck forced me to go to the limits of my endurance."

"A lot of people today, who oppose abortion in any form, ask me if I ever got pregnant during this part of my life. Of course, what they're really asking is, 'did I kill any of my unborn children.' I never got pregnant during the months preceding my filming of *Deep Throat*. I hate rubbers. But I took birth control pills—and they worked."

During one of her "gigs," the appearance of her host and client genuinely shocked her: He was attired in a military uniform inspired by the Nazi aesthetic of the Third Reich. In black, knee-high boots, he ordered, instead of inviting, Chuck and her inside. She wanted to break away and run when she saw a large portrait of Adolf Hitler hanging over the sofa, where it was bathed in a soft pink, almost romantic-looking, light.

The client, who stood six feet, four inches, was tall and husky. Under his curly blonde hair was the square-jawed face of a remarkably handsome man. Chuck introduced her to him as "Heinz," although she had no idea what his real name was, not that it mattered.

"Thank you for bringing the Jew bitch," Heinz said to Chuck, and then demanded of him: "Come into the bedroom."

Left behind, bewildered, in the living room, Linda overheard a brief argument, perhaps about money. When Chuck came back into the living room, he said, "I'll call for you in three hours. Do exactly what Heinz orders you to do."

She waited three minutes until she perceived that Chuck had departed from the corridor outside. Hearing no noise from the bedroom, she tiptoed to the main door and was preparing to open it and run away. But at that moment, Heinz entered the living room. "What is this? Your pimp takes my money and then you try to bolt? You'll not get away with it. Take off all your clothes, Jew Bitch!"

From that point onward, he called her a Jew Bitch every time he issued one of his commands.

After she'd pulled off her clothes, he said, "Get down on your hands and knees and look up at me."

After her acquiescence to that command, he began to disrobe. He looked like a man in his early 50s, although he seemed to have the vitality and physique of a much younger man. His face was deeply tanned and finely chiseled, with a straight nose over a full but firm mouth. His eyes were unclouded and blue, or, as she'd later tell Chuck, "like those of the Nazi soldiers who dropped the gas pellets." He pulled off all his clothes, revealing a hard, flat stomach, big muscles, and a powerful chest covered with blonde but graying hair. His thighs were solid columns. He had an exceptionally large, uncut penis. "Come into the bathroom with me, Jew Bitch."

She trailed behind him, trembling, as she had a rough idea of what was in store for her.

He ordered her to kneel on the bottom of the bathtub, as he stood, spread-eagled, above her. "I've been holding back going to the toilet," he said, "waiting for your visit. I can't hold out any longer. I've had about five beers and I'm overflowing. Drink every drop, or I'll kill you, you Jew Bitch."

Afraid not to obey, she accepted his penis in her mouth. Almost at once, he began to urinate. She swallowed and choked, but continued swallowing mouthful after gulping mouthful of his piss. To her, it seemed like an endless flow. She was crying when "the spigot," as she later defined it, eventually ran dry.

"Now we come to the really exciting part of my evening," he said. "I know a Jew Bitch like you will enjoy it even more than I do. I want you to clamp your mouth onto my anus. Very slowly, some extremely tasty stuff will emerge. Better than Bratwurst. I want you to savor it in your mouth and swallow every lovely turd. Jew Bitches and sometime young Jew Boys were forced to do this during the war."

"I can't do it!" she protested. "It would make me sick."

"Very well," he said. "Stay in the tub." On the sink, he took a cigar, cut it, lit it, and sat down on the toilet stool. We'll negotiate." He began to suck in large amounts of smoke until the cigar developed a fiery red tip.

"Are you sure, Jew Bitch, that there's nothing I can do to make you change your mind?"

"No, nothing," she said. "You're disgusting."

Almost without realizing what was happening, she watched him as he lurched over her. Without warning, he shoved the cigar, with its glowing tip, up her vagina. She screamed in agony as he knocked her back against the porcelain. "Listen to me, Jew Bitch, and listen good," he said. "I've got this wire. If you don't open your throat for me, I'll wrap it around your neck and strangle you to death."

At this point in the 1980s, during her recollection of those events, Linda refused to continue with her description of what happened next during this litany of New York City-based horror stories.

Die deutsche Haltung,
die deutsche Leistung
beweisen
das nordische Rassenerbe!

"It was ghastly!" she said, sobbing.

"But did you do what he ordered?" the researcher asked.

"It was either that or be strangled to death. What would any woman who wanted to live do? Yes, I did what he wanted. I held his turds in my stomach throughout the rest of my time with him. But when Chuck finally came for me at around midnight, I walked down the steps and retched on the sidewalk."

"I found out later that there's a whole cult of people out there who engage in this filthy perversion. There's even a name for it. *Coprophagia*, but don't ask me to spell it."

***

In New York City, over a period of several weeks, one bizarre sexual experience followed another, especially when she encountered two very different techniques from the Far East—the first from ancient China, the second from modern Japan.

Without telling her where she was going or what to expect, Chuck drove her from Jersey City to Long Island, where he headed east. It was dark when he pulled up at a gated mansion outside Southampton. She later learned it was the property of a wealthy Chinese-American industrialist.

After clearing security with the guard at the entrance, the gate was opened. Chuck drove up to the elaborate entrance whose design was inspired by a pagoda.

A ringing of the doorbell brought a very tall, slender young man, who was exceptionally effeminate. He wore a yellow jacket, black pants,

183

and silver slippers, with long pointed toes. After greeting them and bowing at the waist, he ushered them into a side salon filled with rare Chinese artifacts. All the colors were scarlet, except for dark wood and gold items. The boy waiter, with a high-pitched voice and delicate little steps, seated them and served them green tea from a red porcelain antique teapot with matching cups and saucers.

She was expecting an older client, but was surprised when a Chinese man in his late 30s entered the room wearing a red silk robe with gold braid. Linda had feared that her client would be some whiskered old sage with a name like *Chou En-lai* or *Chiang Kai-shek*. But later, Linda remembered him as quite handsome, bearing a close resemblance to the actor Turhan Bey as he appeared in the 1944 film, *Dragon Seed*.

[As their relationship progressed, whenever Chuck and Linda encountered a new client, they described him to one another as having a resemblance to whatever movie star his or her physicality evoked. Other than sex, movies were their only form of entertainment. Taking in double features, they had once sat through fifteen movies in one Miami weekend.

On television, they had viewed Dragon Seed, *a film which had been based on a Pearl Buck novel of the same name. MGM, in a fit of bad casting and bad judgment, had cast such obviously Anglo-looking stars as Katharine Hepburn and Walter Huston as Asians. They had also cast Turhan Bey, an actor of Turk-ish/Austrian ancestry, as a Chinaman in the same film. Linda had remembered him as a rather handsome man, well suited to playing an exotic-looking "for-eigner."]*

Greetings were exchanged. "Welcome, honored lady," the host said. Then he turned to Chuck. "She is all that you said. I do not like it when flesh peddlers misrepresent their merchandise."

"She does everything," Chuck promised.

"What good news that is for me," the host replied. "Women must obey their masters. From talking to you, I know you agree that the only role for a woman on this planet involves bearing children and to serve her master."

"Linda does that great," Chuck asserted.

"You told me she was your wife," the host said. "I especially appreciate American men who turn their wives over to me. I view it as a gift to be handled with great delicacy, like a thousand-year-old egg."

At a clap of the host's hands, the young man in the yellow jacket reap-peared to escort Linda downstairs to what was referred to as "the playroom." Chuck told her he'd booked her for an overnight visit and that he would pick her up after breakfast the next morning. She left the room willingly while she heard Chuck concluding the financial arrangements associated with her visit.

She was led downstairs to a room that looked like a Chinese version of one of those dungeon-inspired "haunted house" movies starring Vincent Price. There were cookies and drinks on a buffet inlaid with jade, and she helped herself. In an alcove was a television set. Flipping it on, she was greeted with Richard Nixon making a speech.

Suddenly, without her being aware of it, "Turhan Bey" was in the room looking down at her. Perhaps he'd entered through a secret passage. He certainly hadn't come through the main entrance.

"My dear child," he said, in a voice with absolutely no accent. "My ancestors, who grew up in Shanghai, practically invented the most exquisite sexual pleasure known to mankind. Please forgive me tonight if I indulge myself in this time-honored ritual. But first, have we made you comfortable?"

She was charmed by his manners. In the wake of her brutal treatment by the Neo-Nazi, she was almost looking forward to some form of sexual encounter

Two views of the Turkish/Austrian Hollywood star **Turhan Bey,** playing it Asian and ethnic in *Dragon Seed*

Lower photo: with **Katharine Hepburn,** who's bizarrely outfitted as a Chinese peasant, in an embarrasing studio miscalculation

with this handsome and very rich client. Perhaps if she performed well, he might invite her back for future weekends in his luxurious mansion.

"I'm so glad to be here, and all of you are so nice," she said. "Your home is beautiful. Lovely things placed everywhere. It's like a museum."

"Thank you so very much," he said. "I'm so grateful you appreciate our humble hospitality. If you don't mind the intrusion, I will need some assistance in giving me my ultimate pleasure," he said.

He sounded a small gong, whereupon the yellow-jacketed waiter or butler appeared from behind a curtain. Perhaps he'd been there all along, eavesdropping on them.

Then the host said, "I don't think I have formally introduced you..." He hesitated. "Let's call him 'Lee.' He used to be my lover until he got far too old. He's a ripe seventeen now."

"It's an honor to meet you, Miss Lovelace," the teenager said. "I'm sure that you will provide my master with the exquisite pleasure he so needs and deserves."

For the first time that night, she looked at this boy very closely. It was not just his high-pitched voice. He had other qualities that evoked a teenage girl—beautiful skin, tiny feet, a small bone structure, and large, dewy eyes.

185

Noticing how she had begun to appraise Lee, the host said, "Of all my lovers, this beautiful boy here was once my all time favorite. I purchased him from his dirt-poor parents in China when he was only five years old. If he were any older, he would not have been suitable for my needs. Of course, he had to undergo vigorous training so he would not develop masculine characteristics. In the beginning, the least masculine movement on his part led to the sting of my lash, which can be deadly. I once accidentally blinded a boy of seven with my whip."

At this point, the teenager bowed low before the host and took each of the fingers of the older man's left hand into his mouth and sucked on them. Then the host patted the boy's head before yanking rather hard on his hair. "My heart was broken when Lee turned fourteen."

Suddenly, she was seized by panic. This was the first indication that her host was a sadist.

"Often in China, we bind the feet of beautiful young girls," he said. "I ordered the binding of Lee's feet when he was five. I also hired two Chinese masseurs to shape his body into the exquisite delight it became. They were marvelous at shaping the tender buttocks of a young boy. Diet and forced feeding were also employed. The skin texture is very important in a young boy. Only the finest of oils and unguents were used upon his golden body. His teachers taught him erotic poetry, songs, and sexy stories to tell me during our foreplay. For years, he gave me untold delight until that awful day when he was fourteen, and I noticed unwanted hair on his body. Because of all those years of training, I did not want to lose him, so I personally castrated him," the host continued. "My hope was that it would delay his masculine development and that I'd get at least three more years of sexual service from him. That did not succeed at first. One night, after making mad, passionate love to him, I seized him and with a dagger I'd concealed, I cut off his entire genitalia. His screams caused me to experience a violent climax without touching myself. Fortunately, I had a doctor hiding behind a curtain. Otherwise, Lee would have bled to death."

"Then, when Lee turned seventeen, he was so incredibly docile, willing to obey any command, so I kept him on as a servant instead of turning him out onto the streets."

"Oh, please," she said, not concealing her alarm. "This isn't going to work out."

"Do not think me cruel," the host said. "I have deprived Lee of certain sexual pleasures, but not all joy. I often insert this large penis-shaped dilatory of ivory into him. He screams, but I know it is a cry of joy—not of pain. The dilatory was used by my ancestors on pre-pubescent boys for more than four centuries."

She rose from her divan. "Forgive me, sir, but you seem to have been taken care of. I don't think I can offer you the pleasure you're seeking."

His face grew stern, his voice harsh. "That remains to be seen."

With a clap of his hands, two muscular, bare-chested young men entered from the rear of the salon. The host barked orders in Chinese, whereupon the men descended on Linda. She struggled against their brute force, but was stripped of her clothing. Fighting furiously, she was overpowered, as one man held her while the other bound her wrists and legs. She was also gagged and tied in such a way as to cause maximum pain.

She was placed on her stomach with knees bent so that her bare feet extended upward. "Ah, my dear," the host said to her. "You resemble a twisted serpent, as depicted in a Chinese painting."

He then removed his robe. Standing beside him, his servant boy also removed his clothing. It was true. The boy had been completely emasculated.

The host arranged himself on a cushion, and the boy tried to make him as comfortable as possible. One of the muscled men handed the host a lithe strip of bamboo.

"While you provide one form of pleasure for me, Lee, with his scented mouth, will lick my body," the host said. "When I get hungry, he will feed me delicacies. I'm a very messy eater, and I let food drool out of my mouth. Lee's only nourishment for years has been what leftovers he can lick from what oozes from the corners of my mouth."

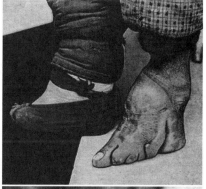

After this shocking pronouncement, the host began to beat her bare feet with the bamboo, the blows falling with the regularity of a metronome. He never hit her twice in the same spot, causing the most excruciating pain. The whipping continued for an hour. Tears were streaming from her eyes, but her screams were muffled. Even if she'd been able to scream at top volume, it wouldn't have done any good.

When the host had to urinate, Lee used his mouth as a latrine. At first, when the host stopped beating her, she thought she'd get a respite. But suddenly, and wordlessly, one of the muscled men took up the rhythm, continuing the beating of

A feminist's bad dream, a podiatrist's nightmare: Two views of the residual after-effects of Chinese foot binding.

her feet.

On occasion, the host spoke to her directly. "It is important that there be no let-up in your punishment. Whenever I tire, one of my men will take over. I think you should know something to give your mind some relief. Otherwise, you might be driven insane. As my ancestors taught me, your ordeal will last for only ten hours. You will not be able to walk at first. The pain will endure for a month, maybe more. It will be but a reminder of the glorious pleasure you provided for your master."

As she would later recall to Reba-Anne Howard, "I guess the human body has a way of turning off when the pain becomes too great. At some point before dawn, I passed out. The next thing I remembered, I found myself in Chuck's car. Instead of that cramped little Volkswagen, he was driving me back to Jersey in a rented van. I was laid out on blankets in the back. My feet not only ached, but my entire body ached. I screamed at Chuck, 'I almost died.'"

"Shut up, bitch," he called back to her. "I got paid $10,000. Never in my life have I earned so much money off one of my damn whores."

***

Throughout the month that followed, Linda could barely walk. If she did, it caused her excruciating pain. She wanted revenge, and at one point, she plotted to cut off Chuck's penis when he was asleep. She'd heard that throughout the course of many centuries, women had done that to men as an act of revenge for some brutal treatment.

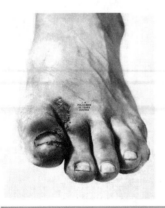

THINK ABOUT WHAT THE VICTIM LOOKS LIKE. STOP THE TORTURE! SUPPORT US.

Amnesty International www.AmnestyUSA.org

LINDA WOULD UNDERSTAND!

(*photo above*): "STOP TORTURE!," an ad campaign from **Amnesty International**, which recognizes the agonies of punishment inflicted (privately) by sadists and (publicly) by some political regimes every year to human feet.

Years later the editorial team assigned the task of researching details of her past life and adventures could never extract any satisfying answer from her whenever she was asked about why she didn't run away. Of course, with her feet aching like they were, she couldn't have gone anywhere.

The only satisfying answer she ever gave involved her belief that Chuck had placed her under some sort of hypnotic trance. Ever since their original coupling in Miami, he frequently hypnotized her, especially as a preface for her role as a vehicle for the fulfillment of sexual fantasies from what he described as his "kink customers."

Since her mobility was greatly diminished, and because she was truly desperate to recuperate, she thought that Chuck would grant her a much-needed and prolonged rest. She constantly reminded him that they had the $10,000 to live on while she recovered from what she called "the worst ordeal of my life. I'd rather have been raped by six sailors who'd been at sea for months."

Her recuperation continued for a week, most of which she spent in bed. During her first three days of confinement, she had to crawl on her hands and knees to the bathroom.

***

During her recuperation in the winter of 1971-72, Chuck left Linda alone in Jersey City during his frequent excursions into Manhattan to investigate a collaboration with any of the dozens of filmmakers specializing in 8mm porn loops. In the course of a meeting with a businessman from Tokyo, he uncovered a possible job for Linda.

Chuck became aware of a secret Japanese-run bordello in Manhattan called *Ketsu*, which, if Chuck had heard correctly, translated as "anus." Later, during his report to Linda, he referred to it as "Jap House."

Wealthy Japanese businessmen during their sojourns in New York would patronize this elegantly furnished townhouse that ostensibly specialized in erotic Japanese massages. Actually, carefully controlled and very discreet prostitution was practiced. The Japanese who visited this super-expensive establishment had grown bored with geishas in their native country and wanted a change of pace, as represented by young American women. During a sales-related appointment Chuck arranged, through his Japanese contact, at *Ketsu,* he screened an 8mm loop, featuring Linda, in the manager's office. Intrigued, the manager agreed to audition Linda. Chuck explained what had caused her aching feet, and the manager was most sympathetic. "We Japanese are so very different from the barbaric Chinese. So many of these decadent ones interpret sadism as an indispensable part of sexual pleasure. In Japan, we do not. We prefer more gentle, more natural forms of lovemaking. We are interested in seeing that our clients and our 'lovemakers,' which can be either a young woman or even a young boy, enjoy the delights we offer here."

Chuck never told Linda the specifics of the deal he'd struck, especially the details about the money involved, but he explained to her that in the work that would be expected of her, she would not have to be mobile, and he emphasized how gentle the lovemaking would be.

Even so, he had to use brute force during his "persuasion." Under threat, she relented.

At Ketsu, it was explained to her that she'd have to undergo several days of training with one of the male employees. Chuck abandoned her to whatever fate awaited her at "Jap House." Her "master" turned out to be a well-educated Japanese masseur who spoke very good English.

Noting how nervous, even terrified, she looked, he tried to soothe her nerves. Within an elegant, but minimalist, décor, he invited her to tea, and began to explain what would be expected of her. "The Chinese, whom I do not admire, might tell a young woman, or perhaps a geisha boy, that 'I plan to stick my hot poker into your overheated oven.' But we Japanese are more delicate. A future lover, or a potential lover, might say to you, 'I am going to seek my peace in your heaven.'"

"That sure sounds a lot better than the ordeal I went through with the Chinese," she told him.

He began to prepare her for the services she'd perform at Ketsu. "We Japanese men, as you probably have heard, are not known for having the largest organs on the planet. We are not Negroes. Some of us have found that the anus, either male or female, provides us with the greatest pleasure."

"I'm an expert at that," Linda said. "I've been trained."

"I am certain that your previous training is something unrelated to what I'll be demonstrating," he said. "Some of our clients, perhaps most of them, will want to be in your bed for six or more hours. During that time, they prefer to keep their penis imbedded in you throughout their entire experience. We Japanese do not like hasty sex."

How to entertain a man, then and now
(left photo) Japanese geisha, late 1870s, and *(right photo, with thanks to Todd Laracuenta)* her modern-day counterpart.

"It sure doesn't sound like you do," she said. "What if a gal has to go to the bathroom?"

"There is a pan in bed to handle urine," he said. "As for your anus, you will need to drink a 'Prep Bowel' compound, a super-laxative that will clean you out the day before. Your system will be washed fresh and clean. That way, your

190

lover can be inside you for hours, with no unpleasant occurrences. Sometimes, he will go to sleep, waking up every now and then to move around inside you. Penetration can continue for hours at a time without climax. Or in some rare cases, before the dawn breaks, a client might have had as many as six climaxes inside you. We Japanese consider such a form of intercourse very restful, very relaxing, and I'm sure you'll enjoy it, too. After the abuse you've suffered from your previous encounters, you will find Japanese men the greatest lovers in the world."

Her teacher did not deceive her. No harm came to her during her hours-long involvement with a Japanese lover. She would never consider them t h e world's greatest lovers, but as she told Chuck, "I sure caught up on my sleep during those long ordeals in bed with one of them. And my system sure got cleaned out frequently. It isn't my favorite form of sex, but it is the least strenuous."

Years later, as a means of interpreting her month-long experience at Ketsu, Linda was asked by her researchers why, if she'd found it so agreeable, she eventually left the establishment.

"I didn't want to leave," she said. "The manager dismissed me. He'd received a shipment of five very beautiful girls from the Dominican Republic, and all the Japanese clients wanted to try out this fresh meat."

Before she left, the manager had told her, "You were very obedient with our clients and did everything requested. However, you received no repeat business, which our other girls get frequently. There was one serious problem with you and, regrettably, it's something you have no control over."

"I really tried hard," she said. "What did I do wrong?"

Nothing, really, except you are far too old for this job," he said. "Our clients usually prefer young girls or very young boys. Prostitution is really a business for the young. Perhaps you'll go back to school and learn some professional skill. I wish you luck. Your man is waiting downstairs. He told me he is your agent, so I turned over your month's wages to him."

"That means I'll never see a penny of it," she lamented.

She was able to walk unsteadily down the stairs, having for the most part recovered from her Chinese torture. Waiting at the bottom of the steps, Chuck didn't even bother with a smile. "Sorry the gig didn't work out here," he said. "It paid good…real good. At least you learned to walk again."

"I don't know what to do next," she said.

"I'll decide that for you," he said. "Within a few weeks, we'll be making loops. I've almost got a deal now. In the meantime, I've lined up a few more jobs for you."

"Not with the Chinese!" she protested. "*Never again!* In fact, from now on, I'll never again order Chinese take-out."

"I'm taking you back to Jersey City," he said. "The place is a fucking pig's stye. You'll need to clean it up. I left food lying around, and the joint's swarming with roaches. Also, we've got bedbugs."

"What a dreary homecoming," she said.

"There's something else: You've got a new roommate."

***

The roommate turned out to be Brandy (not her real name), whom Linda mentioned in one of her autobiographies, *Ordeal.* She claimed that Brandy was one of Chuck's former hookers in Miami and that she had "done several tricks with me in Florida." Brandy had never made any real impact on Linda's life until she moved in with Chuck and her in Jersey City.

"Brandy" was really an eighteen-year-old hooker named Goldie Tibbs. Born in Columbus, Ohio, in 1952, she'd studied dance, been a cheerleader, and had "almost" completed high school before she got pregnant. When she wasn't turning tricks, she was a voracious reader, and never really liked "wasting time" watching television.

Since Chuck and Linda liked to draw comparisons between their clients and colleagues with famous movie stars, Brandy was likened to the blonde-haired movie temptress, Gloria Grahame.

With her pouting upper lip and an expressively arched brow, Grahame had played a sultry *femme fatale* on movie screens during the 1940s and 50s.

Grahame's widest exposure evolved from her 1952 involvement as one of the stars Cecil B. DeMille cast in his *The Best Show on Earth,* which won the Oscar as Best Picture of the Year. Grahame had also crafted some delightful musical interludes as the sexed-up "Ado Annie" in the Rogers and Hammerstein musical, *Oklahoma!,* released in 1955.

At the time Chuck began pimping Brandy, Grahame was still a famous name and face in America, so Linda and Chuck transformed their chief hooker into as much of a Gloria Grahame lookalike as possible. Because that technique had brought Chuck some degree of success in Miami, he hoped to replicate in New York another stable of hookers who resembled movie stars. But as a means of getting his latest enterprise launched, he badly needed cash.

Since Brandy's natural hair color was brown, Chuck ordered Linda to take her to a beauty parlor and to bring her back home as a blonde who resembled Grahame.

For a teenage girl, Brandy was a shock to Linda, particularly in her views about prostitution. She'd acquired eight books on prostitution and was studying every one of them. She told Linda, "If you want to be a rocket scientist, you study for it. Same as if you want to be a doctor, lawyer, or engineer, whatever.

There are three ways to approach this prostitution game."

She outlined them for Linda: 1) the streetwalker, often hooked on drugs, who picks up a client for the evening, often making no more than twenty dollars; 2) the party girl, often a nymphomaniac, who does it for the thrill of it all in addition to the money, or 3) the call girl who uses prostitution to move up the ladder of success until she nails a rich client who might even agree to marry her.

"I plan to have at least three rich husbands in my life," Brandy prophesied. "My alimony settlements will be fantastic. Of course, the final husband I'll bury and inherit everything."

"How are you going to meet all these upperclass guys? Linda asked.

From one of her books, *The Abnormality of Prostitution,* written by Dr. Edward Glover, she read Linda a quote:

"Many people of the highest intellectual and ethical development may find themselves compulsively attached to prostitutes, because only with prostitutes are they capable of sexual potency. With their wives, they may remain completely impotent. You can see that in such instances, the prostitute satisfies a psychopathological demand."

Brandy claimed that she had contacted more than a dozen psychiatrists, promising them free sex if they would hook her up with the right men who needed prostitutes as a means of reasserting their virility. "I've just done this, so I don't know the results yet."

Linda was thrilled to learn, through Brandy, that some of the most famous women in history rose to lofty positions in society because they had been prostitutes or at least sexually promiscuous.

For the first time in her life, she admitted, "I didn't feel dirty. I realized that in a man's world, a woman has often had to use her charms on men, not only to seduce them, but to gain power and wealth through them."

From a book Brandy lent her, she identified a roster of influential courtesans down through the ages, dreaming of using them as role models instead of spending her day watching sitcoms on television. Of course, she couldn't hope to rise to the lofty plateau of her favorites, but in some strange way, these historical women gave her courage that she might find some security in life if she played things correctly. That would begin, she realized, with freeing herself from Chuck and charting her own course.

Brandy, Linda's newest friend and confidant, emphasized her physical similarities to the Hollywood star **Gloria Grahame** *(depicted above).*

***

Brandy slept with Chuck and Linda in the only bed in their small Jersey City apartment. Privately, Brandy had told Linda that "lesbian sex is not my thing unless I get paid for it." But even so, at night, he sometimes pressed them together into lesbian contact, usually guiding Linda's hand to a position over Brandy's nude breast. Even more daring, he would direct Brandy to insert two of her fingers directly into Linda's vagina.

Chuck had a motive for encouraging a context of lesbian familiarity between the two women. He wanted to sell them as actresses in girl-on-girl porno loops. Early one morning, over breakfast, he informed them that he'd arranged gigs for them with a team which included both a photographer and a camera man shooting 8mm loops for private collectors.

The photographer, Ian Cording, who specialized in S&M layouts, occupied a drafty, oversized loft at the corner of 21st Street and Third Avenue in Manhattan. Before their photography session, he defined himself in front of them as a "cinematic smutster."

Born in Queens, Cording was a very short man with a beer belly and a balding head. Before his present incarnation as a "bondage photographer," he, along with his wife, ran a mail order business specializing in "naughty novelties." But by the time of his meeting with Linda, the market, worldwide, for porno loops and "dirty pictures" was mushrooming within America's underground landscape. Almost unknowingly, Linda became one of its early pioneers.

In the 1950s, Cording had specialized in the kind of bondage layouts often associated back then with Bettie Page. "I found my market in these," he told Linda. "Now I deal almost exclusively with layouts for private collectors. I want you gals to live out their fetish fantasies. But I've got to be careful. A guy like me can get into a lot of trouble with the post office."

After offering each of them a cup of morning coffee, Cording stood up. "Time to strip down, girls. Unlike most horny cameramen, I'm not a problem. Every Saturday night, I fuck my wife for four minutes, then turn over and go to sleep. That's enough sexual satisfaction to last me the rest of the week."

Linda took in some of the photos adorning Cording's work space. Some were single shots of women; others encompassed views of men being intently intimate with each other; some focused on women with women; and almost as an afterthought, there were old-fashioned and "traditional-looking" shots of men in erotic positions with naked women.

One corner of the loft was configured as a bondage chamber. It included chains hanging down from overhead hooks, and a wide assortment of whips which evoked, at least for Linda, memories of cowboy, Lash La Rue. There were various torture devices, some reminiscent of medieval times. On his small

194

kitchen table were several bottles of Heinz catsup. As he explained, "We use tomato sauce instead of blood."

"THAT's a relief," Brandy said sarcastically. It was obvious she didn't like Cording.

Although still a teenager, Brandy peeled off her clothing a lot faster than Linda, and seemed more like a professional hooker, in spite of her lack of experience.

Chuck sat nearby, having volunteered his services as both a prop man and as an assistant cameraman, whatever Cording desired. Since Chuck had boasted so convincingly about his skills as a cameraman, Cording eventually assigned him some of those duties while he devoted himself to still photographs.

Cording showed Linda and Brandy a stack of bondage stills, with the intention of having them replicate the poses. Linda looked at one skeptically, that of a young woman with catsup smeared across her bloodied back. To Linda, it looked ridiculous, causing her to wonder what kind of man would get turned on by this obviously posed still. Surely, the allure of the picture derived from whatever fantasies the viewer brought to it—perhaps a mental replication of the beatings that had caused the whiplashes that had disfigured the backside of their victims.

As he arranged the onstage props around them, Cording said, "Our customers range from merchants who hawk diamonds to U.N. diplomats from Nigeria. The guy who commissioned today's shoot is from Saudi Arabia."

The filming of the first loop, entitled *Dildo Rape,* placed Linda in the center of a replica of an elaborate spider web crafted from ropes and pulleys. Cording bound her securely and gagged her. She was then raised off the floor, her arms and legs spreadeagled. As action got underway, a nude Brandy inserted various weirdly shaped dildos into Linda. One was grotesquely spiked with nubs and caused some pain, but Cording applauded and cinematically emphasized the agony on her face.

In the second loop, *She Dances on Her Ass,* Linda was given the thinnest of G-strings and ordered to perform a dance—"as lascivious as possible and with gusto." She shimmied sexily, wearing nothing but a floppy black hat, black stockings, and those stiletto high heels. The trick involved positioning herself on her back on a sofa, from which she gyrated, pushing and retracting her pelvis, without ever rising to her feet.

A third loop, *Down and Dirty,* required Linda and Brandy to "open wide their vaginas for intimate close-ups, and then to plunge each other into scenes of mutual masturbation."

In every scene, Cording ordered them to wear six-inch stiletto heels, even when they had nothing else on. "All my clients demand high heels. No collector wants to see a woman barefooted, unless they're a foot fetishist. It's the number one rule of the game. I get all sorts of requests. One of my clients is turned on by black rubber against a nude white women's body; another wants to see his gals in white underwear—the dowdy, old-fashioned kind his mother used to wear. They pay good for these things, since most often they can't find them on the open market. My weirdest request was from a guy who wanted to be fellated while he stuck a long hat pin into the belly of a pregnant rat."

"Sign me up for that," Brandy said, again showing her sense of sarcasm. As Linda had surmised, Brandy was not impressed with the porn loop business. Linda suspected that as soon as she found another way to survive, she'd go for it.

During their filming of the day's final loop, Brandy sat on the sofa, nude except for high heels and stockings. Linda wore the same wardrobe as she lay across Brandy's lap and received the most stinging bare-butt spanking of her life. Cording kept screaming at Brandy, "Harder! HARDER, GOD DAMMIT! Don't fake it!"

Over dinner that night in the Times Square area, Chuck chose hamburgers and cokes for his two female "stars" while he ordered a steak for himself. Afterward, he suggested they visit a club he'd heard about, the New York Psychedelic Shack, a joint which featured bottomless dancers.

From positions within the audience at the Psychedelic Shack, Chuck sat with Linda and Brandy watching the routine acts of its go-go dancers and strippers. He was obviously bored. During intermission, he went backstage to talk to the manager. An older man, Greg Whitcliff, who'd once worked in burlesque as a baggy pants comic, had hired the dancers and was rather thin-skinned when Chuck criticized his performers.

"You're so wrong," Whitcliff retorted. "I've got the best god damn dancers in New York."

"The best nude dancer in Manhattan is sitting right up front there at the bar drinking with that other gal," Chuck said, pointing to Linda and Brandy.

"Okay, fucker, if your chick is so hot, bring her back here. We'll give her a live audition. The club's packed tonight, every place taken. Your little whore had better be good."

As Linda later wrote, "That night, I did the ultimate flash of my life." She had the lecherous men cheering and whistling, then begging for more. "I did a strip that didn't stop at all. I was naked to my clean-shaven pussy. I did bends, gyrations, bumps, and made erotic moves to drive men wild."

She did not exaggerate, as she was a sensation that night, outclassing the other performers and arousing their jealousy. Brandy had taught her well, all the steps, all the seductive moves.

Linda's finale was the show-stopper. She came out under the main spotlight and, with her fingers, slowly opened the lips of her vagina for all the world to see. Then she announced, coyly but loudly, "The cheapest bill I'll take up here has to have a picture of Alexander Hamilton on it, though I much prefer Andrew Jackson. George Washington's picture is a big turn-off to me."

Although the manager had been skeptical, he was impressed, and he was a man not impressed with burlesque queens, whom he'd studied since he joined the vaudeville circuit at the age of sixteen.

Although he paid his other strippers $150 a week, he offered Linda $250 a week, with the additional understanding that he'd allow her to keep anything the men stuffed up her vagina.

After conferring with Chuck, she accepted his offer. But the very next day, she canceled her commitment, calling Whitcliff and telling him that she intended to leave town and therefore couldn't configure herself as a performer at his "Shack."

***

She had abandoned the gig with Whitcliff because she'd gotten what she was told, loudly by Chuck, was a better-paying job. Based on his previous experience as a crop duster and photographer, Chuck had been offered a contract for an extended aerial photographic assignment. The gig included use of an apartment provided as part of the deal in Bryan, in Southeast Central Texas, not far from the flagship campus of Texas A&M University.

By five o'clock that afternoon, both of them were on a plane headed southwest to Houston, leaving Brandy to pay the rent on the Jersey City apartment with whatever money she earned from prostitution.

After they finally landed in Houston, Chuck checked them into a low-rent motel. Early the next morning, in a rented car, they drove the 92 miles to Bryan. As he drove down the city's Main Street, Linda thought she'd been transplanted back to the year 1950.

She enjoyed the subtropical and temperate winter weather. The apartment was more adequate, better furnished, and cleaner than some places where they'd recently lived, but it was so impersonal that she didn't really relish spending too much time inside it.

In her memoirs, Linda only mentioned that she went to Bryan, but gave no additional information about her trip there. Later, she claimed that "Chuck must have rented me out to every

LOVELACE TRIVIA
for residents of Texas

Question: Where in Texas did Linda live with Chuck during a brief interlude between sex videos?

Answer: **Bryan**, home of Texas A&M!

197

pilot in Texas. I was flying high with every flier, or so it seemed. Every guy in Texas was supposed to be big. Listen to one who knows: The men of Texas have penises that come in all sizes, from teeny-weeny to bull meat."

"A lot of my gigs were arranged in Houston where we spent much of our time. But Chuck also learned that one of four residents in Bryan was black. He set up several dates with these guys. He told them, "Regardless of how big you are, Linda has a deep throat and a take-it-all pussy."

***

After Chuck completed his assignment, he and Linda flew back to New York. Brandy had held onto their apartment and had kept up with the monthly rent. She seemed glad to see Linda, but was much less enthusiastic in her greeting of Chuck. Not realizing the disdain in which Brandy held him, Linda smiled when he said to her, "I bet you haven't had a really good fuck since I went to Texas."

Brandy did not respond.

Reinstalled in Jersey City, with the bright lights of Manhattan nearby, Linda's ambitions evolved into a desire to become a bigtime movie star like Natalie Wood or Faye Dunaway. Linda felt she would have been far better than Dunaway at portraying Bonnie opposite Warren Beatty's Clyde in their big hit, *Bonnie and Clyde,* released in 1967.

"After appearing in a few loops, I was already beginning to think of myself as a film star," Linda recalled in the 1980s. "I was convinced of that when I went to this fortune teller who occupied a hole in the wall off Sheridan Square in Greenwich Village. She thrilled me by telling me that in only a few short months, I would become a movie star whose name would be known on all the continents of the world. And, guess what, she was seeing the truth in that crystal ball of hers. It all came true."

"Brandy warned me that by being an actress in porn films, I could never go legit. But I knew better. I told her that everyone from Joan Crawford to Steve McQueen to Sylvester Stallone had done porno and gone on to spectacular careers in films. Even Marilyn Monroe, I told her, had performed in a porno flick for Howard Hughes. That didn't seem to hurt her career. Maybe rumors of that and her nude calendar were what provided her final push into super-stardom!"

"While I was dreaming all these wonderful dreams, I never imagined that in a few short weeks, I'd make a film that for a while was almost as notorious as *Deep Throat*. And I couldn't even imagine that my co-star would be a German Shepherd."

CHAPTER SIX
The Queen of Porn

"There never was a Linda Lovelace. I'm Linda Lovelace. She got where she got because of my brain, not because of her throat."

—**Chuck Traynor**

During the weeks prior to the filming of the historic *Deep Throat,* Chuck and Linda entered the movie business—well, sort of. In a memoir, Linda admitted to making seven 8mm films, but she starred in nearly fifty more for private collectors, which she chose not to mention. She did claim, "I was something of a comer (no *double entendre* intended*),* I was so damn good."

Sometimes, Chuck worked as a cameraman, and he was one of the most skilled in the business. He'd also taught Linda how to be a still photographer, and she became adept at it. "On occasion, for $75 a day, I also offered my services as an actress, if you know what I mean."

Chuck and Linda entered the field of 8mm porno loops just as the industry was about to take off. "Kook loops," in which Linda specialized, could be found for sale in the rear of several "scumatoriums," including a dive called Exotic Circus at 140 West 42nd Street in Manhattan.

As one commentator noted in *Tales of Times Square,* a customer could purchase loops of "menstruation vampires, bowel movement unloadings; girls fucking horses; Great Danes getting their peckers sucked; whatever. German distributors came up with the most bizarre loops—two wild girls from Hamburg shoving live eels up their snatches and assholes; fish fucking; farmboys fucking cows; man fucking hen; woman sticking arm up cow's ass; man licking 400-pound pig's asshole; or girl taking on a dog, horse, and pig simultaneously."

Even as early as 1968, the mob had muscled in on the burgeoning business. When Chuck and Linda entered the Times Square loop market, one of their distributors had paid $150,000 to the mob for protection between 1968 and 1971.

Kiddie porn, though illegal, was still being sold in the Times Square area until the mid-1970s, when the police really cracked down on its distribution. Chuck had brought along the negative of the kiddie porn loop that he had shot of Linda with the two brothers back in Miami. Without her knowledge, he arranged for it to be distributed in New York. Today, even its possession is against the law, but many child porn fanciers are said to have a hidden copy of it.

During the heady days of the early 1970s, into which Linda wandered, it was easy to round up "a bunch of swingers" to shoot porn. Chuck and Linda were always available to go into rat-infested basements or drafty lofts in Soho. Most of these loops ran from twelve to fifteen minutes and were often sold in the rear of paperback bookstores.

Earning from $200 to $500 a day, a cameraman often doubled as the producer, director, and lighting technician.

A single man with a lone woman didn't sell as well. Variations were the rule of the day, featuring both gay and straight sex in any combination. Most of the players in orgy scenes, male or female, gay or straight, seemed to take on all combinations of sex.

"Unlike the women making $75 a day, male porn stars were paid only $50 a day, and I felt sorry for them," Linda said. "They had to get up with the rooster and raise a hard-on at six in the morning. Sometimes they'd be called upon

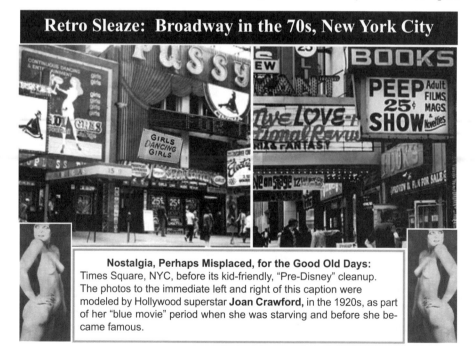

Retro Sleaze: Broadway in the 70s, New York City

Nostalgia, Perhaps Misplaced, for the Good Old Days:
Times Square, NYC, before its kid-friendly, "Pre-Disney" cleanup. The photos to the immediate left and right of this caption were modeled by Hollywood superstar **Joan Crawford,** in the 1920s, as part of her "blue movie" period when she was starving and before she became famous.

to keep raising an erection by ten that night. Not only that, but I would work a guy up to a raging climax, and the director would yell, 'Cut! Not yet!' The poor jerk would deflate, having a cup of coffee and letting his meat droop. Then, back on camera, I would have to work him up again. Sometimes, his climax would be delayed two or three times in one afternoon. Men call that blue balls. Men's lib should look into this injustice. Actors in porn get almost nothing. The men upstairs take all the dough. As for myself, I worked most times for peanuts—or penises, as the case may be."

Journalist William Sherman credits Martin Hodas for introducing the first Times Square peep shows. Before that, Hodas had operated an assortment of vending machines. In a talk with a repair man on Tenth Avenue near 42nd Street, Hodas was told, "You should do something with these old film machines. They were like nickelodeons. The modern peeper show was born that day."

In the aftermath of that dialogue, Hodas purchased thirteen of the machines and installed them in hard-core bookstores in the Times Square area. At first, the loops featured only naked dancing girls. Soon, male customers demanded more explicit fare.

Linda entered the business at this time. "Credit me with aiding the porno takeover of Times Square in the early 1970s," she said. "I helped make Times Square Slime Square."

Some porno filmmakers shot as many as three or four films in just one day. Producers were paid $200 to $500 per loop. Chuck got steady work because he was one of the best in the business at filming an erect penis being inserted into a woman's vagina, often Linda's.

One newspaper reported, "Filmmakers projected images of turgid genitalia and puckered perinea onto 42nd Street." Linda read that. "What in hell is puckered perinea?" she asked Chuck. (*Editor's note: Someone's perinea is the region between the scrotum and the anus in males, and between the posterior vulva junction and the anus in females.*)

So many people entered the porn business that rubber-necking tour bus visitors were invited, for a price, into private studios where loops were being shot. Some producers charged as much as $25 per ticket. Nearly all of the customers were men voyeuristically looking for diversions.

"Whenever we needed money, Brandy and I worked at the Wurlitzer Building on 42nd Street," Linda recalled. "This was a big studio loft that drew a lot of customers, often Japanese and German tourists, but also rubberneckers from the Rocky Mountains or Alabama, wherever.. They thought they were watching actual loops being made, but most times, there was no film in the camera. Whenever Brandy and I saw a group of these rubberneckers descending on us, we started licking each other's pussy, presumably for the cameraman. We most often ended in a sixty-nine. When we tired of sixty-nines, we inserted oddly shaped dildos into each other. Many of these Peeping Toms got so turned on, they unzipped and masturbated while watching us. It was all so very raunchy."

Linda rarely saw any of the films she made for private collectors, since she was never given a print. Years later, she could remember only a few of them. One in particular stood out in her mind. Called *Women Also Shave,* it starred Brandy and herself. "At first, we came into this bedroom where we began to undress," she said. "We shed all of our clothing and stood naked in front of the camera, staring at each other's crotches. This one had dialogue:

BRANDY*: I see you have a razor in your bathroom.*
LINDA: *Many men—and many lesbians, too—want a shaved pussy.*
BRANDY*: You must have been shaved by a hair stylist. I see he left a small line of soft pubic hair near the center, just over the lips of your pussy. This thicket of fuzz looks like a tiny little cock.*
LINDA: *Do you think it looks beautiful?*
BRANDY: *Good enough to eat!*
LINDA: *Then don't just stand there staring at it! Hop on it!*

The film ends with the two women getting onto the bed together and indulging in every form of lesbian love. For a finale, Brandy straps on a dildo for a "brutal fuck," as ordered by the cameraman/director.

Another short Linda remembered making was a take-off inspired by a soft-core loop, *Tambourine Dance,* which cult model Bettie Page had filmed in the 1950s.

"I was hired to do the XXX-rated version," Linda said. "I wore a semi-transparent black bra

Linda's hardcore homage to S&M pinup and international cult goddess **Bettie Page** (*left and center photos, above*) was an XXX-rated reprise of what the vintage stripper had previously filmed in the 1950s as a soft-core but titillating *Tambourine Dance.*

202

and panties. At first, I performed all these shakes and shimmies with maracas. Then I switched to a tambourine. At all times, I wore stiletto high heels. At the end of the lewd dance, I lowered my panties and masturbated for my close-up."

She also recalled that she and Brandy had starred in one loop entitled *Peeping Tom.* "We came into this apartment on a hot summer night and raised a window to let in some air. Inside the room, we stripped down and got on the bed. After kissing and fondling breasts, we got into a wild sixty-nine. At the window appeared the face of a young Puerto Rican boy who was wide-eyed with excitement. He slipped into the room and pulled off his clothes. While we're still going at it, he approached us with a big erection. We let him join in on our fun. Before the loop was finished, this little stud had penetrated each of our three orifices. It was real steamy."

Porn performers Billy Sullivan and Lynn Talbot were genuine swingers. They were legally married and often performed together for 8mm loops. Lynn didn't care who Billy fucked, and he could have cared less who she fucked. The couple, believe it or not, really loved each other and had been making it with each other since junior high school.

Lynn was viewed as America's answer to the French sex kitten Brigitte Bardot. Her long neck flowed into straight shoulders with a forty-inch bosom. A tiny waist gave way to well-rounded hips which tapered into long, stunning legs. She had honey blonde hair, a stunningly beautiful face with pouty lips, and sky-blue eyes with thick lashes.

Billy, her husband, was her male equivalent in every way. The first time Linda worked with him, she was enchanted by him, praising his attributes. "He was a real doll—he was *adorable!*—tall, blonde, and cute. How could a guy who looked like that be starring in sleazy porn?"

"His body was a piece of sculpture, " Linda said. "He worked out in the gym and had this six-pack. Even his legs were beautiful. His prize asset was a long, thick penis, at least ten and a half inches long. I measured it."

"After our first loop, he told me that he rarely found a gal who could deep throat him. On a few occasions, I slipped around and gave him a blow-job. But he never climaxed. He told me he had to save all his blast-offs for the camera or for some of his rich clients. He never climaxed, even in Lynn."

"He screwed women on camera, but as a private sideline, he had a lot of rich gay queens who paid him as much as three or four hundred dollars. No hustler or hooker got that kind of money back in the early 1970s. Oh, did I mention another big asset? A pair of balls that were each the size of a Florida orange? Loops of Billy, some with me in them, are valued today."

Her first film with Billy also starred Brandy. It had virtually no plot. Linda and Brandy were depicted lying nude on a bed when a stranger enters their room and removes all his clothes.

"The two of us kissed him all over and got him sexually aroused," Linda claimed. "I don't care which hole he put it in, there was something magic about Billy."

"One night, Chuck and I were invited to dinner at the apartment of Billy and Lynn," Linda said. "After dinner, Chuck fucked Lynn on the sofa, and I performed all sorts of gymnastic feats with Billy on the carpet. That night should have been filmed. Soon after that, Billy and Lynn headed for California, and we never heard from them again. What a pair!"

Before leaving town, however, Billy and Lynn starred with Linda in their final film together. It was an 8mm "epic" entitled *Yellow Shower*. Throughout most of the film, Linda was depicted having sex in all positions with both man and wife. "We did everything sexually that one man and two women can do to each other," Linda said. "The director told us he needed a socko finish, and he ordered us for the final five minutes of the film to piss on each other. Billy was ordered to lie down on a rubber sheet, and Lynn and I were told to piss on him."

"Although Lynn tried, she couldn't urinate on her husband. That upset the director very much, and he accused her of not being professional. I was called in to do the job. Lynn was told to lie down, and Billy and I were ordered to piss on her. We weren't delivering, so the director sent out for six packs of Budweiser. After drinking all that beer, Billy and I just had to go. We chug-a-lugged until we got it right on film. When it rained, it poured."

Linda later called *Yellow Shower* "insane." As for the people who bought the loop, she claimed "They were so sick."

She continued to wonder why a couple as beautiful as Billy and Lynn rented themselves out to make such "disgusting" films, when either of them, in her opinion, would have been sensational as a legitimate model.

"Billy posing for an underwear ad would have caused a mob riot at Macy's," Linda claimed.

***

Eric Edwards made his first porno film with Linda in a seedy, filthy loft on Manhattan's 42nd St. He later admitted that, "I was scared shitless," mainly because he didn't know what he would be called upon to perform. The Colombo crime family was said to have financed this loop.

The man behind the camera was Ted Snyder, sometimes called "Tom." He dressed in cowboy boots with gold chains around his neck. He wore a gold pinky ring with the name TED spelled out in diamonds.

The film was to star not only Linda and Edwards, but Chuck himself, along with an anonymous red-haired woman "who had red hair in all the right places,"

according to Chuck.

Although Chuck frequently bragged about the size of his penis and his sexual prowess, he proved himself a dud on the set. He couldn't produce an erection for either Linda or the redhead.

For his total fee of forty dollars a day, Edwards was photographed as Linda performed her deep throat specialty on him. He later told an interviewer, "I was amazed that she swallowed me all the way. No woman had ever done that before." She must have liked that sex with Edwards, because she phoned him repeatedly after their initial encounter and wanted to perform in other loops with him later.

Like the woman in the porn flick, Edwards was also red haired. Born in Michigan in 1945, he went from this lowly beginning in films to earn the distinction of having lasted longer in the porn industry than any other performer, either male or female. As one porn fancier noted, "Eric has brought his romantic, touchy-feely sexual style to more than 500 features without losing his erection."

The handsome young actor didn't set out to become the most enduring stud in the history of porn. Attending college in Waco, Texas, he won a scholarship from ABC Television to study at the American Academy of Dramatic Arts in Manhattan. Upon graduation, he hoped for a career as a legitimate actor when his diploma, during his graduation ceremony, was handed to him by Lillian Gish, the legendary star of silent films. He remembered talking backstage with Henry Fonda for fifteen minutes.

After hawking toothpaste and razor blades on television, he starred in a medley of 8mm porno loops. He later told Linda that he blamed his wife for his drift into porn. At the time of their divorce, she'd convinced him that he was a "lousy fuck."

Linda disagreed, asserting "that guy delivers—and how! It's the red pubic hair, I think."

Edwards' biggest exposure came in 1979 with the wildly popular *Debbie Does Dallas,* one of the most popular hardcore features ever released. His three-way romp with Christy Ford and Robin Byrd was seen around the world, although not by as many people as *Deep Throat,* of course.

Edwards remembered that it was Linda, not Chuck, who called to ask him to appear in another loop with her for producer/director "Bob Wolfe." As Edwards later confessed, "Linda liked working with me—or fucking me, I should say."

That was true. She later referred to him as "one of my best lays."

"Bob Wolfe" was an alias name for Lawrence T. Cole. During the rise of porn, he churned out more loops and feature films than almost any other movie producer in history. Although he worked with Linda in the early 70s, Wolfe's heyday would be the 1980s. He was steady and reliable, turning out such features as *House of Strange Desires* and *I've Never Done This Before.* Details associated with his personal history are elusive. Over the course of several months, Linda and Edwards would appear together in several loops for Wolfe, their final efforts becoming especially notorious when they made *The Dog Fucker.*

***

In addition to working on loops with Edwards for Wolfe, Linda recalled a brief stint filming for a cameraman/director known only as "Joe." He turned out to be Terry Drummond, a 30-year-old homosexual from Birmingham, Alabama, who got involved in a sex scandal in his native hometown for photographing high school athletes, without their knowledge, in the locker room.

"Most of his business involved shooting gay guys in action, but he did an occasional straight job," Linda recalled. "When Chuck and I first met him, he was shooting stills for an underground magazine called *More Than Seven Inches.* When he wasn't working in his loft, he spent his spare time at night hunting down hustlers with more than seven inches so he could photograph their hard-ons."

When Chuck and Linda arrived at Joe's studio, his door was opened by a strikingly beautiful late teenage boy—Joe's chief assistant—whose dyed platinum blonde hair evoked Jean Harlow in those movies from the 1930s.

Linda was told that Joe's "epic" would be entitled *Jungle Girl Gets Raped.* The blonde, who introduced himself as "Granger Granger" (an obvious *nom de plume)* took her to the dressing room and asked her to change into a leopard skin outfit that might have been worn by "Jane" in those Tarzan movies

206

with Johnny Weissmuller.

"Don't worry," he said. "It'll be ripped off later." He told her how lucky she was that her two co-stars would be arriving soon. "They are a pair of Mandingos," he said. "You should volunteer to do them for free. In the second loop today, I'll get to have them."

With Chuck's assistance, Linda appeared in the leopard skin, and he tied her up between two *faux* trees. "When your rapists appear, I want you to open your eyes wide like Joan Crawford's in *Sudden Fear,* and really pretend you're afraid." Joe said.

At that point, two tall and rather handsome black men arrived in Harlem-inspired street dress. They quickly shed their clothing as Wolfe chastised them for being late. He didn't even bother to introduce them to Linda.

The scene opened with Linda squirming to escape her bondage. After about three minutes, the two young African Americans appeared on screen dressed in loincloths. One of them rips off Linda's leopard skin. Both men then remove their loincloths and begin to masturbate themselves to massive erections.

THE PERVASIVE EFFECTS OF HOLLYWOOD

Many of Linda's references and points of view were influenced by her exposure to Hollywood, both its gossip magazines and its movies.

Here, **Johnny Weissmuller** and **Maureen O'Sullivan** portray Tarzan with Jane—a coupling that inspired her during her filming of *Jungle Girl Gets Raped.*

Linda later told Brandy, "I was supposed to be afraid, but actually, I was looking forward to it. I'd had interracial sex in Georgia before this."

At first, Linda appeared to resist the assault, but finally gave in to it, screaming for the two Mandingos to "fuck me harder."

After seeing the final cut, Joe retitled the picture, calling it *Once You Go Black, You Never Go Back."*

After lunch, and after their loop was shot, Linda and Chuck decided to stick around to watch "Granger Granger" take on the two black dudes. This loop was shot in a bed with dirty sheets.

Both men attacked the mouth and anus of Granger, fucking him brutally. Joe shouted at him to look like he was in pain and agony, but the platinum blonde was clearly enjoying the assault.

At the end of the shot, he informed Linda, "How many times can a gay guy like me get to enjoy twenty black inches in just one hour?"

Linda's interracial sex loop, which seemingly has disappeared from the radar screen today, was one of the pioneer films in black-on–white porn. An exhibitor in Times Square recalled, "My customers enjoy seeing black men fucking white women, perhaps fantasizing that they're screwing their white daughters and wives. I know it doesn't make a lot of sense, but that was my market. They want to see massive black dicks defiling pretty white girls and making them squeal. I sold a huge number of copies of *Oh NO! There's a Negro in My Mom,* all to lilywhite men."

Gail Dines, who has written and researched the porn industry for twenty years, wrote: "Interracial porn seems strange, given that a relatively short time ago, the thought of a black man just looking at a white woman was enough to work white men into a lynch-mob frenzy. And now they are buying millions of dollars worth of movies that show in graphic detail a black man doing just about everything that can be done to a white woman's body."

***

Three weeks before she made *The Dog Fucker,* Chuck had taken Linda to a private sex club in Brooklyn, where exhibitions were secretly staged for members. There were three acts—first, a pair of lesbians engaged in passionate lovemaking, followed by one woman and two men performing in almost any sexual combination imaginable.

For the third act, Linda was shocked when a very handsome young man came out with a beautiful woman and a large, male, unneutered poodle. The dog was invited into bed with them and eventually lured—"tricked," as Linda phrased it—into joining in a three-way.

First the man gave the poodle what Linda described as a "rousing (rectal) fuck, which put a wide grin on the dog's face." As Linda described it, the woman then crawled around on the mattress, "playing the part of a bitch, woofing and sniffing." She then invited the dog to "climb aboard and sock it to her," which the animal subsequently did.

After the show, Chuck introduced Linda to the manager of the club, asking him if he'd like to hire her as a sex performer in the arena. "She's amazing. You can't believe what she can do. If you want to go back to your office, she'll demonstrate some of her sexual skills."

"No thanks," the burly manager said. "I hire only women I like to fuck. I wouldn't touch your bitch with a ten-foot pole."

Once again, Chuck had failed to successfully peddle Linda's body, and when he got her home, he slapped her around and blamed her. "Your body's just too god damn ugly!" he shouted at her.

***

Although no one, including Linda herself, ever agreed on the number of 8mm porno loops she filmed, Chuck estimated that she performed in a dozen loops for Bob Wolfe at his studio on 14th Street in Manhattan. "He was doing the freakiest films," Chuck claimed.

One afternoon, Wolfe asked Chuck, "Would your old lady want to ball a dog on camera?"

Without hesitation, Chuck shot back, "Sure thing."

"Actually, I'd like to shoot two 'bitches,' so to speak, and one dog," Wolfe said.

"Linda and I are living with this little number, Brandy," Chuck said. "She's eighteen and legal. And hot!"

"Show up tomorrow morning at eight o'clock," Wolfe said. "I'll have the dog here. I've filmed him before."

After meeting with Wolfe at his loft, Chuck returned to Jersey City to inform Linda of her new film role. He gave only sparse details, telling her that it was a dog movie.

"I knew at once it wasn't going to be a sequel to one of those *Rin Tin Tin* or *Lassie Come Home* movies. I wouldn't have to play some Liz Taylor role. Without Chuck saying so, I suspected right away it was one of those dog-on-woman movies. They were all the rage at the time."

She refused, even though she knew she'd receive a beating. She later told Brandy, "Getting one of Chuck's beatings is better than getting raped by a dog."

But after he assaulted her and made numerous threats, including some that involved cutting up her face with a pocketknife, she relented.

As she later recalled, "Our fat, greasy, black-haired director—a reference to Bob Wolfe—got his god damn wish."

What remained was for Chuck to persuade Brandy also to appear in the

LINDA: "IT'S NOTHING NEW" (BESTIALITY THROUGH THE AGES)

left: Woman coupling with a dog, from 17th-century India; *center*: Woman-with-Fido coupling from 16th-century Persia, and *right,* 19th century Japanese watercolor of a woman mating with an octopus by Hokusai Katushika, "The Dream of a Fisherman's Wife"

film. When Brandy returned home from servicing a john in his hotel room, Chuck tried to recruit her for the dog movie, informing her that it was an easy way to pick up $150, minus his commission as agent.

She adamantly refused, asserting that all she'd do with a dog involved either walking it or feeding it.

For the first time since the debut of his association with her, Chuck got rough with Brandy. Linda witnessed it, but Brandy stood her ground. "I'm not going to let some dog fuck me—and that's that."

That night, Chuck crossed the Hudson into Manhattan, trying to pick up another "actress" to co-star with Linda in the upcoming dog movie. His search, which lasted until 2am the following morning, was in vain.

After he left, Brandy began packing her suitcase, telling Linda, "I'm splitting."

"Please stay," Linda pleaded. "I need you."

"I've decided this life is not for me," Brandy said. "I'm going to get a regular job, meet Mr. Right, settle down, and have three kids. I'll forget the past and become a housewife in the suburbs."

By the time Chuck returned to the apartment, Brandy was gone. Linda would never see or hear from her again.

Eric Edwards, the red-haired porno star who'd previously starred in dozens of loops, recalled that in 1971, every porn producer in New York wanted to shoot bestiality movies with dogs. "But often, the dog wasn't willing."

Wolfe hired him to co-star with Linda in the bestiality film.

Wolfe was furious at Chuck for not rounding up another woman. "Okay, we'll shoot it just with Linda." He turned to her. "I hope you're a dog lover." He laughed as if it were some sort of joke.

"I'm terrified of dogs," she said. "I was attacked by a dog when I was only eight years old. I've never gotten over it."

"Oh, shit!" Wolfe said. "Get over it! We'll be ready to roll when that trainer arrives."

Then the elevator door opened and a trainer with a German shepherd entered the loft. To her, all big dogs looked mean, as if they would attack any person, except for their trainers, who got close to them.

The trainer, a young man in his late twenties, was the dog's owner. He introduced the dog to those on the set, saying that his name was Norman. The trainer then assured Wolfe that the dog knew what to do "because I rehearsed him last night with my wife."

Wolfe feared that the trainer's wife might have exhausted the dog.

"Don't worry about Norman," the trainer responded. "Norman can go all day and night."

"Did your wife go down on Norman?" Wolfe asked.

"Hell, no!" the owner said. "Do you seriously think I'd let a wife of mine do such a disgusting thing?"

Linda heard all this. She whispered to Chuck, "He'd let the dog fuck her, but not that other thing. But it's okay for *your* wife to go down on a dog, right?"

"Shut your face," Chuck ordered her.

The attendant brought the German shepherd up close to Linda. The dog frightened her as it growled softly, almost from the inner depths of its throat.

"Don't worry," the trainer said. "Norman is scoping you out."

"We don't have all day," Wolfe said. "Linda, get on that mattress." He turned to the trainer. "Have Norman join her."

As directed, Linda spotted the dog and said "*Ooooooh!*" You could see her mind spinning, as she suggested through her facial expression that Norman might finish the job her boyfriend had abandoned.

"Start feeling the dog's underbelly," Wolfe instructed her. "Get acquainted. Imagine he's a thirteen-year-old boy you're introducing to sex."

Sliding her hand across the dog's belly, she found his cock and began to fondle it. "Get down under it and lick!" Wolfe commanded.

His cameraman called out, "I can't see the action!"

"Get the dog on his back," Wolfe ordered.

The German shepherd obeyed the trainer and rolled over onto his back. Using both her mouth and her hand, Linda coaxed the dog's cock out of its leathery sheath. A small, slim, pink knob appeared, and it slowly began to grow longer, until it evolved into a big, red arrow. As Linda licked and sucked, the dog began to whimper.

Even to Chuck, it was an eerie moment.

After fellatio, Wolfe wanted to see the dog fornicate with her. He ordered that as her next move.

Edwards did not appear in any scene with the dog. He played the role of Linda's boyfriend in the movie, and was seen fornicating with her before abruptly leaving for work. Linda indicated that she had been left unsatisfied.

Edwards said, "As soon as Linda got on all fours, the dog mounted her. That's what dogs do. *Bang, bang, bang.*"

She reached for the dog's cock and guided it inside her. The dog seemed to catch on to what was expected from him. Inside her, he began to hump frantically. The speed was almost unbelievable, like no man she'd ever had before. The dog maintained his momentum, going faster and faster. Finally, he exploded inside her again and again.

Then, almost immediately, the animal pulled out. He sniffed the air around Linda for a few seconds, and then wandered off. The action over, the cameraman shut down his equipment.

Only the sounds of Linda's sobs could be heard in the studio. She'd been humiliated—and defiled.

Edwards later claimed that even though he wasn't needed on the set, he had stayed behind to watch the action unfold. Later, he said, "When the shoot was over, Wolfe told me that Norman had actually ejaculated inside Linda. "The dog pulled out, he smoked a cigarette, and asked for Linda's phone number," Edwards jokingly said.

Later, during an interview, Linda confessed that she was in bed with the dog for a full two hours—"There seemed to be no end to it. I feared Norman would bite me."

She later claimed that she found the loop disgusting and that she would never have sex with a dog again, "even when I'm ninety and can't get anything else."

For "my worst nightmare," Chuck was paid one hundred and fifty dollars.

Months later, when the loop became known to Linda's fans following the release of *Deep Throat,* nearly all the reviews were attacks. One viewer from Chyby, Poland, defined it as "taboo-breaking and utterly sickening." A young man from Tennessee wrote, "What can you say about a grainy, poorly filmed stag film where the best and most attractive performer is a German shepherd?"

Identifying himself online as "Baretooth," one reviewer challenged Linda's claim that she was coerced into making the loop. "If she were, she is one of the best actresses who ever lived. She doesn't hold back, and seems very enthusiastic in what she does. She doesn't seem intimidated in any way, like you would expect someone with a gun pointed at her head to act."

Michael Elliott of Louisville, Kentucky, claimed that Linda in *The Dog Fucker* crossed the line more than the drag queen, "Divine" did in John Waters' *Pink Flamingos,* when "she" actually ate dog shit. "There are several times when the German shepherd appears to be trying to get away in *The Dog Fucker,* yet Linda Lovelace pulls him back into the action before he finally gets it," Elliott wrote.

***

When not making 8mm porno loops, Chuck continued to sell Linda's services to "the kook and perv market," as he defined it. She was for hire to men with abnormal desires that no self-respecting hooker would accommodate.

In the late 1980s, Linda was very reluctant to discuss "this dark hour of my life—at times I thought about suicide."

"There are memories in me so deep I cannot pry them loose," she claimed.

It took great pressure from her super agent, Jay Garon, to get her to reveal details about three incidents that stood out in her mind.

One encounter was significant. It concerned a rare medical condition suffered by one of her clients. When she shared the details of this sexual liaison with Gerard Damiano, during the filming of an 8mm porn loop for him, it indirectly led to an idea that eventually formed the plot for *Deep Throat*.

One night when Chuck drove her to the apartment of Victor Findley, she had no idea of how bizarre her involvement with him would be, and Chuck, as was his way, did not give her a clue about what to expect.

Findley's two-bedroom apartment was beautifully decorated in an extreme modern style, but she was somewhat surprised that all the colors, including the draperies and upholsteries, were either chartreuse or pink. In retelling the story, Linda would define it as "pussy pink."

Over the fireplace were displayed portraits of what she assumed were the owner's mother and father. Both of them looked like very conservative and very rich American aristocrats, based on their expensive clothing and haughty manner.

Chuck spent only ten minutes with Findley, obviously working out financial arrangements, during a period when Linda was in the bathroom. He never told her how much Findley had offered.

When she first met Findley, she didn't know why he'd had a hard time hiring hookers, as Chuck had warned her. He appeared to be in his mid-forties, and he was a rather handsome man, graying at the temples of his brunette hair. He bore an amazing resemblance to the future presidential candidate, Mitt Romney. He had deep blue eyes, a trim and slightly muscled physique, and was immaculately clad, wearing a pink-and-chartreuse dress shirt, and a well-tailored, pin-striped, charcoal-gray suit.

As she sat across from him in his elegant living room, she was obviously nervous, fearing the demands he might make on her. Finally, she asked him, "I have to know before we go into that bedroom. Just what do you expect from me?"

He spoke with intelligence and perfect diction. "Please don't be alarmed. I desperately need sex. It's been two years. I want you to fellate me and I want to penetrate you in the missionary position."

"I've been led to believe that you might have some very odd request."

"Not at all," he said. "If I may be vulgar, I want two blow-jobs and just one penetration of your vagina."

"If you're telling the truth, and if there are no hidden surprises, I can accommodate that, I think. How much time between those blow-jobs do you want…I mean, to rest up a bit?"

"The fellatio can be performed one after the other," he said. "I find you very attractive, a natural hippie free-loving kind of girl."

"I'm not so sure about the free part," she said.

"I know," he answered. "Your husband, Mr. Traynor, drives a hard bargain.

We settled at five-hundred dollars for this two-hour session."

"As you known, that's well above the market price. That's why I'm suspicious that you want something more than you're telling me."

"You'll see," he said, rising from the sofa and directing her into the bedroom. "I'll be in in a minute. You can go in there and pull off your clothes and get on the bed."

Her suspicions were still aroused, but she did what he ordered. Within ten minutes, he came into the bedroom, wearing a pink terrycloth bathrobe.

"You look very lovely, my dear," he said. "But you must have had some dreadful operation."

"I was involved in a car crash," she said. "I hope you don't mind."

"Not at all," he said. "In fact, your imperfection allows me to show you mine. You see, I was born with two penises." At that point, he opened his robe and exposed himself.

She tried to mask the horror on her face. He had only one scrotum, but two circumsized penises. The position of the larger penis was placed in the position of that of the average male and was also of average size, but there was also a slightly smaller penis that grew out of his pubic region, immediately to the left of the larger organ.

"I have been photographed and have appeared in medical journals," he said. "The medical term is *diphallia,* or penile duplication. Will you please satisfy both of my penises? I'm capable of an erection in both of them, and can emit semen from each of them."

As repulsive as it was, she moved to fellate him, working first on the larger penis and then on the smaller one. When fully erect, the principal penis was about six inches long, the smaller one around four inches.

She moved back and forth between the two organs as he lay on his back on the bed. He was moaning and urging her on. His first climax came after only four minutes. Since the smaller penis remained erect, she then fellated it to a climax which occurred within a period of only about a minute.

After time in the bathroom, she came into the living room wrapped in a towel. In his robe, he sat on the sofa, and was filled with gratitude. He treated her most courteously.

Seeing her interest in his bizarre condition, he explained it to her. The first reported incidence was documented by a Swiss physician (Johannes Jacob Wecker) in 1609. Today, *diphallia* occurs only once in 5,500,000 men born in the United States. "I can pass urine through both penises," he said. "My rare condition sometimes appears in pigs or other mammals."

"I've never heard of such a thing," she said.

"There was one case where a man was born with six penises, but they were each the size of that of the average three-year-old boy. In most cases of *diphallia,* men cannot achieve an erection. As you now know, that is not my problem. In one case cited in that medical journal I was in, a man was born with two penises, a third leg, additional abnormalities in the bladder and lower bowel, and a higher possibility of reduced blood flows and infections."

"I'm glad a woman can't be born like that," she said.

"There's also a male condition, a very rare congenital anomaly—in which a man is born without any penis. That's called *aphallia.* Women, too, can suffer *aphallia.* "

"How on earth?" she said.

"*Aphallia* in a woman is when the female infant is born without a clitoris," he said.

As a coincidence, Findley was evoking the medical oddity that played a part in the upcoming script of *Deep Throat,* but with one exception. Instead of having no clitoris, the script of *Deep Throat* would call for its protagonist to have a clitoris bizarrely positioned in her throat, not enveloped within the folds of her labia.

Before Chuck arrived to rescue her, Findley invited her into the bedroom for one final sex act. This time, he wanted to penetrate her vagina with the larger of his two organs, and she agreed. "I just closed my eyes and imagined it was Warren Beatty," she'd later tell Chuck.

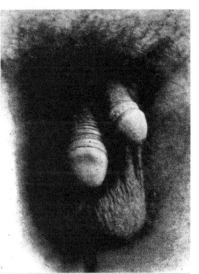

When Chuck picked her up an hour later, she told Findlay good night. He kissed her gently on the cheek. "I have sex every two or three years," he said. "Perhaps months from now, I'll get in touch."

"Perhaps," she said.

En route to Jersey City, she told Chuck, "*that* was one for the books—the medical journals, that is."

***

"For my next gig, Chuck booked me into the twilight zone," Linda later recalled. "This time, he stayed with me throughout the ordeal. Actually, it wasn't all that painful, just weird and creepy, which carries

Diphallia and the Kink Market

Diphallia (multiple penises as a result of a chromosomal misreading after conception) is a rare genetic abnormality *(see nearby pages)* that has challenged experts (including Linda Lovelace) in their field.

215

its own kind of *angst.* ”

The client's apartment was on the Upper West Side of Manhattan. When he opened his door for Linda and Chuck, she gasped in horror. The host, with considerable effort, had transformed himself into Bela Lugosi as he appeared in the 1931 film, *Dracula,* which she had seen in re-runs on late-night television. He wore a black suit and, even though indoors, was in a black cape with a blood-red silk lining.

“Come into my chamber,” he said to them. She was very reluctant to move from her position outside his door. Chuck had to push her forward.

“This is the willing girl I've been telling you about.” Chuck said. “She's just what you've been looking for, I know.”

Sensing her fear, he assured her, “You must not worry, dear girl. I'm a very gentle soul. My name is György Nádasdy—that's Hungarian.”

“Glad to meet you in person,” Chuck said, “and not just over the phone.”

“I bid you welcome,” Nádasdy said.

To Linda, he looked not only like Lugosi, but he had the aura of a walking, talking, breathing, corpse. He wore so much white make-up that his face looked ghostly. As she and Chuck sat across from him, he offered them a glass of blood-red wine. Both Chuck and Linda turned it down, perhaps thinking that a glass might actually contain blood.

“I know Linda is a bit scared, Mr. Nádasdy, but you explained everything to me about what's needed and wanted.” He turned to her. “Mr. Nádasdy will ask little from you. There will be absolutely no pain.”

“I can vouch for that,” Nádasdy said. “In fact, you may derive some sexual gratification from it. I certainly will.”

She was growing more anxious by the minute, as she sensed that blood-letting was involved. She jumped up from the sofa, even though Chuck tried to pull her back down. “I'm out of here. There are limits to what I will do.”

“Perhaps you should explain it to her like we discussed,” Nádasdy said.

“There's nothing to it,” Chuck said. “If you're afraid, I'll stay with you. All he wants is to make a tiny incision in your neck. It will hurt no more than getting an injection. He wants to taste a little bit of your blood—nothing else. He's willing to pay us a great deal of money, and we sure need it. I lost a bundle at the race track.”

Bela Lugosi as Dracula, the Vampire

Everything in the apartment, including the walls and furniture, was painted black. Only the heavy draperies and upholsteries were in a blood-inspired scarlet. Over the large sofa hung an antique portrait of some regal-looking woman in a formal gown that evoked the 16th Century. The portrait added a baroque formality to a room that was otherwise quite bare. Most of its illumination came from a sequence of small red lightbulbs organized into a rectangular frame around the portrait.

It took about fifteen minutes of reassurances from both men before she agreed to submit to this form of sexual expression. "My God," she lamented. "If you stay in this business long enough, you'll meet all kinds."

"Your services with me will be in two parts," Nádasdy asserted. "Each session will last fifteen minutes. As I've agreed with Mr. Traynor, I will pay you $1,000 per session."

Chuck pleaded with her, "Honey, the rent's two months behind."

"Okay," she said, rising from her seat. "But you guys had better not lie to me."

In the bedroom, she was instructed to remove only her blouse and bra. Nádasdy handed Chuck a sharp pointed instrument, which Chuck used as a pricking device to extract a small amount of blood from Linda's throat.

When her newly inflicted wound started to bleed, the instrument was replaced with Nádasdy's sucking lips. Nádasdy remained fully and formally dressed throughout the ordeal.

As she recalled that night many years later, she said, "It was not painful at all…sort of like a nurse drawing blood from your arm. Actually, his sucking, licking lips were kind of erotic. Oops—you'd better not use that. Those words make me look like a sicko, too."

At the end of the first session, Nádasdy disappeared into the bathroom for about half an hour while Chuck and Linda sat on the sofa, staring at that portrait, whose image evoked a painting she'd seen of the Renaissance monarch, Elizabeth I of England.

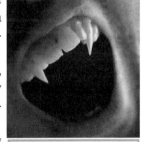

"Count Dracula" emerged from the bathroom, causing her to wonder what he'd done in there. "My dear, I hope it was as we told you it would be…relatively painless."

"It was okay, but I still prefer sucking and fucking for my own sexual pleasure," she said.

"To each his own, my dear," he said. "For the second and final round, you can remain on the sofa and let Mr. Traynor hold your hand for reassurance, if you wish."

Servicing the Vampire Fetish Market

How much of Linda's blood did Chuck's $1,000 fee include?

After another pin prick to her throat, as Nádasdy sucked blood a second time, it was less terrifying than before, as she knew more or less what to expect.

When the session was over, she retreated to the bathroom and found some alcohol, which she applied to her throat. She sealed the wound with a Band-Aid, but the blood had already stopped. Nonetheless, she felt weak.

THE COUNTESS

Two depictions of **Erzsébet Báthory de Ecsed,** 16th-century Hungary's "Blood Countess," the most prolific female serial killer in history.

lower image: British actress **Julie Delpy,** producer, director, and star of the Franco-German film *The Countess,* exhibited in 2009 at the Berlin Film Festival and in 2010 at the Cannes Film Festival.

Back in the living room, Chuck was still sitting on the sofa, and "Dracula" looked immensely pleased.

A bottle of champagne, cooling in a silver bucket, had appeared on the coffee table during her absence. "Let's drink to the successful conclusion of our business deal," Nádasdy said. "You performed brilliantly, my dear. You must have some champagne. When you get home tomorrow, drink some blood-red wine. It will restore the blood I removed from your throat."

She sat on the sofa and stared once again at that regal portrait. "It's none of my business, but just who posed for that portrait? The woman is very beautiful."

"That is my beloved mother, Countess Elizabeth Báthory de Ecsed, a countess born in 1560 in the Kingdom of Hungary. She was a great beauty. My wonderful father was Ferencz Nádasdy, the chief commander of the Hungarian troops in their battle against the Ottomans. No Hungarian had finer parents than mine."

"I don't get it," she said. "How could she be your mother if she were born in 1560?"

"That's simple, my dear," he said. "She was a vampire. I am a vampire. We live forever. Mother would be sitting right here with us tonight had it not been for an unfortunate event. Three months after her burial, her corpse was disinterred, dug up from its resting place. What remained of her heart was cut out of her body and burned, thus destroying her immortality."

At that point, Linda realized that Nádasdy was insane, although she did not fear him. She suspected that he had probably been born around 1895, somewhere in eastern Europe, perhaps

Hungary or Russia.

"I cannot help who I am," he said. "I'm a very rich man, and I've consulted some of the best psychiatrists in America and Switzerland. All of them tell me that the innate sexuality of bloodsucking is an unconscious association of draining semen from the body. They suggest that I want to swallow the semen of men, which would make me a homosexual. I am not a homosexual, since I'm attracted to women. Other know-nothing psychiatrists dismiss my interest as a sexual perversion called 'oral sadism.'"

"Please tell me about your mother," Linda said. "She sounds fascinating. What a beauty."

"I loved and admired her very much," Nádasdy said. "But she had her critics. Some people even today call her the 'Blood Countess' or 'Countess Dracula.' She retained her beauty for years, bathing in the blood of virgins and rubbing her porcelainlike face with menstrual blood. Today, she's the subject of books, films, legends, even toys and games. She's called the most prolific female serial killer in history. She was steeped in black magic and the practice of her religion required her to sacrifice children for bones and blood. Personally, I think that in a free society, people should be allowed to pursue their religion without government interference. She was influenced by her relatives. Her aunt, a lady at court, was a lesbian and a witch. Her uncle was an alchemist and devil-worshiper; her brother could not be left alone in a room with a woman or female child."

"My mother worked at maintaining her beauty. There were those who called her a vain narcissist. She changed her gowns six times a day and spent hours in front of mirrors admiring her beauty. She used all manner of oils and unguents to preserve her porcelain white skin."

"Not knowing that my mother was merely adhering to the tenents of her religion, she was criticized for killing 650 girls between the years 1585 and 1610. Mostly, they were lured into her castle to accept well-paying jobs as

ALL IN THE FAMILY:

Count Ferencz Nádasdy (1555-1604) became engaged to Elizabeth Báthory when she was eleven, and later sired five children with her, three of whom survived.

Known for his cruelty to his Ottoman enemies, he learned many of his torture techniques from his sadistic wife. One of these involved impaling his victims rectally, and slowly, with wooden spikes.

maids. She preferred severe beatings, but sometimes, while her victim was tied up, she ate the flesh off a girl's face. At times, she chewed off and ate their vaginas. Sometimes, she starved a girl to death. She particularly liked to have a girl raped by a hundred of my father's soldiers until she died. Often, she would burn a victim to death. At other times, she liked to slice up their bodies with razors. Another sport involved long needles, stabbing them into the eyes of the young girls. Some stupid books claim she was psychotic. But she was the sanest woman who ever lived, the kindest, and the one with perfect mental health. She was just misunderstood."

"Finally, the villagers demanded that my mother and her accomplices—Semtész, Jó, and Ficko—be brought to trial. Mother did not appear at their trial, and each of the defendants were found guilty. Semtész and Jó had their fingers ripped off their hands with hot pincers before being burned at the stake, and Ficko was beheaded. But mother was assigned to be locked away in a tower, where she languished for four years. There was no light, only a slit in the masonry which entombed her, as a means of passing provisions.

"We are so sorry you lost her," Chuck said, rising from the sofa. "But over the centuries, I heard that millions of people have died because of their religious beliefs."

In the car, on their way back to Jersey City, Linda turned to Chuck. "You really know how to get bookings for me. That Nádasdy belongs in a straitjacket in a mental ward."

***

In her memoirs, Linda admitted to using dildos both in private and in her public performances—even a double-ended variation boasting two "penises" pointing in opposite directions. That dildo functioned as a sort of "see-saw" as each partner took an end as a means of stimulating either the anus or vagina. Linda frequently used such a dildo simultaneously with her friend, Brandy.

During some of her gigs with men, she used a strap-on dildo. She later remarked, "It was amazing the number of so-called straight men who enjoyed me to penetrate them with a dildo, some quite large."

During the late 1980s, she told her researchers about a bizarre movie she'd made for a Japanese house of prostitution, where she'd worked briefly, in Manhattan. She'd been fired because she was too old, and because most of the house's business clients preferred younger, more virginal-looking women.

The manager of the house had learned from Chuck that Linda was "The Mistress of the Dildo," accepting with very few issues all sizes and shapes. He called Chuck and asked if she'd pose for a special film in which she'd be asked to perform alone, accompanied only by a view of a man's hand inserting various dildos, some of them dauntingly oversized, into Linda.

Chuck agreed that Linda would be available for the filming, and even volunteered to allow his hand and arm to be used, on film, as the instrument for inserting the dildos. Consequently, Linda was welcomed back, at least temporarily, to Ketsu, the Japanese whorehouse which had previously fired her. Its director greeted Linda and Chuck, bowing before them. He told them that he preferred to "use my American name, Barry Farber, and not my Japanese name. I do not want to bring dishonor to my ancestors."

A set for the shooting of the film was established outdoors, on a bright sunny day, on a building's rooftop in Manhattan, beside an open-air swimming pool. "Farber" explained the sequence of the script to Linda.

She was to emerge nude from the pool—"like Venus rising from the sea." He had arranged for someone to craft a large necklace out of seaweed, which was draped around her neck throughout that part of the filming.

At that point, a thin Japanese boy in a white jacket came onto the roof from downstairs. He was not formally introduced, but Linda and Chuck were informed that he would be in charge of props, including the dildos, which she hadn't seen yet.

"Farber" then explained to her that in Japan, there were strictly enforced obscenity laws, and that some merchants had gotten into trouble manufacturing dildos that evoked the male phallus. "To get around these laws, and as a means of evading prosecution, manufacturers craft dildos that resemble animals or cartoon characters. These are then packaged and sold as children's toys. Some of these have surfaces which are textured to enhance the pleasure of the user," Farber said. "So just to be clear, it's agreed that throughout this project, only your husband's arm and hand will be seen as he inserts, manipulates, and removes various dildos from your vagina as you lie on a *chaise longue*. You and he will not have a strong direction. There will be no sound, so Mr. Traynor can call out to you—more or less guiding you through your scene."

She was shocked when she finally realized that the dildos had been modeled on the actual penises of animals. She still hadn't comprehended what it was that she would be called upon to do.

"Like the animals themselves, some of the penises will be large, some quite small," Farber said. "A rabbit cannot, of course, measure up against a bull. Mr. Traynor, however, had assured me that you can accept large objects. Before I start filming, would you confirm that?"

"I can," she admitted. "But within reason. My body is that of a woman, which means I can't take a tree trunk up there."

"I understand," he said, giving her a polite smile. It was obvious that he held her in contempt.

"We will begin the film with the insertion of a banana followed by a rather large zucchini," the director said. At the far end of the roof was a steel cabinet, from which the servant boy began to produce the props.

When filming began, the banana was inserted first, then the zucchini, neither of which she found particularly challenging.

The first animal penis presented to her was in the shape of a wolf's phallus, which she quickly compared, size-wise, to the penises of many of her former clients.

Before the afternoon waned, Chuck would insert dildos modeled on a donkey, a horse, a Great Dane, a monkey, a bear, a pig, a rooster, a rabbit, and a duck. "That gives new meaning to 'fuck a duck,'" she said. The bull dildo he inserted was relatively large, but she managed to accommodate it with a minimum of effort.

Some of the penetrations were vaginal, others anal. The director explained that animal porno in Japan is often depicted as a means of avoiding censorship laws. "We have used Russian women as models and we have them perform fellatio on animals. In Tokyo, for example, oral penetration of a non-human penis is not against the law. Actually, a number of animal porn actresses are emerging. They each specialize in bestiality movies."

During a break, Farber told them that many of the Japanese live by harvesting the bounties of the sea. From his portfolio, he showed them the drawing he was going to include as part of the marketing campaign for an animal dildo film. The drawing had been executed by Hokusai Katsushika (1760-1849), an artist who had also painted "The Dream of a Fisherman's Wife," showing a woman being sexually pleasured by an octopus.

IN CASE YOU WERE WONDERING:

1) It's a dildo and

2) It was modeled after the penis of a wolf, and

3) It can be suction-mounted to any smooth, nonporous surface, and

4) it's one of many zoological lookalikes that can be ordered online.

The most gruesome and frightening object that Chuck inserted into her that day was a reptile. It was a large (non-poisonous) black snake. The snake had been heavily drugged, and she was assured that there was no chance of her being bitten. "The snake is alive but practically comatose," Farber assured her.

Years later, she could not identify the exact breed and snake and finally refused to discuss that "horrifying encounter" at all. In fact, she grew angry when she was questioned further. "It happened, god damn it, and that's it. I don't have to relive the most gruesome parts of my life, which I chose to forget."

At the end of the day, Farber announced that he was well satisfied with Linda's performance. In fact, he was so pleased that he began a discussion about sex performance roles he might offer her in his filmmaking future. "I'm working on a script now," he said. "But you can star in it only when you're having your period. We want two versions of the first one, which can be shot during two different months. "One will bear the English-language name: *Running a Red Light.* I want to depict a man having sex with you during your period. The other, to be entitled *The Vampire Lesbian's Supper,* will be a film about a lesbian going down on you during your period."

"What's the other one?" Linda asked in horror.

"This will be for a very special cult," he said. It's defined in the *Encyclopedia of Unusual Sexual Practices* as *Oculolinctus.* Its fanciers get off sexually by licking the surface of a human eyeball."

"Got anything else?" Chuck asked.

"Yes, *Strawman,"* Farber said. "Linda would have to be penetrated anally during the first scene. Then the Strawman comes in, He inserts a straw into Linda's anus and then sucks out the semen. The act is called 'felching.'"

Without checking with Chuck, Linda got up from her chair. "Thanks for everything. Chuck and I will get back to you about those other starring roles."

On the street with Chuck, she told him, "That donkey dildo you inserted into me made me grateful I didn't have to do that live donkey show you were setting up for me in Mexico. As for his other film offers, he can take those and shove it."

"You took all those animal penises with ease," Chuck told her. "I don't know if you're aware of it, but bestiality films are all the rage today."

"Is that the next series you have in mind for me, you bastard?"

Even though they were walking along a crowded street, he hauled off and slapped her in front of all the other passers-by. None of the pedestrians paid any attention to the assault.

***

Linnea Eleanor (Bunny) Yeager, a first-rate photographer and a former pin-up model herself, had once been hailed as "The World's Prettiest Photographer" by *U.S. Camera* magazine. The Pennsylvania-born (in 1930) beauty was one of the most sought-out models in Miami. When she retired from that, she moved her career behind the camera.

Meeting pin-up model Bettie Page in 1954, she, along with photographer Irving Klaw, were the two principal players who transformed Page into the leg-

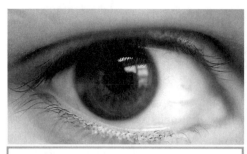

Linda: "It's a sexual perversion known formally as *Oculolinctus*. Don't even ask...."

end she is today. Yeager's photos of Page which appeared in *Playboy* helped make the model a household name, at least among males.

Chuck had two fantasies, one for himself, one for Linda. He wanted Yeager to hire her and turn her into "the second Bettie Page." Chuck's pitch to Yeager involved the perception that those 1950s pictures of Page in "states of naughty *déshabillée*," as the press put it, needed to be updated for the liberated 1970s. He knew that Linda would pose for more explicit and pornographic pictures than Page did.

Linda had also seen Yeager during the mid-Sixties chattering away with Johnny Carson on *The Tonight Show.* Yeager took the famous still images of Ursula Andress on the beach for publicity associated with the release, in 1962, of the James Bond film, *Dr. No.* Linda had also seen Yeager on the screen when she appeared as the Swedish masseuse opposite Frank Sinatra in *Lady in Cement* (1968).

Chuck wanted to hook up with Yeager in hopes of also furthering his own career as a filmmaker. Lenny Camp, a photographer and convicted child pornographer, had known Linda and Chuck in Florida. "Linda followed him around like a puppy dog," Camp claimed. "Ninety percent of what Chuck said was total bullshit. He shared his secret dream with me. He wanted to be the next Hugh Hefner. In fact, at times, I think he thought he was Hugh Hefner. Actually, he was a superpimp—that's all he was."

DEEP THROAT MEETS BUNNY:

Swiss-born beauty **Ursula Andress,** as photographed by Bunny Yeager, on a beach in Jamaica during the filming of *Dr. No*

Chuck had long been intrigued with Yeager. He once told an interviewer, "To a sixteen-year-old, anybody with long blonde hair and big boobs is good-looking, ha-ha-ha."

When Yeager read his comment, she said, "He was always quick to laugh."

Chuck called Yeager, whom he'd known for years, and touted Linda's charms. "This girl is really hot. Photos of her will made everybody forget Bettie Page."

Yeager agreed to meet with her, but was shocked by her appearance. She arrived wearing a cowboy hat, military jacket, faded blue jeans, scruffy boots, and a tangled mess of hair. When she stripped, she revealed her flat chest and this hideous scar that ran all the way down the middle of her chest. "I shot her as a favor to Chuck, but I knew that her pictures were going to be tossed in the trash can."

She hired Chuck as a cameraman on an X-rated 35mm film (*Sextet)* she was shooting. [*Sextet* should not be confused with the film of almost the same name—*Sextette*—being filmed around the same time in 1968. In it, Mae West disastrously made her last film appearance. It was arguably the most jaw-dropping camp classic in history.]

On his second day of working for Yeager, Chuck brought Linda to the studio a second time and asked if Yeager could offer her a role in the film. "She's sweet," Yeager said, "but I don't see that she has any sex appeal." However, as a favor to him, she hired Linda for a brief appearance as an extra. She was depicted fully dressed, sitting on a sofa with two far more attractive and alluring women.

"That was it," Linda later wrote. "No fuck, no suck, no nothing."

She later claimed, "I got the last laugh when *Deep Throat* became the highest grossing porn film in history. As a line from the Connie Francis song might have informed her fans, Who's Sorry Now?"

***

No other jobs for Linda ever emerged from Yeager. Consequently, Chuck applied to Director Gerard Damiano of Damiano Productions for a position as a cameraman. He was hired on the same day he applied for the job.

Damiano's was a name well known to

Two views of **Bunny Yeager,** top a self-portrait from the 1950s, bottom, cover to a collection, released in 2012, of her photos, considered among the best from the golden age of the pinup queens.

Chuck. Born into an Italian Catholic family in the Bronx, he served in the Navy, joining at the age of seventeen at the end of World War II. During the mid-1950s, he opened a hairdressing salon in New York. Later, he claimed that eavesdropping on the conversations of his sexually frustrated female clients set him to thinking that X-rated films could have crossover appeal—and not be geared just to men's smokers.

When Chuck met him, Damiano was churning out pseudo-educational documentaries such as *The Marriage Manual* and *Changes,* both made in 1970, followed in 1971 by *Sex USA.* On the side, he shot straight porn and for quick money, some 8mm loops.

While working at Damiano's studio, Chuck brought Linda by and asked if she could be hired as a script girl. She got the job.

During a lunch break one day, Chuck touted Linda's sexual specialties, especially her expertise as a fellatio artist. "She'll come to your office and demonstrate."

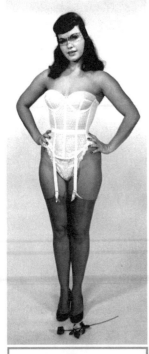

As Damiano later said, "I was feeling horny that day, and my Italian sausage needed servicing, so I told him to bring her in to see me."

"She came in and looked rather shy," Damiano said. "I didn't expect much. Chuck left and I lowered by pants and stood by my desk. She kneeled before me. I'd probably had a thousand blow-jobs in my life, but nothing like Linda's. She practically swallowed me whole and went for the balls, too. She was not only a sword-swallower, but a suction pump. My blast-off had enough power behind it to propel us to the moon. I decided I had to use this hot bitch in a loop."

At the time of Linda's audition as a fellatio expert, Damiano hadn't yet written the script for *Deep Throat,* much less directed it.

As co-star with Linda in the porn loop he envisioned, Damiano chose a handsome young actor with a bushy mustache working for him at the time. He was marketing himself as Harry Reems. He had been born with the name of Herbert Streicher in 1947 to a German-American Jewish family in the Bronx. A former Marine, he pursued an acting career off-Broadway, but the work turned out to be non-existent at the time, and the pay was not a living wage.

Chuck Traynor hoped that Yeager would do for Linda what she had done for 50s icon and S&M bondage queen **Bettie Page** *(photo above).*

Eventually, he drifted into porn, working for Damiano. One afternoon, Damiano approached Reems and asked him if he would perform with "a girl named Linda Lovelace—both anal and fellatio. She's terrific. You're well-endowed but she can handle it."

Reems met Linda the following afternoon. She seemed very nervous until Damiano ordered Chuck off the set—then she relaxed.

No one, not even the director, knew they were filming a sequence for *Deep Throat* that day. But the loop that resulted from the day's shooting would eventually be inserted into the final print of *Deep Throat,* a film whose script had not even been conceived at the time.

Cast and outfitted as a sexy, partially unclothed nurse, Linda entered the hospital room of a patient played by Reems. She pulled back the bedsheet to discover him wearing underwear decorated with depictions of hearts and flowers. His cock was wrapped in bandages, tied at their tip into a bow. Despite the patient's protests, she gets to work at laboriously untying the bandages around his penis. When it fully emerges from its casings, it is stiffly erect, even before she begins to apply the "oral therapy" that's needed to ease his pain.

Gerard Damiano in 1971, then specializing in porn overviews of :"feverish flower children"

As Reems recorded in his memoirs, "Her tongue and lips were everywhere. Then I felt the muscles in the back of her throat opening up. Her head lowered over me. Suddenly, I could feel my cock go right into her throat. I'm like 7 ½ inches when fully erect. But it's 7½ bulky inches that slope conically from a fat circumcised head to an even broader base. She swallowed that and all the auxiliary equipment. I couldn't believe she ate the whole thing! My cock and balls and half my pubic bush were all engulfed in the cavernous deep throat."

He feared for "the source of my livelihood," but she kept going up and down. Damiano later claimed, "We were witnessing a landmark in sexual history."

When it was time to begin filming the anal sequence, Reems suggested some lubricant. She turned him down, wetting the head of his penis, with her mouth, instead. She had no problem taking him through her rear door. "Chuck can put his fist up there," she told Damiano.

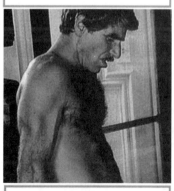

SEMPER FI

Porn performer and ex-Marine
Harry Reems

Reems admitted that he fell in love with Linda that day, but only briefly. "We balled our brains out and fucked every which way."

At the end of the loop, Damiano brought out bourbon for Chuck, Linda, Reems, and himself. "Just out of the blue, I asked her about the weirdest man she'd ever deep throated."

"She told me this incredible story about a client who had two penises, both of which could get fully erect." Damiano said. "I'd never heard of such a thing. I really doubted her, but that weekend at home, I researched it. What she said was true, and I learned a lot more."

"The condition was known as *diphallia,* or penile duplication. I also learned about *aphallia,* which, in the female, means she's born without a clitoris. An idea flashed in my head. The plot for a film I called at the time *The Sword Swallower* was born. But I didn't want our heroine to have no clitoris at all, so I placed it in her throat."

In a magazine interview, Damiano claimed that he wrote the screenplay for *Deep Throat* that weekend. Impressed with her "girl-next-door look," he also said he was determined to cast her even though she'd never acted before. He noted that Chuck made her wear cutoff jeans that were so short and so tight that "the lips of her pussy would hang out. While writing the script, I invented the expression *Deep Throat* and retitled the movie."

While pre-production moved ahead on *Deep Throat,* Damiano filmed a pseudo-documentary on the porn industry, calling it *Sex USA,* a 69-minute movie released in 1971.

Damiano played himself as an interviewer, and Chuck was hired as a cameraman. Linda had a small part, and the film featured some of the leading porn stars of that day, including Tina Russell, her husband Jason Russell, Harry Reems, and Fred. J. Lincoln.

On the set, Linda met Lincoln, who at that period of his career not only appeared in movies but made hot, cheap, porno grinders before moving on to shooting films with bigger budgets. Lincoln later became one of the best-known of all porn producers and was also noted for his provocative comments: "The Republican Party sounds just like the Ku Klux Klan. If you take out 'family values' and put 'Aryan race' in there instead, you've got Hitler making speeches again." Before the 70s ended, Lincoln would direct *Daisy May,* a crude and "rollicking sex-soaked parody" of Al Capp's *L'il Abner,* with lots of "hillbilly humping…and the kinds of old-fashioned sex that makes you proud to be an American."

Lincoln was not impressed with Linda, and would later challenge some of her assertions about being coerced into porn. He also referred to her as "a pain in the ass. While I was trying to conduct business, she'd get down between my legs and unzip me. I didn't care for her, and resisted her cocksucking overtures.

Finally, I told her, 'I just let pretty girls have the honor of doing me.'"

During the context of *Sex USA*, Damiano hosted an awkward round table discussion on censorship and sexuality in America. Himself a filmmaker, actor, director, and Hollywood personality Ron Wertheim appeared at the table with nothing of any importance to say. One segment within the film, whose inclusion would be legally censored today, is the advocacy of having children view pornography as part of their learning experience or sex education.

One reviewer claimed that "the format is merely an excuse to show a group of porn performers, who demonstrate sexual positions and in a voice over share their lurid sexual fantasies. The XXX content is well photographed and edited, upstaging the often stupid round table material. At one point, a gay guy doing voiceovers described the proper method of deep-throat technique, a prophetic preview of what would soon put Damiano in the history books."

On the set of *Sex USA,* Linda met Tina Russell, a porn star she both admired and envied. During her five-year career in the 1970s, this beautiful, highly sexual woman became almost legendary for her appearances in sexvids.

Sexually adventurous housewife roles meeting the postman, or whomever, became Russell's stock-in trade. Admired for her hot session on screen with both men and women, she became one of the reigning queens of the "Golden Age of Porn."

When Linda first met Tina, she had recently married a photographer, John Sanderson, who had also been lured into porn, billing himself as Jason Russell. Since he was an attractive, well-endowed male, his wife suggested that he share his charms with the world. As a couple, they appeared in countless loops which were screened as peepshows in Times Square, and they also were featured in a number of marriage manuals aimed particularly at honeymoon couples who "didn't know all the ropes." Tina also became the star of several hardcore porn features produced in New York.

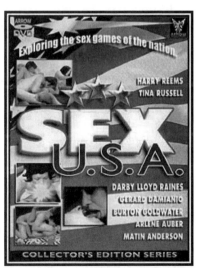

Linda secretly wanted a three-way with Jason and Tina, since she found both of them highly desirable.

She confided to Damiano that if Jason and Tina ever split up, she'd like to date Jason. "I think he's hot, but so is his wife. I wonder if they ever make it with each other since they always seem to be fucking some-

SEX USA, Damiano's pretentious pseudo-documentary about the porn industry. It immediately preceded the production of *Deep Throat*

one else."

Harry Reems recalled working in a loop with Tina, who dressed like a hooker in high heels and a miniskirt—"definitely no bra." He claimed he developed a hard-on right away, until a handsome, slender young man joined them. When Tina introduced Jason as her husband, Reems said his erection dropped like an express elevator. When Jason assured Reems that it was okay to fuck his wife, his erection shot up again.

Tina had attracted a rich fan, a porn collector who paid Damiano $750 to film a lesbian loop with Tina and another woman. Damiano selected Linda for the co-starring part.

"After I made that loop with Tina, I almost became a lesbian for life," Linda said. "The gal knew what she was doing. She should know, as she was also a veteran of live sex shows. In one of her live shows, she took on ten guys, each a volunteer from the audience, doing them one at a time."

The publication of Tina's 1973 memoir, *Porno Star,* motivated Linda to write some memoirs of her own—four of them, to be exact. Critically speaking, however, none of the four could be defined as a genuine, bona-fide autobiography, as each focused only on scattered, carefully selected scenes from Linda's life, never revealing the entire picture.

Regrettably, just after Tina's star rose, it quickly faded from the sky. She and Jason separated. Linda heard rumors from Damiano that she had become a self-destructive alcoholic. On May 18, 1981, Tina died of stomach cancer in Vista, California.

Tina Russell, one of the reining queens of the Golden Age of Porn: Sexually Adventurous Housewife meets the postman, or whomever

Tim Connelly, who had previously filmed a loop with Jason, claimed in the mid-70s that he was anxiously looking forward to meeting Tina. He was disappointed, asserting afterward that she was a mess. "She smelled and she was fat and bloated from booze and dope. Instead of a beautiful chick, I met a troll."

When Linda heard about the encounter, she said, "As God is my witness, I will never let that happen to me. I'm going to die in Beverly Hills, a rich, beautiful, movie star surrounded with six adorable men."

***

During the peak of her fame, after she abandoned the filming of 8mm loops, Linda never looked back on them nostalgically. But in the 21st

Century, some porn industry insiders remembered them fondly, Linda in particular. And years after New York City's cleanup (some say "pasteurization") of Times Square in the mid-1990s, there were even highly vocal advocates praising the virtues of a plan designed to "bring the porn back to 42nd Street."

For Linda, Times Square in the early 1970s was a place of terror, not an oasis of memories associated with some golden age of porn.

As noted by *NickatNite.com*, "Times Square was dangerous day and night. Roving gangs of violent urban youths (i.e., black teenaged males) would occasionally descend on the area in search of prey (usually white people). The many drug dealers there attracted numerous street hookers and junkies (often one and the same), which led to lots of street crime as well. The 42nd Street subway stop was the most violent in the city."

Linda later claimed that she dreaded working in the area, especially for late-night gigs. She said that one night at around 2am, four black men tried to force her into a car at 42nd Street at 10th Avenue. As she told Jay Garon's research team, "They were pushing and shoving me into the back seat, where I knew they would cart me off to rape me. I fought and screamed. I was saved by some white sailors who happened by and took them on in combat. I don't know the end result of that fight because I fled. Maybe the black boys grabbed one of the sailors and took him off to rape him when they couldn't have me. That night, I dreamed those guys had captured me, raped me brutally, and then murdered me."

Many porn fanciers, including Mickey Clifford, preferred Linda Lovelace loops, among others, released in the 1970s before the industry moved to Southern California. "They had natural women on camera back then, hookers like Linda Lovelace. Today, you get nothing but obvious implants, boring tattoos, tongue piercings, and definitely hair color from the bottle. In both straight and gay porn, actors spit into each other's mouths, scream like a lunatic at penetration. On most occasions, you see nothing but gang bangs with a bunch of losers who could not make it in legit films."

"Give me Linda Lovelace any day," claimed Bill Sharpton of Tennessee. "She can put her shoes under my bed, even if her tits are sagging. I'm sure she hasn't lost her Deep Throat talent."

Milas Horne, a theater manager in Kansas City, said, "Southern Cal dominates porn today. But I find their films often lack eroticism. Give me that old-fashioned Big Apple porn of the 1970s. Linda Lovelace was great at it. She was very switchable. She could be submissive in one loop, then dominant in the next. Actually, I preferred her as a dominatrix when she beat the shit out of some victim spread out over her knees. She appealed to all types, from rock-and-rollers to bondage queens. Linda herself, or so I read, once referred to her fan base as 'nonconformist types.'"

***

In his memoir, Harry Reems wrote, "I got a legitimate union job on a C-minus opus starring Troy Donahue. Remember him? You sure won't remember the name of the film: *Without Last Rites.* I never got paid for the job. See what I mean when I say it's the straight, overground world that can rip you off the worst?"

Without Last Rites ultimately led to Linda meeting her screen heartthrob, Troy Donahue. She'd thrilled to "his male beauty" when she saw him on the screen with the big box office star of the day, Sandra Dee.

In an indirect way, *Without Last Rites* led to Troy showing up one day at around noon at Damiano's loft studio. The director introduced Troy to Linda, who was in awe of him, although he looked much older and a lot more rundown than he did when he had appeared years previously with Dee.

A pin-up image of the previous decade, Troy was still blonde, blue-eyed, and blandly handsome, an icon of 1960s pop culture. His popularity had waned almost before it had begun, and she'd heard that he was making low-budget quickies. At six feet, three inches, he seemed to tower over her.

"I've been one of your biggest fans," she said, looking around and being grateful that Damiano had sent Chuck on an errand to buy film.

Troy explained that he'd come to the studio in search of Harry Reems, with whom he'd recently completed their cheapie.

"You entertain Troy in my office, and I'll send a search party out for Reems," Damiano said.

She welcomed the chance to be alone with Troy. In the office, she noticed that he was shaking and seemed extremely agitated. "You look like you need a drink," she said.

"I'd rather smoke some weed," he said.

"I always travel with some pot," she said, reaching into her purse and handing him a joint. After lighting it, he sucked in the smoke with a certain desperation. "Forgive me," he said, "but I started drinking when I turned thirteen in the seventh grade. But after the ordeal I suffered through as a movie star in Hollywood, only painkillers, amphetamines, and cocaine will do—and pot, of course."

After she'd offered him a cigarette, he amused her with stories about his career. "I have this agent, Henry Willson. Gay as a goose. He tried out the name of Troy on Rory Calhoun and James Darren before giving it to me."

"When you made that movie with Rock Hudson, *Tarnished Angels* (1957), I thought you two actors were the best thing since cock was invented," she said.

"I'm glad you liked it," he said.

232

[Years later, she read in a book that Willson had asked Hudson what he thought of Troy. "Great cocksucker, tiny dick," Hudson had responded.]

Actually, Troy had come to Hollywood to become "the next James Dean," even wearing the red jacket Dean had worn in *Rebel Without A Cause.* Autograph hunters often confused Troy with Tab Hunter, another blonde heartthrob, except that Hunter was gay. Although he denied it, Troy was actually bisexual himself.

"I started my career by invading the wet dreams of pubescent girls," Troy confessed. "Many young married women named their first-born male child 'Troy.' Now look at me. When I left Hollywood, I was drinking liquor and taking codeine before every take. I was scared shitless facing the camera."

After their second joint, Troy had grown quite mellow, at least enough to tell her that he'd come to the studio looking for Reems because he wanted a private loop made.

"I hope there's a part in it for me," she said. "I don't know if Damiano told you, but I'm known as the best cocksucker in New York. Ever since you came in here, I've been eying your crotch. I want to know what drove Sandra Dee crazy."

"In *A Summer Place,* I knocked up Gidget, but learned that's a no-no. I pounded her off screen, too."

"I'm better than she is," Linda said, aggressively reaching for his zipper.

"I'm a little bit horny today," he said.

She managed to get his pants and jockey shorts down, checking him out. She tried not to show her disappointment. Later, she'd tell Damiano, "What I encountered looked like a piece of okra. I got a rise out of it, but it never made it to the back of my throat. But did that kid ever blast off—at least a quart of cum. Sometimes, the smallest of cocks deliver bigger loads than the whoppers."

After Linda had gotten "down and dirty" with Troy, he told her the real purpose of his visit. "I'm broke," he said, claiming that he had met this "rich, crazed gay fan. He lives in Connecticut, and he's willing to shell out $10,000 if I'll make a private porno loop for him."

Two views of 50s heartthrob **Troy Donahue**

lower photo: With **Rock Hudson** in 1957 on the set of *Tarnished Angels*

"I'll do it with you," she volunteered.

"You don't get it," Troy said. "He's gay and he wants to see me in action with another guy. I've seen a porno loop Reems did, and I want him to be my co-star."

She looked terribly disappointed.

An hour later, Damiano told Troy that Reems could not be located, but that he had another guy doing a loop "with a chick—and he'd be terrific."

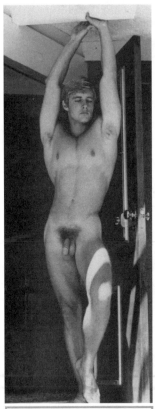

To consumers of hetero porn, he was **Rick Cassidy**, but in his gay films, he identified himself as "Jim."

No record remains, at least none that we know about, of the privately commissioned porn loop he made with **Troy Donahue,** as described by Linda Lovelace

Linda and Chuck were introduced to Rick Cassidy, whom she'd later describe as "a Greek God." He was young, blonde, blue-eyed, and a well-endowed bodybuilder. He and Troy seemed powerfully attracted to each other and huddled together in the corner for about an hour."

When Troy brought the subject up once again with Linda and Damiano, he reported, "Rick's all for it. In fact, he'd looking forward to it."

At that point, Chuck returned to the studio and hastily hustled Linda back to Jersey City. He didn't even learn that Troy Donahue had been in the studio.

A few days later, Damiano screened the Cassidy/Donahue loop for Chuck and Linda. "It was hot," she recalled, "and Rick, not Troy, was clearly the star. I think it turned Chuck on a bit. When he got me home, he fucked me more than once. He never did that. But I suspect he was thinking about Rick and Troy, not me. I began to suspect that Chuck was a closeted gay. The loop would have been great, except for one thing. Damiano should have called it *Sandwich* with me the meat in the middle."

During the months ahead, she noticed that Cassidy went on to become a bigtime porno star, appearing in some one hundred XXX-rated movies. She met him briefly again on the set of the 1973 *French Schoolgirls,* a porn flick that starred John C. Holmes (*aka* Johnny Wadd), hailed at the time as "The King of Porn." Rick also appeared with Tina and Jason Russell and even Harry Reems himself.

Cassidy told her that so much of his mail came from male fans that he was also making gay movies under the assumed name of Jim (as opposed to Rick) Cassidy.

During a break in filming, Holmes approached her. "I've heard about your specialty. I do films for private collectors. Let's get together and do a few loops. Can you really take almost fourteen inches?"

"Just try me," she said.

***

[It was inevitable that the Queen of Porn, Linda Lovelace, would meet the King of Porn, John C. Holmes, since both of them had appeared on the XXX scene at the same time. But whereas she had become porno's first female superstar, based on only one movie, Holmes, in contrast, would appear in some 2,500 movies before his untimely death of AIDS at the age of forty-three in 1988.

Holmes breakthrough movie, Johnny Wadd, *released in 1971, had launched him into his most successful series. In it, and for a fee of $475, he played a "hard-boiled private dick," the character based on Raymond Chandler's creation of the tough private detective, Philip Marlow. This, and other films with the series, would later be on exhibit for the Meese Commission investigating pornography in 1986, at which time both Linda and Holmes would be summoned to testify in Washington, D.C.*

Many producers wanted to hire Linda to deep throat the penis of Holmes, which was optimistically appraised at fourteen inches, although those who measured it claimed that it was thirteen inches (perhaps thirteen and a half), and six inches thick.

As writer John McAbee proclaimed, "In the world of dicks, Holmes was the D-Day, the 1968 NASA moon landing, the JFK assassination, and the invention of television all rolled up in one big, giant cock. His penis truly defined a dick generation that came, but hasn't gone yet."

At least five feature-length scripts were written as potential vehicles for the full-length cinematic pairing of Lovelace with Holmes. None of them was ever filmed.

However, a wealthy homosexual from San Francisco, a man who had previously hired Holmes for sex, hired both performers to make a short loop for his private screenings.

According to Linda: "My sessions with Johnny were filmed in Palm Springs at a private villa. I was told that Liberace, a friend of our backer, would be sent a copy. He was enamored of Holmes, so I was told."

"Before getting intimate with Johnny, I'd heard all these tales about the gals in porn who couldn't take him, and who refused to sample his club."

"But that simple country boy from Ohio proved no big challenge for Linda

235

Lovelace, the expert fellatio queen. I opened up my throat and swallowed him whole. He later told me it was the best blow-job of his life."

"When I got oral with Johnny, his penis grew like Pinocchio's nose. He shot quite a load. Our backer, whose greedy eye lustily took in all the action being filmed by the cameraman, hovered over us. When it came time for Johnny to enter through the rear door, he was about to grease up with Vaseline, I told him, 'No way. I want it natural and rough.'"

"He didn't follow my advice and greased up anyway. Actually, he turned out to be a great lover—very thoughtful, very gentle. He did not break my jaw, he did not split my ass, and he did not tear up my vagina. He's welcome to invade any of my orifices at any time he should desire in the future."

"I liked Johnny a lot, but by the time he got around to wanting me to do those (full length) porn flicks with him, I had bowed out of the game. Too bad. I really liked him."

"When we both kick off, after we're dead, my throat and his dick should be preserved in alcohol in the Erotica Hall of Fame."

Holmes himself would later say, "Unlike Linda Lovelace, no one ever pointed a gun at my head. No one in the porn business ever forced me to do anything I didn't want to do."

Al Goldstein of Screw had plenty to say about Holmes. "He had everything I didn't. He was hung like a horse; me a squirrel is more like it. We're all size queens. I'm not gay, but I thought one day I'd love to suck that cock. Feel that power. Swallow his virility in the same way some African tribes cannibalize their enemy."]

***

"Between jobs, in the months that followed, Chuck and I had run out of money, and we were eating catsup and mustard sandwiches," Linda recalled. "All of a sudden, an offer came in from Damiano. He made me a star overnight. In the next few months, the whole world seemed to be talking about Linda Lovelace. I personally was one of the soldiers who launched America's cultural war."

Linda, responding to a provocative question from porn mega-star **John C. Holmes** *(photo above, with various of his co-stars):*

"Just try me."

CHAPTER SEVEN
The Movie that Changed the World

"Deep Throat poses this question: Can a woman with a misplaced clit find love and sexual togetherness with a man who's hung to the stretch of fourteen inches? Can a girl with a deep throat find deep happiness?"

–Harry Reems

Chuck had heard that Lou ("Butchie") Peraino, son of mob boss Anthony Peraino, Sr., was entering the burgeoning porn business, even though it was illegal. "In the 1920s, booze was outlawed; in the 1950s, dope was, and in the 1970s, porn is, but that's not going to stop us," Butchie said.

Leaving Jersey City that morning with some of Linda's 8mm loops, Chuck had made an appointment to bring her into Peraino's Manhattan office and show him some of her porn. He planned to screen *The Dog Fucker* for the producer.

Once inside the office, it was obvious that Butchie wasn't impressed with either Chuck, Linda, or their films. However, he agreed to see the bestiality loop. Three minutes into the film, he ordered Chuck to turn it off. "We don't do shit like that here. Get out!"

Chuck quickly gathered up his gear and departed with Linda. Out of earshot, she whispered to him, "He thought I was garbage. God, I detested him."

When the doors to the elevator they were waiting for opened, Gerard Damiano emerged. He, too, had an appointment with Butchie that morning. They chatted pleasantly, and he told them about a feature film he was casting. "The title will be either *The Doctor Makes House Calls* or *The Sword Swallower.* It's about a gal who can take the big ones down her throat."

"That's an ideal part for Linda," Chuck interjected.

"But you'd have to convince Butchie in there," she said. "He treated me like I was one big turd."

"I might win him over," Damiano said. "Let's meet around eight o'clock tonight in front of this building. We'll go to dinner and later on to this swingers' club."

After dinner that evening, Damiano escorted them to the private sex club, "Wet Dreams," which had a sign posted: ONLY STRAIGHTS ALLOWED.

By midnight, Damiano had watched Linda fellate six different young men, one of whom was exceptionally well endowed with more than ten inches. "She opened up that throat of hers and gulped it all," her future director said. "She did me but I wasn't that much of a challenge. For the movie, she'd be the ideal lead."

When Damiano proposed casting Linda as the lead to Butchie, he objected almost violently. "It's our god damn money we're wasting on this little hippie girl. The role calls for a bleached blonde with big tits. If she is a gum chewer, all the better. You're not going to waste my Dad's money."

When Damiano invited Linda and Chuck to the studio the next day, he heard the director engaged in a shouting match with Butchie. "Big boobs sell movies!" Butchie yelled. "This Lovelace cunt is flat chested. Besides, I like blondes!"

"Linda is going to be the star of the movie—and that's that!" Damiano said. "It's going to be about a woman whose clitoris is in her throat. She needs a big cock to satisfy her. Most women can't deep throat a guy. Many of them can't take it up the ass without bleeding. Only Linda can do the movie. She can take huge objects in any hole."

Butchie demanded that Damiano film a screen test for Linda "to see if the bitch can talk."

For the test she was asked to recite that old nursery school poem, *Mary Had a Little Lamb.* At first, she gave a dramatic reading, followed by a more mocking version.

LINDA AUDITIONS FOR DEEP THROAT WITH Lou ("Butchie") Peraino

After the test, Damiano told her the part was hers, but Butchie still wasn't convinced.

Fearing that Linda was losing out on the role, Chuck intervened, suggesting that Damiano send Linda into Butchie's office so she could go down on him, and he could witness firsthand her deep throat technique, "up close and personal."

When Damiano proposed the sexual encounter between Butchie and Linda, the producer agreed. "Send the broad in here and have her suck me off. I'll see how good she is."

Before she went in to fellate Butchie, Damiano warned her, "Do a fantastic job on him, convince him you're a real deep throat freak.

238

Otherwise, your ass is in trouble."

She went into his office, finding "the object of my upcoming love making to be in his mid-forties, heavy set, and sloppy. He was loud mouthed, like one of those old-time, cigar-chomping producers pictured in the movies."

For two minutes, he didn't even look up from what he was looking at on his desk. When he finally did, he yelled at her to lock the door and to come over to where he was sitting.

"Let's get this over with," he said. He pulled down his pants and underwear. "Okay, kid, go for it."

Like Damiano, he wasn't much of a challenge, "but I sucked for dear life, and he blasted off after about two minutes. All the while I was going down on Butchie, I imagined I was Marilyn Monroe doing her casting couch bit with some old geaser as a means of breaking into the movies."

When it was over, he rose over her before she could even stand up. He pulled up his jockey shorts and his pants, zipping up. Without thanking her, he said, "Now get the hell out of here! I'm a busy man."

However, during the next few days, he called for Linda when he ate his lunch, which was always a pizza. "I'm giving him head and he's downing anchovies or pepperoni. He hated me, but he sure went for my blow-jobs."

Finally, Butchie green-lighted the project, agreeing to cast Linda as the female star. There were two other lead female roles, and one male lead, but Damiano began shooting without casting them.

Several of the porn scenes were shot in New York before Damiano and his crews, along with Linda and Chuck, transferred to Florida. Linda wrote, "When it comes to studs who can do their thing on camera, New York has always been the place."

Of course, that is no longer true. There's another state loaded with cinematic potentialities for budding porn players: It's called California.

On the set of *Deep Throat,* she said that some of the actors claimed to be "the sturdiest male animals on earth. But once the camera is turned on them, these studs go baby-soft."

In a memoir, she wrote that homosexual actors are the most reliable in producing on-camera erections. "They're the most exhibitionistic. If they're hung, they love to show their wares. They can build a sufficient hard-on, too, as long as it doesn't have to go to work on a girl." She revealed that in *Deep Throat,* there were about a dozen men in the cast,

Butchie's auditor and father, Mafia insider
**Anthony Peraino, Sr.
("Big Tony")**

239

but only six of them were straight guys. She said that the actor who was cast as the psychiatrist in *Deep Throat* "could ball at high noon in Macy's window."

Occasionally, Anthony Peraino, Sr., visited the set "to see how my son, Butchie, is wasting my money." He was always accompanied by five bodyguards, all of them in trenchcoats. Linda likened them to extras in an old Edward G. Robinson movie.

Within the mob, Anthony, Sr. was known as "Big Tony" because he weighed more than 300 pounds. In time, his clan was labeled as "the pornography family," as he was aided by his brother Joe (The Whale) Peraino, Sr., his sons Lou (Butchie) Peraino and Joseph C. Peraino; and his nephew, Joseph Peraino, Jr.

In the *Los Angeles Times,* on June 13, 1982, a report claimed, "Anthony Peraino, Sr., a reputed 'made man' (i.e., officially initiated into the Mafia) was a member of the Joseph Colombo crime family. He police record included six arrests in New York—for gambling, tax evasion, and homicide by auto—but no convictions.

In the late 1950s, Peraino became involved in the burgeoning pornography business. He got in on the ground floor for what turned out to be organized crime's most profitable new business venture since it had entered the arena of narcotics in the 1950s.

Harry Reems came into the studio and volunteered to be one of the actors in the film. Damiano turned him down, but accepted Reems' offer to work as part of the film's production crew for twenty dollars a day.

After the New York-based segments had been filmed, Reems wanted to continue his association with the project from its new base in Florida but Damiano told him it would be too expensive to take him. But eventually, the director agreed to an arrangement wherein Reems would drive Damiano's car from New York to Florida, with the understanding that once he got there, safely and with the car intact, Reems could be part of the production crew for the final segments of the film.

Linda's "Pimpmobile,
Why the 1972 Cadillac will forever be associated with the opening scenes of *Deep Throat*

Eventually, Damiano's blue-and-white Cadillac, the one Reems had driven to Florida from New York, was featured as the car Linda drove in the opening scenes of the movie. She referred to it as "the pimpmobile."

When Chuck learned that Anthony, Sr., would be driving from New York to the new location in Miami, he asked if Linda and he could ride with him. The mob boss agreed, and consequently, the three of them headed south in Anthony, Sr.'s car.

On their way to Florida, Chuck tried to get Linda to service the senior Peraino. Unlike his son, he showed no interest at all, preferring to sleep alone in the motels they stopped at along the way.

At one point, Chuck became so exasperated with Linda, he shouted at her, "Why don't you fondle his crotch while he's driving, unzip him, and give him a blow job?"

Finally, Anthony, Sr., from behind the wheel during the long drive to Florida, gave Chuck a little lecture. "You may not know this, but Italian men don't cheat on their wives. If an Italian gets a good wife, he wants to hold onto her and he will not cheat."

"That was pure bullshit," Linda said. "He just wasn't attracted to me. The moment he got to Florida, he demanded of Damiano, 'Where are the broads?'"

***

The Voyager Inn on Biscayne Boulevard in Miami became the headquarters for the crew and stars of *Deep Throat.*

When Reems finally arrived in Miami with the Cadillac intact, Damiano made good on his promise to employ him, hiring him as a gaffer and grip, but ignoring his pleas to cast him as one of the actors.

Reems wasn't particularly flattered that Damiano could find no actor to play the doctor. "He couldn't have searched far and wide, as he never left the swimming pool and his bottle of Jack Daniels," Reems claimed.

Eric Edwards, years later, asserted that he had been the first actor offered the part eventually interpreted by Reems in *Deep Throat,* but that he had already contracted for a role in a summer stock production at the time. "While Linda was sucking off Reems, I was performing in *The Man of La Mancha.*"

Reems, however, nabbed the role. According to Damiano, "I finally decided to cast Harry as the doctor because no other actor I auditioned could keep it hard. I feared that Harry was overexposed, and I was looking for a fresh piece of meat. As it turned out, it was a good choice, because Linda and Harry had real chemistry between them. He was turned on by her, and she dug him, too. That really pissed off Chuck Traynor, who felt he was losing his grip on Linda."

Chuck obviously noticed the attrac-

Harry Reems,
Deep Throat's horny health industry professional

tion between the two stars. Soon he was referring to Reems as "that asshole." She got several beatings from Chuck for enjoying sex with Reems so much. "But that's what the director wanted!" Linda protested before being slapped hard in the face.

Damiano rehearsed his actors' dialogue until they got it right:

REEMS: *It's not too bad. You should be thankful you have a clitoris at all.*
LINDA: *That's easy for you to say. How would you feel if your balls were in your ears?*
REEMS: *Why, then I could hear myself coming.*

Reems later asserted, "It wasn't really necessary for Linda to open her mouth to say her lines. Any time she opened her mouth, I was there to fill it."

Actually, in the final cut maybe only three different cocks were used for the cum shots, with footage spliced together in sometimes explosive repetitions. "One of those big ones, by the way, was Chuck's," Linda originally claimed.

In later accounts, Linda and Damiano differed in their assessments of Chuck's erections. She had asserted in a memoir that Chuck's erect penis, not his face, was depicted in some shots within the final film. But in contrast, Damiano claimed, "Chuck couldn't get it up on the *Deep Throat* set,"

Damiano seems to have had truth on his side. His claim was bolstered years later, when Linda asserted that Chuck had personally inserted that favorable piece of public relations for himself into her memoirs, and that the appearance of his dick within the film never happened.

***

For Linda, her first day of work on the set of *Deep Throat* turned out to be her best until violence broke out that evening. "Harry loved me, and I thought he was wonderful. The crew treated me with respect, and I was enjoying performing."

At around three o'clock that afternoon, Chuck cornered her. "What in fuck is going on? You've been walking around with a smile all day. I noticed that every time you see a man, your eyes go immediately to his crotch to see how big his package is. You smile at Damiano. But you really come on to that asshole Reems. You're practically salivating every time he walks onto the set."

"You ordered me to pretend to enjoy the sex," she protested.

Later that evening, Damiano threw a drunken party in the motel next to the bedroom Linda shared with Chuck. She wanted to attend, but he refused to let her. For no apparent reason, perhaps jealousy, perhaps out of fear that he was losing control of her, he launched his attack.

"You cunt!" he screamed before socking her hard in both the face and on her chest. "That fucking smile. All day long, that fucking smile. Well, let's see how you smile now." His fist plowed into her stomach. When she collapsed, he kicked her thighs.

"You told me to smile," she shouted back at him. "You claimed I looked too sad."

When he kicked her again, she yelled at him, "You're crazy! You need a shrink!"

"When I finish with you, bitch, you'll be the one in need of a doctor." He attacked her again as she lay on the floor. She rolled herself into a tight ball, trying to protect her breasts and stomach. "Help!" she screamed, hoping that someone at the party next door would come to her aid. The sounds of drunken revelry suddenly stopped. It was obvious that the partygoers could hear her getting beaten up.

Chuck picked her up off the floor and tossed her against the wall. She was certain that the crowd next door heard the crash.

Jumping up, she ran screaming into the bathroom and locked the door. She turned on the shower. When she dared re-enter the bedroom, Chuck was sitting in his underwear, watching a Western on TV.

"May I go to sleep now?" she asked.

"Hell, yes," he said. "I don't give a fuck what you do. You're just a whore. I'm ashamed to call you my wife."

The next day on the set, her make-up did not conceal all her bruises, which later would be seen by millions of people around the world.

***

With Reems and Linda as the film's leads, Damiano went on to cast the two starring female roles, awarding them to Carol Connors and Dolly Sharp.

Born in 1952, actress Carol Connors (aka

243

Carol Kaiser) was one of the four stars of *Deep Throat*, cast as the nurse to Reems' role as the doctor. Between the filming of *Deep Throat* in 1972 and 1986, she appeared in about twenty XXX-rated films, the most visible of which included *The Erotic Adventures of Candy* and its sequel, *Candy Goes to Hollywood*. She is best known for her ongoing involvement in *The Gong Show*, performing as the girl who introduced the show's host, Chuck Barris, every week at the debut of each episode. Later, she married actor Jack Birch, who also performed in porn.

Miss Connors (or Miss Kaiser) is the mother of the Emmy-nominated Thora Birch, a leading child actor during the 1990s, who evolved into more mature performances in *American Beauty* (1999) and the cult film, *Ghost World* (2001).

Throughout *Deep Throat*, Connors, playing a nurse, engaged repeatedly in sex with her boss, the doctor, as portrayed by Reems.

The fourth lead went to Dolly Sharp. An overview of her was posted on-line by an anonymous but accurate fan. It referred to her as "a thick-set strumpet who looked more like a greasy spoon waitress than a sexual superstar." She had fake eyelashes and a curvaceous figure that featured some up-front "bra busters."

Dolly got her start posing for nudist magazines in the 1960s. Prior to her filming of *Deep Throat*, she had appeared in a series of softcore "grinders," the most visible of which was entitled *The Weirdos and the Oddballs*.

In *Deep Throat*, the sexually liberated Dolly takes on the studs after they

Porn diva **Dolly Sharp**

Enraged, on-set, by the intensity of Linda's sexual bonding with her husband

emerge from Linda's bedroom. Some of her "down and dirty" anal expertise was also featured. As one critic wrote, "Dolly proved to be a gal who would do *anything* and *everything* on screen."

In the movie, Linda can get no satisfaction from the many studs she hooks up with, each of whom attack her anally and vaginally. Finally, in frustration, she visits a quack doctor (Reems) whose diagnosis reveals that her clitoris has migrated northward to her throat. Consequently, he inserts his penis into her mouth as a means of delivering a clitoral climax.

Grateful for his accurate diagnosis, the character she plays declares her love for him, believing that he is Mr. Right. She wants to marry him, but he's already taken by his nurse, with whom he's having a torrid affair. He tells her that she needs to find a stud with at least a nine-inch penis, big enough to reach the inner recesses of her throat.

The plot continues with his offer to her of a job as a physical therapist, working with his patients on whatever ails them.

Linda and Reems agreed that the insertion of humor was what helped make *Deep Throat* a super-grosser. In one scene, Linda as a nurse gives an elderly Jewish man a blow-job in his hospital bed.

OLD MAN: *Linda, listen, that was marvelous. Can you come by and give me treatment like that every day?*
LINDA: *Well, I don't know...*
OLD MAN: *Magnificent, Linda. A thing like this, my poor wife, she could never do it.*
LINDA: *I just don't know. It's expensive, and...*
OLD MAN: *Don't worry. I got Blue Cross.*

One of the funniest scenes in the movie was when Helen (Dolly Sharp) receives the grocery boy who has communicated, awkwardly, his attraction to her. He allows him to go down on her. During the course of cunnilingus, she asks him, "Do you mind if I smoke while you're eating?"

Reems said that he felt sorry for the actor who played the grocery boy. He was identified in the film's credits only as "Tony."

"The kid was a nice guy, in his early twenties," Reems said. "He wanted to be a movie star, seen by millions of people. But all they saw was the back of his head, bobbing up and down."

For one scene in *Deep Throat,* Damiano acquired a hollow-core glass dildo for use as a prop in the film. The scene called for one of the actors to drink Coca-Cola from a straw inserted into the dildo's interior. At first, Linda was afraid that the glass would break "and cut me all to pieces."

The coke-filled glass dildo was inserted into Linda's vagina, and the actor began to drink with his straw. But something caused her to burst into

DANGER!

The photo above illustrates a **hollow** (and therefore dangerously fragile) **glass dildo** manufactured in Shenzen, in China's Guangdong Province, near Hong Kong.

LOVELACE'S CONSUMER ALERT:

Take Linda's advice and use equivalent devices at your own risk!

laughter. The dildo shot out from her vagina and flew through the air. (She later referred to it as "a pussy fart".) On impact, the dildo shattered. "My vaginal muscles were doing their job," she later said.

Reems referred to Sharp as "a sex machine" and made the preposterous assertion that "she had the ability to accommodate half a dozen cocks simultaneously."

Sharp insisted that her husband, Billy Sharp, be hired as one of the actors. Consequently, he was cast as the bandit who appears near the film's ending. The script makes clear the premise that the character played by Linda has found her perfect mate, a man whose monstrous cock satisfies her "throat clitoris" to complete satisfaction.

Yet Linda, in the film, returns to her doctor (Reems) the following day, complaining that her beloved has a fourteen-inch dick, and that she wanted only eleven. "Can you help me, Dr. Young? Can't you do something?"

"Nothing to it, Miss Lovelace," the doctor assures her. "We'll operate. We'll cut off three inches."

Behind the scenes around this time as filming progressed, Dolly Sharp one day became furious with her husband during his filming of a love scene with Linda. According to Reems, "Billy and Linda were really going at it, and it was obvious they were digging it. Cannons could have gone off, and they would not have heard."

"When Billy exploded, it was in buckets," Reems said.

"I love it! I love it!" Linda shouted

At the end of the scene's filming, Dolly stormed over and slapped her husband really hard. "She dragged him off the set, and we never saw him again," Reems said.

***

Some of the scenes in *Deep Throat* were shot in the Coconut Grove mansion of Baron Joseph (Sepy) de Bicske Debronyi, the Hungary-born sculptor, royal crown jeweler, aristocrat, art collector, world traveler, movie maker, pilot, wine connoisseur, sportsman, playboy, and *bon vivant*. The raffish expatriate, thanks to his ascots, his silk smoking jackets, and his high-flying sense of ostentatious hedonism, was known as the Hugh Hefner of Miami.

When Linda met him, he was wearing a snakeskin vest, snakeskin pants, and snakeskin boots. "I prefer only rattlesnake skin," he told her. "I like that particular snake because its venom brings a quick death."

Linda was mesmerized by him, and actually wanted to dump Chuck and become his mistress. Damiano had sent Chuck to Miami to purchase supplies when Sepy showed Linda around his mansion. He was a walking autobiography of his own life.

The Baron had one favorite subject and that was himself. He told her he'd been a pilot in the Hungarian Air Force during World War II. "I was once an interpreter for the American Military Mission, as I speak six languages. Later, in Stockholm, I worked with the crown jewelers for the Swedish Royal Family. I designed the brooch that Folke Bernadotte *(Editor's note: Count of Wisborg, Swedish diplomat, and grandson of Sweden's King Oscar II)* gave Princess Elizabeth when she became engaged to Philip."

"I later lived in Cuba, where I became close friends with Ernest Hemingway and Errol Flynn, even Nat King Cole. While I was in Cuba, I supplied blonde American showgirls to Fulgencio Batista before he was overthrown by Fidel Castro."

LINDA'S HUNGARIAN RHAPSODY

MEMOIRS OF A ROUÉ
Romantically *Schtupping* in Coconut Grove

Two views *(top photos)* of the hedonistic socialite
Baron Joseph (Sepy) de Bicske Debronyi

(lower photo) The living room of his famously eroticized house where scenes from *Deep Throat* were filmed.

She was awed by some of the artifacts of his world travels, including 120-pound elephant tusks, two Nepalese temple lion statues, six Tibetan yak-wool rugs, and his brass-plated nude sculptures. Baron Sepy was renowned for his bronze and gold sculptures of famous celebrities, including the controversial 42-inch tall golden statue of a nude Anita Ekberg. "She posed for me, but I think it ended her marriage when it appeared in the August, 1956 issue of *Playboy.* Hefner was a friend of mine."

He also showed her bronze nudes he'd sculpted of Raquel Welch and Brigitte Bardot, both of whom he claimed to have had flings with. Linda didn't know if he were telling the truth.

"You're not making this up, are you?" she asked skeptically.

"Hell, no!" he said. "I'm famous for my seductions of the stars—Lena Horne, Jayne Mansfield, Ava Gardner, Joan Crawford. I had a torrid affair with my fellow Hungarian, Eva Gabor, who threatened suicide when I dumped her."

"I fucked Carmen Miranda. Even

Errol Flynn one night in Jamaica, when I was designing his home. Frank Sinatra, even Barry Goldwater, were friends of mine. Frank and I often fucked the same girl in the same bed."

"After I fucked Linda Christian, she told me that her hubby, Tyrone Power, would love to get fucked by me, too."

"He also threw out the name of Debbie Reynolds, but I didn't quite believe that," Linda said. "Not our sweet Debbie, not Tammy."

"If you're in Miami at Christmas, you must come to my topless Christmas Yuletide party," Sepy told her.

"He was a fantastic human being, and his house [was] a shrine to sex," Linda later claimed. "After I gave him what he called 'the best blow job of my life,' he sampled my other two holes. All this took place in his bed, which was a replica of a Viking ship. The way we moved around in that bed, it was a sail across stormy seas. I proposed marriage to him, but he told me that he already was married, although he wasn't certain which exact wife of his he was actually wed to at the present moment."

Having divorced New York heiress Amy Green Brown, Sepy was actually married to Annette Nordquist, a statuesque Swedish blonde. At the time, he was in the throes of divorce, eventually becoming the first person in Miami to file for a no-fault marriage dissolution under a revised state divorce law activated in 1971.

Sepy fell out with Linda when she "extolled my physical properties" in her 1973 autobiography." I was shocked—shocked, I tell you—at that gal's indiscretion. Please, I can provide better references to my sexual prowess than Linda Lovelace—Lana Turner, Rita Hayworth, and even Tallulah Bankhead. Miss Bankhead and I did it in my pool when she was performing in a Tennessee Williams play in Coconut Grove."

"Sepy did make a prediction that came true," Linda said. "He told me that *Deep Throat* would make me a big name movie star and that I, too, would one day be featured in Hefner's *Playboy.*"

***

The filming of *Deep Throat* wrapped on January 3, 1972. "It would been finished sooner, but several members of the crew got so turned on by the action that they had to excuse themselves to go to the bathroom to take care of their hard-ons," Linda said.

The sixty-one minute movie was very tongue-in-cheek with dialogue and songs. Fireworks go off and bells ring during Linda's onscreen orgasms.

At the end of filming, Linda claimed, "It was no big deal. It'll open and close within the week."

"No, I think you're wrong," Damiano said. "I think we've got something here…something sensational."

"We had our problems during the shoot," Reems recalled. "The January weather acted like London. All the cocks hired, except mine, went limp."

That was only partially true.

Originally budgeted at $18,000, *Deep Throat* ended up costing $25,000 because Damiano wanted original music, including the theme song, "Deep Throat," which he wrote himself.

For the totality of her work as the star of the film, Linda was paid only $1,200, but Chuck confiscated the money and she never received a penny of it.

Damiano told Reems, who was his friend, that the mob had agreed to pay him $15,000 in $500 monthly installments, for his direction.

Reems claimed he "did seven of the nine cum shots in the film." He ended up getting $250 for his work on the film. "I made $35 every time I blasted off on camera." Out of these meager earnings, he had to pay his own airfare back to New York.

In his memoirs, he deliberately misstated the names of the backers of the film, referring to them as Lou and Tony Perry. Actually the real names of the backers were Anthony Peraino, Sr. and his son. Lou, known as Butchie.

The movie concludes with the line: THE END AND DEEP THROAT TO YOU ALL.

***

After making *Deep Throat,* Linda almost forgot about it and pressed on with the emergencies of her life. As she stated, "It would be months before the film would open, more months before anyone would hear about it, still more months before the name Linda Lovelace would become known throughout the world."

She also forgot about Harry Reems, although he had seemed to genuinely love her, albeit briefly. He, too, would become a movie star—a porn star, that is—but a movie star nonetheless. "To me, Clark Gable was a movie star, perhaps Al Pacino or Dustin Hoffman. But Harry Reems?" Linda said.

During their transit back to Jersey City, Chuck picked up a sixteen-year-old hitchhiker who called herself "Ginger." Not a great looker, she took Chuck's bait about becoming a hooker. "Look, you've obviously been giving it away," he told her. "So why not get paid for it?"

After enduing repeated child molestation from her father, with no help from her mother, Ginger had run away from home.

Back in the New York area, Chuck was more determined than ever to make it as a filmmaker. Borrowing an 8mm camera from Butchie Peraino, he set out to make two movies starring both Linda and Ginger. The first one called *The Foot* was a variation of the film she'd shot previously (co-starring with a man) in Miami. The new version of *The Foot* was made with Linda receiving Ginger's foot.

That was followed with *The Fist,* also shot with Ginger, following the exact same plot line, except that this time, Ginger used her fist to probe inside Linda, instead of her foot.

Butchie paid Chuck one-hundred dollars for each 8mm flick, enough money to finance a trip back to Florida. During their last night in Jersey City, Chuck, for his own amusement, tried to promote some lesbian action between Linda and Ginger. But Ginger protested loudly and told him to leave her alone.

Linda admired her rebellious spirit, even though she was just a young girl. Once again, Linda was consumed with the idea that she, too, should be able to run away from Chuck or at the very least, stand up to him.

Before dawn one Monday morning, Chuck, Linda, and Ginger headed south.

During the course of this newest southbound migration, their first stopover was in North Carolina as part of Chuck's long-delayed visit to his neglected mother. Linda dreaded having to confront the woman.

A Star is Born: **Linda Lovelace**

She met them at her front door, a small woman in late middle age with dyed raven black hair and more make-up than a transvestite in a drag show. Her heavy eye shadow made her look like Vampira.

Over dinner that night, she relived her glory days when she was a gun moll for the Mafia. "They called me Flower Lady because I ran a florist shop that was a front for the mob. My career kept me too busy to raise a son, so I dumped the kid at my parents' home," she told Linda.

To her, Chuck was her "Chucky-Poo," and she obviously adored him, bragging about his exploits as both a Marine and a pilot. None of the stories she told about his adventures had anything to do with reality. Perhaps they were fantasies he'd shared with her.

On the second day of the maternal visit, Ginger and Chuck got into a fight over how she was washing a car. Ginger packed her suitcases, hitting the open road, hoping to be picked up by a trucker.

Chuck and Linda would never see her again.

***

Continuing with their southbound trip back to Miami, Linda felt she was back where she had started from, with no hope, no prospects. "I became a hooker again, turning tricks for Chuck."

In the immediate aftermath of her filming of *Deep Throat,* "I went to bed with lots of men—white, black, Hispanics—but they had my body, not me," Linda claimed. "They did all sorts of things to my body, but I was on a cloud far away. For weeks at a time, I didn't know who Linda Lovelace was. Chuck called me his 'old old lady,' but I never felt for a moment that I was Mrs. Chuck Traynor. He was my pimp, nothing else, certainly not a husband."

He warned her that if he ever got arrested again for illegal activities, it would be her duty as his wife 'to fuck anything and anybody, from the judge to all the jurors, to get me out. That's what wives do.'"

He was selling her for $25, but he instructed her to do all sorts of extras for a man. "Lick his armpits, lick anything, including his ass, but try to bring home $45. Fifty dollars would make me love you more."

Every day, she plotted her escape. When he booked her to service a trick at a Howard Johnson's Motel, she began to plot how she might escape. Her longtime friend, Betsy Quinn, lived only a mile from that motel.

After a long separation, she called Betsy, who was still living at the same address, except that she had a new man in her life, Kevin Hodges, who had been a football player in high school. Betsy and Kevin, Linda was told, had jointly produced two girls.

Over the phone, Linda poured out to Betsy her accounts of the abuse she'd suffered from Chuck, and the degrading experiences she'd had serving sexual partners with bizarre tastes and requests.

Her girlfriend shocked Linda when she told her that she and her boyfriend, Kevin, "had seen that god damn dog movie. I told Kevin you weren't really like that."

Linda wanted to ask what she and Kevin were doing renting a movie about a dog fucking a woman, but she didn't dare bring that up, since she didn't want to alienate Betsy.

Throwaway Children

"Ginger"
Porn performer & runaway teen

After a twenty-minute conversation, Betsy agreed that she'd get Kevin to drive to the motel and rescue her. She promised that she'd be in the car with him.

At eight o'clock that night, Chuck delivered her to the motel. He parked at the entrance with the motor running and accompanied her inside the lobby. He pressed the right button in the elevator for her and instructed her "to give it your all—the works. I need money."

She had no intention of servicing the trick, and through a complicated series of evasive maneuvers through the motel's side entrance, she managed to locate the car where Betsy and Kevin were waiting, with its engine running. During their drive away from the motel, and away from Chuck, Linda poured out the horrors of her life.

"We'll do everything we can for you," Kevin promised.

The next few days passed as an unremembered blank in Linda's life. "I lived in their guest bedroom as if I was in a coma," she later recalled. "At any minute I expected Chuck to burst in through the door. I didn't really think I had escaped him."

Betsy's home had been rented from the chief honcho of the local branch of Hell's Angels. It reflected his motorcycle-gang tastes. "The mirrored ceiling in my bedroom and the waterbed suggested that the room had been used for many an orgy. There was a movie projector right near by bed. I didn't know if I were being filmed or not."

After a week, Chuck figured out where Linda was, and began to call Betsy, asserting that Linda had thrown a temper fit when he wouldn't buy her a new car, which was not true.

After refusing to talk to Chuck at least a dozen times, Linda finally agreed to pick up the phone when he called. At first, she didn't recognize his voice. He seemed like a different man, telling her how much he loved her and how he couldn't live without her. "Don't forget you are my wife and I am your husband. We belong together. We can make it work. I'll drive over in about an hour."

Even the sound of his voice terrified her. She screamed into the phone, "I'm never coming back!" She slammed down the receiver.

Based on the fury in his voice the next time he called, "Dr. Jekyll had turned into Mr. Hyde," Linda said. "Suddenly, I was 'The Cunt' again. He told me to go and look outside the window, where I'd spot a red van. I did. I think the van belonged to a fireman who had testified for him on that drug charge, asserting that they were forming a sky-diving club."

"You're not leaving me, bitch, if I have to kill you and Betsy, too. There's a machine gun in the van with grenades. My guys—there are three of them—will blow the place sky high. Betsy's brains will be splattered all over her living room."

He claimed that he was on his way over to kidnap her. At first, she was tempted to call the police, but she knew a search of the house would turn up everything from pot to cocaine, from LSD to mescaline, and all sorts of porno movies.

Kevin was not in the house when she walked into the living room to find Betsy watching TV. "I've got to go back to him," Linda said. "Otherwise, he's threatening to blow up this house and to kill all of us."

"He's been making those threats to me all week," she claimed. "I'm not afraid. You don't have to go. We'll stand by you."

Linda was in the bedroom when Chuck arrived forty-five minutes later. By that time, Kevin had returned with a six-pack. He let Chuck in.

"I've come for my wife," Chuck told him. "My old lady is going back where she belongs."

Both Kevin and Betsy turned to look at Linda, seeking her reaction.

"Linda, do you want to go with this man?" Kevin asked.

"I'd better," she said, "for safety reasons. I've gathered up all my stuff, and I'm sorry to have put you through all this."

Betsy rushed to kiss her. "We're always here for you if you need us."

"She won't ever be needing you again, because this is the last time she's ever running away," Chuck told them.

From the driver's seat of his car, for a long time, he didn't say anything, motoring through the night in an ominous silence. She realized he was seething with rage. "That red van is following us," she said. "Who's in it? It's an awfully big van."

"You might as well know," he said. "You know you've got to be punished. I know you know that. My boys, all good friends of mine, have got to get something out of this for their trouble. It's Saturday night. By the time Monday morning comes, you will have lost count of how many times you were raped!"

***

Linda knew she'd face some kind of ongoing punishment for having left Chuck. In the days and weeks ahead, "I became his garbage dump."

She was back working as a hooker, turning tricks with strange men while he spied on her through a peephole. He also enjoyed exposing her, taking her to a fast-food joint and insisting she wear no underwear. He'd order her to hike her skirt up around her hips, exposing her vagina. Her legs apart, her genitals were clearly visible. He seemed to enjoy the shocked reaction of the other diners.

When driving, he would order her to become topless, and then he'd steer up against any army truck or bus fill with school boys or athletes, seemingly enjoying their hoots and hollers at Linda. One afternoon, when she was sunning herself in a garden, he took a garden hose and inserted it into her anus, then turned the water pressure on to full blast.

Sometimes, he bartered her, selling her to a storekeeper for a pair of binoculars, or whatever. When he needed clothes, he sent her into a store to see if she could service some of the salesmen in the dressing rooms in exchange for free underwear or slacks for himself.

He destroyed anything she liked, as when she was given a suede belt with fringes. He cut it up into small pieces.

One afternoon, her parents finally tracked her down. He'd ordered her to sit naked on the sofa while he watched television.

At the sound of their knock on the door, she jumped up and looked out the window to confront her mother and father. As she rushed for her robe, he blocked her access to it, demanding that she open the door in the nude. In her comments later, while relaying the incident, she said that her parents hadn't seen her in the nude since she was a little girl. He removed his gun from a nearby drawer and told her he'd blow her head off if she didn't open that door stark naked.

Her father looked extremely embarrassed to see his daughter so inappropriately dressed, especially in light of the duration of their absence. Her mother, in contrast, looked at her with utter disgust.

Finally, Chuck threw her robe to her. "Cover yourself! That's no way to go to the door!"

During their dialogues after their long separation, the Boremans revealed that someone had delivered an anonymous message stating that she was in dire need of help. The message had not originated with Linda. Perhaps Betsy had sent it.

Chuck assured the Boremans that everything was all right, and that they were living a normal life together as a loving man and wife.

After twenty minutes of idle chatter, Mrs. Boreman excused herself to go to the bathroom. Within a minute or so, Linda followed her, assuming that Chuck would not break in on them in the toilet.

Once they were alone, Linda blurted out her woes. She spoke of being beaten to "a bloody pulp," and of being forced into prostitution. "Mother, he even forces me to make porno movies, one with a German shepherd. He turns lesbians loose on me. If I don't obey him, he's threatening to kill me."

"Now, now," her mother responded. "You must remember, he's your husband. You must obey him. You also must stop with this obscene talk. If you are going to tell lies on Chuck, at least speak of something that is believable. Sex with a dog? Do you think I'm a total moron? That's disgusting."

"Oh, mother, you don't understand," Linda said.

"There's another thing: Your little boy is beautiful, healthy, and well cared for by his guardians," Mrs. Boreman said. "They're willing to let you see the child if you want to. I'll drive you over to their house."

"Oh, no, I can't," she said. "I'm not living a life that would allow me to properly take care of a baby."

"It's obvious you're a bad wife to long-suffering Chuck," Mrs. Boreman said, "but on top of it all, you're also a bad mother."

When Linda and her mother returned together to the living room, her father stood up and looked at her sternly. "Chuck has told me what you've been doing," he said. "While he's out trying to earn a living and provide a home for you, you're running around with other men."

"Oh, father!" she said, in exasperation. "Why don't you and mother just get out the fucking door and don't come back?"

In tears, she ran to her bedroom. Outside her open window, she could hear Chuck telling her parents goodbye. "She's been a bad girl, a bad wife, but I've stood by her even though she's broken my heart time and time again. She makes up the wildest stories. Maybe I should take her to a psychiatrist. She'll run off with a perfect stranger and have sex with him. I'm afraid she's either going to get some dreadful disease or else meet up with a murderer one night."

"Chuck, we admire you for forgiving her her sins and not divorcing her," Mrs. Boreman said. "You're a good man and a good son-in-law. We trust you to look after our daughter. Maybe she'll find Jesus and grow out of this and cease to be this wild gal."

When Linda heard her parents drive off, she dreaded whatever new punishment Chuck would inflict upon her. She was going to have to pay for cornering her mother in the bathroom and telling her what was really going on in her life. Even though he hadn't heard her exact words, she had the feeling that he had intuitively sensed that she had confessed to her mother many of the most sordid details of their marriage.

There was no punishment that night, He did not even come into the bedroom.

He always woke up before she did, and she came into the kitchen as he was cooking his own breakfast.

He ate in silence. As he rose from his chair, he told her he had to drive into Homestead, a city thirty-five miles southwest of Miami, to buy some more film. "We've got to make some more loops," he said. "You're not earning enough money to keep us in rice and beans."

He returned late that afternoon, at around five o'clock. He presented her with a halter and a pair of skimpy hot pants. "Put these on," he said. "I've got a booking for you tonight."

She didn't like the sound of that. "What kind of booking?" she asked, her suspicions mounting.

"That, my dear wife, is for me to know and for you to find out."

***

That night without explanation, Chuck drove her to Miami's International Airport where a private plane was waiting to fly her to Nassau. There, a limousine waited at the airport to drive them across New Providence Island to the bridge that led to the adjacent Paradise Island. She'd been flown to The Bahamas before by the heiress Joe Carstairs.

In spite of repeated requests, Chuck refused to tell her why she was being flown out of Miami. It was all very mysterious.

In a residential neighborhood of Paradise Island, a Bahamian chauffeur deposited Linda, with Chuck, at the entrance to a villa whose décor was inspired by the Arabian Nights. An Arab boy greeted them and directed them to a lavishly furnished guest cottage. Two young Bahamian men carried their meager luggage to their quarters.

Finally, Chuck filled her in on why she was here. "We're going to make a movie."

"But you didn't bring any equipment," she protested.

"Never mind. Everything I'll need we'll find here."

He wouldn't give her any more information. At nine o'clock, a lavish dinner was served, consisting of exotic specialties along with Bahamian lobster. She hadn't eaten this well since leaving Whale Cay.

The following afternoon, Chuck disappeared into the main house to arrange details of the filming that was scheduled to begin that night.

"Isn't there a script or something?" she asked.

"Don't worry, I will tell you what to do later," he said, before leaving. "In the meanwhile, relax around the pool, get a suntan, enjoy yourself. You can't live like this every day. For anything you want, dial 1 and a servant will bring it to you."

At around sunset, Chuck returned to their cottage, warning her not to eat anything until after midnight. "We don't want you to go in front of the camera with a bloated stomach."

At around 8pm, Chuck led her to a small outbuilding whose interior looked something like a theater in the round. Six elegant divans had been placed around the perimeter of the circle, each prefaced with a table loaded with food and drink.

"What is this?" she asked.

"You'll find out." He led her into a large dressing room.

"Is this where I'm to get into my costume?" she asked.

"There is no costume," he said. "You appear nude in the film."

"How unusual for me," she said, sarcastically.

"Don't give me any lip, bitch."

There was a knock on the door, and Chuck opened it to admit an extremely handsome young man with olive skin and raven-black hair. He had piercing brown eyes so dark they appeared nearly black, giving them an air of mystery. Dark circles below them looked almost like eye shadow. His face looked as if it had been sculpted, with a long and straight nose and a lower lip which was appealingly larger than its upper counterpart. He wore a form-fitting white T-shirt, sandals, and a pair of blue jeans that looked two sizes too small, outlining a massive package.

"Hi!" he said. "I'm Shawn Cole. I'm going to be your co-star in tonight's film."

It was obvious that he'd already met Chuck, who viewed him with a certain jealousy. Chuck moved to answer the door, where a waiter was bringing fresh water.

"Glad to meet you, Shawn," she said.

"Right before I left New York, I saw *Deep Throat.* You were terrific in it. What technique! I'm a porn star myself in West Hollywood."

This was among the first clues that *Deep Throat* had opened. She wanted to ask so much more, but Chuck reappeared, telling them they had to get undressed. Then, quickly, he left to check on the equipment and the lights in the arena.

"What's going on here?" she asked, checking her make-up. "Chuck told me nothing."

"This vacation compound is owned by an oil-rich Sheik from Saudi Arabia. He's on holiday here with his five grown sons. He wants me to bring you out into the arena where I mock you as an American slave. Arabs get off on buying American women as whores. After some sexual acrobatics with me, you're to go down on each of the Arabs, beginning with the Sheik, who's in his 60s. After that, each of them will fuck you on their individual divans. Are you game?"

"What choice do I have?" she asked.

As she'd done before so many other men, she began to strip. Standing six feet tall, Sean kicked off his sandals, pulled off his T-shirt, and unbuttoned his blue jeans, revealing that he wore no underwear.

"My god," she said. "Your dick is gorgeous…and big."

"Nine and a half inches," he said. "I have a dildo on the market modeled after my dick."

He went over to one of the sofas and removed a slave collar with a metal chain from a paper bag resting there. "Forgive me, I've got to put this on you."

"It wouldn't be the first time," she said. As he fastened the collar around her neck, she felt like some big dog being chained.

Shawn reached into his bag and removed his fetish gear.

Chuck came back into the dressing room. "The Sheik and his sons have taken their places. They're eating imported dates and enjoying their drinks." He turned to Linda. "There are only six of them, hardly a challenge for a cunt who took on fifteen fraternity boys from the U of M in one night."

"Okay, we're ready," Shawn said. "I've got it down as to what I'm to do."

"The Sheik is paying us a lot of money for this, so don't you guys fuck it up," Chuck said as a final warning. "There's a clock on the wall over there. Wait five minutes and then I want you, Shawn, to appear, with Linda trailing you in chains."

"Gotcha," Shawn said. Linda chose to say nothing at all. This didn't seem like the kind of film that required rehearsals.

With trepidation, she was led out into the arena like some slave on the auction block in ancient Egypt. She couldn't make out the faces of the six men on the perimeter of her "arena." She did determine that each of them wore white bathrobes, but only the center of the stage was spotlighted.

"I'll try to make it easy for you," Shawn whispered in her ears. "But I have my instructions. Don't take it personally. I actually like you."

***

Two separate cameras were turned on Shawn and Linda to catch the action from different perspectives. With Shawn in control of her leash, she was exhibited under the spotlight shining into the center of the arena. Embarrassed and humiliated, her head was lowered. The kindness and gentleness Shawn had displayed during their initial meeting disappeared before the camera. He jerked her collar, forcing her to raise her head to face her potential rapists.

"This American bitch dog is not worthy of you," he shouted to the Sheik.

"We shall see, we shall see," the Sheik responded in accented English.

Five Bahamian boys in rich silk robes worked the arena, serving the food and refilling the goblets of the Arabs.

Shawn forced her to turn around and to stand before the men with her buttocks exposed. He whispered to her, "Arabs prefer the ass on a woman, and they want to see yours." Then he ordered her to bend over and use her hands to spread apart her ass cheeks. She felt relieved that the men approved, because she heard them, as if in unison, shout, "Ahhhhhh!"

Suddenly, without warning, Shawn began to run around the perimeter of the arena, forcing her, by jerks on her collar, to trot along after him. After a few minutes of this, he came to a sudden halt. Again, she compared herself to a dog,

258

perhaps one competing in some canine exhibition.

"We like to see dancing girls," the old Sheik said. "Make her dance." With that, Shawn backed away. The chain attached to her collar stretched at least ten feet, allowing her room to dance. Remembering routines she'd learned in New York, she began a sensual dance for them.

This continued for five or so minutes before Shawn pulled the chain, causing her to fall onto the floor. She heard the sound of laughter from the audience.

Shawn then led her to a position directly in front of the gathering's patriarch.

"The unworthy slave would like to give your glorious sex the greatest of pleasures," Shawn announced.

She kneeled down before him and took his soft penis, curled up like a snake, and put it in her mouth. Slowly, he began to respond. It uncoiled and eventually penetrated her throat. She worked on him furiously, but his breathing became heavy and irregular, and she feared that he might be having a heart attack. Finally, he exploded, grunting and moaning. He gripped the back of her head until his breathing returned to normal and his penis softened.

"You have a silken throat," he said. "He motioned for her to service a young man who lounged beside him. "My oldest and favorite son," the Sheik said, without putting a name to him.

The oldest son looked to be in his twenties. When he opened his robe, he displayed a well-developed body with six-pack abs. He obviously lifted weights. His penis was relatively small, though it appeared to have a mushroom head. "Eat, dog woman!" he commanded her.

In spite of his undesirable personality, she moved to deep throat him. The session lasted for only about three minutes. "In my home country, I have two blonde boys kidnapped from Vienna. They are better than you. Move on, unworthy dog."

The next son appeared to be about nineteen. Unlike the other, more masculine boys, he was the effeminate son. He wore a gold earring and a gold necklace studded with diamonds and rubies. His almost pencil-thin penis had a small head. Of the sons, she suspected that from a woman's point of view, he was the least desirable. After five minutes, he came in her mouth and quickly removed himself and tightened his robe around him. A young Bahamian boy appeared to refill his goblet. The Arab seemed more interested in the waiter than in Linda, and she just assumed he was a homosexual, living in a land where that was almost a death sentence.

A **Shawn** Lookalike

A set of twins, perhaps no more than seventeen,

were her next challenge. Their looks were as average as their cocks. In a school playground, they would be the bullies. After an argument as to who would go first, one of the twins won out. Linda could easily take him in her mouth, but there was a twist to the game. Normally, she would never gag, but one of these evil twins grabbed her by the throat and slowly, inexorably, began squeezing on its sides, restricting her flow of air. Despite his slowly tightening grip on her throat, she nevertheless felt forced to continue trying to service his brother. When he finally let up and inserted his dick into her mouth, the other brother switched roles and attempted to strangle her as well.

She would later refer to that scene within the larger context around her as an incidence of oral rape and strangulation. For their finale, both of the twins inserted their cocks into her mouth simultaneously, and she brought them to a joint climax.

Then, in full-frontal view of the Arabs, Shawn slapped her, hard, on the face. "Thank the twins!" he shouted at her.

"Thank you, kind sirs, for letting my unworthy self service your glorious penises!" she said.

The final Arab son, who appeared to be no more than sixteen, if that, would become one of the biggest challenges of her career. Unlike the others, he had chestnut-colored hair and was by far the most handsome of the lot. He didn't look like an Arab at all, but the scion of the Sheik's mating with a European woman, perhaps German.

When he opened his robe and exposed himself, she gasped. His penis was a sexual deformity. In her past, she'd known dozens of men with longer cocks, but not since her experience back in North Carolina with Sam Phillips had she seen one that was thicker, or with such a gigantic head. She feared how large it would become when erect.

"You can try, unworthy one," he said to her. "Others have failed."

As his cock began to stir to life, she rushed to take it in her mouth before it swelled up any larger. For the first time, she feared she could not make it.

Pre-cum was already oozing from his penis as she began to run her tongue over it.

"The miserable American Dog Woman cannot satisfy me," the young boy told Shawn.

"She will do it or live to regret it," Shawn responded.

That sent terror flooding Linda's brain, and she truly knew she must succeed, fearing the harm that might come to her if she didn't.

"Once or twice in my country, when I have achieved full entry, the weak flesh of one woman and one boy failed me completely. They had to be carried off to the hospital. For the boy, it was too late. I split his ass open and he bled to death."

260

Very slowly and firmly, she tried to absorb the head. Her mouth opened wider and wider until she didn't think she could stretch it any more. Straining and pushing, she could no longer lick or maneuver with her tongue because it was pressed down so firmly into her lower jaw.

For a boy so young, he had beefy legs. As she struggled with him, he wrapped those legs around her and used his hands and interlaced fingers to grip the back of her skull, using that position to force her face against his groin and his dick even deeper into the recesses of her throat.

She gagged, as waves of nausea almost caused her to retch, a reflex she struggled to control, since she realized that if she did, there would be no escape for her vomit and she might suffocate on her own puke. Through her nose, she inhaled deeply as her jaw seemed close to either breaking or becoming dislocated. She tasted blood and she hoped it was not from him, but from her own throat and gullet.

She tried to jerk free, but he held her within the constricted prison he'd devised, and resolutely pushed himself forward. His thrusts increased in speed and urgency, signaling that he was heading for a fast climax. She got the distinct impression that her throat had begun silently screaming as the connective tissues of her jaws seemed on the verge of snapping.

Suddenly, the jerky thrusts of his pelvis stopped. His penis contracted, then seemed to expand even more, if that were possible. The taste and pungent smell of semen flooded into her mouth, but since his dick quickly diminished in hardness and size, she managed to make room for it as she hastily swallowed his load. As he orgasmed, he screamed with pleasure and perhaps with some kind of pain.

It was over. She'd succeeded. She pulled back. She was free.

But not for long.

"Let the bitch rest before the final conclusion," the Sheik called out to Chuck. "Turn off those cameras."

The boy lay gasping on his divan, not opening his eyes. He started to cry, perhaps with joy that someone at long last had allowed him to climax within one of their orifices.

Back in her dressing room, as she began gargling with Listerine, she told Chuck and Shawn, "From that milk bottle emerged a quart of cream."

XXXXXXXX

A gender-bending re-enactment of Linda's Arabian Nightmare

***

A knock on the door brought one of the Bahamian waiters with a goblet for Linda. She was told to drink it. "How do you like it?" Shawn asked.

"It has a peculiar taste," she said. "I hope it's not poison."

"The Sheik told us it has some oil of hashish, which will prepare you for the ordeal ahead," Chuck told her.

"You'd think I'd had enough *Ordeal* already," she said.

Within the hour, there was another knock on her door, and she was summoned once again into the arena, where Arabic music was softly playing.

A bed had been set up within the perimeter of the arena, guarded by four Bahamian boys. Shawn, with his arms crossed fiercely across his muscled chest, stood beside it dressed this time as a dominant and sadistic master.

The four Bahamians took Linda's nude body and spreadeagled her, with her stomach down, onto the bed, tying her wrists and ankles. One of the young men rubbed some kind of oil or lotion on her anus, pushing some of it inside her with his finger.

Then Shawn removed the collar from her neck. She knew that it was showtime once again. The Sheik and his sons surrounded her from standing positions nearby.

Although the Sheik was encouraged to go first, he refused. "When I was twenty, I could take on a dozen women and perhaps a boy or two as well, all in a single night.... but that was long ago…"

The oldest son mounted her first. He seemed to deliberately want to hurt her, perhaps wishing he could probe deeper than his penis allowed. Once again, he proved his mettle as a three-minute man. Angry that he had climaxed so soon, he grabbed the bullwhip that Shawn had been holding in his role as the slave master. The Arab lashed her three times as she screamed in pain.

"You filthy American dog woman," he shouted at her before pulling his robe back on and stalking off the stage.

The nineteen-year-old, the effeminate one, had a hard time getting an erection. She suspected that, as a means to achieving climax, he was taking in Shawn's magnificent physique and not acknowledging that it was a woman lying spreadeagled beneath him. After his orgasm, he quickly dismounted from her and put back on his robe. "The woman is worse than swine, disgusting."

As anticipated, each of the twins followed, forcing her into simultaneous vaginal and rectal penetrations. She accommodated both of them without anything that might have even appeared like foreplay, and they came in unison. This time, there was no attempt at strangulation. Perhaps their father had warned them that they might kill her. After all, they were no longer in Saudi Arabia, where they could have easily disposed, without consequence, of a dead body.

Her "moment of truth" had come, and she dreaded it. It was time for the ultra-endowed youngest son, the one with the chestnut-colored hair and the milk bottle between his legs. She realized that each of the evening's previous seductions had been preparations for this final onslaught.

The youngest son appeared before her and dropped his robe. He was already fully erect. She twisted her head around to see his upraised pole ready to mount her. Each of the Arabs looked on in fascination for the penetration. Apparently, while she'd been in her dressing room, they had placed bets among themselves.

Two of the Bahamian boys appeared, one taking one cheek of her ass and pulling it in his direction, the other stretching her buttock by pulling it his way. Then, with no other bit of foreplay or preparation, the Arab teenager aimed his heavy cock straight down and rammed it into her.

She let out a blood-curdling scream. Still, he didn't stop. She jerked her body against the incredible pain, and somehow managed to extricate her anus from his huge dick.

He pulled back in anger. "She needs to be taught to obey," he told Shawn. Then he grabbed the bullwhip from Shawn's hands and lashed her buttocks a total of ten times. Her cries, begging him to stop, went unheeded. When she twisted her head to the right, she noticed the two twins masturbating each other, as they took in this eye-popping scenario.

The teenaged Arab then mounted her again. She begged for mercy, but it was obvious that he was resolute about not showing any. He plunged into her so fiercely that her whole body shook. She seemed to feel the pain all the way to her toenails. Again and again, he slammed into her, bursting through until he was buried up to his pubic hair.

"The first time ever," he shouted at his father and brothers, who applauded his triumph. He ground his mammoth engine into her. She felt a snapping sound and excruciating pain unlike any she'd ever experienced before, as if she'd been invaded by some heavy artillery. Her insides were being ground up and crushed. Suddenly, she felt blood bursting and pouring forth from deep inside her.

The Arab teen at that point shouted in joy, "Allah!"

She jerked her head from left to right and back again, not stopping the flow of tears. For her, breathing was difficult. She felt she couldn't take much more of this.

His drives became longer and harder, and, if anything, even more relentless She was dripping with sweat, and so was he. She could feel the slimy wetness of his body, and also the dark depths of his savagery.

She began to lose feeling in her body, as she drifted into dizziness and darkness. The pounding was no longer unbearable. It was as if it was happening to some other woman. After several more minutes of this, from deep within her fog, she heard him scream in ecstasy.

Listening to his rants of joy, she perceived that he had passed his climax, but she wondered if she would be able to walk.

Hours later, as she drifted in and out of consciousness, she realized that the end had not been near at all. Before he eventually dismounted, he'd stayed inside her for the duration of two additional brutal fucks, the memory of which existed only through the pain he'd left.

On the plane back to Miami, she grabbed Chuck's arm. "I'm bleeding to death. As soon as this plane lands, I've got to see a doctor or I'll die."

***

By the time the plane from Nassau landed in Miami, Linda's jeans and panties were soaked with blood. In a memoir, she referred to the proctologist Chuck took her to as "Dr. James." When the doctor asked what had caused her condition, she claimed that she'd been dildo assaulted by a sadistic lesbian, not revealing what she later exposed during her dialogues with Reba-Anne Howard. Even in her memoir, *Inside Linda Lovelace,* she was secretive and coy, referring to "Arab slave traders" only once, giving no additional details.

She claimed that Dr. James reminded her of the movie villain, Peter Lorre. He wore horn-rimmed glasses with thick lenses, and had foul breath and leering eyes. Her anal tissues had been so seriously torn that she required painful stitches.

After her treatment, she remained in agony. Dr. James said, "you must have had a whopper up there. You must tell your husband that you can no longer indulge in any more anal sex."

"Please don't tell him that," she begged. "If you do, he'll insist on it every night."

He looked at her as if he misunderstood. "I'm warning you: Many of my clients are elderly homosexuals who, after years of sodomy, have lost control of their sphincter muscles. This is often an affliction of aging, extremely promiscuous, and rectally submissive gays. You, too, could become incontinent."

Back in the waiting room, Dr. James immediately astonished her by telling Chuck that he was not to engage in anal sex with her, in spite of her request that he not speak of it.

"Did Linda make a deal with you?" Chuck asked.

"What sort of deal?" the doctor asked.

Chuck called him aside and engaged in a whispered dialogue with him, out of Linda's earshot. When Dr. James returned, he told her, "I'll see you every Thursday afternoon after five o'clock, when my nurse is gone. We'll have the office to ourselves, interrupted only by some annoying phone calls from my wife."

At that point, she was certain what kind of deal her husband had made with her doctor. After his examination of her, he'd given her a prescription for Percodan, the existence of which she managed to keep secret from Chuck. "It was seven weeks of Percodan and a series of seven Thursdays fellating Dr. James. Unlike that Arab boy with that mammoth thickness, Dr. James's penis, with its one-inch circumference, was like putting a pencil in my mouth."

When she returned home, Linda walked around for days in acute discomfort, waiting for the stitches to be removed. She vowed no more anal assaults, although that was a promise she made to herself that would not be kept.

After the Bahamian incident, Linda went through a dark period where she engaged in "the debate of my life, all with myself." For a while, she was determined to commit suicide before deciding she'd rather kill Chuck instead. But how to do it?

One time, when he was suffering a diabetic seizure and had collapsed on the kitchen floor, she was tempted to let him lie there and die. She'd seen Bette Davis in the movie *The Little Foxes*—"And that's what Bette did." But eventually, she relented and rushed to his aid.

She once wrote in a memoir that a trick gave her some poison pills, telling her that two of them in a glass of water would kill Chuck instantly. Like so many of her stories, this one left more questions unanswered than answered.

First, what trick kept poison pills in his apartment or house? Secondly, why would she confess to a relative stranger that she was planning to kill her husband; why would he provide her with the means to do it; and why would he implicate himself in the process? She never explained.

Also, according to her memoirs, after several gruesome weeks of trying to decide what action to take, she finally decided to flush the poison down the toilet.

Once again the question arose, "Why didn't she just run away from Chuck since she had endless opportunities to do so?" Her usual answer was that he would track her down and kill her, as he'd threatened to do so many times in the past.

Acquaintances who worked with both Linda and Chuck had their own answer, asserting that he was the ultimate sadist and that she was his long-suffering masochist.

Chuck had found a new way to get free medical treatments through an offer of Linda's services to whatever doctor or medical technician would accept them in lieu of cash. "We visited four professional men in downtown Miami who operated out of the same big building. I can't believe that all of them, each a pro, would accept such a deal from him. But to my amazement, they did."

The next doctor was a dermatologist who treated her when she developed a skin rash on her thighs. "On every office visit I deep throated him until my rash was cleared up. He had a very unusual penis that went from a very thick base to a tiny pin head."

One morning, Chuck woke up with pink eye (conjunctivitis) from a hooker he'd auditioned. He ordered Linda to accompany him to an ophthalmologist who operated out of that same medical building. "He looked like such a fine and decent man I couldn't believe he'd accept Chuck's deal. But he did. I paid off Chuck's medical bill by going down on the guy. His penis was average in size, but bent incredibly to the right. I didn't like it at all."

In the same building were the offices of six lawyers. "Chuck had this sixth sense about searching for the most crooked one," she said. "He made three separate visits to the office without her. On his fourth trip, he asked her to go along. The lawyer had drawn up a contract for her to sign, naming Chuck as her manager. "It's a sort of Colonel Tom Parker and Elvis Presley deal," the attorney said. She thought that meant a fifty-fifty split. Chuck forced her to sign it without reading it. "You've got to trust me, honey," he said.

Years later, she learned, painfully, that she'd signed a contract giving Chuck all her earnings for the next twenty-five years.

One morning, Chuck woke up and came into the bathroom as she was stepping out of the shower. "I can't stand looking at that flat chest of yours one more day. I've found this doctor who does silicone injections."

"I've heard bad things from gals who had silicone injected," she said. "Besides, it's illegal."

"Get dressed, bitch," he said. "By nightfall, you're going to have big tits—and that's that!"

Dr. John Smith (not his real name) was well known by strippers from Key West to Fort Lauderdale. Clients who patronized strip joints wanted to "see those jugs juggling," as one nightclub owner so graphically described. Unlike the other doctors they'd visited, "Dr. Smith" had three nurses working for him.

Obviously, each of those nurses had either been born with very substantial breasts, or had already submitted to silicone injections, and consequently, displayed impressive bosoms. In her descriptions of them, Linda continued her custom of comparing every person she met to some movie star. She decided that the nurses, respectively, evoked Diana Dors, Connie Francis, and Jayne Mansfield.

Chuck came up to the Mansfield lookalike. "Are they

Linda's proctologist, "Doctor James," reminded her of Hollywood's favorite psychotic villain, **Peter Lorre** (photo above)

for real?" he asked.

"Feel free to judge them for yourself," the nurse said.

He felt her breasts for such a long time that she finally said, "Enough is enough, unless you want to book a room for me."

When Linda first entered the office of Dr. Smith, she felt she was back on the set filming *Deep Throat*. "He could be the older brother of Harry Reems, and like my co-star, I suspected the doctor was also seducing his sexpot nurses."

She had a fear of having foreign objects permanently inserted into her, and she shared her concern with him.

"I must have treated one hundred gals in Dade County, he told her. "No harmful effects. There is just one problem. You'll never be able to breast feed your baby, should you have one. But I understand that that's not a problem. Mr. Traynor told me that if you ever got pregnant, he'd have the child aborted. I privately can arrange abortions."

When she returned for the operation, she claimed she was trembling with fright. As she lay on a hospital table, terrified, he gave her a pain killer before he produced the largest needles she'd ever seen. "I was terrified. It was because of the silicone. I was shot with needles on all four sides of both breasts. Those painkillers didn't work. It felt like I'd entered hell."

She claimed that when she finally was allowed to stand up in front of a mirror, her breasts had gone from size 34B to 36C.

Dr. Smith would not accept Chuck's deal, because he claimed the operation was too costly, and he was already sexually satisfied by his three nurses and a wife at home, plus two or three girlfriends on the side.

"That meant that I had to turn tricks to pay for the operation myself," she said. "However, there were a few occasions with Dr. Smith. He was a real breast man. He didn't want oral sex. He liked to insert himself between my newly formed breasts and reach a climax that way, spurting into my face."

In the years ahead, she'd regret that day of the silicone injections, especially when the gel degraded and her breasts became lumpy and painful.

Her operation gave Chuck an idea. In an underground paper, he'd read an advertisement for penile enlargement. "As you already know, I'm big," he told Linda. "But with three more inches, I can have the bitches screaming."

The next week, after making an appointment, Chuck drove her with him for his first injection. The moment she walked into the office, she was suspicious of Dr. E.J. Burns, if that were his real name. When she met the "doctor" himself, she was shocked by what he wore in his office: Plaid pants, a paisley shirt, and a rainbow-colored necktie. She wanted to warn Chuck about him, but amazingly, this so-called doctor and Chuck bonded.

He asked Chuck to strip. Linda volunteered to leave the office, but the doctor wanted her to remain. "You can fellate him to get him erect. I'll need to take exact measurements."

After a thorough physical examination, with much handling of Chuck's genitals, she began to suspect that the doctor was behaving inappropriately. Then, when he called upon her to fellate Chuck, she had a "hard time making him hard."

When Chuck was erect, the doctor spent a lot of time manipulating and measuring his penis. He was told to come back the following Tuesday at which time he would be injected with "a very special substance."

Two nights after receiving the injections, Chuck woke up in the night screaming with pain and clutching his genitals. His cock had swollen as if it had suffered from a hundred wasp stings. He put through an early-morning call to the doctor, but didn't even get an answering service on the line.

Linda drove him to the nearest hospital, where he underwent some surgical procedure, perhaps to have the illegal substance drained and removed.

After the surgery, Chuck refused to speak about it, finding the whole matter embarrassing. No man wanted word to get out that he ever submitted to treatments for penile enlargements.

As it turned out, the doctor, as she suspected, was a quack. Not only did he not have a medical degree, he hadn't even finished high school. He'd set up an office because he liked to work with male penises. He was subsequently arrested.

When Chuck recovered from his botched injections, he drove her to the Humane Society, telling her that it was time for them to adopt a dog.

"It's your choice," he told her. At the kennel, she spotted a female Cocker Spaniel that she found "cuddly and adorable." He had something else in mind, steering her to a big dog named "Rufus," who was about two years old, the result of a mating between a Bloodhound and a Great Dane. "He had the saddest face I've ever seen on any mutt," she later said.

After adopting Rufus, he drove her back to their house and chained him to a tree outside. Rufus looked even sadder.

"Tonight, I want you and Rufus to get better acquainted."

***

"About the last thing in the world I wanted to do was to get fucked by another dog in a porno loop," Linda said. While in New York, she had met Sally Allen, who had previously starred in a number of bestiality movies with large dogs. She gave Linda tips on how to get a dog "hot and bothered."

As a means of sabotaging Chuck's hopes about the dog's potential as a performer, and after assimilating Sally's advice about how to cope with the amorous attentions of a large canine, Linda decided to do the opposite of every tip Sally had given her. Therefore, instead of sub-tly enticing the animal to approach her of its own free will, as Sally had instructed, she made a wrong-minded series of clumsy overtures, includ-ing fondling its genitals, that ultimately frightened, confused, and chased away the befuddled animal.

Rufus backed away from her and didn't want to play. This angered Chuck. "No wonder Rufus won't screw you!" he shouted at her. "You're so fucking ugly, even an animal turns in disgust from the sight of you!"

After her disappointing "failure" with the dog, a call from New York came in at around midnight. It was Butchie Peraino, offering to pay all their travel expenses—first class—if they'd return to Manhattan for interviews. Chuck immediately accepted for both of them.

Rufus looked like this.

But as he talked it over with Linda, he seemed baffled. "Why would any-one want to interview the porn star of some cocksucking movie? Reporters in-terview Jane Fonda, not some porno whore."

Only when Linda and Chuck arrived in New York did the reality dawn: *Deep Throat* was not being interpreted as just another routine porn flick. Al Goldstein, the publisher and founder of *Screw* magazine, had seen the movie and had hailed it as "the very best porno ever made." Pictures in the New York press showed customers forming lines that stretched around the block for en-trance into the World Theater on Manhattan's West 49th Street.

Still not realizing the importance of the film, Chuck at first didn't even want his name associated with the project. He told Linda to refer to him as "J.R., your manager. No name other than J.R. Got that?"

He drew up a long list of questions she might be asked, and gave her, in ad-vance, a rundown of appropriate answers. He came up with such sample ques-tions as, "How often do you suck cock during any twenty-four hour period?"

Her answer, as scripted by Chuck, would be: "If I don't have at least three young cocks in my mouth every twenty-four hours, I go crazy. When I'm not sucking cock, I'm engaged in girl-on-girl action."

Another question with a pre-rehearsed answer from Chuck was "Do you prefer sex with men to sex with women?" (*ANSWER: "For my daily diet, both are vital. If I'm ever deprived of either one, I go crazy."*)

Later, Chuck asserted that his motivation for Linda's journalistic Q&As derived from his desire for a platform from which he could attack the prudery of then-president Richard Nixon, and call for uninhibited sex for everyone from pubescents to grannies.

Before her first interview, he delivered a final warning: "If some newspaper guy—it could be a dyke reporter as well—shows the slightest interest in you, make it clear that you'd like to go down on him (or her)."

Previously, Chuck had told her that only such sex magazines as *Screw* would ever express an interest in interviewing her. But then she learned from Butchie Peraino that *Playboy* had called. So had *Esquire*. So had a reporter from *The New York Daily News*. "And would you believe," Butchie said, "someone from that gray old lady, *The New York Times?*"

Chuck was dumbfounded. "*The Times?* Don't they publish only news fit to print?"

The first big change she noticed in New York came from Butchie himself. She was no longer referred to as "Bitch," or "Cunt." Instead, it was, "How are you, Linda? My, you're looking swell. I hope your hotel suite is okay? Remember to charge everything you want to room service. This afternoon, I'm having four outfits delivered for you to wear to interviews."

Before leaving to meet *Screw's* chief honchos, Al Goldstein and his publisher, Jim Buckley, Chuck warned her, "I hear Goldstein is largely responsible for the success of *Deep Throat*. When you meet him, suck up to him. Get that, Linda? *Suck* up!"

***

In the May, 1972 issue of *Screw* magazine, Goldstein had written:

"The star of the film has fine legs, firm tits, a not unattractive face, and the greatest mouth action in the annals of cocksucking. The girl with the deep throat is almost a Ripley's Believe-It-Or-Not, as she takes the whole joint down her gullet. No, it's not a small-potato penis, but a roustabout rod of ten inches that plummets into the deepest recesses of our lady's oral cavity; down, down, and down it plunges until nothing remains. It seems a miracle."

The interview with *Screw* was conducted a month later in a cold, seventeen-dollar-per-night hotel room. Goldstein found Linda inarticulate, and Chuck answered most of the questions, except for a few.

Linda appeared at the interview in a transparent blouse to meet Goldstein and *Screw* magazine's editor, Jim Buckley. She found Buckley rather reserved and dignified, but Goldstein, in her words, was "a cheap guy—loud, crude, rude, infantile, obnoxious, and dirty."

"My interview was about as dirty as Goldstein looked," she said.

"When I wrote that review that put you guys on the map, I couldn't get over the cum pouring out of your mouth as you sucked off Harry Reems," Goldstein told her. "Your movie gave me eleven hard-ons. That's why on *Screw's*

Peter Meter, I gave *Deep Throat* a hundred. That's our max."

After the interview, Chuck asked, "Listen, Al, you're so interested in cock-sucking, why not try Linda out yourself?

He also asked Buckley if he'd like to sample Linda's golden throat, but he declined. As Goldstein later said, "Jim likes to keep his repressed cock zipped up!"

Of her experience with Goldstein, Linda later wrote, "I numbed myself to that experience."

Goldstein, however, was more articulate in his memoirs:

"Here I was with the world's greatest cocksucker, and yet it was a lonely experience. I had never fucked a woman in the mouth like that. It seemed hostile. I felt alienated. Though I've often felt I was hung like a rodent, I have a slightly above average cock, seven inches, and the fact that it disappeared down her throat interfered with my concentration. I kept thinking, 'Am I that small? Is she that good? Should I cum now?' She then sat on my face in a 69 position, as I was eating her, but not bringing her any pleasure. Her pussy was hairless, which I didn't care for."

Back in Butchie's office, Peraino wanted to know how the interview with *Screw* went. Linda responded, "He (Goldstein) took a picture of me sucking his cock, and it's going to appear in *Screw* magazine."

"The publicity will be great!" Butchie responded.

"On the way here, five men and one woman stopped and asked Linda for her autograph, a first for us," Chuck said.

"Expect more to come," Butchie said. "But first I've got to ask Linda something." He looked sternly at Chuck. "Let *her* answer this time. I want to sign you to make a sequel, *Deep Throat Part II.*"

"I'd love to make a sequel," she said.

"That's great to hear," Butchie said. "Last night, Johnny Carson took an entourage in a limo to see *Deep Throat.* He loved it. He wants to arrange a private meeting between you and him in a hotel suite. He also mentioned something about you going on *The Tonight Show.*"

"Johnny Carson?" Chuck said. "That's bigtime!"

"There's more, Butchie said. "The last call this afternoon came from this British singer. Ever hear of a guy named John Lennon?"

SCREWING WITH AL

Al Goldstein's *Screw* was, in the words of journalist Andrea Balboa, "A response to a burgeoning sexual revolution and to the supposedly air-brushed soft-pedaled sexuality of magazines such as *Playboy.*"

Goldstein's memoir *(photo left)*, published in 2006, was marketed with this blurb from its publisher:

"Like a fat tiger with nine lives, Al Goldstein constantly collides with his own mortality, yet has survived for 69 years, so far. Recently, after finally succeeding in cannibalizing his entire fortune, Goldstein toughed his way through a full year homeless on the streets of New York — merely his latest accomplishment. Al's list of priors involve two dozen arrests, four ex-wives, Mafia hit contracts, thousands of death threats, innumerable medical procedures, and constant legal attack throughout his 34 years publishing *Screw*. Al's blood enemies include politicians, D.A.'s, CEO's, and religious officials.

When Goldstein was acquitted on pornography charges in Wichita, Kansas, in 1978, he flew the entire jury to New York to celebrate at Plato's Retreat, and took them all out to dinner on the anniversary of his acquittal. This landmark victory thereafter insured the right of Americans to view buck-ass naked sex with or without redeeming social value."

Fascinating at Any Age:
Al Goldstein, founder and publisher of *Screw* magazine, in 1991, at his home in Florida
©1991-2012, with thanks to Steven Paul Hlavac

272

CHAPTER EIGHT
Hollywood's Playmate of the Year

Almost overnight, *Deep Throat* and Linda Lovelace became household words. Porno chic was born.

After Al Goldstein's blow-job, *Screw* magazine made Linda "our Marilyn Monroe," featuring her extensively as the new voice of liberated sexuality. "Had I been a faggot," Goldstein said, "she would have become the magazine's Judy Garland."

Writing in *The New York Times,* Vincent Canby said, "The film has less to do with the manifold pleasure of sex than with physical engineering."

Butchie was delighted when he examined the Manhattan box office receipts from *Deep Throat,* announcing that it was outgrossing *Cabaret* (1972), a film which later won eight Academy Awards.

Porn star and porn director Fred Lincoln mocked Linda, claiming that she sincerely believed that people were seeing *Deep Throat* because of her acting. "She's not only a masochist, but a fucking moron!"

Almost overnight, *Deep Throat* opened in three hundred theaters across the country, from Maine to Florida, from New Jersey to Washington State. FBI agent Bill Kelly attended a showing at the Sheraton Theater on Miami Beach. He was accompanied by Jack Roberts of *The Miami News,* who attacked it the next afternoon in his paper, referring to it as "a piece of garbage." In contrast, its rival, *The Miami Herald,* gave it lavish praise as attendance soared.

Celebrities, as well as ordinary people, began to show up at screenings. Barbara Walters, who had never been in a porno house, arrived in a limousine, accompanied by Roy Cohn, the homosexual "red baiter" during the infamous Joseph McCarthy era.

Film director John Waters, no conduit of good taste in moviemaking, picked up a copy of *The New York Times* and was startled to read within one of its ads: IF YOU LIKE HEAD, YOU'LL LOVE THROAT.

Harry Reems claimed "guys like Mike Nichols showed up."

Ed McMahon arrived with six friends and a six pack of Budweiser. After the screening, he stood on the sidewalk in front of the theater, urging patrons to go inside. He had been the one who alerted Johnny Carson, his boss, to go and see it.

The most surprising viewer was Jacqueline Kennedy. She had once been photographed leaving a movie house with Aristotle Onassis after viewing *I Am Curious, Yellow* (1967), a Swedish erotic film. According to a report in *The New York Times,* she openly attended a screening of *Deep Throat.*

Actually, she wasn't so open about it. She went to the theater with author Gore Vidal but entered only after the film had begun. They sat in the back and left hurriedly at the end, hoping not to be recognized. They were seen disappearing into a limousine at the corner.

Truman Capote, who, on a separate occasion, invited Jackie's sister, Lee Radziwill, wasn't so secretive about their visit, even signing autographs as they departed from the theater.

Carson began to use *Deep Throat* as inspiration for his comedy routines. "This is a strange country, isn't it? Judges can see *Deep Throat,* but they can't listen to the Nixon tapes."

On TV, Bob Hope said, "I went to see *Deep Throat* because I'm fond of animal pictures. I thought it was about giraffes."

In a 2005 documentary entitled *Inside Deep Throat,* author Norman Mailer recalled the nostalgia of the 1970s. "Pornography lived in some mid-world between

Pornography that produced lots of *crème* and attracted *la crème de la crème*

Gore Vidal *(left)* accompanied his distant relative, **Jackie Kennedy,** to a screening of *Deep Throat.* On the way out, they tried to keep their visit a secret. In the wake of their viewing, attendance soared.

Truman Capote *(right photo)* accompanied Jackie's sister, **Lee Radziwill** *(left).* Truman, then near the height of his fame, was less discreet, signing autographs in the lobby after the show.

crime and art. And it was adventurous, preoccupying critics, cops, and the courts. Most major distributors were financed by Mafia families."

The respected filmmaker, Fenton Bailey, the producer of *Inside Deep Throat,* said, "*Deep Throat* is like the acceptable face of porn, in which chintzy *whucka-whucka* guitars and ludicrous flavor-savor mustaches have slipped into the socially sanctified category of kitsch. Sure, it's a bad film, but it's better than you would expect from a hump flick, and is actually quite fun in a goofy kind of way. Incredibly, thirty-three years after it was made, it is still the most famous porn title ever."

Bailey also said that Linda Lovelace became as famous as Madonna, but she really didn't want to BE Madonna." He finally concluded that Linda, Reems, and Damiano should not be defined as pornographers, but as "avant-garde bohemian renegade mavericks."

Deep Throat had reopened at the World Theatre in Manhattan on June 12, 1972, three days before a break-in at the Watergate complex in Washington. "Deep Throat" was soon to became the universally accepted name for the otherwise anonymous source whose information, as funneled through *Washington Post* journalists Bob Woodward and Carl Bernstein, eventually led to the forced resignation of a U.S. President.

In 2005, the FBI's former Associate Director, Mark Felt, outed himself as the informant—the one nicknamed Deep Throat—to Bernstein and Woodward. But to this day, the *Deep Throat* association remains the most colorful part of the behind-the-scenes Watergate lore.

Except for its booming debut in New York, the film did not fare well in other cities, opening, for example, in Los Angeles and closing in four days. Theater manager Vince Miranda decided to reopen it at the Pussycat Theater in Los Angeles, but at first it did only minor business.

Damiano was hailed as "The Ingmar Bergman of porno films." Reems interpreted Damiano as "a grown-up Wizard of Oz, a short, jolly, jellybean with a gray goatee and a funny little toupée."

"After working with Bob Wolfe, Damiano was like Cecil B. DeMille," Linda claimed.

On looking back, Damiano recalled, "If it hadn't been for Linda and for the, uh, particular skill she had developed, there wouldn't have been any *Deep Throat.* At the time, my partners said the title was no good, but I was

Pornography and Politics

How an anonymous source identified worldwide as *Deep Throat* ended, in disgrace, the regime of an American President.

Feminist Heavy-Hitters Weighing in on Linda:

(left to right, above) **Erica Jong, Barbara Walters, Nora Ephron.**

adamant. I said it would become a household word. And it has. Not only in the Watergate Case, but last week, we were no. 6 across in *The New York Times* crossword puzzle."

Richard Corliss, writing at the occasion of Damiano's death in 2008, said: "Long before home video, *Deep Throat* took the recently legalized porn films out of the gutter and into the mainstream. It was the *Citizen Kane* of porn. Because of *Deep Throat,* the hardcore movie became a must-see item for the *glamorati*, a topic for serious debate in newspapers and magazines including *Time,* and a fun date for ordinary couples who had never seen a sex movie."

Rock Hudson, who had met Linda in The Bahamas, claimed, "Linda Lovelace put fellatio on the map. Across America, husbands were demanding that their wives go down on them."

Barbara Walters hailed the movie as a "new badge of freedom."

Erica Jong proclaimed that with the release of *Deep Throat,* "Sex came out of the closet."

Not all reviews were raves, including one from writer Nora Ephron. "*Deep Throat* is one of the most unpleasant, disturbing films I have ever seen—it's not just antifemale, but antisexual as well."

One of America's leading movie critics, Roger Ebert, went to see *Deep Throat,* writing, "It is all very well and good for Linda Lovelace, the star of the movie, to advocate sexual freedom, but the energy she brings to her role is less awesome than discouraging. If you have to work this hard at sexual freedom, maybe it isn't worth the effort."

On October 12, 1975, *The New York Times* released a story about how organized crime was hauling in huge profits from *Deep Throat.* It was revealed that Butchie had bought out the interests of Gerald Damiano, who should have been cut in on a third of the profits. He settled for $25,000. When a reporter asked him why so little, he said, "I had a choice—that or get my legs broken or perhaps my throat slit."

Fred Lincoln said, "I heard Lovelace is bitching about how little money she was paid. Hell, when I was in Wes Craven's *The Last House on the Left,* I was paid nine hundred dollars, and I was the jerk who got his dick bit off."

"Then the shit hit the fan," Butchie Peraino said. Mayor John Lindsay, the handsome, charismatic mayor of New York (in office from 1966 to 1973), turned out to have a Puritan streak in him. "I also heard from this *puta* that the mayor was a lousy lay," Butchie claimed.

Lindsay decided to wipe out pornography in New York and ordered the New York Police Department (NYPD) to confiscate a print of *Deep Throat* from the World Theater, where crowds of both men and women had been lining up around the block.

The next morning, headlines blared—MAYOR CRACKS DOWN ON DEEP THROAT. The national media picked up the story, and subsequently, *Deep Throat* made front-pages across the country.

"*Deep Throat* became the most 'in' thing since The Twist"

right figure in photo above: **Chubby Checker**

"Al Goldstein at *Screw* was largely responsible for launching *Deep Throat in New York,*" Damiano said, "but it was Mayor Lindsay who made it a nation-wide success and ultimately, a worldwide hit. Demands for copies of *Deep Throat* were swamping Butchie's office in New York. Almost overnight, he had a major hit worth millions. Linda Lovelace, of all people, became a movie star."

The World Theater decided to fight the obscenity charges. "Overnight, another print of *Deep Throat*

Hours after running this picture *(right, above)* of **Mayor John Lindsay**'s cock on May 30, 1969, the first NYPD police raid occurred on *Screw*'s Manhattan office. Al Goldstein was fingerprinted, charged with obscenity, and held behind bars. "His honor has a fairly huge cock, and it provoked controversy whether it was real, erect, or in repose," Goldstein claimed.

Reportedly, the photograph was authentic, snapped at some unknown date in the New York Athletic Club.

was delivered to the movie house, and showings resumed, because it would take months for the battle to be resolved in the courts," Reems said. "*Deep Throat* became the most 'in' thing since The Twist. Until then, paying porn audiences had been mostly the raincoat-over-the-lap crowd. But here was a hardcore movie challenging the censorship laws. Plump, mink-coated matrons from Mamaroneck and Manhasset, who looked like they were heading for a matinée of *No, No, Nanette,* were lining up to plunge down their five dollars at the box office."

***

From Florida, FBI agent Bill Kelly learned that at the Peraino office in Wilton Manors (a residential neighborhood of Fort Lauderdale), so much money was coming in that "The Perainos have it stuffed in garbage bags—too much to count."

Kelly had evidence that the mob was blackmailing theaters showing *Deep Throat.* Often, a representative would show up at the box office, demanding "five thousand or else."

"Or else" was usually interpreted as a threat to burn down the theater—and more.

As *Deep Throat* forged ahead at box offices across the country, in spite of legal challenges, Kelly asserted, "Where is J. Edgar Hoover now that we need him?"

The homosexual F.B.I. director had died in 1972. When he heard Kelly's remark, Damiano said, "Yeah, Hoover would have tried to shut it down, while saving a copy for himself and his lover, Clyde Tolson, who could be found at home jerking off to it."

"After *Deep Throat,* I was a turn-off to the average type john I had been serving previously," Linda said. "I think a lot of them feared they would not measure up. Overnight, I began to attract a new type of client, although I'd served a few celebrities in my notorious past. But that had been only an occasional thing. After *Deep Throat* became so famous, my phone began to ring. Often a household name was on the phone wanting me to suck his cock."

"These so-called studs might have five inches, but you could count on big egos in all of them. In their peapod brains, they had at least ten inches. Jerry Lewis would be an example of that. On a scale of one to ten, I heard that the showgirls of Las Vegas rated him a one. In the months ahead, I came across a lot of stars who had super egos and small dicks, but I met some real big studs, too."

On the East Coast, Ed McMahon, famous for his nightly introductions ("*HEEEEEEERE'S JOHNNY!*") of Johnny Carson on *The Tonight Show,* evolved into the first major celebrity to discover "the glories" of *Deep Throat* at Manhattan's World Theater.

Linda was a faithful watcher of the show, and had actually found McMahon "more sexily intriguing" than Carson himself. Previously "packaged" as a Philadelphia television personality, McMahon was a husky former Marine aviator cast as an amiable lush who functioned as Carson's straight man and comedic foil and counterpart.

After seeing *Deep Throat,* McMahon praised the porn flick so much that, in a limousine, he escorted Carson to a screening of the movie at Manhattan's World Theater.

Carson was most receptive of the movie, and talked about inviting Linda as a guest on *The Tonight Show.* His nightly appearance was peppered with sexual banter and innuendo, in contrast to the bland, previously established whitewashes of the 1950s and early 1960s. In fact, many critics hailed Carson for popularizing America's sexual revolution. For a while, *Deep Throat* became standard fare for Carson's own peculiar brand of humor.

Although Linda felt that McMahan was the sexier of the duo—"He's probably got more hanging than Johnny"—she found Carson a boyish-looking Iowa native with a disarming grin.

When a call came in from an executive of *The Tonight Show* about a possible appearance by Linda, she and Chuck were all ears. Chuck told her that many a career had evolved from an appearance on Carson's show.

Chuck accompanied Linda in a taxi to the NBC studios at Rockefeller Plaza. She met briefly with Carson's musical director, Skitch Henderson, who quickly determined that Linda had no musical talent whatsoever. Someone's idea about her performing a song in front of millions of TV viewers was quickly buried.

Then McMahon appeared and congratulated Linda on *Deep Throat,* while giving her a wet kiss on the mouth. Privately, he conferred with her, asserting that "after tonight's taping, Johnny would like to have a late dinner with you." He whispered in her ear, "without your husband."

When Linda explained to Chuck that he wasn't invited, he was furious, until Linda suggested, "Johnny's gonna eat more tonight than lobster." Chuck understood immediately. For the next few months, he would always be willing to peddle his wife to a celebrity, particularly to any that could advance her career.

That evening, Chuck disappeared before Carson finished his taping. Carson met with Linda in his dressing room. She was nervous about meeting him, but he had a way of putting guests at ease, as he amply demonstrated every night on his show.

After he'd changed clothes, he escorted her out of the studio and into a limousine, where he took her to an out-of-the-way Italian restaurant, a favorite dive of his.

"No one will bother us here," he told her. "The manager respects my privacy." Over a meal of squid and ziti, he inquired about her past.

She later admitted, "I gave him a sanitized version. Instead of champagne, we toasted each other with a cold beer."

After dinner, he told her he'd like to take her back to his penthouse, "but I have a guest staying there right now."

In lieu of taking her to his home, after placing a call, he arranged for the rental of a suite at the Plaza Hotel As he slipped into the lobby, he wore dark glasses and a hat pulled down over his face. No one recognized him.

In the luxuriously furnished suite, with two bottles of champagne chilling, he told her to make herself comfortable. He kicked off his shoes, removed his coat and tie, and unbuttoned his shirt. Seated on the sofa, he invited her to watch *The Tonight Show* with him.

He gave her a quick kiss on the mouth, but once the show began, it attracted his intense attention. He frowned and even winced on occasion, and was very critical of his own performance. "I missed a chance there," he said. Or else he'd say, "My timing was off on that."

As he watched the show, she observed him. She concluded that it was his boy-next-door charm that made millions of Americans invite him into their bedroom at night. Although virtually everyone in the entertainment industry interpreted him as a New York sophisticate, he still retained that gee-whiz Midwestern quality that made him at least appear non-threatening.

Near the conclusion of the show, she began to slip off her clothing. He hugged her to him, one of his hands cupping her right breast. She hoped he wouldn't conclude that they were silicone.

Hanging out at NYC's **Plaza Hotel** (*middle photo, above*) with **Ed MacMahon** (*top photo*) and **Johnny Carson** (*lower photo*)

280

While watching the show, they had knocked off one bottle of champagne, and she was feeling tipsy.

"Linda," he said in a soft voice. "I could invite you back to the bedroom, and it would be perfectly safe, since I've had a vasectomy. But I'd rather enjoy your specialty."

Slowly, she unzipped his pants as he unbuttoned his shirt, exposing a rather scrawny chest. He couldn't weigh more than 165 pounds, as he was a fairly small man, standing about five feet ten inches. She pulled down his pants and jockey shorts, but he didn't bother to remove them completely. It looked like it was going to be a quickie.

His cock was not impressive, but not too small either, as it rose to attention. It would be no *Deep Throat* challenge to her at all. What she really noticed were his elegant long hands, ideal for a surgeon or perhaps Liberace at the piano. As she fellated him, those beautiful hands rubbed her shoulders and ran their fingers through her hair.

After it was over, he rose to his feet, pulled up his pants, and headed for the bathroom. "There are two bathrooms in this suite. You can use the other one."

In the bathroom, she washed herself and rinsed out her mouth. "His cum had been rather thick, with a slightly nutty flavor." (This very personal evaluation was told to the Jay Garon researchers.)

Back in the living room, he put back on his jacket and tie. "I'm running late," he said. "I have another appointment. That was terrific. I want you and your husband to spend the night and tomorrow night here as my guests. Order anything you want from room service—lobster, caviar, whatever. Ed will make the arrangement for you to appear on my show. He'll call."

At the door, he kissed her good night, but it was the sort of kiss a man might give his daughter. He whispered one final comment. "You're really good at your work…I mean, really good. When I was a Navy air cadet during the war, and about eighteen years old, I danced with Marlene Dietrich at the Stage Door Canteen in Hollywood. She took me home and fellated me, the best I've ever had…until tonight."

After Carson had departed, she called Chuck, inviting him to the Plaza and urging him to accept the TV star's generosity. Within a half hour, Chuck was in the suite, demanding details and ordering lavishly from room service. He was delighted to hear that both of them could occupy the suite for another night.

After the taping the following evening, McMahon arrived in the suite at around 10pm, having communicated that Chuck was not supposed to be on-site.

When she asked him about Carson, McMahon revealed that the person occupying Carson's Manhattan penthouse was Carson's girlfriend. Indeed, Linda would later read that in September of 1972, Carson married former model

Joanna Holland. He'd been previously married to both Joanne Copeland and to Joan Wolcott. "Each of my wives had a name starting with a J" he told his TV audience. "That way, I don't have to change the monograms of J&J on our towels."

Her suspicions were confirmed before McMahon left her suite that night. As she'd later tell Chuck, "Ed is much better hung than Johnny."

Before departing from the Plaza at around midnight, having taken advantage of all of Linda's orifices, he delivered the bad news: "Sorry, Linda, but the producers of the show insist that you're far too controversial to go on. I'm really sorry, because I think you'd be terrific. At any rate, you were great in *Deep Throat.* Good night, sweetheart."

***

In a memoir, Linda mentioned meeting John Lennon, but added no details. Either her editor cut the section, or she was deliberately inarticulate. Jay Garon's associates pushed her into giving complete details.

A rendezvous with Lennon, who had seen *Deep Throat* three times, and Linda was arranged in someone's private apartment. The meeting had been set up through direct communications between Lennon and Peraino's office.

Chuck wanted to be included in Linda's meeting with Lennon, but the Beatle refused, demanding that the rendezvous be private, including only Linda, within an apartment in Manhattan's West Village. She was instructed to ring a doorbell labeled "Apt. C, Dickers," and she was told she'd be buzzed in after identifying herself through the microphone.

In a newly purchased red pants suit, she followed instructions and arrived there at 9pm for a meeting with the fabled figure who, in spite of his youth, was one of the most famous men in the world. Known as "The Magical Minstrel," he had set the tune of the 1960s. His respected biographer, Albert Goldman, writing in *The Lives of John Lennon,* published in 1988, defined the musician as "by turn a man, woman, and child; moralist and immoralist; idealist and cynic; solipsist and exhibitionist; bully and wimp; sadist and masochist; ascetic and junkie; creative genius and plagiarist; master and slave; murderous criminal and crucified victim."

After a young Asian boy welcomed Linda into the antique-filled apartment, she found Lennon very non-threatening. He put her at ease at once, complimenting her on her "acting" in *Deep Throat.* He wore a military style uniform, his midnight black pants rather narrow. His black jacket was adorned with gold buttons up to his neck. His hair was shoulder length, long, and brown. When he saw her noticing it, he said, "I'm thinking of going blonde."

"Oh no, please," she said. "Keep it like it is. I think it's lovely."

"Then I will," he promised. "What bloke could ignore the advice of Miss Linda Lovelace?"

In the living room, she heard Beatles music playing in the background. "I'm hungry," he said. "How about you?"

"I can eat something," she said.

"Good!" He called out to the Asian boy, placing his order first. "I want a toasted cheese and bacon sandwich and a platter of steak—you know how I like it—and fries. But first, bring me a Coca-Cola and a glass of Johnny Walker Blue Label. How about you, Linda?"

"Oh, the steak and fries would do just fine," she said. "And a Coke."

"As a special treat later, I have some hash cakes and a punch that will 'pot roast' your noodle," he said.

Because she ingested some drugs before leaving very early the next morning, she could not remember all that he'd told her for her diary, but she captured enough of his dialogue to give her researchers a flavor of what it was like being alone with Lennon. He did most of the talking.

As he drank his third glass of whiskey, he said, "I've dropped acid and popped pills, as the world seems to know. But I'm also a bloke who loves his whiskey."

After dinner, and after some hash cakes, he asked her, "Would you like me to do my impersonation of Boris Karloff?"

She said that she would. Before her eyes, he transformed himself into the Mandarin of Horror, delivering a five-minute performance in the style of *Grand Guignol*. Somehow, he seemed to make his body gaunt and stooped, his brows sinister.

At the end, she congratulated him, claiming, "You sent chills down my spine. Instead of a music maker, you could have become movie's greatest ghoul."

In a mellow mood, he confided to her, "I've fucked hundreds of birds. Some of my more ardent female fans throw themselves at me. Hundreds of young gay males want to suck out my seed. I find that I can have almost any girl or boy I want, even if the boy is straight. But not always. One night in a club in London's Soho district, I went for my coat. I took my hand and felt up the hatcheck girl's quim. She objected and wouldn't let me fuck her. So I pulled it out,

Vintage whiskeys, psychedelics, and acting improvisations with superstar **John Lennon**

Lennon to Linda: "I'm thinking of going blonde."

283

whacked it a few times, and shot all over the bitch."

The world was growing hazy for her when he described his tour of America. "I flew around with my fellow insects—George, Paul, and Ringo. I was careful not to get locked up in the slammer for violating the Mann Act. I was told by our promoters that it was safer for me to seduce hookers, Las Vegas show girls, or celebrities. Sometimes, I didn't want a partner. I just toss myself off."

"I think we call that jerking off," she said.

"I don't like the word 'jerk,'" he said. "So, Linda you're a celebrity. You're safe. You're not going to sue me, so why not demonstrate your specialty?"

In front of her, he stripped and stood completely nude. She pulled off her top to show off her new breasts, as she fellated him. As she'd later recall, "I've seen bigger uncut cocks, but he grew to a respectable length when he was erect. There was a slight taste of head cheese. I suspected he hadn't washed it thoroughly that day. But I got him off, and I wanted to do a good job, hoping he'd call me back. He never did, by the way."

"I think his curiosity was settled after only one workout. But he thoroughly enjoyed it, or so he said. Instead of kicking me out after he got off, he let me stay for another hour or two."

"As he put on more music, he asked me who my favorite singer was, 'Elvis Presley, before tonight,' I told him."

"Oh, that Elvis," Lennon said. "That bam-bam Caliban. He's a rebel, all passion, but it's just not translatable. He believes in shaking it, even if he doesn't have much to shake."

He spoke about growing up in England. "In 1956, when the Teds took over in London, I couldn't afford all those drainpipe trousers and gunslinger's jackets. So I put my wide trousers on my auntie's sewing machine and made them tight. I also cultivated a greasy quaff and sideboards."

"I think Elvis would call that a pompadour and sideburns," she said.

He even told her what he expected in a wife. "For variety's sake, I expect a wife to supply me with beautiful, nubile young birds—or else, on that rare occasion, a lovely young Tadzio boy with a succulent bum. I also expect, if I demand it, for her to supply me with a very agreeable Japanese geisha, subject to my every whim."

"You sound like some ruler in *Arabian Nights,*" she said, "not that I've read *Arabian Nights.*"

"I could be," he said "because at times, I feel I'm eight different people. A couple of years ago, I had this nervous breakdown and took to bed. I decided I didn't want to talk or eat. I got up only to take a piss or a shit."

She giggled. "I didn't know one of you Beatles actually had to shit any more," she said. "I thought you'd evolved beyond that."

Without warning, he rose to his feet. "This 'Nowhere Man' is sleepy and going to bed. I'd invite you to join me, but I've had enough action for tonight."

"I hope to see you again," she said, getting up on her unsteady feet, grabbing her things, and heading for the door.

"That would be grand," he said, "But if it doesn't happen, know that you carry my seed in your stomach. It will get rid of any blemishes, extend your life for five years, and make your firstborn immensely talented should you decide to become a breeder. *Ciao.*"

"Good night, Mr. Lennon," she said. "I don't know you well enough to call you John."

"And now to bed with you," he said. "May all your dreams be of me—now and forever more."

***

It was almost inevitable that Butchie Peraino would get a call from Hugh Hefner, the publisher of *Playboy*. Naturally, he wanted Linda's phone number.

When the call came in from Hefner, Chuck and Linda were in Florida. They eagerly agreed to travel to his *Playboy* mansion in West Los Angeles as part of a photo shoot whose results would appear in Hefner's magazine. "I loved Linda in *Deep Throat,* but also in *The Dog Fucker,"* Hefner told Chuck over the phone.

With the understanding that Hefner would send his private *Playboy* jet for them, Chuck, through Hefner's staff, coordinated the details of their westbound flight. Noting that Hefner seemed to like bestiality movies, Chuck opted to bring Rufus as part of their entourage.

Linda agreed to pose in the nude for *Playboy.* The photographer asked her to cut her hair again, just like it had been during her appearance in *Deep Throat.*

Dressed for entertaining:
Playboy founder and Lifestyle Guru
Hugh Hefner

"I think it was the call from *Playboy* that caused Chuck to respect my earning potential for the first time," Linda said. "Instead of treating me like I was trailer park trash, he began to view me as a hot property. I never knew how much *Playboy* paid for that layout of me, because Chuck took all the money and didn't tell me."

"From the moment we arrived in Los Angeles for the *Playboy* layout, Hefner had ordered a limousine and chauffeur for us," Linda said. "For the first time in my life, I felt like a bigshot."

When she encountered the setup at the Playboy Mansion West, she said, "I knew this was going to be a class act—no bullwhips or dildos. The *Playboy* photographer treated me like a lady, so courteous and courtly. He used lace—as in Love-*lace*—as a backdrop. Antique lace, that is. He'd shopped half the antique stores in Los Angeles. He put me at ease. He even made me feel I was a vision of loveliness in the sunlight. No one had ever done that to me before."

"Not all the shots were arty," she later confessed. "I had to strike some stupid poses, like sucking my finger instead of a big dick. I had to fondle my fake breasts. In one shot, I was depicted licking my lips as if I'd just tasted a load of cum."

**Bunny-Hopping
at the Playboy Mansions**

(top photo) The original **Playboy Mansion in Chicago** was built in 1899, acquired by Hefner in 1959, and donated to the Art Institute of Chicago in 1974.

(lower photo) **The Playboy Mansion West**, built in 1927, acquired by Hefner in 1971, and famous for its scandalous parties attended by, among hundreds of others, Linda Lovelace.

After she'd posed for the centerfold layout, a young staff member at the mansion showed them around the estate.

The Playboy Mansion West stood on thirty acres in the heart of Holmby Hills, an exclusive residential neighborhood that Hefner claimed was still haunted by the ghost of Humphrey Bogart. Prior to his death in 1957, Bogart had lived nearby. The mansion lay only a block off Sunset Boulevard, which Hefner called "The Boulevard of Broken Dreams."

He had bought the property for a million dollars in February of 1971.

She was awed when she stepped inside the Tudor Gothic building. Guarded by a dozen men assigned to security, the main house was filled with antiques, leather sofas, and lots of overstuffed armchairs. There was even a room for pinball machines, and lots of places to unwind, including a sauna and a Jacuzzi whirlpool. A curved double staircase led to the locked doors of a master bedroom where she hoped the publisher and high priest of *Playboy* would invite her for a sleepover.

Hefner had extensively redesigned the grounds and gardens, creating what he called, "a veritable Eden with waterfalls, fish ponds, and a variety of birds and animals running free. In other words, a Disneyland for adults."

A special feature was the Jacuzzi found in a man-made grotto under a waterfall. During a hot Roman orgy, it could hold as many as one hundred undulating bodies. The "décor" of the grotto was modeled on a cave, famous for its prehistoric paintings, in France.

With Chuck, she explored a landscape inhabited with peacocks, African cranes, macaws, monkeys in trees, rabbits running wild, flamingos, and dogs.

Together with Chuck, she toured the citrus groves, the bathhouse, the greenhouse, the guest cottage, the Jacuzzi, the tennis court, and the game room, which once a week was converted into an orgy room.

No one captured the scene better than Anthony Haden-Guest, writing in *Rolling Stone:* "Hugh Hefner's Playboy Mansion West is a mullioned slab of Old Englishry, a gray gleam of ersatz granite in the Southern California sunlight. To the back, the image dissolves, re-forms. Sexy vicarage metamorphoses to miniature Versailles. Gibbons swing and chatter in the trees, while a couple of house guests foozle with croquet hoops; a quintet of East African cranes lope up a handmade hill, and an associate movie producer hopefully pursues a trio of cuties. Mottled Japanese carp float on one side of a bridge, and on the other, in the bathing pool, another cutie, with the left cheek of her bikini bottom cut into a heart shape, floats on an air mattress."

Both Chuck and Linda were invited back that night to attend a buffet and a movie Hefner was screening for about fifty guests. "I changed my view of *Playboy* that day," Linda said. "Before I came to the mansion, I thought *Playboy* was a dirty magazine my brother-in-law used to jerk off to in the toilet."

"But when I saw all these high-class people there, I changed my mind. I learned that Hefner sometimes attracted really big names like Teddy Kennedy and definitely Jack Nicholson. One night I heard that George McGovern showed up. He was that guy who ran for President against Richard Nixon. In other words, I wasn't hanging out with white trash, baby."

For her first evening appearance at the Playboy Mansion, Chuck even shelled out a hundred dollars to buy a form-fitting, dove-gray knitted dress for Linda.

Before meeting Hefner that night, Chuck came up with what he called "a fun scheme." He escorted Linda around the mansion, inviting the butlers and other servants to see how many fingers they could put

That Naughty Grotto
Orgies at the Playboy Mansion West

inside Linda. She was humiliated by the experience, although the male staff members seemed to regard it as excitement. She later said, "I hoped they washed their hands before serving the guests food and drink."

"On my first night there, I spotted Warren Beatty and Peter Lawford. I didn't get to speak to them, but would in the future. Goldie Hawn was there and so was Connie Stevens."

Blonde-haired Hawn, then in her late 20s and married at the time to dancer Gus Trikonis, seemed to have just discovered Eastern philosophy, claiming that she was "a Jewish Buddhist," although no one seemed interested.

Stevens, who had become famous for playing "Cricket Blake" in the popular TV detective series, *Hawaiian Eye,* had divorced Eddie Fisher in 1969. She entertained guests with her tales about dating Elvis Presley, and much less so, her devotion to the Republican Party. While she was doing that, her former

husband, Eddie Fisher, who was also at the gathering, discreetly obtained Linda's phone number, which he tucked into a secret compartment of his well-stuffed wallet. From her position at the other side of the mansion, Stevens didn't seem to notice—or even care—that her ex-husband was at the same party, on a Bunny hunt.

In a memoir, Linda claimed that within the mansion, she encountered Elizabeth Taylor, but was too afraid to speak to her, perhaps fearing that the

People Linda was likely to have met at one of the Playboy Mansions in the early 70s

Elizabeth Taylor *(top left photo)* **and** *(lower row, left to right)*
Connie Stevens, softcore porn king **Russ Meyer,** and **Goldie Hawn.**

movie diva would interpret her as a trash act. Actually, to the Garon researchers, she relayed a different story, claiming "It was Miss Taylor who spoke to me, breaking the ice. At first, she terrified me, but she was so quick to put me at ease. She looked so down to earth, although she wore a celestial hairpiece and a shimmering gown, plus a diamond-and-ruby necklace."

"Elizabeth may have looked like a regal queen, but when she spoke, she sounded more like a drunken sailor on Saturday night," Linda claimed. "Tanked up on champagne, we got right to the point."

"Hefner screened *Deep Throat* for me," Taylor said, "and was I impressed. I really was. Perhaps if I pay you well, you'll give me lessons. I'm sure Richard Burton would volunteer to be our guinea pig for instructions in how to throat a cock."

"I'd be honored, but I think there are few things I could teach the Serpent of the Nile," Linda said.

"You flatter me, darling, but, believe me, I'm always learning. I usually get rave notices from my men, but I couldn't satisfy Victor Mature. He wanted me to go all the way down. But after gulping down a foot and a half of cock, I gave up."

"I bet I could handle him," Linda said.

"You know what?" Elizabeth said. "I bet you could, too, and he would love it. Would you write down your phone number? I'll have Vic call you. He'll let me know how your session turned out."

"You're not kidding, are you?" Linda asked. "THE Victor Mature?"

"Samson himself."

Linda wrote down her phone number and handed it to Elizabeth, who made a notation on it and put it into her purse. Taylor continued, "Believe me, Victor is the best. I should have married him. Rita Hayworth, Betty Grable, and Lana Turner have told me the same thing. We shouldn't have let him escape our clutches."

At this point, one of the staff approached Elizabeth, telling her that Hefner wanted to see her in the library.

Before tearing herself away from Linda, Elizabeth took her hand and caressed it. "Keep up the good work, my dear. You have many fans in Hollywood. I know for a fact that half the male stars will soon be trying to get in touch with you. Don't expect to hear from the other fifty percent. They're gay."

Although Elizabeth was gracious, her all time idol, Clint Eastwood, was not. "I've worshipped

Victor Mature
Swords, sandals, and beefcake

289

him on the screen for years. He was my dream man. In the coincident of coincidents, he took the empty seat next to me in the screening room where Hefner showed some movie. I don't remember the name of it. All I could think about was Clint Eastwood sitting next to me."

"To my deep heartbreak, he didn't even look at me or say hello. By the time we were thirty minutes into that stupid movie, I decided to take the bull by the horns, so to speak. Slowly, I reached over and placed my delicate little hand on his crotch. I'd seen his package in some movie in which there was a bedroom scene, and he paraded around in a pair of white jockey shorts. From what little I saw, I wasn't expecting John C. Holmes. But I planned to make do with what he had."

"He really insulted me. He very firmly took my hand off his crotch and placed it back in my own lap. That was the end of my romance with Clint Eastwood. No more fantasies about him."

Hefner always made his appearance at around ten in the evening. His drink of choice was a cold Pepsi-Cola. "Joan Crawford would have been proud of him," Linda said. "After all, she was the Pepsi queen."

Hefner was most gracious in greeting both Chuck and Linda. She resented that he spent most of the time chatting with Chuck about kinky sex, and she was horrified that *The Dog Fucker,* starring herself and a German shepherd, was one of Hefner's favorite 8mm loops.

Finally, he got around to complimenting her, telling her that she was much prettier in person than on the screen. "Usually, when I meet a movie star, it's the reverse. On screen, she's a *femme fatale,* but up close and personal, I greet an old hag. Incidentally, Warren Beatty freaked out over your movie. He wants to meet you."

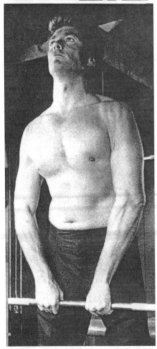

Two views of
Clint Eastwood
(*top photo,* as Dirty Harry
in 1971)

After their first night at the Playboy Mansion, Hefner gave both Chuck and Linda a gold card, which allowed them to come and go from the mansion whenever they wanted. "We joined the rest of the freeloaders to see the movies, to devour the food and drink, to attend the parties, especially those Wednesday night orgies, where *Deep Throat* was a regular feature," Chuck said, as reported later by Linda.

***

For a brief period in her life, Chuck and Linda became "members of the family," as Hefner labeled it, at Playboy Mansion West.

"Just from the way he approached the various girls and bunnies, I could tell Hefner was a big boob kind of guy, but I suspected that all those mammoth tits were made of plastic," Linda said.

The longest time she spent with Hefner, a total of four hours, was in his library. "There was no sex," she said. He genuinely seemed interested in me, Linda Boreman, as a real person. Where I came from, what I felt, what intrigued me. No one had ever paid attention to me before. All they wanted was Linda Lovelace—or, more to the point, her deep throat."

She had taken to speaking of herself in the third person, as if the character she played in *Deep Throat* was a fictional creation and not her.

In front of Hefner, his bunnies, a scattering of movie stars, and assorted flotsam and jetsam of the sex-crazed 1970s, Chuck demonstrated a new trick, using Linda as his victim. "It's called fist-fucking." Then, to the astonishment of the audience, he inserted his fist into Linda's anus.

After gaping at the fist-fuck demonstration, "all of Hefner's guests applauded, just like they'd have done for a dance by Ginger Rogers and Fred Astaire in a 1930s movie," Linda said. "At the mansion, it was always a bacchanal—a word I'd learned only recently—and Hefner was always cast in the role of Caligula. As for Caligula, all I needed to know about him I learned from that Bob Guccione movie eight years later. The hard core stuff in *Caligula* wasn't bad, but I could have done without all those beheadings and disemboweling. To my knowledge, Malcolm McDowell, Peter O'Toole, Helen Mirren, and John Gielgud each made their first porno in *Caligula*. I started this trend of big stars doing porn."

"Chuck and Linda may not have in-

Linda: "At the end of our demonstration, all of Hefner's guests applauded, just like they'd have done for a dance by Ginger Rogers and Fred Astaire.

(top photo): **Astaire and Rogers** in *Roberta* (1935)

vented fist-fucking, but they set off a new craze," claimed Steve McQueen. "It was all the rage for many years, although it put a lot of people, both gay boys and women, into the hospital."

"A lot of voyeurs at the mansion wanted to see me get fist-fucked," Linda recalled. "When they didn't want to watch that, they wanted me to indulge in some lesbian love with one of Hefner's bunnies. No one seemed to want sex like grandma did it."

Every week, Hefner staged "orgy night" at the mansion, the sex often taking place inside a simulated grotto near the pool. Always attired in an elegant bathrobe and/or in silk pajamas, Hefner made his appearance late, after the action was already under way.

"Chuck virtually pushed me at Hefner, but he took his time coming on to me," Linda claimed.

Before Hefner jumped into the pool, she saw him strip down and apply Johnson's Baby Oil to his chest, thighs, hands, and penis. Then he plunged into the water, laughing as he did.

"When Hefner finally joined us in the pool, I wanted to fuck him and give him some head," Linda claimed. "He first invited me to make out with this beautiful gal standing next to me. We started with some lesbian love, and he joined the scene. I felt his much experienced tongue on my clit."

"After he'd had enough of that, he entered me from the rear. The guy really knew what he was doing. He should, after all the experience he'd had. He turned me around and began to screw me royally, down deep and dirty. He went at it for fifteen to twenty minutes. I lost count. We both had a climax together. I'd call that perfect harmony. Some of the famous names I seduced during the height of my popularity plunged in no more than two dozen times—and that was that."

"Actually, I never experienced sex with Hefner the way I really dreamed it," Linda said. "I wanted him to take me up in his private plane and screw me 30,000 feet off the ground. I wanted to join the Mile High Club."

"Sure, Hefner and Linda balled, usually in public and around the pool," Chuck said. "But it wasn't a romantic thing. It was more of an ego trip for him, because Linda was the sex symbol of the moment. *Playboy's* honcho was known for separating sex from romantic feelings."

Hefner was said to own the largest collection of 8mm loops in the world, including porn shot by stars before they became famous. These included everybody from Joan Crawford to Marilyn Monroe. He also collected bestiality films, including loops depicting women fornicating with donkeys and horses. One particularly bizarre loop that Chuck discovered showed a young man getting sodomized by a black stallion.

She was upset to hear that Hefner had seen *The Dog Fucker* several times.

She heard him tell Chuck that his staff at the Mansion had tried several times "to bring a chick and a dog together, but it had not worked out."

Chuck agreed how tricky it was, and then offered to bring their dog Rufus to the Mansion the following night. "Wait until you see how Linda and Rufus go at it," he promised.

"Hefner really wanted Linda to fuck a dog," Chuck claimed.

Although she said that she intended to be ready for the dog, Linda had no intention of letting Hefner witness her getting fucked by Rufus. The following evening, when the dog was brought out to join them at the pool, Hefner and Chuck settled back for some excitement, which they did not get.

Using techniques which had worked before, she came on aggressively toward the dog, acts which this time seemed to frighten him. When Rufus couldn't produce an erection for Linda, Hefner ordered a member of his staff to take the dog to his kennel. But after only one night there, Rufus killed one of Hefner's sheep dogs and nearly chewed another dog to death. The following morning, Rufus was shipped back to a kennel in Miami.

In a *New York Times* article published on September 5, 2004, a reporter claimed, "Linda gained a reputation for her enthusiasm for seducing dogs. She reportedly put on bestiality shows for Hugh Hefner and company at his Playboy Mansion in Los Angeles." Years before, she had denied that, giving her own version of events.

Norman Mailer, the author, had heard of the various entertainments provided at the mansion, and he showed up on a number of occasions. Years later, he admitted that he missed all the fist-fucking and bestiality, but that he had found other diversions there instead.

"Those in attendance often felt swept up in a timeless, spaceless sensation," said Mailer. "One was in an ocean liner, which traveled at the bottom of the sea on a journey whose duration lasted a year."

"You never knew the sexual liaisons you'd have there," Mailer said. "One night, I met Linda Lovelace, who volunteered to give me a blow-job. I think Hef turned her on to me. Now I won't pretend that Linda had read *The Naked and the Dead*. But what did it matter? It was the best blow-job of my life."

"I'm just a nice Jewish boy from Brooklyn," Mailer told Linda. "But James Baldwin claimed I'm a real sweet *ofay* cat, but a little frantic. Allen Ginsberg said I was 'macho folly,' and Chandler Brossard claimed 'I was an unemployed and unemployable Hamlet.' *The Village Voice* dismissed me as 'a narcissistic pest.'"

She had never heard of any of the men Mailer had cited, but found the assessments amusing. At the end of his recitation, he asked her, "And what do the pundits say about you?"

"That I'm the world's greatest deep-throater, although some stupid actor told the press I use too much teeth."

"That simply isn't true," Mailer told her. "You didn't leave one tooth mark on my honorable penis."

"Truman Capote always claimed that he gave a better blow-job than Linda," Mailer claimed. "That Capote was such a bullshitter. One night at a drunken party in Brooklyn Heights, I let Capote go down on me. The mincing little flamer gagged. By far, Linda was a better deep-throater than Capote. Trust the man who knows. Of course, I would have preferred Marilyn Monroe to both of them."

"I rarely went down on a famous author like Mailer," Linda said, "but during my days at the Playboy Mansion, I sucked off a lot of movie stars at some of Hefner's orgies," Linda claimed. "It didn't always have to be at an orgy. On any night, there was sex going on somewhere, perhaps in the hidden corner of the grotto or somewhere on the grounds. On orgy nights, most of the big movie stars disappeared, perhaps fearing they'd secretly be photographed. But many of the stars were very exhibitionistic, guys like Tony Curtis who didn't seem to mind parading around naked in front of people and getting it on. Tony went both ways, and one night I saw him going down on a young actor wannabe. Perhaps he promised the kid a part in his next movie."

Literary prizewinner and bad boy **Norman Mailer**: "Now I won't pretend that Linda had read *The Naked and the Dead*. But what did it matter? It was the best blow-job of my life."

(photo above) **Mailer** as he appeared on the cover of *LIFE* in August of 1969.

"One of my greatest triumphs was the night I got to go down on Tony Curits," she said. "I met him in the pool and we sneaked off under a waterfall into the grotto. He had an uncut dick, not terribly big, but he knew how to use it. He literally fucked my mouth. As he did, visions of his former conquests, everyone from Elizabeth Taylor to Marilyn Monroe, bounced through my head."

"With Tony's creamy gift lining my stomach, we later put on our bathing suits and enjoyed a lobster-and-wine buffet, courtesy of Hefner," Linda said. "Some of the females didn't even bother to dress for dinner, if you get my drift. All of them flirted with Tony. I had drained that guy dry. He amused his admiring flock of young Bunnies by telling them that when Elvis started out, 'He copied my hairdo.'"

Linda recounted that one of her most memorable seductions occurred at the Playboy Mansion during the summer of 1972. Hefner had invited the Rolling Stones for a four-day orgy of sex, drugs, and partying, according to reports.

"I was determined to suck off Mick Jagger, as I was a big fan of his," Linda claimed. "At Chuck's urging, I went after him. Mick wore a bathrobe obviously borrowed from Hefner. It was a terrycloth robe, the color of gold. I came right up to him. 'Mr. Jagger, I'm the world's greatest cocksucker. I want to blow you.'"

He looked at her. "You're a lustful little bird," he told her.

"I don't think he'd seen *Deep Throat* at that time," she said, "but he studied me carefully, then flipped open his bathrobe. 'Go to it, luv,' he said, and I did. I don't know have many times he'd had sex that day. It took him a long time. But he shot off, and I wouldn't release his dick from my mouth until I'd swallowed the last drop."

"Hefner told me that after the Stones checked out, 'My Mansion looked like Rome after the barbarians attacked. Somehow, they even managed to clog the drainpipes. But the boys were fun, if you liked to live in a tornado.'"

"I remember other movie stars there, including Raquel Welch—that stuck-up bitch, Jack Nicholson, and even Groucho Marx. I'd seen Groucho on TV and thought he was very funny. He told me his greatest wish was to be able to get it up again. 'I was born in 1890, but don't tell anybody,' he said. "I took his left hand and let him feel my pussy. He got quite a good feel. After he'd finished, he said, 'I can tell you've just gotten back from the barber.'"

"The orgies, of course, weren't too brightly lit, and you never knew who was piling on top of you," Linda recalled. "I was stoned a lot of the time. One night, I looked up into the face of Russ Meyer. I recognized him from the Hollywood newspapers. He'd made that campy *Beyond the Valley of the Dolls* plus a lot of other movies."

"Late in 1974, I tried to get him to cast me in his picture, *Supervixens*, but he must have forgotten about the free fuck I gave him. Of course, he was famous for casting women with mammoth boobs, and, even with the silicone, I guess I wasn't busty enough."

At this point, Linda became a bit catty. "As for Meyer the Lover, he got to the point quickly enough—a hug, a brief kiss, a touch of my breast, and quick penetration, goodbye, and thanks for the memory."

"No Satisfaction" Superstar
Mick Jagger

Hefner, after the Stones checked out: "My mansion looked like Rome after the barbarians attacked."

"Did you get any turn-downs by any stars? Reba-Anne Howard asked her years later.

"On another occasion, I ran into Angie Dickinson," Linda answered. "I came on to her, but I don't think that at that time, she knew who I was. I'd heard that JFK had fucked her, but my pass was subtle. She just walked away. She may not have heard me, but if she did, I think she had no interest at all in lesbian love."

"I also saw Peter O'Toole strolling the grounds with Hefner, and I wanted Hef to set up something with me and O'Toole. I had fallen in love with him when I saw *Lawrence of Arabia.* But nothing came of it. When I later heard him talking to a bevy of women in the living room, he said, "Hefner's mansion is what God would have created if only he'd had the bread.""

"I once saw Paul Newman wandering about, but I didn't get him that night. Blue Eyes definitely lay in my future. All Paul needs to do is ask Harry Reems if I can handle Jewish dick."

***

One night, she met a lusty Anthony Quinn, who came on to her rather strong. As a frequent movie goer, she had thrilled to his smoldering presence in such movies as *Zorba the Greek* (1964).

One of the first questions this Mexican-American asked her was, "Linda, now that you're a movie star, who is your role model? Elizabeth Taylor, Jane Fonda, or Lucille Ball?"

Anthony Quinn *(photo above)* to Linda: "I fucked everyone from Carole Lombard to George Cukor--now it's your turn to find out what's special about me."

"I want to be a serious actress, but the only roles offered me are in porn," she said.

"In the 1920s, when I was a teen, I did some porn, but I think all the loops are lost today," he said. "At least nothing has resurfaced to haunt me."

"Who was your role model?" she asked.

"Believe it or not, I wanted to be Napoléon, Michelangelo, Shakespeare, Picasso, Martin Luther, and Jack Dempsey, all rolled into one," he said.

"Fortunately for those of us who go to the movies, you became none of the above...but Anthony Quinn."

"That compliment, little darling, will get you anywhere with me," he said.

"Standing before you, I'm ready, willing, and

able," she said.

"Forgive me, but what I have in mind calls for you to be on your knees," he said.

"You're on!" she said. "Let's head for the game room."

After plunging down on Quinn, Linda agreed with the former assessment of his girlfriend, actress Evelyn Keyes, who had played Scarlett O'Hara's younger sister in *Gone With the Wind*. Keyes had said, "There was simply too much of Tony. Yes, down there, too."

"After giving him 'one of my best blows,' he said something strange," Linda said. "He told me that 'until tonight, I've never really felt a man's masculinity was in his penis. But it sure was tonight.'"

"I love reading about the love affairs of movie stars," she said to Quinn. "I fear unfavorable comparisons with your former lovers—Mae West, Shelley Winters, Rita Hayworth, Ingrid Bergman."

"No competition from Ingrid," Quinn said. "She doesn't go that route. You're the best, and I've been fellated every since I was fourteen years old and passed out on L.A.'s Seal Beach. When I came to, an older woman was licking away to her heart's content."

[At the time Linda met Quinn, he was married to Jolanda Addolori, the Italian costume designer.]

A much stranger encounter was with bald-headed actor Yul Brynner, famous for starring in *The King and I*. When he heard that Linda was at Hefner's mansion, he arranged for a male member of the *Playboy* staff to send for her.

Linda, discussing **Yul Brynner**
(photo above)

They met on the grounds, far away from the main house, in a temporary Arabian Nights tent which had been erected in the gardens.

She was shown inside, where Brynner was the center of attention while seated with five other men, perhaps actors, but none she recognized. He had to explain to her that they were smoking opium, and he invited her to join him, but she refused.

"Pot, or perhaps a little cocaine, are my drugs of choice," she said.

"Too bad," Brynner told her. "Opium is life's greatest pleasure."

"You didn't invite me here to smoke opium," she said in front of the other men, all of whom had remained silent and seemed to resent her presence. She suspected they were gay, since Brynner was known for his bisexual tastes.

"He told me that girls have an unfair advantage over men. 'If they don't get what they want by being smart, they can get it by playing dumb.'"

"I've decided the two greatest pleasures in life would be to combine smoking opium with getting a blow-job," he said. "Would you oblige me in what is increasingly known in Hollywood as the Linda Lovelace specialty?"

"I'd love to," she said. She came over to him and got down in front of him. He was wearing a robe which he opened for her, displaying an uncut penis which in her mouth and throat rose to an impressive eight inches. "As he smoked, I blew," she later recalled.

"Someone had told me that starlet in the 1940s, Nancy Davis, now married to Reagan, had been called 'The Fellatio Queen of Hollywood.' Now that she was retired from the game, I wanted to be known as the new 'Fellatio Queen of Hollywood.' During their affair, I could just imagine how many times Nancy went down on Yul, and I was determined to best her."

"Yul really blasted off to the moon, so I think I won the prize. He more or less confirmed it. I looked up into his eyes for approval. 'Better than Nancy?' I asked."

"Tallulah Bankhead was not good at it, but Nancy and Marlene were," Brunner said. "You beat them. For your effort, I'll share a special treat with you."

A bowl of grapes rested nearby. "I'd never done this ritual before," she said. "But he put the grape in his mouth, eating half of it and inviting me to share the other half. It was all very, very sensual. I wondered if he pulled shit like that with another of his lovers, Joan Crawford."

[At the time Linda met him, Brynner was married to the French socialite,

James Caan:

"I'm the kind of guy when work is done who has to blow it off like going to the rodeo, drinking, or whoring."

Jacqueline Thion de la Chaume, but she was nowhere to be seen. They had adopted two Vietnamese children. Linda had also read that in Switzerland in 1965, he had renounced his naturalized U.S. citizenship for tax reasons.]

In addition to Brynner, one of the more regular visitors at the Playboy Mansion was actor James Caan. "He was a little guy, but I found him sexy," Linda said. She claimed she made it one time with Caan, "but I was with three other gals, and I don't think he even knew who I was."

Biographer Mart Martin claimed that Caan seduced "lots of *Playboy* centerfolds, including Connie Kreski, and models." Martin also quoted Caan as saying, "I balled an astounding number…*bam, bam, bam, bam*…in a row."

Linda said that one night she was standing in "that row of Bunny fuckees" when one of the

298

Playmates told her that Caan was "crazy about licking pussy. I spent hours squatting over his face."

"Caan was an amusing guy, and I found he had a powerful sex appeal," Linda said, "even if he didn't know, or seem to know, who I was. Once, sitting around a buffet, he amused his table by claiming that he lost his virginity, at the age of thirteen, in a Miami whorehouse. 'It was taken by a middle aged *puta*,' he said. 'As I fucked her, my ass was eaten alive by mosquitoes.'"

Sometimes, Chuck and Linda joined Hefner aboard his private plane for visits to the Playboy Mansion in Chicago. "In Illinois, we didn't meet much of that movie star crowd, and the parties there were much duller," Linda said. "I couldn't believe it: Some of the jerks in Chicago didn't know who I was, and at the time, I was one of the most famous movie stars in the world. Chuck spent most of the day watching 8mm loops, and I enjoyed the world's best beef Wellington prepared by this wonderful chef."

"I remember meeting Shel Silverstein, the writer and cartoonist. He suggested doing an album of country and western songs with me, but greedy Chuck screwed it for me and the deal fell through."

When she first met Silverstein, Linda did not know who he was, until Hefner explained that he was a singer-songwriter, musician, composer, cartoonist, and author of children's books. In books alone, he'd sold more than 20 million copies, which were translated into thirty different languages.

In 1957, this Chicago-born artist became one of *Playboy* magazine's leading cartoonists. His sketchbook took him to locales which included a nudist colony in New Jersey, whose residents he sketched, as well as to points within San Francisco's Haight-Ashbury district, Paris, Spain, and Africa.

Years later, at his home in Key West (Florida), Silverstein told the author, "I don't know what it was, but there was something that attracted me to Linda. In some ways, she reminded me of Loretta Lynn. I'd written a hit for Loretta called, 'One's on the Way.' For Linda, I somewhat envisioned her potential for a whimsical hit like 'A Boy Named Sue' that I'd written for Johnny Cash. Except in this song, as sung by Linda, she'd have a girl, whom she'd name Henry to help her fight off rapists in the Rocky Mountains."

Illustrator, songwriter, and *Play-boy* cartoonist **Shel Silverstein** *(photo above):*

"When I'm getting a blow-job from a woman, I don't like the husband barging in to direct the scene."

"I tested Linda out, and she couldn't sing. But with the right—and loudest—background music, I came up with the idea of a mostly talkie song about a woman who develops a sore throat after a wild night of partying."

"Of course, there was her technique. She

swallowed a guy whole and even tried to fit in his balls. As an oral artist, she was great sex. I was really turned on by her. My Jewish girl friends in high school wouldn't ever go down on me."

"Linda would have been great recording my cautionary song about venereal disease, 'Don't Give a Dose to the One You Love Most.'"

"In 1962, I wrote a song, 'Boa Constrictor,' about a hapless man getting swallowed by a snake. That folk group, *Peter, Paul, and Mary,* recorded it. I envisioned doing a sort of porno version of it—not dirty, just comedic—with Linda singing about swallowing the boa constrictor. I thought we could put together a comedy-and-song album."

"What screwed the deal?" he asked. "That fucking Chuck Traynor. He started barging in with his demands and talks of percentages. I finally said to hell with the idea, but not until I got a final blow-job from the *artiste* herself, Linda Lovelace."

According to Linda, Chuck had more of a fantasy about Hefner than she did. "He wanted to become Hefner's best pal, sharing Playmates and fluffy-tailed Bunnies," she said. "Hefner, of course, was too smart to get tangled up with a sleazeball like Chuck, and he came to realize that he and Hefner were not going to become fuck buddies or business partners."

Although Hefner was not ready to go into business with Chuck, he did recommend a former Bunny, Delores Wells, as an ideal candidate for the management of their newly created Linda Lovelace Enterprises. Delores turned out to be a savvy choice.

Delores Welles *(photo above)*, a Bunny at the original Playboy Club in Chicago, was Playmate and Centerfold of the month in June of 1960.

In the mid-70s, she was hired as the business manager of Linda Lovelace Enterprises.

When Chuck met Delores, he liked her at once, because "she fitted my chief requirement that all my female employees have big tits."

But it was to Linda that Delores was drawn, finding her unspoiled, natural, and very sweet in spite of her name and scandalous reputation. "When I introduced her to my six-year-old daughter, Linda shed a tear, confiding in me that her great dream involved having a happy marriage and children," Delores said.

When the nude *Playboy* layout of Linda was released, it did not meet with universal approval from the magazine's readers. In the opinion of thousands of men, Linda did not live up to the beauty, glamour, or the breasts of previous Playmates.

A typical criticism came from Larry Wilson,

who wrote: "I was always at a loss to understand the appeal of either Lovelace or *Deep Throat.* She was rather unattractive, not even the usual soft-focus airbrush photography of *Playboy* could make her appealing."

In later memoirs, Linda would present an unattractive portrait of the debauchery at the Playboy Mansion. But Hefner never treated her unkindly. She concluded: "Hefner was a terrific guy. A wonderful guy. He did something that Chuck could never do. He treated me like a human being."

She had a parting, rather blunt, comment: "Hefner knows how to make a girl's cunt feel real good."

Asked to recall her encounters with Hefner, she said, "I think he borrowed a bit of life's philosophy from Peggy Lee and her famous song. He told me, 'If that's all there is, then let's keep dancing.'"

***

Ever since Hefner had informed Linda about how engrossing Warren Beatty had found *Deep Throat,* she was anxious to meet him. When she was fifteen, Beatty, along with Clint Eastwood, had been her dream man. Her previous encounter with Eastwood had been a dud, but she was hoping for a livelier performance with Beatty, who was a frequent visitor to both the Playboy Mansion West, and to the Playboy Club that had opened on the Sunset Strip in the mid-1960s.

Hefner's biographer, Steven Watts, a professor of history at the University of Missouri, wrote: "Beatty was notorious for his sexual conquests. According to an observer, the stunningly handsome, soft-voiced move star would simply approach a young woman, shake her hand, and quietly say, 'Hi, I'm Warren,' at which point she would melt."

Beatty's reputation had preceded him. Film historian David Thomson claimed, "Warren Beatty cannot endure or dispense with the legend of Don Juan."

Linda was convinced that Beatty, according to the gossip columns, maintained the most impressive list of seductions of any male star in Hollywood, beginning with Jackie Kennedy and Elizabeth Taylor, with whom he'd made the 1970 *The Only Game in Town.* In 1967, Linda had seen *Bonnie and Clyde* five times and had thrilled to Beatty's good looks, calling him at one point, "The Sexiest Man Alive."

Beatty's list of his conquests were legendary before and after Linda met him—Leslie Caron, Cher, Julie Christie, Joan Collins, Jane Fonda, Angelica Huston, Bianca Jagger, Diane Keaton, Madonna, Mary Tyler Moore, Christina Onassis, Lee Radziwill, Vanessa Redgrave, Diana Ross, Jean Seberg, Carly Simon, Barbra Streisand, Goldie Hawn, H.R.H. Princess Margaret, Princess

Elizabeth of Yugoslavia, Brigitte Bardot, Candice Bergen, Diane Sawyer, and maybe—just maybe—Tennessee Williams and "that other gay playwright," William Inge.

One night at the Los Angeles Playboy Club, Linda sat at Hefner's table and overheard Playboy bunny "Kevin" Lauritzen speak of her affair with Beatty. She told the table, as she'd later confide to Beatty's biographer, Ellis Amburn: "Warren is a cerebral fuck, not a great lover. He fucks your mind before he fucks anything else. He even convinced me I was a more fascinating woman—and better in bed—than Jackie Kennedy. I've had better lovers. It's not his love making, but the attention he gives a woman. More than any guy I know, he really listens to a woman, and that's a real turn-on. He's the most sought-after date in Hollywood, and the reason is not because of what's between his legs. He reaffirms your femininity, your womanhood."

Another visitor to the Playboy Mansion, Sarah Porterfield, told author Amburn: "Warren would never go to a girl's apartment, because he was so paranoid. He was terrified of hidden cameras that would show them doing it. If he wanted sex with a girl, he always went to the Beverly Wilshire Hotel. The only place he ever did sex besides the Wilshire was at Hefner's mansion. It was safe there. I remember being up at Hef's one day and Warren appeared with a Bunny on each arm. Hef said, 'Have you been robbing the Hutch again, Warren?' I think he was doing Playmates as well."

Finally, Hefner introduced her to her idol, saying, "I'd like your number one fan, Warren Beatty, to meet his number one fan, Linda Lovelace."

At this point, the screen darkens. Linda could be very graphic in descriptions of her sexual encounters. But in a few cases, she simply refused to describe what happened, protecting the object of her affection for whatever reason she had. Even in her memoirs, in some instances, she described her encounters, but refused to identify the names of their famous participants.

Warren Beatty
A universal sex symbol who was "terrified of hidden cameras"

She'd heard that Beatty had "flipped' over *Deep Throat,* "He praised my free-flowing style. Since he didn't come on to me, I believed he was sincere."

Perhaps forgetting what she'd written in an earlier memoir, she reported their encounters differently. She wrote, "Just the thought of Warren touching my hand would create shivers." She also claimed that on several different evenings at Hefner's mansion, Beatty propositioned her and wanted her to go to the Beverly Wilshire with him. "If I ever faced temptation," she said, "that was the occasion. Still, I never went away with him."

Literary agent Jay Garon's researchers refused to believe her. "She consistently denied going to bed with Beatty, even though admitting how powerfully attracted she was to him," Garon said. "She went to bed with every Tom, Dick, and Harry in Hollywood, so why leave Beatty out? I'd bet at least ten thousand dollars she sucked Beatty off. But when she refused to admit something, she was stubborn."

During those same "grilling" sessions, Garon asked Linda if she'd gone to bed with Ryan O'Neal, the other Hollywood Lothario of the 1970s. "She neither confirmed nor denied it," Garon said, "but that Mona Lisa smile on her face more or less confirmed it. Put another way, she had a look of a cat who ate the canary. But we can't be sure, because she wouldn't tell us."

"Everyone in Hollywood knew that Beatty and O'Neal sometimes seduced the same women—Joan Collins, Angelica Huston, Bianca Jagger, Diana Ross, Barbra Streisand," Garon said. "In the case of Linda Lovelace with those two studs, we'll have to give it a maybe. If I were on a jury, I would vote guilty in both cases."

Author Joy Fielding took a rather cynical view of Linda's seductions. "Perhaps she came to feel that ultimately, no one would believe her gruesome memoir, and that she would be dismissed as a woman only out to make a buck, out to out-confess Britt Ekland or Joan Collins, and all the others who'd slept with Warren and Ryan. Perhaps Lovelace feared she'd be laughed at as a woman clutching at the straws of fame that had long since deserted her."

***

At the newly established Linda Lovelace Enterprises, various calls came in, most of which were handled by Delores Wells, as Chuck and Linda were rarely available. Even if Linda were on site, Chuck didn't want her making any deals for herself. He was still her control freak, although it was increasingly clear that his days with her would be over soon.

Many of the calls were solicitations from wannabe actors or even movie stars wanting to line up a date with Linda as a means of sampling her deep throating. Others were proposals for business deals, including movie offers and night club acts, most of which Chuck sabotaged. "If you wanted to queer a deal for me, bring in Chuck and a potential backer who might have done something for my career. After a few minutes with Chuck, a potential producer would flee to the Hollywood Hills."

One call that came in intrigued both Chuck and Linda in equal measure. It was from a rather effeminate male secretary—Burt Lancaster hired only gay males as his secretaries—who wanted to set up a meeting between the superstar and Linda. "It seemed like some sort of movie offer, although I'd heard that his production company, Hecht-Hill-Lancaster, had gone belly up," Delores said.

From a debut as a struggling circus acrobat who had posed for porno, often gay, on the side, Burt Lancaster had evolved into one of the top stars in Hollywood, famous for his intelligence, his magnificent physique, and his brooding good looks.

Known for his competence with both heavy drama and roles as swashbucklers, he had thrilled Linda in *From Here to Eternity* with that "on the beach" scene with Deborah Kerr. "Burt even managed to thaw out that ice maiden," Linda recalled.

Over the coming weeks, she would discover what a complex and paradoxical man he was, both arrogant and sensitive.

She'd heard that he was a "babe magnet," seducing his leading ladies in a pattern that had begun with the sultry Ava Gardner in *The Killers* (1946). When he'd co-starred with Yvonne de Carlo in *Brute Force* (1947), she'd said: "He had a tremendous intensity and was the kind of macho man who says nothing, but takes a girl by the hand and leads her off to his lair."

One of his most famous affairs had been with Shelley Winters, who had co-starred with him in *The Scalphunters* (1968), although their sexual encounters had begun years before that.

Chuck had heard that Lancaster also had "a taste for cock," especially if it was attached to Tony Curtis, with whom he'd co-starred in *Trapeze* (1956). Although that film was a critical success, it was a box office disaster.

Lancaster's biographer, Kate Buford, wrote: "Lancaster's rages, promiscuity, and mood swings suggested some kind of conflict or confusion about his sexual identity, at least."

Linda's defender, champion, and playmate: **Burt Lancaster,** with a rose tattoo on his chest.

The playwright, Clifford Odets, who had scripted the film version of the 1957 *film noir, Sweet Smell of Success,* brilliantly captured Lancaster's mercurial personality:

"There was not one Burt Lancaster, but seven: Inscrutable Burt who, even when he was there seemed not to be; Cocky Burt, utterly confident and maybe contemptuous; Wild Man Burt, with an overpowering voltage of energy and enthusiasm; Big Daddy Burt, the paternal caregiver who took over when weaker persons needed him; Monster Golem Burt who could instantly transform into a cruelty machine; 'Marquis de Lancaster Burt,' the grand

old courtier of precious gestures and mincing words, a caricature of nobility; and, juggling life with grace and mischief and laughter, Hustler Burt, the man who revealed nothing to no one."

Linda saw only the "Big Daddy Burt" side of this volatile star.

Chuck accompanied Linda to the Polo Lounge of the Beverly Hills Hotel for cocktails. But after the first drink, Lancaster suggested that Chuck might seek a diversion elsewhere while he talked privately with Linda.

After he'd left, Lancaster expressed his disdain for Chuck, which afforded her the opportunity to tell the star about the abuse she suffered from him. She immediately won his sympathy, as he was always a champion of the downtrodden, probably owing to his own early hardships in life.

After drinks, he invited her to join him in a bungalow on the hotel grounds. "I've seen *Deep Throat,"* he told her. "You're really good."

Later, in the bedroom, after some preliminary talk, he stripped down and showed off his physique, of which he was proud—and with good reason.

I'm sure my cock comes as no surprise to you," he said. "Both of us have been depicted buck naked in Al Goldstein's *Screw* magazine."

"I saw that," she said. "The shit presented you in what he called 'all your uncut glory.'"

"It's not as small as it looked in that picture, as you can see," he said. "I'm a grower, not a show-er."

As she'd later remember it, "Burt wanted the longest foreplay of any john I've ever had. He was an *Around the World in Eighty Days* kind of guy. The complete works, from his ears to his armpits, even a tongue up his nostrils. He wanted his tits worked over, his fingers sucked, his belly licked and his balls tongued, his thighs and calves devoured, and one toe at a time. I finally got around to my specialty. As I did that, he demanded I jiggle his balls. It was some night."

"Unlike some of the others, he promised to call me soon, claiming he was into three ways," she said. "Most movie stars tried me one time and then no more. But Burt kept his promise in the weeks to come."

"When he learned the Chuck took all her money, including her fee for *Deep Throat* and for the nude *Playboy* layout, he made a deal with her. "I'm giving you six hundred dollars," he said. "Tell that fart you made only a hundred and pocket the rest. Why not open your own bank account? Save up enough money so you can run away from the bastard. Slavery went out in 1865."

Afterward, she said, "I didn't do it right away, but in time, I would do just what Burt suggested. My only regret

Tony Curtis:

"I know too many Hollywood secrets."

305

about Burt is that he didn't become my next husband. What a guy! What a dreamboat!"

[At the time Linda met Lancaster, a native New Yorker, he had recently divorced his longtime spouse, Norma Anderson.]

"If you ever want to get married again, I'm available," Linda said. "As soon as I divorce Chuck, that is."

***

As she was leaving the Beverly Hills Hotel, with Chuck waiting outside in his car, Linda was approached by an elegantly dressed, dark-haired woman. "I recognize you," the woman said. "I'm Jacqueline Susann, and you're Linda Lovelace of *Deep Throat* fame!'"

"One and the same," Linda confessed. "I've heard of you. You wrote *Valley of the Dolls*. That was the only novel I've ever read in my life."

"I'm flattered," Susann said.

"You were in your book's movie version, too," Linda said. "I recognize you: You played a reporter."

"It was such a bit part," Susann said. "I'm glad I left an impression." She glanced at her gold watch. "I'm late and we're both on the run, I'm sure. But I have something I want to talk over with you—let's call it a business proposal. Could you meet me here in the lobby at around one o'clock tomorrow afternoon? We'll have lunch at Chasens. "

"I'd be honored," Linda said.

"It's strictly a private affair," Susann cautioned. "I won't bring my husband if you don't bring yours."

"It's a deal," Linda promised. She was enjoying her new access to VIPs without Chuck's overweening presence.

The next day, with help from Delores, Linda made herself look as much like a Catholic schoolgirl as possible. She didn't want to have lunch at Chasen's with the celebrated novelist looking like a Times Square hooker.

Dressed in "virginal white," she arrived at the Beverly Hills Hotel in a car driven by Chuck. He had wanted to attend the lunch, but she'd warned him that Susann had pre-defined the event as, "No men allowed."

The novelist was not in the lobby at 1pm, so Linda inquired at the reception desk. "Oh, yes, Miss Lovelace," the receptionist said. "Miss Susann requests that you come up to her suite. One of her conferences is running late, and she wants to meet you there."

As the hotel elevator carried her upstairs, Linda inspected herself again in her pocketbook mirror, deciding that her makeup was "Audrey Hepburn subtle," instead of garishly painted like Shirley MacLaine's in *Some Came Run-*

ning.

Linda was shown into the suite by a maid. The chicly dressed Susann was most gracious, kissing her on both cheeks. "I've been having a little *tête-à-tête* with Robert Ryan here," Susann said. "Mr. Ryan, meet Linda Lovelace."

"What a privilege," the soft-spoken, firmly masculine actor said. "I'm familiar with your work." Then the former boxer and model gave her a gentle handshake. He appeared warm, sincere, and intelligent. The only movie of his she could recall was *Clash by Night* (1952), with Barbara Stanwyck and Marilyn Monroe.

As she settled into a chair on Susann's terrace for a pre-luncheon cocktail, Linda gathered that the actor was meeting with Susann to discuss his recent film, *The Love Machine,* released in 1971 and based on her novel of the same name.

The novel, Susann's inside look at the world of television, had been a shocker. It was said to have been based on the life and career of James Aubrey. Nicknamed "The Smiling Cobra" by his enemies, he had been the colorful president, during the early 1960s, of CBS Television and the developer of series, including *Gilligan's Island* and *The Beverly Hillbillies*, which each became an icon of the American *zeitgeist*.

Susann told an amusing story of how she reached the conclusion that only Charlton Heston could play the role of the film's anti-hero, Robin Stone. She had "seen the light" after she admired Heston's bare *derrière* in *Planet of the Apes.* "But Ben-Hur, or Moses if you will, turned it down. Then five other leading men rejected it too—Gregory Peck, Frank Sinatra, Dean Martin, William Holden, and Rock Hudson—before the role went to John Philip Law."

"Don't forget, Jackie, I was also in the movie," Ryan said.

"Yes, Robert played Dyan Cannon's husband."

When Susann left the terrace to answer a call from her husband, Irving Mansfield, Ryan leaned over to her.

"I thought you were very good as that sex therapist in *Deep Throat,"* he said. "It's because you were so convincing in that role that I'd like to meet privately with you."

"Do you call me or I'll call you?"

He handed her a card with his private number. "I've got this problem, you see, and I think you're the gal to solve it."

Valley of the Dolls

How Linda made a sensation at Chasen's with **Jacqueline Susann**

"Did she really look "like a truck driver in drag," as asserted by Truman Capote?

307

"I can work miracles," she promised. "After all, I'm the *real* love machine."

***

Arriving by limousine, Susann and Linda made a spectacular appearance together at Chasen's, where all the luncheon guests quickly checked out the latest arrivals. In hip Hollywood of that day, nearly everyone recognized Susann, and quite a few whispered "It's Linda Lovelace!" *Deep Throat* was being screened in private celebrity homes across Hollywood.

Susann ate very lightly, but Linda took advantage of the menu to order one of the best lunches of her life.

The theme of the meeting soon became clear. Susann was searching for a new subject to write about, explaining to Linda that she based her fictional characters on real people.

"Let me guess the *Who's Who* of *Valley of the Dolls,*" Linda proposed. "Neely O'Hara was Judy Garland, and Helen Lawson was Ethel Merman. Jennifer was Marilyn Monroe, and Anne was Grace Kelly. That Ed Holson character sounded a lot like Arthur Godfrey to me."

"Close enough," Susann said, "but I'll never tell. For a novel I'm planning to write, I want to base it on this sweet, natural-looking girl who makes a porn movie that has all the world talking. When she comes to Hollywood, all the big movie stars want to make out with her. I want to write about her drifting from one man to the other until she meets this handsome, dashing, swashbuckler of a figure, a combination of Errol Flynn and Burt Lancaster. Both the girl and her true love have had notorious pasts, but in each other, they settle down and live graciously ever after as the King and Queen of Hollywood Royalty."

"That's a role I'd like to play," she said, obviously excited by the idea.

"What I'm proposing is for you to meet with me at least once or twice a week and tell me about your sexual adventures," Susann said. "I know you'll be having affairs, or at least sexual encounters, with lots of the stars. I'd also like to know about your past. Where you came from. How did all this unlikely fame descend upon you—stuff like that. Of course, I'll give you a weekly salary for your cooperation."

"I'd love to do that," Linda promised.

"Oh, good, that's wonderful." Susann reached for her hand and held it possessively for an extra long moment. Linda wondered if, like her, Susann had a lesbian streak in her.

She was soon to find out.

But before she left the restaurant that day, she looked up to stare into the face of one of her favorite actors, William Holden, who was just leaving his luncheon table with Natalie Wood at his side. In her view, he was such a romantic idol that she could well understand why Gloria Swanson would rather shoot him in *Sunset Blvd.* than have him leave her for that "dowdy little mouse," Nancy Olson.

After pleasantries were exchanged, Holden said, "I've been watching you two dames from two tables away. Natalie and I were wondering what scheme you two were plotting."

"That secret belongs for the moment just to Linda and me," Susann said.

"My husband, Chuck Traynor, when he was in the military, won a contest," Linda said to Wood. "First prize was a date with you."

"Did he get lucky?" Wood asked, breaking into an impish smile. "There are those who have."

"Not me," Holden said. "Natalie is still holding out on me."

"Yeah, right," Susann said. "Just like she held out on Elvis."

"Enough of this talk," Wood said. "We must go. If he's good, Billy Boy here might get lucky today."

As Holden shook Linda's hand, he slipped a piece of paper into her palm. She discreetly put it into her purse after the two stars had left their table. But, later, after she'd read it, she realized that she possessed the private telephone number of one of the biggest celebrities in Hollywood.

After another drink within Susann's suite, the novelist invited Linda into her bedroom. "I know you haven't had a chance, or perhaps the money, to build up a wardrobe. I'd like to help you." She went to her closet and produced a fur stole. "Try this on."

Linda modeled it before her and approved of how it looked in the mirror.

The next item Susann removed from the closet was a beautifully tailored designer-made cocktail dress in emerald green. "Irving *[a reference to her husband, Irving Mansfield]* bought me this, and I've worn it on three different occasions. In this town, no gal can show up in a cocktail dress more than twice, at the very most."

Linda stripped down and tried it on. "I can make a few adjustments, and it'll look great on me!"

When she removed the dress and stood only in her bra and panties before Susann, the slightly masculine-looking novelist moved in on her.

Within minutes, Linda's undergarments were gone and so, too, was Susann's clothing. In the luxurious bed of her suite, Susann and Linda engaged in a passionate "sixty-nine." Linda welcomed a woman for a sexual change of pace.

As Linda later remembered it, their love-making went on for at least twenty minutes, maybe more. "We had a climax at the same time. It was great."

As Susann rose from the bed, she looked down at Linda. "Welcome to Hollywood, kid," she said.

***

That night, Linda had a violent argument with Chuck, at the end of which she declared victory. "Like a whiny little kid, you're always begging to go along with me to meet the stars. Get real! Do you think that when a movie star summons me to get sucked off, he wants a voyeur like you looking on?"

Even Chuck couldn't counter that argument. He was very excited by the Susann prospect. "When she writes that book, a movie sale is almost guaranteed. I want to promote you as the star of what will be an A-list movie in spite of its subject. You know she'll have a male lead. I think Warren Beatty would be ideal playing me."

"Dream on," she said, sarcastically, a comment which earned her a slap in the face.

***

Her next star encounter, again without Chuck, was with Robert Ryan.

After Ryan telephoned, Chuck agreed to drive her to a private home in Santa Monica. She just assumed that most of her star seductions would be with men who either had girlfriends or wives. Rarely invited to the home of a star, she was usually told, "It's a friend's house." The owner of the building was never identified.

A disturbing mixture of anger and tenderness, movie star **Robert Ryan** never established himself as a romantic lead. But he wanted Linda Lovelace, during the final months of his life, as his sex therapist.

When she arrived at a relatively modest villa, surrounded by a few palm trees, Ryan answered the door himself. It appeared that he was alone within the building. He'd made some sandwiches for her, and had some beer in the refrigerator.

After their small lunch, he told her he was rather despondent over his career. "Every time a good role comes up, it goes to either Mitchum or Lancaster. And if not to them, then to Bill Holden or Kirk Douglas, even though I'm a better actor than all those pansies."

"You indicated you have some problem, perhaps physical," she said.

"About two summers ago, I was cooking breakfast at my place in New Hampshire, and I dropped a pan of bacon grease on my bare foot. I had to go to the hospital. It should have been a routine treatment. X-rays were taken. But during his

310

treatment, the doctor discovered I had *lymphosarcoma*. That's cancer of the lymph glands. It's inoperable."

"Oh, my god," she said. "What in hell did you do?"

"I know I'm going to die, but the way I figure it, I've got to be stoic," he said. "If I'm lucky, I can make it for five years, two of which I've already lived. All they can do is slow down, but not cure, my malignancy. I had to endure this debilitating chemotherapy treatment. It left me very thin and absolutely weak. I kept my illness from everybody except two or three close friends. Otherwise, if word got out, I'd never work in this town again."

"Actually, don't tell Jackie I told you, but when you came by her suite, we weren't talking about *The Love Machine,*" he said. "She has cancer, too, and is undergoing treatment."

"I can't tell you how sorry I am for the both of you, and I won't say a word to her, I promise," she said.

"Linda, this is embarrassing, but the reason I brought you here is I want you to make love to me," he said. "I still have this sex drive, but I've not been able to get it up. I thought you might treat me like that nurse and patient scene you did with Harry Reems in *Deep Throat.*"

She agreed to go into the bedroom with him. As he pulled off his clothes, she felt more sympathy for him than passion, but she planned to perform her specialty as best she could. He seemed to appreciate her tenderness with him.

"It took a long time," she recalled, "but I was finally able to help him achieve an erection. He shot off in my mouth. It was more like a little squirt than a blast-off to Mars, but he was grateful for that."

"Oh, Linda, I have $250 in my wallet, which I'll give to you." Ryan said. "I want you to promise me one thing. You will visit me again?"

"Of course, I will," she said, "I think you're a very attractive man, in spite of what's happening to you."

"Thanks, you sweet girl. Before you go, could I have a real passionate kiss?"

She kissed him, and held him in her arms for about a half-hour.

At the door, wearing nothing but a towel, he said, "If you're game, I have other adventures I want with you."

"I'll be eager to share them with you, regardless of what they are," she said. "I'm always ready for anything."

"That's my girl," he said, before giving her a goodbye kiss.

In the car, she handed over the cash to Chuck. Then, with Chuck driving, they drove from Santa Monica back to Los Angeles without saying a word.

[Ryan did not make it through the final years he'd hoped to live. He died in the summer of 1973. Susann died of cancer in 1978. With Ryan, there would be other encounters during what he defined as "the twilight of my life."]

311

***

Brutalized, kicked, beaten, and degraded, even tortured, Linda Lovelace experienced a rapid change in fortune, which manifested itself during the months ahead. She'd remember it as the most memorable of her life.

"I feel like I'm not just the Queen of Porn, but the Queen of Hollywood, right up there with Elizabeth Taylor herself. I bet I'm bedding more stars than she is."

She couldn't believe the volume of names and addresses she was writing down in her recently acquired appointment book, made of red leather with gold lettering. Telephoning her were a *Who's Who* of Hollywood—William Holden, another call from Robert Ryan, Burt Lancaster, Eddie Fisher ("at least I'll find out what enthralled Liz"), and Victor Mature. And Jacqueline Susann extended another luncheon invitation at the Beverly Hills Hotel.

One call especially intrigued her. It was from Butchie Peraino from his office in New York. In his cigar-chomping way, he was as blunt and crude as ever.

"Linda, baby, would you suck a nigger's dick?"

She hesitated, offended by his question.

"C'mon," Butchie said. "Confess."

"I've been known to…I guess," she answered. "It depends on who it's attached to."

"It's attached to your biggest fan. He's seen *Deep Throat* at least a dozen times. He's practically begging you and Traynor to visit him in Hollywood."

"Who is this guy?" she asked.

"Sammy Davis, Jr.," Butchie said. "Call him. He's salivating, and most definitely wants you to salivate over him."

Sammy Davis, Jr.

"The Devil's Disciple"

312

CHAPTER NINE
What Makes Sammy, the Rat Pack, and William Holden Run?
(Seducing Hollywood, One Inch at a Time).

When *Deep Throat* opened at the sleazy Pussycat Cinema in Los Angeles, Samuel George Davis, Jr. (better known simply as Sammy Davis, Jr.), in sunglasses and a hat pulled down over his forehead, attended the showing by himself. He sat through four screenings, fleeing the theater before dawn. To his closest friends, he claimed, "I'm in love with this Linda Lovelace chick. She's hot and I'm hot for her. I've got to get into that throat of hers and teach her that black guys make better lovers and better basketball players than white dudes."

Before contacting Linda, or at least trying to get in touch with her, Sammy came up with an idea. He decided to rent the entire Pussycat Cinema for one night and invite some of the biggest names in Hollywood.

For the screening, Sammy, of course, invited the Chief Rat of the Rat Pack, Frank Sinatra himself. He suggested to Sinatra that he bring a "hard-to-get chick," if such a dame existed in Los Angeles.

"After watching Lovelace on the screen in action, you'll have your reluctant babe so hot, you'll have her before the night is over."

Sammy later told Dean Martin, "I was shocked when Frankie turned up with his 'date' for the evening. It turned out to be Spiro Agnew, the vice president of the United States."

That night, the Pussycat Cinema saw a brigade of A-list Hollywood stars for the first time in its often tawdry history—Milton and Ruth Berle, Warren Beatty ("with some chick"), Mr. and Mrs. Dick Martin, even Lucille Ball and her husband, Gary Morton. Ball's first husband, Desi Arnaz, was invited, but didn't show up. Among other A-list guests were Truman Capote with a young actor he'd later deep throat himself. Rat Packer Shirley MacLaine attended the showing, as did writer Nora Ephron.

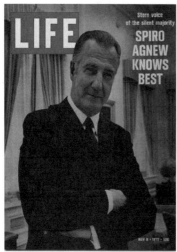

In May of 1973, *Life* magazine's editors got it wrong when they publicized then Vice-President **Spiro Agnew** as the choice of the so-called Silent Majority as a Presidential candidate in the upcoming elections of 1976.

Disgraced and ousted from Nixon's administration for accepting cash bribes, he was, privately, an early fan of Linda Lovelace and her film work in *Deep Throat,* and eventually, through Frank Sinatra, during his shaky tenure as VP, arranged a private meeting with her.

Davis also invited the assembled totals of two different bachelor parties. Bachelor Party no. 1 consisted of Dana Andrews, Forrest Tucker, Ralph Meeker, and Robert Mitchum. The guest list of Bachelor Party no. 2 included Lee Marvin, Aldo Ray, Laurence Tierney, Johnny Weissmuller, Rory Calhoun, and Fernando Lamas.

Sammy figured that watching Linda "do her thing on screen" would make all the men horny. To satisfy them, he imported some Las Vegas showgirls to entertain the men in two different hotel suites after the screening. "I wanted to get an orgy going with these guys and dolls," Sammy said.

At the end of the private screening of *Deep Throat* at the Pussycat, Sammy asked the audience to stay over to see a final, "very special" porno loop. Made in the 1930s, the grainy black-and-white loop was entitled *The Masked Bandit: He Steals Pussy.* In the loop, two beautiful girls were completely naked. The lone male star, who looked very skinny and very young, had his face covered with a black mask, which remained in place throughout the entire loop. Although he had a small frame, the boy in the film, who looked under twenty years old, boasted a prodigious endowment. Unknown to the audience, the actor was a very young Frank Sinatra.

Little did Sinatra know that at the Pussycat, Sammy had ordered a revenge prank on him for a caper wherin Sammy had been an object of ridicule.

Two weeks earlier, at the Sands Hotel in Las Vegas, Sinatra had learned that an elderly man had died as the result of a heart attack in one of the bedrooms. Sinatra asked (and bribed) the manager to help him play a joke on Sammy. The manager instructed his staff to secretly deliver the corpse to Sammy' suite when the star was deep asleep at 3am.

The next morning at around 10am, Sammy sleepily stumbled into the living room of his suite to discover the dead man sitting upright on the sofa. "I shat bananas," Sammy later claimed. "I vowed to myself that I'd get even."

After the screening of *Deep Throat* and *The Masked Bandit,* as they filed out of the Pussycat, all of the guests thanked Sammy for his hospitality and for making them part of the porno chic movement—all except one, and that was Sinatra himself.

Later that night, Sammy told his wife, actress/dancer Altovise Gore Davis, "Ol' Blue Eyes looked at me. No polar night ever had such a chill. I think I've really fucked up big time. I think the only person in the audience who nailed Frankie was Lucille Ball. She probably recognized his dick. Obviously, Frankie didn't appreciate my little joke."

"It wasn't so little," Altovise chimed in, with a laugh.

***

HOMAGE TO A GENIUS:
SAMMY DAVIS, JR.
(1925-1990)

In Memorium, Rest in Peace
The brilliant **Sammy Davis, Jr.**

Top row, left to right:

1. with **Altovise Gore;**
2. as **child vaudeville actor**, in blackface, during segregation; and
3. **in the mid-1970s**, around the time he met Linda Lovelace.

lower photo, left **In 1964, on Broadway,** in *Golden Boy*

Some anonymous woman finally contacted Linda through her Los Angeles office and arranged for both Chuck and her to visit Sammy and Altovise.

Will Haygood, author of *In Black and White: The Life of Sammy Davis, Jr.,* wrote: "Davis was forty-six years old in 1972 and was experiencing something akin to a midlife crisis around the time of *Deep Throat's* theatrical release. The wave of youth, of everything else, was so colossal that Davis had no intention of being left behind."

When Chuck finally realized that he was never going to be Hefner's close pal and that the *Playboy* publisher was never going to share the wealth with him, either in terms of money or women, he focused on this invitation from Sammy.

Before Linda's first visit to Sammy's house, Chuck instructed her, "If he shows the slightest sexual interest, seize the opportunity. Go along with it one hundred percent, even if it means tonguing his black asshole."

With Chuck walking close behind her, she stepped up and rang the doorbell to Davis' residence. A big black bodyguard opened the door and ushered Linda and Chuck in to meet Sammy. Like a high-output dynamo, he jumped up to give her a hug. He seemed to overflow with energy. "I'm a big fan of yours," he told her, before moving on to shake Chuck's hand.

"You're the one with the talent," she told him.

"I saw *Deep Throat* more than fifty times," Sammy told Linda.

"Glad to hook up with you, Sammy boy," Chuck said.

"Sammy is okay but drop this 'boy' shit," Sammy responded. "Us boys in blackface don't go for that."

"Sorry," Chuck said. "It won't happen again."

Altovise stood up and extended her delicate hand to both Chuck and Linda.

A black hipster's amorous adventures in segregated Hollywood

large photos, left to right, above: **Ava Gardner; Kim Novak** ("the lavender blonde"), **Marilyn Monroe**. Two inset photos: their seducer, **Sammy Davis, Jr.**

In her high-heel boots, she rose to a height of nearly six feet, towering over her husband, whom she fondly referred to as "My Beloved Midget."

Linda knew little about her, other than that she was Sammy's third wife. Before, in 1958, he'd married showgirl Loray White and, in 1960, the blonde-haired Swedish actress, Mai Britt.

Sammy had previously seduced such glamour queens as Ava Gardner, Marilyn Monroe, and "that lavender blonde," Kim Novak. In looks, Altovise rated somewhere way down the ladder from those screen goddesses, but she had been a talented dancer and possessed a kind of quiet charm and subtle grace. Linda quickly surmised that Sammy's invitation had not been Altovise's idea of a good time.

In the late 1950s, mobsters in Las Vegas had kidnapped him and threatened to put out his other eye if he didn't stop dating Columbia's big star, Kim Novak. They had been motivated, and paid, by studio mogul Harry Cohn, who had contacted and ordered them "to put the scare of God into the little nigger."

As a means of appearing to cater to their demands, "I married Loray right away, but it was never consummated," Sammy claimed. "After six months, I got rid of her for $25,000."

But he was still partial to blondes and in 1960, he married Mai Britt, a Swedish actress who had had a brief career in Italian films, became his second wife. When Sammy wed Britt, Frank Sinatra was his best man. The marriage, however, virtually ended Britt's film career. Sammy's career survived, despite a barrage of neo-Nazi pickets, including one that materialized in front of the Lotus Nightclub in Washington. A sign claimed, "GO BACK TO THE CONGO YOU KOSHER COON."

Before his arrival at the Davis/Gore home, Chuck had been anticipating an orgy, but nothing like that happened. It was a purely social evening, as Sammy told amusing stories of his early career in show business. At one point, he screened the film version of *West Side Story* (1961). During the musical numbers, he jumped up and danced in front of the screen.

At the time of Linda's introduction to Sammy, he was organizing a telethon for the promotion of seat belt safety. When he learned about Linda's near-fatal car accident from years before, on the Taconic Parkway in New York State, he asked her to be on the show. The understanding was that she would declare, on camera, that if she had had her seat belt on, she would not have been seriously injured.

"Trophy Wife" Blonde
Mai Britt:

Her marriage to Sammy virtually ended her film career

Chuck was against the idea, because mention of her scar tissue might come up, thereby damaging her image as a sex goddess.

Somehow, being in Sammy's presence gave Linda more confidence than she usually had. In defiance of Chuck's instructions, and consistent with her wishes to make media appearances not related to *Deep Throat* or other aspects of the porn industry, she informed the entertainer that she'd be delighted to appear on his telethon.

During the course of the foursome's evening together, Sammy told amusing stories about the Rat Pack, especially ribald and often unflattering stories about Sinatra and Peter Lawford. Throughout the evening, Chuck constantly steered the subject around to sex.

At one point, Sammy pointedly asked him, "Are you as a married couple into a certain diversions every now and then?"

"We're into anything," Chuck responded.

Sammy probably interpreted that literally. But at the time, instead of proposing anything specific, he simply said, according to Linda, "I can dig that scene myself."

To the surprise of both Chuck and his wife, the evening evolved into a series of events that were more or less typical of a Hollywood dinner party—pre-dinner drinks, followed by a fabulous meal prepared by a Hong Kong chef, and then a movie in a private screening room. Linda found both of their hosts gracious and charming.

Linda noticed that the fingernail of the pinkie finger of Sammy's left hand had been painted with scarlet nail polish. She asked about it. "Later, much later, little darling," he said. "I'll tell you about it when I know you more intimately."

When Sammy, the next day, pitched the idea of having Linda on the Telethon to its producers, they adamantly rejected the idea. He was extremely disappointed, and too embarrassed to confront Linda directly with the news, so he had Altovise call her and apologize.

Sammy himself phoned Linda a few days later and invited her to another dinner at his home. "This time, we'll have some real entertainment," he promised.

Frank Sinatra *(upper photo)* was not amused.....

Although nothing sexual had transpired the first night between the two couples, on the second visit, things were different.

After dinner, Sammy screened Frank Sinatra's porno movie, the same loop he'd arranged to screen at the Pussycat Cinema after the preview of *Deep Throat.*

After seeing the porn loop, Sammy explained that Sinatra had been filmed in it in New York City sometime around 1934, when he was young, impoverished, feuding with his parents (who had thrown him out of their house) and trying to "make a go of it," in show biz with few prospects in sight. He'd left Hoboken with only ten dollars in his pocket. He'd made the film during an era when he'd been virtually homeless, sleeping in a sleazy all-night movie theater near Times Square.

"In a men's room, a stranger, who shot blue movies for a living in the Bronx, spotted Frankie's big whang at the urinal and offered him a job," Sammy said. "It was the first time Frankie ever held a hundred dollar bill in his hand."

His sexual partner in the film was "Dawn Day," also known as Betty Joe Calahan, who had once performed a strip act on Miami Beach with a boa constrictor.

"The loop was supposed to have appeared as a segment within a 1970 film anthology entitled *Hollywood Blue,*" Sammy said. "It featured loops of movie stars who had made porno before they became famous, and it included segments with nude versions of Joan Crawford and Chuck Connors. Frankie got wind of how the producers planned to include his loop within their anthology. He threatened to sue them, and the producers subsequently removed his loop from the context of their film. But I acquired a copy of it."

Leaving Chuck and Altovise to their own amusements in the living room, Sammy took Linda's hand and led her into the bedroom. "It was at least two hours before he got around to having sex with me," she said.

In her diary, she recorded some of his exchanges with her: "I make no bones about it," he said. "When they started making porno, I became an avid collector. *Deep Throat* is my favorite, and you're my favorite porno star."

He also told her, "If God ever took away my talent, I would be a nigger again."

Then he asserted: "Complete ugliness, utter ugliness, like mine, is most attractive. Yes, I'm convinced that a really ugly man, in the end, seems attractive."

He laughed at what New York Daily News columnist Robert Sylvester had written about him: "God made Sammy as ugly as he could, and then hit him in the face with a shovel."

He also talked about his early days as a child vaudeville star, working with his father and uncle. "One day, some authority came backstage to check up on me to see if I were working underage. I put on a stage mustache and pretended I was a midget."

Before going to bed with Linda, he played her some of his original musical tapes. "Christ," he said, "how my voice has changed."

Finally, he began to strip. But it wasn't the usually awkward scenario of a man removing his clothes, a situation with which she was intimately familiar. Sammy performed as if he were a stripper in an erotic night club. Before he pulled down his shorts, he said, "Wanna see what Jean Seberg was crazy for? Even Tempest Storm, went for it, claiming I was better than either JFK or Elvis. If Liberace were in the room with us now, he'd go bat shit." Then he pulled down his shorts, as his penis flopped into view.

"Sammy was well hung," as Linda recalled, "but perhaps not quite as much as he thought he was. One blow-job was not enough for him. He'd wait a little and then demand another. I gave him my best work, and he really responded. Like so many stars I'd fellate in the future, I got high praise."

As she later learned, while she was spending all that time alone in his bedroom with Sammy, Altovise and Chuck were having intercourse on the sofa in the Davis family's living room. From what Linda perceived, without actually being told, the mating was not successful.

Linda expressed sympathy for Altovise. "I think she would have preferred to be alone with her husband. She was going through these sex scenes just to please her husband—that was obvious. Her motive might have been to please Sammy, but my motive involved keeping Chuck from putting a bullet in my head."

Before she left that night, Sammy presented Linda with a gold medallion to wear around her neck. It was inscribed, "To Linda, from Mr. Dynamite."

"I've given only ten trusted people that same medallion," he told her. "It is reserved for my very special friends, of which I include you as one."

"Sammy," Linda claimed, "looked like a savior to me. Just being in his company kept me out of other situations." By "other situations" she was no doubt referring to "gigs" that Chuck might have forced her into.

After two weeks of heavy dating with Linda, Sammy made a special request to her. He frankly admitted that Altovise detested Chuck and didn't want any more sexual encounters with him.

"Does she want another man?" Linda asked. "I'm sure Chuck can round up some attractive hustler. I noticed in Hollywood you can find a dozen on any block."

"No, she doesn't want another man," Sammy said. "She wants you. And I want to watch."

"I didn't know she was into that, but I don't mind putting on a show. I've been with women many times before. To me, sex is sex, regardless of gender."

"I'm delighted you feel that way," he said. "Let's rejoin Chuck and Altovise in the living room. As you know, guys like to watch gals get it on."

Within the hour, Altovise and Linda were nude in front of their fully dressed men . To Linda, as she remembered it, Altovise was a bit awkward and didn't seem all that thrilled to be performing before her husband, a porn star, and a man she loathed.

Linda knew she'd have to be the aggressor. She began by kissing her fully on the mouth, as she fondled the nipples of her breasts. "It took a while, but I finally turned her on. Her legs parted, and I used my hands to explore the moist region that was starting to pulsate."

Soon, she moved below, kissing Altovise's thighs, her tongue finally reaching out and licking the outer lips of her labia.

"After that, it was easy," Linda said. "I'd heated Altovise up, and soon, she was doing to me what I'd been doing to her. Sammy and Chuck loved it. They seemed transfixed. By evening's end, Sammy took me back to the bedroom for my specialty. Chuck was the only one that night who didn't unzip. He was just a voyeur."

***

Throughout their relationship, Sammy was constantly presenting Linda with gifts—sometimes elaborate presents, at other times some relatively simple trinket. When he gave her one of the first Polaroid cameras, it became a fascinating new toy for her.

"I put it to use right away," she said, "beginning with Sammy. He let me photograph his big erection. Not his face. Over the next few months, I would photograph the hard-ons of some big-name stars. No star would allow me to photograph his face. But I took pictures of their cocks at full masts. Most of the guys seemed to enjoy posing. I think all actors are exhibitionists anyway."

"I kept the pictures in this small little leather suitcase, which was stolen from me in a hotel room about three years later," she claimed. "The damn thief never knew what he made off with because no faces were shown. If he'd known who had been pho-

CHANGING TECHNOLOGIES
PRODUCE
IN3TANT INDICCREET PHOTOS:

The Polarold SX-70, first introduced to American consumers in 1972

Linda: *"I sure made use of this camera. It was amazing how many stars would display it all for me...no faces, however. Desi Arnaz was proud to do it. So was John Ireland and Fernando Lamas...and the beat goes on. I had the best collection of male nudes in Hollywood, but, alas, I didn't get to keep them."*

tographed, it could have been worth a gold mine. I'm not a blackmailer, but those pictures were worth something."

On some nights, Sammy tantalized her with the possibility that he might put her in one of his shows in Las Vegas. "I could see the marquee. Sammy Davis, Jr., appearing with *Deep Throat's* Linda Lovelace. We'd be a smash. A real sensation. On other nights, he suggested acts so wild she was certain no hotel or casino in Vegas would stage them.

Sammy contacted the well-known classical and modern dancer Frances Davis, who had performed during a period of her life with Katherine Dunham's modern dance troupe in Paris. Married for nine years to trumpeter Miles Davis, she had appeared with Sammy in the Broadway version of three different plays, *Mr. Wonderful, Porgy and Bess,* and *Shinbone Alley.*

She later claimed that her marriage to the "Prince of Darkness was intolerable. Even a gilded cage is still a cage." She divorced him and moved to Los Angeles to reinvent herself, teaching dance.

Sammy eventually hired Frances to teach Linda the rudiments of stage presentations. "He wanted to get something going for her, but she didn't have any talent," Frances said. "She began with voice, then went on to movement, followed by dance lessons. What fun, teaching Linda Lovelace pelvic movements. But eventually, she (Linda) stopped showing up for classes."

Altovise came to resent all the attention her husband was showing Linda. "I already know how to dance." During the course of more and more evenings, Altovise was not at home, dining out with friends.

According to Linda, "Even though I was constantly going down on Sammy, he explained to me that in his fashion, he was still faithful to Altovise.

Sammy's point of view was: "For the big thing, the missionary position, I save myself for Altovise. But with blow-jobs, it's different. It could be anybody, man or women."

One night, just after Linda and Chuck arrived on the Davis family's doorstep, Sammy said, "You just missed Altovise. She's gone for the evening, but sends her love."

The night began along lines equivalent to others they had spent, starting with drinks and a screening of some new porn loops that Sammy had acquired from a distributor in San Fernando Valley.

When Chuck went to the bathroom, Sammy talked privately with Linda in a low voice. "Your husband got off a few times with Altovise, but he doesn't join us in any action. Tonight, I was thinking about Chuck joining us in a three-way. I want to try some cocksucking myself."

A sudden thought occurred to Linda, who saw how she might extract some small token of revenge on Chuck for all the weird gigs he'd forced on her.

She told Sammy, "Chuck loves to get his cock sucked. He'd love it if you'd practice on him."

As a super-macho former Marine, Chuck referred to homosexuals as "fags." Later, privately but in front of Linda, he'd label Sammy as a "nigger fag."

"It looks like I'm in luck tonight," Sammy said, before Chuck came back into the room.

The next loop Chuck would screen was an S&M scene where one woman was tied up while being assaulted by three lesbians. Linda knew that the film would provide the kind of visuals that would give Chuck an erection.

Sammy sat next to Chuck on the sofa and ever so gently lowered his hand over Chuck's crotch. At first, Chuck lurched back and almost pulled away.

"Finally, it dawned on Chuck that this was Sammy Davis, Jr., a big time star, and he wanted some action," Linda said. "Chuck was completely star struck and would do almost anything a movie star wanted. He settled back, realizing he was in for the duration. Sammy unzipped Chuck's pants, and his erection popped out. Chuck even raised himself up off the sofa, allowing Sammy to pull down his pants and shorts."

"Sammy really went to work on it, and Chuck glared at me like he could kill me," she said. "It was hard for me to believe that this was Sammy's first time. He went to work on that dick like a professional whore. Although he'd been horrified at first, Chuck finally settled back and got lost in the action on the screen."

"Then the inevitable happened. He blasted off inside Sammy. Later that night, as we were leaving, Sammy slipped Chuck his standard gift of five-hundred dollars. But he had a different instruction on this particular night."

"From now on, I don't want you to cum during the day," Sammy announced. "When you get here, I want the full blast. So save it for me. On your next visit, you'll go into the bedroom with Linda and me. While she blows me, I'll blow you. I think I can develop a taste for white dick."

"Whatever turns you on, Sammy," Chuck said.

Although Chuck had presented a cooperative smile in front of Sammy, Linda knew that once the door was shut at home, he'd turn menacingly onto her. She was aware that a beating loomed, but she couldn't resist a final quip. "From this night on, you're going to help me earn some of those five hundred dollars from Sammy."

"Shut your face, bitch!"

Later that night, she revealed that Chuck "flipped out" when he got her home. "He beat the shit out of me, but I'd given him just a taste of his own medicine."

***

323

In contrast to her other celebrity encounters, which were always conducted in secret, Sammy openly escorted Linda to major functions where other stars gathered. He didn't seem at all ashamed to be seen with her. Of course, some of his introductions were followed by snickers. Sammy didn't care, although the put-downs embarrassed Linda.

Sammy once took her to an exclusive fashion boutique in Beverly Hills and outfitted her in a stunning white satin gown with a sable wrap. "The kind that Lana Turner appeared in in the 40s," Linda said. "I looked gorgeous."

To match her outfit, Sammy dressed up in a white tuxedo with white gloves, even a white top hat.

"A lot of big name movie stars were at this charity event at the Beverly Hills Hotel," Linda said. "I was dazzled. Sammy literally knew everybody. The competition was great but we lit up the room."

"We met Fred Astaire," she said. "He didn't proposition me. Nor did he turn me on. I'd heard that he was mostly gay anyway and had once had an affair with Randolph Scott. According to Sammy, Scott had been the lover of Cary Grant. Grant was at the party and I met him. But I held little interest for him. I don't think he regarded me as a class act."

"I did meet Dennis Hopper there," she said. "He looked drugged and came on to me."

"While Sammy was talking to fellow Rat Packer Joey Bishop, I was invited out on the terrace with Hopper. He had a joint, and we shared it."

As they smoked, he told her that his former buddy, James Dean, and he were once into peyote and grass. "Back then, it was something you couldn't even mention to your closest buddies."

"Well, we can now," she said. "You don't look like the kind of guy who carries around just one joint, so hit me again."

Hopper asked her to come to his hotel suite at around eleven o'clock the following morning.

"I think Natalie Wood and Ursula Andress would be a tough act to follow," Linda said.

"Don't worry," he told her. "From what I've seen on the screen, you've got them both beat."

Before going back into the ballroom, he surveyed the scene. "I can count fifteen starlets in this room that I've had. There isn't a starlet around that I can't have. As for stars, they're harder to get."

"I'm a star," she said.

"And you can be had," he said, kissing her lightly on the lips. "I'm looking forward to our rendezvous."

Abandoned by both Hopper and Sammy, Linda remained on the terrace alone for a while. She felt too stoned to walk back into the room.

Suddenly, a voice behind her spoke. "I'd heard you were here tonight, but I couldn't find you."

She'd know that voice anywhere, having heard it countless times on TV coping with Lucy. It was Ricky Ricardo.

She turned around to star into the drunken face of Desi Arnaz.

Before they were interrupted by Sammy and his hastily assembled party of five, Arnaz and Linda had agreed to spend the weekend together in Palm Springs at a private villa. "Don't worry," he said. "There's a thousand in it for you."

***

Slipping away from Chuck and Sammy the following morning, Linda kept her appointment with Hopper. But to her later researchers, she didn't have much to say about the encounter.

"There's not much to tell," she said. "He answered the door in the nude. I don't know why all those big stars went for him. I agreed with Howard Stern's later assessment. He'd seen Hopper's penis on the screen and compared it to the size of an elevator button. I didn't give him a deep throat. His dick came nowhere near my throat."

"We smoked two joints, and he told me he got hooked on drugs when he was eight years old and living on this farm in Kansas. 'I used to sniff the gasoline fumes from my grandfather's truck,' he claimed. "

As he stood at the doorway kissing her goodbye, he whispered to her, "You're a hell of a lot better at cocksucking than I am. When I used to sleep over with Jimmy Dean, he'd always demand that I suck his cock."

"I'd like to have sampled Jimmy," Linda said.

Dennis Hopper in 1971	**James Dean** (1931-1955) a year before his death.
Linda: *"Big star on the screen, little star when the pants came off,"* Linda claimed. *"He told me, 'I'd rather give head to a beautiful woman than fuck her, really."*	Linda: *"He was dead long before I hit Hollywood, but I'd have chased after him...He should have been the lead actor in* Last Tango in Paris—*not Brando!"*

"Too bad he passed on before I hit town."

"Yeah, too bad," Hopper said, shutting the door behind him.

***

When Sammy left town on some night club engagements, followed by television appearances in New York, Linda had time to accept some invitations from other celebrities who had been pursuing her.

Nancy Leigh Semin, who wrote an academic examination of Linda Lovelace and her influence on feminist thought and the porn industry, stated:

"The Playboy Mansion was not the only place where Linda attracted a crowd of celebrity admirers. Her fellating talents also captured the attention of many celebrities who went out of their way to sidle up to her at a party to introduce themselves, including Warren Beatty and Joe Namath."

Just how extensive that list of celebrities was came as a shock to several researchers when Linda agreed to "tell all."

According to literary agent Jay Garon, "I'm very aware of celebrity hook-ups in Hollywood, ever since I was George Cukor's 'boy' in the 1940s. I think it's safe to say that Linda had more sexual contact with male movie stars than any other female star in the history of Hollywood—and that includes Marlene Dietrich, et al."

Sammy had monopolized so much of her time that she hadn't returned all the calls from male stars wanting to perform her specialty on them. "One thing I concluded in the months ahead was that almost every male movie star had one favorite subject…and that is himself."

Since he knew there would be money involved, Chuck agreed to drive Linda to the villa in Palm Springs where Desi Arnaz had said he'd be staying for the weekend by himself.

Even during his famous marriage (1940-1960) to Lucille Ball, he consistently sneaked away for weekends with other women. He'd been known for seducing young nurses in particular—in fact, it was Linda's appearance as a screen nurse in *Deep Throat* which had piqued his interest. He also seduced local pickups in whatever town he was in, starlets, and on occasion, some really big stars like Ginger Rogers, Betty Grable, and Lana Turner.

Insider Hollywood viewed him as a switch hitter. He'd had dalliances with actor Cesar Romero; Lorenz Hart, the lyricist; and Richard Kollmar, husband of columnist Dorothy Kilgallen.

When Linda, with Chuck, arrived in front of the villa in Palm Springs, he let her out of his car and drove off to check into a seedy motel, where he spent his free time pursuing hookers in town for the weekend holiday trade from Los Angeles.

A Mexican houseboy led Linda out to the villa's pool area, where Arnaz had just emerged from the water, wearing a flimsy G-string that clearly revealed his fat Cuban salami.

"Hi, Linda," he said. "Why not pull off everything and jump in with me."

"It's one hot day, so I think I will," she said, taking off her simple sundress. She wore no bra or panties and jumped in with him.

He held her close and tongue kissed her while fondling her vagina. "We're going to have one hot time—and I'm not talking about the weather."

Arnaz's reputation had preceded him before he hooked up with Linda in Palm Springs. Cesar Romero, his longtime friend, who was always madly in love with him, claimed, "Desi loved sex. He couldn't get enough of it. He didn't know the difference between sex and love. To put it bluntly, love was a good fuck. He could get that anywhere."

Arnaz had his own special view of marriage. "As a Latin man, I have a double standard. What is good for me is not good for my wife. Your wife is your wife. Fooling around in no way affects your love for her. Your relationship is sacred and a few peccadilloes mean nothing."

After a lunch of Mexican specialties, Arnaz took Linda into the master bedroom for a siesta. He'd had four beers at lunch and was a little high. She slept in his arms until she felt a "stirring" sometime between three and four o'clock.

He whispered to her, "With those much experienced lips and tongue of yours, I want you to discover every erogenous zone on my body."

That body was not as lean and tight as it had been in the 1950s. A gray patch of hair separated his breasts, and he had a bit of a beer belly. But she tackled him, exploring strange new territory to excite him, including the areas behind his thighs and calves.

Lucille Ball with **Desi Arnaz**

"Plenty to keep secret about."

"He particularly liked love to be made to his rosebud, and he adored armpit licking. Finally, I got to the salami itself, only to discover that when he reached his climax, he was a screamer."

Throughout their long, hot three days and nights together, he showed no interest in either her life or her background. But he talked a lot about himself, details of which she'd later record in her diary.

Although Arnaz's time in Palm Springs had ostensibly been configured as a holiday, he spent

327

a great deal of time around the pool chatting by phone to show-biz executives in Los Angeles and New York. He flaunted his nudity as he took call after call. "He was really dynamic," she said. "Thank God the phone cord extension was long, because he did a lot of pacing as he talked. His movements were almost acrobatic. At one point, he flopped down on the *chaise longue* and buried his face in his hands. Obviously, that had been a disappointing call."

At twilight before dinner one evening over *Cuba libres,* he discussed his life growing up in Cuba. "I lost my virginity to the family cook when I was twelve. I learned about sex in the brothels of Santiago. The *putas* down there weren't good at blow-jobs. That's one of the reasons I booked you here."

"When I arrived in Florida, I had to clean shit from canary cages and for a while I delivered very bad pizzas. I went to high school with Al Capone, Jr. Finally, I decided to become a musician. Eventually, I got hired by Xavier Cugat at the Waldorf-Astoria in Manhattan. But he paid me so little money I had to steal food from the hotel kitchen."

Only on his final night did he speak of Lucille Ball, whom he'd divorced. "I tried to be faithful to her, but girls throw themselves at me. I remember when I appeared in a club with the Copa Girls, eight of the most gorgeous dames you'd ever seen. I couldn't decide which one to fuck first."

Sitting back one afternoon behind rhinestone-rimmed sunglasses, he smoked a Cuban cigar and claimed, "For a little Hispanic kid, I did all right. I knew everybody from Eleanor Roosevelt—I think she wanted me to fuck her—to Judy Garland. That one definitely wanted me to fuck her."

Since he talked so freely about his sex life, she asked him, "What was your weirdest sexual experience?"

"File this under *Believe It or Not,"* he said. "But would you believe it was a blow-job from the Director of the F.B.I., J. Edgar Hoover? Lucy and I used to double date with Hoover and his lover, Clyde Tolson. One afternoon at the Del Mar Racetrack, he gave me a blow-job in the men's room while an FBI security detail guarded the entrance."

"Imagine that," she said. "The director of the F.B.I., a homosexual! Wait till I tell Chuck."

"Hoover and I used to attend the racetrack together every time he came to Los Angeles," Arnaz said. "He always called me. Incidentally, as you now know, I have something in common with a horse."

She later claimed that "Desi exaggerated only slightly."

At the end of what had been a wonderful weekend for her, he was telling her goodbye at the villa's front door. "But he had to go and ruin it for me," she said.

"I really prefer blondes," he told her. As if to make a point about Lucille Ball, he said, "That's blonde, not a redhead."

328

"Since I'm neither one, guess I'll be heading out," she said. "Bye-bye, Desi."

***

On the Tuesday after her long weekend with Arnaz, she returned the phone call from William Holden, reflecting upon how, in the 1940s, during the period when Arnaz had been pursuing showgirls, Holden had been pounding Lucille Ball, or so she'd been told.

In his screen-familiar voice, Holden invited her to his plush apartment that afternoon. She could think of nothing else until the appointed time.

She had read lots of gossip about Holden, even learning that he'd once had a torrid affair with Jackie Kennedy. He was known for having seduced some of the great celestial beauties of Hollywood, notably Grace Kelly and Audrey Hepburn. But what really turned Linda on were rumors of his affair with Susan Hayward, with whom he'd co-starred in *Young and Willing* in 1943. In spite of fierce competition, the flame-haired beauty, Hayward, had remained Linda's all-time favorite, even more so than Barbara Stanwyck, Holden's co-star in *Golden Boy,* that 1939 picture in which he'd played an emotionally wounded boxer.

When her screen hero had starred in *Picnic* in 1955, Holden had complained to the press that, "I'm too damned old and too conservative to do a striptease." However, within that film, he went through with the part anyway and titillated horny straight women and gay men with his beefcake scenes. The way Linda calculated it at the time of their meeting, Holden was at least seventeen years older than he'd been during the shooting of *Picnic,* so she wasn't anticipating a body in its prime.

From the gossip columns, Linda also learned that Holden was one of the best friends of Ronald Reagan. She didn't exactly know how to ask Holden, but she wondered if he could fix her up with Reagan, a formerly washed-up, B-list actor who, since 1967, had been serving as the 33rd Governor of California. Although happily married to

THE UNTOUCHABLES (SACRED MONSTERS)

Left photo: Director (1924-1972) of the FBI, **J. Edgar Hoover** and his Assistant Director and long-time companion, **Clyde Tolson.**

Nancy Davis Reagan at the time, Linda wished she could go down on Reagan. During her tenure as a starlet at MGM, Nancy had been known as "The Fellatio Queen of Hollywood."

As Linda brazenly said to Sammy Davis, Jr., one night, "I want Ronald to compare my skills with those of Nancy—and then decide who is the *real* Fellatio Queen."

"Sounds fair enough to me," Sammy responded.

At the time Linda hooked up with Holden, he was at a low point in his career, having received unenthusiastic reviews and low box office attendance for his 1971 film, *Wild Rovers*, in which he played a cynical, saddle-worn outlaw leading a band of doomed gunmen.

But what intrigued her far more was his casting as the lead in a blood-drenched western called *The Revenger* (1972), in which he set out to kill those who had massacred his family. She wasn't particularly interested in the picture itself, but she was anxious to learn if he had resumed his World War II affair with his co-star, Hayward, who still looked ravishing, despite her age (55) at the time of its filming.

William Holden, with **Barbara Stanwyck** in *Golden Boy* (1939)

When Holden opened the door to his apartment, Linda quickly ascertained that they were alone. He kissed her on the cheek, and she could smell liquor on his breath. In Hollywood, he was widely identified as an alcoholic. Although he seemed anxious to get down to business, he chatted pleasantly with her about his career and answered a few questions.

"It must be thrilling to a man to play love scenes with all those movie queens—Susan Hayward is my all time favorite."

"Well," he said. "It is and it isn't. By the time Susan and I completed *The Revengers,* we were both getting a little long in the tooth. Over the years, kissing movie stars can be a lot of fun, especially if their names are Audrey Hepburn, Grace Kelly, or Deborah Kerr."

"But it can be hell, too. I made this film with this big-busted Italian star. We had a love scene to shoot after lunch. She adored pasta with heaps of garlic. Instead of kissing her, I was nearly overcome with the stench."

Holden, stripping, with **Kim Novak** in *Picnic* (1955)

"Surely, he wasn't referring to Sophia Loren?" Linda wondered, but was too polite (or intimidated) to ask. Holden had starred with Loren in *The Key* in 1958.

He continued: "I starred once with an actress who was three months pregnant at the time and shall remain nameless. We had this love scene in which we were told to be really passionate. As we began the scene, she started to vomit. Then, after puking and some Listerine, it was back again to shooting that fucking love scene. I think she used up a whole bottle of Listerine before the director called 'cut.' It's hell kissing a woman between pukes."

"Another famous star I did a kissing scene with had just had a temporary bridge cemented into her mouth. During my intense tongue-lashing, the god damn bridge fell out."

He stared at Linda intently. "I'm sure that in your work fellating penises, you've had your mishaps, too."

"I sure have," she said. "Would you believe with a man who had two, not one, dicks, or even a celebrity like John Lennon, who had head cheese?"

"Let's define kissing and fellating as occupational hazards," he said. "Now it's bedtime." In his bedroom, he removed all his clothing and lay down on the bed. "Please do your thing," he said.

"I'll do *your* thing," she said.

As she later recalled, "Holden had a very decent size cock, which was difficult to get hard, but I managed. All those years of heavy drinking had taken a toll. I finally got him off, but I earned my paycheck. I had to turn my mouth and throat into a suction pump."

After he'd climaxed, he rose quickly from the bed and headed straight for the shower. As she remembered it, "William Holden was the cleanest actor I ever made love to. Good hygiene was not his problem. He later told me he took at least four showers a day, including one before sex and one right after sex."

"Ronnie Reagan and I don't always agree politically, but he's a compulsive shower taker like myself. Before and after Nancy goes down on him, he heads for the shower."

Before leaving the bedroom, Holden, with a red towel wrapped around his midriff, reached into the drawer of his nightstand and handed her three one-hundred dollar bills. "I don't mean to offend you by offering you money, even though you're a movie star. But all actors are whores. We sell our bodies to the highest bidder."

William Holden playing a gigolo for faded film diva **Gloria Swanson** in *Sunset Blvd.*

Holden with **Sophia Loren** in *The Key* (1958). Servicing Tugboat Captains "who never get torpedoed."

Holden with **Susan Hayward** in *The Revengers* (1972) "Her adieu to the screen."

Linda attempted, through Holden, in vain, for Reagan to compare her fellatio skills with those of his wife Nancy. **Ronald Reagan** with **Nancy Davis** in 1952.

After she'd showered, she came back into the living room, where she found him sitting in an armchair and having a drink.

"Forgive me," she said. "But I'm dying to ask you one more movie trivia question. Did you make love with Gloria Swanson off screen when you guys made *Sunset Blvd.?*"

"For years, I denied it. I told everybody I didn't. But now it's time for me to confess. I did fuck that egomaniacal midget. When I was young and had first arrived in Hollywood, I became known for throwing mercy fucks to older actresses. You name the babes, I had them— Constance Bennett, Kay Francis, Loretta Young. But today, I go mainly for the young stuff."

After another drink, he showed her to the door. She hesitated. "I'd love it if you'd call me again. It's not every day that a gal gets a chance to suck the cock of the great William Holden."

"I have an idea," he said. "I've got this buddy, Richard Widmark, and he and I get together about every three weeks and raise hell. I'm seeing him Monday night. Want to come along?"

"I'd love to," she said. "He's a real dynamo on screen."

"Linda, my dear girl, you bring out the devil in me. Forgive this unusual request, but it's long been a fantasy of mine. When I get together with Richard on Monday, would you perform a double suck on us?"

"Of course, I will," she said. "I've always believed that two cocks in a gal's mouth are better than one."

"I'll invite Dick," he said. "We've got a date."

***

Alert to the fact that Eddie Fisher had been the most successful pop singles artist of the first half of the 1950s, selling millions of

332

records and hosting his own TV show, Linda had played phone tag with him since their inaugural meeting at Hugh Hefner's Playboy Mansion West. She finally got him on the line. He was in Las Vegas.

He invited her to fly from Los Angeles and to join him in Nevada, were he was appearing onstage nightly in a song-and-dance *schtick*. He relayed the details about where she should pick up her pre-paid air ticket.

Linda expressed how eager she'd be to see him. That was indeed true, but she lied when she told him that he was her all time favorite singer. "Actually, my heart still belongs to Elvis," she told Delores Welles, continuing to nurture her fantasies about "The Pelvis" long before they eventually met.

She informed Chuck that she'd be traveling to Las Vegas alone, and that he could not accompany her. Although belligerent, he had more or less resigned himself to the reality that he would not be invited, except to the home of Sammy Davis, Jr., on most of her "dates." Before she left to visit Fisher, Chuck instructed her, in his words, as relayed by Linda, "to get as much out of the little Jew as you can."

At the Las Vegas airport, Linda connected with the limousine that was waiting for her. Hired and paid for by Fisher, the driver maneuvered her to her suite at Caesar's Palace. Two bottles of champagne were waiting, along with a welcome note from Fisher informing her that he'd be joining her in the suite sometime after midnight.

After a long bubble bath, she worked on her face and body to make herself as sexy and appealing as possible. In a deviation from her usual pattern, she painted her mouth a flaming shade of red.

When Fisher entered her suite, she was startled to see how he'd deteriorated since the last time she'd seen him. They entered briefly into casual dialogue with one another, but after a sudden knock on the suite's outer door, Fisher invited a man inside who carried a black medical bag, and who looked like a doctor. Fisher then told Linda to "make herself comfortable" in the suite's living room, and that he had "some business to take care of." Then he ushered the man, alone, into the bedroom, closing the door behind them. She suspected that the man was giving Fisher an injection, or injections, in his buttocks. The man left soon afterwards, nodding curtly to Linda on his way out.

About thirty minutes later, Fisher emerged from the bedroom, shaking and looked haggard. "Things didn't go well tonight," he said. "I was told I'm not singing well, and I missed my cues. My timing was completely fucked up. I even forgot the lyrics to songs I've sung a thousand times. The house was only half full, and the manager told me that former fans were coming to my show just to see how low the former *Mr. Elizabeth Taylor* had sunk."

"You'll bounce back bigger than ever," she reassured him. "Sinatra did it, and you're a hell of a lot better as a crooner than he is."

As she interacted with him, she didn't know if she was reacting to the broken man before her, or whether she was still dazzled by his reputation. During his heyday, he'd had affairs with everybody from Marlene Dietrich to Mia Farrow before she became Sinatra's wife. Judy Garland had gone over the rainbow with him, and later, he'd moved in on another of Sinatra's women, the dancer, Juliet Prowse, who had previously shared her charms with Elvis Presley.

Some of Fisher's seductions had been from outside the world of show-biz. They included Pamela Turnure, press secretary to Jackie Kennedy, and Virginia Warren, the daughter of U.S. Chief Justice *[from 1953-1969]* Earl Warren. Most compromising and controversial of all, Fisher had shared the sexual charms of the notorious Judith Campbell Exner, an Elizabeth Taylor lookalike who had simultaneously sustained sexual liaisons (and political secrets) with both President John F. Kennedy and mob kingpin Sam Giancana.

Fisher had even managed, at least briefly, to sleep with Nathalie Delon, the wife of Alain Delon, the actor voted around that time as "the sexiest man in France."

On a more bizarre note, both Noël Coward and Fisher's rival, the bisexual Richard Burton, had admired and perhaps penetrated Fisher's well-shaped buttocks.

A dedicated movie buff like Linda was anxious for insights into Fisher's fabled marriage (1959-1964) to Elizabeth Taylor, but he had little to say on the subject. "Sexually, Elizabeth was every man's dream. She had the face of an angel and the morals of a truck driver. But who am I to judge after the life I've lived?"

Crooner **Eddie Fisher**, "torn between two lovers" in 1958, with wife-to-be **Elizabeth Taylor** *(left)*, and wife-of-the-moment, **Debbie Reynolds** *(right)*.

"I dug Elizabeth Taylor in bed," Fisher claimed. "Or anywhere else, including the back seat of a limousine. Taking Debbie to bed was like having sex with your little sister."

Once, the then-married (1955-59) Fisher and Debbie Reynolds had reigned together as America's Sweethearts, but that had more to do with publicity than reality. Fisher later claimed, "I never loved Debbie Reynolds."

In retaliation, Reynolds shot back, comparing her former husband to "an elevator that can't find the floor."

That night in Las Vegas with Linda, whatever the doctor injected into Fisher seemed to have improved his condition to some degree. At least he was no longer shaking. But he was still in a depressed mood.

"You're still young," he said, "but I'm in my forties and have this awful fear of growing old. You'll face that someday yourself. All stars do, and in your own special way, you're a star unlike any other star I've ever known. Every day, I feel that time is my own worst enemy. Or maybe I'm my own worst enemy."

Throughout these interchanges, Fisher had remained fully dressed, and she admired his clothing. "It cost me enough," he said. "I stopped off in Hong Kong on this tour in 1969, and I purchased 155 tailor-made silk suits, 185 silk shirts, and 50 pairs of silk pajamas. I never had any sense of money. I buy jewelry for my friends, both men and women. I once paid a small fortune for a black pearl necklace for Elizabeth which turned out to be paste. I had this custom-made Bentley convertible that Greg Bautzer, that rich attorney and starfucker in Hollywood, admired. So, guess what? I gave it to him. I lend money crazily when I have it. In three months alone, my cocaine bill came to $200,000. No wonder I'm going bankrupt."

Finally, Fisher got around to the main point of the evening—sex. "Sex and drugs," he said, "are my two favorite things. In the past few years, I've been fulfilling my sexual fantasies—having sex with two women at the same time. With cocaine, a three-way becomes even more exciting. In the 1950s, I was known as 'the Coca-Cola kid' because of my TV show. Today, I'm known in Hollywood and Las Vegas as a cokehead."

SHOW-BIZ DATES FROM THE HIGH SOCIETY A-LIST:

top: **Eddie Fisher**, boy singer,

lower left, **Virginia Warren**, daughter of Supreme Court Justice Earl Warren, and *(lower right)*

Pamela Turnure, Press Secretary to then-First Lady, Jacqueline Kennedy.

"I hope you don't mind, but I've invited this showgirl I know to join us in our festivities tonight. She's gorgeous and, oh yes, bisexual. From what I've heard, you do women as well as men."

"You heard that right," Linda said. "It's okay with me, providing you deliver the cum shot to me."

"I'll deliver it personally, deep down in your talented throat," he promised.

When the doorbell rang shortly thereafter, she was introduced to "April Showers," who had brought the evening's stash of cocaine. She told Linda, "I adore coke more than sex."

Because of her figure, her flexibility, and her large breasts, the blonde beauty had been passed around show business royalty. Fisher asked her to recite some of her more famous conquests.

"You name them and I've had them," she boasted. "Elvis Presley and Frank Sinatra are at the top of the list, followed by Bob Hope, Milton Berle, Louis Armstrong, Johnny Carson, Bing Crosby, Tony Curtis, Xavier Cugat (I had a hard time finding it), John Huston, and Nicky Hilton. Nicky is proof that all men are not created equal."

Linda then joined in what Fisher defined as "our cocaine supper." When their shared experiences of that night ended, both women remained on-site in Fisher's suite for a sleepover.

[When Jay Garon's researchers grilled Linda about that three-way, she was rather vague. "I was too stoned to remember, but it was your typical threesome, with two women and a man. When it's with two men and woman, it's very different, of course."

Garon pressed her to "end the debate" about Fisher's endowment. Some biographers have equated his equipment with that of King Kong. In contrast, when Debbie Reynolds appeared on a nationwide talk show, she contemptuously held up two fingers to indicate that the size of his penis had been exaggerated.

"It was somewhere in between two different opinions," Linda said. "It was far less than all those claims made by writers, but quite a bit more than Debbie claimed. Being Jewish, Eddie was circumsized. But, in my opinion, the rabbi got hungry and bit off too much foreskin. I understand they actually use their mouths to bite off an infant's foreskin."

"Some do, some don't," Garon responded.]

The next day, after a late rising, and after kissing both women goodbye, Fisher left for a one o'clock luncheon date with some casino bigwigs. He told them that he wouldn't be back until after midnight, and that in the interim, they were welcome to use the hotel facilities, including the spa. "After that workout last night, it will rejuvenate you. April's already been taken care of. But as for you, Linda, I'm allowing you to go into this wonderful dress shop down in the lobby and charge up to five hundred dollars worth of merchandise. See how generous I am?"

Before April and Linda left the suite, a call came in from Chuck. Sammy Davis, Jr. had phoned from New York and wanted her to call him back.

French pinup, actor
Alain Delon

"The sexiest man in France, a cuckolded husband."

336

When she got Sammy on the phone, his familiar voice asked, "Who loves ya, baby?"

After a few minutes of chit-chat, he got to the point. "Frankie's in Vegas. As you know, he's seen your movie, and he wants to hook up with you. How about it?"

"Oh, I'd love to meet him!" she said.

"Here," he responded. "Write down this number and call him before three o'clock this afternoon. Don't mention it to Eddie."

"Agreed," she said. "And Sammy, hurry back. I miss you. Are you being faithful to me up in wicked New York?"

"Yeah, right," Davis said. "And if you believe that, I've got this bridge to Brooklyn to sell you."

Before she put through a call to Sinatra's suite, April made a proposal of her own: "Let's skip the spa, honey. I want you to go with me on a gig. It's with a famous star. He slips into Las Vegas on occasion and likes to have more than one showgirl at a time in bed. He's seen your movie. Everybody in Las Vegas has seen your movie. Somewhere in this town, it's being shown twenty-four hours a day. Now don't be surprised when I reveal his name. He has a squeaky clean image, but that's just to protect his hero reputation with thousands of young American boys who worship him."

She searched her mind for an entertainer with a large following of American boys. But before she could come up with an answer, April blurted out. "LET'S GO FUCK ROY ROGERS, BABY!"

***

The squinty-eyed, wholesome-looking Roy Rogers, dethroned "King of the Cowboys," was not the heroic looking singing cowboy she'd seen on *The Roy Rogers Show* on NBC television.

When Linda first met him, he was in his early 60s and had lost that boyish Western charm he'd once projected. Actually, he had been born Leonard Franklin Slye in Cincinnati, Ohio, in an urban tenement, in 1911.

A former fruit picker and a refugee from the Dust Bowl and its associated hardships, he'd finally made it big in California knocking Gene Autry off his cinematic saddle. By 1943, Rogers had become the biggest Western star in America.

As a long-term consumer of fast food, Linda had also consumed many a grilled beef burger at various branches of the Roy Rogers restaurant chain.

April had already revealed to her that Rogers had a Dr. Jekyll and Mr. Hyde personality. To the public, he pretended to be a deeply devoted family man, faithfully married to actress Dale Evans, dubbed "The Queen of the Cowgirls."

He had a darker side to him that came out on his secret visits to Las Vegas, where he booked hotel suites under the name of Leonard Slye and patronized Las Vegas hookers. Many of these showgirls spent only one night with the cowboy protesting afterwards, "Never again!"

That had not been the case with April, who had been with him several times by the time she introduced him to Linda. When she met him, Linda lied to him, telling him that, "My all time favorite song is 'Don't Fence Me In.'"

She went on to say, "I always liked you more than Gene Autry. You're much handsomer and sexier than he is."

"Thanks, Little Lady, but shucks, I think ol' Gene is one of the best ol' boys in the whole wide world. Sure, we've been competitors, but that's show biz, the name of the game. And thanks to the Good Lord, I came out on top. Yep, I've done mighty well for myself. Oh, sure, me and Dale have had our ups and downs, our share of grief over the years, but we try to let Him keep us sensible and calm in tragedy. Because if He is for you, who's against you?"

April, by now, knew Roy well enough to cue him to relay to Linda his oft-repeated favorite anecdote. As such, the cowboy told them how he met Marilyn Monroe, then known as Norma Jeane Baker, during the late spring of 1946 in Las Vegas.

"Trigger and I were asked to lead the Helldorado Parade, an Old West themed thing, through downtown Vegas. Louella Parsons and Hedda Hopper even came to Vegas to cover it for the press, and this skinny little pop singer named Sinatra had flown in to be its Grand Marshall. But the fucker didn't show up. He had fled to Chicago."

"There I was, leading all these parade floats, covered wagons, Indians on the warpath in all their regalia. I was at the time starring in a film whose name was officially spelled as *Heldorado* (1946), with a single 'l.' Its name had originally been spelled with two 'l's, but censors were afraid of the Hell part, so they deliberately misspelled it to avoid censorship."

"Actually, the plot of *Heldorado* was prophetic in its forecast of what's going on in Las Vegas today. I was cast as a ranger who helps the government track down racketeers making off with untaxed earnings from gambling."

"Norma Jeanne was standing in the crowd beside the parade route. She caught my eye. I thought she was a beauty. I pulled Trigger to a halt and hoisted her up onto my saddle. I took her for a ride as the onlookers, many in old-timey Western clothing, looked on. Very discreetly, Norma Jeane felt my crotch, and I knew the bitch was hot to trot."

"Dale Evans, my future wife, was also in the parade a block behind us, so I had to be discreet. Then I invited Norma Jeane to join me and the movie crew for a hoedown barbecue that night. It was staged at what was then the old Frontier Hotel on the old Los Angeles highway, now called the Strip."

"Somehow, I managed to slip away with Norma Jeane for about thirty minutes. I didn't bang her, but she gave me the best blow-job of my life. Up to then, it was the first time ever. None of my girlfriends, especially Dale, would ever do that to me, and I loved it. Now in Las Vegas, I have no problem getting that treatment. And now, here I am sitting with Linda Lovelace, the champion artist of all blow-jobs."

Linda felt anxious that afternoon about whether she'd be able to handle both Sinatra and Fisher on the same night without one alerting the other, so, acknowledging to herself that time and her energies were limited, she stood up. "Well, it's about time to ride 'em cowboy."

Roy Rogers in 1948 as part of a promotional tour through Bloomingdale's Department Store in New York City.

She'd later recall, "That was just something to say. I didn't know he'd take me literally."

"In the bedroom, Rogers, April, and I stripped jaybird naked," Linda said. "For those pecker checkers, he had an uncut penis that measured no more than six inches, and I call that average size."

In her first memoir, she came up with the most unlikely name for Rogers. She called him "Saul." But by the time of her interviews with Reba-Anne Howard, she had reverted to using his real name.

"To get Roy really hot, I went down on him while April rimmed him," Linda claimed. "He was screaming *YIPPEEEE!* in ecstasy. He really dug that, 'cause he didn't get it at home. I brought him close to climax, but he always held back. He had a special way he liked to get off."

"He ordered me to get on all fours, and then he fucked me doggy style," she claimed, "while whopping my ass really hard but not hard enough to make me scream out in pain."

From her many months with Chuck, Linda knew that slaps did not necessarily leave bruises.

When her time with him was over, with a sore ass, and with a collected fee of three hundred dollars, she said goodbye to the singing

During his peak, **Roy Rogers** received 1.5 million fan letters a year.

cowboy. At the door, knowing that she would probably never see him again, she said, "For the first time, I feel sorry for Trigger."

"I understand," he said. "When I'm in the saddle, I ride rough. I should be called Hopalong. Happy Trails to ya, partner!"

***

Because Chuck almost never bought any clothes for her, Linda tried to enlarge her wardrobe whenever she had the chance. Consequently, before her pre-arranged rendezvous in Sinatra's suite, Linda stopped off at a fashion boutique within Caesar's Palace, wanting to take advantage of the $500 credit which Fisher had arranged for her. She'd flown into Las Vegas wearing a dress Jacqueline Susann had given her for performing lesbian sex with her. As Linda had quipped to April, "A gal has to do what a gal has to do to get ahead, even if it's giving head."

Because of a sale in effect at the boutique, Linda was able to buy three glamorous outfits with Fisher's credit voucher. She had wanted April to help her select the right wardrobe, but the hooker refused. "You don't want me, honey," she said. "I've got whore's taste, and you'll want to show up looking like a lady when you call on all these bigtime movie jocks."

Although Sinatra was best known for his A-list seductions, including a former First Lady, Jacqueline Kennedy Onassis, he'd been known to have seduced dozens of Las Vegas showgirls and New York City hookers, even waitresses he casually picked up, too. Nonetheless, Linda somewhat naïvely envisioned her rendezvous with Sinatra as the "biggest gig of my life."

The length of Sinatra's list of affairs was staggering, and included Lauren Bacall (whom he jilted), Zsa Zsa Gabor (whom he'd raped), heiress Gloria Vanderbilt, Lee Remick, Elizabeth Taylor (whom he'd impregnated, leading to an abortion), Natalie Wood, Lana Turner, Grace Kelly, dancer Juliet Prowse (who ditched him for Elvis, Marlene Dietrich (who fellated him), Shirley MacLaine (who was more of a pal than a lover), Kim Novak, and inevitably, Marilyn Monroe, who had desperately wanted to marry him. He had even shared Judith Campbell Exner with both Sam Giancana, the Mafia strongman, and President Kennedy.

[Even before Linda Lovelace got involved with Sinatra's penis, a bevy of other Hollywood insiders had already expressed their opinions about it: Jeanne Carmen, Marilyn Monroe's best friend, said that Sinatra's penis "was like a watermelon at the end of a toothpick." Jazz age legend Billie Holiday, after experiencing it "close up and personal," had proclaimed, "Not bad for a white boy." Fellow Rat Packer Peter Lawford had relayed a story around Holly-

wood that stated: "Ronald Reagan, so I hear, once bragged to Sinatra that he had eight inches. Our Chairman of the Board shot back at Reagan, 'I've got that much soft.'" In a widely publicized quote, Sinatra's former wife, Ava Gardner, claimed, "There's only ten pounds of Frank, but 110 pounds of cock." And perhaps wittiest and most deeply steeped in the ethos of the entertainment industry, Judy Garland, after she fellated Sinatra, drunkenly accused him "of trying to break my jaw so your records will outsell mine." These comments, amplified by gossip transmitted by an armada of show girls, call girls, and casual pickups, combined into a canon of beliefs about Frank Sinatra's penis that were already firmly in place before Linda Lovelace ever entered Sinatra's orbit.]

At the reception desk at the Sands, a bodyguard was summoned to escort Linda up to Sinatra's suite. When they reached one of the upper floors, the guard ushered her in "to meet Frankie."

"Hi, babe," Sinatra said. He was seated and having a drink on the terrace of his suite. "This lowlife here is Sid Luft. I'm sure you've heard of him."

She had not, but pretended that she had. "I'm honored to meet you, Mr. Sinatra," she said in as demure a voice as she could manage. She lied when she told him, "You're my favorite singer."

"All I ask, Linda, is for you to keep me out of those memoirs you'll write in the future," Sinatra said. "It seems that every chick who's ever come into contact with me wants to write about me, or sell something to the tabloids. If I'd had as many love affairs as they give me credit for, I'd now be speaking to you from a jar in the Harvard Medical School."

She soon realized she had interrupted the closing moments of a business discussion Sinatra was having with Luft. Both men ignored her as she was seated. The bodyguard brought her the Coca-Cola she had requested.

Luft and Sinatra chatted together for another few minutes before she realized that Luft had been the husband *[during a tumultuous thirteen year period beginning in 1952, with many separations]* of Judy Garland, although she found it impossible to believe, as she'd later tell April, "that a great star like Judy Garland would marry a fat toad like Sid Luft. He looked like one of those Damon Runyon characters from that Marlon Brando movie, *Guys and Dolls*. Frankie was in that picture, too."

Sinatra and Luft talked together about one of Garland's most pathetic performances, a setback which occurred at Las Vegas' Flamingo Hotel Showroom on New Year's Eve, 1957.

"It was a disaster," Luft said, "the worst Judy ever had. We'd actually arrived for the Christmas holiday shows, but Judy was in no condition to go on. She'd just performed five weeks of shows in London, including a command

341

performance for Queen Elizabeth. She was popping pills and drinking. She had signed a contract with the Flamingo, and the managers insisted that she go on."

"The Las Vegas press had reported that when Garland appeared on the Strip, she was 'worn out and alarmingly fat,'" Luft said. "Excessive drinking had caused her to retain large amounts of body fluids, and she looked bloated, like a drowned corpse found floating at sea. On opening night, December 26, she'd lost her voice. Couldn't warble a note. I had to cancel all shows until New Year's Eve."

"On New Year's Eve, I sat at the head table watching the drama unfold," Sinatra said. "My heart went out to Judy. Before I got swinging again, I, too, had some bad nights in gin joints, just like Judy. But at Judy's show, the drunken bums started yelling insults at her. I wanted to kill them. In the middle of her number, 'Get Happy,' one goon hollered, 'SHUT YOUR FUCKING MOUTH, BITCH! YOU CAN'T SING ANYWAY, AND YOU'RE TOO FAT!' I jumped up and knocked the shithead in the mouth. She had some loyal fans there that night, but the drunken crowd was against her. Then five cunts with their sagging tits rose from their table and came onstage with Judy in the middle of her trolley car number. They began dancing the hula. At that point, Judy fled from the stage."

"We took the next plane back to Los Angeles," Luft said. "The Flamingo sued, but lost in court."

Finally, Sinatra diverted his attention to Linda. "Welcome to show business, doll. Are you sure you want to make this your profession?"

"I think I do," she said. "There's talk now of my putting an act together for Vegas."

"Let me stage it," Luft said. To Linda, he seemed drunk. "The climax, no pun intended, would be when you let Frankie 'come out,' no pun intended, and you give him history's greatest onstage blow-job for a 'blast-off,' no pun intended."

"Get out, you bum," Sinatra said. "I don't even know why I agreed to have a drink with a lowlife like you. You fucked up Judy's life, and I'll never forgive you for that."

Turning to Linda, Luft said, "Judy fucked up her own life." Then he looked at Sinatra. "See you around, pal."

After Luft's exit, Sinatra said, "Sid's a bum, but at least he was a better husband than that fag, Mark Herron, who Judy married in 1965. Judy told me that even after five months of marriage, their relationship was never consummated. Guess what? Herron was getting fucked, or else fucking, Peter Allen, who was married at the time to Liza, Judy's daughter. You figure it out. Welcome to show business."

Linda was anxious to shift the dialogue away from Garland and onto herself. "Sammy told me you saw *Deep Throat* at the Pussycat and liked it."

"Oh, hell, let's face it," Sinatra responded. "It's a shit movie, but I admired your technique. Dietrich knew how to do it, but Lana told me, 'don't put that big, old, dirty thing in my mouth.' It ain't dirty, baby. Other than Bill Holden and Ronnie Reagan, I take more showers than anybody."

Fifteen minutes later found her in Sinatra's bedroom, where both of them removed their clothing at the same time.

"For him, it was easy. All he had to do was drop the terrycloth robe he was wearing. At last, I came face to face with that Italian salami. It lived up to its billing, especially when I skinned it back and attacked the head. It grew and grew. I swallowed every inch and nibbled at his pubic hair. From the sounds coming from that crooner's throat of his, he really dug it. He shot such a load that if it had been deposited in Ava Gardner's pussy, she would have had triplets, I'm sure."

"I lied when I told **Frank Sinatra** *(photo above)* that he was my favorite singer—Elvis was," Linda said. "But Ol' Blue Eyes had 'The Pelvis' beat in one important department."

After sex, Sinatra, like William Holden, headed for the shower. But, unlike with Holden, he invited her to join him. "After I'd washed all his vital parts, I gave him a first-class rim job under the running water. He loved it and told me that some whores refused to do that."

As he dressed into a tuxedo, he asked her to his show, telling her he'd let his bodyguard escort her. "Unfortunately, I can't seat you at the head table. It's already booked by June Allyson and Dean Martin. Those two are carrying on, but I warned them to cool it in public. They're sharing a suite, but I've sent a man and a woman to sit with them tonight as beards."

Even though Sinatra had urged discretion, Linda noticed that Allyson and Martin at the head table were rather obvious about their intimacy.

The next day, one reporter wrote, "The shenanigans of Dean Martin and his 'tag along,' June Allyson, America's former sweetheart, raised plenty of eyebrows. Frank Sinatra needs

Judy Garland during the course of her marriage (1952-1965) to her "bulldog," **Sid Luft** .

Linda on Luft: "Judy might have deep throated him--and she could have him."

to tell his friends to 'get a room.'"

"Before he went on stage, Frankie gave me my marching orders," Linda said. "He told me to go to the suite after the show because, as he said, 'I missed a few holes to plug.'"

As she'd later recall, during her reminiscences with Garon's researchers, "We made a night of it, and he let me sleep with him. After deep throating him one more time, I told him that he should have been my co-star in *Deep Throat*. He interrupted my blow-job to have sex the old-fashioned way. He plunged in and didn't seem to want to pull out. What a deep dicking I got before he blasted off like a rocket launch."

She continued: "Right before dawn, I found some missile entering my rear door. By this time, he was pretty tired. I think he was in the saddle for thirty minutes. He was some kind of man, the kind rarely found among all the wimps out there."

"Finally, he turned over. 'I've got to get some sleep…alone,' he said to me. 'I left a thousand dollar bill for you on the coffee table. You're good, babe. Princess Grace, my long lost love, should fly you to Monaco for lessons. You guys can practice on Prince Rainier. I'm sure he'd love it.'"

"Thanks, Frankie," she said. "You're a great guy…no, not that, *the* greatest!"

Until her exit from Sinatra's suite, Linda, if she could be believed, had forgotten all about Eddie Fisher. Arriving back at Caesars Palace, she went to the reception desk, where she was told that Fisher was not receiving visitors. There was, however, a note and a baggage ticket, with instructions that she could retrieve her luggage from the porter.

The young man at the hotel's reception desk stared at her: "You're Linda Lovelace, aren't you?"

"Yes, I'm in a hurry," she responded, humiliated at the way Fisher had handled her, although she realized that because of her disappearance, she'd asked for it.

"I get off in thirty minutes," the young receptionist said. "We could slip upstairs to an empty room. There have been a lot of check-outs this morning."

"You're sweet," she said. "Maybe next time."

In a taxi en route to Las Vegas' airport, she found herself crying and wasn't sure why. Having been confronted with a choice between Fisher and Sinatra, she felt she'd made "the only real choice."

Before her exit from the lobby of Caesars Palace, she had opened her luggage to confirm that her new wardrobe was there, and it was. As she'd later tell Chuck, "I didn't get cash from Fisher, but I enlarged my wardrobe."

Linda's acquisition of more clothing did not interest Chuck. Instead, he demanded to know how much money she'd gotten from Sinatra. Since he was angrily insisting, she decided to admit to having received a thousand dollars from him, but claimed that she had spent most of it on items associated with her stay in Vegas and her return journey back to Los Angeles.

As she relayed to Chuck, "Eddie must have been furious with me, because he called the airline and canceled the return portion of my ticket. I had to spend some of the money to pay for my flight. So much for the former Mr. Elizabeth Taylor, and he bragged about how generous he was. I bet he soaked Elizabeth for millions when she had to get rid of him."

Months later, when Linda returned to Las Vegas to perform in her own show, she made several attempts to get in touch with Sinatra. Secretly, she day-dreamed that he had been so turned on by her that he might want her to divorce Chuck and dump Sammy Davis, Jr. On three different occasions, she left messages with the receptionist at the Sands.

One of her notes read: "I'm still waiting by the phone, Frankie, you big lug. Just give me a call day or night, and I'll come running, just like Shirley MacLaine in your film, *Some Came Running.*"

Her messages, if they were ever delivered at all, were never answered. "I guess Ol' Blue Eyes," she said, "has found other more amusing attractions."

***

Linda's next film commitment would be for a gig in New York, but before she left Hollywood, she was able to work in one-night stands with two big stars (at the same time) and a weekend in Laguna with three other stars too. "I felt like the Queen of Sheba," she said, "getting requests from all these Hollywood hunks even if one of them was ailing."

Her reference was to Robert Ryan, who was suffering the agonies of advanced cancer. Nonetheless, he called her, inviting her to spend a weekend in Laguna with him "and with two of my best buddies, Ray Danton and John Ireland."

Dean Martin *(left)* and **June Allyson** *(right)*

Lana Turner said "my friend June fell for Dean big time and was a regular ringsider night after night at his act in Las Vegas. I've had Dean myself and knew what a lucky gal June was."

[Linda would later learn that this trio of actors had met in 1957 when producer Harold J. Kennedy mounted a Los Angeles production of Jean Giraudoux's very avant-

garde Tiger at the Gates, *first published in 1935, a play which defined Girau-doux as a transitional figure between classic and modern French drama. "I would pay you for the privilege of reading such beautiful words," Ryan had told Kennedy at the time*

Also included in the cast were Mary Astor and Marilyn Erskine, who, like their male counterparts, agreed to work for the Actors Equity minimum pay of forty dollars a week. From that time on, Ryan, Ireland, and Danton had been "bonded at the hip as drinking and fucking buddies."]

At the time, Chuck was seeing "some other woman," and Linda wasn't in the least bit jealous. Instead, she was relieved that someone else was fulfilling his sexual fantasies and needs because she just wasn't interested. In fact, by this time in her life and career, she'd come to regard Chuck as physically repulsive.

She drove herself to Ryan's villa in Laguna, where the actor himself answered the door dressed in Bermuda shorts and a white T-shirt. He certainly was no longer the muscled man in an undershirt who had grabbed Barbara Stanwyck and made love to her in *Clash by Night (1952). [Incidentally, Stanwyck at this period of her film career was seducing her co-star, Marilyn Monroe.]*

Ryan gave her a quick kiss and welcomed her, showing her to her own bedroom inside his house. Before her inaugural meeting with Danton and Ireland, she showered and put on a bathing suit, although still self-conscious of her scar.

Thirty minutes later, out by the pool, Ryan introduced her to the two Hollywood hunks, each of whom wore only the briefest of bathing attire. Danton amply filled out his pouch, but Ireland, widely rumored to be the most lavishly endowed actor of the 50s, looked as if he'd bundled some socks together and stuffed them into his crotch.

After telling her how glad he was to meet her, Ireland disappeared for a pre-lunch siesta, and Ryan went into the kitchen to prepare some soup and sandwiches for lunch.

That left her alone with sexy, virile Danton, who had mesmerized her on the screen with his good looks when he had appeared in an MGM film with Susan Hayward, playing her doomed lover. Hayward had been starring at the time in a biopic (*I'll Cry Tomorrow,* released in 1955) of the destructively alcoholic big-band singer, Lillian Roth.

"When you died on the screen, I cried a little," she told Danton. "I just knew Susan would never find another man like you."

"You really had a crush on me and Susan thrilled you, too," he said. "Did you know that that fiery redhead often fucked her leading men? At the same time, she held men in contempt, claiming she'd like to fry all of us in deep fat."

"She didn't mean that, or she wouldn't have seduced so many of you," Linda responded. "I worship her. Seen every film she's ever made. As for you,

346

Mr. Danton, I think you and your baritone voice and that well-built body of yours makes you one of the sexiest men ever to grace a movie screen."

"Well, well," he said. "This must be your lucky day, 'cause you'll find out if I live up to my billing. Ever since Bob told me he'd invited you down for the weekend as a party favor, I've been looking forward to you devouring me. Let's knock off a quickie before lunch, with more to *cum* later. I know that last remark can be interpreted two different ways."

Danton showed her the way to his bedroom, then left her alone for a moment while he went into the kitchen for a brief discussion with Ryan.

As she pulled off her clothes and freshened herself for Danton, she was well aware that since 1954, he'd been married to the gorgeous Julie Adams, whom he'd met when she was a contract player at Universal.

Years later, when Linda was asked by Garon's researchers to recall her sessions with Danton, she said:

"He was dark and dangerous, an incredibly stunning man, very masculine. When he took off that skimpy bathing suit, I was confronted not with the biggest cock in the world, but the most beautiful. It would take a Michelangelo to carve a cock like that."

"When he was nude on the bed, I attacked his nipples like lamprey," she said. *"Within seconds I had him moaning. I ate everything, including tonguing his navel, as I set about to discover his hot spots. Even his rosebud was not only tasty but gorgeous as well. His balls had a wonderful masculine aroma and actually had their own kind of beauty, and I don't think most men's balls are beautiful."*

"My dreamboat nearly came in my mouth several times, but I kept slowing him down because I wanted to keep sucking for as long as he could hold back. His strong hands eased my head up and down."

"I think he was thrilled and flattered at the sounds escaping from my throat," she said. *"I enjoyed him immensely. I sucked on him like a woman being given a ripe juicy orange after going without water in the desert for two days."*

"His cock was at least eight inches—long and uncut," she said. *"It was ridged with little veins snaking just under his satiny skin, pumping blood into it."*

"After he'd climaxed, he gave me a gentle kiss, promising he'd fuck me later that night," she said.

***

At lunch that early afternoon, Ryan proved he was not destined for a career in the kitchen. The men drank beer and ate Campbell's soup and ham sandwiches before retiring to their quarters after agreeing to meet later, at twilight.

It quickly became clear that at this point in their weekend together, it would be John Ireland's turn to entertain and be entertained by Linda. She'd seen very few of Ireland's films, and had never included him among her favorite actors. She'd heard talk at parties that he had been born in Canada, that he was known for his skill at portraying angst-ridden protagonists in *film noir*, and for his substantial genital endowments.

For those in the know, that became obvious beginning in 1948 with the release of *Red River* starring John Wayne. In the picture, Ireland compared the "size of my gun," with that of pretty boy Montgomery Clift, privately nicknamed "Princess Tiny Meat" in gay circles. The scene was a "wink" to the size of Ireland's penis.

When Ireland starred with Joan Crawford in *Queen Bee* (1955), she told friends that "John has the biggest cock in Hollywood, and I should know. After all, I was married to that jawbreaker, Franchot Tone."

[The high point of Ireland's career came in the 1949 movie All the King's Men, *a political drama based on the life and career of Huey Long, the former governor of (1928-1932) and U.S. Senator from (1932-1935) Louisiana. The film had won an Academy Award for Best Picture of the Year, and Ireland was also nominated for an Oscar as Best Supporting Actor.*

Ireland gave a forceful performance as the hard-boiled newspaper reporter,

Jack Burden, who evolved from a devoted disciple of the autocratic political boss Willie Stark (a metaphor for Huey Long, as played by Broderick Crawford) to a cynical trailblazer and denouncer of the Stark (i.e., Huey Long) regime.]

Linda recalled that Ireland, in the bedroom, "took off that jock strap-like bikini and stood before me. With clothes on, he was not particularly good looking. But when he stripped down and displayed what he called 'The Monster,' I think he could have had any man or woman he wanted."

As he lay nude on the bed, he told her, "I still get fan letters from women for whom size matters. Most of them request a plaster impression of my nose. I guess they're too polite to ask for a replica of my dick. All of them write about my 'virile' nose."

Hero or villain on screen, **Robert Ryan** was a man of deep undercurrents.

"In movies, as in life, he ended up on the short end of the stick," Linda said.

"I've heard that men with big noses have big cocks," she said.

"That may not be true in all cases, but as you can see, it's true for me. Maybe that association got started with

Cyrano de Bergerac."

[Cyrano, known for his ugliness, the size of his nose, his sense of poetry, and for his power as a seducer of women, was the mythical protagonist of what originated as a 17th century French play with several later French and English-language variations.]

"At that point, Ireland started to play with himself," Linda said. "Then he looked up at me. 'You really like to suck dick, don't you, kid?'"

"It's my specialty, my reason for living," she responded. Of course, she was exaggerating as a means of increasing his desire. "Staring me in the face was a foot-long piece of meat. It was very thick. But I knew from experience that I could handle it."

She managed to go all the way down on what she'd later call "his log," expanding her throat muscles. "Usually, the bitches can't get beyond the head," he told her, as she gasped for breath. She went up and down on him for nearly thirty minutes. He kept uttering, "Suck my dick, baby."

She claimed, "I did just that. I didn't need to be told what to do. A muffled gurgle or two came from me as he'd re-enter my throat. All in all it was perhaps the most memorable facefuck of my life."

To Garon's researchers, she said, "I never went to bed with the King of Hollywood, Clark Gable, since he died twelve years before I became famous. But if cock size is the measure of the man, John Ireland should be crowned the new King of Hollywood."

***

When the Laguna house party reunited that same day in the late afternoon, Ryan, looking very tired, remained supine on the living room sofa and didn't walk out to the pool. Ireland sat on a *chaise longue* at the far end of the pool, reading a script.

Like most actors, Danton was eager to talk about himself after he and Linda anchored themselves at the bar, having drinks. "I think I

Two views of **Ray Danton** in *Beat Generation* (1959) *(lower photo,* strangling **Fay Spain)**

Two views of **John Ireland**

(*lower photo,* with **Joan Crawford** in *Queen Bee* in 1955.

"I was not exactly what you would call a Hollywood pretty boy," Ireland said. "But once I took off my pants, I could have anybody, male or female, in Hollywood. Crawford couldn't get enough of me."

arrived in Hollywood at its decline; otherwise I might have become a big star like Rock Hudson," he said. "But I had a good run of it. I have this Kirk Douglas cleft chin, the dark hair, the olive skin, and I'm fairly good-looking, so whenever a director needed a stock-in trade virile type, he rang me up."

The New York born actor had made a career of playing gangsters in "B" movies. Linda had first seen him in 1959 as "The Aspirin Kid" rapist in *Beat Generation.* But he had appealed to her more memorably in *The Rise and Fall of Legs Diamond* (1960), and *The George Raft Story* the following year.

"I know why you were selected to play Legs Diamond. You do have great legs—great everything, if you ask me."

"Thanks, he said. "I appreciate the build-up. Right now, I seem to be at the twilight of my career, grinding out trash, often horror flicks, in Europe."

"Before dinner that night, Danton took me in for some more deep throating," Linda said. "He also screwed me. He might have played villains on the screen, but in the sack he was very loving, not violent. It was a seduction without intense feelings on his part, but a powerful attraction on my part. I really dug this guy, but in some ways I felt he was behaving like a professional gigolo, doing everything to satisfy the woman and not just trying to satisfy his own needs. When he came, I fear I held on to him a little too long when he tried to get up. As far as I was concerned, he could have stayed on top of me forever."

"When he came out of the shower with a towel wrapped around his waist, I did something stupid. I asked him if I could become his steady girl. He looked startled."

"Now, now, gal," he said. "You better go see John or Bob. I've got to get some sleep. I couldn't make an arrangement with you. I'm in love with my wife, and I've got to be faithful to her."

***

350

She'd later recall her final time in bed with Ireland:

"He wanted some more deep throating and continued to be amazed that I could take all of him. But he also got down and dirty with me, ordering me to 'suck my balls and eat that fuckin' asshole.' After a lot of fun and games, he was raring to mount me."

"His teeth were clenched and he grunted at each thrust. In and out he went, ramming harder with an increasing ferocity. His eyes glistened and his face contorted as he shot, his lips coming down on mine."

"All I can say it that when John Ireland fucks a woman, she'd gonna get the screwing of her life. He should have won that Oscar, not as a supporting player, but as a star, for that is what he is, at least in bed. I'm sure the likes of Joan Crawford, Shelley Winters, and especially Joanne Dru would back me up. In the afterglow, he did tell me that he nearly split poor Monty Clift open when they were making Red River *together. That's what a guy or a gal gets when they take on more than they can handle. Fortunately for Linda Lovelace, that is not a problem."*

***

Shortly before midnight, Ryan entered her bedroom a few hours after Ireland had retreated to his own room. Danton had left the house to have some drinks at a beachfront bar.

"In my bed, Ryan had the desire, but not the stamina. I couldn't get a rise out of him. Finally, he asked me to hold him in my arms instead. I did that for about half an hour. He was crying, but ever so softly, with an occasional moan. He knew he was dying."

"He'd made love to many beautiful and famous women in his day, not just Marilyn, but Joan Bennett, Gloria Grahame, Janet Leigh, Claire Trevor, Ida Lupino, quite a lot. But now he knew it was all over. The cancer, he told me, was on the warpath again. There were precious few days left for him, maybe a matter of months or even weeks. For all I knew, his sexual contact with me, limited though it was, might have been his last time with a woman."

***

At around 10am on Sunday morning, as Danton and Ireland still slept, Ryan gave her six-hundred dollars. "The boys chipped in and also thanked me for arranging for you to show them a good time."

"Having had a good time was something he could not claim for himself," she said with a sense of regret during her latter day confessions with Reba-

351

Anne Howard.

Ireland and Danton, however, had made her weekend memorable. As for Ryan, she felt great sympathy for him, as she kissed him on the cheek, but she didn't know what to say to him, so she blurted out the first thing that came into her head. "Good luck. I know you'll pull through."

Driving north from Laguna, back toward Los Angeles, she had cause to wonder what all her encounters with the stars were heading to. But, as she'd recall, "I was not one for a lot of self-analysis, so I turned off by brain and turned on the music."

***

Another memorable evening began at William Holden's plush apartment, where he'd summoned her back for a repeat performance, this time with his close friend, Richard Widmark. When she got there, Holden gave her a kiss evocative of the one he'd planted on the delicate lips of Audrey Hepburn in *Paris When It Sizzles* (1964). "In that one I had to take care of Audrey *[A reference to Audrey Hepburn]* and also perform stud duty to Marlene Dietrich on the side," he'd told her.

Holden looked hung over from the night before, and it was obvious that cocktail hour for him had begun before lunch. He chatted with her while watching the TV News at the same time. Politically, he was a conservative, and complained that Richard Nixon was setting back the Republican Party two decades. "Ronnie should have been elected president instead of Nixon."

She knew, of course, that he was referring to Ronald Reagan. He had never acted on her request to set her up on a date with Reagan, and she knew he never would. But at least she was getting to service Widmark, and if she performed brilliantly, she suspected that Holden would set her up with other male stars as a party favor.

When Widmark arrived, he was cold sober and still fairly handsome for a man "on the shady side of his fifties," as Linda put it. He was well groomed and in reasonably good shape. Holden had warned her that Widmark at first came off as rather subdued, but that "with enough booze in his gut, he has a wild side to him."

She didn't interpret Widmark as the menace he presented on the screen. He seemed "rather pulled together," as she put it, "and definitely not the giggling sociopath villain," Tommy Udo, as he appeared in the 1947 *Kiss of Death,* where he pushed a wheelchair-bound Mildred Dunnock down a flight of stairs to her death.

During an interlude when Holden and Widmark talked with one another, ignoring her, they seemed to be re-creating the four hell-raising months they spent together in Baton Rouge, Louisiana, during the sweaty, hard-labor filming of *Alvarez Kelly* for Columbia in 1966. Patrick O'Neal had co-starred with them in the film, and Janice Rule had played the female lead.

[Alvarez Kelly had been based on the real life "Beefsteak Raid," a September, 1864 fracas that involved procurement of food supplies during the peak of the U.S. Civil War. Cattleman Alvarez Kelly, as played by Holden, is commissioned to deliver a herd of cattle to the Northern (Union) Army during its military forays into Virginia. However, at the successful conclusion of a cattle drive that had begun on the western frontier, the animals are confiscated, and Kelly is kidnapped by Southern (Confederate) forces led by a raider portrayed by Richard Widmark.

Eventually, in a series of events complicated by the arrival of a southern belle played by Janice Rule, Kelly is coerced to re-direct the cattle toward Confederate consumers, who are starving during a Union blockade of Richmond. In a convincing portrayal of male bonding for mutually beneficial ends, Kelly

(Holden) teaches Widmark's men how to drive cattle. Then, they proceed to capture and re-direct the herd, despite the efforts of an alert Union officer , as portrayed by Patrick O'Neal.]

"That communist, Edward Dmytryk directed it, and I was none too happy to be working again with him," Holden said. "I'd had a small role in his *Million Dollar Legs* in 1939 when I was getting started in the movie business. On that one, I got to fuck Betty Grable offscreen. Dmytryk was among the blacklisted 'Hollywood Ten,' because of his support of the Reds."

"I was one-eyed in that film," Widmark said. "The highlight came when I got to shoot off one of Holden's fingers. God dammit, that was fun."

"We were typecast," Holden said. "Me as a cynical, opportunistic, and charming kind of guy, with Dick here as a tough and ruthless rebel."

"Things got really shitty when Ardis served you with divorce papers," Widmark said. He was referring to actress Brenda Marshall (known offscreen as Ardis), the only person Holden ever married.

Two views of
Richard Widmark
lower photo: as a giggling sociopath in *Kiss of Death* (1947)

Linda: "Was Widmark faithful to his wife? Yeah, right."

"Let's don't go there," Holden said. "The script was shit and my horse hated me. I took him riding in the Bayou country and he threw me into a swamp. I could have been eaten by alligators. When I got back to the set, I rolled up that script and shoved it up the nag's asshole."

"I always make it a point to screw a gal in every country I visit, or every state if I'm in America," Holden said. "In Louisiana, I bagged Janice, even though she played Dick's gal in the movie. She was balling Steve McQueen, who was also in Louisiana filming *Nevada Smith.* Janice, Steve, and I got real drunk one night. Steve invited me back to their hotel suite. An hour later, Steve was asking me to go first with Janice, and I did. I found out later that the guy prefers 'sloppy seconds.'"

"I know Steve McQueen!" Linda said. "Been there, done that…"

"I found out that Dick here used to be a drummer," Holden said. "He came down with the flu, and I bought a snare drum for him to practice on during his recuperation. When he went to the Playboy Club in New Orleans, the guys let him play with them in the band."

Widmark rose to his wobbly feet as Holden was already standing. "Our four months of being together was the equivalent of fifteen years of friendship," Holden said.

"Tonight, with your help, Linda, we're going to get to know each other as we've never known each other," Widmark said. "We want to have sex with you at the same time."

"I've been warned," she responded. "Off to the bedroom with you and off with those stuffy clothes. I want you guys naked for my workout."

As she would later recall, "Neither of them was John Ireland, so I did double duty and brought both of them to a roaring climax at the same time. At first, I thought that these two macho males, very straight, would feel awkward standing side by side with their hard dicks rubbing up against each other. But they seemed to enjoy it, and were amazed that I could deep throat both of them at the same time. I enjoyed it too, It was all very decadent, like so many other scenes in my life.

Feeding the Confederacy:
Holden *(left)* and **Widmark** *(right)*
in *Alvarez Kelly* (1966)

Throughout six weeks of salmonella poisoning in Louisana, Holden was tended to by Widmark at his bedside. But Widmark never expected to get as close to Holden as he did when Linda took both of them on at the same time.

But the evening wasn't over yet."

Later, Holden announced that their threesome would be moving on for a night on the town.

En route to the Los Angeles Playboy Club, Widmark explained to her that Holden often liked to bring home as many as five Bunnies at a time. "Then he goes and takes a shower—he's the cleanest man I know—and he comes back into the living room with a towel wrapped around his waist. He does a very sexy striptease and at the last minute flips off the towel and flashes the family jewels. The Bunnies scream."

"And you told me you felt too old to do a striptease in *Picnic* and that was in 1955," Linda said to Holden.

Arriving at The Playboy Club, Widmark asked if he could play drums in the band for a while. The musicians agreed, welcoming him. It was even announced that, "By special arrangement, Richard Widmark will be playing drums tonight."

For a part of the evening Holden went on a Bunny hunt.

For about thirty minutes, Linda sat alone at a table, feeling that even though she was the most sought-after woman in America, in her opinion, she was still neglected while Widmark and Holden pursued other sexual interests.

"You're Linda Lovelace," she heard a drunken male voice say. She looked up into the face of Scott Brady. That handsome, good-looking former lumberjack and prizefighter had gone on to become a movie tough guy in various action films.

"Oh, my god, Scott Brady in person!" Forever a movie buff, she said, "I loved it when you played the Dancin' Kid in *Johnny Guitar*. Imagine having Joan Crawford and Mercedes McCambridge fight over you."

"Joan got me," Brady said. "She's only one-quarter dyke. Mercedes is one hundred percent dyke. Can I join you?"

"I guess it's okay," she said. "I'm actually here with William Holden."

"I see," he said. "The A-list. With me, you'd be dating from the B-list."

Three views of
Scott Brady
(Middle view is from 1971)

"On the screen, I was often in the saddle; off screen, I was also in the saddle—just ask any gal on Hollywood Bouldvard."

She found Brady extremely sexy, as he was known for being one of the few actors of his generation who appeared on screen showing off his big basket in tight pants.

"I'm here with my older brother, Lawrence Tierney," he said. "I'm sure he'd like to hook up with the both of us for some action."

"I can't because I've got to hang out with Holden until later," she said. "I haven't gotten my paycheck from him."

"Oh, I see," he said. "What about tomorrow night?"

"Please give me a raincheck," she said. "I'm flying to New York in the morning."

"Larry and I will be in New York in a few days," he said. "I'll call you and let's get together. Probably with Larry. All of us can have some fun."

"I'd love that," she said. "I'll be staying at The Plaza."

"We'll call you and set up a date," he said. "Ever have two brothers at the same time?"

"You wouldn't be the first," she said. "I'm a very experienced woman."

"You're preaching to the choir. I saw *Deep Throat.* I gotta go. I don't want Holden to catch me here. He might cast me in his next picture, and I don't want to piss him off."

"I'll be waiting to hear from you and Lawrence," she said, and she meant it.

Leaving the Playboy Club at around midnight, Holden was deeply intoxicated, but insisted that he drive the car they'd come in.

Widmark whispered to Linda, "He's drunk, and I call him Leadfoot, but he always wants to be in the driver's seat."

Holden seemed to have no control of the car, and she feared he'd have an accident. He was going much too fast. A light rain was falling and visibility was bad. Without warning, he ran a red light, and then sideswiped three parked cars in a row.

"Fuck!" he shouted, opening the car door and jumping out. "Linda, take the wheel! You're sober. I can't be caught drunk in another accident. I'll pay you well. I'll taxi home." And then he was gone, leaving Widmark and Linda alone in his car.

"Do what he said," Widmark said. "I'll explain later. They won't do anything to you. Bill's too vulnerable. Please do it! There's a reward in it for you."

Within minutes, a dome light was flashing as a squad car pulled up beside them. Then a young patrolman jumped out from his car's passenger side. "Get out of the car," he ordered.

She did as he said, although she was trembling. "What happened?" the second officer asked.

"I don't know," she said. "Somebody ran out from between two parked cars, and I swerved in the rain to keep from hitting him."

"You don't look drunk," he said, after shining a flashlight into her face. "Let me see your license." He studied it. "Say, you're Linda Lovelace, aren't you?"

"Yes," she said, "and I'm riding with Mr. Richard Widmark, who will vouch for me."

The policeman shined his light into the car and recognized Widmark. "I'm a great fan of yours, Mr. Widmark," he said.

By then, the other cop had approached and looked her over. "I saw *Deep Throat,*" he said. "I enjoyed it."

Thinking fast, she said, "While your partner here writes the ticket, maybe we could go for a ride. There must be some dark street nearby at this time of night."

"Okay, Jack," he said. "You handle it. I'll be back in thirty minutes."

"Got it," the other cop said.

She knew what to expect. He drove in his cop car a block or two, and then turned into a dark, deserted street. "I'll keep a lookout while you do me," he said, unzipping his fly.

She reached into his pants and was pleasantly surprised to find a most generous cock, which she worked to its most rigid position.

"Sucking against the clock, I did my best, a real good lube job, and soon he was shooting off."

After he'd zipped up, he said, "We'll drive back and get my friend. He deserves a chance at you, too."

"I'd love to do him," she said. "Both of you are so good looking!"

The exact same scenario unfolded with the other cop. Within the hour, both police officers had driven off, and she got back into Holden's car with the by-now impatient Widmark.

The right side of Holden's car was badly scraped and its front fender had been bent, but otherwise, it was in good condition for driving.

Back at Holden's apartment, they found him passed out on his bed. "I know Bill," Widmark said. "He's out for the night. Can you stick around till morning?"

"Sure," she said. "I'll call my husband. My plane doesn't leave until late tomorrow afternoon."

Pouring himself a drink, Widmark explained why Holden couldn't afford an involvement in another car accident.

"Bill's in love with death," Widmark said.

Reporter Bob Thomas echoed that belief in *Golden Boy,* his biography of the star. "It had started when William Holden was a boy, with backyard stunts that exasperated his mother. The feats on Suicide Bridge, the dangling from high windows, the obsession with speed, the fascination with wild and dangerous places, the insistence on doing his own movie stunts."

"Bill's luck ran out in Italy in the summer of 1966," Widmark said. "Bill was behind the wheel of his silver-gray Ferrari, going about 120 miles an hour on the *Autostrada* between Florence and the Tyrrhenian coast. In the car with Bill were Sarah West and Susan West, the granddaughters of Anita Loos, the author of the original book version of *Gentlemen Prefer Blondes*."

"Suddenly this junky-looking Fiat 500 appeared in front of him in the passing lane. He couldn't stop in time. He swerved to the right, but it was too late. The Fiat was totally wrecked. This textiles salesman, Valerio Giorgio Novelli, was killed instantly. Bill and the girls were okay, but he was later charged with manslaughter. He got off on a suspended sentence. He paid the guy's family $80,000."

"Oh, shit," she said. "I understand now."

Widmark kissed her goodbye and promised to call on her again, but he never did. After phoning Chuck and explaining what had happened, she fell asleep on Holden's sofa.

It wasn't until 11am that a nude and disheveled Holden stumbled out of his bedroom, looking like he'd spent a week, without sleep, in a barroom.

"Thanks for saving my ass," he said. "I realize now I can trust you, and I'll definitely call on you again."

That was a promise he'd keep.

"Before I take a shower, I have something for you," He removed a painting that had been hanging on a wall of his apartment, thereby revealing the presence of a previously hidden safe. "Here's $2,000," he said. "I'll call you when you get back from New York."

"Thanks," she said. "I'll be waiting for you. What an evening!"

"I say, 'what an evening' nearly every night of my life," Holden responded at the door, giving her a kiss goodbye.

***

At 5pm that afternoon, Linda sat with Chuck in the first-class compartment of a flight headed to New York City, courtesy of tickets provided to them by Butchie Peraino.

"I think this sequel is going to be big, bigger even that *Deep Throat*," Chuck told her. "You're going to make a fortune. You've been climbing that mountain long enough. You're going to reach the top. You'll be Queen of the World."

CHAPTER TEN
Hollywood's Most Sought-after Hooker

At Linda Lovelace Enterprises, Delores Wells informed both Linda and Chuck that "deals are coming in over the transom." Several movie producers had phoned, suggesting that they join Linda and Chuck in setting up a jointly controlled production company for the manufacture of porn films, thereby eliminating their need to rely on mob money for financing.

Naturally, there were deals for Linda Lovelace T-shirts depicting her with her mouth open wide. One entrepreneur wanted to manufacture Linda Lovelace posters exposing her bare ass. Another idea involved production of a Linda Lovelace Candy Bar, a confection shaped like a penis with a scrotum. When ingested and bit, "cum," in the form of a sugared and creamy substance would explode (suggestively) into the consumer's mouth.

A magazine publisher wanted her to write a *Lovelace Advice to the Lovelorn* column every month, concentrating, of course, on sexual dynamics between men and women. He submitted two sample questions which he thought might interest the readers of his publication:

1. How many inches should a man have as a means of really satisfying a woman, and
2. Does the taste of a man's semen vary according to what he ate during the previous 48 hours?

Linda had her own ideas about a product she wanted to endorse. It was for throat lozenges. "Can you see me now? I could hold up a box of these cough drops. I could say, 'Ladies, you can suck cocks all day while hubby is away, and you won't even be hoarse if you use one of these cough drops after each *deep throat* orgasm.'"

Still under the threat of legal rumblings nationwide, *Deep Throat* had been denounced by some of the nation's leading film critics. Judith Crist, writing for *New York Magazine,* referred to it as "Idiot Filmmaking." In the *New York Review of Books,* Ellen Willis stated that *Deep Throat* was "witless, exploitative, and about as erotic as a tonsillectomy."

On their first day back in New York, Chuck and Linda left their suite at the Plaza Hotel for a meeting with Butchie Peraino about the upcoming filming of *Deep Throat Part II*. Peraino was following a recommendation from one of his lawyers that if the courts ruled that the original version of the movie was obscene and consequently slapped injunctions against screening it, "We'll make two more versions—one an X-rated film like the original, the other soft core enough to get an R rating."

During the meeting, when the discussion turned to the fees involved, Linda was ordered to leave the room while Butchie and Chuck negotiated terms.

Chuck never told her how much she'd be paid. Years later, she read in a newspaper the details of what her deal involved. She (or rather, Chuck) was given $40,000 up front in cash, plus five percent of the film's net profits. Even if the latter had derived from legitimate studios, they would have been difficult to monitor, but considering their origins within the accounting labyrinths of the Mob, their collection, if earned, would be almost impossible. She was aware that the director of the original *Deep Throat,* Gerard Damiano, was eventually coerced into abandoning his previously negotiated percentage of the profits and settle instead for a flat fee of $25,000, even though the Perainos were making millions off the film.

On the first day of the shoot, Anthony Peraino, Sr. ("The Godfather") came onto the set to deliver some advice to the film's two stars. "As for you, Linda, keep sucking those big pricks right down to the short hairs. As for you, Harry Reems, I want you to fire off that fat prick of yours, and I want to see some cum on the girl's cunt, or I'll cut off your fucking balls."

Instead of Damiano, Linda and Reems were introduced to their new director, Joseph W. Sarno, an American film director and screenwriter well-known for soft- and to a lesser degree hard-core "sexploitation" films made in the U.S., Germany, and Scandinavia. When Sarno was asked by Butchie to direct *Deep Throat Part II,* his first question was, "Will I go to jail?"

Chuck and Sarno knew each other from the days when he'd first come to Miami to shoot soft-core porno. "They weren't exactly friends, and Sarno warned Chuck that he was not to interfere in production in any way, but he was allowed on the set, "provid-

Director **Joseph W. Sarno,** pictured above in 1968, was the founding father of the American "sexploitation" film and a driving force in the sexual revolution of the late 1960s.

360

ing you keep your fucking nose out of my business."

One week before his first meeting with Linda, Sarno reviewed *Deep Throat* at a private screening. He later told Linda, "I was shocked at how blatant it was."

For *Deep Throat's* sequel, he came up with a very different idea, that of a screwball comedy poking fun at both sex and the Cold War. Russian spies would attempt to steal secrets from the FBI and the CIA.

Once again, Linda was cast as a nurse in the employ of the libininous Dr. Jayson (Reems). She no longer had her clitoris in her throat, but she could "suck information out of any spy alive." At one point, she tangles with a female spy named Sonia Shinobitch, who in the film exhibits more than just lesbian tendencies.

As the week progressed, Linda learned more about Brooklyn-born Sarno (1921-2010). He was the king of sexploitation films in America, including *Sin in the Suburbs* (1964) and *Moonlighting Housewives* (1966). Noted for scenarios addressing issues associated with sexual anxiety and accented with "artistic" input which included careful attention to staging and stark contrast of light and shadow, his films did much to break down the taboo against erotic content in American cinema.

In a review of his career, *The New York Times* claimed that Sarno "bridged the gap between the nudist and nudie-cutie films of the late 50s and early 60s and the hard-core genre that developed after *Deep Throat.*"

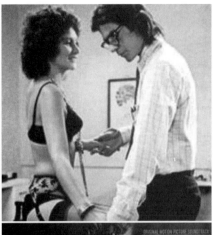

Deep Throat Part II, released in 1974, and starring Linda, was a murky reprise of the original.

It is not to be confused with *Deep Throat II*, which was released in 1987 and in which Linda did not appear.

361

Linda found Sarno far more fascinating than Damiano. The son of a bootlegger and a mother who was a socialist labor organizer, Sarno had led the kind of gritty life reflected in his films.

Filming on *Deep Throat Part II* began early in 1973, although it wouldn't be released until a year later.

Nearly every male or female porn actor in New York showed up for auditions. Among those finally selected was a talented and sexy actress, songwriter, and singer, Andrea True, who ultimately became one of the disco queens of the 1970s, especially because of her best known release, in 1976, of a dance tune, "More, More, More," which peaked at #3 on the *Billboard* chart.

DISCO FEVER

Sexy, resilient, and talented disco singer **Andrea True** (1943-2011), was noted for her ability to transcend her origins as a porn star. Here, Disco Queen Andrea performs her all-time disco hit, "More, More, More."

The third wheel in a *ménage à trois* which also included Linda Lovelace and Chuck Traynor, Andrea was variously identified onstage and on screen as Inger Kissin, Singe Low, Sandra Lips, Andrea Travis, and Catherine Warren.

She came to New York in hopes of becoming a mainstream film star, but got "waylaid" into porno. Throughout the 70s and into the 80s, she made at least sixty hardcore films. Like Linda, True later turned her back on porn, asserting that she'd rather be a waitress than make porn.

Although none of her subsequent singles ever topped "More, More, More," she made a lot of money with other songs such as "N.Y., You Got Me Dancing" and her album *White Witch.*

During the filming of *Deep Throat Part II,* Linda claimed in a memoir that Chuck, True, and herself formed a short term *ménage à trois* within their temporary home at the Plaza Hotel in New York City. True later denied it ever happened, but it appears to be accurate.

Linda told Sarno, "Chuck fucks Andrea in the ass at night while I go down on her. We show her a good time, but she doesn't reciprocate all that much."

True also spoke to Sarno about what was going on. Years later, at his home in Key West, Florida, Sarno quoted her as saying, "Chuck is a lousy lay, but Linda is hot."

Over the years, Linda watched as True hit it big as a disco singer. "She made the crossover into a legitimate medium, which I tried to do and failed. Ultimately, the only thing True and I had in common was that we both attended all-girl Catholic schools."

When interviewed in True's apartment on New York City's Upper East Side, she remembered

362

Linda as 'being rather quiet, soft spoken, and actually pretty with her curly hair. Except for me, none of the cast got to know her. She didn't mix easily with company. Believe it or not, in spite of her reputation, she was rather shy."

"My role in the film was expanded when Linda could not remember some of her lines. She was stoned throughout most of the shoot, and didn't really seem to care. Sarno kept changing the lines, the plot, everything, and Linda became so confused that I think she finally said to hell with it."

Reems echoed True's opinion: "So many changes were made that I finally didn't know what the film was about. Every day Sarno came to me with new lines. I don't think he knew what he was doing. It was total confusion from day to day."

"It wasn't Sarno's fault," Linda said. "Butchie Peraino and his dad, Tony, constantly demanded changes. They were trying to make another moneymaker like *Deep Throat,* but it was obvious that it wasn't going to happen.'

Sarno claimed that he shot hard-core scenes for an X-rated version and turned them over to Butchie Peraino to decide if, legally, he dared insert them. These pornographic scenes were never inserted into the final versions, Butchie claiming that subsequently, someone stole them from his office. "Frankly, I don't know what happened to them," Sarno said. "Butchie was such a liar. At any rate, those X-rated clips never resurfaced."

Despite her denials, True was in the suite at the Plaza when there was a loud pounding on the door early one morning at 4am. In his bathrobe, Chuck answered the door to discover some FBI agents.

True remained inside the suite's bedroom and did not enter the living room during the FBI's visit, as she was not under investigation and not specifically summoned.

But Linda got dressed and, with Chuck, confronted the agents.

She later surmised that the FBI came specifically to make a deal with Linda. As prosecution against the screening of *Deep Throat* intensified throughout America, she was asked to give state's evidence against the film's producers, the Perainos, in exchange for immunity from prosecution.

True claimed that the FBI agents met with Chuck and Linda in the living room at the suite in the Plaza Hotel for at least two hours. "They never told me what it was about, but it was obvious. To save her own skin, or to avoid jail time, Linda became a turncoat. To my knowledge, it was her first betrayal of the porn industry. More betrayals from her were yet to come."

***

Within her suite at the Plaza, Linda picked up the receiver of her phone. Thinking it was Chuck, or perhaps Butchie Peraino or Joseph Sarno, she said,

"It's Linda."

"Good, I've finally reached you," came a husky male voice on the other end. "At last, Linda Lovelace. I'm Victor Mature. Elizabeth Taylor, one of my favorite people, recommended you."

"She remembered!" Linda said. "I met her at the Playboy Mansion in Los Angeles. I thought an important person like that had forgotten all about me!"

"Elizabeth is loyal to her friends," Mature said. "I called your office in Hollywood, and they said I could reach you at the Plaza. I'm in town and lonesome, and I thought we might get together today."

"That would be great!" She was hoping to see Mature without Chuck finding out. He and Andrea True had gone off someplace, but didn't want to tell her where. She secretly suspected that he wanted to become True's agent.

Would three o'clock this afternoon be okay?" he asked. "I think it's called *Love in the Afternoon.*"

Ever the movie buff, she said. "I think Gary Cooper and Audrey Hepburn have already done one." She was referring to the 1957 film, *Love in the Afternoon,* directed by Billy Wilder.

"I'll be there," he said, hesitating. "I hope you don't have a sore throat today."

"From what I've heard about you, you'll give me a sore throat," said Linda. "Just kidding."

[In the early 70s, when Linda met Victor Mature, his film career had already drifted into a twilight zone. Born in 1913 in Louisville, Kentucky, he was the son of Austrian parents. In Vienna, his father had been a scissors grinder, but in America, he went into the refrigeration business. As Mature recalled, "I had a choice. I could either sell ice boxes in Kentucky or go to Hollywood and become a movie star."

Right before heading for California, he took a job as a candy salesman. In

Victor Mature

fact, before going west, he packed two suitcases filled with candy bars so he would have something to eat until he found work. He rented a garage, which was half burnt out, for eight dollars a week. That left him with exactly eleven cents, and he needed forty-seven cents a day for food.

One afternoon, as he was walking down Hollywood Boulevard, a homosexual director spotted him and solicited sex from him. As Mature later recalled, "After he raved about the size of my dick, he passed me around the Hollywood homo set. But when I became a movie star, I told studio publicists that I had washed dishes and waxed floors at the YMCA for a living."

During the day, he studied acting at the Pasadena Community Playhouse, and he also married a struggling actress, Frances Evans. His big break came in 1940, when he was cast opposite Carole Landis in One Million B.C. *Thanks partly to his muscles and his charm, Mature became an overnight sensation. Landis fell for him, but so did a lot of other Hollywood stars, including Betty Grable, Rita Hayworth. Gene Tierney, and Lana Turner. "I was the new boy in town," Mature recalled.*

During World War II, he served in the Coast Guard. Oleg Cassini snapped a picture of him lying nude in his bunk, with his thick penis hanging over the side. The candid snapshot was widely reprinted and later sold underground around the world. Author Gore Vidal asserted that if the Nazis had seen that nude of Mature, "they would have surrendered three years earlier."

Back in Hollywood after the war, Mature was dubbed the Lush Lothario, the Technicolor Tarzan, or the Overripe Romeo. "I was also called a ham," he said, "uncured and uncurable."

His great triumph came in 1949 when Cecil B. DeMille cast him in the title role of Samson in Samson and Delilah *opposite Hedy Lamarr, with whom he had a torrid affair.]*

When Mature arrived at the door to Linda's suite, he was in his early 60s and not as fresh as when she'd seen him on the screen. But he still had a muscular frame and hadn't lost his toothy smile, those thick lips, and that slick wave of hair.

Years later, she'd recall her impression of him as they enjoyed a drink together. "Many movie stars, at least those I'd met, lived in a world of illusion. But Vic was very outspoken and realistic, both about Hollywood and himself. At times, he could also be brutally honest and very frank. He told me, 'Critics are always saying I can't act. Hell, that's no scoop. All anyone has to do is see one of my movies, and they'll know I'm no actor."

"I come from New York, so this is my hometown," she said. "I heard you grew up somewhere in the South."

"I didn't do well at school be-

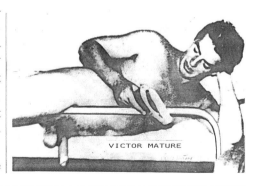

Victor Mature at ease, aboard a U.S. Coast Guard vessel in 1942

When film director Cecil B DeMille called on a nude Victor Mature in his dressing room, he later said, "Vic measured up to the role of Samson in all departments."

cause I had this habit of biting my teachers until they bled," he said.

"Are you married now?" Linda asked. "Not that it matters one damn bit to me."

"I got my last divorce in '69," he said. "Not that long ago. I'm in between marriages. The trouble is that I can't get along with a wife and, when I have one, I can't live with her."

"I hope you didn't have to struggle for as long as I had to," she said.

"One thing I must concede about Hollywood," Mature said. "A pretty boy doesn't have to go hungry."

"You were fabulous in *Samson and Delilah,* but I loved you even more in *Demetrius and the Gladiators* because you starred with Susan Hayward, my all-time favorite. I worship Susan."

"I certainly didn't worship her, but I fucked her. I usually end up fucking my leading ladies or male co-stars if they're gay or bisexual. When I made *The Robe* in 1953, I plowed both Richard Burton and Jean Simmons. Then I turned down *Untamed* in '55 with Tyrone Power and Susan. The way I figured it, I'd spend so much time trying to satisfy Ty's sexual demands and pumping Susan, I wouldn't have anything left for the camera."

"Elizabeth told me you were too much man for her," Linda said.

"She may be right," he answered.

"Once, Elizabeth flew all the way to Morocco to get deep dicked by me. Her husband *du jour,* Michael Wilding, and I were making this horrible bomb, *Zarak* (1956), with big tit Anita Ekberg. One afternoon, Wilding came

Marital Infidelity in a Hollywood simulation of Afghanistan

Victor Mature *(turbaned figure in the Zarak poster, top left)* generates tabloid headlines offscreen on the set of *Zarak.*

bottom left: **Anita Ekberg**
bottom right: **Michael Wilding,** husband at the time of
Inset photo: **Elizabeth Taylor**

366

back early from the shoot and caught me in bed pounding his wife. She rose up in the bed and shouted at him, 'I'm getting fucked by a *real* man.'"

"Regrettably, news of our affair broke in *Confidential,*" he said. "I still remember the headline: WHEN MIKE WILDING CAUGHT LIZ TAYLOR AND VIC MATURE IN ROOM 106. That exposé ran in the summer of 1956."

All this talk ultimately led toward the bed, which was still unmade from the previous night. "We never got around to the missionary position," Linda said. "He could have that with hundreds of girls. With me, he wanted to be deep-throated, then rest up for an hour, and then get deep-throated again. Even at his age, he had the stamina of a bull."

According to Linda, Victor had a very thick cock that measured six and a half inches soft, rising up to 10 ½ inches when aroused. "I should know, I measured it," she said.

He told her that when he returned to Hollywood, he'd have to call Elizabeth to thank her for the connection.

As Mature was leaving Linda's suite—no money was exchanged—she asked what his next picture would be.

"I've just finished this spoof called *Every Little Crook and Nanny (1972).* The title alone reveals how far I've fallen. It may be years before I get another role."

He was right. In 1976, he was cast in *Won Ton Ton, the Dog Who Saved Hollywood.* When *Samson and Delilah* was remade as a movie for television in 1984, Mature played Samson's father, a piece of casting which marked the closure of a Hollywood career.

***

Jacqueline Susann had been unable to reach Linda in Hollywood for a repeat performance of their lesbian romp. During one of her visits to New York, the novelist heard that Linda was living at the Plaza and called her to be her luncheon guest in the Plaza Hotel's Palm Court at 1pm. Linda was eager to rendezvous with Susann, hoping for some news about her latest project, which might ultimately lead to an A-list movie role for her. "It's my way out of porn," she'd announced to Chuck, who urged her to go to the luncheon and to pump Susann for any useful information.

Most celebrities kept Linda secretly out of sight, avoiding being photographed or even seen in public with her, but Susann boldly paraded into the Palm Court with Linda at her side. As heads turned, whispers were heard across the room.

Susann usually spent a luncheon talking about herself, but this time, she seemed to want some specific information. "You must be getting some amaz-

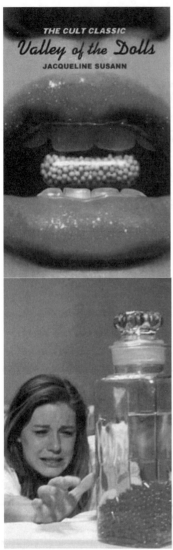

THE CULT CLASSIC

Valley of the Dolls

JACQUELINE SUSANN

Linda had counted on her life story being the inspiration for Jacqueline Susann's (then unnamed) next novel, even though **Patty Duke**'s *(lower photo, with the star playing a pill addict)* career had been almost wrecked because of her appearance in the film version of Susann's *Valley of the Dolls* (1967).

ing offers," she said.

"At least some very bizarre ones," Linda claimed. "Only yesterday, this marketing promoter wanted me to sell him any of my used bath towels, with instructions that I should pay special attention to drying my vagina on them. He thinks he could get good money for them."

Susann laughed, although it wasn't quite a laugh, more of a knowing chuckle. "That's an amazing coincidence. In my novel, *The Love Machine,* I describe this lovesick girl who carries around a towel that her lover had used the night before."

The novelist quickly switched to self-promotion. "You and I have had hits that the whole world knows about," she said. "I hate riding subways in New York—I'm strictly a taxi girl—but I went down into the underground and rode the trains just to see who was reading *Valley of the Dolls.*"

"When it was the number one best-seller for weeks, my husband, Irving Mansfield, was with me promoting the book in Atlanta. He took me to the intersection where Margaret Mitchell, who wrote *Gone With the Wind,* was killed by a speeding car in 1949. Irving asked me to step out into traffic and get a little bump from an oncoming car. I was to pretend it was a near-fatal incident and to collapse on the street, and that I should continue the illusion that I was seriously hurt during my transit to a hospital in an ambulance. Irving's belief was that the story would break that I was fighting for my life after being hit by a car on the exact same spot where the creator of Scarlett O'Hara was fatally injured."

"I flew on promotional tours to every big city between New York and San Francisco, from Boston to Miami," Susann said. "I made three dozen TV appearances in a week, and twice as many radio shows. I lived out of a suitcase in hotel rooms while working eighteen-hour days.

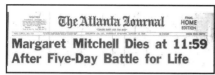

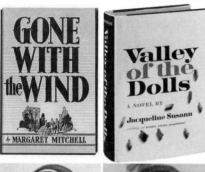

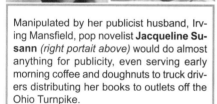

Manipulated by her publicist husband, Irving Mansfield, pop novelist **Jacqueline Susann** *(right portait above)* would do almost anything for publicity, even serving early morning coffee and doughnuts to truck drivers distributing her books to outlets off the Ohio Turnpike.

But she bolted when Mansfield wanted her to get hit by a car on the same streetcorner in Atlanta where **Margaret Mitchell** *(left portrait above)* had been fatally injured.

One thing I learned….Being famous is no picnic."

"I'm learning that for myself," Linda answered.

"At least I've got Irving as my business manager, but I understand your Chuck Traynor is a psychotic shit. You'll have to free yourself from his clutches…sooner than later. I have a dear friend, Joyce Matthews. She married Milton Berle two different times. Uncle Milty, as he's called, is the world's most self-centered man. He always tried to control every aspect of Joyce's life. I'm sure he'll be getting in touch with you for fun and games."

"Chuck controls me, but he's been treating me better since I started earning big bucks for him. I'm his meal ticket."

"How long will that last?" Susann asked. "Monsters revert to their true nature sooner than later. But now, my dear, I have to bring up something unpleasant. First, I want to tell you that I don't write dirty books, in spite of what critics say. I object violently when people claim that *Valley of the Dolls* is a dirty book. It isn't. Actually, it shocked my mother, but she defends me anyway. She claims that all great writers, including Tennessee Williams and Norman Mailer, write dirty today. It's part of the changing readership of America."

"I went to my publisher and pitched the idea of writing a *roman à clef* about you," Susann said. "I wanted to tell your story, all the degradation, the humiliation, the pain you've suffered along the road to becoming a household word. Instead of a dirty book, I wanted to write a true book. You understand. Well, to cut to the chase, my publisher defines any story based on your life as a dirty book."

"You mean, the deal is off?" Linda asked. She almost burst into tears. She'd been counting on being the inspiration for Susann's next novel.

"I don't write about graphic sex," Susann said. "My publishers think that even though I don't describe sucking and fucking, the subject matter of a pornographic star would in itself be pornography. After all, you'd have to describe, graphically, some of the situations you found yourself in."

"I worked on this sequel to the movie version of *Valley of the Dolls,*" Susann contined. "My scenario was provisionally entitled *Return to the Valley of the Dolls.* Everybody at the studio said they loved it, but then, without warning, Russ Meyer made *Beyond the Valley of the Dolls,* and it was a disaster. It had absolutely nothing to do with my scenario."

"I met Meyer," Linda said. "In fact, he fucked me at Hef's Playboy Mansion."

Always eager for gossip, Susann asked, "How was the sex?"

"Not good," she answered. "He's hung up on big breasts. He likes to get off fucking a woman between her breasts. Not my scene."

Looking at her watch, Susann rather abruptly asked, "Is your suite free this afternoon?"

Still disappointed at the collapse of her dream about how her experiences might be featured in an upcoming Susann novel, Linda lied, telling her that Chuck and some business associates would using the suite for the rest of the afternoon and evening. "Perhaps tomorrow we can arrange something," Linda said, having no intention of following through with that vague offer.

"Despite the collapse of our literary collaboration, I was hoping we could still be friends," Susann said.

Wistfully, Linda responded, "I've read about your friends. Doris Day is my favorite. She's not only a great singer, but a damn good actress. You're lucky to have her as a *very special* friend."

"To my knowledge, Doris doesn't go that route," Susann said. "Of course, you never know."

"I wish I had a good friend like Doris," Linda said. "Actually, I don't have any friends at all."

"That is not unusual," Susann said. "Believe it or not, many famous people have no close friends. They are just surrounded by people who get a paycheck every week."

"Let an old pro in show business give you some advice," Susann continued. "Decide on an image and stick to it. If the facts of your life differ from that image, then change the facts, make up some new 'facts,' or else dodge the issue completely. If you're famous as a cocksucker, then stick to that."

Regrettably, during the months ahead, as she watched her career turn into ashes, Linda would not follow Susann's very sage advice.

***

As he had promised back in Los Angeles, Scott Brady, in his late 40s at the time, called Linda at the Plaza and set up a date, which met with Chuck's approval. "He's not paid too highly, but you should get a tidy sum, especially if his crazy brother, Lawrence Tierney, joins the party."

Brady asked her for dinner at a very unfashionable Ukrainian restaurant in Manhattan's East Village, which had been discovered and frequently patronized throughout the late 1960s by hippies. Together, they feasted on beer and stuffed cabbage.

[Consistent with his image on the screen, Brady was a mixture of good looks, obvious virility, and a sexy toughness. Linda remembered him mainly from his starring role as the Dancin' Kid with Joan Crawford in Johnny Guitar *(1954), a campy cult classic. She'd also followed his TV series as Shotgun Slade from 1959 to 1961.*

Linda's only real competitor for the role of Hollywood's most successful and promiscuous starfucker, cult film goddess Liz Renay, had already gotten to Brady.

As Renay herself reported directly to the author of this book, "Brady was bisexual and had fucked a lot of sailors in the Navy. He told me that whenever he couldn't get a gal, a hot young boy's ass would do just fine. He also claimed he'd screwed Yul Brynner when they made Port of New York *back in 1949. My opinion of Brady as a lover? I think he could give a woman multiple orgasms even if he was raping her."*

Born Gerard Kenneth Tierney in 1924, the younger of his family's two brothers, he had changed his name to "Scott Brady" at the debut of his career as an actor. During World War II, he'd evolved into a boxing champion. After the war, he built up his body working as a lumberjack. He sometimes bragged, "There's one part of my anatomy I never had to build up. I was born with it."

Anne Bancroft, his former co-star in The Restless Breed *(1957), confirmed the assertions Brady had made, relaying to the author of this book, "Scott was proud of his equipment, and well he should have been."]*

After stopping off at a bar for some after-dinner drinks, Brady hailed a taxi and took Linda back to his hotel. Years later, Linda couldn't remember its name, but it was definitely not first-class. His lodgings were dreary, with cabbage rose wallpaper, but at least it had a private bathroom, unlike some of the seedy joints she'd stayed and worked in before.

Linda had assumed he'd made a lot of money on his TV series and that he'd be living in a grander style. Perhaps he was being careful with

Scott Brady
in his TV series as
Shotgun Slade

his money.

After using the bathroom and inviting her to do so, he suggested that both of them strip down. As he pulled down his jockey shorts, he seemed rather proud of the size of his cock.

She also stripped and lay down on the bed, trying to figure out what he wanted from her, sexually.

Wasting no time, he said, "Doll, I'm raring to go." Skipping her lips, he assaulted one of her nipples and then the other. He bit very hard on her right nipple.

"That hurts!" Linda protested.

"And you love it!" he said, kissing her hard on the mouth. Then he grabbed her hand and lowered it onto his crotch. "Big enough for you, baby?" he asked.

Brady's tongue moved down over her ribcage. He sucked and licked her navel before he plunged into her vagina, biting and tonguing her.

Suddenly, he was moving north, cupping her head with his two strong hands. "Now me," he said. "You had your fun. It's my turn."

She recalled, "It went on for at least fifteen minutes, maybe more. One thrust down my throat after another. He liked it rough—fun for him, but hard on the woman."

After he climaxed, he headed for the bathroom, where he called out to her: "Kid, you're good. Nearly every women I know can't hold up to what you did, but that's the way I like it."

"I mean to satisfy," she said, although her throat ached.

Back in the bedroom, he dressed hurriedly. "I talked to Larry this afternoon. He's very anxious for you to come by and see him—say, at around 7pm tomorrow night. I wrote down the address—it's on the coffee table."

Covered with a sheet, she expected some cash. But Brady didn't bring up the subject. "Use the room for as long as you want, but lock the door when you leave."

"Do you want me to get dressed and go with

top: **Scott Brady,** with a gleam in his eye

bottom: **Jeanne Crain** *(right)* with **Jane Russell** *(left)* prove that *Gentlemen Marry Brunettes* (1955).

you?" she asked, sitting up.

"Not now," he said. "The night is still young, and I've got a hot but very secret date with Jeanne Crain. We made *Gentlemen Marry Brunettes* together in 1955. Did you catch that one?"

"No, I didn't," she said. "My loss, I'm sure."

***

Brooklyn born and emotionally unstable Lawrence Tierney, Scott Brady's older brother, was often referred to as "The Bad Boy of Hollywood." Born in 1919, and far more talented than Brady, but much more volatile, he was known for his screen portraits of mobsters and hardened criminals. His most famous screen appearance was in the title role of the 1945 *Dillinger.* This tale of "bullets, blood, and blondes" made him a star. *The New York Times* called him "Not so much an actor, but a frightening force of nature."

Tierney got his start posing for underwear ads for Sears & Roebuck's catalogue, but they were judged obscene and he was fired. The editor of the catalogue told him, "We do not want to give our male customers penis envy."

Over the years, Tierney got frequently involved in fistfights and bar brawls—some of them very serious—and on a few occasions, he landed in jail.

Then in his mid-50s, he arranged to meet Linda at one of Manhattan's best known watering holes, P.J. Clarke's, a perpetually crowded late 19th-century landmark on Third Avenue that *The New York Times* once described as "The Vatican of Saloons." A self-admitted alcoholic, Tierney seemed to have already consumed more than his capacity when she sat down with him for dinner.

As they talked, he told her he had such a bad reputation in Hollywood he wasn't getting many offers. "I don't want to go back to my former job in New York—driving a horse-drawn carriage through Central Park."

After he congratulated her on her fantastic success with *Deep Throat,* he told her, "I'm desperate for work. I am tempted to pitch the idea of doing a porno flick with you. I've got the dick for it, and you've certainly got the throat for it. I really want to work. More than that, if I don't get work, I'll go under."

"If you know a director who wants a two-fisted, hell-raising man, who can play a real tough guy and mean it, call me, and I'll come running, drunk or sober," he said. "As for my brother Scott, you might not know this, but he's a closeted fag."

At one point, he stood up and started loudly reciting the metaphysical poetry of the English Renaissance satirist and priest, John Donne (1572-1631), to the patrons at P.J. Clarke's, who seemed to regard him with a mixture of fear, contempt, and amusement.

When he sat down, she brought up his films again. "I hear you were the meanest guy in pictures."

"I'm not really mean unless a *puta* pisses me off," he said. "Then I might circumsize her." In his early 50s, he radiated an aura of menacing intimidation. After too many drinks, he stood up again and said, very loudly, "I've got to take a piss real bad. Would you guide me to the head?"

"I'll guide you there, but after that, you're on your own, big guy."

Three young men at the bar had been eyeing their table all night, checking out the still handsome, rather famous, and very loud movie star. When he went into the toilet, all three men left their bar stools and followed him.

Within a few minutes, she heard him shout, "You fucking cocksuckers, what are you staring at? I'm sure you've seen a man's dick before." As she'd later learn, he became so infuriated at the most aggressive of the men that he'd turned from the urinal and pissed on him.

Reacting to the disturbance Tierney was creating, one of the bouncers walked into the urinal and asked Tierney to leave the establishment.

The fistfight that began in the men's toilet erupted into the bar. "I'll leave, you fucker," Tierney shouted at the bouncer. "But, first, a present." He hauled off and smashed his fist into the bouncer's face, knocking him down.

Jumping to his feet, the bouncer was ready to fight back until two of the waiters restrained him.

Out on the sidewalk in front of P.J. Clarke's, she hailed a taxi and headed with Tierney to his hotel, the Penn Post, a seedy dive near Penn Station.

The Penn Post was even seedier than Brady's hotel. Linda stripped down and got on the bed, as he staggered around the room trying to get undressed. Seeing the scar on her chest, he said, "Welcome to the club. I got one of those

Question: Who gets away with loudly reciting the 17th century metaphysical poetry of **John Donne** *(left photo)* within "the Vatican of NYC saloons," **P.J. Clarke's** *(center photo)* during a drunken public outing with Linda Lovelace?

Answer: One of his era's baddest Hollywood Bad Boys, actor **Lawrence Tierney** *(right photo)*, brother of Scott Brady. "When he's sober, which is rare, he's quite bright. When he's drunk, which is most of the time, he's liable to push a gal to her death through an open hotel window."

myself. One night I kicked down the door of my girlfriend's apartment and caught her fucking this nigger. I took him on. How in hell was I to know he was a streetfighter with a switchblade?"

"We've got a sink here, but no toilet," he told her. "It's in the hall, and there's no way in hell I'm going out there. The hallways are filled with cocksuckers because downstairs is a gay steamroom."

A drinking glass was positioned on the nightstand. He reached for it and began to urinate in it. After he'd filled it up, he tossed its contents out the open window.

She heard someone yell and curse from the sidewalk below. That didn't seem to bother him. He filled another glass the same way and tossed its contents out the window, too. This time, she didn't hear anyone yell.

Too drunk for sex, he fell onto her in bed. She somehow managed to work her head down to his groin and almost desperately tried to pump some life into his limp penis. She lavished great quantities of saliva on the unresponsive cock. She licked his balls to simulate him. But nothing happened. He pushed his head back into the softness of the pillow, but didn't wake up.

She finally lay beside him, having abandoned her hopeless quest. "Perhaps later when he wakes up," she thought.

When she herself awakened, it was already 10pm, and she knew that Chuck would be furious at her. She lay without moving by Tierney's side, listening to his snoring.

Another hour passed, and she decided it was time to go. She'd had to pay the food and liquor bill when he'd stumbled with her out the door of P.J. Clarke's, and she had almost no money left in her purse.

She was reluctant to return to the Plaza from her hardworking evening's endeavor with no money. On the sofa, she spotted the actor's wallet. Feeling underappreciated for her time and services, she removed about a hundred and fifty dollars, leaving him with twenty dollars in his wallet.

It was at this point that Tierney woke up for a full view of what she was doing. "You fucking whore!" he shouted at her, rising from the bed. He rushed over to her position on the sofa and grabbed her by the hair. Suddenly, his strength had returned. He dragged her to the open window and tried to push her through it to the sidewalk below.

She screamed and fought back, finally freeing herself from his clutches, letting his money fall to the floor.

She escaped into the hallway and raced down the stairs and out into the street. With so little money, she took the subway back to the Plaza.

A few years after her violent altercation with Tierney, she read that he'd been arrested and questioned by New York City police in connection with the death of his 24-year-old girlfriend, who had plunged from the window of her apartment to her death below. Tierney told the police that as he came into the room, "she just went out of the window."

Linda's reaction was sarcastic. "That gal went out the window with a push from Tierney, and I'd bet my left nipple on that."

***

Late one night, Sammy Davis, Jr. phoned Linda at the Plaza Hotel from a location in Chicago, where he was appearing at a club. After her filming of *Deep Throat* and its sequel, he had promised to help jump-start her career whenever a chance for greater stardom arose. He did say, however, "There can be no greater stardom than the original *Deep Throat*. How many hits like that can a star have in one lifetime?"

He told her that John Derek had slipped into New York and wanted to discuss a possible movie deal with her. "It could be a big break for you and could possibly open up the door to more A-list films."

She thanked him profusely and told him once again how eager she was to hook up with him after their return to the West Coast. "We'll spend a few days in Hawaii together," he said. "You'll love it. Some guys I know want to meet you. Don't worry. They're all gorgeous and each of them is a big deal."

"That's a tantalizing prospect you're dangling in front of me," she said.

"When I meet up with you, I've got something else to dangle before you," he said. "Gotta go. Love you." Then he hung up.

Derek called in the late morning and a dinner rendezvous was coordinated at a restaurant he liked on Greenwich Street. "I'm in town, but keeping it quiet," he said. "I understand that Chuck Traynor is your manager, so bring him along."

That indicated to her that their upcoming dinner would be devoted to business and not necessarily followed by a sexual tryst.

She wondered why he had sounded so secretive until she remembered something she'd read in a fan magazine: Derek had previously been married to Linda Evans until he met Ursula Andress and had fallen in love with her. Back in 1962, when Chuck had taken Linda to a screening of the James Bond 007 movie, *Dr. No.,* Linda had been stunned when Andress appeared onscreen wearing a white bikini. At Hefner's mansion, she'd also seen the nude photos that Ursula had posed for and which had appeared in *Playboy* in 1954. She told Chuck, "I feel insecure. How can I 'stack up' against a gal like Ursula?"

When Ursula launched a long affair with the much-married French actor, Jean-Paul Belmondo, Derek moved on into the arms of the sixteen-year-old Mary Cathleen Collins, whom he referred to as "jail bait." To avoid child molestation charges, he lived with her in Germany until she reached the U.S.'s legal age of eighteen. He would later configure himself as her Svengali, turn-

376

ing her into "Bo Derek," who would create a sensation in 1979 when she starred in Blake Edwards' sexy comedy, *10.*

At the restaurant, Linda and Chuck came face to face at table with "the man of my dreams." She had long considered Derek "a knockout," with his dark, curly hair, classically beautiful face, his liquid eyes, and trim swimmer's physique. Although approaching fifty at the time of his meeting with Linda, he appeared in excellent shape.

Born with the name of Derek Harris in 1926, he was a true son of Hollywood. His father, Lawrence Harris, had been a silent screen filmmaker, and his mother, Dolores Johnson, was a minor film actress.

Before breaking into movies, Derek had been a male hustler, satisfying the sexual demands of closeted Spencer Tracy and other usually male movie stars. Tracy lived in a bungalow on the estate of director George Cukor, who had also been a client of Derek's.

As he grew older, Derek pursued romances with both Shirley Temple and Elizabeth Taylor, seducing only the latter, even though Elizabeth was still a self-proclaimed "child in a woman's body."

Chuck was delighted to meet Derek, who, surpassed only by Hugh Hefner, was one of Chuck's most compelling role models. At the time, Derek was living a life that Chuck could only dream about—that is, seducing and photographing some of the world's most beautiful women.

As they ordered drinks, Derek explained how he and Sammy Davis had become friends. "I know to some we appear like the odd couple, but we were drawn together by our love of beautiful women."

Derek said he had met Sammy when director Marc Lawrence had cast them together in a 1965 film, *Nightmare in the Sun.* Derek played a hitchhiker trying to evade a murder charge. Sammy had appeared at the beginning of the movie as a truck driver with whom Derek hitches a ride. According to Derek, "My beautiful Ursula was the star of the picture, and Aldo Ray played the villainous sheriff."

"The movie closed before it opened, or that's how it seemed at the time." Derek said. "Sammy told me that he couldn't even persuade his best friends, Frank Sinatra and Peter Lawford, to go see it."

Throughout their dinner, Derek expressed his belief that once its legal challenges had been satisfied, *Deep Throat* would greatly affect future movie projects. He felt that when censorship issues were relaxed or removed altogether, filmmakers, scriptwriters, and directors, would, in the future, feature frequent and very graphic depictions of sex, even in A-list mainstream films.

"We've come a long way, baby, from the days when Lucy and Ricky Ricardo could not be shown sleeping in a double bed—only twin beds could get past the censors."

Chuck was anxious to see how he and Linda would fit into Derek's new vision.

Derek outlined the scenario of a movie he wanted to shoot on the Caribbean island of Nevis. "I know this beautiful setting that would make the ideal backdrop. The plot would revolve around Linda, who inherits this old inn following the death of her young husband, who gets killed by a shark. Two young men, both divorced, check into her hotel to recover from having been robbed by their ex-spouses."

"During their month-long vacation, with lots of nudity, both men fall in love with Linda," Derek said. "Instead of the usual 'Peter Lawford loses girl to Gig Young shit,' both men would win the girl, all three of them eventually sharing her double four-poster," Derek said.

"That sounds hot," Chuck said. "Have you lined up the two male leads? Or will they be unknown?"

"That's the whole point," he said. "I don't want unknowns. I've talked to a lot of people in the industry. In the late 70s and 80s and beyond, they think soft core—and eventually hard core—sex scenes will become standard fare in movies."

"What if an actor is hung like a rooster?" Chuck asked.

"That's not my problem, but for some guy who's not proud of his thing, we can always get a well-hung actor for the genital close-ups. In my film, I want all three of my stars—that means two men plus Linda—to have names which are known throughout America. Linda has already achieved that name recognition. As for the actors, I've been negotiating with Aldo Ray and in an unusual casting call, with Bo Belinsky."

As a movie fan, Linda knew who Ray was. She had found him "maddeningly attractive" when he'd co-starred with Rita Hayworth in *Miss Sadie Thompson* (1953). She asked Ray who Belinsky was.

(left to right) **John Derek** and his lover **Ursula Andress** and her lover, **Jean-Paul Belmondo**

378

"I'm a big fan of his," Chuck said. "I'll tell you all about him later."

"Just one question first," she said. "Is this Bo guy handsome?"

"No," Derek said flatly. "He's gorgeous."

The evening ended with brandy, as Chuck agreed for Linda that she'd co-star in an upcoming movie tentatively entitled *Ménage à Trois*.

Then Derek invited Linda to a studio on West 34th Street, where he wanted to shoot some provocative stills of her.

"We'll be there," Chuck assured him.

Derek looked annoyed. "Just Linda. I don't like to photograph my women when their husbands are looking on. It inhibits the artist in me."

***

When she arrived, alone, at a loft where Derek was filming, she was hauled upstairs in a rickety elevator by a janitor who rode with her to the top floor of a seedy building that looked old, decrepid, and drafty. He used his key to let her in, locking the door behind her. "Mr. Derek said to go to the back."

As she walked through the studio, toward a dressing room, she heard the sound of running water. Derek seemed to be taking a shower.

She called out to him, and he responded, telling her to come on in.

Dripping wet, he stepped out of the shower in front of her. Despite his middle age, she was mesmerized by his almost perfect body. Her eyes immediately gravitated to his penis. Although it wasn't the largest she'd ever dealt with, it ranked up there with that of Ray Danton's as one of the world's most beautiful.

When he saw that she was obviously enjoying the sight of his body, he allowed her time for a long overview of his pumped-up pecs and a broad-shouldered frame that had tanned to a mellow bronze. Slowly, he began to dry himself with a towel, paying special attention to his cock, which began to harden in front of her.

"I hope you don't mind, but I always take director's privilege," he said. "I like my female star to work me over so I can better understand her moves to re-capture on camera."

"That's one of the better excuses," she said, moving toward him. "Here, let me dry your back."

"You can dry more than that," Before she'd finished toweling him, he was fully erect. He shifted his weight from one foot to the other, as his balls finally settled in their pouch after her excessive toweling.

His breathing quickened as her fingers crept up his chest, settling on his nipples. As she fondled him, she noticed that a silvery drop of pre-cum had appeared on the head of his penis. She kneeled before him and took it in her mouth. He smelled of coconut. It must have been the soap.

Soon, he was feeding her tonsils, finding his own rhythm. As she gently squeezed his balls, he assaulted her for a good ten minutes, maybe more. His pulse quickened, and his body grew feverish. She was ready when the floodgates opened. "Here it comes."

It was an announcement she didn't need. She realized that she had already stayed on him long past her time, but for some reason, she couldn't let his penis go. She later confessed, "John Derek tasted delicious. There is no food in the world that competes with the aroma of this manly man."

Finally, she was forced to let him go.

"Let's get dressed," he ordered her. "Aldo Ray is here. I heard him come in."

***

Although Aldo Ray had aged somewhat from the last time she'd seen him on the screen, he still possessed his husky good looks and that distinctive gravelly voice of his. She later defined it as sounding "like he was gargling Listerine." He evoked a battle-toughened jarhead who had just led his Marine platoon through rigorous training. While Derek went to fetch fresh coffee for them, she had a chance to chat with this macho actor. He complimented her on her performance in *Deep Throat.*

"I can return the compliment," she said. "You and Bob Ryan were wonderfully white trashy in *God's Little Acre* (1958)."

Both of them lamented the serious health issues facing that cancer-stricken actor.

"I also saw you in *The Green Berets* (1968) with John Wayne," she said. "You guys were terrific."

"If only the commie critics had thought so," Ray said. "I see Duke about three times a week. We go to the same health club. Although in public he attacks sexy movies, in private he's more tolerant. He lambasted the hell out of *Midnight Cowboy,* calling it filth, but when the lights go out, Duke is pretty X-rated himself. He's fucked everybody from Joan Crawford to Clara Bow, from Marlene Dietrich—"the best lay I ever had," he said—to Paulette Goddard and Carmen Miranda. He even let John Ford give him blow-jobs when he was trying to break into movies."

"I figured that Wayne wasn't a goodie-Two-Shoes," she said.

"The Duke has seen *Deep Throat* and wants you to service him at our health club where we have a private room," Ray said. "I spoke to him last night. Forrest Tucker will be there, too."

"I'd love to meet the Duke and Tucker," she said. "Talk about macho!"

"Duke won't be a challenge for you," Ray said, "but that Tucker whang would clog the Holland Tunnel."

"I'm sure I can handle him," she said.

"Okay," he responded. "We'll have a little party when we get back to Los Angeles."

When Derek returned with the coffee, he spent the first five minutes talking about the two pictures in which they'd appeared together. They included Ray's first film, *Saturday's Hero* (1950) and the more recent *Nightmare in the Sun* (1965).

Finally, Derek relayed the very rough scenario that he wanted them to act through on camera: "I need some hard-core stuff. Don't fake it. I want it to be real. Don't worry about the final cut. Linda, begin with some heavy kissing, then work your way down Ray's chest and deep throat him like you did Harry Reems."

"I've got nine inches," Ray said.

"I can handle that," she responded.

"Even though I know you'll want to, don't explode in her throat," Derek warned. "I want you to deep dick her after the deep throating."

"I'm your man," Ray said. "I've posed buck ass naked before, back when I was a hairless youth. Nudes of me are sold from under counters at every dirty book store in America. George Cukor, my former director, has a large blow-up of me *hanging* over his toilet stool. When I worked with him, he wanted me to save all my gooey stuff for him, so he cast me with two dykes."

[*Ray was referring to Judy Holliday in* The Marrying Kind *and Katharine Hepburn in* Pat and Mike, *both released in 1952.*]

"I want to shoot the scene hard core," Derek said. "Nothing fake. I want you guys to actually do it on camera. Of course, the decision of what footage gets used in the final cut, depending on the legal climate when my film is released, is entirely up to me. Now I want you both nude on the bed."

"It wouldn't be the first time," she said.

He turned to her. "Begin with some heavy tongue kissing. It would be really hot if he spits in your mouth at some point. After enough of that, start licking and kissing his hairy chest until you reach The Promised Land, at which point you'll do your thing."

"I want to get in your throat," Ray said.

"Linda can take it down to the pubic hairs," Derek said.

"Actually, I'm looking forward to it," she said.

While they talked, a black cameraman from Harlem was setting up the scene. Derek told them that his specialty involved photographing 8mm loops of blondes in bondage being raped by black men.

Ray did not hesitate pulling off his clothes. He hadn't exaggerated the size of his penis, which was about five inches limp.

As she remembered it, "Aldo and I forgot all about Derek and his camera-man. We went to it. That guy really knew what to do in the sack. He was completely uninhibited. When Rita Hayworth made that movie with him—the one where she played a hooker—she should have taken Ray home with her. At least he'd be a better choice than some of those losers she married, including that Prince what's-his-name?" *[The reference, of course, was to Prince Aly Khan.]*

Derek kept them working until way past lunch, until he was satisfied. "It's going to be great," he said. Then Ray moved on to another appointment, as Derek coached Linda on her upcoming scene with Bo Belinksy, scheduled for the following morning.

"Derek was really gung-ho," Linda said, years later. "Both Ray and I be-

MÉNAGE À TROIS

THE XXX FILM THAT ALMOST HAPPENED, BUT NEVER DID,
co-starring **Linda Lovelace** *(left)* and movie star **Aldo Ray** *(right)*, with direction by
John *("I want to shoot the scene hard-core")* **Derek.**

lieved we were on to something big that would make Hollywood forget all about Brando's upcoming *Last Tango in Paris.*" According to Derek, 'With heavy sex scenes interspersed into an A-list story line, we were going to change the way most movies are made.'"

[Aldo Ray's on-camera work with Linda, as filmed by John Derek, never evolved into a marketable film. Ray did, however, appear in porn at the twilight of his career. In the late 70s, he was one of the stars of the X-rated Sweet Savage, *which led to his expulsion from the Screen Actors Guild for having accepted work in a non-union production. At the time, he'd been forced to take any job offered as a means of maintaining payments on his costly health insurance.*

He died in 1991 of throat cancer, having just starred in Shock 'Em Dead, *a film that showcased porn star Traci Lords, of whom Linda was jealous, and the fallen matinée idol, Troy Donahue, with whom Linda had, as she phrased it, "tricked many moons ago."]*

***

When Derek had first mentioned Bo Belinsky to Linda as a possible co-star with Aldo Ray and her in *Ménage à Trois,* she had never heard of him. But before her screen work with Bo, she learned quite a lot about him.

As it turned out, Chuck was a big fan of Belinsky, a celebrity baseball player identified in the tabloids as "The Playboy Pitcher." His pitching prowess as a rookie with the Los Angeles Angels had catapulted him into a glittering life surrounded by Hollywood movie stars, Las Vegas showgirls, and New York models.

[On the West Coast, Bo's red Cadillac, later a gold one, was often seen cruising up and down the Sunset Strip. On his arm, heading for the latest club, was his movie star du jour—perhaps Ann-Margret, Connie Stevens, or Tina Louise—cuddled up beside him in the front seat.

As a baseball star in Los Angeles on the evening of May 5, 1962, Bo attracted the attention of the sports world at the newly opened Dodger Stadium, or "Chavez Ravina," as the stadium was known among the Angels, who shared the space with the Dodgers. Against the Baltimore Orioles, Bo threw a 2-0 no-hitter for his fourth straight victory game of the season. It was the first no-hit game ever pitched in the California major leagues. Overnight, Belinsky's name became a household word, in large part because of all the publicity that Walter Winchell, then the most popular syndicated columnist in America, churned out about him. "The lefty with the outstanding fastball and screwball is destined for the Baseball Hall of Fame," Winchell had predicted.

From his status as a one-time pool hustler born in 1936 on Manhattan's Lower East Side, Bo had become a celebrity. Winchell arranged for Bo to meet another big fan of his, J. Edgar Hoover, the deeply closeted gay director of the F.B.I.

One afternoon, when Bo was in the nation's capital for a game against the Washington Senators, two FBI agents came into the clubhouse after a warm-up before the big game.

As Bo would later inform Derek and others, he was escorted by G-men to F.B.I. headquarters. "I wondered what I'd done. As arranged by Winchell, I met Hoover himself. He thought I was terrific. He took me to this firing range, and I got to shoot some machine guns. Later, he invited me to this private club where he had booked a steam room all to ourselves."

"He came into the steam room with a towel wrapped around his waist," Bo said. "But I came in buck-ass naked because I knew what he wanted. I can get a hard-on without touching myself, and I apologized to Hoover for my grow-ing erection."

"That's nothing to apologize for," Hoover told him. "If anything, it's some-thing to brag about."

"I knew I had to make the first move, so I stood in front of Hoover, who was seated on a wooden bench. My dick was two inches from his mouth. If that wasn't an invita-tion, I don't know what is. He gave me a blow-job, sucking like a baby denied milk for a week. He was drooling."]

When Linda came together with Belinsky, he was still in his hell-raising days, long before he sobered up and became a Born Again Christian.

Chuck had told her that Bo's career was in decline. "In sports, at least, he had a short reign. By '64 he was pitching—and not all that well—for the Philadelphia Phillies before going on to other clubs. But sexually, he became one of the most notorious swingers of his day, and was seen out with a different chick every night. For seven months in 1963, he was engaged to Mamie Van

Doren, that Marilyn Monroe clone. Eventually, he fell into drug and alcohol abuse."

Linda vividly remembered her first meeting with Bo at Derek's studio. "He might have been in decline in professional sports, but he sure looked good enough for me to eat," she later said.

Derek explained that for the first scene he envisioned for the two of them, he needed access to a secluded beach. "We'll have to film it in California."

What he wanted to create was a rip-off of that famous beach scene between an adulterous Deborah Kerr and Burt Lancaster in the 1953 *From Here to Eternity.*

"Derek seemed to delight in ripping off that movie," Linda said, "because he claimed he was originally set to play the role that went to Montgomery Clift."

"I want you to go a hell of a lot farther than Lancaster and Kerr ever even thought of," Derek told them. "I want you to make love like they did, but at some point, I want that swimwear of yours to come off. I want to see some hot sex and I want to see that both of you are really into it."

Partly because there was no immediate access to a beach, Derek wanted to spend the day shooting still photos of them in the nude to see what kind of chemistry they shared.

"That's okay with me," Bo said. "Linda has already exhibited her charms, and in my way, I have, too. In the 60s, half the sports photographers in America shot my dangling dick in whatever locker room I was using at the time. I heard that at my peak, those nudes of me were among the best-selling underground pictures in America. So if all those vendors are making money off my dick, why can't I?"

"That's the way to look at it," Derek said.

As Linda recalled, "Bo and I didn't have sex or actually climax that day, although I would have loved to. Bo was something else. Mainly we posed in hot embraces for Derek's camera. He wanted stills. Bo got hard right away. When Derek went away to take a piss, Bo whispered in my ear what he'd like to do to me, and we made a date for the following evening."

"When Derek came back, he shot more stills for at least an-

This is how John Derek imagined the visuals of the xxx-rated film he was making with Aldo Ray, Bo Belinsky, and Linda Lovelace

photo above: **Burt Lancaster** and **Deborah Kerr** in *From Here to Eternity* (1953)

other hour and then let us go, saying that he thought that we'd been great together." He also told us that he'd like to film a three-way with Aldo, Bo, and me. I told him, 'I can't wait for that to happen.'"

"Maybe we'll have to have several scenes with the three of you," Derek said. "After all, the picture's title is *Ménage à Trois,* although I've been advised that it should probably be retitled *Threesome* since a lot of dumb Americans might not know what a *Ménage à Trois* is."

She accepted a date with Bo for the following evening, with the understanding that their meeting would occur at P.J. Clarke's on Third Avenue, the scene of her earlier disaster with Lawrence Tierney.

Inside the bar, no one seemed to recognize her, perhaps because she wore a red wig.

[During the course of a marketing project that lasted no more than a week, Chuck at the time was configuring her first as a redhead, to see how that went over, and then as a blonde. Both experiments were defined as failures, and Linda eventually went back to her natural hair color.]

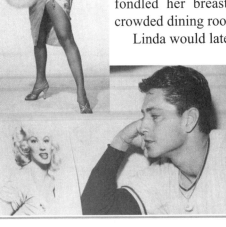

It seemed, however, that every person, male and female, in P.J. Clarke's knew who Bo Belinsky was, even though his sports career was in decline. As he worked his way to their table, about a dozen of his fans asked for his autograph. And as they consumed their beer and hamburgers, one well-stacked blonde approached their table and asked the baseball player to autograph her breasts. He refused but told her he'd squeeze them instead. As he fondled her breasts, she squealed in delight as the crowded dining room watched.

Linda would later reminisce about her eight-hour sex marathon with Bo Belinsky "as one of the most memorable fucks of my life. We fucked and sucked, then took a breather and resumed after a smoke or a drink. By 2am, he'd completely satisfied me. But at 5am he was still pumping. I've never known a man like Bo Belinsky. What's the male equivalent of a nymphomaniac?"

In her memoirs, *Playing the Field,* Mamie Van Doren would also extol the sexual prowess of Bo, to whom she was engaged on April

Two views of **Mamie Van Doren**
top photo: in *Teacher's Pet* (1958)

lower photo: **Bo Belinsky** pines for **Mamie**

Fool's Day of 1963, breaking it off by Hallowe'en.

Linda agreed with Mamie's assessment of the athlete, which went like this: "Bo was a ladies' man, fully aware of his powers and with little inclination to curb them. I melted into his muscular arms, and we kissed with a growing passion. He was deep chested, lean, and trim, and we reached greater and greater heights of ecstasy."

Mamie also agreed with Linda about how Bo could actively and aggressively participate in sex all night. "What Mamie didn't write about was Bo's dick," Linda claimed. "It was a wonderful love machine, if I can steal a phrase from Jacqueline Susann. It was plenty big for the job, but not grotesque. He had developed a way of moving inside a woman that hit all the right spots. I don't know how he did it. He certainly could use that prick of his to bring a woman to multiple orgasms."

"One night between fucks, he named some of the movie stars he'd seduced without attracting press attention. He cited Lee Remick, Ava Gardner, the doomed Sharon Tate, and Jayne Mansfield, Mamie's rival."

"All of them went down on me," Bo said. "All except Lana Turner. She doesn't give blow-jobs. But you're the best, Linda. Your throat is like a suction pump."

"When I first took Marilyn Monroe to bed," Bo continued, "she said I was as good—or better—than another baseball player she'd known. Guess who she was talking about? If I hadn't fucked up my career, I could have become bigger than Joe DiMaggio."

When Bo finally released Linda at 8am the following morning, he asked her for another date with him for that upcoming evening. "I heard you do three-ways, and I'm into that, too."

"I've been known to play along," she said. "Who's the lucky gal?"

"Judy Campbell," he said, matter-of-factly. "An Elizabeth Taylor looka-like."

Linda hadn't known who Bo Belinsky was, and she certainly didn't know who Judy Campbell was, either. "But I was about to find out." Years later, Linda would recall her experience with Bo and Campbell to Jay Garon's researchers.

"At the time I came together—forgive the pun—with Bo, I began to feel that I was a vital link in this gigantic daisy chain that stretched from coast to coast. I'd meet one man who would turn me on to another. I was passed along like a bucket of water in a fire brigade. I certainly was putting out a lot of fires. Bo told me that 'every male movie star, athlete, or politician should have a chance to spend at least one night with Linda Lovelace.' Chuck had destroyed my self-confidence, but I was regaining it by the bushel."

Most the daisy chain described by Linda channeled her to sexual episodes with men, but on a few occasions, to women as well. For variety's sake, Linda was anxious to meet this mysterious Judy Campbell, especially if she looked like Elizabeth Taylor, whom Linda had considered a goddess since their meeting at Hugh Hefner's party.

***

Bo invited Linda to his hotel suite at least an hour before the arrival of the mysterious "Judy Campbell." It would allow time for him to fill her in on the background of this controversial dark-haired beauty.

[In the years to come, Linda would become well acquainted with the personal history of Judith Campbell Exner. When she was 18, she had entered into a marriage (1952-1958) with a minor Hollywood actor, William Campbell, a violent and abusive alcoholic. In 1960, thanks to an introduction from Frank Sinatra (who, along with Eddie Fisher, had also been one of her bedmates) she entered into an on-again, off-again, 18-month affair with then-Senator from Massachusetts John F. Kennedy, which continued on and off through the early years of his tenure as U.S. President. Those intimacies, with their associated security risks, transpired more or less simultaneously with her status as a girlfriend of the Chicago mob boss, Sam Giancana, and as an occasional sexual playmate of one of Giancana's henchmen, Johnny Roselli. Much later, from 1975 to 1988, Judith was married to a professional golfer, Dan Exner.

In the mid-1970s, when Judith was summoned before a U.S. Senate investigating committee, she became a notorious (and much-loathed) media sensation, and ultimately, the second-most-famous mistress of JFK's, ranking—in terms of fame—just a notch behind Marilyn Monroe.

After the exposure of her affair with JFK in the press, Judith became the first person whose personal history represented a direct and scandalous attack upon the fragile myth of Camelot.

Although Mamie Van Doren revealed the link between Belinsky and Judith in her memoirs, that revelation went almost unnoticed by the press, despite the volume of ink that the media used in its exposés of JFK and his obsessive womanizing.

"Somehow, I never appeared on the radar screen," Belinsky told Linda. "One night, when I was in Washington for a game, Judy came right to my bed at the Mayflower Hotel, her cunt still warm from having just fucked the President at the White House. That night, I got JFK's sloppy seconds.]

Campbell's affair with Bo began in 1960, the year that Senator Kennedy ran for president, surviving through the remainder of the Camelot era and enduring as a "sometimes thing" into the 1970s. As Bo later confessed, "We rarely were in the same town. When we were—say, in Chicago—we stayed together in the same hotel and set the sheets on fire. Once, we even talked about mar-

388

riage."

"Judy said I was a far better lover than the President," Bo said. "She gave me a #10 rating, ranking the President at the lowest level of #1 because he was much too quick on the draw."

"Judy also told me that the President had claimed to her that he was interested in bedding Mamie, even though I was engaged to her at the time," Bo said. "Through Judy I sent a warning to the President not to come sniffing around Mamie or else I'd make him real sorry."

"Judy reminded me that there was this security outfit called the Secret Service that prevented retribution from jealous boyfriends or husbands."

[In later years, Jackie Kennedy called Judith "a user, a manipulator—common as dirt!" But Linda, in the early 70s, almost a decade after JFK's assassination and before the media frenzy associated with her investigation by the U.S. Senate, found her "unassuming, very nice, and, oh so polite."]

Frank Sinatra's valet, George Jacobs, referred to Judith as "the perfect Eisenhower-era pinup of the girl next door." After very briefly chatting with Judith, Linda could understand why Jacobs had formed such an opinion of her.

Knowing what was coming up in the bedroom, Judith was very frank and upfront with Bo and Linda, feeling that she was speaking to safe company. Judith asserted that it was Frank Sinatra who had originally turned her on to the pleasures of three-ways.

According to Judith, "In Las Vegas, he [Sinatra] invited Marlene Dietrich to his suite when I was sleeping over. Marlene liked both men and women, so we had a grand old time. President Kennedy, on July 11, 1960, brought Marilyn Monroe to a suite where I was entertaining him during the Democratic National Convention in Los Angeles. He told me he was highly nervous about the convention and needed Marilyn and me to help him relax. We did our job. My romp with

Judy Exner

RENT GIRL: In the early 1960s, as part of a scandal that would break in the news media after the assassination of JFK, one of the mid-20th Century's most notorious and reviled women, **Judith Campbell Exner** *(center photo),* provided courier and sexual services to the U.S. President and to key ringleaders of organized crime.

389

Judith Campbell Exner

Linda Evaluates Her Three-way

At least a decade after the assassination of JFK, Linda found herself as a member of a three-way whose participants included baseball icon **Bo Belinsky** (*photos left and right, above*) and the sexually notorious **Judith Campbell Exner**. Shortly afterwards, Exner was dragged to the floor of the U.S. Senate for a belated investigation associated with JFK's connections to the Mafia.

Linda later recalled her three-way with Bo and Judy Campbell: "I missed out on President Kennedy by at least a decade. But at least I got to seduce him as part of an extended daisy chain—that is, JFK fucked Judy who fucked with Bo who fucked with me. I guess that makes me part of history."

Marilyn and Jack was a hell of a lot more fun than being with Frank and the aging Dietrich, who was almost 60 at the time."

"Sex with Bo and Judith wasn't kinky at all," Linda later claimed. "We stuck to the usual stuff, fucking and sucking. Judith didn't go down on me, but I enjoyed her. Before the dawn broke, Bo, with his stamina of a bull, had fucked both of us, although preferring me to deep throat him while he went down on Judith. Of all the men I've ever known, Bo was the best for handling two women at once, because his thing would not go down. DiMaggio was known for going one round, but Bo seemed to enjoy at least six climaxes in just one night. Before I met him, I didn't think men could do that—and certainly not one named Chuck Traynor."

"After that night, I never saw Bo or Judith again," Linda said. "But I hope they have good memories of me. I think I showed them a hell of a time. Judith made all the right moves, but was not too experimental. But oh, that Bo...I nicknamed him 'Tiger.'"

"I also never saw Derek again after New York," she said. "He never raised the money to film *Ménage à Trois,* although I thought it would be hot at the box office. Derek didn't need me. He had another Bo *[Bo Derek].* Sadly, his film ventures with her failed, too."

Linda was referring to *Tarzan, the Ape Man* (1981); *Bolero* (1984), and *Ghosts Can't Do It* (1990). Ultimately, his movies provoked laughter and ridicule from audiences.

"My conclusion about Derek is that he belonged in someone's bed making love instead of wasting time directing pictures."

***

After the film experiment with Derek, Linda and Chuck remained another two weeks in New York. Andrea True, who had been sleeping with them, arranged to introduce them to a friend of hers, David Zentner at Pinnacle Books.

"I was moving on," True later said. "I had my own deals and film offers, but I knew they needed money. As a farewell, I hooked them up with Dave. *Inside Linda Lovelace*, published by Pinnacle Books in 1973, would be the first of Linda's so-called memoirs. Chuck told me he was given a $40,000 advance. I bet Linda didn't see a penny of that. For a finder's fee, I insisted on ten percent of the profits, which was granted."

A ghost writer was hired to listen to some of Linda's recollections, although Chuck—who consistently maintained that "I created her"—dictated most of this *faux* memoir, especially the oft-repeated exaggerations of his own sexual prowess. The name of the ghost writer was never revealed, although within the pages of the book, Douglas Warran was thanked for his "editorial assistance," and Chuck Traynor was acknowledged as "the creator" of Linda Lovelace.

In the book, she races through a few pages of her heavily edited early life. After only fifty pages, the book evolves into a sex manual and how-to guide, relaying Linda's points of view about various sexual techniques, including vaginal control, anal manipulation, and deep-throating techniques and secrets. There's also a vanilla-coated section about the filming of *Deep Throat* and her discovery by the world at large.

Nancy Leigh Semin, in her 2006 doctoral dissertation on Linda, wrote, "More interesting than what Linda included was what she omitted."

In her first memoir, instead of revealing details about her private life, Linda took up a lot of space configuring herself as a sexpert, even discussing cock quality and cock size in a style evocative of Dr. Ruth (Westheimer). "Sometimes the smaller ones get harder," Linda claimed. "Guys who are well hung are often egotistical to the point of no finesse."

Since her memoir was short and rather skimpy, she included within its context a chapter entitled *LINDA LOVELACE'S SEXUAL MANUAL (For Tired Lovers),* in which she gives advice on how to become a blow-job artist.

At the time of its publication, most newspapers and magazines didn't review it, interpreting it as nothing more than a publicity tirade. However, *Newsweek* was intrigued that Linda as a young girl had wanted to be a nun.

The English feminist, novelist, and essayist Angela Carter (1940-1992) defined Linda as a "prisoner in a cage whose bars are composed of cocks. She has been so thoroughly duped she seems quite happy there. Each age gets the heroine it deserves, and by God, we deserve Linda Lovelace." Carter went on to emphasize that the publicity triumph of Linda Lovelace unfolded during the pre-AIDS, sexually explosive 1970s.

Although Linda may have wanted to write a "tell-about" memoir, she didn't. She never named the majority of her famous clients, although she did obliquely refer to a few, assigning them nicknames.

At parties stretching from Malibu to Beverly Hills, based on her oblique and usually confusing memoirs, *tout* Hollywood tried to figure out the identities of the movie stars who had acted out their sexual fantasies with her. Speculation was rampant at nearly every Hollywood gathering and among ladies who lunch. Among the handful of celebs cited by Linda in her memoirs was a hard-riding "Saul," who got in the "saddle" and treated Linda like Trigger. He was the easiest for most members of the reading public to figure out: It was Roy Rogers, King of the Cowboys, with whom she'd had a fling in Las Vegas.

Linda's episode with "Dave" was a last-minute addition to the book, an editorial decision that was activated when the editors interpreted her written accounts of involvements with celebrities as a bit on the skimpy side. It was decided by her editors that she had to document, or at least mention, a few, es-

When Linda's first book of memoirs was ghost-written and published, her scandalous but oblique references to a "jungle boy" she code-named "Dave" set off speculation as to who he really was.

At first, speculation centered on the most famous of the many actors who played Tarzan, **Johnny Weissmuller** *(left photo)*, who boasted a string of Hollywood seductions that had earned him a nickname, "The Big Swinger." Then, speculation shifted to **Lex Barker** *(center photo)*, pictured above with **Monique Van Vooren** in *Tarzan and the She-Devil (1953)*.

The early speculation was incorrect. She was actually referring to **Jock Mahoney** *(right photo)*, the only middle-aged man to ever play Tarzan in the movies.

pecially some of the more bizarre encounters.

When the book was published, it made references to the "athletic sex" of a Hollywood stud who Linda identified as "Dave." Swinging from ropes suspended from hooks in the ceiling, it evoked for some readers the most famous of movie Tarzans, Johnny Weissmuller. But that guess was wrong.

There was also speculation that "Dave" could have been a reference to the super hunk, Lex Barker, once married to Lana Turner. But since he had died in 1973, he wasn't doing much swinging with Linda in the wake of the release of *Deep Throat* in 1972.

It was through a date arranged by John Derek that Linda paid a visit to the famous Hollywood stuntman, Jock Mahoney. "He's a bit weird, but harmless," Derek said. [*Derek would later hire Mahoney as a stunt coordinator for his own version of* Tarzan the Ape Man (1981), *starring Bo Derek with Miles O'Keeffe and Richard Harris.*]

A daredevil pilot during World War II, Mahoney had drifted to Hollywood after the war. There, he executed stunts for Errol Flynn, John Wayne, and Gregory Peck.

Originally, Mahoney had wanted to replace Weissmuller on the screen as Tarzan, but the mantle of jungle boy had been awarded to Lex Barker instead. In 1960, Mahoney auditioned for the role of Tarzan once again, but Gordon Scott was chosen in his place.

Standing six feet, four inches, and weighing 220 pounds, Mahoney was finally allowed to play the Ape Man in 1962 in *Tarzan Goes to India.* The following year, he found himself again in a loincloth for *Tarzan's Three Challenges,* this one shot in Thailand. At the age of 44, he became the oldest actor ever to play the jungle king. The producers wanted a younger Tarzan for their next film.

David Fury, who wrote *Kings of the Jungle,* said "Mahoney turned out to be one of the best Tarzan actors, and it's a shame he didn't get the role until reaching his middle 40s. A 30-year-old Mahoney as Tarzan, with his great skills as a stuntman and the intelligent fire of a Greystoke in his eyes, might truly have been the answer to Edgar Rice Burroughs' quest to film his fictional hero as he had created him.'

"Derek calling Jock a bit weird was an understatement," Linda claimed. "Jock had never met a sex toy he didn't like, and he collected them from all over the world. China and Japan produced some that were really bizarre. I visited him three times. He always appeared in a loincloth, which came off soon enough, and he wanted me to dress as Jane."

"Overseeing all the action was a Cheetah who shrieked all the time," Linda said, "especially when we fucked. In Jock's playpen in the basement of a secret address in West Los Angeles, he liked to swing on this big vine. When I was a girl watching Tarzan movies, I was always hoping to get a glimpse of the good-ies when he swung on that vine in only the loincloth. I never saw anything in the movies. But Jock didn't wear a jockstrap, even though he was called Jock. When he swung on the vine, I saw everything, and there was a lot to excite a gal."

"The strangest contraption was this chair from Hong Kong," Linda said. "It had been made with a hole in its seat, and was suspended from the ceiling by three ropes. Jock would spin the chair around until the ropes were tightly twisted. I got in the chair and placed my vagina over the hole. Jock lay on his back on a raised platform and produced a large erection."

"He then released the taut ropes holding the chair. As he did, the chair began to spin around his cock, which was already inside me. It was an incredible sen-sation. That was *screwing* in the truest sense of the word."

"For the finale, every time I visited, I went into this jungle-like shower that he'd built in his bathroom. He lay down on a rubber pillow on the tiles. He did-n't need the water from the nozzle of the rain shower. The golden shower came from me, and he demanded that I target it between his nipples and his power-ful chest. In my less experienced days, I couldn't pull off that stunt. But I came to piss like an expert. I equated it to an actress having to turn on her tears for a crying scene on camera."

"Did I mention that Jock loves porno movies, but with a difference?" she asked. "He screens them on a rear projector that shows the action through a large aquarium full of fish. He gets to see the beautiful fish swimming by up front and the hot sex scenes in the rear. As I said, Jock was a bit weird. I didn't tell you what his favorite porno movie was. It was about a young girl who had a clitoris in her very deep throat."

LINDA REMEMBERS: "Jock never met a sex toy he didn't like."

Jock Mahoney *(above)* suspended, in *Tarzan Goes to India (1962)*

Linda enjoyed her fling with Ma-honey just in time. In 1973, he suffered a stroke while filming an episode of *Kung Fu.* He recovered, but never regained his original stamina during the years ahead. He often had to use a wheelchair.

"Jock Mahoney would not be the only Tarzan who *lay* in my future," Linda said. "One more Tarzan, younger and hand-somer, loomed. I truly learned the meaning of 'Me Tarzan, you Jane,' but I never per-fected the Tarzan yell like Carol Burnett, al-though these two Tarzans certainly gave a gal something to shout about."

***

Linda's points of view as expressed through *Inside Linda Lovelace* set off even more speculation in Hollywood when she identified an (otherwise un-named) actor as "Super Cock." At least some of the energy fueling the specu-lation about the identity of "Super Cock" involved Linda's widely discussed intention, through Linda Lovelace Enterprises, of launching a series of "the most sensational porno movies ever made," with the implication that at least some of them would feature, or at least try to feature, A-list movie stars. This plan dissolved after she changed her focus and began attacking porno and its premises.

Consequently, she and Chuck interviewed what she claimed were "dozens of possibilities" as potential male co-stars, but the one actor she wanted to work with was known in Hollywood as "Super Cock." She had seen an 8mm hard-core loop he'd made before he became famous. As she described the actor's appendage, "His prick measures in at a fat nine inches when it's soft, and more than a foot long when it's hard. It has a circumference of about eight inches. That, my friends, is one big cock."

Even Jay Garon's researchers in the late 1980s could not get her to divulge the actor's name, because a deal with Super Cock was never negotiated. She did, however, give a tantalizing clue, claiming that he became famous on TV playing the best pal of the juve-nile lead in a situation comedy that ran for years.

"Back then, he was just a kid, but he grew and grew, and grew some more, becoming the man he is today." Linda said.

Confronted with her refusal to divulge his name, the alert and super hip Jay Garon, from his headquarters in Manhattan, reviewed, with-out success, many possibilities of who that celebrity could be.

Eventually, one of his assistants, without any proof at all, suggested that it might—"just might'—be Henry Winkler, who was best known for his role as "The Fonz," a leather-clad greaser and auto mechanic in the televi-sion sitcom, *Happy Days*. The Fonz (aka

HAPPY DAYS
"It's **that** big...or is it?"

Henry Winkler was the erroneous target of Hollywood gossip that sur-mised, incorrectly, that he was the man mysteriously referred to by Linda in her memoirs as "Super Cock."

395

"Fonzie") was the best pal of the all-American boy, Ron Howard.

But Winkler was shot down as a possibility when a researcher discovered that the long-running TV series first aired in January of 1974, and Linda's memoir had been published the previous year. In reaction to that, Garon and his researchers continued to sift, without success, through all sorts of possibilities, and although Linda would name other stars, for some quirky reason of her own, she stubbornly refused to divulge the identity of "Super Cock."

According to her: "I didn't want to release his name because his phone would be ringing off the wall," she said. "My God, if he was known, every time he went to the men's toilet, he'd cause a stampede. I couldn't ruin his life that way, because we never actually worked together, and I would be unfairly taking advantage of him."

"I made repeated calls to him, but they were never returned," she said. "I think he wanted to escape his porn past now that he had a reputation for delivering what was known as 'family fare' on TV."

***

After the filming of *Deep Throat Part II* was completed, just as Linda and Chuck were organizing their departure from New York, Sammy Davis, Jr., breezed into town and invited her to a black tie party in his hotel suite. "It's strictly A-list baby, and that's where I put you."

"Oh, Sammy, I've missed you so," she said.

"I've missed you, too, baby, and I can't wait to hook up with you later. In fact, I want you to come over at eight o'clock, an hour before the party begins, and we'll have time to make some music together."

"I'll be right over," she said. "In a new white gown I've acquired. Virginal white."

"I always go for white girls in white dresses," he said. "Incidentally, Altovise will be at the party too. She sends her love. And somebody else does too. One of your greatest admirers."

"Who might that be?" she asked. "Richard Nixon?"

"No, Deano Martin," he said. "He saw *Deep Throat* and dug your acting. In fact, he asked me, 'Do you think I can get Linda to do that to me?'"

"Tell him I will, indeed," she promised. "I'll go down on him like gangbusters."

"Fine. I'll tell him," he answered. "Gotta run. See you at eight."

Linda decided not to tell Chuck about the party, as she wanted to arrive alone as a free agent. Fortunately, he was in Greenwich Village, trying to promote some deal.

Sammy had told her that Richard Burton and Elizabeth Taylor—"cuddly close friends of mine"—would be at the party, along with Liza Minnelli, Lena Horne, Danny Kaye, and Laurence Harvey. "I invited Frank, but he's out of town."

"When you see him again, tell him I'm still waiting for him to return my phone calls."

"Oh, Frankie, he's such a busy guy. You know with all the holes in the world to fill with that cock of his, he can't get around to all of them."

"I know," she said, with just a touch of bitterness.

***

Exactly at eight o'clock, an hour before the scheduled arrival of the other guests, when Linda was ushered into Sammy's suite, he had just emerged from the shower. He came into the living room wearing a terrycloth robe that was wide open, exposing himself at half mast.

"As you can see," he said, looking down at his penis, "Killer has missed you." Then he signaled to her what he wanted.

Even though she'd outfitted herself in her new evening gown, she glided to her knees to deliver him one of her most spectacular blow-jobs—"if I had to say so myself."

After he'd climaxed, he said. "God, I've missed that." Then he picked up the receiver of the ringing phone. "Oh, thanks," he said, before putting down the phone. He turned to her. "Freshen up real quick. Altovise is back from shopping. I want you sitting on the sofa looking regal. I'll be in the bedroom getting dressed."

When Altovise came into the suite's living room from the hallway outside, she'd just returned from purchasing a new gown to show off at the party. She was polite but not overly enthusiastic about seeing Linda again. After ascertaining that Linda had already been given something to drink (a Coca-Cola), she, too retired to the bedroom to dress for the party. By then, the bartender and a pair of waiters had arrived. The bartender asked for her autograph. The waiters each appeared to be gay and had little interest in her skills. One of them asked her, "When are you going to make a film with Johnny Wadd? I saw him in *Blonde in Black Lace* (1972). He's going to become the biggest star in Hollywood."

The waiter was referring to the "Big Dong" of porn, John C. Holmes. "Johnny and I will be getting deep down and dirty soon," Linda assured him.

After nine o'clock, the guests seemed to fill up the room so quickly she became lost in star gazing. As host, Sammy was clearly the star of the evening. Pontificating a bit, he made it clear to everyone that Linda Lovelace was his special guest. He also sounded off about her cultural significance.

"*Deep Throat* is shooting down taboos that have existed in this country forever," he told some of the assembled guests. "Suddenly, it's become acceptable to take your wife or girlfriend to an X-rated film. Someone had to be the first across the line, and Linda led the parade."

"High-class and artistic sex films are on the way," Sammy predicted. "*Deep Throat* is paving the way for upcoming A-list films such as *Last Tango in Paris.*"

"Of course, all actors can't perform in them," he continued. "Many guys I know will turn down parts in sex films because they're ill equipped. I won't name them." Then he flashed his famously infectious smile. "Of course, as some of you ladies know, that is not my problem."

"There are women with wrinkled breasts who won't be burning any bras on camera. One 'superstud' I known, one of the reigning kings of the box office today, would be laughed off the screen if he ever showed his pee-pee to audiences."

With no hot Hollywood properties offered them, **Elizabeth Taylor** and her aging flame of yesteryear, **Richard Burton**, took to the Broadway stage in a revival of *Private Lives* (1983).

After the curtain went down, Dame Elizabeth was sleeping with a 55-year-old Mexican lawyer, the paunchy, balding, and rather ugly Victor Gonzalez Luna. He gave her a $250,000 diamond and ruby engagement ring and wanted to marry her.

He planned to run for President of Mexico. "You'll show Nancy Reagan that you, too, can be a First Lady."

As Sammy later recalled in his memoir, *Hollywood in a Suitcase,* "In the early seventies, you couldn't get through ten seconds of a conversation at any Hollywood gathering without referring to the latest X-rated film. Guys would stand in corners at parties all night talking about the significance of every shot in *Deep Throat.* It was fashionable to know the actresses like Linda Lovelace and invite them to the house."

When the guests of honor, Elizabeth Taylor and Richard Burton, arrived, all attention shifted from Linda.

After thirty minutes, Sammy motioned for her to come over to meet the famous couple, not knowing that Linda had previously been introduced to Elizabeth at the Playboy Mansion West.

"Help!" Sammy said to Linda. "Elizabeth Taylor is trying to talk my diamonds right off my fingers." Then he provocatively introduced her to Burton. "He's the most brilliant actor on the planet, but he's making all those toilet movies these days."

At that point, Elizabeth smelled Southern fried chicken, and she grabbed Linda's hand. "Let's have some of that."

Sammy winked at Burton: "Elizabeth knows

the absolute truth. Only niggers know how to make Southern fried chicken."

As Elizabeth began chowing down on some chicken legs, she turned to Linda. "Vic raved about your performance." She was referring to Victor Mature.

"I'm glad to hear that," Linda responded. "I really enjoyed that man."

"Another of my former trinkets, Fernando Lamas, also wants to meet you," she said.

"I'd be thrilled."

"Fernando and I made *The Girl Who Had Everything* (1953) together," Elizabeth said. "He once had a fling with Evita Perón and then moved on to seduce half the stars in Hollywood. As for *The Girl Who Had Everything,* how wrong that title was for me. I was broke and deep in debt at the time, mortgage and all." After the chicken feast, Elizabeth excused herself to go to the bathroom for emergency repairs and to remove the chicken grease.

Burton took the opportunity to step up beside Linda. "I'm often praised for the on-stage words that flow from my so-called golden throat. As I've seen, you've also got a golden throat. Elizabeth and I are going back to the Coast soon. If you'll slip me your number, we could get together and compare throats."

"Or something," she said. Writing down her number, she handed it to him. "Meeting up with you will be my biggest thrill."

"Not the biggest, my dear," he said, "but the best."

Taking her by the arm, Sammy maneuvered Linda through the crowded party, passing Liza Minnelli on the way. Linda would later meet with her in Las Vegas. He introduced Linda to a very buxom fading blonde beauty on the sofa, who was sitting with a startlingly handsome mulatto. The way they were cuddling and holding hands, Linda assumed they were lovers.

Liz Renay seemed to be some sort of celebrity. The young man was identified as "Pupu," or, more formally, "Pupu Junior."

Renay invited Linda to sit beside her on the sofa after Sammy disappeared into the crowd. Before he left, he said, "Larry wants me to retreat into the bathroom for a quickie. He's such a cocksucker."

Linda figured that he was referring to actor Laurence Harvey.

"Oh, that Larry," Renay said. "He's known in Hollywood as 'Florence of Lithuania.'"

"Darling, we really must talk," Renay said to Linda. "Sammy told

Liz Renay in 1977 in John Waters' *Desperate Living* (1977)

399

me you're flying back to Los Angeles. So are Pupu and myself. I've got a deal to pitch to you. It's from my dear pal, Mickey Cohen. Surely you've heard of him."

"Who hasn't?" she answered. "*Variety* calls him the celebrity gangster."

"He's certainly a celebrity," Renay said, "but Mickey wouldn't like that gangster bit."

"I'll explain everything in Los Angeles," Renay said. "When you get back there, he wants to send a limousine to drive you to a villa he uses in Palm Springs. I'll go with you. So will Pupu, whom you can get to know more intimately. There's two thousand dollars in it for you, maybe more if Mickey decides to give you a diamond ring."

"Now you're talking my kind of money," Linda said.

Pupu reached for her hand. "I look forward to revealing my secret talents."

"I certainly am game for hearing more about this deal," Linda said. "After all, I'm a working girl. In the meantime, I'm going to get Sammy to tell me just who you two lovely people are."

"If he doesn't, we'll tell you ourselves," Renay said.

At that point, Davis returned to retrieve Linda. "Watch those two," he said jokingly, "or you're liable to lose your virginity. Dean Martin has arrived. He wants to meet you. Come along."

***

"The very handsome **Laurence Harvey** seduced Elizabeth Taylor in *Butterfield 8* (1960), but he didn't even give me a handshake, much less a tumble," Linda said.

"He once propositioned John Wayne and Princess Margaret's Lord Snowdon. He was a bit drunk when he told me that he was a better cocksucker than I was."

Years after that party, Jay Garon's researchers wanted to know a lot more about Linda's sexual liaison with Dean Martin. Garon was well aware of Martin's reputation as a Hollywood Lothario who had previously bedded June Allyson, Pier Angeli, Judith Campbell Exner (when she wasn't involved with JFK , Sam Giancana, or Johnny Roselli), Catherine Deneuve, Dorothy Malone, Ann Sheridan, and two of America's most famous blonde bombshells—Lana Turner and Marilyn Monroe.

Dean's former comedy partner, Jerry Lewis, had proclaimed, "The most beautiful broads went crazy for Dean. In truth, I fucked more than he did; but it was always like they wanted to burp me."

"Frankly, it was no big deal with Martin," Linda later confessed. "That's not a reference to his Italian salami, which was way, way more than average. He didn't bother with a lot of preliminaries. When the party broke up, he lured me into the spare bedroom next to where Sammy slept with Altovise."

"He pulled off his clothing and got into bed with me, where I worked him over. I hit all the right spots and got him off one and a half times. The second blast wasn't so powerful. Guess what he did? He turned over and went to sleep."

"The next morning, I tried to talk to him. He wasn't really nasty, but looked bored and wanted to get on with his day. He told me, 'If you wanna talk, see a priest.' Then I got a pat on the ass and a goodbye."

"He just wanted the famous Linda Lovelace blow-job, so he could be one of the Kings of Cool in Hollywood—and that was it. Actually, he did leave something behind. In the bathroom I found a container of Percodan, and drugs like that always come in handy for a gal like me."

***

Back on the West Coast, an assortment of engagements and gigs had piled up for Linda's attention, but two of them were especially pressing. "My god, if this keeps up, I'll need an appointments secretary."

Her first obligation involved Sammy Davis, Jr., and as such, she agreed to meet him before any of the others. Her most dazzling invitation was from the public relations department at Columbia Pictures, who wanted to enroll her as the guest of honor at the upcoming premiere of *Last Tango in Paris* (1972).

[Last Tango in Paris was an avant-garde Italian film directed by Bernardo Bertolucci and released in 1972. Its gritty portrayal of emotional turmoil and sexual violence evoked various forms of censorship and worldwide controversies. Starring Marlon Brando, Maria Schneider, and Jean-Pierre Léaud, it depicts a grieving American widower's anonymous sexual affair with a young Parisian woman who's about to be married, and who kills him when he declares his love for her and breaks the anonymity which had previously been rigidly enforced as the backdrop for their fling.]

Nude, **Dean Martin** relaxes on a circular moving bed in *The Silencers* (1966), part of the Matt Helm series.
"

"Judith Campbell told me he gave her some of the best sex she'd ever had," Linda claimed. "All I got was a slam bang, thank you, ma'am."

***

Dressed entirely in black, Sammy appeared tense and agitated the evening of their West Coast reunion. As part of the logistics of this particular night, he had instructed that Chuck remain at home. "We're embarked on an adventure," he said. "You'll get paid for your services. I jacked the fee you'll be given up to two-thousand dollars. I know you're a working gal, and you've got bills and rent to pay."

"I'm game," she said, although she was mildly disturbed.

In the back of a limousine, he told her, "Evil fascinates me. I feel it lying in wait for me. And I wanted to experience it personally and head-on. I'm ready to accept the wildness, the rolling in the gutter, the having to get up the next morning and wash myself clean."

"What in hell are we heading into?" she asked.

"He held up his pinkie, which he'd re-painted a shade of scarlet. "You once asked me about this. It's a secret code by which one Satanist recognizes another. Tonight you're in for a thrill: I'm taking you to our Los Angeles branch of the Church of Satan."

***

Sammy shared some of his sexual fantasies with Linda, admitting that his church "is not for the faint of heart."

She was puzzled. Why was his church not for the faint of heart? What did the priest there do? Stage human sacrifices, like the Aztecs did in pre-Columbian Mexico?

"Sammy frightened me at times, although he never hurt me," she later said. "But deep down, I thought he was a super-freak."

[Years later, there was evidence that Sammy didn't take Satanism all that seriously, viewing it as an amusing diversion. He was quoted as saying: "My fellow Satanists weren't really Satanists, but bullshit artists, and they'd found an exotic way they could ball each other and have an orgy. And get stoned. It was all fun and games, filled with dungeons, 'dragons,' and debauchery, but not really dangerous. As long as the chick was happy and wasn't really going to get anything sharper than a dildo inside her, I wasn't going to walk away from it."]

Jake Austen, in his article "Sammy Devil, Jr.," wrote: "Sammy started his personal relationship with Satan during a 1968 visit to The Factory, a Los Angeles nightclub he partially owned with Peter Lawford, among others."

One night, according to Austen, Sammy was invited to a private party at The Factory, where he encountered a group of men and women, each with their pinkie painted in red nail polish, signifying their allegiance to the Church of Satan.

Since then, Davis had been a regular member of their "coven." The other

Satanists knew the details of his relationship with Linda, and requested that he bring her by for participation in a ceremony.

Once within their midst, Linda was introduced to the notorious Anton Szander LaVey (1930-1997) a Chicago-born writer, occultist, musician, the founder of the American branch of a Satanic cult, and author of *The Satanic Bible.* Like Yul Brynner, he shaved his head every day. Although in the years before his death, he became grotesque, in the early 1970s he looked, in the opinion of Linda at the time, quite handsome and sexy.

Sometimes defined as "The Black Pope," he had been born to a Russian father and a Ukrainian mother. For that night's special event, LaVey had flown down to Los Angeles from San Francisco.

He privately told Linda that Sammy wasn't the only major movie star associated with his church. "We've found a number of secret members who practice our rites." Among his claims was that while playing the organ in a Los Angeles burlesque house, he had sustained a brief sexual affair with a then-unknown Marilyn Monroe during the late 1940s. "I was only seventeen at the time."

Before the debut of services scheduled to begin at midnight, LaVey showed Linda a feature length documentary entitled *Satanis: The Devil's Mass (*1970), whose footage included overviews of the rituals and references associated with LaVey's congregation.

When he spoke, he sounded like a man ritualistically intoning a public sermon. "Sex is sacred. There is nothing wicked about it. We must wash away our pre-Judeo-Christian tradition and revert to ancient religious concepts. At our church, we view sex as part of a healthy life. It is something to be desired, experienced, and acted upon. To hell with this family values

"There is a beast in man that should be exercised, not exorcised."
—Anton Szander LaVey

the **SECRET LIFE** *of a* **SATANIST**

America's leading Satanist, **Anton Szander LaVey**, liked to seduce movie stars of either sex. he claimed to have seduced Marilyn Monroe, although her biographers doubt that. But he definitely had an affair with sexy **Jayne Mansfield** *(see lower picture above).*

Sammy Davis, Jr. and Peter Lawford also participated in the bisexual rituals at LaVey's church, but LaVey suspected that the pair was doing it for the sex, not because of any religious devotion. Linda Lovelace was hired one night as the love goddess of that evening's ritual, the recipient of "The Devil's semen."

shit. We are our own family with our own values. In our church, we often ritualize sex and make it part of our ceremony. We work with gods and symbols from many religions—Greek, Celtic, Egyptian, Aztec, and Hindu. We are not a stagnant religion, but an active, changing, adapting, and growing form of polytheism, ever expanding."

"What does polytheism mean?" Linda asked.

"Worshipping more than one deity," LaVey answered. "We live in more than one world. We can pierce the veil separating the physical from the spiritual world. Welcome to our world. Tonight, we are staging our annual worship of Astarte. In our ceremony, you will function as the incarnation of Astarte."

"Never heard of her," Linda said.

"She was the great goddess who was worshipped as far back as the Upper Paleolithic Era *[also known as the Late Stone Age]* around 25,000 B.C. Astarte's last temples were closed in 500 A.D. We are bringing her back! She was the goddess of fertility and sexuality. Pictorial representations show her naked. Her symbol was Venus. The Greeks would refer to her as Aphrodite."

"Every year, ten of my priests, and also myself, appear before Astarte and

LINDA GOES TO MIDNIGHT MASS
(PRIMORDIAL REPRESENTATIONS OF THE ETERNAL FEMALE)

Pre-Christian cults in regions across the ancient Mediterranean and Mesopotamia celebrated the Procreative Power of the Eternal Female with names that included Astarte, Isis, Ishtar, Hathor, Aphrodite, and Venus.

Some scholars argue that these fertility cults survived late into the Christian Era through the thinly veiled attribution of mystical powers to Mary, the Mother of Christ, and Mary Magdalene.

Inevitably, Linda Lovelace, one of the most visible symbols of female sexuality alive at the time, got involved in a modern-day covens celebrating, in one way or another, these pre-Christian (pagan) symbols.

plant their seed in her. Because of your special skills in fellatio, we have decided that instead of regular intercourse, our young priests will plant their seeds into your throat. All of them, including myself, are extremely well-endowed, but Sammy assures us that you can handle even the largest of men."

"You are to appear before our priests in their private chamber wearing only a horned headdress."

"I'll be your Astarte," she said.

In one of the dressing rooms, a young priestess gave her a robe crafted from flimsy white material and placed a horned headdress on her. Then she was passed an inscribed gold chalice from which she was told to drink the red wine it contained.

She'd later tell her researchers, "The bitch must have put something in that wine. I didn't feel faint, but lost in space, as if I didn't have a care in the world. Then I was led into this room where ten nude men stood in a circle. Each of them could have posed for a statue of Adonis. In fact, as a coven of men, they were the most beautiful I'd ever seen. LaVey stood in back of them."

"Then that so-called High Priestess removed my robe. Attired in just my horns, I was directed into the center of the circle, where she motioned for me to kneel on this red satin cushion. Red seemed to be the favorite color of this church. The first priest, a real cute guy, stepped forward and presented his dick to me. It was erect. Call him John Holmes, Jr. One by one, the priests came before me, depositing their offering deep in my throat. I feared I'd gained weight after all that protein was pumped into me."

"Actually, I sort of enjoyed them," she recalled. "They were gorgeous compared to the old cranky priests I met when I was a Catholic schoolgirl. The tenth priest told me to hold his semen in my mouth and not swallow it because it would be needed for the final ritual with the love goddess."

"Then I was placed on a slab of white marble covered with a red satin cushion," she said. "A nude LaVey appeared before me and eased himself down on me. He was already fully erect. As

"Mary was the Mother of Jesus Christ, and I was about to become of the mother of the Devil's child," Linda proclaimed when she became pregnant after a fertility rite by Anton Szander LaVey, the high priest of America's Church of Satan. I'd seen *Rosemary's Baby,* and I knew what to expect."

She was referring to **Mia Farrow**'s performance in the 1968 Roman Polanski film in which Farrow *(above)* is the unsuspecting young wife whose husband becomes involved with the Satanists and an agent of their plans.

405

he entered me, he tasted the semen in my mouth. This priest obviously had had a lot of practice. He delivered one of the great fucks of my life. In my confusion and with my light head, I feared that, despite my birth control regimen *[Linda maintained a regular cycle of birth control pills]*, I'd give birth to the Son of Satan!"

"Suddenly, all the men were gone," she said. "The priestess came for me and took me back to the dressing room. I asked for Sammy, but he'd already gone home. A black hearse was waiting to deliver me back to Chuck. In my purse on the way home, I counted twenty one-hundred dollar bills. I decided to give Chuck a thousand dollars, secretly keeping the other thousand as mad money."

"Later, when I became pregnant with LaVey's kid, I used part of that money for an abortion," she claimed. "There was no way I was going to give birth to *Rosemary's Baby.* My kid would probably have been born with a red tail."

***

The following day, Linda said, "Only one night back in California, and I'm already into all this weird shit. Church of Satan. What a joke! It's just an excuse for those guys to get their rocks off."

Although she wouldn't admit it, Linda Lovelace was jealous of the sultry beauty, **Raquel Welch.** At the premiere of *Last Tango in Paris,* Linda appeared in a see-through gown so shocking that she distracted the paparazzi away from the more beautiful Raquel.

As part of her first A-list appearance before *le tout* Hollywood, she bought herself a chic boutique dress made of crocheted red wool. "Parts of it were see-through," she said. "I had no secrets that night. Thinking it was too racy—one of those 'Hello Officer!' outfits—I put on a gold lamé G-string to cover my pussy." This was the outfit she opted to wear to the premiere of *Last Tango in Paris.*

"For my grand appearance, Columbia sent a gunmetal gray Rolls-Royce to pick me up," she said. "I was sorta turned on by the chauffeur and volunteered to give him a blow-job while he drove me to the theater."

According to Linda, in response to her offer, the uniformed driver said: "I've let Rock Hudson, Clifton Webb, George Nader, Monty Clift, and Roddy McDowall blow me, but never a woman. I don't think I can even get it up for a woman. I call their vaginas the wound that never heals."

"Okay," she said peevishly, somewhat insulted. "Forgive me for living."

Her arrival at the premiere created a sensation. Microphones were shoved in her face, and the "paparazzi went wild," she claimed. "They could photograph your regular old movie star any day, but here was a chance to get at Linda Lovelace. I noticed that Raquel Welch was pushed aside in favor of me. Besides, Raquel is looking more like a great-grandmother every day. I'm the hot new girl in town. All the male stars want me to suck their cocks."

With press agents from Columbia Pictures positioned on either side of her, she sat through the screening of *Last Tango in Paris*. Shortly after her arrival, prior to the screening of the film itself, she'd been asked if the release of *Deep Throat* had paved the way for a sexy A-list movie like *Tango*. At the time, not having seen the movie, she didn't have a ready answer.

To the public and in front of the microphone, she kept her mostly negative reaction to the film to herself. But to Gary Sheehan, who was there that night and who worked for Columbia, she was frank:

"The movie's too long, at least by an hour. Brando is a good actor—in fact, after his work in *A Streetcar Named Desire,* he's one of my favorites. But

Linda's secret wish was to have starred in the role that **Maria Schneider** played opposite **Marlon Brando** in his controversial film, *Last Tango in Paris (1972)*.

Before attending the premier of the film, she'd read in *Variety* that in the wake of the sexual revolution that had swept over the U.S. in the late 1960s, *Last Tango* had ushered in porno chic .

"Brando and this Schneider kid didn't usher in porno chic," Linda said. "I, Linda Lovelace, did. The biggest question of the day was did Brando and Schneider actually 'do it' on camera."

"If those same people asking that had seen *Deep Throat,* they wouldn't be asking if Harry Reems and I actually did it."

throughout the movie, he was constantly acting, and we, the public, were aware of his *acting* the character instead of *being* the character."

"So, all of a sudden, Linda Lovelace is a method actor and movie critic?" Sheehan asked.

"And the sex scenes were pathetic," Linda continued. "They lacked one important ingredient…and that is sex itself. Frankly, with all its advance publicity, I was disappointed."

"I hope that during interviews, you'll not share that opinion," Sheehan said.

"I'll keep my mouth shut," she responded. Then, realizing that that could be misinterpreted, she added, "Unless some hot guy wants a blow-job. For me, the ideal movie would have been a *Deep Throat* with higher-quality filmmaking. Or a *Last Tango* with a lot more sex. It's like the two pictures—the two mediums, I mean, porn and A-list films—need to merge. Just ask John Derek. Instead of *Deep Throat* or *Last Tango in Paris*, we need a picture that could be called *Deep Tango.*"

At that moment, the other representative from Columbia, Jack Boone, descended from an upstairs office.

"Miss Lovelace?" he said. "Our most important VIP is waiting in the manager's office. He's seen *Deep Throat* and would very much like to meet you. In fact, he's convinced that you should have played the female lead in *Last Tango* instead of Maria Schneider."

"He sounds like my kind of man," she answered. "Lead the way!"

After about five minutes of climbing stairs, maneuvering through long hallways, and opening door, she was ushered into the foyer of the theater manager's office. Standing before her with an extended palm was the star of the picture, Marlon Brando.

"Introductions aren't needed," he said. "We've seen each other's movies, and we know who we are."

She smiled at him. Instead of taking his hand, she kissed his cheek and said. "You might know who you are, but I'm just finding out who Linda Lovelace is. Perhaps you'll help me."

"My noble tool has always been ready, willing, and forever able to help a Damsel in Distress," he said.

CHAPTER ELEVEN
More Stars Than There Are in Heaven

Within a fews hours of meeting Marlon Brando, Linda was chatting with him in his living room. He was very articulate and wanted to talk about what was happening in the film world, especially after the nearly simultaneous releases of *Last Tango in Paris* and *Deep Throat.*

"I was all ears," Linda later said.

"You noticed I left at the end of the film and didn't give interviews," he said. "I don't trust reporters. They're all panty-sniffers, they'll distort your words, embarrass the hell out of you, and end up destroying you if you'll let them. I have every right in the world to resist turning the insipid protocol of my life into a running serial you find on bubble gum wrappers. You can't take sensitive parts of yourself and splatter them around like so much popcorn butter."

"I'm not good with interviews, especially when a reporter mentions a movie called *The Dog Fucker,*" she said.

"I heard about that," he said, "but I haven't seen it. Nor do I plan to. But you shouldn't be ashamed of it. Reporters, as if they would know, claim I lost my virginity when I was nineteen to Estrelita Rosa Maria Consuelo Cruz, a married woman from Colombia. They're full of shit. I've had my own experience with bestiality, not with a dog, but with a friendly goat on the plains of Nebraska where I grew up. That's how I lost my virginity. From that day on, I preferred goat's milk to that from a cow. Actually, to confess, I really prefer milk from a mother's breast who has just birthed an infant."

It was inevitable that the talk would soon turn to *Last Tango in Paris,* which most of Hollywood was discussing that night. "I don't mean to insult your intelligence, because I know you're a smart girl, but did you understand what *Tango* was about?"

"Frankly, I didn't," she confessed.

"I don't know what it's about, either," he said. "Bernardo Bertolucci, its director, claims he knows. He's going around Hollywood telling people that *Tango* is about the reincarnation of my prick."

"Whatever that means," she said. "Some of the lines were really great, even if I didn't understand them. Like when you told Maria Schneider, 'Let's just say we're taking a flying fuck on a rolling doughnut.'"

"I even allowed the bitch to mock my not altogether fallen body," he said. "Remember when she told me during a segment of the film, 'In twenty years, you'll be playing football with your tits.'"

"One episode never got into the movie. I was supposed to play a scene in the Paris apartment where my character of Paul meets Jeanne, and I was to be photographed in a frontal nude. It was such a cold day that my penis shrank to the size of a peanut. It simply withered. Because of the cold, my body went into full retreat, and the tension, embarrassment, and stress made it recede all the more. I realized I couldn't play the scene this way, so I paced back and forth around the apartment, stark naked, hoping for magic."

"I've always maintained a strong belief in the power of mind over matter, so I concentrated on my private parts, trying to will my penis and testicles to grow. But my mind failed me. I was humiliated, but not ready to surrender yet. I asked Bernardo to be patient. I told the crew I wasn't giving up. But after an hour, I could tell from their faces that they had given up on me."

"Bernardo wanted to film Maria and me actually having sex, but I refused. I told him that I didn't want our sex organs to become characters in the film. There was, however, one scene of buggering. I used butter as lube. But we were faking the actual sex, simulating orgasms....stuff like that. Perhaps you've heard of Norman Mailer."

"His circumcised dick has, indeed, invaded my throat," she said.

"Good to hear that," he said. "After Mailer saw *Deep Throat,* he said to the press, 'Brando's cock up Schneider's real vagina would have brought the history of cinema one huge march closer to the ultimate experience it has promised since its inception—that is, to embody life.'"

Brando continued, "Bernardo briefly considered configuring *Last Tango* as a homosexual drama, with me playing a middle aged man who gets sexually involved with a handsome younger man. At the time, I wanted to go for the gay scenario. I'd met and slept with this young actor—a real beauty—in New York. Christopher Reeve.

He's twenty or so now, but he still looks thirteen. He has a beautiful, very trim swimmer's build, not too well developed, a perfect Tadzio."

[Brando was an early devotee of Christopher Reeve, who, in 1978, with a vastly beefed-up body, would appear in a star-making turn in Superman. *In 1982, he would play a sinister gay lover in the film adaptation of* Deathtrap.]

"The worst fallout I had from appearing in *Last Tango* came in court from my former wife, Anna Kashfi," he said. "She was fighting me for custody of my son, Christian. She told the judge that in *Tango* I played 'a sexually maladjusted and perverted person who utters obscene, foul, shocking, and distasteful profanities.' She even tried to introduce a snapshot of me, back in 1952, performing fellatio on my former roommate, Wally Cox."

"So, you're no stranger to fellatio yourself?" she asked.

"You got that right," he said, "and I admit it freely. I am not ashamed. Of course, I'm not the expert you are. Kenneth Anger, who wrote that silly book, *Hollywood Babylon,* tried to get his publisher to run that picture of Wally and me, but was turned down. But I predict that someone, probably after I'm dead, will run it in a more liberated era."

[Marlon Brando spoke prophetically. Danforth Prince, in Blood Moon's 2005 Brando Unzipped, *was the first publisher to ever run the forbidden photograph, a closeup view of Brando, in profile, "going down" on an erect penis. As a former female bedmate of Cox told Prince, "That's Wally in that photograph all right."]*

When Linda went to bed with Brando, she was joining a long line of conquests who included James Dean, Marilyn Monroe, Tallulah Bankhead, tobacco heiress Doris Duke, composer Leonard Bernstein, and the novelist, James Baldwin.

"Every trick I ever turned in Hollywood or New York was different," Linda recalled, "But even with that as a premise, there was always some variation with Marlon, some of them unique. He wanted me to give him a blow-job, but only after he'd buttered his dick. Perhaps that was a direct result of his using butter on Maria Schneider's asshole before sodomizing her in *Last Tango."*

At the time, Marlon's ex-wife, Anna Kashfi was going around Hollywood claiming that,

Christopher Reeve

(*shown in Deathtrap, above*) was Brando's early lover and his star choice when *Last Tango* was at first envisioned as the story of a middle aged man involved with a younger man instead of with a young woman.

"Physically, Marlon is not well appointed. He screens that deficiency by undue devotion to his sex organ."

"Actually, it wasn't as inadequate as she claimed," Linda said. "It was about average sized—five and a half inches, not six inches as some claim—and that was okay. What Kashfi failed to mention was that he was rock hard, so hard I felt I was going down on a bar of steel. After all the limp penises we gals have to face, we should at least give Marlon credit for that."

Marlon himself had frequently claimed, "I've never been circumcised—in fact, I'm opposed to this barbaric practice—and my Noble Tool has performed its duties valiantly through thick and thin and without fail."

"I can testify that Marlon was telling the truth," Linda said. "In fact, over a period of a month, we had five dates until that final night—the one that ended in disaster."

***

Brando often liked to visit the raunchy Malibu Cottage, bashed-up, much-abused watering hole overlooking the Pacific, where Marilyn Monroe once took John F. Kennedy before he became President. It contained only a dozen bar stools and a few scattered tables placed on its sawdust-littered floors. After midnight, it was known for wild scenes where Steve McQueen was a regular visitor.

A former patron during the 1960s, Jayne Mansfield, once claimed, "You could take your pickups there—you know, blue collar types with dirt under their fingernails and a big sausage in their jockeys—and no one asked questions, no one judged."

As part of Brando's fifth date with Linda, which turned out to be his last, he took her on a late night visit to Malibu Cottage. Unknown to him, Lee Marvin had bribed the bartender fifty dollars to phone him if Brando came in.

Ana Kashfi, during her divorce proceedings from **Marlon Brando,** filed a motion in court to introduce "the forbidden photograph" (*above*) of the actor performing fellatio on Wally Cox when they were roommates.

[Their animosity on the set of The Wild One *(1954) had almost led to fistfights. What had most recently goaded Marvin into attacking Brando was a remark repeated at a Hollywood party at the home of Jean Peters, an actress*

412

best known today for having married the demented billionaire, Howard Hughes.

Actually, Brando was repeating a criticism he'd heard from director Joshua Logan, who had helmed Marvin in Paint Your Wagon *(1969). "Not since Attila the Hun swept across Europe, leaving five-hundred years of total blackness, has there been a man like Lee Marvin."*

Hollywood partygoers, known as they are for gossiping, wasted no time reporting the put-down to Marvin. "I'm going to beat the shit out of Brando," Marvin vowed. "And now I know where to find him."]

Before her chance encounter with Marvin, Linda had seen only three of his movies, including *Cat Ballou* (1965), for which he won an Oscar for his interpretation of a drunken gunman and his psychotic twin, a desperado with an artificial nose. She'd also seen him in *The Wild One,* in which he'd co-starred, albeit a lot less famously, with Brando.

A tough former Marine, Marvin was lean and mean, with a cool, mocking air about him that suggested menace. He spoke in a gravelly voice that evoked, at least for Linda, Aldo Ray. He was contemptuous of some of his previous film roles, asserting, "I've played everything from a beanery cook to an ass-kissing colonel named 'Slob.'"

As critic David Thomson wrote: "Marvin's career is central to the role of violence in American cinema. As a personality, Marvin eventually dropped insensate cruelty for stoical self-defense. At his best, he was without sentimentality, mannerism, or exaggerations, frightening in his very clarity."

Marvin stood six feet, two inches and seemed like one frightening *hombre* when he barged, drunk, into the Malibu Cottage, looking forward to a fistfight with Brando. "Marvin's on the rampage tonight," Brando told Linda when he spotted Marvin entering the bar. "Here's a hundred," he said. "Take a taxi home. I'm slipping out the back entrance. I'm a lover—not a fighter."

When Marvin was told that Brando was at a table at the darkest rear of the bar, he staggered toward Linda. "Hi," she said. "I'm Linda Lovelace, and you look like my kind of man."

"Where's that fucker Brando?"

"When he saw you come in, he ran out the back door," she said. "When faced with a real man, he becomes a yellow belly. He probably jumped into the Pacific and swam halfway to China by now."

"The guy's such a pansy," Marvin

"Lee Marvin (*photo above*) had gun and could travel, but the 'gun' I'm talking about was in his pants," according to Linda Lovelace said. "I should have done him in years ago."

"Sit down," she said. "Who needs that cocksucker Brando when Lee Marvin's in town? Not that I have anything against cocksucking."

"Year, I hear you're the world's greatest. What were you doing tonight? Giving him some pointers?"

"Something like that," she said. "I was slumming."

"I was going to mop up the floor with that fucker, but I'd rather be with you. I bet, in addition to that magic throat of yours, you've got the prettiest little clit in the room."

Accepting the fact that Brando had eluded him, he ordered a round of drinks for them. She tried to make small talk to distract him from his killing mission.

"When I was a gal in school, I thought anyone named Lee was Chinese and ran the laundry on the corner," she said.

"Look at me," he said. "Do I fucking look Chinese? I was named in honor of General Robert E. Lee of the Confederacy. He was my first cousin, four times removed."

"Forgive me for asking, but are you as tough as you look on screen?"

"I've got my sensitive side," he answered. "When I was a teenager, I wanted to be a violin player. I was a bad boy, though. Got kicked out of three different schools before I joined the Marines. I won the Purple Heart. I'll show you my wound."

He stood up, unbuckled his pants, and pulled them down along with his white jockey shorts. "See that wound on my ass cheek? It was from machine gun fire. It severed my sciatic nerve. I almost got my ass blown off!"

At that point, two rather effeminate men paraded by. "Mr. Marvin, thanks for taking down your jockey shorts. So now we know, the rumor about you is true."

"Get along, little doggies," he said,

When they were gone, she said, "I think half the bar tonight is filled with gay men."

"Don't put them down," he answered. "I don't know if you read the January, 1969 issue of *Playboy,* I think I was the first major actor in Hollywood to stand up for gay rights. That takes *cojones.* If you back the gays, everyone says you're gay, too. Cowards like Sinatra, shits like that, wouldn't take a public stand supporting gays even after the Stonewall Riots in New York. When I get my cock hard, I know anyone in his right mind would like to suck on it. How about you, Linda?"

"Ever since you sat down, I've been wanting to devour every inch of your body," she said. "You saw what I did to Harry Reems in *Deep Throat.* For us, that will be just the opening act. I will transport you to Nirvana, wherever that is. I owe you one. You've rescued me from that jerk Brando, who was boring me to death with his pontificating."

Marvin looked at her lasciviously, his face not fully concealing his desire. "Okay, chick, it's a deal. I can kill Brando some other night."

On their way out the door of the Malibu Cottage, he told her, "When I was young, I never got my share of the action. I'm gonna make up for that oversight tonight. Babe, you're going to get fucked every which way known to man."

"A promise I'll hold you to," she said, getting behind the wheel of his car and taking the keys from him.

***

In the bathroom of Marvin's home, as she freshened herself, she noticed a movie poster advertising *The Professionals* (1966), a taut Western drama where four soldiers of fortune were employed to go after a Mexican varmint. She already knew, intimately, two of that film's actors—Burt Lancaster and Robert Ryan—and, as she related later, she had a flash of irony about how she was about to get more intimately involved with a third, Marvin himself.

Back in his living room, she discovered Marvin pouring himself another drink. He offered her one, but she refused. She mentioned that she knew Lancaster and Ryan, and she spoke of the cancer eating away at Ryan's body.

He suggested that they should set up an appointment and call on him, and she agreed. "Unlike Brando, Burt and Bob were easy to work with."

This new reference to Brando touched yet another nerve in Marvin, who said, "When we made *The Wild One,* we hated each other on sight. When the creep wasn't on the set, I imitated him, using a girlish lisp and placing my hands on my hips. I paraded around like a fairy."

"When the picture was wrapped, I told a reporter that Brando was the biggest piece of shit on a stick in Hollywood, where the competition is keen."

[Subsequently, when Brando was asked about Marvin by the same reporter, he said, "Marvin's an asshole, both on and off the screen. As an actor, all he can do is toss a cup of scalding coffee into poor Gloria Grahame's face." He was referring to the 1953 The Big Heat, *which contained just such a scene, which has now entered the pantheon of all-time screen portrayals of a sadist.]*

One critic wrote, "In *The Wild One,* Marvin was Mercutio playing opposite Brando's Romeo."

The two rivals hated each other both on and off the screen. Producer Stanley Kramer told the press, "The trouble is, Marvin wants to be Marlon—and he's not."

Back in Marvin's living room, the actor went for another drink. "I've learned a bitter lesson," he said. "Never shack up with anyone with lower billing than yourself. I'm going to follow that advice in the future. On *Raintree County,*

I fucked Elizabeth Taylor. Talk about star billing. She came on to me. You were the star of *Deep Throat,* so you're safe. I don't think you're going to sue me like that cunt Michelle Triola."

[Linda had read in the papers that Triola had been Marvin's live-in girlfriend from 1965 to 1970. When he dumped her, she sued him, seeking common property rights according to California law. In court, she claimed that Marvin had impregnated her three times, paying for two of her abortions. While carrying his third infant, she'd had a miscarriage.

The case was still pending at the time of Linda's hookup with Marvin in the early 70s. Ultimately, in 1981, in the California Court of Appeals, the actor would prevail over his former girlfriend.]

To Jay Garon's researchers, Linda did not go into any details about her sexual relations with Marvin. As she said, "I can re-create it in a single line: Did you ever see one of those wildlife documentaries shot in Africa in which a lion, the King of Beasts, attacks a zebra for supper?"

***

Robert Ryan was staying at the house of some unknown friend, and when Marvin and Linda arrived there, a housekeeper led them up the steps to his bedroom. After a knock on the door, Linda and Marvin were admitted inside. There, Ryan was propped up in bed, looking considerably weakened from the treatments he'd recently received for cancer.

His face brightened when he saw his visitors. Linda kissed him gently on both cheeks, and Marvin not only shook his hand, but clasped it together with his other palm, holding it in a warm embrace.

"I'm getting better every day," Ryan told Marvin. "When you see our director, John Frankenheimer, tell him I'm looking terrific."

"Indeed, I will," Marvin said.

"As they talked, Linda was startled to learn that Ryan had recently signed a contract with the American Film Theatre to shoot another movie with Marvin. Filming was soon to begin on Eugene O'Neill's dark journey into a man's psyche, *The Iceman Cometh.*

"Along with Fredric March, each of us has agreed to do the thing for $25,000 each," Marvin said.

"What's the play about?" Linda asked.

"Self-delusion and death," Ryan answered. "It's four hours long. Alcoholic lost souls drift about in a hazy cloud of rot-gut booze, going in and out of stupors, trading apprehensions about their pipedreams and visits from the Iceman."

"I can't wait to see you guys pull that one off," she said, bewildered by

416

what she'd just heard. "My movie was simpler. The girl's got her clitoris in her throat and needs a man to satisfy her."

Both of the men laughed.

As Marvin and Ryan talked, she realized that this unlikely pair shared a long and detailed film history with each other.

"When filming begins, you gotta help me, Bob," Marvin said. "I'm a bit shaky these days. Chalk it up to my personal crises.'

"I'll be at your back," Ryan said. "Just like I was when we made *Bad Day at Black Rock* (1955)."

Marvin turned to Linda. "Our director, John Sturges, said that whereas I suggested badness, Bob here was downright *dangerous.*" He looked at Ryan resting on his pillows, exhibiting a sickly greenish tint. "I believe that you're one of those actors like Edward G. Robinson who will get better and better with each new picture. You'll lick this cancer thing. Your greatest roles are ahead of you."

"I don't know about that," Ryan said. "When you and I did *The Professionals,* I appeared in many scenes, but the fuckers gave me only twenty lines of dialogue. I was a scenic backdrop."

"Who in Hollywood has won them all?" Marvin asked. "Sometimes, it's all about taking home a paycheck."

Ryan smiled. "We mopped up the floor with Charles Bronson and Ernest Borgnine when we did *The Dirty Dozen* (1967), didn't we, Lee?"

"Those were some of our more memorable moments on screen," Marvin said.

"What did you think of it, Linda?" Ryan asked.

"I haven't seen it yet, but before the week is out, I'll somehow manage a screening. It sounds terrific."

Realizing that Marvin and Ryan wanted to talk privately together about their previous films, Linda began to drift off. Sensing that, Ryan suggested she go downstairs and out onto the patio.

"If you've ever sat in a theater and watched Bob Mitchum, wondering what his dick looks like, here's your chance to find out," Ryan said. "He's lying there beside the pool, buck naked."

"Excuse me," she said. "He was always one of my favorites. I used to go to his movies hoping he'd take off his shirt."

"Hop to it, gal!" Marvin said.

Macho and emotionally complex
Robert Ryan

417

***

Robert Mitchum lay nude on a *chaise longue* beside a swimming pool. Linda's eye went immediately to his rather large cock before moving up to his familiar face. Here was the ultimate screen tough guy, once called "a slab of beef," exposing himself in all his glory to her hungry eyes. She was enthralled.

Rugged, barrel-chested and cleft-chinned, he looked at her through hooded eyes, with an insolent gaze.

"You must be Linda Lovelace, and I think you know whose puss this is?" he said. "Perhaps you agree with that jerk who said I look like a shark with a broken nose."

"You're one shark I wouldn't mind devouring me," she said.

"I'll take that as a compliment," he said. "Usually, I don't reveal so much of myself to my fans."

What she knew about him came mostly from movie fan magazines. His bad boy image had been fueled by ample use of liquor and drugs. He had once been sent to jail on a marijuana charge.

During the Depression, Mitchum had ridden the rails as a hobo and had been imprisoned as part of a chain gang in Georgia until he escaped. He'd been a migrant fruit picker, a boxer, a beach bum, and a songwriter. *Confidential* had exposed him as a male hustler catering to the gay trade when he was trying to break into movies.

Before Marlon Brando, before James Dean, and before Clint Eastwood, Mitchum was the hipster antihero who invented screen cool.

"Let's get one thing straight," he said. "All the stories about me are true. The booze, the brawls, the broads—all true. Frankly, I'd like to sleep all day. When I first got to California, I lay on the beach at Venice, drinking beer all day and rolling drunks. But when I got into the movies, I had to at least open my eyes. I'll confess how I did that. I sprinkled hot sauce on tobacco and chewed it."

She wanted to give him head right away, but then decided that it might be better to be discreet. Eager to join his roster of A-list sexual conquests, she wanted to be numbered among Carroll Baker, Shirley MacLaine, Lucille Ball, Gloria Grahame, Rita Hayworth, Jane Greer, Jane Russell, Sarah Miles, and inevitably, Marilyn Monroe.

Mitchum was blunt: "What do you do when you're not sucking cocks?"

"Struggling to find some niche in the entertainment business that doesn't have to do with cocksucking."

"That's a noble quest," he said. "Good luck. But I hope you haven't abandoned cocksucking forever, at least not before I get my turn."

"Are you kidding?" she asked. "I could never give it up until I've had you.

After all, you're my favorite calypso singer, far better than Harry Belafonte."

At that point, Marvin came onto the patio, "Good god, gal, Bob is an actor—not a singer."

"But the gal is right," Mitchum said. "I've made records. In 1957, I recorded an album of calypso vocals for Capitol. It was called 'Robert Mitchum—Calypso Is Like So!'"

"I still think you guys are bullshitting me," Marvin said, before one-upping them with: "Did I tell you that during the 50s I regularly visited the White House to fuck Mamie because Ike was impotent?"

The talk quickly shifted to Ryan and his illness. Mitchum pointedly asked, "Do you think he can hold up long enough to finish a movie, especially one as grueling as that Eugene O'Neill shit?"

"I hope so," Marvin said.

"Ryan and I have been friends ever since we made that *Crossfire* movie back in 1947," Mitchum said. "That commie, Edward Dmytryk, directed what were called 'the three Bobs'—Robert Young, Robert Ryan, and this Robert who's now displayed in all his glory before you."

"It was a great picture," Marvin said. "Gloria Grahame, the gal whose face I disfigured with the hot coffee, was in it too."

"Actually, the picture was supposed to be about violence and prejudice directed at homosexuals," Mitchum said. "But in those days, the Code wouldn't even allow the word 'homosexual' to be spoken on screen, so the script was changed to reflect violence against Jews."

"Dmytryk also directed Ryan and me in *Anzio* (1968)," Mitchum said. "We've been pals for years—That's why I'm so sad that he may soon leave us. Ryan is not a man you love, but one you respect."

"I think it's probably better to be respected than to be loved," Marvin said.

"I told Ryan that he'd go on forever," Mitchum said. "But he's too smart to believe me. He knows he's dying."

"That fucking director, Budd Boetticher," Marvin said, "told the press that 'the three toughest guys in movies are Robert Michum, number one, of course, followed by Robert Ryan and Jack Palance. I guess that shit never heard of a guy called Lee Marvin."

As a girl going to the movies, Linda was thrilled when **Robert Mitchum** took his shirt off. When she met him, she was even more tantalized, as he also had his pants off.

"The whole world's heard of you," Linda chimed in.

"Friends of Ryan, people he hasn't seen in years, are calling and visiting him," Mitchum said. "That's a bad sign. It happened with Bogie. And the Angel of Death is about to show up, so I'd better wrap a towel around myself."

"Who's the Angel of Death?" she asked.

"That's what we in Hollywood call Katharine Hepburn," Mitchum said. "She has a weird habit of making appearances at the dying moments of key Hollywood figures such as Ethel Barrymore and Bogie."

"I never saw that picture you made with her," Marvin said. "*Undercurrent* (1946), wasn't it?"

"Not a lot of people saw it," Mitchum said. "It was my worst *film noir.* On the set, Hepburn told me, in that lilting Bryn Mawr voice of hers, 'You know you can't act. If you hadn't been good looking, you would never have gotten a picture. I'm tired of playing with people who have nothing to offer.'"

[Years later, Mitchum denied that Hepburn had ever said that to him.]

"*[Film director]* Mervyn LeRoy, came up with a different judgment," Mitchum continued. "He told me, 'You're either the lousiest actor in the world or the best. I can't make up my mind.'"

Suddenly, a houseboy came out onto the patio to announce that "Miss Hepburn has arrived, and Mr. Ryan is coming down to have tea."

"I'd better put my pants on," Mitchum said. "The sight of a dick would probably cause Hepburn to faint. I don't think she's ever seen one before."

***

"I was in Trinidad making *Fire Down Below* (1957) with Rita Hayworth, who played a shady lady," said **Robert Mitchum**. "I learned to sing calypso, and later, how to hit all of Rita's hot spots."

Photo above: Album cover of **Robert Mitchum Calypso is Like So**.

With the imperial air of a reincarnated Eleanor of Aquitaine [*a character she had brilliantly impersonated in 1968's* A Lion in Winter], Katharine Hepburn breezed into Ryan's living room. Except for a slash of red lipstick, she was dressed in a pants suit the grayish color of a battleship. Ignoring everybody in the room except Ryan, she rushed to his armchair. "Have no fear," she said. "I have brought remedies. Follow them, and you'll be cured. Spencer once faced a cancer scare, and my remedies saved his life."

[She was referring to Spencer Tracy, with whom she'd long maintained a platonic

420

relationship.]

After some opening pleasantries with Ryan, who had welcomed her, she turned to face Lee Marvin, Robert Mitchum, and Linda, addressing them as if they were an audience. "I discovered this divine creature *[meaning Ryan]* in 1960, when I asked him to appear opposite me at the American Shakespeare Festival in Stratford, Connecticut. Bob is a damn fine actor, better than Olivier who is only about posturing. As for Burton, he's not in love with Elizabeth Taylor, but with the sound of his own voice." Suddenly, she seemed to intently focus on Mitchum. "Oh, it's you," I noticed that you did not heed my advice and give up acting as a career."

"Miss Hepburn, may I present Lee Marvin," Mitchum said, gallantly.

"I have heard of you," she said, "but I don't go to see your kind of movies. I saw you only once on the screen. Actually, I sat through *Ship of Fools* (1969) just to see Vivien. I really should have played Scarlett O'Hara—not her. In *Ship of Fools,* you seemed perfectly cast as that bigoted, has-been ballplayer. Of course, Vivien stole your drunken scene—the one where you made a clumsy pass at her. She literally ate up the screen. As for you carrying off that Oscar in 1965 for *Cat Ballou,* even you must admit that Burton in *The Spy Who Came in from the Cold,* or even that Olivier creature in *Othello* really deserved the prize."

"Fuck them both," Marvin said. "I won—and that's that."

"I see you've been in Hollywood long enough to forget any manners you might have had," Hepburn said, primly.

"Miss Hepburn, this lovely lady here is Linda Lovelace," Mitchum said.

"Lovelace," Hepburn said. "Such a beautiful name. And whose little sweetie might you belong to?"

"Actually, I'm Mr. Marvin's girlfriend today, Mr. Ryan's girlfriend yesterday, and, if my luck holds, Mr. Mitchum's girlfriend for tonight."

"A woman who sleeps around..." Hepburn said. "At least you're honest about it. I admire honesty in any person, especially a woman. Most women lie about everything."

"Linda's an actress, too," Mitchum said. "She's the star of *Deep Throat.* The whole country's talking about it. It's frontpage news."

"My dear, even *I* have heard about this film," Hepburn said. "I don't plan to see it, although that impish little black devil, Sammy Davis, Jr., in-

Robert Mitchum told Linda, "the real reason **Hepburn** (*above*) doesn't like me is because I have a dick—and not a pussy."

vited me to a screening at the Pussycat Theatre, wherever that is."

"Let's face it," Ryan said. "All of us must launch ourselves some way into show business. Linda chose the unusual route of showcasing her oral-genital specialty. If nothing else, we must admire her spunk."

"If that's what it's called, then let's admire it," Hepburn said at the same moment that the houseboy walked in with the tea.

Hepburn proved herself a world class tea drinker. Up to now, Linda was not the type of woman who normally attended formal tea services in the late afternoon. Carefully, she watched what Hepburn did with the tea service, and imitated her.

Although Hepburn devoted most of her attention to Ryan, discussing some of the more radical methods of curing cancer, especially a bizarre diet she was promoting, she did focus on Linda every now and then with undue interest. Under Hepburn's gaze of evaluation, Linda grew distinctly uncomfortable.

When Linda excused herself to go to the bathroom, Hepburn followed her. "Those teacakes make a wreck of my lipstick," she said. "We girls need to freshen up."

In the bathroom, Hepburn was very forthright. "If you could visit me tomorrow afternoon after four, I have a job for you. It pays well." She looked her up and down. "You do like girls, don't you?"

"In equal measure with men," Linda said.

Hepburn reached into her purse and handed her her card. "My address is on this card. Call an hour before coming over. I prefer you to keep our rendezvous an absolute secret."

Half an hour later, Hepburn, Mitchum, and Linda paid their final farewell to Robert Ryan.

The stricken actor seemed mellow and sensitive. "I see trees and flowers and pretty girls," he told them. "I see beauty that I used to be oblivious to. I see things with a much fresher eye. And, actually life is much better enjoying it day to day."

***

For Linda, it was a night to remember. When she sat down to record it in her diary, much of it seemed a blur. After dinner at a little bistro run by Rodgers Brackett, a former TV producer and the onetime lover and mentor of James Dean, in Santa Monica, Linda drove Marvin and Mitchum to the Malibu Cottage. Fortunately, Brando was nowhere to be seen that night.

"I walked along the beach with Mitchum," Linda recalled later. "Even though he'd been jailed for possession of marijuana, he still carried three joints with him. We left Marvin, drunk, at the bar, and Mitchum and I sat on the beach in a blaze of marijuana smoke."

"He rose from the sand, pulled down his pants, and skinned it back for me with an invitation. 'Have a ball,' he told me. And I did."

"It was one juicy thick piece of meat, and I enjoyed servicing him. With him, I wish it could have become a regular thing, but I doubted it would happen. So many of these male stars seemed to want me for only one workout—and that was that. A girl has to be realistic about these things. Fortunately, there were so many fish to fry in Hollywood, I never really got hung up on just one guy."

"Just as soon as I'd finished, Mitchum got up and stood right in front of me and took a horse piss," she said. "He didn't bother to turn around. I suspected he was a real exhibitionist. Later that night, I would have an iron-clad confirmation of my suspicion."

"You give one hell of a blow-job," he said. "Far better than Marilyn, whom I got to enjoy when we made *The River of No Return* together."

Then he invited her to sit on the sands enjoying his final marijuana cigarette before going back to the Malibu Cottage to retrieve a drunken Marvin.

"My buddy, Rory Calhoun, and I bonded with Marilyn. Rory and I both knew what a jail cell looked like from the inside. We shot most of that film around Jasper, Wyoming, and also at Banff Springs, near Lake Louise in Western Canada. The director, Otto Preminger, spread the word that Rory, Marilyn, and I were having a *ménage à trois*. The creep at least got *that* right."

"My most memorable evening was when I fucked Marilyn for the first time in the ass. That all began when Marilyn approached me with a book on sexuality. She asked me to explain to her what the author meant by 'anal eroticism.' Could you believe it? A gal who'd been around the block like Marilyn had never been fucked in the ass before? She later bragged to half of Hollywood that I was an expert at 'back door entry.'"

"I didn't get a total rave from her, though," he said. "She later said I should watch out for that bad breath, and she also claimed I was a lousy kisser. Who in hell did she think I was? Errol Flynn?"

Holding Mitchum's hand, Linda slowly made her way back to the Malibu Cottage, where

Marilyn Monroe and **Robert Mitchum** made *River of No Return (photo above)* on location with Rory Calhoun.

Marilyn's husband at the time, Joe DiMaggio, arrived on the scene and warned the two actors, "If I find either of you has been fucking my wife, I'll cut your dicks off while you're sleeping."

423

loud music blasted into the night, competing with the waves of the Pacific.

What she saw horrified her. "A completely nude and wasted Marvin," she later wrote. "He must have finished off two bottles of liquor. With the jukebox blaring, he was dancing, naked, on top of the bar, performing a hula. I later heard that he'd danced nude on a bar at the Kawaii Hotel in Hawaii during the filming of *Donovan's Reef* (1963). The gay boys loved watching his dick flop up and down, as did a number of horny women."

Efficiently and quickly, Mitchum took control of the situation, helping Marvin off the bartop and removing his own shirt to cover Marvin's nudity.

"We got him into the parking lot and into a car," Linda said. "Even though I was stoned, I became the designated driver. Once in front of Marvin's house, we had a hell of a time getting him up the steps to his bedroom. But we finally managed. Mitchum is one strong guy."

"Before that, I'd had some stupid fantasy about dumping Chuck and becoming Marvin's live-in girlfriend, now that he'd dumped Michelle Triola. But when I saw how fucked up and what a drunk he was, I decided that wasn't a good idea. Besides, I suspected that, like Chuck, he had a violent streak in him."

Before leaving, Mitchum went into Marvin's kitchen and removed a bottle of catsup from the refrigerator.

"Is that next on the agenda?" she asked. "You're going to cover your dick with catsup and invite me to eat the burger raw?"

"Not at all," he answered. "We're going to a wild party," he said. "When I get there, I'm gonna strip, splash catsup on my chest, and enter as a plate of steak tartare."

***

Armed with his bottle of catsup as they drove away from Marvin's house, with Linda at the wheel, Mitchum directed her to 9402 Beverly Crest Drive. "We're going to a pool party at Rock Hudson's house, a place he calls 'The Castle.' It used to belong to Sam Jaffe, the producer. Universal bought it and gave it as a gift to Hudson. I wish someone would make me such a gift."

"I've known Rock for years," Mitchum said. "He's gay, of course, but so is every other male star in Hollywood. He's a great guy."

"I know," Linda said. Then she explained to Mitchum the bizarre circumstances in which she'd met Hudson and Sal Mineo on Joe Carstairs' private island in The Bahamas.

"Rock is famous—should I say 'notorious?'—for his pool party bacchanals," Mitchum said. "My pal, Rory Calhoun, will be there. You never know who's going to show up. Rock prefers his guests to arrive in skimpy costumes—actually jaybird naked, hence, my Grade A beef costume I've chosen tonight."

424

"What about me?" she asked.

"I noticed you were wearing a G-string," he said. "Take off everything except the G-string. At least the beaver will be concealed."

"If you, a big-time star, are willing to show up wearing only catsup, then I'm game for the G-string."

Parking in front of Hudson's Castle, they stripped down for their entrances. The houseboy who opened the door for them didn't even look shocked, accustomed as he was to nudity during the course of his day-to-day activities there. "Good evening, Mr. Mitchum," the boy said. "You and your Lady friend are most welcome. Mr. Hudson told me to expect you."

A lot of noise was coming from the pool area, where music was playing. On the way out to the patio, she discovered a large statue of Michelangelo's *David* and a marble replica of a little boy peeing into the pool. At least twenty-five young men in various states of undress were either lounging beside the pool or cavorting within its waters.

Word spread quickly that Robert Mitchum had arrived in the nude, and a virtual ring of fans and onlookers formed quickly around him, with Linda more or less pushed off to the side.

After a few minutes of Mitchum proudly showing off his dick to an admiring audience, Hudson came to the rescue. The good-looking and rather tall star was wearing a pair of bathing trunks and walking with a cane.

"Hi, Bob," he said. "How's it hanging? Don't answer that. I can see for myself." Then he turned to Linda and kissed her on the cheek. "I'm not going to be burned at the stake, this time, am I? That Joe Carstairs…She should be locked up. She scared Sal and me half to death."

Someone spread the word that the young woman accompanying Mitchum was none other than Linda Lovelace, star of *Deep Throat.* As Hudson led the way to the pool house, opening onto a view of the party, she heard it repeated endlessly, in whispers, "That's Linda Lovelace with Bob Mitchum."

Inside the pool house, Hudson said, "You guys put on a great show, but I bet you'd like some robes and flip-flops."

After they dressed, he guided them into the gigantic living room of his main house. "I decorated it in a style called 'Early Macho,'" he said.

She took in the African masks, the zebra skins, the wall-mounted hunting trophies, and the ten-foot-long davenport sofa. "That was rescued from the set of *Pillow Talk* (1959), that comedy I made with Doris Day," Hudson said.

Behind the sofa, she spotted two young men intertwined together in a sixty-nine position. "Oh, ignore them," Hudson said. "One of the straight guys who came here tonight said he wanted to try gay sex. That's always happening around here. He told me that sucking cock wasn't so much different from sucking on a woman's nipple." He led them into the library, still hobbling on his cane.

"What happened to you?" she asked.

"Bob knows about it," Hudson said. "I'm recuperating. I recently filmed a movie called *Showdown* (1973) in New Mexico. I had to drive this beautiful vintage automobile on loan from Laurence Rockefeller. The brakes failed, and I crashed into a concrete wall. I suffered a concussion, fractures on my left leg and both arms, and I cracked a rib. A fine mess I was. I had to take to bed for six weeks."

As Mitchum and Hudson talked, she noted how whenever two actors came together, they often spoke about when they came to Hollywood and how much better the town was then than today.

"Maybe I'm getting old, but even my pool parties are starting to bore me," Hudson said. "Actually, I loved the good old pre-lib days. Life was a lot more fun back then."

"Don't leave out the awesome fact that we were younger then," Mitchum said.

"I think both of you guys still look terrific," Linda said. "Either or both of you could put your shoes under my bed any night of the week."

"I thought I'd get my chance at the handsome hunk, **Rock Hudson,** who in The Bahamas had preferred Sal Mineo to me," Linda said.

"If we made that 'suck-and-fuck' movie he wanted, I'd get him on camera..at least. He told me he was going to make Brando in *Tango* eat crow."

"The uglies are taking over the business," Hudson said. "Most actors, when I hit town, had to be good looking—Rory Calhoun (who's here tonight), Tab Hunter, Farley Granger. Troy Donahue, Robert Wagner, Guy Madison. Now directors are screaming for Dustin Hoffman and Al Pacino, neither of them the best-looking men in Hollywood. I wouldn't go bed with either of them."

Finally, Hudson began paying some attention to Linda, telling her how much he had admired *Deep Throat*. "I can't tell you how many people in Hollywood are waiting for the outcome of that court case against your picture, waiting for its outcome as a precedent for how the legalities of porn will be defined in the future."

"It's a new day out here," Hudson continued. "I know two smart business guys, Lud Gerber and Harry Weiss, who are promoting the debut of *Huge, Inc.,* an enterprise catering to a gay and mostly male clientele. Hudson paused to smile. "It must have been named after me."

"They're buying up bars, steam baths, and a

426

male hustler-on-demand enterprise they're defining as an 'escort service.' And they're planning to produce gay porn for the homosexual market. These guys predict that in the 70s and beyond, porno—both gay and straight—will become the biggest industry in the San Fernando Valley."

In her first memoir, *Inside Linda Lovelace,* Linda wrote that one of the biggest stars in Hollywood wanted to make "a fuck-and-suck movie" with her, but she didn't reveal his name. During later revelations, she claimed that the unidentified party was Hudson himself.

In the wake of the fame associated with both *Deep Throat* and *Last Tango in Paris,* Hudson had assigned somebody to work on a porn scenario that would star himself. At the time, his screen career was fading, and Universal had offered him a key role in what eventually became a popular TV series, *McMillan and Wife.*

"But he wanted something more, something to really attract the attention of the world," Linda said. "He seemed jealous of all the publicity Brando was getting for *Last Tango.*"

Hudson told Linda and Mitchum that his commercial vision of a changing cultural landscape had also been inspired by the 1971 release of the controversial British film, *Sunday, Bloody Sunday.*

[In that movie, the depiction of a love triangle as directed by John Schlesinger, a middle-aged woman (as played by Glenda Jackson) loves a much younger bisexual man (as played by Murray Head) and so does the character played by Peter Finch. Finch's portrayal of a late middle-aged homosexual was noteworthy for the time in its premise that he was not particularly upset by his sexuality, and—other than his unrequited love for Murray—relatively well-adjusted. TRIVIA NOTE: Making his film debut at the age of 14 in this film was the then-uncredited child actor Daniel Day-Lewis. For a fee of £2, he played a hoodlum who vandalized expensive cars parked outside his local church.]

Sunday, Bloody Sunday was a 1971 British film that had starred *(left to right)* **Peter Finch** (Vivien Leigh's lover), **Murray Head** *(center)*, and **Glenda Jackson**.

Rock Hudson wanted to create an American version, co-starring himself, Linda and Sal Mineo, that would depict bisexuality but make *Sunday, Bloody Sunday* seem like a harmless garden party.

"So far, here's how my film might go," Hudson said that day in his home to Linda: "I'm a successful business man devoted to my wife, whom I married in college. She's very natural-looking, a rather unassuming girl who looks and emotes a lot like you. At my office,

I hire this assistant—I'm thinking of Sal Mineo, whom you know already. He turns out to be a skilled seducer who lures me into homosexuality."

"As a result, my world comes apart, but I can't resist him. There would be very graphic sex scenes between you and me and between Sal and me. As you know from our time together in The Bahamas, Sal and I are very well hung, so we wouldn't have any of the problems Marlon experienced in *Last Tango*. At one point during the film, after you learn about Sal's affair with me, you lure him into your bed, too."

"I'd go for that!" she said.

At this point, Michum chimed in: "I wouldn't go for that kind of shit myself, 'cause I'm an old-fashioned kind of guy. Of course, if it was 1944, and I looked like I did back then, I'd be the first actor taking my clothes off and showing it hard."

"Well, sign me up," Linda said. "Any time you're willing to go into production, I'm ready and raring to be your co-star."

At that point, Rory Calhoun walked into the library wearing a pair of snug jockey shorts, a costume which made Linda realize why Marilyn Monroe was so attracted to him during her filming of *River of No Return* with him back in 1954.

"I heard that Linda Lovelace was in the building," Calhoun said. "Hello, Linda, I'm hoping that you can disprove the most famous quotation I ever made."

"What's that, Rory?" she asked.

"I once said, 'the trouble with Hollywood is that there aren't enough good cocksuckers around any more.'"

***

After sex with him—an experience she later defined as far too brief—Rory Calhoun became yet another man she wanted to configure as her full-time lover. Compared with Chuck, a man with whom she was increasingly disillusioned, each of her recent conquests looked like Princes.

She knew that Calhoun was married. In 1971, she'd read that he'd wed a journalist, Sue Rhodes in the immediate wake of his bitter divorce, after twelve years of marriage and three children, from glamour queen Lita Baron. In court, Baron had charged that Calhoun had had adulterous relationship with some seventy-nine women, including Betty Grable, Marilyn Monroe, and Lana Turner.

His response was, "Heck, she didn't even name half of them."

[In an exposé in Confidential, *Linda had read that at the age of thirteen, Calhoun had been sent to reformatory school in Ione, California, for stealing*

428

a revolver. After a few months, he escaped, robbed three jewelry stores, and stole a car, driving it across state lines, a federal offense. He was recaptured and spent three years in the Missouri State Penitentiary at Springfield, Missouri, a prison defined by Time *magazine as "the bloodiest 47 acres in America," before being transferred to the California State Prison at San Quentin. It was there that he was paroled shortly before his twenty-first birthday.*

After that, Calhoun worked as a coalminer, lumberjack, and cowboy, before hitting Hollywood Boulevard "selling my big dick to any buyer with the money. One day back in 1943, when I was riding my horse through the Hollywood Hills, I came across this five-foot five-inch matinee idol who was cruising along the cacti and chaparral."

"I figured I'd better display my talents, so I got down from my horse and took a piss. When Alan Ladd saw what I had hanging, I was launched."

Calhoun's road to stardom passed within the orbit of the gay talent agent Henry Willson, "The man who invented Rock Hudson," and who had discovered a number of other pretty boys who each became prominent on the Hollywood scene in the 50s. Willson quickly became famous and notorious for peddling (and bedding) the male flesh of, among others, John Derek, Clint Walker, Robert Wagner, Troy Donahue, Tab Hunter, and Guy Madison.

Willson fell madly in love with Calhoun, whose real name was Francis Durgin, and [temporarily] renamed him "Troy Donahue." Somehow, that name didn't fit, so he "re-knighted" him as "Rory Calhoun, The Dark Prince." Soon after, Calhoun was photographed with blonde goddess Lana Turner, who shared Willson's fondness for good-looking, well-endowed young men.

Within a week, Willson had Louella Parsons on the phone, claiming, "I've discovered the next Clark Gable, the most exciting man I've ever met."

Linda had first thrilled to Calhoun on the screen when he'd appeared alongside her favorite actress, Susan Hayward, in With a Song in My Heart.

Calhoun admitted that, "I didn't always score. When I made That Hagen Girl, *with Ronald Reagan and Shirley Temple, I had heard that Ronnie was gay. In the studio men's room, I stood by him to take a piss, which is what he was doing. But I produced a big hard-on real*

Unknown to the general public even to this day, **Rory Calhoun** may have seduced more female stars--and quite a few male ones too--than any other actor in Hollywood, including Errol Flynn. Conquests included both Marilyn Monroe and Linda Lovelace.

quick, and turned it in his direction. He practically fled from the toilet before zipping up."

Reagan may have fled from the latrine, but few other A- or B-list actors and actresses turned Calhoun down. In all, he estimated that he'd gone to bed with nearly 200 movie stars, "only one-fourth of whom were men.]

After performing her specialty on Calhoun at Rock Hudson's house that day, Linda recalled, "When one has Rory Calhoun, who needs caviar and champagne?"

"I called him several times, but he never phoned back," she said. "Usually, when one of my dates didn't call me back, I just moved on to the next big game. But with Rory it was different. There was real chemistry there. But in the end, unfortunately, I think the competition was too keen for me."

***

During the late 1980s, Linda was very reluctant to discuss what happened when she visited the great and legendary screen diva, Katharine Hepburn, for tea and other amusements. "No one will believe me," she said. "Everyone thinks that she and Spencer Tracy are carrying on this torrid affair, even though both of them are homosexuals. Of course, their closest friends, people like George Cukor, that director, know that the great love between those two is platonic. But the unwashed public still likes to believe what they've read in all those movie magazines of the 1940s and 50s."

Rory Calhoun and **Shirley Temple**, as they appeared in the 1947 picture, *That Hagen Girl*, which had co-starred Ronald Reagan, who didn't want to make the picture. At the end of the filming, Calhoun told his agent, Henry Willson, "Shirley missed out on my 8 1/2 inches."

In later years, Linda didn't miss one single inch.

[What a difference a quarter century makes. Today, Linda's revelations about Hepburn's lesbian liaisons would fall on more sophisticated ears.

Hepburn died in 2003. In the wake of her death, at least three major biographies were published. The most thorough investigation of her lesbian life, including details about her longtime affair with the American Express heiress, Laura Harding, was documented in Katharine the Great, A Lifetime of Secrets Revealed *(© Blood Moon Productions, 2004).*

Other biographers, including one written by veteran Hollywood writer James Robert Parrish, also weighed in with tales about the deeply closeted

430

lesbian life of Katharine Hepburn. Dozens of tabloid exposés followed, as well as several outings of Hepburn on TV. On the popular ABC-TV talk show, The View, *co-hostess Joy Behar loudly asserted, "Everybody knows Hepburn was a lesbian."*

Friends of Hepburn claimed "she would turn over in her grave" if she'd lived to see the prestigious New York Times *out her in not one but in two separate articles, exposing her penchant for hiring "rent girls."*

In both its Sunday Styles section and in a book review, the public learned about Hepburn's hiring—with the stipulation that "there not be any blemishes anywhere on their bodies"—of female prostitutes to service her sexual needs.

Other major exposures resulted after a handsome former Marine, Scotty Bowers, then eighty eight-years old, wrote about his days as Hollywood's most famous pimp. He made arrangements for major stars to meet and have sex with beautiful young women or handsome men. Many of these studs worked at his notorious filling station—hence, he entitled the published version of his memoirs Full Service. *In his book, Bowers graphically described his liaisons with the bisexual but deeply closeted Spencer Tracy, an actor frequently and almost obsessively cited by Hollywood press agents for his (mostly fictional) long-term sexual dalliance with Hepburn.*

Scotty's other sexual partners included—according to him— the gay director of the F.B.I. (J. Edgar Hoover) and the gay, much disgraced, former King of England, Edward VIII, who abdicated his throne to marry "the woman I love." Edward's wife, Wallis Warfield Simpson (known worldwide after her marriage to Edward as the Duchess of Windsor) shared Hepburn's fondness for sex with beautiful young women.]

In anticipation of her visit with Hepburn, Linda had read a profile about her…several, in fact. One writer asserted that Hepburn's voice "rose above the mainstream, like a lace hem being lifted above the mud." It was a voice that actually intimidated Linda, who feared she'd do something "socially incorrect" in the presence of such an august person. When she sat down with Hepburn, the actress seemed as cold and sexless in person as she did on the screen. She had the breeding and posture of an American aristocrat.

"You have the most wonderful voice on screen," Linda gushed. "And in person, too."

"Actually, Spence [Spencer Tracy] says I always talk like I have a feather up my ass."

Mostly, Linda and Hepburn talked about movies. Some of the diva's statements startled Linda. "I love movies, but I disapprove of them," Hepburn asserted.

Knowing that she had once been married, *[to the obscure photographer, Ludlow Ogden Smith]*, Linda asked Hepburn if she had any children.

The actress looked astonished at such a question. "My father didn't want me to make babies. I'm not a breeder, like some cow in the field."

"I may be proper, but I'm not a prude or some dried-up old prune. I was the first major actress to sing the word shit on Broadway when I was the lead in the Broadway musical *Coco.*" [based on the life of French designer Gabrielle (Coco) Chanel.]

Before taking her to her bedroom, Hepburn warned Linda, "Whatever transpires in that bedroom must remain an absolute secret between the two of us—and I must insist on that. My privacy is my own, and I am the one to decide when it shall be violated. I'm tired of some two-bit whore like Margaret Sullavan spreading across Hollywood that I'm a 'dikey bitch.'"

"What Henry Fonda saw in Sullavan, I will never know." Hepburn said. "To Hank's credit, he did say, 'she castrates a man, makes him feel like two cents—and two inches.'" Hepburn went on to claim that "Sullavan got back at him, spreading around town that Fonda was a 'fast starter but a lousy finisher.'"

"To hell with Sullavan," Hepburn told Linda. "She knew about truck stop pickups long before Betty Grable made them fashionable."

[Only when pressured by Garon's researchers did Linda reveal a few of the details associated with her liaison with Hepburn.]

"The sex was very mechanical," Linda claimed. "Without any feeling or passion whatsoever. Perhaps it brought some relief to Miss Hepburn's pent-up emotions. But not for me. It did absolutely nothing."

"She was just a client, a very famous one, but a client nonetheless. She gave me five hundred dollar bills so crisp I felt they'd just been printed. Even if she called me back for a repeat performance at some other time, I would not have gone. She never did call me back, and I was glad to be rid of her. The male stars wanted me, but I got almost no calls—except for a notable exception here and there—from the dyke community in Hollywood."

***

One night, Sammy Davis, Jr., who had become one Linda's "regulars," suddenly announced that he and Altovise would be flying from Los Angeles to Hawaii for a vacation, and that he had arranged first-class tickets so that Linda, with

Chuck, could accompany them as part of the experience. "I booked a suite at the Kahala Hilton," Sammy said. "The four of us can live together."

During their airborne transit from Los Angeles to Honolulu, Sammy opted to occupy the first-class seat next to Linda's, with Altovise and Chuck sitting in a pair of first-class seats several rows behind them. The seating, at least officially, made it easier for Sammy to discuss some issues privately with Linda en route

"We'll have a grand old time," Sammy had promised them. "One of my best friends will be in Hawaii at the same time. Sometimes, I let him go down on me, but he can't open up his throat like you do. Perhaps you'll give him some lessons."

"I'll try," she said.

"He's a dedicated cocksucker and pussy eater, depending on what night it is," he said. "You may have seen him in the movies. He's Peter Lawford, a charter member of the Rat Pack."

"You mean the guy who was President Kennedy's brother-in-law?" she asked.

"One and the same. I want you to eat Peter while he eats me. But before that, take him out by the pool and teach him some technique. I'll have two well-hung waiters running food service to and from our lodgings. You can both practice on them as guinea pigs."

"It sounds far out, but I'll go for it," she said. "I always thought Lawford was very handsome—at least he used to be—although he's a bit too cultured and British for the likes of me. But knowing that we're both cocksuckers will break the ice."

The foursome's first night in Hawaii was all about partying, drinking, dining, and enjoying music and dancing. Even though he was having problems with the Internal Revenue Service and was constantly overspending, Sammy splurged on extravagant gowns for Linda and Altovise. "I'm lucky if I can get Chuck to buy me a doughnut," Linda confided to Sammy.

Beginning with the westbound flight to Hawaii, when Sammy insisted on sitting up front with Linda, she noted that Altovise's attitude toward her had changed for the worse. As if to punish her husband, she was shopping more and more during the day, running up extravagant bills that her husband could ill afford.

Chuck had been assigned to drive Altovise around the island, although her distaste for him had not changed. Being the lesser partner within each of their respective relationships, both Chuck and Altovise seemed to accept their second-class status. Sammy obviously controlled the purse strings, and dictated what his entourage would be doing throughout the course of their time together.

Linda was receiving increasing numbers of offers, which she delayed responding to, but she was bringing in money and providing Chuck with a lifestyle he'd never known before. He no longer tried to control her every movement, and he had stopped abusing her. If anything, he began to view her as a precious commodity which he planned to exploit as her commercial potential grew. He had high hopes for the success of the release of her upcoming movie, *Deep Throat Part II* and the publication of her first memoir, *Inside Linda Lovelace.* He predicted, "We'll make millions." She, however, wasn't that certain.

One afternoon, when Chuck was driving and escorting Altovise on yet another shopping expedition, Sammy lounged on their private terrace with Linda. Although he usually bounced around like a broken electric wire in a hurricane, he seemed subdued and very serious on this particular afternoon.

He informed her that Peter Lawford would be arriving in Hawaii in just two days. "Although he and Pat *[Patricia Kennedy Lawford]* are divorced, I think he's still banging Jackie on occasion. He doesn't want to cut off ties with the Kennedys completely. You know, they have kids, stuff like that. Peter is a total bisexual. I think his ideal sex life would involve having Jackie and Sal Mineo in his bed at the same time every night."

All day, Sammy seemed to have had some troubling thoughts on his mind. Finally, he revealed what was bothering him. "Little darlin'," he said, taking Linda's hand. "I've been fighting my feelings for you, but they're growing more serious day by day. I don't think I can live without you."

"You don't have to," she said. "I'll always be there for you. Just call and I'll come running."

"Maybe I want more than a gal I can ring up whenever the impulse occurs," he said. "I want a more serious commitment. You see, I've fallen in love with you. I want to spend the rest of my life with you. That means I'll have to divorce Altovise, and you'll have to divorce Chuck. I do care for Altovise, and I don't want to hurt her. As for Chuck Traynor, it's obvious you don't give a rat's fart for him, and I can see why. Let's face it: He's a user and a bastard. The only reason I invite him here is because of you."

"The idea of marriage never occurred to me," she said. "I must admit I'm shocked."

"When you have me in your throat, I come alive—no pun intended," he said. "I'm in ecstasy. Altovise can't do that for me. Also, I find I can talk and unburden myself to you. I can even confess to you that at times I hate Frank Sinatra, and that I'm very jealous of him. It's clear to me you're not pretending, that you actually love to listen to my stories about my adventures in show business."

"Frankly, I think I bore Altovise. Also, I saw the way she was making love to you. I think she digs women more than men, and I've had that suspicion for a long time. I have to face it: You turn me on more than the guy she calls her midget. God, I hope she's not referring to my dick. No, she couldn't be…"

Suddenly, Linda sensed the presence of someone. She looked up and stared into the hostile face of Altovise, who had unexpectedly returned early from her shopping trip. Apparently, she'd eavesdropped on Sammy's declaration of love.

He looked up just in time to see Altovise put her hand over her mouth and run to their shared bedroom. "Oh, fuck!" he said, rising quickly and going after her.

For about an hour, she heard screams and denunciations. When Chuck came in midway through the worst of it, she didn't relay the full details, saying only that Altovise and Sammy were having domestic squabbles because of all the money she'd been spending. Linda suggested that they go down to the bar until the fight had abated.

In the bar, about thirty minutes later, a waiter indicated to Chuck that someone had asked to speak to him on the phone. Chuck moved away to answer the call.

When he returned, he said, "It was Sammy. Altovise is leaving him, and he wants me to take her back to Los Angeles, now, with all her purchases and all her luggage."

"I'm going to stay here in the bar till you guys have gone," Linda said. "I don't want to go back upstairs now and get involved. It might go badly and screw up the deals we're planning with Sammy."

"You're right," Chuck answered. "We've got a tiger by the tail, and we'd better not let go. Also, I've got business to attend to, including finding out from Delores what offers have come in. We've got to start capitalizing off them in a big way. I'm sick of this five hundred or a thousand dollars a night shit."

Linda returned to Sammy's suite a few hours later, finding him sitting alone, still outfitted in his swimming trunks. She felt vaguely uncomfortable being alone with him as she was usually with him when there were other people around.

He didn't seem upset that Altovise had left him. Finally, he said, "She'll come back. She doesn't have any other place to go. I'm the man in this relationship, and I'll do what I fucking want."

"At least I'm glad you packed Chuck off," she said. "I'm getting so I can't stand him."

"I've got some great news for you," Sammy said, getting up from his chair to pour himself another drink. "Peter is arriving tomorrow. We'll be sharing this suite with him. Right before I got off the phone with him, I told him, 'You're in for a treat. It's no bullshit. Linda, without a doubt, is the best cocksucker in the world.'"

During their vacation in Hawaii, **Sammy Davis, Jr.,** *(above)* wanted Linda to give Peter Lawford lessons in deep throating.

***

For a prospective bridegroom, Sammy surprised her. He'd proclaimed his love for her and wanted to marry her, yet he seemed to continue a pattern of dangling her before his friends or associates as if she were some kind of trophy.

She had long ago decided that everybody in Hollywood, male or female, had their fingers crossed whenever they pledged fidelity at a marriage ceremony.

For years, an avid devotee of Hollywood gossip, Linda had followed the trail of Peter Lawford, especially his role as pimp to President John F. Kennedy and his antics as a charter member of Frank Sinatra's Rat Pack.

Although he had been ostracized from the Rat Pack by Sinatra, Lawford still found a loyal friend in Sammy. Sammy threw work at Lawford whenever he could, including, in 1966, a gig for a small role, paying $15,000, in *A Man Called Adam.*

Lawford's biographer, James Spada, wrote: "Every day held little deaths for Peter. He coveted film roles but didn't get them. He accepted small parts in minor pictures to meet the bills. And prodigious bills they were. He couldn't completely give up the trappings of wealth and power he had so enjoyed as John Kennedy's brother-in-law."

During his heyday at Camelot, **Peter Lawford**, according to his biographer, Larry Quirk, was frequently vilified as "a playboy, opportunist, bisexual, nymphomaniac, drug addict, alcoholic, and pernicious sycophant to both Frank Sinatra and the Kennedys."

In Honolulu, Linda Lovelace found him "all that and more!"

[In 1968, Sammy and Peter Lawford had been in London together, co-starring in a contrived British comedy entitled Salt and Pepper, *a parody of the current craze for James Bond 007 films. Directed by Richard Donner, it featured Lawford and Sammy as night club owners in London's Soho district. The trouble begins when two "baddies" turn up at their joint to inaugurate the overthrow of the British government. Confusingly, whereas Lawford had been cast as Cris Pepper and Sammy as Charlie Salt, the names of the characters they played, based on their skin colors, should have been reversed.*

In London, Lawford and Sammy were spotted

riding matching minibikes, waving to gawking onlookers. Sammy's license plate read SALT 1 and Lawford's proclaimed PEPPER 1.

In the midst of "Swinging London" of that era, in a scene dominated by both optimism and hedonism, they established new records for partying at such trendy discos as Alvaro's on Kings Road in Chelsea.

Journalist Christopher Booker, a founder of the archly satirical Private Eye magazine, described the social revolution of the swinging sixties like this: "There seemed to be no one standing outside the bubble, observing just how odd and shallow and egocentric and even rather horrible it was."

Experimenting with drugs and sexual freedom, Lawford and Sammy shot their movie during the day and partied all night, experimenting with drugs and sexual freedom, the latter often without being gender specific. Sammy indiscreetly told a reporter for a London tabloid, "Our lifestyle is stimulating, frightening, fun."

At all the hot spots in Soho, they appeared wearing love beads, Nehru jackets in tones ranging from chartreuse to pink, pork chop sideburns, long hair, and bell-bottoms. Sewn onto Lawford's blue jeans a patch read: GET YOUR SHIT TOGETHER.

Back in Hollywood, Lawford had left behind a long and provocative list of lovers, male and female, that contained more A-list celebrities than any equivalent list in town: Lana Turner, Ava Gardner, Marilyn Monroe, Nancy Davis (Reagan), June Allyson, Lucille Ball, Judy Holliday, Grace Kelly, Lee Remick, Elizabeth Taylor, Merv Griffin, Roddy McDowall, Tony Curtis, Van Johnson, Robert Walker, Tom Drake, Noël Coward, and Jacqueline Kennedy Onassis. Of course, Sammy, too, figured among Lawford's intimate conquests.]

Linda was anxious to meet Lawford, but Sammy had already warned her, "Peter doesn't look exactly like he did when he appeared in *Little Women* back in 1949."

The most vivid memory Linda had of Lawford was not based on any of his movies, but from a television appearance when he had introduced Marilyn Monroe at the star-studded fund-raising gala at Madison Square Garden on May 19, 1962, the celebration of President Kennedy's up-

In her memoirs, Linda had written about having a sexual three-way with the mysterious "Salt" and "Pepper," but refused to divulge their names.

Years later, she revealed that "Salt" referred to **Peter Lawford** (*right figure in photo above*), and "Pepper" referred to **Sammy Davis, Jr.** (left). The two stars are depicted above in a scene from their spy movie, *Salt and Pepper*.

Insiders in Hollywood, however, had known who Salt and Pepper were years before Linda finally got around to identifying them.

coming forty-fifth birthday. Before millions of viewers, after not appearing in the spotlight after her first introduction *[She was still getting ready, high on pills, and flustered with anxiety]* Marilyn finally appeared onstage *[in white ermine and wearing the tightest-fitting dress ever seen in the history of A-list Hollywood].* Her tardy appearance, rich with stage-fright jitters for almost everyone involved that night, prompted Lawford, with a hint of exasperation, to announce to the world at large, "Mr. President, the late Marilyn Monroe." Then, haltingly and to everyone's shock and in some cases, outrage, she sang the world's most notorious rendition of "Happy Birthday, Mr. Pres...i...dent."]

There were many questions Linda wanted to ask Lawford, especially about the late president and his relationship with, and the mysterious death of, Marilyn Monroe. But Lawford made it abundantly clear from the beginning that the subject was off-limits. "I'm constantly being offered big bucks for my autobiography, and I desperately need the money, but I'm not going to write it. *The National Enquirer* has already offered me $100,000 for serialization rights to the book, but I turned them down."

Linda and Lawford chattered pleasantly about their mutual friend, Hugh Hefner.

"He is my good chum," Lawford said. "In fact, he sets aside one of his bedrooms as my own private boudoir. It's decorated entirely in black and with mirrors on the ceiling and on all four walls. The bedroom is soundproof and has a stereo console housed within this mammoth round bell. By dialing "33" on the bedside phone, one of Hefner's butlers will arrive, supplying everything from condoms to champagne to one or more of the Bunnies. Sometimes I request one of the handsome young studs Hefner employs mostly to service his distinguished female guests."

At Madison Square Garden, **Marilyn Monroe** *(right)*, after having been introduced by **Peter Lawford** *(left)* sang "Happy Birthday" to JFK.

Later that night in his suite at teh Hotel Carlyle, she gave JFK his real birthday present.

When Linda's first memoir was published, it wasn't hard for inside Hollywood to figure out to whom her oblique references to "Salt and Pepper" applied.

As biographer James Spada noted, "All Lawford was interested in was oral sex. He no longer even attempted traditional intercourse and could reach orgasm only after several hours of fellatio. He had become primarily a voyeur," as Linda soon found out.

Fully aware of Lawford's waning sexual powers, Sammy had secured some sort of aphrodisiac in

438

Hawaii that brought renewed life to Lawford's often dormant penis. As Linda wrote in her memoir, "Their specialty is sandwich games, and I've been in on them when they lasted three to five hours. I might be on top of Pepper, face-to-face. His cock is in my cunt. Salt lies on top of me in the same direction and fucks me in the ass. Then we switch position, with Salt on his back, fucking my ass, while Pepper takes the top position. I've taken both cocks in my mouth at one time, and have also taken them both in my ass—together, I mean."

However, Lawford's renewed sexual vitality didn't last long. One night after one of these marathon sessions, he developed a seizure. The house doctor was called. After a thorough examination, the doctor concluded that the drug Sammy was administering to Lawford had endangered his life and had almost catalyzed a fatal heart attack.

After that scare, Lawford went back to a more limited role of simply performing cunnilingus on Linda—"at least my tongue is still in working order"—and being a *voyeur* as she otherwise performed fellatio on young men he met on the beach.

Linda always believed that her "sexcapades" on the Hawaiian beach during her holiday there with Lawford were inspired by the example of Sebastian, the unseen and morally bankrupt protagonist of *Suddenly, Last Summer,* the 1959 film based on a play by Tennessee Williams. In the movie, the character played by Taylor had been used as bait by her cousin, Sebastian, as a means of luring young men to his room, where he'd perform fellatio on them.

The most iconic movie still from Tennessee Williams' ***Suddenly, Last Summer*** featured **Elizabeth Taylor**, clad in a provocative white bathing suit, looking up and into the crotch of a young man on a beach.

In the movie, her cousin, a symbolically rich but otherwise faceless character named Sebastian, had sent her to the beach to procure young men for him.

On a beach in Hawaii, Peter Lawford was inspired to use Linda Lovelace as bait in his search for young men to seduce.

For Lawford and Linda, Sammy had arranged the use of an elaborate private cabana-style tent that was erected directly on the sands of the beach. "I don't need any more sun," Sammy told them. "This here nigger is black enough already."

During the day, Lawford requested that Linda cruise up and down the beach, looking for "well endowed young men who filled out the pouches of their bathing suits."

According to Linda, "Before we left Hawaii, I must have

brought at least twenty young studs back to our tent. As long as any of them got a blow-job from Linda Lovelace, they didn't mind putting on a show for Lawford. Sometimes, after the men had climaxed, they generously allowed Peter to lick them clean."

One day at the beach, when Lawford wasn't turning tricks, she learned that he, too, was considering making a movie whose theme would be inspired by the recent success of both *Deep Throat* and *Last Tango in Paris.*

"It's called *The Sun Seekers,"* he announced. "Set on the French Riviera during the 1930s, its two leads are roughly based on F. Scott and Zelda Fitzgerald."

She had never heard of them.

"The husband is a world famous novelist, but he's addicted to decadence and alcohol," Lawford announced. "The wife is mentally ill and addicted to sex. The two spend every week of every month seeking out fun spots. I envision nudity in the film and rather graphic sex. The couple often share their tricks together. They have no particular gender preference in mind during their seductions."

"That sounds like a hot film," she said. "I'd be ideal for the girl's part."

"Thanks to your specialty, I think you indeed might be."

Like so many movies dreamed up in Hollywood by stars, directors, or writers who at the time were influenced by drugs and alcohol, *The Sun Seekers* was never made.

***

Back in Los Angeles after their return from Hawaii, Sammy never told Linda how he had reconciled his marital difficulties with Altovise. But she noticed that during the next few times she visited him, his wife made it a point to have another engagement.

Even Chuck had curtailed his visits to Sammy. It would be months before she found out why.

Chuck had begun seeing another woman, a beautiful blonde named Marilyn Chambers, an actress who was destined to become the second most famous female porn star of the 1970s. Linda would learn a lot more about Chambers later.

Once, during one of her visits at Sammy's, Linda found herself face-to-face with Altovise in the hallway as she was leaving. In a sharp, rather mocking voice, Altovise said, "I'm leaving you two love birds alone. Enjoy, enjoy, enjoy!"

On occasion, Sammy still discussed love and even marriage with her, but he became increasingly vague. "If we ever do get married, you'll have to per-

440

form your specialty on me first thing every morning, and last thing every night."

In spite of what he said, she felt that Sammy was growing bored with her and that he wanted to move on to other conquests.

There was even speculation that Sammy had become emotionally involved with Marilyn Chambers, whose 1972 performance in *The Green Door* had created a sensation. This fresh-faced blonde had appeared beaming at a baby on boxes of Ivory Snow, a brand of laundry detergent manufactured by Proctor & Gamble. The advertising slogan associated with the product (and presumably, with its spokeswoman, too), defined it as "99 and 44/100 percent pure."

Behind the Green Door was a pornographic film about a woman who is abducted, taken to a theater, and ravished (much to her delight) in front of an audience of both men and women. It, along with *Deep Throat,* are today cited as among the first X-rated films to gain wide mainstream distribution.

Linda had heard that Chuck, during one of his prolonged absences from her, was living with Chambers, so she just assumed it was her husband who had linked Chambers up with Sammy.

In spite of Sammy's slow drift away from her, he still treated Linda politely, although he no longer showered cash and expensive gifts on her, as he'd done lavishly before.

***

One day, an invitation came in from Liz Renay and "Pupu" for a stay at their rented villa in Palm Springs. Linda eagerly accepted, with the understanding that both William Holden and Burt Lancaster wanted to "party with me when I got back." She didn't know what kind of celebration either of those actors had in mind.

In Hollywood, there's always someone waiting in the wings to replace you.

In Linda's case, that someone was **Marilyn Chambers**, who ironically became the second wife of Chuck Traynor following his divorce from Linda.

Proctor & Gamble, the industrial giant which had hired Chambers as the fresh-faced blonde who appeared on boxes of Ivory Snow, soon learned that Marilyn was a lot less than "99 and 44/100 percent pure."

When Chambers' film, *Behind the Green Door*, was released, the ad campaign which had featured her as a smiling "young mother with child" went down the drain.

Along with *Deep Throat*, Chambers' film helped establish a mainstream market for pornography.

441

When the cult film goddess, **Liz Renay**, known as a Marilyn Monroe lookalike, was voted "The World's Most Beautiful Woman," there was widespread disagreement in Hollywood.

There were those who thought Audrey Hepburn, among dozens of other competitors, was more beautiful.

Regardless, Renay's phone rang off the wall with calls from men wanting dates.

Among them were Errol Flynn, John Payne, and Steve Cochran.

Photos above: Two views of **Liz Renay**

Before her departure for Palm Springs, Sammy filled Linda in to the degree he could on the background of Liz Renay.

"She's the biggest starfucker who ever hit Hollywood," he said. "If you keep going at the rate you are now, you might one day top her record."

Born in 1926 to Christian evangelist parents in rural New Mexico, Renay was far older than Linda, but in her heyday, she'd been designated by some members of the press as "The World's Most Beautiful Woman" and hailed as a love goddess. But her reputation included far more than that: She was the most notorious and promiscuous actress ever to step off the train at the Los Angeles railway station. When she won a Marilyn Monroe lookalike contest her date book filled up quickly.

When Linda had first met Renay in New York, she'd already published a memoir, *My Face for the World to See* (1971), some of which had been penned during her three-year stint in prison, She had served time (1961-1964) for violating the terms of her probation for perjury in Mickey Cohen's 1959 tax evasion case. She later said: "I have paid a dear price for the mistake I made, and I hope the public will be forgiving. I wanted to protect Mickey. I felt I owed him that. I couldn't deliberately hurt someone who had been nice to me."

Renay's memoirs were more titillating than revelatory, but her writing style shared something in common with Linda's. In their respective memoirs, neither actress listed or defined all the celebrities they'd screwed, perhaps for legal reasons, or perhaps for fear of reprisals, at the time.

Renay dated from both the A- and B-list of movie stars. The sexual conquests she had sampled along with Linda included Desi Arnaz, Marlon Brando, Scott Brady, Rory Calhoun, Sammy Davis, Jr., William Holden, John Ireland, Burt Lancaster, Dean Martin, Lee Marvin, Victor Mature, Robert Mitchum, and Robert Ryan. Linda told Sammy, "I want to compare notes with her. And I want to hear

442

what she says about Sinatra."

Renay's greatest love, or so she had claimed, was Glenn Ford. Although she had been married eight times, no one ever seemed to remember seeing her in public with one of her spouses.

Sammy knew a lot less about Pupu: "Actually, his name is Pupu, Jr."

[Renay's escort, Pupu, Jr., might have been the son of "Pupu Sr."(Jean-Pierre Roux), who had been born before World War I through the union of a "brown Créole belle" and a "colonial from the mainland of France" in Martinique.

Pupu Sr. had evolved into an exotic and awe-inspiring figure standing six feet, four inches with a sculpted physique and enormous self-confidence. In the French West Indies, he had become legendary for his endowment, often appearing as a sex performer in various stag shows.

When he arrived in Hollywood, he opened a male bordello that catered to both homosexuals and aging female movie stars.

Pupu Jr.'s mother was believed to have been the 1940s film goddess, Maria Montez, who had died in 1951 when she stepped into the scalding hot water of her bathtub, an action which catalyzed a heart attack. Her lovers had included Darryl F. Zanuck, Orson Welles, the "Sarong Actor" Jon Hall. She eventually married the handsome French movie star, Jean-Pierre Aumont, next to whom she is buried at the Montparnasse cemetery in Paris.

Born in the Dominican Republic, Montez is still known today as one of the queens of cinematic camp, mainly because of her starring role in films which included Cobra Woman and Ali Baba and the Forty Thieves, *both released in 1944.*

During his marriage to Elizabeth Taylor, it was revealed that Michael Wilding, the bisexual British actor, had had a torrid affair with Montez.]

As she packed to head for Palm Springs, Linda wondered about the new adventures that awaited her there.

"With Pupu and Liz, and maybe with Mickey Cohen dropping in, you're headed for some wild weekend, gal," Sammy said. "Come back alive."

A STREAK OF VENUS

Liz Renay was nearly fifty years old when, in 1974, she pulled off all her clothes and, as part of a publicity stunt, streaked down Hollywood Boulevard. Some 5,000 to 10,000 men (estimates vary) turned out to witness and record the experience.

She later said, "On my tombstone, I want it writ:

**LIZ RENAY,
CONNOISSEUR OF MEN.**"

"Guys have called me everything--whore, slut, Princess, Queen, Mona Lisa, Goddess, Aphrodite. That's okay, as long as they keep calling me."

"This Pupu and Liz sound like fun," she said. "I wonder if I'll have to deep throat anyone during my stay with them. "

"In Palm Springs," Sammy said with irony, "nothing like that's ever been known to happen."

***

In the desert resort, a Mexican houseboy led Linda to the large swimming pool where a nude Liz Renay sunned herself on a *chaise longue*. Beside her lay an equally nude Pupu. Her attention was immediately drawn to his elongated penis. Noticing where she was looking, Pupu said, "I take after my father."

Although Renay was forty-seven years old, her body and large breasts were in excellent shape for a middle-aged woman.

Pupu went to get some cold drinks and to check up on how their lunch was coming. Linda accepted Renay's invitation to strip down and enjoy the sun. Without hesitation, she did.

"Pupu looks like he'd make some girl a great friend," she said.

"He's as good as he looks," Renay answered. "I'll send him to your bedroom tonight for some deep throating. I'm sure you agree that a huge cock can't always be trusted. I've known men with such oversized dicks that they injure their partners. I've done research on the subject. Only twenty percent of the female population demands a big cock. The other eighty percent is satisfied with an average sized cock. What counts the most is achieving and sustaining an erection."

"Actually, based on my unscientific research, I'd agree with you," Linda said.

"Speaking of large appendages, your breasts are huge."

"You can feel them if you wish," Renay said. "They're real."

Linda fondled her breasts, envying them.

"I'm known for having the best breasts in Hollywood," Renay said. "They are larger than Marilyn Monroe's. She was just a 34, though she claimed she was a 38. I'm a 44."

"Mine are fake," Linda said. "I never got by on my breasts. I had to use what God gave me and that was a deep throat."

"You're lucky," Renay said. "Many gals don't know how to give a decent blow-job."

When Pupu returned with the drinks, Renay said, "Suck him hard! You won't believe the size of his thing."

Without hesitation, Linda fell on her knees onto the matting and produced a magnificent erection from Pupu.

During the course of his marriage to Elizabeth Taylor, British actor **Michael Wilding** carried on an adulterous affair with another actress, Maria Montez, of the Dominican Republic.

Questions still remain.

"Don't bring him off," Renay said, sharply. "I have other uses for him today before he spends the night with you."

Very reluctantly, Linda withdrew her suction pump. Pupu looked irritated at being cut off.

An hour later, after Linda had showered, she put on a robe and ate with her hosts on the patio, feasting on tacos and guacamole.

Renay informed her that she'd spoken to Mickey Cohen, who was paying the rent on their villa, and that he'd be by for a visit tomorrow after ten o'clock in the evening.

Downing a beer, Renay discussed her loyal and enduring friendship with Cohen. "We go way back. I still remember our first date in the 1950s. We rolled down Hollywood Boulevard in his bulletproof Cadillac Eldorado."

"Like Al Capone, Mickey was eventually trapped by the IRS. He was tried for income tax evasion and sentenced to fifteen years in prison. I, too, had to spend three years in prison, with all the dykes chasing after me, because I wouldn't rat on Mickey. Prison ruined my career, but I did it for him."

Linda learned that Cohen only recently had been released from the Atlanta Federal Penitentiary. In the wake of his release, and until the end of his life, he commented widely about the physical conditions under which prisoners had to live, including foul toilet facilities, skimpy, flea-infested mattresses placed on rusty cots; food that was often spoiled; and brutality from the armed guards.

In one of the villa's guest bedrooms, Linda slept for a few hours until the houseboy knocked on her door, suggesting she get ready for dinner on the town with Pupu and Renay.

Within the hour, all three of them were dining at what Renay told her was Frank Sinatra's favorite restaurant in Palm Springs, although Linda later couldn't remember its name.

Five tables away, she spotted the very famous face of Senator Ted Kennedy dining with two unknown women and another man.

Renay told her, "The Kennedys are on the outs

Maria Montez was known as both the Queen of Technicolor and a 24-hour-a-day actress, skillfully re-inventing herself as a sexually desirable exotic in B-grade movies which stand today as monuments to over-the-top escapist camp.

with Sinatra. He's become a Republican. He and Sammy are now brown-nosing Nixon and Spiro Agnew, of all people."

Linda had read that Kennedy was a womanizer, and she wanted to know how to hook up with him. She confided her dilemma to Renay.

"I'll handle it," Renay said. She signaled to her waiter.

Ordering one of the restaurant's best bottles of champagne for Kennedy's table, she asked the waiter to bring her a blank card, instructing Linda to write a note to Kennedy. Renay dictated what it should say:

Dear Teddy,
I think you're a handsome lug, better-looking than your brothers were.
You're my dream man. I hope you'll call me tomorrow. My throat...OOOPS!
I mean door...is always open to you.
XX
Linda Lovelace

At the bottom of the card, Renay scribbled the phone number of their villa.

Then the waiter delivered the champagne with its note. After reading it, Kennedy blew her a kiss across the room and signaled he'd call tomorrow.

A few hours later, back at the villa, a nude Pupu suddenly appeared in her bedroom.

As Linda later recalled, "Of all the men who've had sex with me, Pupu ranks up there at the top. He came on like gangbusters. 'You want cock, baby...well, you're going to get it,' he said. He kicked the door shut with his foot and practically tossed his crotch in my face. I went to work on it...and how!"

"I opened my throat and swallowed him," she said.

"'Even with all her experience, Liz can't go all the way,' he told me. That made me work all the harder. Speaking of hard, it was a fucking steel bar. I barely had room to move my tongue, his cock was that big."

"He wanted everything he had all over his body sucked, and he returned the favor. I lost count of how many orgasms I had. He fed his prize into every hole he could find. He was a rough lover without being violent, if that makes sense."

"During our marathon, he kept a bright light on all the time," she said. "He wanted to see my face during his assault on me. When it was all over, he paid me a compliment. He said. 'Never have I seen a woman's eyes cloud over like yours. I've never seen a woman's head thrash as violently as when you had a foot of cock stuffed in you. I drove you crazy, and you did the same for me. Too bad I can't do this to you every night. But my dick is my bread winner, and I've got to spread it around.'"

"The next morning, before joining Liz for breakfast, Pupu sorta ruined it for me. He gave me a compliment, I guess, but it was rather insulting: 'You were pretty tight for a whore,' he told me."

***

The following evening, Mickey Cohen, the famous gangster, arrived in Palm Springs to reconnect with Liz Renay and to meet Linda.

Although she feared she'd be encountering some psychotic killer, Linda found Cohen "a true gentleman," the same assessment Liz Renay later made in her second memoir, *My First 2,000 Men.*

During the hour Linda spent talking and drinking with Cohen, she dubbed him "the celebrity gangster." He name-dropped a lot, and he had powerful or famous friends. Sammy Davis, Jr., was his friend, as were Red Skelton, Lena Horne, Jerry Lewis, Walter Winchell, Redd Fox, Don Rickles, even TV newsman Mike Wallace.

He was immaculately groomed and manicured and wore a tailor-made suit that looked like it cost $3,000. His smell was of English Lavender, his favorite cologne.

Among B-girls and Las Vegas dancers, Cohen was known for "his way with women." His sexual prowess was frequently and loudly attested to by Renay herself.

Although Linda understood that she had met Cohen during his dotage *[he would die of cancer in 1976],* she didn't see what women saw in him, other than mob-based power and money. He'd been a boxer, bodyguard, blackmailer, pimp, gambler, haberdasher, restaurateur, racketeer, and crook. He hobnobbed with the Rat Pack, including Frank Sinatra, and he was known for ruthlessly and efficiently following the orders of Mafiosi bigwigs who included both Sam Giancana and Lucky Luciano.

Linda just did not see what all the excitement was about. When he pulled off his expensive garments and lay down nude in the middle of the bed, his dick to her looked just as short and stubby as the rest of his body. "There was no love making,"

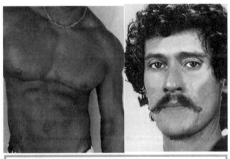

Linda later claimed that **Pupu Jr.** *(represented by the left-hand photo),* was once hired by a wealthy collector to make a private 8mm loop with **John C. Holmes** *(right)* and his enormous appendage.

Perhaps they did, but no such loop has ever surfaced. It is assumed that this film remains in a private collection somewhere in the West.

she claimed. "Love had nothing to do with it. He wanted to sample my fellatio talents. I worked him over as best I could, giving him great head. He seemed to have a hard time reaching climax. Eventually, he pounded my rear. Physically, he looked like he was on his last days. Certainly he was slowing down from the little stud who had pounded strippers Candy Barr and Tempest Storm."

"He got up, thanked me, went to the bathroom, took a quick shower, got dressed, and left two thousand dollars on the night stand. Good pay."

Renay joined them in the living room after each of them had tidied up.

Cohen was not above bragging when he suggested that Linda might want to develop a nightclub-style showcasing of her talents in Las Vegas.

"I was once connected to this club, Slapsy Maxie's in the Miracle Mile district of Wilshire Boulevard in L.A," Cohen said. "As a means of getting Dean Martin and Jerry Lewis launched in '48, I invited the A-list—and the fuckers showed up. You name them, Bogie, and his Baby *[Lauren Bacall]*, Jane Wyman *[without Reagan]*, James Cagney, Clark Gable, Gene Kelly, Barbara Stanwyck, Fred Astaire, Rita Hayworth and Orson Welles, Carmen Miranda, Al Jolson, Judy Garland accompanied by Mickey Rooney, Spencer Tracy without Katharine Hepburn, even Greer Garson and William Powell. June Allyson, a big star at the time, went backstage *[for a meeting with the then not-very-well-known]* Dean Martin, and was fucking him by midnight. The nympho fell madly in love with him."

"Later, Joan Crawford told me, 'Martin obviously is the handsome one, but I bet Jerry Lewis would make the better lover.' Sinatra had a different take on their stage appearance that night. He said, 'The Dago's lousy, but the little Jew is great.'"

"You get an act together, kid, and I'll see that all the big names turn out," Cohen promised Linda.

"If there's one think Mickey knows, it's how to fill up a room," Renay claimed.

It was a promise never to be fulfilled, in large part because Linda never developed an entertainment-style showcase, suitable for mainstream viewing in Las Vegas, that the gangster could really back.

In the wake of their sex act, Linda thought Cohen might have more important things to do, but he stayed another hour talking about his glory days. After those years of humiliation in prison, he wanted to re-establish his power and prestige among the *Mafiosi* by reviewing some of the accomplishments of his influential past. Among the events he took credit for was the launching of Richard Nixon on his long and eventful road to the White House.

"Hell, when Tricky Dickie was running for the Senate seat in California back in 1950, his chief fundraiser, Murray Chotiner, approached me," Cohen claimed. "He told me that if I could raise enough mob money, Nixon would keep the rackets committee boys off me when he became Senator. So I booked the Banquet Room at the Hollywood Knickerbocker Hotel and invited 250 boys from the gambling interests in Vegas, those on the shady side of black. All of them showed up and contributed to the pot. We got Nixon launched, and he never double-crossed us."

Cohen became very bitter when he spoke of those years in prison. "Somehow, I managed to put up with the brutal guards, the rotten food, the endless boredom, the bedbugs in my cot. What got me was having to live in close quarters with all those god damn cocksuckers. They didn't go after me, but they had a field day with straight guys cut off from pussy. Prisons are nothing but one great big male bordello."

"Don't get me wrong," he said. "As a Jew, I can't be too bigoted. After all, the fags ended up with the Jews on the way to the gas ovens in Germany."

"I'll let you in on a dark secret of mine," he said. "I've never told anyone. My credentials as a straight man are well known. But the greatest piece of ass I ever had, other than that delivered by Miss Renay here, was the tight boy ass of Sal Mineo."

"Hell, I didn't even know you knew him," Renay said. "Sal Mineo, of all people."

"Liz, my darling, when a guy has fucked Sal, he's had the best. He was such a fine young man."

Cohen glanced at his watch. "I've got to be going. But, listen, gals, I make promises I plan to keep. I've already promised you, Linda, to fill up a room with celebrities if you open with your own act in Vegas. As for you, Liz, I know I'll be dying soon. In my will, I'm leaving you my sex tapes. If you use them for blackmail, they'll be your old age money."

"And as you already know, I've got hot stuff—Lana Turner with my boy Johnny Stompanato, Marilyn Monroe, June Allyson, Desi Arnaz, Rita Hayworth, Elizabeth Taylor, even Clark Gable one night in

Gangster-at-large **Mickey Cohen** (both photos above) was once the bodyguard for Bugsy Siegel, who was murdered, and a friend of Jack Ruby, who assassinated Lee Harvey Oswald.

He carried out the order of Mafiosi bigwigs while associating with Hollywood's royalty: Lana Turner, Marilyn Monroe, Frank Sinatra, and Jerry Lewis, among many others.

He lived by his own interpretation of the Golden Rule: "I have killed no man in the first place that didn't deserve killing."

Palm Springs. I've got all three Kennedy brothers, but I've never blackmailed them. Teddy's in Palm Springs now. Maybe I should call on him."

"Or maybe he should call me," Linda said.

"I'd love to have those tapes," Renay said. "If for nothing else, my own listening and viewing pleasure. But now, as a favor to me, your true love who ruined her movie career and went to prison for three years for you, I want you to fulfill a final request."

She turned and looked at Linda. "And this involves you, too, sweetheart."

"Your wish, my command," Cohen said. "What star do you want to get your revenge on?"

Renay's lip quivered, as if she were still in love with the star who had dumped her. Finally, she said, "I checked. He'll be in Palm Springs for three more nights."

"Well, name the fucker who treated you wrong," Cohen said.

"Glenn Ford."

***

Liz Renay drove Linda to the hotel in Palm Springs where Senator Edward (Ted) Kennedy was staying. Renay herself then drove to the hotel where Glenn Ford was staying to deliver a note to him. Although it had been signed by Linda, it had been dictated by Renay. She'd been Ford's former lover, and in some ways was still in love with him.

At the reception desk, Linda was granted clearance to go to Ted's suite. En route, she was escorted by a bellhop.

Like his brothers, John and Robert Kennedy, Ted was drawn to the pursuit of beautiful women. Max Lerner, the syndicated columnist, compared his preferences to "the archetypal figure of the forbidden temptress, Astarte, who is dangerous and seductive."

Linda could easily relate to that. After all, when Sammy Davis, Jr. had escorted her to a secret coven of the Church of Satan, she had been designated as the love goddess, Astarte herself.

Lerner, in years to come, would also accurately sum up some of Teddy's points of view. "He had Jack's attitude toward women: To triumph as often as possible, but to keep from yielding his heart and commitment. They both had difficulty in relating with any emotional depth to a woman, or seeing her as anything more than sex object and a field for conquest."

Linda first met Ted more than three years after that summer night in 1969, when he was involved in a fatal automobile accident on Chappaquiddick Island off the coast of Martha's Vineyard, killing Mary Jo Kopechne. Since then, hounded by close and constant scrutiny from the press, the Senator had tried, sometimes in vain, to maintain a low profile.

Linda had grown up with an appreciation for the glamour and wealth of the Kennedy brothers. After meeting Judith Campbell, Linda told people, "Had I lived at a different time, and would have been old enough, I would have gladly gone to the White House to give Jack blow-jobs. I bet his thing never crossed Jackie's lips. She looks too prim for that."

Before she was allowed into Ted Kennedy's hotel suite, a bodyguard frisked her, searching for concealed weapons. When she finally was allowed to join Ted on his private patio, he said, "Sorry you had to be felt up. But I get daily death threats. One arrived last week. It read: YOU'RE NEXT. BULLET IN THE NECK."

The reference, of course, was to John F. Kennedy's assassination in 1963 and Robert F. Kennedy's assassination in 1968.

"How dreadful to live under such a threat," she said. "I'm so sorry."

"At least you're here to make love, not war, with me," Ted said.

"You've got that right, big guy," she said, accepting his invitation to sit down and have a cold drink.

She was astonished to see him eating three cheeseburgers delivered by room service. He offered her one, but she politely refused.

Some magazine editors once voted this photo of **Senator Teddy Kennedy** as "the sexiest photo" of him ever taken.

"I always have to watch my diet. When I was growing up, my mother, Rose, called me 'cheery and chubby.' Around the house I was a second-class citizen compared to my brothers. I have a compulsion for eating too much, drinking too much, and having too much sex," he said. "I also have this preference for walking around nude except for my long-tailed Oxford shirt. And never with underwear."

Linda asserted that "his scandalous past didn't bother me one bit. Of course, I was sorry that Mary Jo Kopechne lost her life back in 1969 in that accident on Chappaquiddick. But I didn't know the whole story."

"What I did know is that I wanted one of the Kennedy brothers, for bragging rights if for no other reason, and some jerks had already shot down JFK and RFK before I got my chance--and that seriously pissed me off."

That functioned as his wardrobe that day. He still retained his shirt, but when he shifted his legs, she noticed that he'd stripped off his jockey shorts, which lay on a nearby *chaise longue*. Noticing the direction of her eyes, he said, "I always believe in getting down to action. It's so awkward having to get undressed in front of someone, especially taking

"Teddy was my consolation prize."

off your pants and fumbling around with your shoes and socks."

"But you're going to finish lunch, aren't you?" she asked. "I mean...before we get down to business?"

"I don't know how you manage to be married and still lead a life of sexual adventurism," he said. "I've always interpreted marriage as a drawback with many obstacles."

"You never had a spouse who pimped you out," she shot back.

"Can't say that I did," he answered, smiling. "Actually, instead of listening to my straight-laced mother, Rose, when I got married, I took the advice of my big brother Jack. He said 'Wedding vows or no wedding vows, Teddy, you should continue to sleep with as many women as I do.'"

"I have this friend in Hollywood—you know of him, Jack Nicholson," he said. "I spoke to him this morning and told him I was meeting you. He liked your film, *Deep Throat.* I think I should introduce you guys."

"He was terrific in *Easy Rider* (1969) and in *Five Easy Pieces* (1970)," she said. "I'd love to meet him. He's real macho."

"Actually, you may be sharing a jail cell with Jack," he said, only slightly in jest, but with a certain sincere ring to his words. "I understand that prosecutors are moving ahead, not only going after the people who made *Deep Throat,* but after Jack, too, for appearing in *Carnal Knowledge* (1971)."

"You've got to be kidding," she said.

"I'm not. Republicans will go after anything. Can you imagine the day when we start jailing actors like your friend, Harry Reems? If the creeps in Washington try to rough you up, call me. I'll grab them by the balls, and I can squeeze really hard."

Some of the prosecutors in Memphis also wanted to arrest **Jack Nicholson** and send him to jail for his performance in *Carnal Knowledge* (1971), along with the backers of Linda's *Deep Throat.*

Depicted nude in the photo above, Nicholson played a hysterical "boy-man" terrified of commitment, a symbol of male sexual arrogance tinged with frustration.

"Actually, I'm off the hook," she said. "I agreed to testify for the state. That means I walk, although they can call on me to give evidence whenever they want. I hope they don't, though."

"I'm really glad to hear that," he said. "That was a smart move on your part. I think their talk about prosecuting *Carnal Knowledge [The 1971 sex comedy directed by Mike Nichols, and starring Jack Nicholson, Art Garfunkel, Candice Bergen, Ann-Margret, and Rita Moreno]* is just that...talk. But you never know with the GOP. The 'Good Old Party' hasn't been

452

good since Lincoln was shot."

"A few months before he was an actor in *Carnal Knowledge,* Jack directed his first movie," Ted said. "It was called *Drive, He Said* (1971). Even *Life* magazine wrote about his casting protocols. There was a small role for a cheerleader with some nudity involved. Apparently, Jack told that *Life* reporter that he had to find an actress who was 'the kind of girl who feels good naked and is completely relaxed about it.' Consequently, he arranged for some one hundred girls to audition, naked, with him before finally awarding the role. We don't have that much fun in the Senate. Who would want to get naked with Jesse Helms? And now that my brother is out of the White House, who would want to get naked with either Jimmy Carter or Richard Nixon?"

"Well, when you become president, you can change that back to what it was when your brother was in the White House," she said.

"I'll run for President again, perhaps in 1978," Teddy said. "That is, if Jack Nicholson doesn't decide to run against me."

"You're joking, aren't you?"

"I don't know if I am or not. When Jack was campaigning for Lyndon back in 1964, he flew around cities with a suitcase stamped with a big bumper sticker labeled NICHOLSON FOR PRESIDENT."

After swallowing the last of the three cheeseburgers and the rest of his coffee, Ted was ready to go, heaving himself to his feet and directing her to his bedroom.

As she later recalled, "I gave Teddy a good time, at least I think I did. He called me back the following two afternoons he was in Palm Springs. He didn't have the world's biggest dick, but it was adequate for the job. At least I kept it rock hard. He was also a bit hung over, so it was difficult milking him."

"I sorta liked him. In some strange way, he seemed rather caring and compassionate. I was hoping he might reward me with something, but he didn't. Maybe he thought it insulting to offer me money. I don't know. I got the impression that the Senator did not pay for sex, since it was readily available to him. Still, I was honored to have served him. As a good, loyal American, I believe in doing what I can for the aid of my country."

"After all, he was a Kennedy. Had I been called upon to service Nixon, I obviously would not have been as enthusiastic."

"When I was with Judy Campbell, she told me that one night in Las Vegas, she had turned Ted down when he wanted sex from her. I think he often got sloppy seconds passed down from his older brothers. At least I didn't turn him down. As proven by the card I sent him in that restaurant in Palm Springs, I was the aggressor, the one who propositioned him first."

[Almost every month from then until Teddy's death in 2009, new rumors continued to emerged about Ted, "The Lion of America's Liberal Left."

Years after meeting him, Linda had lunch with actor Jack Wrangler (born Stillman), who had become the hottest and most visible gay porn star in America, and who had also appeared in X-rated straight films too. Oddly enough, he was married to the former big-band songbird, Margaret Whiting, who seemed to readily forgive him for having so many boyfriends.

Wrangler had met with Linda to discuss their making an X-rated movie together. He informed her in advance that his policy, as regards cum shots, would involve substituting a straight male actor for the filming of their genital-to-genital close-ups. "But for the blow-jobs, I can probably get it up in advance before shoving it down your throat," he told her.

During the course of their luncheon, he told her that at Studio 54 in Manhattan, he'd seen a drunken Senator Ted Kennedy getting a blow-job from Andy Warhol in the bowels of the club. "I also heard that he indulged in kinky stuff at orgies in the home of Jack Nicholson," Wrangler claimed.

By the time dessert arrived, Linda had begun interpreting Wrangler as a turn-off and rejected the idea of ever working with him.]

At the time of their final meeting, and after she'd delivered her last blow-job to Ted, he had a question. "You know, it never occurred to me to inquire about your politics. Are you with *us* or with *them?*"

"Had you won the nomination, I would have voted for you, no doubt about that. Nixon turns me off. Poor Pat."

As Kennedy told her goodbye, and after making that pronouncement, she had no idea that within a few days, she'd be sharing intimacies with one of the Senator's most implacable political enemies.

Linda might have been the Queen of Porn durng the early 70s, but **Jack Wrangler** *(photo above)* was the King of Gay Porn at the same time, helping to launch a vastly expanding industry.

Even though they met to discuss the possibility of some creative film work together, Wrangler and Linda didn't click.

Consequently, the "God and Goddess of Porn" never struck a deal.

***

As she was leaving the Kennedy suite, Ted Williams appeared. The Senator introduced the baseball great to Linda.

She was hardly a baseball fan, but knew who Williams was.

[Theodore Samuel (Ted) Williams (1918-2002), often described as "The Greatest Hitter who Ever Lived," played most of career as the

left fielder for the Boston Red Sox (1939-1942) and again from 1946-1960). His baseball career was interrupted twice by service as a U.S. Marine Corps fighter-bomber pilot. At the time of his retirement, Williams ranked third all-time in home runs, right behind Babe Ruth and Jimmie Foxx. Although he remains a household name to baseball fans everywhere, he enjoyed something approaching cult celebrity status in his home town of Boston, and a decades-long friendship with Ted Kennedy, long-time senator from Massachusetts.]

Apparently, Williams and Kennedy were supposed to attend a party somewhere within the hotel. The Senator bowed out, claiming he had to get some sleep. "After my time with Linda, I have to recuperate."

Williams had heard of *Deep Throat,* but had not seen it yet. And whereas the Senator could not show up at any large, mainstream gathering with Linda on his arm, he suggested that Williams escort her downstairs in his place. Not having seen the movie, and perhaps because he didn't fully realize who she was, Williams agreed.

Who she attended the party with that late afternoon and early evening in Palm Springs evolved, over time, into one of those mysterious and unclear ambiguities within Linda's memoirs. It caused a great deal of speculation as to the identity of the athlete she seduced that night.

Years later, she confessed to Garon's research team that one of her sex scenes in Palm Springs, as she had previously described in her book as having transpired with a football jock, actually took place with a baseball player (Ted Williams) and not with a football player, in contradiction to what she'd written in her memoir.

The immediate speculation was that she was writing about Joe Namath, who was widely pursued by women. To confuse her readers even more, she described a party where she did indeed meet Namath.

She remembered seeing him surrounded by women "and lapping it up like a proud peacock. I had heard so much about this guy that I was curious if it was just press-agent bullshit or if he really was a good ball."

She told Jay Garon's researchers that

Linda's memoirs suggested that she had sex with a horny football player, a known womanizer. Linda's fans assumed she was talking about Joe Namath, who was blazing a seductive trail across America.

But in private, she later admitted that the unnamed athletic hero she had referenced was baseball hero **Ted Williams**.

"I had two Teds in a single day, Ted Kennedy and Ted Williams."

"Williams struck out."

she actually met Namath at a party one night in Los Angeles, not in Palm Springs.

He came up to her and said, "You're Linda Lovelace, aren't you?"

She snapped back, "What a fantastic opening line. Wow. You didn't think of that all by yourself, did you? You must have had that written for you."

In contrast to what she wrote in the memoir, she claimed that she and Namath indulged in small talk only for a minute or so. Then he spotted a very beautiful woman across the room and drifted off.

So according to Linda's later revision of a statement she'd made previously in her memoir, it was Williams, not Namath, who wanted to seduce her as the sun went down over Palm Springs. "Our time from beginning to end in his bedroom took all of five minutes," she said. "The first minute was spent circling each other like two champion players before the big game."

"I walked over and unzipped him to find a limp cock. I went down on it. It wasn't a big tool, but it got hard real quick. At its full glory, it wasn't very long. I gave him a couple of good, long, hard sucks when the sonofabitch let go and came. A river of come went shooting out and trickled down my white silk, see-through dress."

He quickly zipped up his pants, telling her, "I'm a fast comer."

"As if I needed to be told that," she later said.

For her final conclusion about Williams, she said, "The guy may be good at hitting home runs, but when it comes to scoring, he's the biggest zero around."

***

The next afternoon, she rang the bell to a hotel suite. The door was opened by one of the most recognizable faces in the world. "Hi, he said, I'm Gwyllyn Newton, but you can call me Glenn Ford."

The day before, she'd sent him a note, delivered by Renay but signed by her, to Ford's suite, asking if she could call on him. He'd responded by phoning her at the Mickey Cohen villa and invited her by.

He was still handsome, though aging, as he was born in 1916. As he showed her around his lodgings and offered her a drink, she found him quite courtly, although she'd read that his former co-star in *A Stolen Life* (1946), Bette Davis, had called him "a son-of-a-bitch" and a "shithead."

He'd been famously married to the actress-dancer Eleanor Powell. When Linda met him, his career was in decline. Or, as Clifford Odets, the playwright and lover of Cary Grant, wrote: "It is an easily won bet that in a few years, Glenn Ford will get just like the other movie people: Bored, sprawling, careless, an overly relaxed fallen angel—they are all affable boys out here, almost tramps."

As one critic described his fading charms: "Glenn Ford could be brooding, menacing, heroic, taciturn, wise, foolish, amiable, dull, sardonic, and, for a period in the 1950s, he had just the right *persona* to make it as a box office attraction, at least during the Eisenhower era."

Before Linda's first meeting with Ford, Liz Renay had described her first encounter with him. She'd met him at a gala honoring the designer, Edith Head. "He was drunk and seated between Lucille Ball and Zsa Zsa Gabor, but blowing kisses at me. He later introduced me to the dyke designer herself. I was wearing a ruby red satin outfit that fitted me like a second skin. The dress swooped down so low it was deliciously obscene. I wore no bra, and the satin clung to my nipples. When Head checked me out, she told Glenn and me that mine was one bra she wouldn't have to pad, as she'd done with so many other stars. She looked down at Glenn's crotch. 'I've also had to stuff many a male jock strap with cotton,' she said."

"That won't be necessary in my case," Ford informed her.

As Linda was getting dressed in white to meet Ford, Renay advised her, "Don't fall for the devilish mother fucker. He's a hit-and-run lover. He'll break your heart before he chases off to his next young beauty."

Renay continued: "Glenn will make you feel like Queen for a Day. His best line is when he'll tell you, it was 'love at first sight.' He may even propose marriage to you. With that line, he's lured many a starry-eyed starlet into his bedchamber where they'll see more stars when he makes love to them. Yes, he's that good, the bastard. His smooth talking is his major tool of seduction, that and the big rod he packs in his pants."

"In spite of what he says in that smooth voice of his, he's just stringing you along," Renay continued. "It's a game he plays. Every chick he meets falls madly in love with him. It's an ego trip for him. He can sweet talk the panties off any gal in Hollywood. The gay boys go crazy over him, too, doing his hair, his makeup, massaging him, dressing him, and begging him to let them suck that beautiful rod of his."

In spite of Renay's warnings, Linda was thrilled to be in the suite with Ford, who was wearing a pair of shorts. Like

Two views of **Glenn Ford**,
Lower photo: romancing Gilda
(Rita Hayworth) in 1946

most actors, he wanted to talk about himself. He asked her how she was lured into the porno business, and she told him that originally, she thought she was going to be a clothes model.

"I got my start as a male model, too," he told her. "It was no ordinary job. I had to put on this jump suit and bail out of an airplane at 2,000 feet. While I was undressing and pulling off all my street clothes, the photographer took a picture of me with my cock and balls hanging out. I understand that picture of me jaybird naked hangs in the bathrooms of most of the gay men in town. I hope they enjoy looking at what they can't have."

"I've never seen that nude," she said.

"No problem," he told her. "You'll get to see the real thing…up close and personal."

"I've always thought of you as a man on a horse," she said.

"That's how I got my start even before the modeling gigs. I worked as a stableboy for Will Rogers, the famous cowboy, when I first came to America. Horseshit and I are old acquaintances. I watched all the big stars come to Will's ranch in the Pacific Palisades for polo games. Clark Gable, Spencer Tracy. I was determined one day to join their ranks and become a big star myself."

"I spent three hours with Glenn," Linda later told Renay. "He wanted fellatio. He wanted the front door, the rear door, rimming, armpit lapping, toe sucking, the works. He was a great lover, and I adored his cock. In between our lovemaking, when we stopped for a rest, he talked about his love affairs, unlike Frank Sinatra, who is close lipped on the subject."

"After I gave him a great blow-job, he rested up before the next round. Then he took hold of his meat, and said, 'Rita [Hayworth] couldn't get enough of this. Neither could Judy [Garland], who got mad at me when I wasn't up for a fourth round. Debbie [Reynolds] was more restrained. Eva [Gabor] treated it like a Hungarian salami.'"

"Margaret Sullavan, that whore, told me that I had nearly three inches more than her former husband, Henry Fonda," Ford claimed.

"After Barbara Stanwyck broke up with that fag, Robert Taylor, she called me. It was Christmas Eve, and she asked me to come over. When she opened the door, she was wearing this pink 'Baby Doll' négligée and holding a glass of champagne for me. 'Come in, Glenn. Take me right away to my bedroom and make me a woman again,' she said to me."

Years later, as Linda recalled, "After he fucked me in the baby-making way, he talked of future plans."

"I like Westerns, and I've made a hell of a lot of them," he said. "Right now, I'm negotiating about doing a TV Western series. You might be terrific in it, and I could get you the role of a cowgirl. It's not a star part, but you're a natural beauty who'd look fabulous in the outdoors."

458

"Today in Hollywood, a lot of glamour queen in Westerns look like they've just stepped out of a Max Factor showroom on Rodeo Drive. They're not convincing on a horse. I mean, did you really believe my former shack-up, Joan Crawford, in a Western? 'Bloody hell, no,' as we used to say when I was growing up in Québec province."

Before she left, he made her a lot of promises, but when she called the next day, she was told he was not in his suite. She phoned again the following afternoon, and a man at the reception desk informed her, "Mr. Ford is out for the day."

Trying one final time, she called him on the third day, only to be told that "Mr. Ford left early this morning for Los Angeles."

Over a drink with Renay, Linda told her, "I can't say you didn't warn me. Glenn and I are not going to ride off into the sunset in any Western TV series. Dale Evans can safely keep her title as Queen of the Cowgirls. She's also welcome to keep that cowpoke, Roy Rogers. One ride with him in the saddle was enough for me."

"You'll see Glenn again," Renay predicted. "In a few weeks, he'll show up for more of your special talents. I know him well. Except this time, I'll get my revenge on him."

"How?" Linda asked.

A steely determination crossed Renay's face. "You'll see when the time comes."

***

Liz Renay and Pupu Jr. were planning their return from Palm Springs to Los Angeles.

She had some business with the real estate agent in Palm Springs who had rented them their villa. She was gone for about two hours, which allowed Linda a chance to enjoy Pupu for a final time. This time, he wanted only a deep-throating, the successful completion of which challenged even an expert like her. She'd later proclaim, "Pupu had enough for three men."

When Renay returned from her errand, she seemed excited. "Honey, I've got another gig for you. Glenn Ford is a tightwad, but Frank Sinatra, as I know from personal experience, is most generous.

I ran into Brad Dexter, who's temporarily living in Frankie's villa in Rancho Mirage *[an upscale resort and residential community a few miles southeast of Palm Springs.]* He's talked to Frankie, and he has a job for you—actually two separate engagements. You'll probably get two thousand dollars if you perform the sexual services you do so well."

"Actually, I think Brad wants to seduce you, too," Renay said. "He loved

Deep Throat."

"Who in hell is Brad Dexter?" she asked. "I've never heard of him."

"He's one of Frankie's best friends, a real handsome actor. He was married to Miss Peggy Lee. If you take the job, I'll fill you in on Brad."

"Who will I have to service?" she asked.

"Two real bigshots," Renay said. "Brad is sworn to silence, but I think we're talking A-list here."

"I could do worse," she said. "Call this Brad boy and tell him I'm his gal."

As Renay and Linda were packing in preparation for vacating their rented villa, Renay described Dexter in such glowing terms that Linda was intrigued and looking forward to meeting him.

After kissing Pupu and Renay goodbye, with promises to meet up again real soon, Linda migrated to the villa owned by Frank Sinatra.

Dexter was still handsome and in good physical condition. He greeted her in his bathing suit, and she admired his physique, which he'd kept in good shape, despite his status as a man in his mid-fifties.

Square-jawed, like Charlton Heston, and broad shouldered, Dexter had strong sex appeal for both men and women. Film critics called him, "the sweetest meanie ever to slug a hero or tussle with a lady." A bisexual, he'd had affairs with Marilyn Monroe, whom he'd first seduced when they made *The Asphalt Jungle* (1950), and the deeply closeted Paul Newman.

The actor invited her for a late breakfast, which was served by a maid on the patio next to a swimming pool.

"I have a house guest," Dexter said, "one of my all time best friends. He's a late sleeper. By the way, he says he knows you. Met you at Hefner's Playboy mansion."

"I met so many guys there," she said. "Who is he?"

"You'll find out later," he said. "It's a surprise."

During the week she was to spend with Dexter in Frank Sinatra's villa, she learned a lot more about him. Although she didn't remember the actor's name, she recognized his face at once from a Western movie, *The Magnificent Seven* (1960), in which he'd appeared with Yul Brynner (one of her earlier conquests), Steve McQueen (an even earlier conquest), James Coburn, Charles Bronson, Robert Vaughn, and Horst Buchholz.

Dexter was known for his brief and stormy marriage to singer Peggy Lee, which had lasted from January to November of 1953.

At the time Linda met Dexter, he was married to Mary Bogdonovich, the Star-Kist Tuna heiress, since 1971. But she was nowhere to be seen.

His friendships with Sinatra began when Dexter saved the singer from drowning on May 10, 1964 during production of the World War II film *None But the Brave* on the Hawaiian island of Kauai. Sinatra had been swept out to sea by the outgoing tide and had nearly drowned until plucked to safety by Dexter. Sinatra and Dexter later co-starred in a second film together, *Van Ryan's Express* (1965).

"When I produced this British spy thriller, which wasn't much of a thriller, *The Naked Runner* (1967), Frank and I fought," Dexter told Linda over morning coffee. "He refused to finish the film, and it was hell getting it completed. Frank fired me when I couldn't put up with his nonsense any more. We've only recently made up."

"I really love Frank Sinatra, and he loves me," Dexter told her. "Don't get the wrong idea. Frank and I are just close friends. He's still pissed off that I saved his life. He would have preferred it if he'd saved my life because then *I* would have been beholden to him."

From one of the bedrooms emerged the mysterious house guest. He was completely nude.

"Linda," he said. "We meet again."

It was Yul Brynner.

***

As Linda would later recall, "Yul Brynner and Brad Dexter were about as intimate as any two actors could be. Sticking your dick in another man is as close as two guys can get. They also like women, too. That's where I came in."

After *The Magnificent Seven,* Brynner and Dexter had made three more movies with each other, including *Tara Bulba* (1962); *Kings of the Sun* (1963), and *Invitation to a Gunfighter* (1964), none of which Linda had seen.

During his breakfast with Dexter and Linda, Brynner managed to at least cover his genitals with a large orange bath towel. "For some reason, Frank prefers the color orange," Brynner said. "I needed a pair of underwear. I looked in his drawer. Would you believe Frank has his jockey shorts dyed orange?"

Although very close, Dexter and Brynner also teased each other. "I told you, Linda, I love Frankie as a friend, but Yul here has long had the hots for him. Too bad Frankie won't give Yul a tumble."

One of Andy Warhol's prized possessions was this nude of **Yul Brynner,** a large version of which he hung in his living room.

A bisexual actor, like so many other Hollywood stars, Brynner won praise from many of his conquests. Deborah Kerr called him "Very, very handsome and very very sensual."

Linda agreed with that.

"Hope never dies until it dies," Brynner recited in his native Russian tongue, a phrase which he then translated for them.

After breakfast, Linda learned that Sinatra's "big name" guest would be arriving the following day. The two actors tantalized her by not revealing who it would be. "I'll give you a clue," Dexter said. "He was the most publicized actor in the history of the world during the 1960s."

"Not only that, but he says he's met you before, but only briefly," Brynner said. "I think he wants to get better acquainted."

As she remembered, "I'd been given a powerful clue with the phrase 'most publicized actor' thing. I'm a movie buff, too, and I should have gotten it, but I didn't. I was soon to find out, though."

According to Linda, "By mid-afternoon, Brad and Yul, along with yours truly, stripped down and swam nude in the pool," Linda said. "We had a real good time. I was already familiar with Yul's dick and Dexter's held out a meaty promise."

Before nightfall, all three of us were in bed together," she said. "I knew what was in store. We spent a good two hours there, and we covered all fronts, meaning if anybody had a hole, it got stuffed, or licked. Both men reached my throat. Although those two guys were middle aged, they still had a lot of man left in them...and a lot of sperm, I might add. Both of them made great sexual partners for men or women, and both of them had had Marilyn Monroe. Now I was getting the best of them."

Two views of **Brad Dexter**

Linda: "He was a handsome hunk of a man, a Serbo-Croatian. When we'd fuck, he'd sometimes switch to his native tongue as he goaded me on."

"In addition to seducing stars like Marilyn Monroe, he also went for some of his leading men, or so claimed Liz Renay."

lower photo: with **Evelyn Keyes** in *River City*

Later, over drinks around the pool, Dexter said to Linda, "Now that you've had Yul again, when he isn't stoned on opium, do you understand why he broke Marlene Dietrich's heart? Not only that, but Nancy Davis told me he's a much better fuck than Ronnie."

"Although that may be true, Brad," Brynner cautioned him, "let's keep things like that our secret. People don't know my real life, and they're not about to find out."

In spite of the polite warning, a drunken Dexter continued teasing his friend. "Do you know what Yul has in common with Mickey Cohen? Both of them claim that Sal Mineo has the best ass to fuck in Hollywood."

Later, she couldn't remember all the inside Hollywood gossip she heard during her sojourn with Dexter and Brynner at Sinatra's villa. But she felt she was getting personal information not available within the scandal-seeking tabloids and certainly not within the movie magazines. One story she remembered for no other reason than its pathos:

Dexter told Linda and Brynner that in 1964, he and Sinatra shared a villa in Italy, where they were shooting *Van Ryan's Express*. Ava Gardner, Sinatra's former wife, was also there, filming *The Bible* with George C. Scott, with whom she was having a torrid, sometimes violent, affair.

"Frankie and I lived at this villa on the Via Appia outside the center of Rome," Dexter said. "One night, he invited Ava *sans* Scott for dinner. She got so drunk, he told her to take one of the bedrooms upstairs and sleep it off. He watched in dismay as she staggered up the steps. After she'd gone, he turned to me and said, 'Ava's the only dame I ever really loved in my whole life. Look at her now. She's forty-two years old, and looking it, and she's nothing but a falling-down boozer.'"

Before lunch the following day, Linda spent two hours working on her dress and make-up in preparation for this visitor who had specifically wanted to meet her again after their original brief encounter.

She was sitting in the living room, "artfully arranged," as she remembered it, when the guest arrived. Brynner and Dexter were out by the pool, *sans* bathing trunks.

The houseboy led the way. She looked up to star into the face of Richard Burton.

To her surprise, on his arm was a beautiful black woman, a real stunner.

***

Richard Burton gave Linda a quick kiss on the lips before disappearing into a bedroom with his black beauty. He looked exhausted and far older than his forty-eight years.

As Linda recalled, "His lovely brown belle didn't appear too friendly. Burton wasn't too anxious to hang out with Brad and Yul either, and even less with me. He wanted privacy. He kept his girlfriend under wraps, and didn't join us for dinner either. We were collectively sharing Sinatra's villa, but we seemed to have divided into two different camps."

"I had expected that I'd be summoned to Burton's bed that night, not knowing he'd arrive with company," Linda said. "Instead, I slept between Brad and Yul, and we had another wonderful romp."

At around 2am, I heard Burton shouting at his bedmate," Linda said. "She seemed to have pissed him off royally. But we heard no sound from her. It seemed like a one-way fight to me. I bet if he'd been with Liz Taylor, he would have a knock-out, drag-out prize bout."

The next morning, she called Sammy Davis, Jr., who was anxious to know what was going on at Sinatra's villa. She told him about Burton arriving with a black woman.

"I don't know her name. We weren't introduced. She's very pretty, I'm certain about her measurements: Bust 36", waist 23", hips 36". She stands about five feet two inches and weighs some 120 pounds, maybe less. By the way, I always believe in 'sizing up' my competition."

"Dick and I have no trouble crossing the color line," Sammy said. "I'm not sure who this gal could be. It might be Jean Bell *[sometimes credited as Jeanne Bell]*. We in the African-American community know who Bell is. She was the second black woman to appear as a centerfold in Hefner's *Playboy*...during the autumn of 1969, if memory serves.

[Sammy may have made a good guess, but it appears that he was wrong about the identity of Burton's date. Bell's romance, a three-month affair, with Burton wasn't until 1975, as exposed by columnist Earl Wilson.]

Late the following morning, the mystery woman was seen leaving in a limousine specifically summoned to Sinatra's villa to fetch her. Dexter and Brynner had gone off somewhere. "I don't know where they went, they didn't say," Linda said. "Everyone associated with Sinatra's villa came and went with no explanation. I hung out waiting for Burton to appear. Eventually, at 1pm, he emerged from his bedroom wearing an orange bathing suit for a vodka lunch."

"You must have borrowed that bathing suit from Sinatra," Linda said. "He loves orange in his wardrobe—orange shirts, orange pants, no doubt orange condoms."

"Elizabeth Taylor told the press that she got an orgasm listening to the voice of **Richard Burton**," Linda said.

"He was a bit worn out by the time he got to me, having done everyone from Laurence Olivier to Barbra Streisand. I was one in about a thousand."

"No doubt," Burton said. "Maybe Frank suffers from citrus deprivation like British sailors of old, or limeys as they were called." When the maid served him grapefruit, he pushed it away. "I need a drink more than Vitamin C."

"I'm sorry I didn't get to meet your friend," Linda said.

Burton ignored that and indulged instead in some idle chit-chat until he asked what he had seemed to really want to know. "Forgive me, but I won't even suggest that your clitoris is in your throat, although it appeared to be in that movie of yours. But I really must know one thing. Do you like to perform fellatio more than you like for a bloke to plow your quim?"

"I like to be fucked as much as the next girl," she said. "But I enjoy giving head. I like to please a man, and it's exciting to have a man implode down my throat."

"I never quite got the hang of cocksucking, although I did enough of it during the war," he said. "I had a homosexual period then, but it didn't take. Today, I prefer a young man only on the third Thursday of any month. Otherwise, I'm strictly a Bluebeard."

"I read that was the name of your last picture, *Bluebeard,* shot in Budapest."

"You're absolutely right," he said. "When the director, Edward Dmytryk, went looking for a ladykiller like Bluebeard, he thought first of me. That's called type casting. That devil surrounded me with beautiful temptations to make me forget my wedding vows—Raquel Welch, Vira Lisi, Joey Heatherton, Nathalie Delon—she's the wife of Alain."

"Eddie Fisher told me about his affair with Delon's wife," Linda said.

"So, Eddie's got around to her too, with that little circumsized dick of his. Elizabeth accused me of having affairs with all these women, although I think I missed one. I'm experiencing seven-year itch."

"As for Elizabeth, she's experiencing the rages of turning forty. I threw a birthday bash for her in Hungary. Noël Coward told me it's impossible to live with any actress when she turns forty, although how that old sod would know that is a mystery to me."

"Forgive me for asking, but does Liz know you're here?"

"I don't think so," he said. "Actually, I don't think she gives a damn. We're tired of each other. She's back running around with her fags—Peter Lawford, Roddy McDowall, Laurence Harvey. All of those guys have had me, so why not? As actresses in Hollywood age, they become fag hags. All the straight blokes are chasing after the young stuff."

"Elizabeth and I are not only tiring of each other, but even the tabloids are bored with our exploits. With my career going into a sinkhole, I've been able to obliterate my thoughts in a stormy sea of vodka. But even that has its downside. As a man veers dangerously close to the age of fifty, there is little toleration for his drinking. When you're in your twenties or even your early thirties, you can get away with it. After that, you're nothing but an old drunk."

"Well, if Liz decides to divorce you, I'm sure that half the women in the world will line up to take her place," Linda said.

"You flattering little doll," he said. "I think divorce is inevitable. I've thought about it. I'm going to give her *carte blanche.* If I know the greedy bitch, she'll take everything. I will return to England with no diamonds, no yacht, no bank account, no art collection, nothing, except the impressive collection of books she once gave me. The only way I'll be able to survive is by my own talent, and there's precious little of that left now."

"I don't believe that," she said. "I bet you have a lot of life left in you."

"That's why I wanted to meet you," he said. "You've got to prove to me I do. With my black beauty last night, I was impotent. I blamed it on her. You may have heard me cursing her. But it wasn't the bitch's fault. She couldn't do it for me. With you, I have high hopes. Surely the world's greatest blow-job artist can make my overused tool come alive again."

"Please, let me try," she said. "Shall we go to the bedroom?"

"In a minute, my love," he said. "First, I need to tank myself up with more lubrication."

Thirty minutes later found a nude Burton and a nude Linda together in bed. The sheets hadn't been changed from the previous night, and Burton had completely wrecked Sinatra's bedroom.

"I began by kissing him with plenty of tongue," Linda said. "He was a great kisser. At least he could do that. I always like to kiss a man's neck, all of his neck. But on the back of Burton's neck I discovered craters the size of those on the moon. They were like sinkholes with blackheads. Talk about a turn-off!"

"Later, I faced that uncut Welsh coalminer's dick," she said, "the very same one that had enthralled the love goddess of the world. I found it difficult making it rise up. The size was perfectly adequate for the job, but nothing you would write home about."

"I was determined to prove to him that he wasn't impotent," she said. "The effort exhausted him, not to mention me. He slept for four or five hours before getting up to join Yul and Brad for a night of vodka. I stayed up as long as I could, but ended up sleeping in the spare bedroom that night by myself."

"Three famous movie stars and me, the reigning porn actress of my time, and I'm sleeping alone. Burton didn't even leave me a diamond. Sinatra, however, ordered Brad to give me two thousand dollars. At least I got *something* from it."

Her final memory of Richard Burton occurred the following morning as she watched Brynner and Dexter escorting him to a waiting limousine, the two actors flanking him and propping him up every step of the way.

Afterwards, turning back to the villa, she had the day to herself, as Dexter and Brynner had informed her that they were going somewhere.

She welcomed the time alone as a means of making her skin and her allure as seductive as possible. Dexter had told her that Sinatra's final guest—"One of the world's most important men"—would be arriving late the following morning.

***

President John F. Kennedy, in 1961, stated, "Long after he has ceased to sing, Frank Sinatra is going to be standing up for the Democratic Party." The crooner himself had proclaimed, "I'm a lifelong Democrat."

How wrong both men were.

Shirley MacLaine once said, "Frank hated Nixon with a deep vitriol."

For years, Sinatra had also detested Ronald Reagan, referring to him as "a bozo, or *Bonzo,* and a stupid bore," a reference not only to his politics but to the movie Reagan had made. It was *Bedtime for Bonzo,* a harmless little 1951 comedy which is often cited as "the pinnacle of absurdity" in Reagan's career. In it, he played a professor who treats a chimp as a human child in a scientific experiment associated with heredity.

Years of being rebuffed by the Kennedys, including a feud with Attorney General Robert F. Kennedy, had taken its toll on Sinatra's loyalty to the Democrats. He had wanted to be named U.S. Ambassador to Italy, but JFK had passed him over.

Sinatra referred to RFK as "that fuckin' cop," a reference to his previous history of prosecuting the Mafia. When RFK was assassinated in 1968, Sinatra said. "I'll shed no tears."

In an act of revenge against the Kennedys, Sinatra supported Reagan when he ran for re-election as Governor of California in 1970.

Sinatra was still denouncing Nixon, a Republican, as late as July of 1970.

In the White House, the Republicans eventually decided that "Sinatra can be had," meaning he could be lured, time and circumstances permitting, into the Republican ranks.

President Nixon spent Spiro Agnew as his agent to woo Sinatra, despite the fact that by that time, Nixon was already disgusted with his vice president. Privately, he told his aide, Charles Colson, "These two sleazeballs from crooked Mediterranean stock should talk each other's gutter language."

Agnew flew at once to Palm Springs, where he invited Sinatra for a round of golf at a local country club. The game of golf led to a bonding that climaxed in an Italian dinner that night. At a club, it turned out that the Vice President had been hooked since the 1940s on the crooners of the Big Band era, adoring the music of Jo Stafford, Peggy Lee, the Andrew Sisters, but mostly the sounds of Sinatra himself. Regrettably it was never recorded, but Agnew on the piano occasionally accompanied Sinatra as he sang three of Agnew's favorite songs— "Star Dust," "I'll Never Smile Again," and "Smoke Gets in Your Eyes."

In the months that followed, Agnew visited Sinatra in Palm Springs some eighteen times. At the Pussycat Theatre in Los Angeles and in Sinatra's den in Palm Springs, they had watched *Deep Throat* twice. Although Agnew was generally faithful to his wife, Judy, Sinatra suggested that he could, if Agnew were willing, arrange a "date" for him with Linda Lovelace.

"Even the most faithful husband likes to knock off a piece now and then," Sinatra told Agnew. Sinatra later revealed to Brad Dexter what he'd said, and subsequently, it was Dexter who made the final arrangements for the "historic" meeting between Agnew and Linda.

The rendezvous was scheduled to take place in Sinatra's guest quarters, which the singer had, a decade previously, remodeled and enlarged for a visit from then-President John F. Kennedy—a visit that never materialized.

[At the last minute, in a decision that was bruited remorselessly around Hollywood, Robert Kennedy, the Attorney General, demanded that his brother cancel his stopover in Sinatra's home because of Sinatra's mob associations. Kennedy, with Marilyn Monroe, ended up in bed together at Bing Crosby's guest cottage instead. Ironically, RFK's decision to switch venues didn't seem to take into account the fact that unlike Sinatra, Crosby had been a lifelong Republican.

Infuriated by what he perceived as a snub and an insult, Sinatra switched his political loyalties from the Democrats to the Republicans--so much so, in fact that during the waning months of Nixon's reign, Sinatra was so closely linked to his administration that the Secret Service assigned him the code name "Napoleon."

In the aftermath of all this switch-hitting, Gore Vidal asserted, "Sinatra became a neutered creature of the American Right, an Italo-American Faust. But his deal with the Republican Devil got him nowhere."

Surprisingly, Sinatra's loyalty to Agnew would survive during the political upheavals ahead, even after the Watergate stigma exploded and the media associated an important anonymous witness to the illegalities of the Nixon camp with a nickname ("Deep Throat") lifted directly from the name of Linda's infamous movie.

Sinatra lent Agnew money and stood by him even after his resignation, in disgrace, on October 10, 1973, as U.S. Vice President, pleading no contest to tax evasion charges from the IRS.

But all of that disgrace and disappointment lay in Agnew's (dismal) future on the sunny day

"Deep Throat (or somebody using that name) brought down the Nixon administration," Linda said.

"But months before that happened, I deep throated his potential replacement. I wish **Spiro Agnew** *(photo above)* had not been a crook and would have replaced Nixon as president."

"If that had happened, I would have volunteered to be for him what Marilyn was to JFK."

he arrived at Sinatra's compound in Rancho Mirage for a holiday in one of its guest cottages. In honor of his visit, Sinatra had re-named the building "Agnew House."]

Linda didn't know until the last minute the identity of the politician she'd be entertaining. Ushered inside by Dexter, three Secret Service agents had arrived to check the layout and security of Sinatra's compound in Rancho Mirage, a routine procedure for them. Since the men were not identified to her, she did not know they'd been assigned to their duty by the White House.

She was asked to remain in her bedroom at the time of Agnew's arrival. She would later learn that this mysterious politician was traveling without his wife.

Dexter told her he'd summon her later. Almost as a footnote, he added, "Frankie is still that little kid from Hoboken who likes to get patted on the head by Presidents. But Lyndon Johnson wasn't impressed with Frank like Nixon is. He gave him a cheap tube of lipstick with the White House seal on it. LBJ told him that flashing that lipstick as a gift would make him a big man with the ladies. Frankie was deeply insulted. He later told me, 'I don't need a tube of lipstick to impress a broad.'"

"Are you telling me that Nixon is here?" Linda asked Dexter. "I despise him. Are you telling me I'm supposed to suck off Richard Nixon, something I'm sure that even Pat has never done."

"Not quite, but you're going to be asked to go down on—potentially at least—the next President of the United States. Right now a poll I read showed that at least thirty-five percent of Americans want this guy to become the next president, and he hasn't even announced himself as a candidate yet."

"Okay, the time has come," she said. "Just who in hell is this big shot?"

"It's Spiro Agnew."

***

The morning after her session with Agnew, Linda was driven in a sleek black limousine from Sinatra's estate in Rancho Mirage back to Los Angeles. She interpreted the event as the stylish prelude to her upcoming publicity tour in New York for the release of her book, *Inside Linda Lovelace,* and for her movie, *Deep Throat Part II.*

She'd later confide to Liz Renay, "I gave Agnew two blow-jobs—one before dinner and another right before midnight. He was most polite, although he kept his shirt and socks on. At least he pulled off his panties and shoes."

"How was it?" Renay asked. "Tell Mama."

"It was the kind of uncut meat you might find on thousands of Greek fishermen—not too big, but not too small either. To my knowledge, this was the first blow job of his life. He moaned and groaned like he was going out of his mind, and he became almost hysterical when I attacked his rosebud with my tongue. I don't think he'd ever had a tongue there before. It drove him wild."

"God, he was the cleanest man, like William Holden and Frank Sinatra. Those guys take so many showers, they must reduce the water supply in California. Maybe he was doing it just for me. I don't think he uses it all the time, but he found a bottle of Chanel No. 5 in Sinatra's bathroom and sprayed it around his groin."

"I didn't get to JFK like Marilyn did," Linda continued, "but if Agnew prevails in 1976 and actually gets elected, I too, will be able to say I've sucked off a President of the United States. Brad Dexter told me that the '76 race will probably pit Agnew against Teddy Kennedy. Regardless of who wins, I'll still be able to bill myself as the 'mistress' of a sitting president, even though that's a bit of exaggeration."

"In show business, honey, we call it poetic license," Renay said. "Every actress who has ever published her memoirs knows what I'm talking about."

Linda would be amazed, "completely balled over," as she'd later proclaim, when the 1976 race for the White House began.

It wouldn't be Ted Kennedy or Agnew running for President, but Linda herself seeking that high office, pitted against President Gerald Ford and a peanut farmer from Georgia, Jimmy Carter.

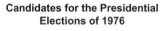

Candidates for the Presidential Elections of 1976

Republican **Gerald Ford** *(left)*
Democrat **Jimmy Carter** *(right)* and
center,
THE FELLATIO QUEEN OF AMERICA!

CHAPTER TWELVE
A Throat That Needs To Be Cut

The Mayor of New York, John Lindsay, had ordered that *Deep Throat* could not be shown in movie houses within the city limits.

But in August of 1972, a New York City jury ruled that *Deep Throat* was not obscene. Yet even after that ruling, anti-pornography crusaders sued Mature Enterprises, the owner of the New Mature World Theater on Manhattan's West 49th Street, on a charge of promoting obscenity. The trial occurred shortly before Christmas in 1972.

Some critics were called to testify, and most of them maintained that *Deep Throat* had social value because it "showed sympathy for female desires." One critic testified that the script contained humor and was "filmed with clarity and lack of grain." In opposition, a dissenting professor from New York University said, "I do not see how you can spoof fellatio by showing continuous performances of fellatio."

In dozens of public forums, the debate over *Deep Throat* continued. As one social critic phrased it, "Hardcore filmmaking was making overtures to the mainstream (and vice versa), as the sexual revolution of the 60s was trickling down to suburbia, and as first-wave feminism was demanding that its roar be heard, and that women's rights included the right to sexual pleasure on women's own terms."

Outside the courts, cultural warriors in both camps continued to issue their own opinions during Linda's "blitz of star fucking." [Chuck's words] in Hollywood.

Erica Jong, the sexually liberated novelist and social commentator who had created her own controversies after the publication of *Fear of Flying,* attacked the graphic sex of *Deep Throat.* "I was appalled at how offensive the idea of a woman with a clitoris in her throat was. How patriarchal."

Naturally, the squeaky clean singer, Pat Boone, of the 1950s, attacked *Deep Throat* as immoral and indecent. But most entertainers in Hollywood, including both Jack Nicholson and Warren Beatty, defended it, citing the First Amendment and rights of free speech as justification.

Despite its many defenders, Manhattan Judge Joel J. Tyler, after viewing the film, apparently the first porno movie he'd ever seen and by now a target in the early efforts of New York City to cleanse Times Square of its seamier elements, upheld the ban on *Deep Throat,* issuing the court's final judgment in March of 1973.

On the wrong side of cultural history, Tyler called the film "a nadir of decadence, a feast of carrion and squalor…and a Sodom and Gomorrah gone wild before the fire."

"This is one throat that deserves to be cut," he wrote. "I readily perform the operation by finding the defendant guilty as charged." Then he levied a fine of $100,000 against Mature Enterprises.

In response, the World Theater posted a marquee—JUDGE CUTS THROAT, WORLD MOURNS.

[Even judges reconsider their earlier verdicts, Years later, in 1991, Judge Tyler, during an interview with the New York Law Journal, reconsidered his judgment, saying, "If I were to write that appendix today, I would be deemed a fool, given the substantial change in our outlook."]

Judge Tyler's ruling only added to the cachet of the film. Mature Enterprises appealed Judge Tyler's decision. In Albany, at the Court of Appeals, his right-wing decision was overturned. The effect, in essence, was to legalize hardcore porn in New York State.

As newspapers proclaimed, "The floodgates were opened." One critic wrote, "If *Deep Throat* has been proven in court to have socially redeeming value, then virtually ANYTHING qualifies."

Despite the film's court victories in New York, serious legal challenges to *Deep Throat* were popping up in more conservative regions of the country with very different verdicts. A jury in Binghamton, New York, ruled that the movie was not obscene. A trial in Chicago led to a hung jury with a mistrial declared.

And so it went, from city to town, with *Deep Throat* emerging in triumph from some courthouses, and condemned by others.

Judicial rulings sometimes varied even within the same states. In Houston, a jury declared that *Deep Throat* was protected by the First Amendment. But in San Antonio, a theater was shut down when Linda's movie was defined as obscene.

Not since 1915, after the release of D.W. Griffin's *The Birth of a Nation,* had a film faced so many legal challenges. A total of twenty-seven states eventually banned *Deep Throat* within a climate whose outcome involved the manufacture of thousands of copies which were illegally transported across state lines and screened at private parties and within private homes.

The Perainos reaped the majority of profits spinning out of *Deep Throat,* but not without some mob-connected competition. In Los Angeles, beginning in 1973, an unrelated video pirating ring copied *Deep Throat* many thousands of times, along with dozens of other porn titles. Anthony ("The Animal") Fiato claimed, "We made *mucho dinero* from this fellatio flick. Even though the film was mob connected and protected by some of the East Coast Crime Families, we still grabbed some of the local porn purveyors and we would tell them, 'If you complain to New York, you will die here in Los Angeles.'"

More confusion was sowed on June 21, 1973, when the Supreme Court of the United States issued its judgment in the *Miller vs. California* case. The decision reiterated that obscenity was not protected by the First Amendment and established the Miller test for what constitutes obscene material.

The appellant, Marvin Miller, operated one of the largest mail-order businesses on the West Coast, dealing in pornography, and conducting a mass-mailing campaign to advertise the sale of "adult material."

"The immediate effect of the Supreme Court decision," said Bob Guccione, founder and publisher of *Penthouse,* will be to drive a multi-billion-dollar industry underground—and that means graft and crime in the real sense. It's the same thing as a return to Prohibition."

The High Court removed from the language of the law the clause about "utterly without redeeming social value," which had long been the favorite loophole for pornographers. Under the new law, any prosecutor wishing to ban a sexually explicit work no longer had to prove it was utterly without value; it merely had to lack serious literary, artistic, political, or scientific value to be considered obscene.

That meant that magazines such as *Penthouse* and *Playboy* or a film such as *Last Tango in Paris* might be judged obscene in towns where right wingers or religious zealots were in charge of legislating local morality.

After that ruling came down, the producers of *Deep Throat Part II* debated whether they should craft several different versions of that film, each with differing degrees of hard-core obscenity, with the understanding that reels could be selected or switched, depending on the laws and legal rulings that were in effect there at the time. The producers eventually abandoned that idea, opting instead to remove all of the hardcore scenes from that movie, fearing that subsequent lawsuits would mushroom if they didn't.

But before the producers arrived at that policy, Linda, who was still evaluating hard-core porn offers from her base at Linda Lovelace Enterprises, told a reporter that her future involvement in triple-X films "would be like a pie. Any hard core segments could be sliced and cut *[in advance of screenings]* in cities or towns where there was trouble brewing about obscenity laws."

Ominously, the FBI also became involved in the prosecution of *Deep Throat.* Agents had seized copies of the film and had analyzed many of its frames in their labs. They also interviewed Linda and the film's other actors as well as its producers.

Mark Weiner, a constitutional law professor at Rutgers-Newark School of Law, said, "Today, you can't imagine authorities at any level of government being involved in obscenity prosecutions of this kind. The story of *Deep Throat* is the story of the last gasp of the forces lined up against the cultural and sexual revolution, and it is the advent of the entry of pornography into the mainstream."

Most of the FBI's probe was centered on persons and theaters in New York City, but agents across the nation, from Detroit to Honolulu, also got deeply involved.

Under the Freedom of Information Act, the 498-page FBI file on *Deep Throat* was eventually made public. For reasons whose motivations remain baffling to most observers today, all of Linda's testimony within the file had been rendered unreadable ("whited-out") in ways akin to what scholars might have expected from a recently declassified high-security file from the CIA.

Ultimately, officials at virtually every level of government tried to prevent screenings of *Deep Throat*. And although Linda's movie and its interconnected obscenity trials dragged on for years, stopping the tide of new attitudes and legalities about obscenity became a losing battle.

In a bizarre twist, as lines of movie-goers waiting to see *Deep Throat* diminished, the flick was revived because of a burglary that took place on June 17, 1972 within the Watergate complex in Washington, D.C. In the political upheavals that followed, the nickname "Deep Throat" was assigned to an otherwise anonymous informant, a Nixon-administration whistleblower who met several times with reporters Bob Woodward and Carl Bernstein in the bowels of a parking garage.

[Howard Simons, Managing Editor of the prestigious Washington Post, *is the media mogul who coined the otherwise anonymous informant's code name as "Deep Throat." The informant's pronouncements from the shadowy depths of a D.C. parking garage added a heady whiff of cloak-and-dagger intrigue to the Watergate reportage. They also reinforced the "celebrity quotient" of Linda Lovelace, contributing to her status as the best-known porn star of all time.]*

In 1974, Linda immodestly asserted, "*Deep Throat,* with me as its star, brought down the Nixon presidency. Not bad for a little Catholic girl from Yonkers."

[It wasn't until three years before his death, in 2005 that Mark Felt, who had been Assistant Director of the FBI at the time of his retirement in 1974, would reveal himself to the general public as the whistleblower whose testimony had been so crucial to the unraveling of the Nixon Administration. Despite previous denials, Felt, at the time of his "confession," was ninety-two

years old, and presumably didn't care anymore about preserving the secrecy of his alter ego from the general public.]

As part of a deal Linda made with government prosecutors, when she agreed to give state's evidence in her film's obscenity trials, she would no longer be subject to prosecution. She was, however, obligated to make what evolved into a total of sixteen separate court appearances, including one particularly disastrous episode in Albuquerque, New Mexico.

To the fury of the judge, she appeared an hour late in court wearing no makeup and with her hair in rollers. Perhaps stoned, she rambled, sometimes incoherently, repeating her earlier, oft-repeated allegations that "When you watch *Deep Throat,* you're seeing me getting raped with a gun pointed at my head." She would spend the next two decades echoing that tired line, which virtually no one in Hollywood or the porn industry believed.

At each of her appearances at various obscenity trials nationwide, she was asked for her autograph by attorneys on both sides.

Prosecutors soon ascertained that she was "very, very flaky."

Chuck Traynor was especially skeptical of her testimony. "Archie Bunker called his Edith a dingbat. I'd call my Linda the same."

Bill Kelly, the special FBI agent who was directly responsible for investigating *Deep Throat* over a period of three years, never went after Linda. He was more interested in the mob money behind it. He later said, "All those peo-

"It took two Deep Throats to alter the cultural and political life of America," claimed author Gore Vidal. The Watergate scandal broke at the peak of popularity of Linda's film.

Nicknamed **Deep Throat, Mark Felt,** assistand director of the FBI, was the unnamed informant, who helped bring down the Nixon administration with his revelations to reporters Bob Woodward and Carl Bernstein.

However, his identity would not become known until 2005, three years before his death. Felt is seen above at various stages in his life, including how he looked *(lower right)* when he emerged from the darkness to let the world know who he was.

ple connected to *Deep Throat* were either immoral or amoral—a lot of them with mid-Mediterranean backgrounds, *ha, ha, ha.*"

Even though Linda ultimately gave testimony that could harm him, Harry Reems continued to defend her, although he "pooh-poohed" her claims of being forced to do porn. "She's a beautiful person," he claimed. "She had that magnetic ability to draw in an audience or anybody in a room directly to her. That twinkle of the eye, that real smile without phoniness or presumptuousness. She's a sweet, sweet girl, a very together person. She's not super bright, and she's not an actress, but she's totally open and free sexually."

Despite injunctions from judges banning the film in twenty-three states, injunctions that were ultimately overturned, *Deep Throat* ultimately legitimized pornography, as millions of American consumers became devotees, some of them addictively.

***

Of the many trials spinning around *Deep Throat,* the one that had the most far-reaching consequences took place in Memphis, Tennessee, the home of Elvis Presley. A series of grand jury indictments began on August 15, 1974, a process that would eventually fill up 1,000 pages of court documents and testimony as various distributors involved with the filming and release of *Deep Throat* were cited. Most of the charges involved the transport of the film across state lines.

Since Linda had volunteered as a witness for the State, she was not indicted. Amazingly, in Memphis, she was not called to testify, either, because of her previous statements before juries in other states. Behind the scenes, prosecutors had privately evaluated her as "a walking time bomb liable to explode at any time." Her reputation as an opponent of censorship had also been clearly noted by all sides of the debate.

At first, it had appeared that the distributors of *Deep Throat* would be the most difficult to prosecute. The film had been distributed, literally, from the trunks of cars by mob-connected "runners," couriers who had hauled the reels of *Deep Throat* from town to town across state lines.

Eventually, however, an undercover government agent succeeded in penetrating the film's distribution network. His name was Phil Mainier. On March 6, 1977, *The New York Times* reported that two of Mainier's severed fingers had been found inside his abandoned car. Later, the rest of his body was discovered in a shallow grave in Ohio.

Partly as a result of Mainer's slaying, Anthony Peraino, Sr., the financial backer of the movie, along with his son, Louis (Butchie) Peraino and some other distributors of the film, went on trial in Memphis for Interstate Transport

476

of Obscene Material.In a somewhat arbitrary decision, of the various actors in the film, only Harry Reems was fingered for prosecution.

Why Memphis? Because technically, based on the laws of that time, Interstate Transport of Obscene Material was prosecutable in any state the material passes through. And Tennessee at the time was a stronghold of Charles Keating, a semi-fanatical and spectacularly corrupt lawyer, banker, and financier whose notoriety would one day extend far beyond the fame of his association with Linda Lovelace.

Charles Keating, from his base in Memphis, had emerged as the most visible anti-porn crusader in the history of America, serving as a dissenting, and the most rabidly conservative, member of the President's Commission on Obscenity and Pornography.

In 1958, in his role as founder of the anti-obscenity group known variously, throughout its life as Citizens for Decent Literature, Citizens for Decency, and/or Citizens for Decency Through Law, he had testified before the House Judiciary Committee about mail-order porn, asserting that it "was capable of poisoning any mind at any age and of perverting our entire younger generation." Working closely with conservative authorities in the Catholic Church, he cited pornography as "part of the Communist conspiracy to destroy the United States."

His organization would grow to 100,000 members in 300 chapters nationwide, deluging members of Congress, officials in the Catholic Church, and regional politicians with some 40 million letters on behalf of its anti-porn positions.

In their designation of Linda as the symbol of a nation gone wrong, "Jezebel" and "Whore of Babylon" were two of the milder names assigned to her. One preacher asserted that she'd "sold her soul to the Devil in the hopes of dragging the rest of God fearing America with her in her journey to the pits of Hell."

In hypocritical contrast, Keating himself was *[wrongly]* defined by his constituents as "Mr. Clean." In defiance of the American trend, Keating evolved into the only member of the President's Commission on Pornography to dissent from its seventeen other members. Each of them had recommended that all laws against adults buying porn should be repealed. Keating, however, violently objected.

Charles Keating

A corrupted and very dangerous Puritan, configuring Linda Lovelace and homosexuals as the symbols of a nation gone wrong.

[The first film that Keating succeeded at suppressing, at least temporarily, was Russ Meyer's soft-core Vixen! *(1968) in Ohio. A few years later, according to reports at the time. Keating had "gone ballistic" after his first viewing of* Deep Throat. *More pervasive and longer-lived than his obsession with porn was Keating's fanatical endorsement of federal policies to persecute homosexuals: "All homosexuals should be prosecuted, sentenced, and thrown into jail." Keating never explained who would finance the incarceration of millions upon millions of American gays and lesbians, and how the government would suppress the inevitable bloodbaths that would ensue.]*

Linda came to view Keating as her "arch enemy," and delighted at his eventual downfall in the aftermath of his key role in the Savings and Loan scandals of the late 1980s—at the time the largest scandal in U.S. banking history. In 1990, he was indicted by the State of California on 42 counts related to having duped customers of the Lincoln Savings and Loan into buying worthless junk bonds. A sales manual from this period of his administration urged Keating's staff to "always remember that the weak, meek and ignorant are always good targets."

His subsequent trials and convictions, followed by appeals, have been the subject of entire books.

In the final count, Keating spent only four and a half years in jail. When his conviction was announced, Linda, with a sense of jubilation, asserted, "Harry Reems and I did not serve one day in jail, unlike Keating, the Perainos, and all those other mob figures linked to Deep Throat.*"*

The most controversial defendant at the Memphis trial was Reems. Among other citations, he faced charges of having "committed sodomy, fellatio, and cunnilingus."

The Hollywood community, in particular, was outraged by the charges against him. Dennis Hopper told the press, "This is the first time in U.S. history that an actor has been arrested and tried for merely playing a part."

Having earned virtually no money for his participation in Deep Throat, *Reems faced a legal bill that would grow to at least $150,000—and maybe a lot more.*

The author of this book helped to spearhead a drive in New York City to raise money to defray Reems' legal fees. Contributions were received from actors who included Laurence Olivier, Richard Burton, Paul Newman, Rock Hudson, Joan Blondell, and such authors as Arthur Miller, Tennessee Williams, Gore Vidal, and Truman Capote.

In an episode of blatant hypocrisy, Reems had to defend himself in a TV interview against a "morally outraged" attacker, the notoriously corrupt Roy Cohn. Cohn had vindictively functioned as Senator Joseph McCarthy's chief assistant during the anti-communist witch hunts of the early 1950s. A closeted homosexual and a close friend and collaborator of FBI Director J. Edgar Hoover, the ever-combative Cohn became a legend for shady dealings that frequently ran very close to the edge of the law.

After Cohn's death in 1986 from complications associated with AIDS, one of the largest collections of pornography in New York was discovered at his residence. It included a framed nude photo of Reems hanging in his bathroom, and three copies of Deep Throat.

Bruce Kahmer, the attorney for Reems, claimed, "It wasn't an obscenity trial at all, but a racketeering and tax evasion trial." Those allegations certainly did not involve Reems, however, who had to spend his own money for his appearance in Deep Throat, having been paid "peanuts" for his work before and behind the camera.

The FBI's Bill Kelly said that after talking to Reems at the trial, he defined him as "A Cat on a Hot Tin Roof. He was friendly to me, thinking perhaps I was going to protect him from the Perainos. Actually, I was trying to put him in jail."

There was rampant speculation that Reems would be repeatedly gang raped if he was sent to jail.

The trial in Memphis began on March 1, 1976. The chief prosecutor was Larry Parrish, an assistant district attorney working in cooperation with the FBI, the IRS, and the U.S. Justice Department. In all, the government spent a million dollars trying to protect "the moral standards of the citizens of Memphis."

Parrish, the Memphis prosecutor, functioned as an Elder in that city's First Evangelical Church of Christ. Early in his career, he had aggressively earned a reputation as "the bogeyman of porn." Reems referred to him as a zealot for having tried a dozen obscenity trials in

Prior to their legal harrassment of the stars of *Deep Throat*, prosecutors in Memphis wanted to throw into jail, for years, the stars of **Carnal Knowledge**, presumably because of their depiction on screen of their carnal knowledge.

top photo, left to right: **Art Garfunkel, Candice Bergen,** and **Jack Nicholson** along with (*lower left*) **Ann-Margret** and (*lower right*) **Rita Moreno.**

one year.

In what could be considered as legal overreach, Parrish had seriously debated the merits of arresting the stars of Carnal Knowledge—*Jack Nicholson, Art Garfunkel, Rita Moreno, Candice Bergen, and Ann-Margret.*

"If we can jail these famous actors, it will send a signal to the rest of Hollywood to make no more movies like Carnal Knowledge," *Parrish claimed.*

"I'm looking at at least twenty years each for both Nicholson and Garfunkel," Parrish is alleged to have said. "Maybe less for Ann-Margret and the other gals."

Porn producer Fred Lincoln referred to Parrish as "a maniac," although the State of Georgia agreed with Parrish that Carnal Knowledge *was obscene. "But Georgia is known for placing on the bench the most ignorant and bigoted judges in the nation, at times outranking Alabama and Mississippi as regards who can be the most stupid," claimed reporter Steve Trumball.*

When Parrish was called a prude, he told reporters, "I'm not a eunuch, but a red-blooded American male. Referring to the defendants in the Deep Throat *trial, he said, "If you dance, you must pay the Piper, and I'm the Piper."*

Based on what was revealed during the trial, Reems was quoted as saying, "I started hearing about people being killed; baseball bats on projectionists' heads; money going to The Bahamas, and I soon realized that I was mixed up with the wrong crowd. Every day in court I sat on the witness bench, I'd move a little farther away from them."

At the beginning of the trial, the jury was friendly to Reems until they were collectively transported by bus to a movie house in a downtown neighborhood of Memphis. When the hearing resumed, they stared at Reems with hostility, interpreting him as a sexual pervert.

Back in the courtroom, Parrish offended some members of the court by being too graphic in his questions. "Did you seem Reems take his penis out and ejaculate all over Miss Lovelace? Did you see his semen run from her eyes into her mouth as she licked it with her lips?"

As regards the outcome of the Memphis trial, in a story published in The

New York Times *on May 1, 1977, a reporter wrote: "Federal District Judge Harry W. Wellford passed sentences on the men convicted in the* Deep Throat *obscenity trial. Distributors sentenced were Carl Carter, Anthony Novello, Michael Cherubino, Mario DeSalvo, Joseph Peraino, Sr. (brother of Anthony), and Louis*

("Butchie") Peraino. Fines ranged from $1,500 to $10,000, and sentences varied from two years (with five months suspended), to a five-year probation with no jail time. The judge delayed sentencing Anthony Peraino, Sr., because he'd fled the country. No one saw him again until around five years later.

The Federal jury in Memphis, which Reems defined as "the buckle of the Bible Belt," convicted him of conspiracy for his role as the doctor in Deep Throat. He faced five years in prison and a $10,000 fine.

The famous attorney, Alan M. Dershowitz, a deeply respected professor of criminal law at Harvard, referred to Reems' conviction as an outrage and subsequently orchestrated Reems' successful appeal. "Here is an actor who works on a film when the type of work he was doing was constitutionally protected. One year later, the Supreme Court changes its ruling and the actor is charged with a crime."

Gerard Damiano Film Productions was also indicted, but the director, like Linda, had agreed to give state's evidence, so no charges were ever filed against him personally. Gerard Damiano Productions, however, was fined $10,000.

The defendants each appealed their case to a higher court. Their retrial was conducted in Memphis in 1978, at which time Reems was dropped as a defendant. The other defendants lost their appeal.

In 1981 and in poor health, Peraino, Sr., returned to the United States from his self-imposed exile in Italy and turned himself in to the authorities. He was fined $15,000 and sentenced to ten months in prison based on his 1976 conviction and for jumping bail.

Mario DeSalvo had been the international distributor of Deep Throat. He would be tried and judged as not guilty. He ended up, however, paying the ultimate price. In Italy, hoping to collect a greater share of the film's box office receipts, he made a strong appeal to Tony Peraino, Sr. For his impudence in having demanded more money, he ended up as "fish food," according to FBI special agent Bill Kelly.

Tony Peraino's brother, Joseph Peraino, Sr., along with his son, Joseph Peraino, Jr., may have escaped lightly in the courts, but their bosses, the Colombo crime family, determined their ultimate fate after discovering "we're getting ripped off" from the massive amounts of money generated by Deep Throat, which, despite its travails in Memphis, continued raking in vast sums around the world. Millions of dollars worth of box office receipts were deposited in the Cayman Islands.

Joseph Sr. ("the Fat Guy") and his son ("the Whale) became highly visible targets, as each was obese. Even the Colombo crime bosses defined these two fatties as having been "bottom feeders all their street lives."

Federal law enforcement authorities claimed that on January 4, 1982, the Colombo bosses sent two of their associates—"Big Sal" and "Junior Lol-

lipops"—*to the Gravesend neighborhood of Brooklyn to assassinate the Joseph Perainos. Senior and Junior.*

Caught in the crossfire as the Perainos desperately sought shelter from the pursuing hit team, a former nun, 53-year-old Veronica Zuraw (formerly known as Sister Mary Adelaide), was fatally shot in the head as she folded laundry in her home. Joseph Jr. died in the gunfire.

Miraculously, Joseph Sr. survived. Doctors claimed that he survived because of the many layers of fat ensconcing his body. In the aftermath, however, he was paralyzed for life.]

***

[In 2012, forty years after the release of Deep Throat, *a final mystery associated with its saga was finally clarified,*

That year, a District Attorney from Upstate New York, a former Bronx prosecutor, finally admitted that he had been the actor, identified in the film's credits as "Gus Thomas," who had starred with Linda and Reems in the 1974 sequel to Deep Throat. *Democrat Mark Suben confessed to his involvement in the film after a Syracuse (New York) television station broadcast a photo from a YouTube video featuring a porn actor who looked suspiciously like him.*

Prior to his 2012 election, Suben had consistently denied having appeared in any porn flick, charging that his political rivals were attempting to sully his reputation. After his "outing," he apologized for his "bad judgment" during his involvement as a player in adult films. Suben, who has also served as a judge,

said, "I am shocked and embarrassed to be confronted with an indiscretion of my youth. I humbly apologize to my family, friends, my staff, and my supporters."

Amazingly, today, descendants of the Perainos are living in luxury mansions and driving custom-made cars because of Linda's talented throat, even though her own life ended in poverty.]

Vote!

Linda Lovelace for President!

Mark Suben *(both photos above)* for District Attorney!

482

***

[After his trial in Memphis and during its subsequent appeal, Reems became an honored guest of Hugh Hefner at the Playboy Mansion West in Los Angeles. He was also seen "hanging out" in Malibu with actor Steve McQueen, both of whom had had the honor of screwing Linda.

McQueen was a bisexual, as revealed and detailed in Blood Moon's 2009 biography, Steve McQueen, King of Cool. *McQueen had complained to his female biker friends "If I had a dick as big as that of Harry Reems, I would no longer have a case of penis envy."*

Until he got his life back together again, booze and drugs took a toll on Reems. A few years after the trial, he was spotted panhandling beside Sunset Boulevard in Hollywood.

Later in his life, Reems, reared as a Jew, converted to Christianity and became a real estate broker living in a ranch house in Park City, Utah, a ski community that's the site, every year, of the Sundance Film Festival.

Some residents of Park City today have no idea that the aimiable local real estate broker was the very visible porn star who, in the 70s, "plowed" his way through more than a hundred hard-core movies, including the seminal Deep Throat.

On looking back, Reems said, "Nobody under fifty even knows who I am now. Unless you're a porn historian , and then you're really sick."

Fellow porn actor Fred Lincoln also delivered a judgment about Reems. "The kid wasn't a great actor, but he sure was a great fucker."

Over the years, Reems remained in very limited contact with Linda. "She was always jumping on the next bandwagon," he said when he heard she'd become a feminist and an anti-porn activist. He donated $1,000 to a fund in 1987 to help pay for her liver transplant. "There was no consistency to her life direction," he said.

The after-effects of Deep Throat *were long lasting and continue to this day. Writing in* Time *magazine, Richard Corliss said: "Porn doesn't affront contemporary community standards: It is a contemporary community standard. For the weary businessman, it's just a combination of Viagra and Ambien."*

A turning point came in 1982 when "porn went video." In the United States today, more than 800 million porn videos are purchased, downloaded, or rented each year—and not just by men. In spite of their family values stance, most of the consumers are from Red States.

Critics and social commentators, deep into the latter 20th Century and into the 21ˢᵗ Century, were still writing about Deep Throat. *In 1981, Gay Talese, au-*

thor of Thy Neighbor's Wife, *a study of sexual behavior in the United States, claimed "What was special about* Deep Throat *was that it required of people to expose themselves, to go into a theater, to be seen walking in or out. That was a revolutionary act in the 1970s."*

Many sex researchers today directly trace the rise in frequency of oral sex in America to Linda Lovelace's Deep Throat. *According to a report issued in 2012 by Indiana University, the increase in the acceptance and frequency of oral sex is the single biggest change in American sexuality over the past sixty years.*

When Alfred Kinsey published his first sexual study in 1948, only thirty percent of men said they had received oral sex from a woman. In 2012, ninety-one percent of men asserted that they had been fellated by a woman sometime in their past. And in Kinsey's 1953 study on sexual habits of American women, twenty-five percent of women claimed they had received cunnilingus at one time or another from a man. In 2012, eighty-eight percent of women reported receiving oral sex.

And according to the University's report, "bicurious" men are on the rise, some fourteen percent of American males reporting having received fellatio from other men.

"Porn chic lasted through the 70s and 80s, creating such "big stars" as John C. Holmes and, later, Traci Lords. Of course, tragedy sruck with the AIDS epidemic. As journalist Humphrey Knipe asked, "What happened to porn chic and the sexual revolution? It caught AIDS and died."]

***

Once extricated from all of his legal penalties, a freed Butchie Peraino was ready for business again. With all the millions he'd made for his share of *Deep Throat,* he headed to Hollywood, wanting to become a player in the film industry. There, he launched Bryanston Films, hiring directors, technical crews, and screenwriters, usually paying top dollar. For example, a script that he could have bought for $10,000, he paid $100,000.

Actually, Bryanston Films never completed an original movie, although the company spent a lot of time debating where its filmmaking energies should go.

One of the company's first executive decisions involved Linda Lovelace.

At the Bryanston headquarters in Los Angeles, Linda arrived with Chuck for a meeting. At the entrance, echoing Gloria Swanson's line at the moment of her supposed comeback in *Sunset Blvd.*, she told the security guard, "Without me, there would be no Bryanston Films," a reference to the millions Peraino had

484

already made from *Deep Throat.*

The meeting did not go well. Butchie was shocked when Linda demanded that she appear in upcoming films exclusively as a legitimate (*i.e. non-porn*) actress.

She shocked Butchie and his cohorts by telling them, "I'm tired of porn. I won't be making any further appearances nude, and cocksucking is out—no more, never again, *finito.*"

As Linda, ruefully, later recalled, "I never became the Queen of Bryanston Films." *[She would, however, be approached one final time to appear as a porn actress for the company, at which time she again refused.]*

Albert S. Ruddy, the producer of *The Godfather,* later said, "It was widely known within the film industry that Bryanston was controlled by the mob. Many legitimate producers did not want them to distribute their films."

Eventually, Bryanston Films redefined itself as a national distributor, rather than a producer, of films. Butchie, through Bryanston, eventually acquired the rights to distribute *The Texas Chain Saw Massacre* (1974). Some fifty million film-goers saw it, although it was banned in some states and in some countries abroad. It is remembered today as one of the most gruesome, bloody, and violent films ever to emerge from Hollywood.

When its profits were divided, the backers of *Chain Saw* got only $8,000. When they sued to collect their rich reward, Bryanston Films had declared bankruptcy.

But before that happened, more or less simultaneous with the release of *Chain Saw,* the studio released two additional movies, *Andy Warhol's Frankenstein (aka Flesh for Frankenstein; 1973)* and Bruce Lee's *Return of the Dragon (aka The Way of the Dragon; 1972).*

The most controversial and artistically credible film Bryanston ever released was *Coonskin* (1973)*,* a racially provocative combination of live action scenes and animated cartoons which is accepted today as the masterpiece of its avant-garde director, Ralph Bakshi.

Born in 1938 in Haifa, in what was at the time the British Mandate for Palestine, Bakshi was a respected director of both animated and live action films. In 1972, the year before he created *Coonskin,* he'd made his debut feature film *Fritz the Cat,* the first animated movie to ever receive an X-rating. It became one of the most successful independent animated features of all time.

Bakshi would later become even better known for such films as *The Lord of the Rings* (1978). Based on J.R.R. Tolkien's 1955 fantasy epic about the inhabitants of "Middle Earth," it used a hybrid of live action footage with cartoon animation, crafted in innovative ways that were unique, even revolutionary, at the time.

Coonskin arrived at Bryanston Films with impressive credentials: Ruddy, of *Godfather* fame, had been its producer.

The very avant-garde *Coonskin* faced negative reviews and rising hostility, most often from people who had not seen it. With some justification, Linda asserted, "The money I made for those boys at Bryanston is paying for *Coonskin's* distribution, so I might as well go and see it."

Consequently, she attended a screening at New York's Museum of Modern Art. When she got there, she found herself surrounded by a protest group from the Congress of Racial Equality (CORE), led by the Rev. Al Sharpton, who had not seen the movie. With Linda listening, he told the press, "I don't go to see shit; I can smell shit."

Fearing a riot, Linda turned away and never saw the film. She later attacked the Perainos for trying to promote racism.

Actually, the passions and rage associated with the release of *Coonskin* were misguided. The NAACP later described the film as a satire and supported it. The movie, for those who had soldiered on and watched it, turned out to be very pro-black and won praise from such activists as director Spike Lee. After seeing it, Richard Pryor told a reporter, "I think it's great."

Bakshi later said, "I get e-mails from fans all the time, most of whom can't believe I'm white."

The release of *Coonskin* catalyzed one final offer from Bryanston films to Linda. Someone on its staff came up with a proposal for a hard-core porno movie featuring Linda and her friend Pupu, Jr., who still operated as Liz Renay's sometimes lover. "We'll piss the hell out of those who still resist miscegenation," claimed a Bryanston manager.

Years later, Linda admitted that she never considered that offer seriously, even though she admitted, "The film probably would have caused riots while packing them in at the box office. It would have been a sensation."

During later years, Linda told Jay Garon's researchers, "If I had made a deal with the Devil *[an obvious reference to Butchie]*, I might have ended up making millions while I was still a hot property. At the time, I blamed Chuck for fucking up every deal that came our way, but I see now that perhaps I shared some of that blame by not continuing, on film, with the Linda Lovelace image that the public had come to expect."

***

Linda's latter day sentiment was almost certainly reinforced by the failure of her second movie, the much-edited, frequently censored *Deep Throat Part II*. Critical reviews had been devastating, and it had been a failure at the box office. One critic had asked, "Did grown human beings make this film?"

"We feared legal challenges, so ultimately the sequel was denuded of both nudity and sex, and its comic situations didn't work," its director, Joseph Sarno, later asserted from his home in Key West. "Fans came thinking they would see Linda deep throating a lot of well-hung studs. They left the theater in disappointment."

Harry Reems delivered his own review: "The picture was a turkey of the lowest order, a disaster at the box office. It couldn't have happened to a pair of creepier creeps or lousier lice." He was referring, of course, to the Peraino brothers, with whom he'd tangled frequently during production. He referred to Tony Peraino, Sr., and his son, Butchie, as "stereotypical thugs, trying to instill fear into everybody."

When presented with the February, 13, 1974 issue of *Variety,* Linda was devastated. Critics had slammed her, writing, "*Deep Throat Part II* is the shoddiest of exploitation film traditions, a depressing fastbuck attempt to milk a naïve public. Audience ire is likely to be aroused. Amateur night quality from truly awful performances from Lovelace and a cast of N.Y.-based hardcore regulars. They drown through Joe Sarno's hackneyed script and direction to a number of raunchy tunes on the soundtrack, all keyed to remind viewers that the leading lady can do something special, even if she can't do it with an R rating. *La Lovelace* can do one thing, but she doesn't do it in this pic. In fact, she doesn't do much of anything but mug as she stumbles through a witless plot about espionage and randy psychiatrists."

At a restaurant in Malibu (California), Linda granted an interview to Bruce Williamson, the movie critic for *Playboy.* She told him, "The second *Deep Throat* will be a backward step if they take out the hardcore in the wake of the Supreme Court's ruling on obscenity. I don't want to back away. I'm not looking for a big Hollywood career. I'm a porno star. I just want to be Linda Lovelace."

But in contradiction of what she told *Playboy,* she *was* trying to establish a career in the mainstream (non-porn) entertainment industry, and as such, made several (ultimately failed) attempts to become an A-list actress.

By the end of 1973, she refused to give any more interviews to porn magazines. When they got word of this, *Playboy,* by Christmas of 1974, had begun referring to her as "The Shirley Temple of Sex." That nickname emerged in the wake of Linda's telling *E!,* "I wasn't doing sex scenes. That's all! If that's what directors wanted, they were out of luck!"

In June of 2008, at the Hollywood F.A.M.E. Awards, Steven Hirsch, owner of Vivid Entertainment, announced that he was producing a remake of *Deep Throat* entitled *Deeper Throat.* But Arrow Productions, the owner of *Deep Throat's* original copyright, objected, as it didn't like the proposed film's new cast and its deviation from Gerard Damiano's original storyline.

When Arrow withdrew its permission for a remake, they forced Hirsch to rewrite his movie to avoid a lawsuit for copyright infringement. Consequently, Hirsch concocted a revised title: *Throat, a Cautionary Tale,* releasing his film in the spring of 2009.

To further confuse consumers, another all new porn film—this one entitled *Deep Throat II*—was released in 1987. Completely unrelated, except by innuendo, to either of Linda's previous *Deep Throats,* it had an entirely different cast and a different director. Unlike Linda's disastrous *Deep Throat Part II* from 1974, which because of fears of legal repercussions had been stripped of its hard-core scenes, this one was, indeed, XXX-rated.

In the 1987 version, two male stars, each famous at the time in the world of porn, were included in the cast—Ron Jeremy and Jamie Gillis. And in that film, the role that might have been Linda's, if circumstances had been different, was played by an actress billing herself as "Scarlett Fever."

***

Arriving in New York with Chuck, Linda was not overly concerned with any of the films which had been conceived as spinoffs from the original *Deep Throat* since she had no financial interest vested in any of them.

Pinnacle Books, a publishing venue established in New York in 1974 and subsequently acquired by the Kensington Publishing Group in 1988, had booked her on a promotional tour for publicity associated with the publication of her (so-called) memoirs, *Inside Linda Lovelace.*

"Its title certainly spells out what it's about, doesn't it?" she asked the editors at Pinnacle.

During her time in their office, she learned a new word making the rounds, a word inspired by her ability to control her gag reflex that was later cited by *Time* magazine on October 27, 2008 in an article written by Richard Corliss. As explained to Linda by an editor at Pinnacle, "Your specialty is now known as a glo-job" *[i.e., 'glottal fellatio,']*. You'll go down in the dictionary, honey."

In New York, Linda and Chuck contacted Gerard Damiano, who had directed her in *Deep Throat.* He brought her up to date about how her name and its connotations were being commandeered by producers of a new crop of porn flicks currently in production.

Some of these had spliced in loops of Linda performing fellatio on various actors. The most visible of these included *Linda Lovelace Meets Miss Jones* (1975), which hoped to capitalize off the fame of Damiano's own *The Devil in Miss Jones* (1973), which had co-starred Harry Reems and Georgina Spelvin. Two years later, it was joined in the marketplace by *Confessions of Linda Lovelace* (1977).

As Damiano explained it, "We tried to get you to star in it *[The Devil in*

Miss Jones], but no one could track you down. I think you were in Hawaii or some place. Instead, we cast Georgina Spelvin, who's thirty-six and a bit long in the tooth for porn. We paid our cook, Claire Lumiere, a hundred dollars for letting us film a lesbian scene with Georgina."

Damiano went on to explain that *The Devil in Miss Jones* was playing nationwide, usually as part of double feature alongside *Deep Throat.* "The films, as a double feature, are breaking box office records. We're being taken seriously and both of my films, including the one I made with you, are being artistically appraised."

He carried some reviews from mainstream newspapers in his pocket, most of them about the newer of the two films, *The Devil in Miss Jones.*

Variety, which had previously panned *Deep Throat Part II,* wrote, "With *The Devil in Miss Jones,* the hard-core porno feature approaches an art form, one that critics may have a tough time ignoring in the future. It can be compared to the plot of Jean-Paul Sartre's *No Exit.* Gerard Damiano has expertly fashioned a bizarre melodrama. Its opening scene is so effective, it would stand out in any legit theatrical feature."

Damiano then read from another critic, Peter Michelson, who wrote, "*Deep Throat* and *Devil in Miss Jones* have a minimal but still sufficient artistic interest to distinguish themselves from the rest of the genre." William Friedkin wrote that *Deep Throat* and *The Devil in Miss Jones* "are the two best erotic motion pictures ever made."

When Linda realized the full implications of these reviews, she burst into tears, realizing that from a career standpoint, she'd made an awful decision. Whereas she was being scalded by the critics for *Deep Throat Part II, The Devil in Miss Jones* was being applauded.

Immediately, she blamed Chuck for not having transmitted Damiano's original offer to her.

Playing across the country on a double bill, *Deep Throat* and **The Devil in Miss Jones** were hailed as the two best erotic films ever made. Both were directed by Gerard Damiano.

Linda learned only belatedly that had Damiamo been able to reach her, she would have been offered the starring role in Damiano's second film. The honor (or dishonor) went instead to **Georgina Spelvin**, who is seen above about to tongue-kiss a snake.

When Linda saw the snake scene, she asked Damiano: "Is sex with a snake also called bestiality?"

For the first time in their relationship, she slapped his face. In the past, he had been the one who administered the blows.

Probably because all of this was unfolding in a public restaurant, Chuck did not slap her back, much to Damiano's relief. Instead, Damiano said, "Had we been able to contact you, and had you accepted the role, you'd truly have consolidated your position as the Queen of Porn. But now, you've got big competition from Georgina, and even bigger competition from Marilyn Chambers. *Behind the Green Door* is going to be big. You could have had that one, too."

"I've heard of Marilyn Chambers," she said, looking squarely at Chuck, whom she knew was having an affair with her. "What about you, Chuck? Have you heard of this Chambers cunt?"

"I've heard of her, but that's all," he answered.

Both Damiano and Linda knew that Chuck was telling a lie. But neither confronted him. She told Damiano that she was in New York to promote her book, and promised that she'd entertain future film and theatrical offers more seriously.

"With that in mind," Damiano said, "there are three guys who'd like to talk to you about touring in a road show," Damiano said. "They are also the best-built hunks in New York City."

"Is it porn?" she asked.

"Not exactly, but their show is aimed at the same audiences Mae West attracted."

"I won't let this chance pass me by," she said.

***

Her book tour promoting *Inside Linda Lovelace* kicked off at the Gaslight Club on MacDougal Street in New York City's Greenwich Village in October of 1972. Steamy, dark, and subterranean, the Gaslight Club had originated as a bar, café, and coffee house which had previously showcased such Beat Generation poets as Allen Ginsberg. After a change of administration and venue in 1971, it also featured, early in their careers, relatively unknown entertainers who included Bill Cosby, Bob Dylan, and, also in 1972, the same year as Linda, Bruce Springsteen.

Linda's book signing there evolved into a disaster.

Based on many of her earlier statements, Linda had frequently denied that she'd ever appeared in a bestiality film. But the always-pugnacious Al Goldstein at *Screw* magazine knew differently, and he showed up at her press conference fully prepared to expose her lies.

The exposure of public figures had already been established as a sales-generating tradition among the editors of porn magazines. The most notorious example of that occurred when Larry Flynt, publisher and founder of *Hustler* magazine, printed photographs of Jackie Kennedy Onassis sunbathing in the nude on the privately owned (by her then-husband, Aristotle Onassis) Greek island of Skorpios.

Ms. Onassis' humiliation was enhanced when she learned that it had been her husband who had organized the photos, secretly paying a member of the paparazzi to set up the shoot with a long-distance lens from a sequestered part of his island. Onassis later revealed that his intentions involved "taking my high-class broad down a peg or two."

Linda was hardly a high-class broad, but Goldstein, who had originally publicized both her and her role in *Deep Throat,* had become disenchanted with her. She later claimed that Goldstein's bitterness was the result of her refusal to appear in a movie he was producing, "because I didn't like the script. After I turned that down, he turned on me," she said.

As Goldstein well knew, a film distribution company had purchased the rights to *The Dog Fucker* and was promoting it as a vehicle starring Linda Lovelace. In nationwide ads for *Deep Throat,* the question was asked, "How far does a girl have to go to untangle her tingle?"

Mocking that ad, the promoters of *The Dog Fucker* were publicizing the slogan, "Linda Lovelace, star of *Deep Throat,* untangles the Tingle of Fido!"

Goldstein showed up at the press conference at the Gaslight Club, waiting patiently for the question-and-answer period. He had brought ample evidence, including photographs, corroborating his allegation that Linda had co-starred with a dog in one of her previous sex films.

Early in the event, Chuck had confronted Goldstein, informing him that grand juries were trying to nail Linda on an obscenities rap based on that dog-fuck gig.

During his attempts to persuade Goldstein to stop, Chuck emphasized that Linda's image as an A-list porn star would be ruined if it got out that she'd been involved in some aspect of the bestiality trade.

Goldstein, however, refused to stop. At the press conference, he waved the incriminating photos and shouted: "Linda! In these hands are pictures of you being fucked by a dog!"

Someone called for a security guard to evict Goldstein from the venue. He later claimed, "Three goons threw me out. I was now considered the enemy. Only in America could a cocksucker go so far."

Goldstein and his allegations weren't her only embarrassment at the press conference. Other members of the press began grilling her about some of the mysterious allegations published within her book.

The revelations in her memoirs were controversial to the point of being incendiary. They involved her claim that she and Chuck had once participated in a sexual four-way with a famous (but unnamed, at least by Linda) Hollywood-connected mother-and-daughter team.

Linda had written that the mother had been a professional model accustomed to erotic poses, and that she had appeared in many girlie magazines. Chuck, she wrote, had snapped some pictures of the mother and daughter having sex, and eventually asked if he could join in the fun. When the mother agreed, "Chuck dove in between them like he wanted first prize in an apple-ducking contest," Linda wrote.

In her memoir she asserted that she, too, had joined in, stating that as Chuck seduced the young girl, the mother juggled his balls.

In her memoirs, in reference to the mother/daughter gig, Linda had delivered some genuinely graphic details, including an assertion she made, in writing, that the mother performed cunnilingus on her daughter, as Chuck sodomized her, and a description about how, during the days ahead, both Chuck and she had allegedly colluded in a series of sex romps with the mother/daughter team.

But despite the energy and conviction with which she made this revelation in her book, she adamantly refused to identify the

Lana Turner *(top photo)*, recipient of lurid publicity throughout her career as a movie star, came in for even more bad publicity after the publication of *Inside Linda Lovelace*. In that so-called memoir, Linda had claimed that she and Chuck had engaged in four-way sex with a famous mother-and-daughter team in Hollywood.

After the fatal knifing of Lana's gangster lover, **Johnny Stompanato** *(bottom photo, center)*, **Lana** *(left figure in bottom photo)* became the most famous mother and daughter in the film colony, chiefly because of the flood of stories surrounding Stompanato's murder at Lana's house and the subsequent debate about which of the women had killed him.

The rumors persisted even though Linda denied that she'd ever met Lana Turner or **Cheryl Crane** (right figure in bottom photo).

mother-daughter team, even at the press conference under intense questioning from members of the press.

"Was it Lana Turner and Cheryl Crane?" one reporter asked, even though Linda's description of the couple did not fit the profile of either Lana or her daughter, Cheryl.

[In October of 1972, Lana and her daughter were the most famous mother-daughter combination in Hollywood.]

"Of course not!" Linda protested. "I have never met either Lana Turner or her daughter!"

Cheryl Crane, daughter of actor-restaurateur Stephen Crane, was reported to be a lesbian. On April 4, 1958, Cheryl, at the age of fourteen, was alleged to have stabbed her mother's gangster lover, Johnny Stompanato, to death in her mother's home. In court, Cheryl claimed that at the time, she was protecting her mother from violence.

However, over the years, many insiders, including Howard Hughes and Frank Sinatra, came to believe that it was Lana who stabbed Stompanato, her daughter taking the blame, with the understanding that because of her status as a minor, she'd receive only a light punishment.

More than a decade later, even in the presence of Jay Garon's research team, Linda refused to identify the mother/daughter duet.

Members of Garon's team, including this author, finally surmised that Linda's references in her book were not references to Lana and Cheryl, but to Liz Renay and her beautiful, tragic daughter, Brenda Romano.

Linda often hung out with both mother and daughter and on many occasions assisted them with their wardrobes during performances of their joint strip act in Las Vegas. Many men in the audience believed that Renay was appearing not with her daughter, but with her sister.

Chuck Traynor, much later in his life, also

Some Hollywood insiders immediately rejected the rumor that Linda and Chuck had had a four-way with Lana Turner and her daughter, Cheryl Crane.

The more likely mother-daughter combo was cult film goddess **Liz Renay** *(left)* and her daugher, **Brenda Romano** *(right)*.

Chuck had snapped the pair in erotic poses during their joint performances in strip acts in Las Vegas, and Linda frequently hung out with them.

But she never admitted that they were the mother/daughter team she had referred to in her memoirs.

493

refused to identify the mother and daughter, yet he was known to have taken erotic pictures of both Brenda and her mother. He sold these candid shots to private collectors turned on by the idea of a mother and daughter making love to each other.

Garon told his researchers, "For our proposed book on Linda, for legal reasons, we cannot name the mother and daughter, but we're allowed a little harmless speculation. I can be pretty sure that it wasn't Sara Taylor and her daughter, Elizabeth (Taylor), although Sara was known for some lesbian romps during her younger days when she was an actress on Broadway."

***

At the end of the Linda's press conference at the Gaslight Club, a reporter, prompted by the loud accusations of Al Goldstein, confronted Linda with a photo from *The Dog Fucker*.

"Can't you plainly see?" Linda responded. "The girl in the photo is obviously not me, but some Chinese woman."

There were no other incidents during the remainder of Linda's promotional tour of *Inside Linda Lovelace*. But in 1976, she ran into additional trouble because of her memoirs. Pinnacle tried to issue a new edition of her book in the United Kingdom, as reprinted by an English publisher, but based on their own censorship standards of the time, the British government brought obscenity charges against Linda, her book, and the British publisher.

Prosecutors claimed that the memoir had no redeeming social value. The publisher's defense countered that the book was "technically instructive" as a sex manual.

Linda, assuming that no harm would come to her, did not fly to London for the trial, even though she was cited as one of the "conspirators" who had made *Deep Throat*.

Finally, after five hours of deliberation, the jury in London found that all of the persons involved in the making of *Deep Throat,* including Linda herself, were NOT GUILTY.

This London trial would represent the last time that Linda herself would be named in any prosecution for her starring role in *Deep Throat*.

"I'm free at last!" she said on hearing the verdict. "But a guilty label of some sort will follow me for the rest of my life."

***

In Miami, when Linda was working as a prostitute pimped to the public by Chuck, she'd had sex with three aging musclemen who operated a local gym.

494

That experience had turned her against weightlifters. In her memoir, *Inside Linda Lovelace,* she attacked bodybuilders, defining them as "bulging globs of rocklike muscle" and referring to them as freaks. "What is it to achieve such a phony physical look by lifting those silly weights?" she had asked. "I'd rather ball the circus fat man than the freak who lifts weights." She also charged that most weightlifters are "all muscle and no dick. That's one muscle they can't beef up."

She later regretted making such a generalized slur on weightlifters. The day after her press conference, Gerald Damiano drove her to a gym in Brooklyn to meet three of the Entertainment Industry's most famous bodybuilders. Even though Damiano had no theatrical experience, he'd been commissioned with the development of a musclebound show starring Linda as hostess, with hope of organizing a nationwide tour. He predicted that the show would run in Las Vegas for an entire winter season.

At the gym, she was introduced to three of the most famous physiques—Mickey Hargitay, Gorden Scott, and Steve Reeves—in the world. She was thrilled to meet them. "They were big and beautiful, such handsome hunks. To judge from the packages revealed in their bikini wear, they were big in all departments."

"All three of them were a treat for a hot-to-trot dame or a gay guy," Linda said. "All of them had seen *Deep Throat* and each of them praised my technique, which I was more than willing to demonstrate whenever any or all of them wanted an audition."

The sweaty men showered, dressed, and invited Linda and Damiano to join them in their transit from Brooklyn to the hotel suite the men were sharing at the Waldorf-Astoria

The year 1955 brought a new Tarzan to the screen in the form of actor **Gordon Scott**, who made his film debut in *Tarzan's Hidden Jungle.*

"He was no doubt the most pefectly developed man who ever appeared on the screen," Linda proclaimed. "I told him I would return to porno if he'd appear as my leading man, but he said no. Handsome? He was a dreamboat."

"I later found out that Gordon, like me, had turned a few tricks in his day."

in Manhattan. Damiano privately filled Linda in with details about who these men were. "Steve and Mickey look like fabulous studs, but it's that Gordon Scott I dig the most."

"Cool down, gal," Damiano warned her. "You're getting overheated. Wait until we get back to their suite."

During her introduction to Scott, he invited her to feel his nineteen-inch upper arms. She later told Damiano, "I wanted to feel something else that was bulging out of his bikini."

[At the time, Scott was forty-seven years old, having been born in 1926, but he was in such great shape, he looked no more than thirty-two. He'd kept his six-foot, three-inch body in superb and highly trained condition.

When Lex Barker, Lana Turner's handsome hunk, abandoned the role of Tarzan he'd been focusing on, producer Sol Lesser gave the role to Scott. Even though Scott privately referred to Lesser as "a cheap prick," he became the next screen Tarzan, making five films between 1955 and 1960.

Prior to filming, when Scott had stripped down for a loincloth fitting in the wardrobe department, one of the gay men there suggested that Scott would also need a heavy duty jockstrap—"or else you'll be flapping in the wind."

Born in Portland, Oregon, Scott was a German-American bodybuilder who became "Hollywood's King of Muscle Men," as stated by Mr. Young America *magazine. Drafted into the Army in 1944, he had to have a special uniform made to fit his muscular body.*

He became the only actor to portray Tarzan as both unworldly and inarticulate, but also, in a reversal from earlier trends, as well educated and speaking perfect English, as the series' creator, Edgar Rice Burroughs, had originally intended.

Scott's biggest success as the man of the jungle occurred as a result of his 1959 film, Tarzan's Greatest Adventure, *in which a young Sean Connery played the villain.*

After his Tarzan roles ended, Scott moved to Italy, where he became a popular star in some sword-and-sandal epics, wherein well-muscled heroes were featured as various Greek and Roman players. In Italy, he met Steve Reeves, and together, they made a film, Duel of the Titans (1961), *in which Reeves played Romulus and Scott played Remus. The two musclemen became intimate friends and lived together whenever they could.*

A rich homosexual in England became so fascinated with Scott and Reeves that he invited them to his estate in Surrey, where he convinced them to make a gay porno film for him. His obsession compelled him to offer them a fee of $100,000, a vast amount of money in the early 1960s. This secret film has never surfaced.

When the public inevitably grew tired of sword-and-sandal epics, Scott was hired for a series of "spaghetti Westerns" in Italy before returning to the States, where his career was at its twilight.

As he related to Damiano, "I'm anxious for a new gig. Let's face it: It's money, money, money that makes the merry-go-round go round."

In contrast, Mickey Hargitay, born in Hungary in 1926, had won the Mr. Universe title in 1955. He was the same age as Scott, and in equally good shape. Linda was particularly intrigued by his status as husband of the deceased movie star, Jayne Mansfield, who had died in a horrible automobile accident in Louisiana in 1967.

An underground Resistance fighter in Hungary during World War II, Hargitay had come to the United States and worked as a plumber and carpenter before spotting Steve Reeves on the cover of a bodybuilding magazine. That photograph inspired him to begin lifting weights and ultimately led to his acquisition of the Mr. Universe title.

Columnist Walter Winchell proclaimed that "What President Eisenhower did for golf, Mickey Hargitay did for bodybuilding."

When Mae West was auditioning candidates for her musclemen revue, Hargitay showed up for inspection. Mae was very interested in seeing what each man "had in his bread basket," so she ordered each of them to

"I'm a big girl, and it takes a big man to satisfy me," said **Jayne Mansfield** *(right figure in lower photo)*. Her husband, the Hungarian bodybuilder **Mickey Hargitay** *(in both photos above)*, fitted the bill perfectly, even though Jayne had to steal him from the aging Mae West.

"Jayne and I had something in common," Linda later said. "We seduced two of the same men, both Mickey and Anton LaVey of the Church of Satan. Of the two, I'd take Mickey any day. What a man!"

"Jayne had appeared in the February, 1955 issue of *Playboy*, but when I appeared, I sold more copies," Linda said.

497

strip before her. She later proclaimed, "Mickey was built in all the right places."

He was hired, but one evening, during a performance in Washington D.C., his involvement with the show began unraveling in the aftermath of Jayne Mansfield's arrival in the audience. After spotting him onstage, she told the waiter, "I'll have a steak and that tall man on the left."

When Mansfield began appearing in the audience every night and subsequently launched an affair with Hargitay, Mae became furious at the idea of losing her live-in lover to a younger blonde. When Hargitay, backstage, revealed to the press that he'd be leaving the show to run off with Mansfield, Mae sent

her other muscleman lover, Paul Novak, to prevent him from making further disclosures. That led to a fistfight, an altercation widely publicized in the press. One New York reporter asserted that Hargitay and Novak were battling over a pair of "female impersonators," referring, of course, to Mansfield and Mae, who, in their exaggerated femininity, did suggest drag queens.

The third muscleman, Steve Reeves, who was born the same year as Scott and Hargitay, was also in excellent shape. His luster had dimmed somewhat from the days when he earned such titles as Mr. Pacific (1946 and 1947), Mr. America (1947), Mr. World (1948), and ultimately, Mr. Universe (1950).

When **Steve Reeves** (pictured above at various stages of his career) met Linda, his movie roles had ended. That left him available to pursue some creative showbiz proposals with Linda and a duet of other musclemen.

According to Linda, "I'll say this about him. He wasn't all muscle. There was one big part of him he didn't develop in a gym."

"More pecs than acting talent," his critics had asserted. His most famous appearance, which had launched his film career, was his title role in Hercules, filmed in Italy in 1957. This led to a series of historical epic films, each of them shot in Italy. At the peak of his box office allure, he became the highest paid male actor in Europe, sharing honors with Sophia Loren, Europe's highest-paid female star at the time.

As part of a bad career decision, he rejected a proposal that he be cast as the lead in A Fistful of Dollars (1964), *because Reeves did not believe that the Italians knew how to make Westerns. The star-making role was eventually awarded to Clint Eastwood.*

Reeves also rejected the role of the first incarnation of James Bond in Dr. No (1962), *a part which eventually went to Sean Connery. Whereas Mr. Muscles had made $250,000 per picture with his Hercules-like characters in Italy, he had been offered only $100,000 to play Secret Agent 007. The muscleman regretted his rejection of Agent 007 for the rest of his life.*

When the allure of his previous films faded at the box office, Reeves capitulated, appearing in an Italy-based spaghetti Western entitled A Long Ride From Hell (1968).

After the collapse of his film career, Reeves returned to America and purchased a ranch near Escondido, California with his earnings. Relishing his incarnation of kitsch and beefcake, gay men remained his loyal fans, and each week, for a few years at least, he continued to receive a hundred or so letters from them.]

During his semi-seclusion at his ranch, Reeves conceived the idea of a sexy road show which would include a coven of bodybuilders, including not only Hargitay, but his longtime and most intimate friend, Gordon Scott.

Reeves had seen Mae West's muscle-bound show featuring Hargitay as one of its stars, and he was inspired by the revue. After watching *Deep Throat,* he came to believe that Linda Lovelace should be designated as the female star in a show loaded with bawdy innuendos about male genitalia. Soon after that, he got in touch with Damiano, who agreed to

Mae West *(center, of course)* toured in a ribald nightclub act with two leading bodybuilders, **Paul Novak** *(left)* and **Mickey Hargitay.** She configured each of them as her lovers until she lost Hargitay to another blonde, Jayne Mansfield.

Unlike all of Mae's other lovers, Novak stayed with her till the very end, which came for the aging diva in 1980. He even planned the details of her funeral.

direct the revue saying, "It's almost certain that I can get Linda to co-star in it thanks to you slabs of beef."

In their suite at the Waldorf-Astoria, Linda learned more about the revue and her interest was piqued. It would definitely be a rip-off of Mae West's commercially successful muscleman revue, the original of which had opened in Las Vegas during the summer of 1954. Mae had entitled it, "I'd Like to Do All Day What I Do All Night."

In her act, Mae featured nine "*athaleets*" imported from Muscle Beach at Venice, California. In her autobiography, she referred to her co-stars as "a magnificent herd of males."

For Linda's 1973 restaging of the Mae West revue, "the men will do the stripping," Reeves told her. "You, as the lone female, will be fully and lavishly dressed."

"Your costumes will be fabulous!" Damiano added. "Take, for example, a diaphanous top, accessorized with an ermine stole and a black plumed headdress. And you'll be a sensation in a black sequined gown with a net midriff. Very classy, very Marlene Dietrich."

"A script writer is working on the revue right now," Reeves said. "In essence, it will be a show devoted to the glorification of the penis, with lots of wit, satire, and humor, both subtle and bawdy. One of the show's highlight will be when all of us muscle guys come out onstage in sequined jock straps in different colors and do a dirty boogie."

"Only guys who can fill out a bikini pouch will be hired," Scott said. "We'll show as much as the law allows. The theater will fill up every night with straight women and gay guys. Instead of evaluating breast sizes on women who strip, it will be women and gays evaluating dick sizes."

"The show will open with us naked under terrycloth robes," Hargitay said. "Our backs will be turned to the audience. In a lavish costume, you'll walk out and one by one and slowly evaluate our dicks for the audience. For example, when you see my dick, you'll announce to the audience, 'That's a bridge I could take all the way to Honolulu.'"

"When you evaluate me," Reeves said, "I want you to purr, 'I can see that you grew up in the redwood forest.'"

"As for me," Scott said, "You can say, 'I've always understood how Tarzan carried his own vine to swing on.'"

"We'll have musical backup numbers," Damiano promised. "The highlight of the show for you, Linda, will be when you come out and deliver a fifteen-minute dissertation on the penis. It won't be serious. It'll be stand-up comedy. The audience will go wild."

"Say no more," Linda said. She rose to her feet. "I'll do it! Now, Gerard, if you'll excuse us for the night, I have to audition these big lugs."

As Linda later recalled to Jay Garon's researchers, "I've had a lot of sexual experiences in my life, many of them awful. But I will always remember that night with Gordon, Mickey, and Steve. Right before exiting from the living room, they stripped down for me, and I pulled off everything too."

"The three of them circled me on the living room carpet. I was on my knees. I looked up to see three of the finest dicks God ever created. They were rock hard. I took my time going from one to the other until the final blast-off from this unholy trio. They tasted wonderful and they shot off like Vesuvius erupting."

"That was only the beginning. We went into the bedroom for a replication of *Wild Nights in Babylon*. Everybody did everybody else, and for one night of my life, I felt like I was Queen of the Universe, in bed at the same time with Hercules, Tarzan, and the Hungarian Rhapsody."

[By the late 1970s, Linda had changed her opinion of muscle men. Someone showed her a frontal nude of Arnold Schwarzenegger. She was impressed. "It looks like a gal could get a rise out of that Vienna sausage. I'm sorry he wasn't around very much when I was the party favor of Hollywood."]

The next day, Chuck still had not returned to their suite at the Plaza Hotel. She didn't know where he had been. Nor had he called. She enjoyed the time away from his overweening presence.

At three o'clock that afternoon, an unexpected call came in from Fernando Lamas, who had been given her phone number by Linda Lovelace Enterprises in Hollywood.

"Elizabeth Taylor suggested I give you a call," Lamas told her.

"I thought a busy lady like Miss Taylor would have forgotten about me," she said.

"She's a very loyal person," Lamas responded. "She always remembers her friends and likes to spoil them with special treats."

"Is that what I am?" she asked.

"From what I hear, you're that and more," he said. "I'm staying at the Sherry-Netherland Hotel, just across Fifth Avenue from you. I could be there in no time. Are you free?"

Because Linda didn't want to be interrupted by Chuck if and when he returned, she agreed to meet Lamas at his hotel. "You've got me between engagements," she told him. "And yes, I'm available."

"THE GIRL WHO HAD EVERYTHING"

"After dolling myself up and within the hour," she later recalled, "I was sitting across from Fernando in his hotel suite. Despite the fact that he was fifty-eight years old, he was still a male beauty in exquisite shape. He was immaculately dressed in tailored clothing. I wore a Chanel dress and looked respectable, not like some cheap whore the way Dolly Parton dresses."

To Linda, Fernando Lamas used to be one of the most exciting men on the movie screens of the 1950s and 60s.

[Born in 1915 in Argentina, Fernando Lamas was the archetypal playboy—in fact, he claimed, "I got into movies because it was a chance to meet broads." By 1942, he was already a film star in Buenos Aires. Before the end of World War II, he was involved in a torrid affair with Eva Perón, who, in 1946, would become the First Lady (some said "co-dictator") of Argentina, the wife of military strongman Juan Perón.

During the early 1950s, Metro-Goldwyn-Mayer imported Lamas to Hollywood as a Latin Lover archetype. Soon, he was swirling Lana Turner around the dance floor in a popular and frothy remake of The Merry Widow (1952). *At night, he was occupying Lana's bed. "I'm a handsome Latin and a wonderful lover," he bragged. "The difference between Latin and American men is that the Latins give you a little more of everything. More headaches, more temper, more tenderness."*

"**Fernando Lamas** certainly turned me on to Latin lovers," Linda confessed. "I can thank **Elizabeth Taylor** (*pictured in top photo getting slugged by Lamas*) for fixing me up with him."

"He really did have something in common with those bulls from Argentina."

The gay actor, Cesar Romero, who tried on several occasions to fellate Lamas, said, "He's a very beautiful man in love with himself."

In 1953, Lamas would romance Elizabeth Taylor both on and off the screen in The Girl Who Had Everything. *She praised his "gaucho charisma." Later that same year, he was romancing MGM's "Million Dollar Mermaid," Esther Williams during the filming of* Dangerous When Wet, *one of her better movies. He proposed to her, but she rejected his offer. "You've got a lot of fucking yet to do. Come back in ten years."*

Lamas actually waited until 1969 before returning to marry Esther, to whom he was still married when he was two-timing her with Linda Lovelace.

By the time Lamas and Linda came together, he was a legendary star, based to some degree on his provocative antics on the Broadway stage during his co-starring performance, with Ethel Merman, in the musical Happy Hunting *(1956). The script had called for him to give Merman a passionate kiss. Once, after an argument with Merman and after delivering it, Lamas walked to the edge of the stage and, showing an obvious disgust, pointedly wiped his mouth. He told reporters, "Kissing Merman is somewhere between kissing your uncle and a Sherman tank."*

That was not the only antic that attracted audience attention away from Merman. As her biographer, Brian Kellow, wrote:

"Irene Sharoff designed a white suit Lamas was to wear in the show. His penis size was already the stuff of Hollywood legend, and he requested that Sharff design his costume as tight as possible so he could show off his endowment. The result didn't satisfy him, and he ordered the pants to be recut for maximum effect. His ploy worked. On opening night in Philadelphia, he stepped out onstage in the dazzling white suit. A chorus of gasps, from both men and women, swept over the theater. Nobody looked at Merman, and she was furious."

Lamas never wore underwear. As he explained it, "I am hung very high—that is, my dick is located high on my pubic bone. It makes my thing look like it goes on forever."

Linda was soon to find out that he was not exaggerating.]

As she talked with Lamas over drinks in his suite, the conversation quickly shifted to a film project he was working on—a project with a possible role in it for her. It seemed that every actor she met was developing, at least in his head, some film project. She didn't know how long her commercial viability would last after the failure of *Deep Throat Part II,* but she was still a hot item as long as those millions kept pouring in from the original *Deep Throat.*

'I've gone to bed with some of the most stunning women on the planet, and married some of them, including Arlene Dahl, but no one was more of a thrill to me than Evita, and she'd make a blockbuster subject of a film," Lamas said.

(top photo) **Eva (Evita) Perón** is shown in the 1950s with her husband, **Juan Perón**, the dictator of Argentina. She is also depicted *(lower photo)* in Paris during her infamous rainbow tour of Europe, when the Pope received her, but the Queen of England refused, referring to her privately as "that former prostitute."

When Fernando Lamas was a rising movie star in Buenos Aires during World War II, he had a torrid affair with Eva.

Subsequently, she became a driving obsession of his for the rest of his life.

"Evita said I was her greatest lover. She'd once been a *puta,* so she'd known many men with whom to compare me."

Linda knew almost nothing about Eva Perón, but he showed her a framed and autographed picture of her, which he frequently carried around with him in his migrations from hotel to hotel.

"But I don't look like that," she protested. "Why not try to lure Grace Kelly out of retirement? If not her, perhaps Eva Marie Saint? There are quite a few porcelain blondes out there."

"Actually, Evita will not appear in this movie," Lamas said. "It would begin on a date forever embedded in my brain: July 26, 1952, when my beloved Evita entered immortality.

Lamas then outlined the plot for *Los Descamisados (The Shirtless Ones).* This was a reference to Evita Perón's political base during her power years in Argentina, the low-income, working class Argentines who provided the bulk of her political support.

"In the film, I will play Evita's chief mourner, a poor, struggling craftsman eking out a meager living for me and my peasant wife, a role that would be ideal for you. My obsession begins in a flashback when Evita is visiting the poor. She was a saint. She would put her hands on lepers and often kiss the poor and let them kiss her back. One day, she spots me in a crowd and plants a kiss on my lips. It changes my life forever."

"Taking you, my wife, with me, I follow Evita to her every appearance, soon becoming sexually obsessed. I begin to regularly demand that you fellate me while I hold up and gaze lovingly upon a photo-

504

graph of Evita. Your head would be shown bobbing up and down on me, but there would be no actual depiction of genitals."

"My obsession grows greater day by day. In our humble home, I have a fading wreath which had rested on her casket and later been plucked from her funeral procession. The film will highlight the Hispanic preoccupation with death and the dignity and splendor associated with it."

"The Argentine people planned a vast memorial for Evita, and I volunteer to help build it for free. Soon after, a famous sculptor spots me and asks me to pose nude for a statue to represent all the *descamisados*. The statue would be larger than the Statue of Liberty."

"Then her grieving husband, Juan Perón, is overthrown by a military coup during the *Revolución Libertadora*. Perón flees the country *[for, among other places, Madrid]* and for sixteen years, Evita's corpse disappears. During all this time, I search in vain for it."

"Finally, her corpse is discovered in a church in Milan, where it had been falsely labeled as the body of another woman, María Maggi. Wax copies had been molded from her body, and a rumor spread that one of them was in the home of an Italian soldier who was using it for sexual purposes. You, my wife, travel to Milan with me as a loving woman who is sympathetic and indulgent to my obsession. I break in on the soldier while he is fornicating with the wax replica of Evita. I stab him in the back during the throes of his passion."

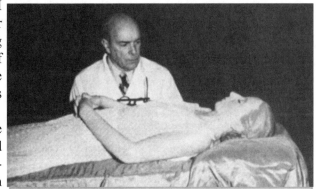

"Then we flee from Milan to Madrid where Evita's embalmed body has been turned over to the now-in-exile Juan Perón and his third wife, Isabel Perón. They have placed Evita's corpse on a platform in their dining room in Madrid, close to the table where they eat—weird as it admittedly is, that's what the Peróns in

Here, **the embalmed corpse of Eva Perón** is seen shortly after her death in the summer of 1952. Millions of her "shirtless ones" went into mourning.

Dr. Pedro Ara *(the male figure in the photo above)*, credited as one of the world's greatest embalmers, oversees the preservation of "my masterpiece."

Fernando Lamas, when he met Linda, proposed a screen role for her, wherein she'd play the role of his Argentinian wife.

Lamas, as a downtrodden but fiery revolutionary, would demand that his wife (Linda) would indulge him in the necrophiliac fantasies his character would associate with the former First Lady of Argentina.

exile actually did with her body in real life. In the film, however, one night, when Juan and Isabel are out of town for a weekend in Toledo, I break into their flat. Ava Gardner lives in the flat upstairs. I spend all night lying on top of Evita, loving her and protecting her embalmed body. A maid catches me the next morning. Screaming and calling for the police, she chases me out."

"The film will end when Evita's body is returned in triumph to Buenos Aires and buried in the Barrio Recoleta in a tomb so secure it could survive a nuclear attack."

"In my role as an ardent fan who worships her memory, every day I bring fresh flowers I have gathered and often stand for one to three hours in front of her tomb, even in stormy weather. In the final scene I am shirtless, bringing flowers to her tomb even on the coldest nights, enduring any hardship to prove to Evita that I am the most loving and the most enduring of her thousands upon thousands of *descamisados.*"

At the end of Lamas' recitation, Linda said, "I'm up for it. It's about time I played a faithful wife, since I'm not exactly one either in real or in *reel* life."

Years later, she would recall her sexual intimacy with the still-handsome Latino star. "He had something in common with the bulls on the *pampas* of Argentina. I wanted to do everything with him, but he requested fellatio. Perhaps he was auditioning me for the role of his fellator wife in his upcoming film. He told me that insofar as sex scenes were concerned, only the back of my head bobbing up and down on him would be depicted in the movie."

"He was a sexual dynamo. After fifteen minutes of rest, he demanded another blow-job. He told me that 'love is always better the second time around.' I went on licking and sucking everything he had, even the most hidden spots, and he went crazy. I'm sure there is no rare steak in Argentina that tastes as good as Fernando Lamas. I milked him dry, and he told me I would be perfect for the role. No money exchanged hands between Lamas and me that night. What I did was an act of love on my part."

Like so many proposals in Hollywood, the dream of Lamas interpreting the role of a *descamisado* went the way of the Peronistas' plans for construction of an "indestructible tomb that would survive the millennia" for Eva Perón.

Years later, Lamas had stoically accepted his failure to raise the money for his film, saying, "The best things in life are those that are only dreamed."

***

In New York a few days later, over dinner, Damiano revealed some surprising news: Butchie Peraino had provided them with two first-class ticket to fly to the French Riviera for the Cannes Film Festival. "He wants you to use your star power to beef up foreign distribution deals for *Deep Throat,* especially in the film markets of Western Europe. There's still a lot of money to be made from that suction pump you call your mouth."

"I'll jump at the chance," she said. "I've never been to Europe before. But I'm not doing it as a means of making more money for Butchie. He's already made millions off me. I'll do it to advance my own career."

"Don't forget that he fucked me, too," Damiano said, "Bigtime. But I'll go with the understanding that I'll be promoting a deal for myself. I've already got some interest from Roger Vadim."

"Is that someone I should know?" she asked.

"My God, woman, you need to get out more," he answered. "He's a famous French movie director. He married three of the most beautiful and seductive women on the planet—Brigitte Bardot, Catherine Deneuve, and Jane Fonda. Right now, he's in the throes of divorce from Fonda."

"I'd better check him out," she said.

"Well, he'll certainly be checking you out," Damiano predicted. "I learned that Vadim has this secret fetish. In addition to seducing beautiful women, he likes to fuck transsexuals. He once told this magazine writer that, "Men who have lost their dicks really get off receiving the cocks of men who still have their jewels.'"

It was inevitable that a rundown of her sexual adventures with the three bodybuilders would emerge before dessert was served. "I talked to Steve Reeves this afternoon," Damiano said. "Incidentally, on a scale of one to ten, Steve, along with Gordon and Mickey, gave you a ten. They thought you were terrific."

"I can't wait to go on the road with them with the revue," she said. "I want you to book a suite for the four of us. In fact, I've decided that four ways are always best. The worst is a three way with one man and two women. The man wears out too soon."

"Forget about sex for a moment," he lectured her. "We're talking business. Anyway, Steve said this old English queen wants to meet us when we attend the festival at Cannes. He lives in this huge villa at St-Jean-Cap-Ferrat. He wants to be the angel for our show."

"Angel?" she asked in amazement. "Sounds like we should have a role for the Devil. Maybe Sammy Davis, Jr. will go for it if the part is big enough."

"My dear girl," he said, "Don't you know anything? 'Angel' is the sucker who puts up money to finance a show. So in addition to our three originals, we need six more muscled, well-hung guys. This queen—we don't know his name, maybe he's an English earl—is hot for bodybuilders. He finances them as they travel from country to country competing for titles. In other words, these Hercules types sing for their supper."

"His current boyfriend, Steve told me, is Mr. Junior Germany. For the show, he'll shop us his favorites—one from England, another from Spain, and the remainder from Italy, Germany, Finland, and Austria."

"I certainly hope he lets me audition them," she said. "If they're anything like Steve, Gordon, and Mickey, I'm in for a treat."

"I'm sure they'll be even better than our boys and twenty years younger," he said. "I just know he'll let you audition them if you let him watch."

"He'll get an eyeful."

"The good news is we can slip out of town without Traynor," Damiano said. "He would only cramp your style and interfere with the deal."

Chuck had already flown back to Los Angeles, telling Linda that he had to tend to business at Linda Lovelace Enterprises, evaluating all the new offers that had come in for theatrical and film roles and for merchandising proposals.

"He might indeed be doing that," she said, "when he's not fucking Marilyn Chambers. He obviously can get it up for blondes more than he can for brunettes like me."

"To hell with him," Damiano said. "We don't want him tagging along with us to Cannes."

Two days later, Linda sat in a first-class seat on an Air France jet bound for Paris. Damiano occupied the seat next to her. Butchie had agreed to cover all their travel expenses, including the bills for their hotel suites. He told Damiano that when they arrived at the International Airport at Nice on the Côte d'Azur, a limousine would be waiting to haul them off to the Carlton Hotel at Cannes.

Based on the many millions he'd collected from his distribution of *Deep Throat,* Butchie had agreed to bankroll a $10,000 budget, most of it earmarked for gowns and accessories associated with Linda's appearances at Cannes.

Damiano had been given the address of a Left Bank outlet that sold designer gowns from such French fashion icons as Christian Dior and Coco Chanel. "Movie stars, French countesses, Princess Grace, whomever, can wear a gown only two or three times," Damiano said. "They don't dare be photographed wearing it any more than that. This outlet I know sells second-hand fashions at cut-rate prices. You'll be a sensation in anything they'd sell you. Your phone will be ringing night and day."

"I'm so excited," she said, as her plane landed in Paris at Orly Airport. "I don't think I've ever sucked a French dick before."

CHAPTER THIRTEEN
Last Tango in Hollywood

After shopping at the discount stores of Paris, Linda transported a suitcase of secondhand dresses aboard a flight to the airport at Nice, where a limousine waited to transport her and Gerard Damiano to their lodgings. They were driven westward along the Côte d'Azur to the resort of Cannes, where a suite awaited her at the very posh Hotel Carlton.

In her capacity as "show horse" for Bryanston Films, Butchie Peraino had booked a suite there for Linda, but had reserved "only a maid's room" for Damiano.

Exhausted, Damiano wanted to sleep for a few hours, agreeing to meet her for dinner at around eight, followed by their appearances at some private parties and film screenings.

"Will *Deep Throat* be shown?" she asked.

"Yes, at midnight," he said. "You'll get all the guys so hot, you'll have to go from row to row taking care of them, especially if they're international distributors."

After a few hours of rest, she showered, made up her face, and wandered downstairs into the lobby of the Carlton in a stunning champagne-colored Christian Dior dress. She didn't really know any of the producers and directors milling around, but within an hour, she was certain to meet a movie star, either coming or going from the Carlton.

How right she was. Within ten minutes, as she'd relate in a memoir, she encountered Rex Harrison. He came up to her—or, as she'd later recall, "came on to me was more like it."

"Tell me it's a mirage!" Harrison said with his clipped English accent. "The young beauty who thrilled me so in *Deep Throat,* not to mention what it did to one part of my anatomy."

She was stunned to meet him. As she later said, "I would think that an international star like Rex Harrison would have something better to do than watch *Deep Throat.*"

"Mr. Harrison, I'm delighted to shake your hand," she said. "I just loved you as Professor Henry Higgins in *My Fair Lady.*"

"I guess the whole world did," he said.

"I'm not necessarily here promoting *Deep Throat,*" she said. "Today, I'm selling Linda Lovelace more than just that movie. Everybody seems to be selling something here."

"True, true, my dear," he said. "But I've always found Cannes festivals like farting into cotton wool."

The British actor, **Rex Harrison**, nicknamed "Sexy Rexy," wooed **Audrey Hepburn** on screen in *My Fair Lady* (1964).

But at the Cannes Film Festival, a chance encounter in the lobby of the Carlton Hotel led to an assignation with Linda Lovelace.

"I've never done that, and I've never attended a festival," she said. "But I hear it's a place to make deals."

"That, too," he said, "although screwing around with wannabe starlets seems the primary goal on most peoples' agenda."

"Is your present wife in Cannes with you?" she asked.

"She's not, and thank you for asking. I think I understand the motive behind your question, and I'm flattered."

"My husband is in Los Angeles," she said. "A creep called Chuck Traynor."

"A creep," he said. "I see. Hell only knows there are a lot of them, and most of the buggers are here in Cannes for the festival. But speaking of marriage, though, I have always felt that the happiest married men I know have a wife to go home to, *not to go home with.* I vowed never to fit into the life of some woman. She has to fit into mine."

"Actually, as a wife, I'm beginning to adopt that motif for myself," she said.

"A liberated wife who's free to make dates outside the home—my favorite," he said. "Let's test the extent of your freedom. Would you be free to have a drink with me in my suite, this evening at six?"

"I'm not only free, but I'll count the hours," she said.

"See you then, you talented sweet thing, you. Forgive me. I'm late for an appointment."

Before her rendezvous with Harrison, Linda invited Damiano to her suite after his rest, telling him about her chance meeting with Harrison.

"Be careful with him," he said. "He's dangerous."

"Earlier, when he was married to Lilli Palmer, he had this adulterous affair with an actress named Carole Landis," Damiano said. "She was a pinup favorite of G.I. Joes, but short of talent. She fell for Sexy Rexy, but in 1948, just after she spent the night with him, she overdosed on sleeping pills when the cad dropped her. The fallout over her death, and the fact that he delayed calling the police for several hours after he found her body, caused such a scandal that Harrison fled Hollywood for the safety of the Queen's bosom in London."

"I read that he had affairs with Gene Tierney, Linda Darnell, Vivien Leigh, and Lana Turner," she said. "But those gals haven't seen what he looks like today. He certainly doesn't look as good as when he played Caesar in *Cleopatra* (1963) with Burton and Taylor."

'But he's still a big name, and you'd better pay homage to the dick that fucked Scarlett O'Hara," he said.

"I agree. So I'm off for my audition with what the movie mags used to call 'Tyrannous Rex.'"

***

The sixty-five year old actor who welcomed her into his suite at the Carlton looked like he'd survived many a disaster, both professional and personal. She'd always remember his eyes and would have agreed with the assessment of his doomed ex-wife, Rachel Roberts. "Rex's eyes are like embrasures in a medieval fortress behind which archers fired arrows and poured boiling oil."

An often slovenly dresser herself, Linda was stunned by the perfection of his wardrobe and his immaculate grooming. She was grateful she was attired in a designer gown and not in her usual cowboy hat, faded and ragged jeans, and boots.

The press agreed with Linda's evaluation of Harrison, claiming that he had "the look, the cut, of *le milord anglais.*"

Over champagne, he told her that his true character was best demonstrated by the title of a Preston Sturges comedy he'd released in 1948, *Unfaithfully Yours.* "If you didn't see it, don't worry," he said. "I couldn't get any of my ex-wives to go see it, either."

"Why do they call you Sexy Rexy?" she asked provocatively.

"I think Coral Browne dubbed me that while rejecting my advances during the play we did together, *Heroes Don't Cry,*" he answered. "But everything I learned was from this black belle when I was a young gent in Liverpool. She'd once worked in a whorehouse in Kingston, Jamaica, and knew how to perform acrobatic acts handed down from generations of African lore."

Years after her experience with him, Linda was relatively inarticulate in her descriptions of Harrison's special qualities as a man. Her editors often wished she'd described him as well as the actress Nancy Olson, who played "the girl" in *Sunset Blvd.*

"I found him very English," Olson said. "The perfect image of an English gentleman. Very independent, very opinionated, very judgmental, very male and arrogant, but in the best sense of the word."

Shortly before Linda's death in 2002, she read the most finely tuned description of Harrison. It had been written by Patrick Garland, the stage and film director. He wrote:

"Rex always appeared relaxed and elegantly turned out. This was part of his innate allure for women, a sensitive maleness, complemented by the low, enticing timbre of his cascading voice, which could 'roar you as gently as any suckling dove,' and the choreographic grace of his movement. It was the eloquent music of his sinuous voice, the swoops and barks and sudden, heart-stopping plunge of his tone, and the pantherine grace of his half-pouncing, half-floating walk which ploughed such furrows in feminine hearts."

After reading that, Linda said, "I should have met him years ago, when he was really like that."

Her own time with him, and very brief it was, was not at all romantic, according to her. "After we'd talked a bit, he rose to his feet, looking at his Rolex. "It's getting late, and I've got two appointments tonight. I want you to make love to me like you did to that bloke in your movie."

Then he stood up in front of her and unzipped his tailored Savile Row trousers and presented an average sized, uncut English cock. As Linda related later, "I got down on my knees and worked on him for a good fifteen minutes. When he didn't cum immediately, I reached into his pants and jiggled his balls, finally bringing him off."

After it was over, he said to her, "That was very nice, Linda. I must confess something. My critics say in private life I have a very direct tongue, and I say what I think, especially the truth, and I don't give a damn for the consequences. I asked you to come to the suite because of that braggart, Richard Burton. He's been going all over the West End, telling people you gave him a blow-job in Palm Springs. The next time I run into the bugger, I want to match his claim."

"Did you know that when I made *Staircase* with him in 1969, wherein we played a pair of homosexual lovers, that that sod, Burton, actually wanted me to bugger him in his dressing room? He told me that if I did that, we'd make our scenes together as lovers more believable. How cheeky of him. I told him I didn't think I could get it up for him."

"Well, I suppose I should be honored that you got it up for me," she said.

"Well, now, *My Fair Lady,* I must freshen myself a bit to appear in public as my witty, debonair, charismatic self, as the press so often says about me."

After bidding him good night, she practically ran down the hall to her own suite to rinse her mouth out thoroughly.

Years later, she said, "You can be *bloody* certain that I won't write glowing reports about Harrison in my memoirs. After looking that one-eyed snake of his in the eye, I decided it wasn't something that would ever make *me* commit suicide."

***

At dinner, Gerard Damiano had told Linda that Maria Schneider, the baby-faced, voluptuous co-star of *Last Tango in Paris,* was in Cannes.

In the French press, an article had appeared linking Linda with Maria. One Nice newspaper defined them as film pioneers setting a new standard in sexually explicit films, hailing both *Deep Throat* and *Last Tango* as symbols of the sexual revolution.

As in Hollywood, European producers, directors, and writers were predicting that in the future, A-list films would meet porn "half way along the bridge to a new type of cinema that would depict couples of any sexual persuasion in bed together."

Damiano suggested that Linda call Maria, who was also staying at the Carlton. "I bet you two gals would have a lot to talk about, beginning with Marlon Brando," he predicted.

After dinner, Linda somewhat reluctantly dialed Maria, who answered the phone herself. Unlike Linda, she was not staying in a suite, but in a small single room. She'd been paid only $4,000 for her performance in *Last Tango,* so she was operating on a tight budget.

Maria seemed delighted to hear from Linda, and each of the actresses congratulated the other on her respective film. That led to an invitation from Linda for Maria to visit her suite.

Within thirty minutes, she appeared and was welcomed into Linda's living room, where she'd ordered a bottle of champagne from room service.

Answering the door, Linda was dressed in a see-through black *négligée,* a recent acquisition from Paris, which had been paid for with Butchie Peraino's *Deep Throat* money. "We meet at last," she said to Maria.

Whereas Linda was dressed seductively, the *Last Tango* star was attired very simply in a dress the color of pink champagne. She kissed Linda on both cheeks.

As predicted, the talk centered around Marlon Brando, with several references to *Last Tango's* director, Bernardo Bertolucci.

"Both of them treated me like a sex symbol," Maria said. "I hated it. I don't want to be treated like that. There's more to me than that."

"That's so amazing," Linda told her. "I feel the same way about myself."

"I want to be a serious actress," Maria said, "but after those sex scenes with Marlon, no one will ever see me in any other capacity. The same thing will happen to you after *Deep Throat.*"

"Marilyn Monroe had the same problem, that of wanting to be taken seriously as an actress, because to the world of her era, she was just a sex doll," Linda said.

"Marilyn never escaped that image, and I fear the same fate awaits me, and perhaps you, too," Maria said.

"At least you got to work with one of the most acclaimed actors on the planet, Marlon Brando," Linda said. "I've deep-throated him, although it didn't go very deep."

"Marlon is overrated, and much of *Tango* is kitsch," Maria said. "Bertolucci as a director is also overrated, a fat, sweaty man manipulating me. It was Marlon's idea to apply butter on his prick before he sodomized me. Actually, he didn't sodomize me at all. All of it was faked. He never got it up, not even once, on the set."

Maria Schneider *(above, in a publicity shot for Last Tango in Paris)* and Linda Lovelace where the snickered-about talk of the Cannes film festival, as producers and distributors mulled over their respective roles in *Last Tango* and *Deep Throat*.

Instead of launching a competitve war, these two sex symbols ended up in bed together.

And the arrival of Maria's father made three.

"From my experience in porn," Linda said, "I've learned that the penis is the most unreliable of all organs."

"To be truthful, I felt raped by both Marlon and Bertolucci."

"Those are my sentiments exactly," Linda said. "I tell people who see *Deep Throat* that they're watching me get raped."

"After the scenes he put me through, Marlon did not apologize," Maria said. "People think we were actually fucking onscreen, but we did not. Marlon eventually became a father figure to me. He kept telling me that I reminded him of his daughter Cheyenne. If you ask me, I think he's in love with Cheyenne him-

514

self."

"One thing our films brought us, for better or worse, is fame," Linda said.

"That, too, has its downside," Maria said. "I can't handle the circus every time I step out the door. I've been doing drugs, mostly pot and coke, and on occasion some LSD and heroin. It's my escape from reality."

"I often go up in smoke myself," Linda said. "In Hollywood, you can't arrive anywhere without the host offering a snort of coke."

"Is your husband in Cannes?" Maria asked.

"No, and I don't want the bastard to be here, either," Linda said. "When I get back to Hollywood, I'm thinking of leaving him. Are you with someone now?"

"I am having an affair with a man right now," Maria said. "More about that later. If you don't mind, I've asked him to drop by later tonight, and I told him I'd be here, with you. Frankly, I much prefer sex with women, as I don't trust men. I reach out for sex, but only when I want it—in fact, I find you very attractive."

"The feeling is mutual," Linda said.

"As you know, *Last Tango* was about an older man having sex with a younger woman," Maria said. "Although Marlon and I didn't make it, I'm now reliving that scenario with another father figure. In the film, my character of Jeanne was supposed to be a Lolita, but more perverse. Guess what? The mystery lover in my life is my real father, Daniel Gélin. He abandoned us when I was a baby, and never publicly acknowledged me as his daughter until recently, after I became famous. I hope you have a sense of irony. Daniel is one of Marlon's most ardent lovers. They've been balling together, as you Americans say, for years."

Linda was startled. "I can hardly believe that. Such a coincidence."

She was eager to know more, and Maria carefully repeated that the famous French actor, who at the time was fifty-two years old, was her biological father. "He went from selling cans of salted cod to appearing with Marlene Dietrich and her lover, Jean Gabin, in *Martin Roumagnac* (1946). In the early 50s, he had an affair with a beautiful model, Marie-Christine Schneider. I am the result of their love mating."

As Linda would later recall, "It seemed inevitable that Maria and I would wind up in bed together. We loved fondling each other's breasts and masturbating one another before we got down to a serious sixty-nine. Maria went at it with more enthusiasm than I did, and she was good at it. She kissed me all over on the inside of my thighs. When she stuck her tongue deep inside me to massage my clitoris, I was transported to heaven. I did her, too, and it was fun and exciting. Even as I was doing it, I thought of the camera. If some cameraman had caught Maria Schneider and Linda Lovelace having sex together, it

Off-screen lovers, **Marlon Brando** *(left)* and French actor **Daniel Gélin** *(right)*, had both appeared on screen as Napoléon, Marlon in the Hollywood film *Désirée* (1954) and Gélin in the French film *Napoléon* (1955).

Gélin was the father of Maria Schneider, Brando's youthful co-star in *Last Tango in Paris*.

At the Carlton Hotel in Cannes, Linda later recalled, "Daniel, Maria, and I had a wonderfully incestuous time. I'm sure that if Marlon had been in town, he, too, would have hopped into our bed--*That Marlon!*"

would probably have become one of the hottest bestsellers around. After all, we were the two reigning sex symbols of the world, at least for a brief time."

It was at around 2am when a buzzer sounded within her suite at the Carlton. "That must be my father, Daniel. With your permission, I'll let him in. If you wish, you can learn what Marlon Brando found so exciting during all these years. And dare we ignore Marlene Dietrich and the great Jean Cocteau? I suspect that Brigitte Bardot, who has always been very good to me, has also enjoyed my father's sexual charms."

The buzzer sounded again as Maria, naked except for a large Carlton Hotel bath towel, answered the door. Rather high on alcohol, Gélin made his entrance into Linda's suite, kneeling on the carpet in front of her, kissing her hand like some French knight during the age of chivalry.

Gélin, along with his daughter and Linda, spent the first hour talking and drinking. When he learned that Linda had been sexually intimate with Brando, he spoke nostalgically of the actor whom he had seen only infrequently in recent years.

She was surprised to learn that Brando, during a brief residency in Paris in the late 40s, had shared a two-bedroom apartment with him on the quai d'Orléans.

"Christian Marquand and I shared a room in the same apartment with Brando and Vadim," Gélin said.

"What a coincidence," Linda said. "My director of *Deep Throat,* Gerard Damiano, is in Cannes, and he's been dying to meet Vadim. Is he also here?"

"Maria and I are going yachting with Roger tomorrow morning," Gélin said. "I'm sure he'd be delighted if you came along, perhaps with your director, too."

Daniel Gélin

"That would be wonderful," she said. "I might get to meet Jane Fonda."

"Perhaps not," Gélin said. "But back to when I lived with Marlon in Paris. Christian *[Marquand]* and I in those days were the Robert Taylor and Tyrone Power of France. Marlon was in love with both of us. He had sex with Christian in the afternoon, and me in bed with him at night. Of course, all of us had beautiful women on the side, whom we picked up randomly and discarded just as quickly."

"As an amusing coincidence, both Marlon and I, in the mid-1950s, played Bonaparte, me in France in *Napoléon* (1955) with Michele Morgan, and Marlon in Hollywood with Jean Simmons in *Desirée* (1954)."

[Gélin was a visible fixture during the existentialist craze that unfolded within Paris' post-war St-Germain-des-Prés scene, centered around such writers as Simone de Beauvoir and her lover, Jean-Paul Sartre. And for a brief period, Marlon became part of the new hot jazz generation in Paris that was launched in the aftermath of the Nazi occupation of France.]

"After we booted the Nazis out of town," Gélin said, "I taught Marlon to play the tom-tom, and we got bookings in some boîtes on the Left Bank. We enjoyed too much alcohol, and we experimented with cocaine and heroin. Our main goal was sexual freedom. The gender of our partner didn't matter—why should it? Both a penis and a vagina can bring satisfaction if put to the right use. We were eager to break the sexual taboos imposed on us by a restrictive society."

As she'd been by Marlon, Linda was mesmerized by Gélin and his accented charm. By 4am, Gélin, his daughter, Maria, and Linda were in bed together, having sex.

As she'd later recall, "I was never someone who condemned incest. After all, I'd been involved in brother-on-brother sex, mother and daughter sex, whatever. At one point, Gélin sodomized me, like Marlon was supposed to have done with Maria in *Last Tango*. While Gélin was doing that, I was going down on Maria. It was wild, and before dawn we'd done everything."

"It was a rather sleepy group of passengers who descended the next morning onto Vadim's yacht," Linda said. "I decided at the last minute that I didn't need Damiano, so I left him behind."

"As I was ushered aboard, I met Jane Fonda's then-husband, Roger Vadim," Linda said. "He was in a bikini so revealing it was what the French call...I forget, whatever. In English, it translates as 'sex-hider.'"

Vadim kissed her on the lips, and ushered her to the far end of the yacht to meet what he called "my blonde goddess."

At first, she thought she was Brigitte Bardot, but the woman's identity led to quite a different surprise.

The American transsexual and Andy Warhol star, **Candy Darling** *(photo above)* quickly managed to seduce French director Roger Vadim.

To the world, Vadim was known for marrying the three sexiest women on the planet—Brigitte Bardot, Jane Fonda, and Catherine Deneuve.

He also preferred kinky sex with transsexuals like Candy. If none were available, a transvestite would suffice.

***

Almost immediately after Vadim welcomed her aboard, he "French-kissed me."

Breaking away, he then asked, provocatively, "Does that mean I've sucked a thousand cocks by proxy?"

She opted not to answer, but thanked him for his invitation for her to come aboard. "It's all so romantic here," she told Vadim.

"As you'll find out later, so am I," the director said.

Vadim had also kissed both Maria Schneider and her father, Daniel Gélin. He'd then motioned for his crew to set sail for an overnight jaunt westward to the once-sleepy seafronting resort of St-Tropez, which Vadim's first wife, Brigitte Bardot, had helped to make famous.

After that, Vadim introduced Linda to the onboard "blonde goddess," identifying her as "Candy Darling." Linda asserted that she was delighted to meet her. But before lunch, she slipped away and asked Vadim, privately, "Who is this thing who calls herself Candy Darling?"

"She's an Andy Warhol star," he answered.

"Never heard of him, either," she said.

"Candy is a male-to-female transsexual," Vadim said. "I like to fuck transsexuals; if I can't get one, a transvestite will do. But mostly, I prefer real women, of course, as my list of international seductions proves."

"She's so feminine," Linda said. "It must be the hormones."

"Candy is also the muse of the protopunk band, 'The Velvet Under-

On board a yacht off the coast of Cannes, Candy Darling and Linda Lovelace vied for the attention of **Roger Vadim** *(photo, right)*.

When I came aboard, he kissed me," Linda said. "Later that night, I French kissed everything he had."

Later, when she was asked, "What was it like fucking Vadim?" Linda gave the most enigmatic answer: "He is both French and Russian. I much prefer the French side of his dick to the Russian side."

518

ground,'" Vadim said.

Over a champagne lunch, Vadim invited Linda to sit beside him. But when Candy emerged from below deck, she instructed Linda to move over. "You're occupying my place," she told her.

"Now, now, Candy," Vadim lectured her. "You know that jealousy is a bourgeois conceit. Thanks to the revolution of the 1960s, we're now free to indulge in sexual freedom. I, for one, believe in an open marriage. Just ask Jane Fonda. Whereas having sex outside marriage is not a betrayal of your spouse, falling in love with another person is quite a different matter. As for me, whenever someone coveted one of my three beautiful wives, I graciously stepped aside for a while. Call it Gallic politeness."

During lunch, Linda could hardly take her eyes off Candy, who was a beautiful blonde with a pretty face. It was hard to imagine her ever having been a young man.

"Oh, sweetheart," Candy said peevishly to Linda, "Please stop staring at me. Can't you figure it out? I'm a cross between Kim Novak and Pat Nixon, with the First Lady's nose."

After that, Linda shifted the focus of her gaze to Vadim, whom she found "quite handsome in a French sort of way."

Vadim was only half French, as his father was Russian. During the war, his widowed mother ran a hostel in the French Alps, sheltering Jews and other fugitives fleeing from Nazi Germany. His first film, *Et Dieu…Créa La Femme (And God Created Woman),* released in 1956, had made Vadim rich and Bardot a star.

Film critic David Thomson captured Vadim's elusive personality:

"It takes an empty-headed intellectual debauchée to enjoy so many pretty maids in the flesh and on celluloid, to watch them pass by him one after another, and yet persist with films that have all the suspended animation of a masturbatory dream. Scolds claimed that he disrobed so many of his own conquests to taunt us, and to make his prowess notorious."

Linda had already seen Vadim's film, *Barbarella* (1968), starring Jane Fonda, whom he had married in 1965. Film critic Molly Haskell had asserted, "Vadim is Fonda's Svengali, and as Josef von Sternberg was to Marlene Dietrich, he was ahead of his time in portraying female sexuality on the screen."

According to Vadim, "Jane was certainly a pioneer in playing sexually compromised characters, as she did in *Klute* (1961), which, as you know, won the Oscar for her. Playing a call girl, she brought orgasms to the screen, real or faked. But you, girls, Linda and Maria, have certainly taken up where Jane left off. That's why I want to talk to you about this film project."

"I'm working on a new script," he said. "I want to work with Brigitte again. I'll cast her as a rich Parisian lesbian who controls young women the way a

ET DIEU...
CREA LA FEMME

In English, the film was billed as *And God Created Woman,* but it was Roger Vadim, not God, who created the French sex kitten, **Brigitte Bardot** *(depicted in both images above),* whom he later married.

One of the great disappointments in Linda's lackluster career was the abandonment of a French film project in which she would have starred as Bardot's lesbian lover.

wealthy Sultan dominates the young girls of his harem. I was thinking of using Maria here as one of Brigitte's playmates, but it might be more dramatic if she had two lovers, both you, Linda, and Maria."

"The film is about a woman who has lots and lots of money, but who ends up bored, restless, and searching for some new depravity as a means of extracting herself from an otherwise dull existence of diamonds, couture, and young women at her beck and call," he said.

"I would love to play in a film with Bardot," Linda said. "It would clean up at the box office. I can see it now: BARDOT & LOVELACE & SCHNEIDER GET HOT TOGETHER

"I have many reservations about doing another sex film," Maria said.

"If Brigitte goes for it, I know she can talk you into doing it, too," Vadim said.

Throughout the course of this dialogue, Candy was more or less ignored. Eventually, she chided Vadim, "I hate it when you talk about other films that won't have a part for me. I'm still bitter that I didn't get to play in Gore Vidal's *Myra Breckinridge (1970).* I would have been ideal in the role of a transsexual—not that witch Raquel Welch."

"I was in Maui when I heard the bad news that I was not going to direct *Myra Breckinridge,"* Vadim said. "I would have cast Candy in the title role. Imagine directing Mae West. What camp!"

"Back in Hollywood, I upstaged that Raquel creature at the premiere of *Last Tango in Paris,"* Linda said. "The bitch probably detests me."

"But she still admires your talented throat," Candy chimed in. "As a matter of fact, everyone here, including Roger, has swallowed a few dicks in our day. Isn't that right, Daniel?"

"My, my, we're being *provocateuse* tonight," Gélin said. "But I suspect that all of us have gone down on *une belle bitte* from time to time."

"Not me so much," Maria said. "I'd much rather eat pussy."

That night over dinner on the deck of the yacht, Candy tried to dominate the evening. She kept urging Vadim to produce the film version of a 1964 off-Broadway play by Tom Eyen, *The White Whore and the Bit Player*, she'd performed in.

"I remember the exact words of one of my reviews," she said. "Some guy wrote that 'with her teased platinum hair and practiced pouts, Miss Darling looks like her character and resolutely keeps her acting little-girl-lost. The role-playing aspect works to her advantage. She could, after all, be a male lunatic pretending to be the White Whore.'"

"That's charming," Linda piped up. "I wish somebody would write something charming about me other than about my cocksucking."

Candy became increasingly drunk as the night progressed. At one point, she stood up, shouting, "LOOK AT ME! I AM A SELF-CREATION! Reinvention, of course, is at the heart of gay culture. I was told not to become a drag queen. So I became a transsexual instead. Mother didn't warn me against that."

Much to the annoyance of Candy, Vadim invited Linda to share his cabin that night. Once inside the room, as he undressed, he told her, "I want all the oral treatments. None of my wives has ever completely satisfied me in that pursuit. You understand I can get all the pussy I want. Tonight, however, I want fellatio from the expert."

She later revealed, "I loved Vadim's dick. Maybe it was a bit on the thin side, but it was magnificent. Before dawn, he delivered three loads. Around two o'clock, we were joined by Gélin, which made it all the more exciting. His dick was quite similar to that of Vadim's After that night, I hoped that more Frenchmen lay in my future, especially Alain Delon and Jean-Paul Belmondo."

On deck the next morning, Linda encountered Maria, who had spent the night with Candy. "How did it go?"

"A new horizon for me," Maria said. "I've never eaten transsexual pussy before."

***

A few days later, during the eastbound drive with Gerard Damiano from Cannes to the villa at St.-Jean-Cap-Ferrat of the mysterious backer of the muscleman show, Linda lied to her colleague about where she'd been. Rather than revealing that she'd opted not to include him aboard the yacht with Roger Vadim, Maria Schneider, Daniel Gélin, Candy Darling, and the others, she falsely asserted that Rex Harrison had invited her for an off-the-record liaison at a private villa. En route, Damiano reiterated his disappointment in failing to contact Vadim. He had wanted to persuade him to get involved in a project of his, a scenario that would star Brigitte Bardot and Alain Delon. *[That scenario was never concretized, dying, like so many other film projects, undeveloped and untested.]*

The identity of this mysterious backer of the muscleman show would remain unknown. Damiano and Linda didn't even know if he were a member of the English aristocracy. All they knew is what Steve Reeves told them—and that was "the old guy's loaded, and they call him 'the Earl.'" During his younger days, he had almost obsessively attended bodybuilding contests around the world, selecting young men he wanted to sponsor.

Damiano learned that the Earl then signed a contract with a young man, or young men as the case may be, offering each of them $100,000 a year to come and live with him at his villa. Other than their daily exercises to keep them buffed, the young men agreed to submit to being fellated at least once a day. Very few cash-strapped bodybuilders ever turned the Earl down.

Arriving at the Earl's sumptuous villa, Linda likened the building to the abode of a Sheik from Morocco. "It was straight from the movies," she said. Ushered inside, they were given two bedrooms in which to freshen up and make themselves ready for a lunch at one o'clock.

"Gerard and I had lunch alone on a terrace overlooking the Mediterranean," Linda said. "The Earl did not appear until 2:30pm, when he joined us for a cognac."

There was no sign of any bodybuilders, although Linda had hoped these musclemen would join her for lunch. Steve Reeves had claimed that the Earl kept at least five musclemen in residence all the time, and that he paid the expenses of these athletes to various bodybuilding contests around the world.

Relying heavily on a gold-handled cane, the Earl finally appeared, wearing a Savile Row suit better suited to a London winter than for a hot day on the French Riviera. He moved toward their table on unsteady legs, slowly seating himself and greeting them. Then he asked the butler for a cognac.

"I'm told not to drink, that it will hasten my death, but what in hell do I care? In fact, I think I might welcome death."

Reeves claimed that he learned that the Earl had been born in 1894, which would make him about eighty years old.

"He looked that and a bit more," Linda recalled. "His face was incredibly wrinkled—no facelift for him. It was a weathered face that was perhaps young-looking in 1917. All of his physical charms had faded with the snows of yesterday, except for his eyes. They were blue crystals and seemed to penetrate a person like an X-ray."

"I could just imagine the hundreds of bodybuilders who had removed their posing straps for his expert blow-jobs. He was probably a better cocksucker than I was, as he'd had more experience. Reeves told us that the Earl no doubt had sucked off half the British troops in the trenches when they battled the Kaiser's soldiers during World War I."

"Forgive me for being so indiscreet," the Earl said to Linda. "I do not like women because body odor offends me, except when it comes from a sweaty, drunken sailor. But, of course, I realize that a woman is essential to pull off a road show like Steve Reeves proposes. I haven't seen him in years. When he was in his twenties, I used to suck him off regularly."

Then the Earl outlined his own vision for the road show which Damiano had been commissioned to direct. "America was always my favorite country," he said. "I lived there during the Second World War. San Francisco, a great city. I became friends with Tennessee Williams, whom I met there. He wasn't much of a playwright, with his silly melodramas, but we agreed on one thing: There was nothing better than a soldier, marine, Air Force pilot, or sailor headed off in the morning to face possible death in the Pacific. To haul one of those boys into bed the night before they sailed, perhaps for their last fuck on Earth, was always a dynamic experience. In instance after instance in those days, I enjoyed the best sex of my life. My wasted life, incidentally, has been devoted to only one thing—the pursuit of sex."

Later, in his living room, the Earl waxed nostalgically about his world travels and his adventures. He told them that his trip to America would be his last to any country. "It's my *adieu* to the world. After that, I will come back to my villa to die."

"When I was a young man, like Howard Hughes in the 1920s, I financed a few silent pictures," he said "Of course, my stars had to sing for their suppers. I made that clear to whatever director I hired. I got Valentino in my bed one night. I also seduced John Gilbert. He was Greta Garbo's lover, though she was mostly dyke."

"Gilbert was romantic on screen, but not at all in bed. But at least I had him. My friend, Noël Coward, spent the night with Gilbert and got nowhere. Chasing him really wasn't worth it. I did enjoy William Boyd and Gary Cooper. Coop was the best. Bedding Ramon Novarro wasn't even a challenge." Then he turned to Linda. "Now that I've confessed my transgressions, who are some of the big names you've bedded?"

"Frank Sinatra, Sammy Davis, Jr., Robert Mitchum, Burt Lancaster, William Holden, Glenn Ford."

"An impressive list," the Earl said. "I only wish I had been in your high heels. I know you've had Steve Reeves, Mickey Hargitay, and Gordon Scott. I had them, too. Only I seduced them when they were in their twenties and full of more spunk."

"Right now, I've got my eye on this young bodybuilder from Austria," he said. "Arnold Schwarzenegger. I think he'll be big in the competitions. I plan to invite him here and offer to sponsor him because I know he's in need of money. With my help, he can become Mr. Universe. I'm never wrong about these things."

During the hour the Earl spent discussing the financing of the musclemen show, Linda sunbathed on the terrace, removing her top. Before the Earl retired for his afternoon siesta, he came out onto the terrace. "To some men, not me, you look rather enticing. For that reason, I must warn you. During the show, don't try to suck off my boys. They're under exclusive contract. Their dicks belong to me for one entire year. When that is up, they can take their $100,000, plus whatever they earn from your show, and run off and fuck anybody they want to, even a woman, although the idea of one of my boys putting their cock into a vagina repulses me."

"Before I retire for the afternoon with one of my picks, I'll introduce you to them in the gym where they're working out," the Earl said. "Even though they're from different countries, I prefer that all of them look as if they just stepped out of a Tom of Finland drawing."

She didn't know what that meant, so he explained it to her.

"Tom of Finland is the pseudonym of the foremost master of gay erotic art. His real name is Touko Laaksonen, and he's rather ugly. But the men he draws are very butch and handsome, super masculine, with such types as leathermen bikers, cops, soldiers, sailors, lumberjacks, hardhats, cowboys. All of them gay stereotypes."

In the Earl's private gym, each of the men, attired in a posing strap, was working out. Linda was thrilled to take in the sight of them, and regretted that the Earl was standing directly beside her with his gold cane and lusty eye.

Later, she recalled, "Each being from different European country, the men's faces were different, but not surprisingly, their bodies looked virtually the same, as if they'd been made from the same mold. I remember them and their hairless bodies so well. Each was powerfully built, a muscular Hercules, with a ripped stomach, thick arms and legs, beefy shoulders and biceps, all that from pumping iron every day. They had no tan lines so I knew they sunbathed in the nude, probably under the watchful eye of the Earl."

"My favorite was Mr. Junior Germany," she said. "Prussians are said to have blue yes, but his were green, almost a spring green, bright and with a gleam in them. I could tell he wanted me, but that damn Earl was standing guard. When we toured with the show, I knew I was going to get that hunk of beef. I couldn't wait to run my fingers through his sandy hair, which in the Riviera sun, looked platinum. He stood six feet, three, and he was the handsomest of the lot. He could have posed as a poster boy for Hitler."

"Unlike Mickey, Gordon, and Steve back in America, all these European bodybuilders were young, each with a body tuned to perfection through weightlifting. They were flawless, with silky smooth skins. Two of them had large rubbery nipples, the other were more modest but still suckable."

"The Italian, who had been Mr. Rome, was olive skinned. He eyes were dark blue. Didn't real Italians have brown eyes? His nose was long and straight, with a slight point. I think they call it a Roman nose. He had the longest dark lashes of any man I've ever known, and very curly black hair. His lower lip was slightly puffier than his upper one, and he had a dimple in his rounded chin. I suspected he was the youngest of them all, perhaps a teenager. When he looked at me, his dancing eyes were filled with desire. Or did I imagine that? For all I knew, he was a fag."

***

In New York, after her return from Cannes, Damiano and Linda heard the bad news from Steve Reeves: Shortly after their visit, the Earl had died of a heart attack. Linda was devastated, because of all the projects being developed, that show was the one she most wanted to perform. All those musclemen and the gorgeous gowns she would have worn were reason enough for her to dream about starring in just such a show.

She wondered what was to become of all the musclemen at the Earl's Riviera estate. Perhaps some of them would find other sponsors.

Reeves assured everyone that he'd find another "angel" for the show, but he never did. "It was a dream only to be dreamed, like so many other projects offered to me," she said. "Like James Dean, ninety percent of the people in Hollywood regularly and frequently walk along 'The Boulevard of Broken Dreams.'"

***

"Back in Hollywood, Chuck Traynor gave me a chilly reception and told me what I already knew," Linda said. "No important live act, advertising deal, film, or sponsorship arrangement had been finalized. Everything was unfocused, everything was still pending."

"My datebook, however, had filled up, and I figured that at least as far as sex gigs, there was some money to be made. William Holden was about to throw a party for the male cast of *The Devil's Brigade* (1968), and he promised me I'd clear $2,000 if I worked his little gathering, although I was sure to end up with a sore throat."

She accepted Holden's offer of including her as part of the evening's entertainment, scheduled for the upcoming Saturday night.

As Holden told her, "I invited Carroll O'Connor and Michael Rennie, but they won't be in town. But get this: You'll get to meet, close up and very, very personal, Dana Andrews, Cliff Robertson, Vince Edwards, Richard Jaeckel, and James Craig."

"What a mouthful!" she said. "I'm looking forward to it!"

Before the end of her second day in California, she'd scheduled other appointments, too. "John Derek called from New York and gave me the number of Nicholas Ray," she said. "Nick was still interested in making some porn. And Aldo Ray called me back about that invitation to his health club, where he promised that I'd get to meet John Wayne and Forrest Tucker."

"Burt Lancaster had also phoned, wanting me to drive to Malibu, where he and Tony Curtis were staying at a beach house. I'd already had both of them, but each of them was up for a repeat performance. The subject of money never came up, however, and my bank account was low. It costs money hanging out and talking about deals, here and abroad."

"My strangest invitation came in from Sammy himself, who was back in Los Angeles," Linda claimed. "He wanted me to go with him to a shooting range to meet Chuck Connors, the guy who had starred with him in the hit TV series, *The Rifleman.* I had already seen Chuck naked and shaking it at our bar on North Miami Beach, when my Chuck had shown those porno loops made by stars before they became famous. But seeing Chuck Connors on the screen and in person were two different horses. I knew he'd be older, at least in his fifties, but I bet he was still hot. On another note, Sammy was no longer inviting me to his home. I just knew Altovise was behind that."

Shortly after her return, Linda arranged a luncheon date with Liz Renay, who was still dating Pupu. Linda pointedly asked her friend, "What about your husband? Aren't you married?"

"Oh, darling, I can never remember," Renay said. "I'm either married or between marriages. Who are you to throw stones? When was the last time you schlepped into bed with Chuck Traynor, not that I blame you."

"*Touchée,*" Linda said. "That's a new word I learned in France."

During their lunch, it became clear that Renay clearly wanted revenge, or something, on Glenn Ford for dumping her so unceremoniously when she was "madly in love with the skunk," as she phrased it.

"I got to know every inch of that handsome devil," Renay said. "We rolled in the hay on my first date. I became his 'Angel,' and he became my Prince Charming. He inserted his dick in every orifice I had or between my breasts. I must say that of all the men I've seduced, he had the sweetest-tasting cum, as you are by now well aware."

"Glenn knows how to make wild, passionate love. Kisses, sweet nothings, in a gal's ear, during all that *après-sex* pillow talk. As you yourself experienced, he's a hard-driving pounder who will leave you screaming at orgasm time. After sex, we always talked over drinks, sometimes for hours at a time, about his big plans for the both of us."

"But he never took me to the hotspots like George Raft did when he dated me," Renay claimed. "He even denied to a reporter that he knew me. He was between marriages at the time, so a wife at home was not the reason for his blackout of me in the press."

"All of his talk about helping me was just make believe," Renay said. "Glenn is a non-paying trick, nothing more. I didn't really lose. At least I got to enjoy some of the best sex I've ever had—and that's something, isn't it?"

"So, as you told me before, you want me to have sex with Glenn in front of a concealed camera?" Linda said. "I like Glenn, and I don't really want to do this, but you're the only woman friend I have in the world. I don't like being a party to blackmail, however."

"I'm not sure it's actually blackmail," she said. "That's not yet been decided. Maybe it's blackmail, but not necessarily for money, though I could use some. I'll be very frank with you: If he knows I've got him on film having sex with you, I might use it as a weapon to get him back in my bed doing his duty. and I'm probably still in love with him to the degree that I'm resorting to this."

"You mean, a kind of sexual blackmail?" Linda said. "Well, maybe I could go along with that, if you want his dick that much. But he left Palm Springs with no forwarding address."

"Leave that to me," she said. "I'll have a personal letter delivered from you to him at his home. It'll be an invitation for a rendezvous with you in this suite at the Beverly Hills Hotel, whose bill will be taken care of, never mind by whom. I know the guy had some real sexual thrills with you. He's always horny. He'll come running, or cum in some way, at least."

Although reluctant, Linda agreed to go through with it. Within a few days, Ford called her, apologizing for having left Palm Springs without getting in touch with her. He accepted her invitation.

A few hours before Ford's anticipated arrival at the Beverly Hills Hotel, Renay reviewed the layout of the suite with Linda, showing her where the camera was concealed.

Linda, too, wanted a repeat bout with Ford, even if she had to participate in this secret filming.

She'd learned long ago that Mickey Cohen often blackmailed stars who had been filmed during sex, and she hoped Renay wouldn't turn over this loop to the gangster. Renay promised she wouldn't. But as Linda

Hell hath no fury like a woman scorned:

Liz Renay

527

later said, "Is there anybody in Hollywood you can trust? It's the world's stab-in-the-back capital."

***

By 8:30pm in the pre-paid suite at the Beverly Hills Hotel, Ford proved himself once again as a skilled lover, as so many women in his past or future could testify. Some of them included Linda Christian (who had married Tyrone Power), perhaps Hope Lange, Carol Lynley, Maria Schell, Connie Stevens, and Joanna Copeland Carson, ex-wife of Johnny Carson. In revenge, or because of a personal grudge, Carson had made so many cracks about Ford on *The Tonight Show* that the actor contemplated suing the TV host.

His very touch sent an electrifying thrill through Linda's body, just as it had done in Palm Springs. Her excitement was enhanced because the sex act with him was being filmed. Little moans of pleasure escaped from her much-used lips, and his breathing grew heavy as he headed toward home. At the pivotal moment, she cried out in ecstasy as he twisted and bounced on top of her.

After sex, he didn't talk, but fell asleep for about an hour before he woke up to find her staring lovingly into his face. "Shower with me and then I want to end the night with an around-the-world from you."

She wondered if there would be enough film in the camera to include all that.

Everything went smoothly until the very end of the evening, at about 2am. As a fully dressed and fully satisfied Ford was telling a robed Linda goodbye, she blurted out the wrong remark:

"I love you, Glenn Ford," she said.

"Hey, girl," he said. "We'll have none of that. Take care. Gotta run."

[Editorial note: One can only surmise about the fate, the whereabouts, and the ultimate purpose of this alleged sex tape. But one wonders whether word of its existence ever trickled back to Ford, and whether in the aftermath of any attempt to blackmail or coerce him, it contributed to the eventual downfall of Linda Lovelace's hopes and dreams for a continued career among the moguls of Hollywood.]

Feeling guilty after that evening with Ford, followed by his brush-off, she never asked Renay for a screening of the loop of her having sex with the actor. She really didn't want to know what Renay planned to do with the loop. She had hated it when she'd been publicly exposed as the star of *The Dog Fucker,* and under ordinary circumstances, she disliked entrapment of people.

***

528

A few days later, during her drive to Malibu, she had other actors on her mind, namely Burt Lancaster and Tony Curtis, who as a team had made two of her favorite films together, *Trapeze* in 1956 and *Sweet Smell of Success* in 1957.

At the small beach villa where their meeting had been scheduled, she found both Curtis and Lancaster in the nude. "We were sunbathing on the roof," Lancaster said. "Tony and I didn't bother to put on our clothes because you've already seen what we have."

"And how good it looks," she said with a bit more enthusiasm than she felt. "After all, these guys didn't have that much to show," she'd later claim.

Out on the terrace overlooking the Pacific, she stripped off her clothes and snorted cocaine with them, compliments of Curtis. He had yet to become an addict.

From their talk, she judged that both Lancaster and Curtis had been lovers for years. They obviously liked to tease each other. Both Linda and Curtis spoke of growing up in New York, she in Yonkers, Curtis in the Bronx. Lancaster, too, was a New Yorker, having been born on East 106th Street in Manhattan's East Harlem.

"When I was born, I was called the runt of the family," Lancaster said. He flexed his muscles. "Look at me now."

"Who would want to look at you, Burt, when I'm around," Curtis said. "After all, I was the prettiest boy in Hollywood in the '50s."

"Well, I'm not the prettiest gal in Hollywood, but I have a certain talent," she said.

"We know that, and that's why you're here," Lancaster said.

"Linda and I met at Hef's Playboy mansion," Curtis said. "Believe it or not, even though I'm a known sex offender, I sometimes stay in my room there, alone like a hermit. Of course, any time I want, I can go downstairs and be surrounded by beautiful women, each of whom find me desirable."

"Neither Tony nor I can exactly qualify as a saint, though," Lancaster said. "I guess I'm the guy who went to bed with the leading lady—even if it was after the movie was finished."

Combined with the cocaine was marijuana, which made the unholy trio rather confessional. The conversation veered toward relating stories about their respective "first times." Linda admitted that she was the object of child molestation on a camping trip by a friend of the family. "And I loved every inch of it," she said. "I was no victim. This was one kid who wanted to be molested."

Lancaster said that he grew up in an era when "girls put a lock on it. I hung out with this gang of six boys and one cocksucker. We kept that blonde-haired, rather pretty boy busy. He loved it, and we did, too. Even back then, I decided a hole was a hole was a hole."

"My life only began when I entered a movie theater by myself," Curtis said. "I was one cute guy. I really came to see the picture show, but I always found an older guy in the seat beside me. His fingers wandered. While I watched Betty Grable, he was on his knees on that sticky floor giving me head. I really lost my virginity with a woman in a Panama City whorehouse when I was only seventeen and in the Navy."

"When I first came to Hollywood, all the beautiful women and all the gay guys were after me," Curtis claimed. "I got no rest. I even met up with a pervert like Burt here. He was the first guy to invade my rosebud. He was already a big star, and I was forced to give in to him."

"Yeah, right, and you loved it, bitch," Lancaster said.

"How did you guys meet?" Linda asked.

"I made my movie debut in this *film noir* thing called *Criss Cross* (1949)," Curtis said. "It starred Burt and Yvonne De Carlo. I was on the screen for about two minutes doing the rumba with Yvonne. Even though I was only an uncredited bit player, I was so good-looking I ended up fucking both stars."

"Or getting fucked by one of them," Lancaster corrected him.

"You see, Burt and I worked out at the same gym and became rather intimately acquainted with each other's anatomy. Although I was afraid Howard Hughes might cut my nuts off, I started dating Yvonne. After a few nights, we landed in the sack. The thrill of stripping her was indescribable. Having her naked with me under hot sheets with a scenic view over Los Angeles was like winning lottery. Thus began my romance with sweet, sexy Hollywood."

In one of their most famous films, **Sweet Smell of Success** (1957), **Tony Curtis** (left) played a smarmy press agent who'd do *anything* to curry the favor of a ruthless, all-powerful newspaper columnist, as played by **Burt Lancaster** (right).

Lancaster's character was based on the real life media mogul, Walter Winchell.

"The script called for me to do anything for Burt, and he took that literally when the studio shut down for the day and he summoned me to his dressing room," Curtis claimed.

Years later, Linda got the opportunity to witness a repeat performance.

"I never told you this, kid," Lancaster said, "but I got to fuck Yvonne two years before you did when we made *Brute Force* in '47," Lancaster said. "I drove her home one night when her parents were asleep. I had her in the backyard under an oleander bush."

"I always say that being a Johnny-cum-lately is better than no cumming at all," Linda told Curtis.

"And you'd better believe it," he answered.

"Well, you two guys have

certainly succeeded at a long-term open relationship—it's survived for years through wives, adversity, lovers of any gender…and me," she said.

"There were rough spots," Curtis claimed. "When I made *Operation Petticoat* (1959) with Cary Grant, Burt didn't speak to me for months after he found out I was shacking up with Cary."

"Well, he wasn't exactly jealous—he was just punishing you for your poor taste in men," Linda said jokingly. "Actually, I met Grant at a party Sammy Davis, Jr. took me to. I said hello and Grant looked at me like I was a pig's liver left out in the sun for too long."

Linda continued: "I've gone to bed with every star who's ever asked me. I think it would be very embarrassing to turn down a big movie star, even if you're already a big movie star yourself, like you guys."

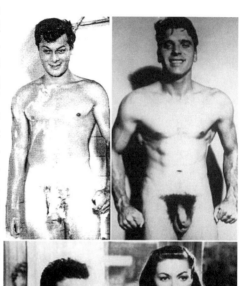

"It is," Curtis claimed. "I once attended this party in London that was thrown for me by Marlene Dietrich and Rex Harrison. I told Marlene that I was heading for Paris. She said that she was, too, and that she'd be staying at the George V. She asked me to call her for a rendezvous after ten o'clock any night of the week. I never did. After all, she was fifty-five years old."

"I also turned down Elvis Presley when he first came to Hollywood," Curtis claimed. "He is a closeted bisexual, you know. He copied my hair-do and some of my mannerisms. I think he idolized me. Or else wanted to be me."

"Elvis is at the top of my list of the men I want to seduce," Linda said. "One night, I'll get him, and tell you guys what it was like."

"I never fucked Elvis," Lancaster said, "but I'd like to. Unlike Tony, I was more chivalrous with Marlene and banged the hell out of

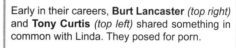

Early in their careers, **Burt Lancaster** *(top right)* and **Tony Curtis** *(top left)* shared something in common with Linda. They posed for porn.

In the publicity still *(lower photo)* from *Criss Cross*, Lancaster, pictured with **Yvonne De Carlo** and Curtis each conducted secret affairs with the film beauty whenever her billionaire boyfriend, Howard Hughes, wasn't looking.

her."

"Hell, Burt, you'd screw Marie Ouspenskaya, and she was born a decade after the Civil War," Curtis said. "You even got off fucking Shelley Winters, that big, brassy, loud, blonde bitch from Brooklyn."

"I did have to slam the door in Monty Clift's face when we were shooting *From Here to Eternity,*" Lancaster said. "He couldn't get enough of me. When I finally told him, 'You've had enough,' he turned on me. He told this reporter that I was 'a big bag of wind and the most unctuous man he'd ever met.'"

Talking in such an intimate and personal way with Lancaster and Curtis made Linda feel she was part of insider Hollywood. She hoped her adulation from the stars would go on forever, but feared that it wouldn't unless she developed another star vehicle like *Deep Throat.* "I didn't fully realize it at the time," she later said, "but the Linda Lovelace juice had a 'sell by…' date written on the bottle."

"Burt and I can talk freely around you," Curtis said to Linda, "because we know you're a fellow fucker from the A-list. Take the film we did in '63 called *The List of Adrian Messenger.* I bet you've had all five of the stars in the film. That means me and Burt here, but also Frank Sinatra, Bob Mitchum, and Kirk Douglas."

"I've yet to get around to Douglas," she said. "All in due time."

"There's a lot to be said about being bisexual, don't you think, Linda?" Lancaster said. "The world knows you're a skilled fellatio artist. But I also hear you're an expert at cunnilingus. Perhaps even better than Tony and me. Which do you prefer?"

"Right this minute, your two dicks," she said. "Let's go upstairs. We're wasting valuable time."

"Don't worry about Tony wetting the bed," Lancaster said.

"Cut the crap!" Curtis said. "That was decades ago, in the Bronx."

***

Linda's life was beginning to change for the worse. "Hollywood hates a failure, and you're only as good as your latest picture," she said. *"Deep Throat Part II* was ridiculed and it bombed at the box office. After that, film offers were slim. I had two or three vague commitments, none of which was very promising."

"I went with Sammy Davis, Jr., to this seedy-looking shooting range, where I met Chuck Connors. He and Sammy were good friends."

Up until then, Linda didn't know that Sammy, partly based on his appearance in westerns, was one of the finest gun twirlers in the West. He'd been one of Connor's favorite guest stars on episodes of his hit TV series, *The Rifleman.*

In one episode (#131; *Two Ounces of Tin)*, Sammy had been cast as a gunman with a killer's reputation and a burning hatred for all lawmen.

When she met Connors, she found him still handsome, tall, and emitting an aura of rugged masculinity. He was in his early fifties and no longer the "hottie" she'd seen in a porno loop in North Miami Beach, sodomizing some young man in the days before he became a star in both the worlds of baseball and on film.

As for his taste in music, Connors was big into the sounds of what might be defined as "retro-nostalgic." The late "big band" sound of Glenn Miller was his favorite, followed by the music of Sammy Davis, Jr., and then Frank Sinatra.

"I stood around for two hours watching them practice shooting," Linda said. "Finally, it was over. Sammy talked to the manager of the range, while Chuck went into the back and took a shower. It was a hot day. Sammy came to me and told me that Chuck was ready for me. I was ushered to a private room in the rear of the clubhouse."

"When I entered, the windowless room was rather dark, with only a small lightbulb," she said. "Chuck's still attractive body stood before me, wrapped in a bath towel. Without any preliminaries, he dropped the towel and lay down on a table with matting, presumably used for giving shooters (no pun intended) a massage after target practice. It was obvious he wanted a blow-job—no chit chat, no foreplay, no missionary sex, and no tongue kissing."

"Unlike many other stars, Chuck really carried around a big bat between his legs," Linda recalled. "Even at his age, he still could pound his meat into me as he'd done when he'd made porn. I really worked him

Around Hollywood, **Chuck Connors** *(right)* and **Sammy Davis, Jr**. *(left)* were known as the odd couple.

Connors, a former performer in both gay and straight porn, was the star of the hit TV series, *The Rifleman (1958-1963)*, but Sammy was known mainly for his skills at singing and dancing. Few of his fans knew that he was among the fastest guns in the West.

Years after the series ended, Linda got involved with each of their respective guns. Young actor and former Mousketeer **Johnny Crawford** *(center)*, according to Linda, missed out on all the fun.

over. I knew he'd been to bed with Liz Renay, and although I like Liz, we were also competitive starfuckers. I wanted him to claim afterward that I was better than Liz."

"He blasted off like a rocket to the moon—and that was that. Giving him that blow-job got me all hot and bothered, but he didn't take care of me. I guess I'd have to leave it to Sammy later that night to satisfy me."

"Don't get me wrong. Chuck was a real nice guy. I just wish I'd had more of him. He sure had the right kind of assault weapon. But I guess half of Hollywood already knew that, so he must have been kept pretty busy."

"Sammy told me that by now, Connors was too big and powerful to have to drop trou for famous male stars the way he did when he was first launching himself in Hollywood."

"Goodbye, Chuck baby, and thanks for the memory. Cum again (this time, pun intended)."

***

"That night, Sammy drove me back to his home," she recalled. "The place was empty—no Altovise, although I knew they were still together. He was distracted, and I understood that he had a lot of money problems, career issues, troubles with the IRS."

After dinner served by a houseboy, we retired to his bedroom. I was shocked that he didn't want his usual blow-job. He made love to me in the old-fashioned missionary position. Normal sex, the first time ever. He wasn't trying to get rid of me. We were in bed for hours, and he held me tenderly, kissing me and telling me how much he loved me and wanted me for his wife instead of Altovise. "

"Who knows what happened after that night," she said. "He and Altovise were together until the end. Maybe she put her foot down. No more Linda Lovelace."

"That night marked the end of our romance. We never went to bed together again. He saw me at a couple of parties in Las Vegas and Hollywood, but our affair was over. Sammy was a good man, at least to me, and he did me a few favors, including one big one when—a few weeks later after I dumped Chuck Traynor—he passed me along to another man,"

"It took me a while to realize that my thing with Sammy was really over, and I loved him in my own way."

"I got the shock of my life, though, when Liz Renay told me that Sammy had discovered a new porn star. It was asshole Chuck Traynor who had set Sammy up with a new fuck buddy, my chief rival, Marilyn Chambers. Not only was she banging my husband and my friend and lover, Sammy, but she was kicking me off my throne as Queen of Porn, too."

***

After Chuck Connors, Linda set up yet another date within a sports venue. This one was in Burbank, Los Angeles, with Aldo Ray, with whose anatomy she already had a working relationship.

There, at the Lakeside Country Club *[which was defined by* The Hollywood Reporter *as one of the Entertainment Industry's top seven golf courses for the ongoing cachet of the dealmaking and star power of its members],* she was about to meet his pals, John Wayne and Forrest Tucker.

When she got there, Ray offered her a drink and told her to wait on the terrace. Wayne and Tucker were finishing a round of golf. It was understood that when he was ready, Wayne would receive her in the clubhouse within a private room that was used for massages. Tucker, followed by Ray, would follow in intervals of about thirty minutes each. "Save the last kiss for me," Ray told her with a slight smirk.

Before her visit to this trio of actors, Linda had telephoned Liz Renay, who had previously been intimate with Tucker but not with Wayne, for advice.

Wayne himself once said, "Women scare the hell out of me. I've always been afraid of them." Nonetheless, he had wandered into the boudoirs of Clara Bow, Marlene Dietrich ("the best lay I ever had"), Paulette Goddard ("Wayne was no Charlie Chaplin"), Carmen Miranda, and Claire Trevor, his co-star in *Stagecoach* (1939).

Renay, through her contacts with Las Vegas showgirls, Los Angeles prostitutes, and an array of minor actresses, knew the penis measurements and performance skills of virtually every male star in Hollywood, even the few she hadn't personally seduced.

Renay warned Linda not to get her hopes up for Wayne. She brought Linda up to date on all the gossip. His former co-star, Joan Crawford, who had made *Reunion in France* with Wayne in 1942, said, "Once you get him off the horse and out of the saddle, you've got nothing."

Director William Wellman told the press, "Wayne walks like a fairy. He's the only man in the world who can do that—and get away with it."

The only known report of Wayne's penis had come from a U.S. Serviceman. Exempted from military service because of a family deferment, Wayne had flown to the South Pacific Theater in 1943 and '44 touring U.S. bases there. His tent-mate on the USO tour was a serviceman who often saw Wayne nude.

"I must confess," he told an off-duty newspaper reporter. "I was a bit surprised to see that he had a very small (conservative even in that respect) uncut penis."

The "golden age" film director, John Ford, who had seduced Wayne when he first arrived in Hollywood in the 1920s, had warned Wayne's co-star, Maureen O'Hara, that there wasn't much there, as she reported in her memoirs.

Linda later admitted that at the Lakeside Country Club, she wasn't expecting much when she opened the door that led to a private, dimly lit massage room where a freshly showered Wayne was waiting for her with a bath towel wrapped around his midriff. He was drinking from a glass tumbler. A bottle of Wild Turkey rested on a table nearby.

"Just the gal I've been waiting to see," he said in well-known patterns which resembled something between a drawl and a growl.

"Glad to see you, too," she said. "At least I get to meet the great John Wayne."

"Not so great any more," he said. "I once made a film back in '31 called *Girls Demand Excitement.* At my age, I'm more like a film I made in '32, *The Hollywood Handicap.*"

At sixty-six years of age, after a hard-living, hard-drinking life, he certainly didn't look like the handsome cowboy who had stunned audiences when he'd changed his name from Marion Morrison to "John Wayne" prior to his starring role in *The Big Trail* (1930).

Pulling off his towel, he revealed the penis that had disappointed silent screen star Clara Bow. Lying down before her, he said, "Go to it, gal. Bring life to that tired old thing." Then he reached for her head with his hands, which were almost twice the size of the hands of the average male. She went to work.

She later had little to say about their interchange. "Except for the penile difference, I was virtually repeating the same gig I'd just had with Chuck Connors. Then, suddenly, it was over.

Wayne got dressed, thanked her, and went to join some of his drinking buddies. Within fifteen minutes, a hot, sweaty, and horny Forrest Tucker entered the massage room. Immediately, he grabbed and kissed her. "Do you want me to shower first?"

During her brief chat with **John Wayne** *(photo left)*, Linda told him that she wanted to become a legitimate (i.e., non-porn) actress, but that she was very discouraged so far.

He told her, "Don't give up. When they tried giving me dramatic lessons, the teacher told me, 'Young man, you'll never be an actor in a hundred years.' I agreed with him wholeheartedly. If you can't act, develop a style, a persona that people can relate to, and then play yourself in picture after picture."

He also told her, "Monty Clift sucked my dick one drunken night when we made *Red River.* He gagged. You didn't gag at all, gulping it down with the greatest of ease. It's more flattering to a man when the cocksucker gags."

"Not at all," she said. "I like the smell of you now…a real man."

"That's my girl," Tucker said.

"In complete contrast to that dud they called Duke, Forrest Tucker was a beast of a different stripe," she said. "He was Hollywood's incorrigible gunslinger in more ways than one—and what a gun! Gun is not the right word. A cannon would be more like it."

James Bacon (1914-2010), the Hollywood columnist who received a star on the Hollywood Walk of Fame in 2007, wrote that "Tuck's big cock was the chief tourist attraction at Lakeside. As Tuck lay passed out drunk on one of the massage tables up front, a stream of members, along with their invited guests, paraded into the locker room for the unveiling. There was the lifting of the towel and a lot of ooohs and ahs."

Another Hollywood columnist, Bill Smith, likened Tuck's penis "to a baby's arm holding an apple."

Today, "Tuck," for those who remember him, is known mainly for his 1958 role as the Southern gent who makes *Auntie Mame* (Rosalind Russell) a rich widow, and for his role in the TV spoof sitcom, *F Troop*, which ran from 1965 to 1967.

Linda had immediately liked Tuck. "He wanted love every which way and complimented me about how I could take him in all three of my holes."

"I can't find many gals who are up for that," he said. "Sometimes when I take off my pants, a gal screams and runs. Others go crazy for me."

"Men like Wayne dropped me after sampling my skills," Linda said. "But Tuck was different. He called me for at least five more dates before I left Hollywood."

On the Lakeside Golf Course which Linda visited for the "servicing" of **Forrest Tucker** *(photo above)*, she heard about a famous golf match between the cowboy star and the actor/comedian Phil Harris. Aiming for the 17th hole, Tucker teed off, his ball hitting the green only a foot from the hole.

It took Harris three shots to come within four feet of the hole. Since he was so close to winning, Tucker wanted to declare victory and move on. Harris, however, was adamant, demanding that Tucker complete the shot.

"God damn it, Phil," Tucker said. The Chief (a reference to his penis) can make the fucking hole."

Harris reached into his baggy pants and withdrew five $20 bills. "You're on," Tucker said. He unbuttoned his pants, pulled out his mighty "club," fell to a position on his hands and knees above the turf, and scored a perfect bull's eye with his swinging dick.

Of all the men I've sampled in Hollywood, Tuck was the most masculine," she recalled. "A real man's man, Duke Wayne got him cast in his biggest hit, *The Sands of Iwo Jima* (1949). Both men were Barry Goldwater supporters, very conservative. But once the door was shut, Tuck wasn't conservative at all. As he said, 'The Chief' likes to get down and dirty. He called his dick The Chief. He was a son of the Depression era, and sometimes talked about his past. His father died of mustard gas poisoning in World War I, and his mother was a 'tough old broad and former burlesque queen.'"

"He was a rough-and-tough kind of guy, a hard drinker and a womanizer. Hollywood needs more men like him. He should have gotten all those tough roles Wayne did, but the public wanted to see pictures with that so-called Duke. Actually, I wanted to marry Tuck and become his sex slave, but I knew that was never going to happen. My loss...."

***

"I think the director, **Nicholas Ray** *(photo above)*, if he'd signed me on, could have made an actress out of me. I'd seen most of his films. But he turned his attention to Marilyn Chambers. She seemed to always have her shopping cart in my personal grocery store--Chuck Traynor, Sammy Davis, Jr., and Nicholas Ray."

Linda later revealed, "I did hear from Ray four months before he died of cancer in 1979. His note to me read, 'Among my many sins is my failure to respond to your urgent pleas. You wanted me to make you a star. I knew I couldn't. At that time I had lost my sense of wonder. Without it, I was nothing. No good to you, no good to myself.'"

"'See you in Hell.'"

Linda was having no success getting in touch with Nicholas Ray, although John Derek had assured her that he was still interested in making an XXX-rated movie with her. But she could never get him to call her back in spite of the repeated messages she left for him.

Ever since she'd seen James Dean in *Rebel Without a Cause* (1955), he'd been one of her favorite directors.

Linda allowed her fantasy about Ray to run wild. She even envisioned that she might become the new woman in his life, thereby adding herself to a list that included Marilyn Monroe, Jayne Mansfield, Sal Mineo, Natalie Wood, and James Dean. Linda had read that he'd even seduced Joan Crawford when he'd directed her in the camp classic, *Johnny Guitar* (1954). Ray had shown a knack for keeping illustrious company, and Linda fantasized that she might become something through Ray both on the screen and in his private life.

[Nicholas Ray had directed one of her alltime favorite movies, Rebel Without a Cause (1955), *starring James Dean. From the movie magazines, Linda had learned that Ray's first wife had been actress Gloria Grahame, whom he'd married in 1948, but divorced in 1952. He had discovered her in bed with his thirteen-year-old son, Tony Ray.]*

As a heavy user of drugs and alcohol, the occasionally unstable Ray had found himself increasingly shunned by the Hollywood film world during the early 1960s. Derek had told her that Ray needed to produce something artistically revolutionary as a means of calling attention to himself, and Linda believed that she was the actress to help him do it.

She informed her errant husband, Chuck, "I'm sure Nicholas Ray and I can come up with something to make the world forget about Brando's *Last Tango."*

Like Ray, Linda had become a heavy marijuana smoker, and to an increasing degree, she relied on drugs such as cocaine to get her through the day. She suspected that she and Ray would be compatibly allied in their mutual drug use.

Linda even concocted a rather ridiculous notion that both of them might rescue each other from their drug dependencies. By the 1970s, Ray had become a heroin addict. In addition to that, he snorted coke, smoked hash, and took LSD. Included with that list were vast quantities of alcohol.

Linda became one of those women who actor-producer John Houseman referred to when he said, "Nicholas is a potential homosexual with a deep, passionate, and constant need for female love in his life. This made him attractive to women, for whom the chance to save him from his own self-destructive habits proved an irresistible attraction."

Although Nicholas Ray never returned repeated calls from Linda, she finally heard from some strange, unidentified man. "Stop pestering Mr. Ray. There's no film deal. Forget it!"

[Linda was terribly disappointed to read in Variety *during the spring of 1976 that Nicholas Ray was about to make a thriller entitled* City Blues. *Norman Mailer, one of Linda's former conquests, announced that he had agreed to play a supporting role in the film. As the film's star, Ray had selected Marilyn Chambers. At the time, although Chambers was the highest paid star in porn,* City Blues *was conceived as an R-rated, not as an X-rated, movie. In response to questioning by the press, Ray said "I have no trouble with Marilyn's past performances in such porn as* Behind the Green Door."

Raving about her talent, he claimed that she was "a great actress right up there with Garbo and Katharine Hepburn. I had once considered Linda Lovelace, which would have been a moronic choice. She has only one talent, and we don't need to go into that. She is no actress."

He also announced that the male co-star of the film would be Rip Torn, a handsome actor who had played Judas Iscariot in King of Kings *(1961), Ray's "Super Technirama-Technicolor" overview of the birth, life, betrayal, and Resurrection of Jesus.*

Linda was deeply humiliated that Ray had not selected her as the lead in City Blues, *and she was enraged that he had singled her out as an actress devoid of talent. Later, when she read that financing associated with* City Blues *had collapsed, she was anything but disappointed.*

Unfortunately for Linda, the publicity associated with that (failed) project had served to remind everyone in the film industry that Chambers was the recipient of roles that might have gone to Linda "had I not fucked up my career. I wanted the acclaim that Chambers was getting. As for her becoming Chuck Traynor's second wife, she was welcome to that asshole."]

***

At this point in her life, entries in Linda's rich, lush diary ended. "I was too stoned most of the time to write down what was happening to me. The next two or three years of my life passed as in a blur. I can only remember them like notations made on a sketch pad and reviewed twenty years later."

[The whereabouts of her diary is not known today. She reportedly sold it to a private collector in the early 1990s for $23,000 when she was desperate for money. According to her, the collector, a wealthy man, had told her that he wasn't particularly interested in her or in her early life, but in her descriptions of some of his favorite male movie stars, about whom he had always entertained sexual fantasies.]

She did recall what she defined as "my last sexual gig in Hollywood." For $2,000, her earlier conquest, William Holden, hired her to perform fellatio on five of his honored guests at a reunion party he was throwing. Each of those guests had appeared onscreen with him in *The Devil's Brigade*, a gritty war hero movie released in 1968.

[The Devil's Brigade, directed by Andrew V. McLagen, was a somewhat clichéd World War II drama about reckless U.S. and Canadian recruits who were whipped into a creditable fighting force. Formatted in Panavision, and filmed with the 3rd U.S. Army Special Forces Group at Camp Williams, Utah, the film was interpreted as overly long by many critics who thought Holden's talents were wasted. The film—in addition to the other names noted below—also featured Richard Dawson, Andrew Prine, Patric Knowles, and among several others, Harry Carey, Jr. The cast also included Gene Fullmer, the World Middleweight Champion boxer; Paul Hornung, the NFL running back; and for its female interest, the very attractive Gretchen Wyler. Its marketing trailers advertised it as "What they did to each other was nothing compared to what they

The Devil's Brigade
Linda's Last Big Deep Throating
Gig as a Party Favor in Hollywood

Cliff Robertson:
"Come fly with me."

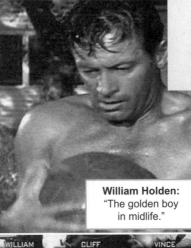

William Holden:
"The golden boy
in midlife."

James Craig:
"'B' star on screen, but
an 'A' star off."

Dana Andrews:
"Hot, hung, and drunk."

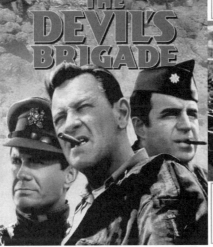

Richard Jaeckel:
"He also fucked
Paul Newman."

Vince Edwards:
"This former porn star
and I played 'Doctor
Casey' together."

"I sucked off all its big stars, but the movie sucked." Linda claimed. "Reviewers wrote that Holden was 'wasted' as the star of **The Devil's Brigade.** He was wasted the last night I spent with him, too, but it was an honor to seduce Barbara Stanwyck's *Golden Boy* and Norma Desmond's gigolo."

did to the enemy!"]

The male guests at the reunion she attended included actors whom she viewed as "heartthrobs"—Dana Andrews, James Craig, Vince Edwards, Cliff Robertson, and Richard Jaeckel.

"To tell the absolute truth," she later said, "It was pretty much a working gig, and I can't remember one of their cocks from another. Obviously, they were average sized or slightly better in size. But not one dick really stands out in my mind...well, maybe one did."

"Although some of them, such as Dana Andrews, born in 1909 (I looked it up), were getting on up there in years, they were still hot men and desirable. In some ways, Dana stands out more than the others, not because he was sixty-four years old, but because he was drunk, so he took the most work."

"Bill Holden treated me nice, and was a real gentleman. When I serviced him, he was also rather drunk."

"I thought Richard Jaeckel was pretty hot, even though he was forty-seven (I looked that up, too!)" she said. "I always remembered him shirtless in *Come Back, Little Sheba* (1952), in which he played Terry Moore's boyfriend, Turk. Lancaster was in it, too, but I'd already had him more than once."

"Then there was Cliff Robertson," she said, "the most elegant of all the guys. At age fifty, when he was still very handsome, he was married to that rich bitch, Dina Merrill. I used to eat her Post Toasties for breakfast. The only film of his I'd ever seen was *PT 109* (1963), after JFK personally selected him to play himself as a young naval officer during World War II."

"I missed Cliff's Oscar winner, *Charly* (1968), and his interpretation of Joan Crawford's younger lover in *Autumn Leaves* (1956). Perhaps Crawford should have played his mother. Forgive me for being catty. I do remember that Cliff's dick tasted good. If he flashed it in a gay bar, he wouldn't have been turned down. But it wouldn't have caused a stampede, either."

In *Autumn Leaves* (1956), **Joan Crawford** took on a young lover, **Cliff Robertson**, both on and off the screen.

"I got him off the screen," Linda said. "He had one of the tastiest dicks I ever swallowed."

"Of all the guys at that party, he smelled the nicest. He was a favorite of mine, a real gentleman. He told me he was a certified pilot, and invited me to fly with him to Catalina Island one day. I got caught up in other projects, and we never got around to it. I think I missed out on something there."

[On September 11, 2001, Cliff Robertson was flying in his

542

private plane at 7,500 feet above Manhattan's World Trade Center when the first Boeing 767 struck the complex's North Tower. Air Traffic Control ordered him to land immediately at the nearest airport. Despite the position of his plane at the time, he was never suspected of being part of the plot, of course.]

"James Craig was sixty-one when he climbed into bed with me. When he first came to Hollywood in the 1940s, or so I'd heard, he was hailed as the next Clark Gable. If I remember correctly, he had the thickest cock of all of Holden's 'Brigade.' I read somewhere that Gore Vidal wrote, 'James Craig, wherever you are today—old, tired, decrepit, flabby, or gray—you're still welcome to put your shoes under my bed any night of the week.'"

"That same assessment goes for me, of course. I would love to have been fucked by him back in the days when Hedy Lamarr and Ginger Rogers were getting their feline claws into him. But believe it or not, although I'd heard of him, I never saw one film he ever made."

I guess that if I had to select the hottest man at the reunion that night, it would have been Vince Edwards, who was only forty-three at the time I blew him. He was in the best shape of all the guys and still very handsome. He'd played that brooding surgeon in that TV series, *Ben Casey,* and I sort of had the hots for him back then."

"After he shot off in my mouth, he told me that he'd never appeared in a porn film but that he'd posed nude for a gay collector back when he was young, dumb, and struggling."

"He surprised me when he told me he was a singer. Like Robert Mitchum, I didn't picture Vince as a singer. But he invited me to come the following Saturday night to hear him at The Troubadour in Los Angeles. He also told me that he'd recorded six record albums in the 60s. Again, I left town and didn't get to hear him sing."

"Thank god Holden gave me my $2,000 early in the evening. When I saw him for the last time, he had passed out on the sofa in his living room. Vince was still in the back bedroom sleeping things off, and the other members of the Brigade had drifted off to other adventures."

[The frequency of William Holden's alcoholic binges would increase as the years went by. On November 16, 1981, he died violently, having passed out drunk and hitting his head on a coffee table on the way down. His decaying body wasn't discovered until several days later.]

"That night, when I staggered out of Bill Holden's apartment, I had so much protein in my belly that I feared I'd gained twenty pounds. Each member of Holden's *Brigade* was husband material—but not for me, it seemed."

"The next day, the phone stopped ringing," she said. It seemed like nobody in Hollywood wanted to get sucked off by Linda Lovelace. I guess I was old news."

"But the day after that, Sammy called," she said. "We still kept in touch on occasion, but not between the sheets, if you know what I mean. He'd never done anything for my career, but he still wanted to help out. That Sammy, in spite of his flaws, was one hell of a nice guy. He told me he was setting up a meeting with a man who could get my career 'rocking and rolling. 'He wants to meet you tomorrow. His name is David Winters.'"

Movie Stars Who Never Got to Sample Linda's Specialty

"In *Gentlemen Prefer Blondes,* Marilyn sang about how we all lose our charms in the end. I didn't hang around Hollywood long enough to get to these hotties on my list of guys I wanted to seduce over the years. They really missed a thrill. Any of them could have *cum* up to see me anytime: Burt Reynolds, Alec Baldwin, Antonio Banderas, Nicholas Cage, Sean Connery, Kevin Costner, Tom Cruise (I'm not too sure about that one), Dolph Lundgren, Al Pacino, Robert De Niro, Johnny Depp, Michael Douglas, Harrison Ford, Richard Gere, Mel Gibson, George Hamilton, Woody Harrelson, Charlton Heston, Don Johnson, Tommy Lee Jones, Rob Lowe, Nick Nolte, Peter O'Toole, Anthony Perkins, Sean Penn, Brad Pitt, Arnold Schwarzenegger, Sidney Poitier, Tom Selleck, Sylvester Stallone, John Travolta (well, maybe), Robert Wagner."

—Linda Lovelace

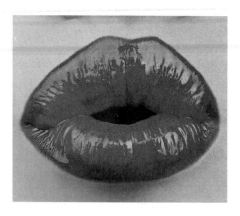

CHAPTER FOURTEEN
Flicker, Flicker, Little Star

"Every woman should know a David Winters at least once in her life."
—Linda Lovelace

Deep Throat had established Linda as an American icon, and the mention of her name continued to open doors. Hugh Hefner still welcomed her at the Playboy Mansion, where she continued to create a stir.

She'd officially changed her name from Linda Boreman to Linda Lovelace in the Los Angeles Superior Court.

Journalist Molly Parkin interviewed Linda right before her star fell from the sky. She wrote that in the film world at that very moment in time, only four female stars could raise hard-backing cash—Barbra Streisand, Liza Minnelli, Glenda Jackson, and Linda Lovelace.

Linda had never heard of David Winters, a Londoner "born and bred." However, he was a famous name in Hollywood, having become a naturalized U.S. citizen. As a child, he had appeared in more than one hundred TV roles and commercials, and had performed on Broadway as "Baby John" in the original stage production of *West Side Story.*

When Linda met him, he was a dancer, choreographer, producer, director, screenwriter, and actor, having either directed or produced more than four-hundred TV specials, motion pictures, or series.

As a choreographer, Winters had taught dance to both Diana Ross (of whom Linda was jealous), and Elvis Presley (whom Linda adored). He had choreographed four Elvis Presley movies and also the 1976 film *A Star is Born* with Streisand. He had been a frequent guest on variety shows and specials, including *The Milton Berle Show,* and in the late 1960s, he had directed two episodes of *The Monkees.* In 1971, he'd helmed Paul Newman, Kirk Douglas, and Dean Martin in an ABC television documentary on the history of auto racing. In 1973, he worked with Douglas again in a TV adaptation of *Dr. Jekyll and Mr. Hyde.*

When Linda met Winters in 1973, despite his amazing list of credits, he was only thirty-five.

"I wanted something new and different," he said, "and that didn't mean doing an act with Mitzi Gaynor. There could be a bit of a spin to this Lovelace gig."

`"When Delores Wells showed me a a compilation of Linda's press material, there were several shots of her going down on men," Winters said. "I thought I'd better get the hell out of Linda Lovelace Enterprises. But then, Linda walked in, looking like a teenage girl from some school in Kansas. A sweet little face, a few freckles—really charming, very unassuming. She was also very polite, rather demure."

At first, Linda was somewhat in awe of Winter's flamboyant dress. Chuck had met him first, and he erroneously told Linda, "this guy's a fag."

When he first stood up to greet her, she noticed his tall boots, which evoked Douglas Fairbanks, Jr. in the 1947 Betty Grable film, *The Lady in Ermine*. His ruffled green velvet chemise looked as if it had been acquired in the 16th century, and he wore stretch pants that were flared and belled at the bottom. When

he removed his wallet to hand her his card, she heard the little bells on it jingle.

"David won my heart when he compared me to Marilyn Monroe," Linda said. "He told me that Marilyn survived the nude calendar scandal and went on to a big career. David felt that I, too, could survive my porn past and go on to become big." Of course, Winters left out the fact that Monroe was an extremely talented actress, whose charismatic personality had captured the imagination of the world.

Chuck was still in charge of her career, and he told Winters that they had a booking for a show in Miami. "But she's got no act, no talent," he warned Winters.

Later that afternoon, Winters drove her to a studio where he, too, discovered that she couldn't act, couldn't dance, couldn't sing or tell jokes. He hired a colleague, Joe Cassini, to work with her. "At least teach her some fucking dance steps," Winters said.

Another colleague, Seth Riggs, was

Linda Lovelace took off her jeans and decked herself out in finery, as if trying to compete with the remade Audrey Hepburn in *My Fair Lady*. On the right *(top photo)* is **David Winters**, the new man in her life.

In the lower photo, **Paul Newman** *(left)* sports a jacket decorated with the logos of his sponsors, while **David Winters** dresses flamboyantly during their filming of a documentary about race-car driving.

546

hired to give her "a basic singing lesson. As it happened, Riggs couldn't see them right away at his home studio, so Linda, with Winters, waited outside in his car.

During the delay, her hands began to travel, and he soon produced an erection which the unfastening of his zipper freed for her. In his car, she performed fellatio on him for the first time.

Riggs was an odd choice as a singing coach for Linda, as he was very religious and kept pictures of Christ and crucifixes hanging on the walls of his suburbanite home.

Later, after an hour of singing practice, Riggs told Winters the bad news: "Linda sucks…I mean, as a singer."

After working with some of the top talent in show business, Winters was bewildered. "I just don't know what to do with you."

Her show was scheduled to open in Miami at the Paramount Theater on November 1, 1973. Like so many shows staged in the past, Winters had hired singers and dancers for back-up. "But back-up for what?" he asked. Then, so that she could work within a structured framework, he brought in writer Mel Mandel to turn out a scenario for her involvement in the show.

"I need you to work your magic with me," Linda told him.

He later said, "I was challenged by her, and I felt I might come up with something new and exciting. I was sort of mesmerized by her. In her very odd way, she was quite fascinating, or at least very unusual for me."

During rehearsals for the show, Linda and Winters launched an affair. He reportedly found her the best sex he'd ever had.

In the summer of 1973, in the midst of all this, Linda decided to bolt from Chuck. The break came when he began to interfere with production, trying to make decisions better left to a pro like Winters, who knew what he was doing theatrically. Chuck did not. "The only thing the shit knew was how to impose his will on me," Linda charged. "What really gave me the courage to leave Chuck was that David had become the man in my life. He's my protector."

Later, she claimed it was something that Mandel said to her that motivated her to leave. "I'd rather be dead than not living," Mandel had told her.

At the time of her break from Chuck, she was sharing a cottage with him in Malibu. When he was out of town, she went to the cottage and frantically packed her possessions. Winters drove her to the Beverly Hills Hotel, because he knew she couldn't hide out at his house. "That's the first place Chuck will come looking for you," he told her.

When Chuck realized that Linda had left him, he was seen driving around Los Angeles "looking for my god damn wife." His companion on the front seat of his car was an M-16 rifle.

Chuck even called Butchie Peraino to send two men from the mob to threaten Winters. But Linda interceded and persuaded Butchie "to call off your boys. "It was like some scene from a Cagney movie," she later recalled.

Eventually, Chuck gave up, mainly because he decided he could make more money off Marilyn Chambers than Linda. "Lovelace is a washed up, an over-the-hill has-been," he told his associates. "Marilyn Chambers is where it is today. I'm gonna marry her."

[Chuck's marriage to Marilyn Chambers would be filled with long separations, as she maintained dozens of other sexual liaisons. "He promised me the world and delivered nothing," Chambers said. "I could never escape my history of porn and get more legitimate work. He failed me like he failed Linda Lovelace. I heard he constantly beat the shit out of her. He didn't do that to me. He might have figured that I was his last meal ticket."

The marriage, officially at least, lasted until 1985. By then, Chuck had disappeared from the radar, and was reportedly living on a broken-down ranch somewhere in Nevada—and going blind.

At the age of 64, on July 22, 2002, Chuck died of a heart attack in Chatsworth, California. Three months after Linda herself died as the result of a car accident in Denver, Colorado. Barbara Boreman, Linda's sister, later said during an interview that she was disappointed that "Traynor died before I could kill him."]

Long before her separation from him, Linda had given up on Chuck Traynor. Eventually, he stopped ranting about her and devoted his attention instead to his lovely new girlfriend and future wife, Chambers.

On September 29, 1973, Linda's attorney, Harvey Strassman, appeared in Santa Monica Superior Court to end their disastrous two-year marriage. In her petition, Linda cited "irreconcilable differences," but did not outline the litany of abuses inflicted on her by her husband.

In the wake of his bitter divorce from Linda, Chuck told *Time* magazine "You gotta trade in your old car when it can't make the hills."

As compensation for her upcoming cabaret appearance in Miami, it was agreed that Linda was to be given $15,000 a week. Her contract called for her to appear nude at one point during her act.

As she gained more independence from him, Chuck wasn't the only casualty. Soon after their separation from him, she notified the Paramount Theater in Miami that she had changed her mind about her starring in the upcoming show, and that she refused to get involved with it in any way. Chuck had arranged the deal, and as she told Winters, "Here's my chance to throw a goodbye fuck in his face,"

LeRoy Griffith, producer of the Miami show, immediately filed a $75,000 lawsuit against her, charging breach of contract. A Florida attorney, and a graduate of the University of Miami, Phil Mandina, also sued Linda for $19,500 for nonpayment of legal fees. He had rendered legal services to both Linda and Chuck between January and September of 1973.

Even though she'd violated her contract and had walked out on her pre-arranged commitment to the Miami show, she still maintained, "I want to forge ahead with my career."

In addition to the percolating disaster in Florida, Winters faced other Linda-associated challenges. One day, she announced to him that she would no longer appear nude, either in film or on the stage. "For god's sake, she was a porno star. Audiences would pay to see her only if she were nude, and preferably sucking cock."

Despite the difficulties that she presented to him, Winters still tried to carve out a theatrical career for her. "I became Svengali and a Henry Higgins in her life, both privately and professionally."

"When I was with David, I had an awesome time," Linda recalled. "I met a lot of people—Bob Hope, Lucille Ball, Paul Newman, Milton Berle, and, most of all, Elvis Presley. He took me to my first play, Richard Chamberlain in *Cyrano de Bergerac.* I saw *Grease* in Manhattan. I also saw the Alvin Ailey Dancers. I became cultured, I guess. I'd never been cultured."

"I secretly wished that I had the talent of Ann-Margret or perhaps that heifer, Raquel Welch. But I didn't. I was who I was. I was Linda Lovelace, and poor David had to make do with what he had. In spite of the Miami fiasco, he did not give up on me."

"Disrobing was off, singing and dancing were out," Winters said, "so that left on-stage dialogue. I booked Linda as the star of *Pajama Tops,* a bedroom comedy. We were to open in Philadelphia at the New Locust Theater, with the hopes that it would be the launch pad for a nationwide tour."

As an artistic vehicle, *Pajama Tops was* a bad choice. Even at the time of its debut in the 1950s, critics did not interpret it as a hot property. In the meanwhile, the sexual revolution had arrived, transforming the play into an outdated period piece.

Advance word got out that Linda was not going to appear naked. Even on opening night, less than half the seats were filled. "In the nights ahead, we had more people on stage than in the audience," Winters said. "Also, Linda mangled many of her lines."

Linda appeared onstage in *Pajama Tops* as a character named "Babette Latouche." She recalled, "For the critics, there is no happier moment than when a porn star tries to keep her clothes on and play it straight. It's like going to a shooting gallery with a Howitzer."

The critics weighed in, including William B. Collins of the Knight Newspapers, publishers of *The Miami Herald.* "Linda Lovelace, star of the world-famous movie, *Deep Throat,* carries out her threat and goes on the stage. A whole month of acting lessons has left her a blissful amateur." Larry Fields of the *Philadelphia Daily News* asserted, "*Pajama Tops* brought a new bottom to the American theater, and I don't mean Linda Lovelace's."

Another critic, Jonathan Takiff, summed up the views of many members of the audience: "Rarely in my years of play-going experience have I been so moved to leave the theater as at last evening's opening of *Pajama Tops.*"

All the critics conceded that Linda had absolutely no talent as a performer, except, of course, for her special skill at fellatio.

Pajama Tops closed in less than a week. The play failed, according to Winters, "because the men in the audience felt cheated that Linda did not strip down and show her tits and ass."

***

Then, Winters came up with another idea: If theater audiences wouldn't turn out for Linda, maybe college boys would. At the annual Harvard Lampoon Celebrity Roast, she was a hit with the young men at Cambridge, who designated her as "America's Sweetheart." She accepted the "Wilde Oscar" award from them for her role in *Deep Throat.*

Some six-thousand students at Harvard turned out to greet her, and there was a big parade for her. "I felt like a queen. It was the happiest day of my life. I wasn't even named worst actress of the year. That honor went to Ali McGraw, who truly deserved it. Did you see *Love Story?* What schmaltz!"

"Robert Redford was voted worst actor of the year. I thought he was very handsome except for that lump on his face. I may be completely wrong, but I suspect he's not very well hung. I asked Liz Renay, but she said she's never slept with him either."

"He didn't show up to accept his award," Linda said. "Such a pity. I would have tried to seduce him, although he once said that he fooled around a lot as a teenager and is no longer interested in loveless sex. Sinatra was quoted a saying it was a pity that Redford couldn't marry his true love—himself. At the time Redford was filming *The Way We Were* with Barbra Streisand. I'm sure that hag got her claws into the Sundance Kid."

"*Deep Throat* was not voted worst picture of the year," she said. "That honor went to Brando's *Last Tango in Paris,* and he deserved to be on Harvard's shitlist. Imagine not being able to get it up for the director. Harry Reems certainly never had that problem."

"My most frequently asked question on the college circuit was, "Do you still have your tonsils, Miss Lovelace?""

Since Linda had been such a smash hit with (mostly male) college students, Winters booked her on a tour of some two dozen college campuses, including

550

Northeastern University in Boston, where she participated in a debate on pornography. She charged $4,000 for each appearance. Winters wrote all her lines. On every campus she advocated sexual freedom, which was a very popular idea with the students. For the film industry, Linda had some advice— "Make love, not war on screen. Cool it with the violence. Save some of that testosterone for the bedroom."

Her appearance sometimes provoked violent criticism, especially when she invaded Redneck Country. Many faculty members at the University of Alabama were shocked, during the spring of 1974, when Linda talked about homosexuality and sex-change operations. Many of her lectures ended with a prize being offered—a date with Linda Lovelace. "I became America's leading expert at giving blow-jobs to college boys," she later confessed. "It was fortunate that David and I had an open relationship, free to fuck anybody we wanted."

***

In January of 1974, Winters and Linda planned to take a nightclub act they had partially organized and named *The Big Gun* to Las Vegas. It had originally opened in Los Angeles but had been shut down by the police. Vegas was relatively permissive about what could be staged, so she and Winters opted to move ahead with plans for the production there, instead.

The production called for her to appear onstage in a blonde wig reminiscent of Jean Harlow. She had wanted the script to evoke Marilyn Monroe, but the writer had insisted on references to the platinum blonde of the 1930s instead.

The male lead had not yet been cast. Linda had seen Howard Hughes' *The Outlaw* (1943), and she wanted an actor who resembled Jack Buetel as he'd appeared as Billy the Kid opposite big-busted Jane Russell. The highlight of the show would occur when Linda, as Jean Harlow, actually fellates Billy the Kid onstage.

During the show's planning stages, Winters paid to fly Linda to Las Vegas as an incentive for potential backers of the show. Because of his close connections with The Riviera, a free hotel suite awaited them.

Reading the Las Vegas newspaper the following morning, Winters noted that Elvis Presley would be appearing there at the Hilton. Winters was always bragging about his personal and professional connection with Elvis.

"I'm sure half a million people also make the same claim," she had chided him.

"Okay, I'll prove it to you," he said. He picked up the phone and within ten minutes was connected directly to Elvis.

"The way they chatted on the phone, it was obvious that they were friends," Linda recalled. "I practically wet my pants with excitement. We were invited

551

to this late show, and we could get together with him in his suite later that night. I was finally going to meet Elvis the Pelvis. I'd been creaming in my jeans over that dude since the 1950s when I was just a girl."

Before the show, Col. Tom Parker came by and warmly embraced Winters. "Loved your movie," the colonel then said to Linda. "You don't look naughty at all. Sorta innocent."

"I thanked him," she later said, assuming he meant that as a compliment.

Later that night, the house lights dimmed and Elvis was announced. As the curtain went up and the lights went on, he bounced into view wearing a fringed white jumpsuit with gold braid.

Although he no longer looked like the fantasy man of her dreams, "he shook his hips, wiggled his ass, and did bumps and grinds with his pelvis," she later said. But she noticed as he'd aged that he did all his familiar stage maneuvers with a kind of self-satirization.

At the end of his second show that night, Linda and Winters visited Elvis in his suite In its living room, she noticed a lot of security guards hired by the hotel and a milling crowd of flotsam and jetsam. She wondered if Elvis knew all the people in his quarters.

A guard came for them and ushered them into the innermost of Elvis' private rooms. Of all the stars she'd met in Hollywood or Las Vegas or even Miami, she had always claimed that Elvis was her biggest thrill. As a very young teenager, she'd plastered her bedroom walls with his pictures.

Here was her dream man in person, and he was not only shaking her hand, but kissing her on both cheeks. She took in the vision before her. It didn't quite match those pictures on the wall. He was very overweight and looked puffy and bloated.

"David and I talked to him for about fifteen minutes," Linda said. "It was all about aikido and karate, shit like that. After thirteen years of hard work, Elvis was proud to have earned a seventh-degree black belt in karate. He had aged and his face showed it. A lot of hard living was reflected in that face."

Linda: "Despite his weight, **Elvis Presley** could still wiggle those hips on stage. Off stage, he was better at karate than in bed."

"David had already told me that Elvis claimed to have seduced at least a thousand women before his marriage to Priscilla."

Soon, they drifted through the open door into Elvis' bedroom. On the bed, Liza Minnelli sat next to Linda. "On the other side of me sat Alice Cooper. David was also on that bed. So was Chubby Checker of all people. We were on the 13th floor of the Hilton. Everybody, it seemed, was on that bed except

552

Elvis himself."

Then Elvis approached, stood by her, and placed his hands on her shoulders, as if to massage her back. "Of all the people in the room, I was the one he touched, and that gesture obviously wasn't lost on David—but he didn't seem jealous."

"Before the night ended, he had guys who worked for him practice karate with him," she said. "One of them would lunge toward him with a knife, and Elvis would throw him on the floor. Before we left that night, he'd shown his skill to us with at least five guys, and I was impressed. A lot of guys on his staff must have had sore asses getting thrown on the floor. Sore asses... Forgive me, Linda Lovelace can't say anything anymore that doesn't have a sexual meaning."

She later asserted that as she sat on Elvis's bed, she fantasized that everyone was gone except for the two of them. "I thought to myself, what would happen if we got together to ball? I would be fucking and sucking a dream, not a man. No matter what, I could never forget that it was Elvis. Elvis Presley! I would probably be sucking his cock and thinking, WOW! This is Elvis Presley's cock. I would probably laugh. After all, how can you fuck a dream?"

To her surprise, when Winters excused himself to go to the bathroom, Elvis whispered to her, "Be here at three o'clock tomorrow afternoon."

That was an engagement she planned to keep.

Whereas she may have broken a date with Eddie Fisher, she sure as hell wasn't going to be a no show in the bedroom of Elvis Presley. She wanted to be alone with her dream man, overweight or not.

Mercifully, Winters had scheduled an appointment for himself the following afternoon, and she slipped away to the Hilton. "A guy from Elvis' Memphis Mafia took me right up to his suite and into Elvis' bedroom. The King of Rock 'n' Roll was lying on his bed wearing a pair of white silk shorts with red polka dots on them. He was watching a Western on television. At last I saw that nude stomach of his. He looked like he'd had too many chocolate milkshakes, but he still looked sexy."

"Come on in, sugar baby," he said. "Daddy is waiting for his gal."

"Oh, Elvis," she said, "I'm thrilled to be here."

"Now, honey, come up with a better line than that," he said. "I hear that one all the time. I'd rather you be thrilled when you leave Big Elvis after sampling Little Elvis."

"I love those shorts of yours," she said. "Now I know what to buy you for Christmas."

"Years ago, this guy named Bill Black bought me a pair of shorts like this when he found out I didn't wear underwear," Elvis said. "He thought they were a sort of joke, but I fell in love with them. I've been wearing white silk drawers with red polka dots ever since."

"Then he looked at me real serious like," she said.

"Speaking of panties, I gotta ask you the big one." He said. "Are you wearing white panties? If not, I can get one of my boys to bring you a pair."

"You're in luck," she said. "I nearly always wear white panties."

"Another thing," he said, sitting up in bed. "It's very important to me that some of your pubic hair peeps out over the elastic band holding up those panties."

"Your luck has run out," she said. "I shave. There's no pubic hair to peek out at you."

"Well, for today, at least, it doesn't matter," he said, "because I don't plan to fuck you, but to do something else. But if you and I get serious in the future, you've got to let that pubic hair grow back."

"To keep coming back to you," she said, "I'd grow a beard."

"You don't have to go that far," he said, "but I've got to ask you a final question. Have you ever birthed a kid?"

She lied to him, telling him she had not.

"Never?" he asked. "That's good. Whenever I hear that a woman has birthed a child, it's a complete turn-off for me."

"Priscilla, then, must be really hard up for dick after giving birth to Baby Lisa Marie."

"If you don't mind, sugartit, I'd rather not go there," he said. "Okay, doll?"

"Sorry."

He reached for her hand, pulling her down to him to kiss her.

"If we're not going to fuck today, what are we going to do?" she asked. "Don't I appeal to you?"

"It's not that," he said. "Little Elvis is not in working order today. I have this problem. A week ago, Natalie Wood was here. I fucked her endlessly, but she couldn't reach a climax. I have this delicate foreskin. It tore and I bled. I still have this slight abrasion. So I want you to suck only the head. You won't be able to deep throat me."

"I guarantee I can get you off by sucking only the head," she promised. "After all, they don't call me Linda Lovelace for nothing."

It was at this point that she looked down and saw that he'd already produced an erection amid the garden of all those polka dots. Actually, she'd seen that erection before, as had millions of other fans. In the 1962 movie *Girls! Girls! Girls!,* Elvis had produced an erection when he was singing and dancing with costar Laurel Goodwin. Viewers who looked carefully had spotted his hard-on encased in a pair of black pants—something the film editors had missed.

"Finally, he pulled off those shorts, and I got to see the erection without it being covered by fabric," she said. "He was uncircumsized and about six inches, hard," she said. "But it was Elvis Presley's cock and worthy of sucking, even if I was confined just to the head. I hoped that some day in the future, he'd summon me back for 'the works.'"

As she was leaving, one of the Memphis boys—she didn't know his name—pointedly asked her, "How was The King in the sack today?"

"I didn't get fucked, if that's what you mean," she answered.

"The same thing happened the first time I brought Natalie Wood into his bedroom," he said. "After twenty minutes, she stormed out, complaining, 'Your boss is all hands, no action. If Elvis calls me back, he'd better be ready to fuck me.' Then she looked around the room at us Tennessee boys, and said in a rather loud voice, 'I think all you guys are homos.' I had to rip off her pedal pushers and fuck her right there on the carpet. The bitch criticized my performance, but at least I proved to her that I wasn't homo."

Two weeks after their encounter at the Vegas Hilton, Linda received a present from Elvis. She opened it to discover two big, blousy velvet shirts with a note saying that he'd worn both of them at two shows on September 26, 1956, at the Mississippi-Alabama Fair.

"One day, you can sell them for a lot of money," he wrote. "One is in romance red, the other in heartbreak blue."

***

Winters also knew another headliner performing in Vegas during their stay there, Liza Minnelli, and he spoke to her the following afternoon. She invited them to her midnight show.

As Linda came into the showroom, she was besieged by autograph seekers after word spread that Lovelace was heading for a ringside table. Winters graciously introduced her to two of his show business friends, Paul Anka and Alice Cooper.

It was not a good audience that night, as many male members of the crowd had consumed far too much liquor. Liza bravely carried on, although many of her songs were interrupted by praise shouted at her—"You're better than Judy, kid!" or "We love you, Liza!"

At the end of the show, the manager approached them, informing Linda and David that word had spread that "Linda is in the building." Consequently, an unruly crowd of fans and autograph seekers had gathered outside the hotel.

"Surely, they want Liza and not me," Linda told the manager.

"No, they're screaming 'Linda,' not 'Liza,'" he said.

The manager escorted Linda and Winters backstage, where they paid a courtesy call on Liza before heading out the back door. During their brief meeting, Winters *[with Linda]* and Liza agreed to have dinner together the following night at ten o'clock.

Linda was thrilled to have met one of her idols, whom she believed was a better singer than her mother, Judy Garland. She didn't say that, however, not wanting to sound like one of those loudmouthed drunks in the audience.

Dawn was breaking over Las Vegas when she and Winters returned to their complimentary suite at the Riviera. Waking up in the afternoon, Winters called Liza, inviting her to go with them after their upcoming dinner that night to a midnight show to hear Frank Sinatra.

Linda was overjoyed. Even though she'd previously serviced both Spiro Agnew and Richard Burton at the singer's villa in Rancho Mirage, Sinatra still hadn't responded to any of her notes, even though he had, at least through his surrogate, Brad Dexter, paid her for her services. But she hoped that if she appeared in his dressing room with Liza and with Winters accompanying her, he would at least acknowledge her.

Early that evening in the living room of the suite she was sharing with Winters, her companion was entertaining two men and a woman who were strangers to Linda. According to what Linda later recalled, "A man named 'Max' wanted to hire me for a weekly fee of $15,000 for my appearance at one of Las Vegas' nightclubs."

Winters, according to Linda, had immediately countered, "Offer us $100,000 a week, and we might talk business."

In the bathroom, Linda, with her hair in curlers, was getting ready to migrate, with Winters, to the MGM Hotel to meet the singer Fabian before their dinner date with Liza.

In her bra and panties, she entered the living room to retrieve her gown from the living room's closet. As she did, the door to their suite was thrown violently open.

A dozen policemen rushed in with their revolvers drawn. She screamed.

"It's the police!" the chief cop called out. "All of you, get on the floor." He turned to Linda. "That means you, cocksucker!"

Although she protested that she wasn't dressed, he forced her onto the carpet. Winters, along with "Max," "Marianne," and "Jimmy," were ordered to lie face down on the floor, too. Each of them was immediately handcuffed.

Then the cops tore through the apartment, opening drawers and throwing their contents onto the floor. In the bedroom, one policeman found a stash of cocaine and various amphetamines in the top drawer of a chest.

Linda begged one of the cops to let her go to the bathroom to urinate, but he refused. "Dopers like you always like to go to the bathroom to flush more evidence down the toilet," he said. "If you've got to piss, piss your pants. The carpet is thick."

After about fifteen minutes, he finally allowed her into the bathroom, but he insisted on standing directly beside the toilet, watching her and listening as she urinated. He'd removed her handcuffs and allowed her to put on a dress, but he refused to let her take the curlers out of her hair.

"In a matter of hours, I'd gone from feeling like the Queen of Las Vegas to being treated like white trash," she said. "Here I was meeting Elvis, Liza, Anka, and Alice Cooper. The next minute, I'm hauled off in handcuffs to jail."

Regrettably, before they reached the jailhouse, news of her arrest had spread to the media, whose reporters and photographers waited for her arrival. The next morning, she'd be splashed on frontpages across the country.

Inside the jail, she was searched by what she called "a burly lesbian who practically masturbated me, claiming female dopers often stash cocaine in their vaginas."

"One asshole cop thought my Pursettes were heroine," she said. "I had to explain to the shithead that I use them for my periods. He seriously pissed me off. I told him I'd give him my phone number. 'The next time I get my period, I'll call you so you can come over and lick me clean.' He slapped my face. I was going to charge police brutality, but maybe I had it coming for being such a smartass."

"To get even with me, the fucker handcuffed me to the trashiest-looking hooker the police had rounded up that night," Linda said. "The bitch looked like some fifty-year-old drunk who'd been walking the streets since 1930…at least. The cop told me, 'This hooker has the clap so bad you can smell it a mile away.' I felt humiliated. I was a bigtime star being treated like some animal. I was thrown into this holding cell with about eighteen hookers, all of whom recognized me. Then the bitches surrounded me, asking me about my technique and wanting me to name all the stars I'd ever fucked. One thing was for sure: All of these whores had seen *Deep Throat.*"

In her past, she'd fellated crooked cops in Miami. "At least they were clean-cut, and one of them was an Adonis. But these creeps in Vegas were redneck pigs. No wonder people hate cops. They were unshaven, loud-mouthed, and dirty, and they treated people, even innocent people, like dirt. David managed to put through a call to Minnelli. I heard him say, "Hi, Liza. We can't make dinner. We're in jail."

"Somehow, word reached Elvis that we were in jail, and he ordered his manager, Col. Tom Parker, to come to our rescue," Linda said. "Col. Parker was well connected to the crooked cops. With just a phone call from him, our $7,000 bail was posted and we were released."

Later, she charged that drugs had been planted in their suite by some informer. "Maybe the chief wanted to make a name for himself and get on the frontpage. He was showing how tough Vegas police were on porn and drugs.

Who knows what the shit was doing—I was his victim."

After her arrest, she maintained a deeply cynical view not only of cops, but of all government officials, including mayors, governors, senators, whomever. "The corruption goes right up the food chain, ending with Richard M. Nixon. "He's full of crap, the number one tight-ass in the world."

"The only policeman I ever knew, a kind and sweet man, was my father," she said. "He didn't even like to give people a ticket."

In the aftermath of her arrest, she had to make eighteen return trips to Las Vegas and even pay $500 for a lie detector test. "In all, I ran up $20,000 in legal fees for a false arrest. I'd been set up. Someone had planted that dope in our bedroom."

A hearing was set for July 25, 1974, and she was told that, if convicted, she might face a six-year prison term.

Fortunately for Linda, the drug charges against her were eventually dropped. Winters also went free.

She later admitted that she snorted cocaine to give her a kind of false confidence. "Without it, I was scared, scared of everything, scared of being alone."

***

Winters invited Linda to accompany him to the April, 1974, Academy Awards.

She stole the show from all the big stars, arriving in a golden coach pulled by four white horses and accompanied by two footmen. She appeared on the red carpet in a leopard skin bikini, holding a Great Dane (Winters' own pet) on a leash.

After that, Winters flew her to his native London, where *Deep Throat* had encountered many legal problems because of government censorship. The publicity associated with that battle, as played out in the British press, had made her a household word.

At the fashionable Ascot Races, Winters pulled the same flashy stunt he'd orchestrated at the Oscars, having her arrive in a golden coach pulled by white horses. "We thought the bloody Queen had arrived," said actor Peter Finch.

For her debut at Ascot, she wore a mammoth black sun hat decorated with large feathers from birds of prey. Her see-through blouse revealed her breasts. Many at Ascot were shocked, although "the gents" applauded. *The Daily Mirror* referred to her appearance at the races as "a winning double"

The next day, she put on a pants suit that was transparent. As anyone could see, she wore no panties. "I saw a bald beaver," claimed an English lord.

For a reported ten thousand pounds, Linda told *The News of the World* that "in addition to the 'tricks I've turned,' I also seduced a perfect 100 celebrities, many of the most famous names in America." The *News* hyped her story by advertising it in large blow-ups on the sides of London's red double-decker buses.

For their transportation around London, Winters rented a Rolls Royce with a license plate that read PENIS.

"The Queen was quite a snob," Linda told a reporter. "She didn't even invite us for tea at Buckingham Palace."

***

Back in the States, Winters was having a hard time getting another gig for Linda. He asked Mel Mandel to write another "autobiography" for her, which he bashed together in three days.

The slim, 140-page paperback that was eventually published in 1974 was entitled *The Intimate Diary of Linda Lovelace*. Disguising his involvement in the project, Mandel used the pseudonym "Carl Allin." The second book didn't fare as well as the first, but it stirred up even more controversy.

Whereas Chuck Traynor had been praised in the first memoir, in *The Intimate Diary of Linda Lovelace,* she referred to her former husband as "Chuck the Schmuck," citing the violence he'd subjected her to.

"I was forced to have sex with strangers for pay. I was a party favor given freely to celebrities, who I cannot name for legal reasons. I was not free at all. I was his profitable little sexual zombie, and he wasn't about to give me up without a fight. He searched for me everywhere, and I had to go into hiding. When he went after me, he carried a flight bag concealing a semi-automatic revolver."

Chuck denied the charge that he'd ever kept her a prisoner. In the April issue of *Screw* magazine, he said, "I was raised in the country, and I don't consider it a beating if you slap your old lady for something. To me, that's a sign of closeness. When your old lady does something wrong, or when she gives you too much lip—I don't really consider that beating up."

Linda, working with Winters, did what she could to generate sales for her second memoir, *The Intimate Diary of Linda Lovelace.*

In her first memoir, *Inside Linda Lovelace,* Chuck had been a great seducer. In her second memoir, Chuck became a sexual dud and Winters became the world' greatest lover. It even contained a graphic insertion of Winters' power in bed:

"With a tremendous thrust, he put his surging, gorgeous cock inside me. A pulsating jackhammer that kept driving, driving, driving, plowing into me, over and over."

Although she consistently camouflaged the identity of many of the personalities she discussed in her book, it was relatively easy to decipher the identity of "The King of Sex" who she described as a man ruling over a magazine empire.

As she described intercourse with Hefner, she wrote:

"Then he began to fuck me. A nice, deep, slow fuck which had me gasping after fifteen minutes. The average guy gives you about twenty-five thrusts with his cock before he comes. But the King was a master. I bet he must have thrust over two hundred and fifty solid times before he finally let go."

When questioned about that flattering description, Hefner responded, "Miss Lovelace and I are just friends."

***

"It didn't take a rocket scientist to figure out that the chapter Linda devoted to Mr. Dynamite was our own beloved Sammy," said his fellow Rat Packer Dean Martin.

In one section of her newest book, Linda claimed "Mr. Dynamite really dug getting head. In the seven months of so that we saw each other, I gave him head many times. I fucked him straight just once. That's right: Just once, and he was great."

She even asserted that she would have been happy leaving Chuck and living with Sammy and his wife, Altovise, as part of a *ménage à trois*. "We were practically living together, anyway," she wrote. "I dug them both. We could have been happy together. I would have given him head while she was giving me head, and we could switch around every night."

The most controversial sex scene in *The Intimate Diary* was even more provocative than Linda's description of her seduction, with Chuck, of the mother-daughter combo that she had inserted in her first memoir. It involved an episode wherein she asserted that she had once functioned as the centerpiece of a "sexual sandwich" whose end pieces were a celebrity father and his famous son.

When she revealed that both of her bed partners during that episode were famous Hollywood actors, that limited the field somewhat for Hollywood-watchers who were interested in deciphering the enigmas. The chronologies of many potential candidates, eliminated them as possibilities. *[Examples of that included the John Barrymores, Senior and Junior. Senior died in 1942. Other father-son combinations, such as Kirk with Michael Douglas, were simply dismissed as extremely unlikely and/or ridiculous.]*

When Linda published her third memoir, *Ordeal,* in 1980, she included a phrase that said: *[In my previous book] "They [the publishers] invented a sex scene with a father and a son, both of them supposed to be famous Hollywood actors."*

However, her friend at the time, Liz Renay, told the author: "That allegation was not invented. Linda told Pupu and me that one night, she had sex with Paul Newman and his son, Scotty."

When probed about it by Jay Garon's researchers, Linda would neither confirm nor deny the father-and-son incident. "That episode has caused me enough trouble already, and I don't want to talk about it."

"We'll leave it to the reader to form his *[or her]* own opinion," Garon said.

[Renay's claim that Linda's sex act transpired with the Newmans, father and son, became more credible when it was revealed that David Winters was a friend of Paul Newman and had worked on a documentary about race-car driving with him. Hollywood insiders assumed that Linda had been introduced to Paul by Winters.]

Actually, the introduction evolved through another connection, Carol Studden, Scott Newman's girlfriend. The beautiful young girl had applied for a job at Linda Lovelace Enterprises, where Linda had befriended her. She liked Carol immensely and began hanging out with her. Linda told Renay, "David is often gone, and, believe it or not, Linda Lovelace often sits at home these days—and the phone doesn't ring."

Knowing Carol meant being introduced to Scott, who was heavy into drugs and alcohol at the time. Linda found him a handsome six-footer, weighting 180 pounds and rather good looking. "He looked very fuckable to me," Linda revealed to Renay, "and I was anxious to give him head. Carol could join us if she wished. The couple had a very open relationship, it seemed to me. Like many kids in those days, they went either straight or gay."

Living resentfully in his famous father's shadow, Scott was deeply troubled. He'd been cast in Paul's picture, *The Towering Inferno* (1974*)*, but only in a small part as a fireman. He told Linda, "I don't have his baby blues, and I sure as hell don't have his talent. And I don't have his luck either. What do I have? Only myself, and that's nothing."

She tried to reassure him. At first, she thought he was the son of actress Joanne Woodward, but he told her he was Paul's only son, having been born to his father's first wife, Jackie Witte. "All the rest of his semen made girls."

She learned that Scott was a daredevil and had performed 500 parachute jumps on camera. A college dropout, he'd been frequently arrested in a drugged condition. One night, he assaulted a police officer and

Although publicly denying it, Linda Lovelace may have been involved in one of **Paul Newman**'s deepest, darkest secrets.

kicked him in the head. Paul rushed to the rescue, posting bail, and hiring a lawyer.

He told Linda that he'd gotten into violent confrontations with Paul when he refused to give up drugs. Eventually, in a fit of something approaching megalomania, Scott demanded the role of the Sundance Kid opposite Paul's Butch Cassidy, but the part, of course, went to Robert Redford instead.

One drug-sodden weekend in Laguna, Scott confided to Linda that he had really wanted to be a singer. She believed he needed to try something different from acting, since he couldn't compete with his father as a film star. She called Liz Renay, who, in turn, phoned Mickey Cohen, who still had some club connections. A weekend gig was set up for Scott at a Los Angeles nightclub. Refusing to capitalize off his father's fame, he opted to bill himself as "William Scott."

On the night of Scott's lackluster singing debut, Linda attended with Renay and Pupu. After the show had started, Paul quietly seated himself in the audience, wearing a disguise, to hear his son. Linda didn't learn that he was there until the show ended with only mild applause from the half-filled seats in the audience. "The kid's no good," Renay whispered to Linda. "Pupu can sing better."

Backstage in a dressing room that seemed to double as a toilet, Linda was introduced to Paul Newman. "He flashed those baby blues at me and I was a goner."

Scott had been very disappointed that his girlfriend, Carol, was sick with the flu and couldn't attend his opening. Renay and Pupu had been invited to a party at Frank Sinatra's house. Linda was sorry that she wasn't included. "After showing him a hot time one night, he's just dumped me," Linda complained to Renay.

FATHER VS. SON

"I live in the shadow of a star," claimed **Scott Newman** *(left photo)* about being the son of a celebrated actor, Paul Newman.

On the right, **Scott** appears as a fireman in one of his father's famous pictures, *Towering Inferno (1974)*. Scott played a minor part, envying the success of his famous father, who shared the film's lead--and most of its publicity--with Steve McQueen.

Seeing that she was not being escorted, Scott asked Paul if Linda could hang out with them for the rest of the evening. Paul smiled—or was it a smirk?—and agreed to let her come along.

She later wrote, "I knew that the two of them were supposed to be very hostile to each other, and fan magazines put out a lot of stuff about how they didn't even talk to each other."

The next day, she informed Renay, "I think Paul and Scott needed me as a referee. They sure got along last night. We had too much beer in this little eatery, and in the car, I provided some pot, and so both of them puffed and went up in smoke with me. We were heading south to this late-night club, but Paul was afraid that Scott would be arrested again, along with both of us, too. "

"So we stopped at this seedy motel for the night. I put through a message to David, and Paul made three calls to some people. Scott put through a call to Carol who complained about having to stay in bed and miss all the fun."

Linda later complained to Renay that, "I couldn't make up my mind which of those drunks I found the most appealing. I hoped for a chance to work my magic on each of them."

After some initial awkwardness among this party of three, "I found myself being sucked and fucked by two generations," she'd later record in her memoir. "At one point, I was giving head to Junior, and the old man was giving it to me nicely in the ass. We all came together. I could feel Junior's cum in my throat and Senior's cum in my ass at the same time. It was terrific."

She claimed that the three of them rested a while in the same bed. In her memoir, she wrote: "The next thing I knew, the son slowly bent his head down and very tenderly began to blow his old man. And his father began to cry, tears streaming down his cheeks."

She confided to Renay that she had then decided that her presence at this reconciliation between a father and his son "didn't need me anymore. Three's a party, you know. What a party! But it was time to go. I quietly got dressed and slipped out of the room. The hotel desk called me a cab to take me back into Los Angeles."

After that, "I got involved in my own life and didn't see Carol and Scotty anymore," Linda claimed. "Sometimes Carol and I talked on the phone, as we really liked each other."

"I remember the date she called me," Linda said, "and I sensed her panic. It was November 20, 1978."

"I think dear Scotty started committing suicide the day he was born," Carol told Linda. "Well, he's succeeded." Then she put down the receiver, and Linda never heard from her again.

Linda read in the papers that day that Scott Newman had died of a drug overdose.

***

For several months during the mid 1970s, Linda's love affair with Winters flourished. She defined it in a not very original style, "We lived high on the hog. I guess anytime we wanted something extravagant, David signed my name to it. Of course, eventually, creditors had to be paid. There came the rub. There was not enough money. We were always in debt."

"I had to provide the money," she claimed. "At first, I thought David was rich. I mean, he'd produced all these successful shows with stars like Rudolf Nureyev, Nancy Sinatra, Ann-Margret, and Lucille Ball."

"But one night after dinner, he confessed to me that he was six million dollars in debt. That was more money than I could even conceive. After all, he was talking to a gal who'd lived off mustard and catsup sandwiches made with stolen bread."

"We had big plans, big dreams, but nothing seemed to be working," Winters said. "There were offers, but Linda was very stubborn with her continued insistence—'no porn, no nudity, no cocksucking.'"

"It all came down to the Bentleys," she said. "With my money, David ordered two of them. The one put in his name was paid for. I learned after our breakup that the one in my name was merely leased."

"Don't get me wrong. Life was great. For a while, I really loved David. But, like many couples, we grew tired of each other. He is a talented, sophisticated, intriguing personality. Some of the biggest names in Hollywood called him a friend—not just Elvis. He knew the big names like Bob Hope and Milton Berle."

Of all her nights with Winters, the one that stood out in her mind was the evening her parents came to visit. Winters and Linda were living luxuriously in Beverly Hills when her parents, John and Dorothy Boreman, flew in from Florida. She drove her expensive Bentley to the Los Angeles airport to meet them.

There was no talk of how she had become such a celebrated star, although through some source, perhaps her sister, she had learned that her father had gone by himself to see *Deep Throat.* Her mother was in denial, and had refused to have that movie mentioned in her household.

To greet them, Linda dressed tastefully in a beautiful Chanel dress she'd picked up secondhand in Paris, although it still looked new. She'd planned a special dinner for them. To show off her familiarity with *tout* Hollywood, she suggested that "David could invite three of your favorite stars to dinner—but not Elvis, because he's touring."

Mrs. Boreman suggested Jimmy Stewart, Gene Kelly, and Lillian Gish.

564

Linda promised her mother that she'd present Winters with the names of the persons she'd requested. She'd never heard of Lillian Gish. Amazingly, all three stars accepted, perhaps out of curiosity because Linda was still the talk of the town.

It was unlikely that Miss Gish had seen *Deep Throat,* but Linda learned that both Stewart and Kelly had. It seemed that Miss Gish had at least heard of the movie—who hadn't? "My dear," she said, during her introduction to Linda, "D.W. Griffith had censorship problems with our *The Birth of a Nation* when it first came out in 1915."

There is no record of what this bizarre grouping of people talked about over dinner.

Even though she'd never heard of it, Miss Gish was more fascinating to Linda than either Jimmy Stewart or Gene Kelly. "David told me that Kelly was a fag," she later said to Liz Renay.

Gish, the defining face of the silent screen, sat across from Linda. Her sad, heart-shaped face, pursed lips, and yearning eyes evoked a Hollywood era long gone by.

[Lillian Gish was born in 1893 and lived until February 27, 1993, nearly reaching her 100th birthday. She and her younger sister, Dorothy Gish (1898-1968), began acting onstage as children. Both of them made their film debuts in 1912 working in shorts.

Lillian would make her last film, The Whales of August (1987), *opposite Bette Davis. When its director, Lindsay Anderson, complimented Miss Gish on her close-up, a jealous Davis had snapped: "She should know how to perform a close-up—after all, she invented the close-up!"*

As Linda remembered it, Miss Gish complimented her on "a perfectly enchanting evening" and noted that "female stars today have to take off all their clothes. In my day, a woman showing her ankle was considered *risqué.*"

Gene Kelly promised to teach her to dance as a means of helping her stage a musical revue in Las Vegas, but he never did.

After dinner, she welcomed a few minutes alone with Stewart when she wandered alone with him in her garden.

As a movie buff, she'd

At a dinner party, **Lillian Gish** *(both photos, above)* told Linda, "Back in the days of the Silents, D.W. Griffith and I also had censorship problems."

learned of his long roster of A-list seductions, beginning with Margaret Sullavan and going on to Ginger Rogers, June Allyson, Olivia de Havilland, Marlene Dietrich, Jean Harlow, Rita Hayworth, Katharine Hepburn (of all people), Jeanette MacDonald, Norma Shearer, Lana Turner, Loretta Young, and Grace Kelly.

Even though Stewart had been born in 1908, he still looked alert and kiddish. Everybody seemed to like him—and so did Linda. A Hollywood columnist had estimated that before Stewart entered World War II, he had seduced 262 different Hollywood glamour girls.

At a private dinner party, Linda wondered if all those rumors about **Gene Kelly** were true. "He didn't even ask me to suck his cock!"

Stewart sensed that she might be trying to arrange, at a later time, a date with him, and he quickly put a stop to that. "You're a pretty girl. When I see a pretty girl, I look and look and look some more. Even as you grow too old to do anything, you still don't stop looking."

"I see," she said. "Too bad for me."

"No, my little dear. Too bad for old Jimmy here."

She later recalled, "Ever since I got to Hollywood, I'd been working my way through mostly the older stars. But reality dawned: Many of them were sitting home at night in front of their TV sets, dreaming of the days when they visited Grace, Lana, and Marilyn."

***

The **James Stewart** *(both photos above)* she'd remembered on the screen and the James Stewart she encountered at her home came as a bit of a shock to Linda.

As David Winters' ideas for promoting Linda as an actress began to dwindle, so did their relationship. However, he came up with a final idea, promoting her as the centerpiece of a film entitled *Linda Lovelace for President,* an all-around flop that was eventually released, disastrously, in 1975.

The political platform she'd endorse as part of the publicity associated with the film called for "free love," and the ersatz political party hastily defined to back her

566

was defined, for media purposes, as "The Upright Party." As news of the endeavor inevitably made its way through the late-night talk show circuits, some comedians joked that it should have been named the "On Your Back Party" or the "Down Your Throat Party."

The movie's creative team was impressive: Writer/producer Arthur Marks also functioned as its (uncredited) director. In addition to a vast string of previous movie credits, Marks had directed or would direct episodes of such TV shows as *I Spy, The Dukes of Hazzard, and Starsky and Hutch.* Marks was also involved in launching the *Perry Mason* series on TV.

Drawing from a budget established at $800,000, *Linda Lovelace for President* was filmed on the campus of the University of Kansas in Lawrence, Kansas, and at Swope Park in Kansas City, Missouri.

In the film, Linda runs for president on a campaign slogan, "A vote for Linda is a *blow* for democracy."

Marks rounded up some very talented back-up actors, including Micky Dolenz of The Monkees (who played a near-sighted bus driver). Chuck McCann, playing "the assassinator," added comic relief. Also in the film was comedian Vaughn Meader, who played a preacher who lusts after Linda.

[Meader had become instantly famous for his impersonation of JFK in a best-selling comedy album, The First Family. *Released in time for Christmas of 1962, it became the fastest-selling record in the history of the United States, eventually selling 7.5 million copies. In the aftermath of Kennedy's assassination in November of 1963 it was yanked from shelves as the nation went into mourning. Still in his 20s, Meader sank into instant obscurity. His film with Linda had been envisioned, regrettably, as his comeback from obscurity.]*

To publicize the film, Linda was flown to Washington, D.C., where she was photographed outside the gates of the White House, handing out bumper stickers. In the

A team of creative, successful entertainment industry pros got involved in an attempt to make *Linda Lovelace for President* a success.

One of them was **Vaughn Meader** *(top photo, imitating JFK in the early 1960s)*, the comedian in charge of **The First Family**, a bestselling recording that lampooned the Kennedys until the president's assassination in 1963 abruptly killed its sales nationwide.

But even Meader and his talented cohorts couldn't rescue Linda's disastrously unfunny race for the White House.

background behind her, Gerald Ford sat uneasily in the Oval Office, his days as President numbered.

According to a deal worked out with Marks, Linda would receive $25,000 up front, plus a percentage of the profits. At the beginning, she warned him, "No sex, no nudity." Although he seemed reluctant, he orally agreed to her terms. But halfway through the production, he announced to her, "Linda, we're ready for the fuck-and-suck scene."

She was furious, claiming that she wouldn't do it, and that an agreement had existed between them.

"Read your contract," he told her.

She later claimed that she was heartbroken that Winters didn't defend her against the demands Marks was making. "He'd been my knight in shining armor, the slayer of California dragons, the last line of defense against the sharpies, the conmen, and the sleaze artists."

The next day, once again, she refused to disrobe for a sex scene. But Marks insisted that she remove her clothes. Again, she refused. Then he fired her. "You'll never work in movies again," he warned her.

Back in her dressing room, she read her contract, which stated that during the filming, she would agree to follow the "artistic" direction of Marks.

Finally, she had to compromise. "There was no actual sex on camera, but some brief nudity," she said.

Opening in the summer of 1974, *Linda Lovelace for President* was featured in *Playboy*, Hefner devoting ten pages to it. Among all the films opening that week, *Variety* tepidly rated Linda's movie at Number Eleven. Getting few reviews, it died from negative word of mouth, flopping within a few days.

As a movie reviewer, Linda could at times be her own worst critic. As she'd done with *Deep Throat Part II*, Linda publicly reviewed her own *Linda Lovelace for President*. "It was a worthless piece of shit, unbelievable and terrible. As an exploitation movie, it was one of the dumbest made. It was so bad that I can't remember the names of the so-called actors in it. It was R-rated, R for ridiculous."

Critic Eric Henderson viewed the characters in the film "as a handful of lame stereotypes—militant Negro, bull dyke, limp-wristed fag, ironing Chinaman, neo-Nazi."

Many critics suggested that Linda in *Deep Throat* had produced an erection in thousands of its viewers, but in her latest film "she is a boner-kill."

Henderson wrote: *[In* Linda Lovelace for President*]*, "We get a nine-minute 'oral history' (snort, chuckle) of the film's production from executive producer Arthur Marks. It's a pathetic, haphazard history, but at least Marks gets a few digs in at Linda Lovelace for being allegedly unprofessional and (in his opinion) not particularly good looking. Sounds like someone got left with blue balls on the casting couch."

As part of the marketing associated with the film, it was actually proposed that she run for President. Her campaign tour, whose itinerary took the shape of an erect penis, was plotted on a map.

A "ballot/petition" was inserted among the end pages of every copy of *The Intimate Diary of Linda Lovelace,* urging readers to cast their vote for her as the next President of the United States. Ultimately, she received 25,000 unvalidated votes, with the tacit understanding that votes had been funneled through the publisher and not through any official voting stream. She lost, of course, to Jimmy Carter in the elections of 1976.

During her *faux* political campaign, she made a widely publicized comment about the presidential race between Gerald Ford and Carter: "I can look at a man who is fully dressed and can accurately estimate his dick size. I have this uncanny, God-given ability. If the road to the White House was based on dick size, Ford would have retained the Presidency. As for that peanut grower, Carter, have you ever seen an unshelled peanut? You get the idea."

In 1976, at the end of her so-called presidential run, she said, "My trying to become president was just a joke, yet another joke to bring ridicule to me. I'm no fool, although some people say I am. No one seriously thought I was ever going to occupy the Oval Office. It was clear to me that not only was I not going to become President, it was doubtful that I was even going to be Linda Lovelace any more. My whole life was spinning out of control. Though there would be a few more feeble attempts at stardom, I began to realize that dream was out of my grasp, though I still got offers to do porno. I had to find some way to move on with my life. There was always the prospect that I could become Linda Boreman again, though I knew I could never escape my infamous past."

***

Although it never reached fruition, Winters made one final deal for Linda after he returned to Hollywood with her after the wrap of her *For President* effort.

Italian film producer, Ovidio Assinitus, was in Hollywood at the time, and he contacted Linda as the possible star of his next film, a work he had already entitled *Laure.* Although he didn't have a script in hand, he assured Winters it would be based on the *Emmanuel* book series, which had erotically detailed the life of an "exotic" European swinger.

The deal sounded promising, as Sylvia Kristel, a Dutch actress, had filmed the 1974 erotic film *Emmanuelle,* which had been already projected as the first of what was envisioned as a series. The Dutch/English film director Just Jaeckin, a long-time resident of France, had cast the willowy, brunette model and former beauty contest winner as the wife of a French diplomat in Bangkok. As the plot evolves, she has a series of adulterous affairs while her husband is at work.

Early gossip associated with the film's release had designated it as a triumph of soft-core porn. After its opening in Paris, it was hailed as a "triumph of feminism," thanks mainly to a scene in which Emmanuelle climbed on top of her husband during intercourse. Some critics had defined *Emmanuelle* as a "respectable alternative" to both *Deep Throat* and to Marilyn Chambers' *Behind the Green Door.*

Winters viewed *Laure* as a possibility for a prestigious movie role for Linda. Assinitus told Winters he believed that Linda's name alone would attract an international audience. The producer was willing to pay Linda $120,000, the highest amount she'd ever received for anything, a sum that dwarfed that $1,200 she didn't get for *Deep Throat.*

Filming was to begin in the summer of 1974. Linda signed a contract,

Among the dozens of film projects proposed to Linda was a follow-up, almost a sequel, to the successful 1974 erotic cult film *Emmanuelle,* which had brought great international success to actress **Sylvia Kristel** *(photo above).*

Kristel regretted she never appeared with Linda, but credited her with helping change censorship laws. Without Linda as a co-star, Kristel went on to appear in other films such as *Lady Chatterley's Lover* (1981) and *Mata Hari* (1985), playing on her reputation as an erotic film star.

"She had the kind of career I wanted, but didn't get," Linda later lamented.

thereby ensuring her involvement in this ill-fated project, but not realizing until later how or what she had obligated herself to. When filming actually began, her relationship with Winters had ended.

For the most part, her love affair with Winters had been peaceful, although she did charge in one of your future memoirs, *Ordeal,* that "he beat me up." But, unlike her marriage to Chuck, violence had never poisoned her months with Winters. In retrospect, in a sad voice, she said, "My love for David was a perfect bubble, but bubbles do burst."

After the breakup, Winters said, "I remember all the good times we had, and I still have a soft spot for her in my heart. She was a nice person, just a simple girl who really wanted to be loved for herself and to settle down with a guy and have a family and grow old together. The girl that I knew, in reality, was really Linda Boreman, not Linda Lovelace."

***

Heading back to Florida, Linda was due in court to face several charges, all of which were for damages caused either by her failure to pay a bill or failure to appear in a show for she she'd previously contracted her services.

On the plane to Miami, she read several clippings that had accumulated in the office of Linda Lovelace Enterprises. One from the *Boston Phoenix* had piqued her interest. "At last, someone believes me," she said.

Gerard Damiano had addressed an audience of college students in Boston. He charged that "Chuck Traynor was a nothing. He had no personality, no charm, no brains. He was just a user of people, and he used Linda Lovelace. He gave her nothing and abused her. He was very brutal with her. Many times she'd come on the set of *Deep Throat* and be completely black and blue."

She was elated that someone was on her side, believing her and speaking out in her defense. Too often, she'd failed to get people to listen to her.

Even though she'd left Chuck and had divorced him, the ghost of his presence still haunted her. She had nightmares about him, as if expecting him to arrive on the scene any minute and threaten her.

One of the passengers on the plane to Miami, a middle-aged man, recognized her. "I saw you in *Pajama Tops* in Philadelphia," he said. "I was disappointed. I thought it was going to be a nude play."

"Well, it wasn't," she snapped. "I got the kind of reviews an Egyptian president would get in Tel Aviv."

In the aftermath of being sued by Miami's Paramount Theater for breach of contract, and in a separate case, for her failure to pay for the legal services of Florida lawyer Phil Mandina, she boarded an airplane for Miami. In a courtroom there, she lost both cases and was ordered to pay the theater $32,000 and the lawyer $19,500.

During her time in Florida, she opted to visit her parents. When she arrived at the Boreman's home in Davie, near Fort Lauderdale, she found it overcrowded. Her mother, Dorothy, told her she'd have to sleep on the living room sofa because her room was occupied. Then, with her mother out of earshot, her father, John Boreman, whispered to her, "I went to see *Deep Throat* and walked out halfway through it to vomit."

Living in what had been her bedroom were her older sister, Jean Boreman, Jean's boyfriend, Larry Marchiano, and their infant son, Larry Paul. She learned from John that Larry and Jean were unmarried and had been living together for three years. But she was also told that they were on the verge of breaking up.

She'd met Larry years before when she'd lived in Westchester County (New York) and worked briefly in a boutique in the hamlet of Shrub Oak.

Before her arrival at the Boreman home, Larry had told Jean and her family that he'd remembered Linda as a "snooty, stuck-up bitch." Amazingly, when he was re-introduced to her, he had never heard of either "Linda Lovelace" or

Deep Throat. Jean later explained, "Our mother had ordered that no mention in her household ever be made of that *'vile and filthy picture.'"*

Larry had lost his job on Long Island as a cable TV installer, and he'd been supporting himself working part-time in Miami as an apprentice plumber and living with Jean and the Boremans.

"When I first saw Larry again, I played the big movie star and dropped names like John Wayne and Richard Burton," she said. "But I soon learned Larry wasn't impressed with that. We finally were open and honest with each other, beginning when both of us admitted we were flat broke."

Although Linda Boreman hadn't impressed Larry, Linda Lovelace appealed to him immensely. "It wasn't just about sex," he reportedly said. "I like her as a person. I was just a blue collar guy out of work, but she took an interest in me. Things pretty much had wound down between Jean and me. We thought the baby might hold us together, but it wasn't happening."

Over the course of several days, she began to learn more about Larry, who had avoided the draft in 1965 and subsequent military service in Vietnam. At the New York draft office, he'd announced, "I'll kill you if you make me kill somebody else." Consequently, he was designated as 4-F. A psychiatrist wrote on his medical report, "A hopeless psychotic."

Linda's biggest night out with Larry changed both of their lives. She felt she could ask him out on a date without making Jean jealous, since they were planning to separate anyway. She called Sammy Davis, Jr., when she read in *The Miami Herald* that he was appearing at the Diplomat Theater on Miami Beach. Sammy was his usual friendly self and invited them to the theater as his guests.

Larry eagerly accepted her invitation, but she soon was made to understand that she had to buy him a suit of clothes. Both of them enjoyed Sammy's show and then went backstage, where Sammy kissed her and shook Larry's hand.

Over the span of a few minutes, Sammy quickly ascertained the status of their lives. "Linda's had a lot of bad breaks," Sammy told Larry. "She needs a strong man in her life, a real man around the house, which she didn't have in Chuck Traynor and in David Winters, who used her. You look like that kind of man to me, and I'm never wrong about these things. Will you consider flying to California and looking after her?"

"Oh, Larry," she said, "That would make me so happy. You could be my manager."

"I know nothing of running a show business career," Larry said. "But I know how to unplug your toilet if it gets stopped up."

"Listen, she's been with sharpies who knew too much about show business," Sammy said. "She needs someone to plow through things and find out who's robbing her."

"That I could do," Larry said.

Sammy went over to a leather pouch and removed $5,000 in one-hundred dollar bills. "Take this money. It'll get you guys to California and stake you a bit."

Dorothy Boreman was furious and cynical when she learned of Larry's decision to dump one of her daughters and begin a live-in relation with another. "You're abandoning her sister with a baby while you run off to shack up with my other daughter? Isn't that pretty?"

Arriving with Linda in Hollywood, Linda and Larry took a taxi to her rented cottage. Once there, he found the place a disorganized mess. He was not sleeping with her at this point, and bedded down that night on the sofa. The next morning, he began to look over her mail, which consisted almost entirely of unpaid bills and what he recalled were "the most ridiculous offers you could imagine."

Linda's first obligation, according to the terms of her contract, involved embarking on a publicity tour "promoting that dumb movie, *Linda Lovelace for President."* At first, Larry was reluctant to get involved until he discovered that she'd get paid $2,500 a week, with all expenses paid. She suggested that because she was certain not to make any more money from the movie, they might as well live it up and charge everything to the production.

The tour opened in Vancouver, where she occupied the Howard Hughes Suite at one of the city's most upscale hotels. They feasted off shrimp, lobster, and champagne.

According to Linda, while watching television, they held each other and then made love. "It was a wonderful experience," she recalled. "That night, I found the man I wanted to spend the rest of my life with."

In New York City, in a sojourn configured as part of the publicity tour, Linda and Larry went to visit the publisher of *Inside Linda Lovelace* and demanded $32,000 in overdue royalties. Larry had calculated that that was what was owed her from the publication of her first memoir.

She learned that the publisher had already sent a check for that amount to Chuck Traynor. Then, to her horror, she discovered that she'd previously signed a contract granting Chuck one-hundred percent of her gross income for the rest of her life.

By the time she and Larry flew back to Los Angeles, another obligation, this one contracted by David Winters, awaited them. She had agreed to film *Laure,* and she was due in Rome to meet with the producers.

"With no script in hand, and with no knowledge of what we were getting into, Larry and I took our free tickets and headed for Italy."

***

In Rome, the producers of *Laure* had reserved a luxurious suite at the very posh Grand Hotel for Linda and her "boyfriend."

David Winters, who had written himself into Linda's contract for *Laure,* also winged his way to Rome and met with Linda and her new love in their suite. These two rivals came together for the first time, but no record exists of the exchanges that passed between them.

Later, when she and Larry walked the streets of Rome, she at first felt that Mussolini's Fascists were still in control. The political reality, however, was far different from that. Italy had become the target for international terrorists, and there was not only a heavy police presence in central Rome, but helmeted soldiers and armed Jeeps were positioned within each of the city's major squares, including in Piazza di Spagna and Piazza Navona.

Strike fever had also hit the land, as labor tested its muscle and organized walkouts practically every day. Often the Roman waterworks cut off the flow of water in the middle of Linda's shower. Whenever that happened, instead of using water to brush her teeth, she used the complimentary champagne from her refrigerator within the suite.

The producers and director of *Laure* conversed rapidly in French or Italian, using very little English, but were nonetheless most gracious to her when they met. She felt that the movie would go smoothly based on her first encounters with them. From what she gathered, *Laure* was "a beautiful love story."

In a memoir, she recorded that her understanding was that she would play the role of either an anthropologist or an archeologist. She was wrong on both counts.

Eventually, she learned that her role in the film was that of an ethnologist. That sent her to the dictionary, where she learned that meant a person engaged in a science that divided human beings into races, their origin, their distribution across the planet, their relations with other people, and their characteristics.

Then she was told that many of her scenes would be filmed in a jungle in the Philippines, Italian wardrobe staffers came by to outfit her with pith helmets, bush clothes, and white safari jackets.

"I wouldn't call it type casting," she told Larry. "Me cast as an ethnologist." Even after looking it up, she still wasn't certain what kind of profession that was.

After reading the draft of the still-uncompleted script, she noted to her dismay that some scenes involved soft porn, obviously calling for her nudity. The next day, presumably after ranting with Larry about it throughout the night, she and Larry informed the producers that she refused to appear in such scenes.

The backers of *Laure* were horrified. The French director asked her, "Are you the real Linda Lovelace? Didn't you do a little more in *Deep Throat* than show brief nudity?"

As Winters himself knew very well, the producers could get 100,000 fully disrobed actresses to replace Linda in *Laure,* each of whom would be a better thespian than Linda.

Relations began to deteriorate when one of the producers and his big-busted bimbo arrived for dinner at their hotel. As the evening progressed, the producer began to send out signals about how the four of them might get to know each other more intimately. When she could stand his insinuations no more, Linda stood up, shook their hands, and thanked them for a charming evening. "Come along, Larry," she said.

Later, she told him, "That ugly frog thought I was an international whore. Well, he learned better."

After that (failed) dinner at The Grand Hotel, negotiations with the producers sank. They simply could not believe that America's leading female porn star would not perform in the nude. "Hell," one of them said, "We can even get Sophia Loren to take off her clothes, and she's the biggest star in Europe."

"Who does this little dime store prostitute, Miss Linda Lovelace, think she is?" a producer asked.

Finally, Linda and the film's backers reached a compromise. The star role would be recast, with Linda assigned a minor role. "Don't worry," the director said. "You can be fully clothed in all scenes." He looked at her with disdain and then said rather sarcastically, "You will wear pants in all your scenes. That way, you will not even have to show a nude ankle."

For a month, Linda and Larry lived in Rome in style, with the producers of *Laure* picking up their hotel and food bills. They spent their days sightseeing, eating, and sleeping. "We did some other things, too," she said.

***

She was alone in their suite at the Grand Hotel when a call came in from Vittorio De Sica, the celebrated Italian film director. She had never heard of him, but he told her that he wanted to cast her in the lead of his next movie. Over the phone, he sounded cultured and charming. She agreed to meet with him that night at eight in his suite at the Excelsior Hotel. Fearing that Larry might be jealous, she made up some other excuse for abandoning him that evening.

In the meantime, she talked to Winters, who informed her that De Sica was among the top two or three most famous film directors in Italy, a leading figure in postwar neo-realism. Four of the films he'd directed had won Oscars, including *The Bicycle Thief (1948),* which today is listed as one of the fifteen most influential movies of all time.

That evening during their encounter in his suite, De Sica still possessed his

Continental charm, but he looked ill to Linda. When not drinking champagne, he coughed frequently. He was most gracious to her.

"I fear my greatest artistic triumphs are of yesterday," he said. "I have this very bad habit: I lose large sums of money gambling. Any day now, I think the Mafia will eliminate me if I don't have a big hit. I lowered my standards when I directed Kim Novak in *The Amorous Adventures of Moll Flanders* (1965), I've just completed *Andy Warhol's Dracula* (1974). But even famous directors have to eat and pay off their gambling debts."

He explained that he was no longer trying to win another Oscar for Sophia Loren, a reference to her appearance in *Two Women* (1961), but that he wanted to make "a movie that will earn a bundle of lire." He asked her if she'd seen Tennessee Williams' *The Roman Spring of Mrs. Stone (1961)*, starring Vivien Leigh.

"I never miss a Warren Beatty movie," she told him.

Italian film director **Vittorio de Sica** *(photo above)*: "I was ill and never got to make that movie I had envisioned. It would have starred Linda Lovelace, Rossano Brazzi, Marcello Mastroianni, and Vittorio Gassman. It would have packed the cinema houses, at least in Italy."

"I was warned that Linda can't act. That would not have been a hurdle for me. After all, I had previously directed Kim Novak in *The Amorous Adventures of Moll Flanders*."

He explained that the film about *Mrs. Stone* had inspired his development of a similar but very different script. "As you know, in *Mrs. Stone*, an aging but very wealthy actress comes to Rome and takes up with a handsome young gigolo, Mr. Beatty. After the war, many German women, even American women, flocked to Rome to find Italian stallions. Of course, the Nazi women had lost their husbands or boyfriends in the war and needed to find replacements."

He told her the plot of his newest film project would be different. It called for her to play a nymphomaniac from a small town in the American South. "Your profligacy has made you an object of shame and derision, even though you've inherited millions from your timber baron father. You come to Rome to escape from your past and to satisfy your desires."

"Unlike the dynamic in the Tennessee Williams play—an older woman meets a younger man—in my movie you will be a younger woman seeking middle aged men because you're secretly in love with your dead father. Of course, there will be the obligatory scene in flashback where he is seen entering your bedroom with lascivious intent when you're still a twelve-year-old girl."

"In my film, you're not torn between two lovers. Instead, you take three men who were each left destitute at the end of the war," he said. "They have their pride, but no money, and they agree to rent their bodies to satisfy the lusts of this demanding American heiress. The plot involves how the four of you live together in your sumptuous villa on the Appian Way. It's all here: The love, the intrigues, the betrayals, the exploitation, the humility of the men being your sex slave—just as it was in the glory days of Rome. You'll have a fabulous wardrobe, of course," he said.

"Will there be any nude scenes?" she asked.

"There will be scenes of you making love to each of these handsome men, but only your legs and your back will show. This will be a mainstream, R-rated feature film—no porno, although a bit of soft core, perhaps."

She started to raise her usual objections even to that moderate request, but never expressed them. De Sica interrupted and told her that she'd be paid $200,000 for starring in the movie. Since she was desperately in debt, she accepted, on an impulse, without checking with anybody.

"This is marvelous," he said. "We'll have an international hit."

"By the way, who are these three other actors?" she asked.

"Italy's finest," De Sica answered. "Rossano Brazzi, Marcello Mastroianni, and Vittorio Gassman."

"I've never heard of two of them, but I do read movie magazines. Wasn't Gassman the guy who married Shelley Winters?"

"One and the same," he answered. "If you wish, I can arrange for these fine gentlemen to come here tomorrow night at eight o'clock to meet with you. You'll find their charm devastating. Of course, they're not as young as they used to be, but they are still sexual dynamos, still what American teen-aged girls call heartthrobs."

"I really want to meet these guys," she said. "I heard gossip about how Gassman also had an affair with Elizabeth Taylor when they made *Rhapsody* (1954). If both Liz and Shelley went for him, he must still be something."

"I think you'll agree that all three of these men are not only big on talent (and fairly big in some other departments), but they ooze charm through every pore."

"I can't wait."

***

As arranged by De Sica the following night in his suite at the Excelsior, Linda came face to face with "the three most charming men I've ever met"— Vittorio Gassman, Marcello Mastroianni, and Rossano Brazzi.

577

Before meeting them, she'd done a bit of biographical sleuthing. She even deciphered their ages: Brazzi was 58; Gassman 52; and Mastroianni, her favorite, was the youngest at the age of 50.

Since 1940, Brazzi had been married to the Baroness Lidia Bertolini, who, over the years, had turned a blind eye to his outside indulgences with other women. This son of Bologna always tried to seduce his leading ladies, especially in his American films, or so Linda had heard.

In De Sica's suite at the Excelsior, Linda pointedly asked Brazzi, "Is it your policy to seduce your female stars? Since I'm going to be starring with you, I want to know. Now. No bullshit, please."

Brazzi admitted to the charge. "In Italy, I nearly always succeed," he said. "With American movie stars, it was hit and miss. I got lucky with the very beautiful Jean Peters when we made *Three Coins in the Fountain* (1954). Her husband, Howard Hughes, neglected her shamefully. I also went after Katharine Hepburn in *Summertime* (1955), even though I did not find her particularly appealing. What do you Americans say? 'She's a bit long in the tooth?' Later, I found out that I would have had a better chance with her if I were a woman."

Linda: **"Rossano Brazzi** *(photo above)* may not have been Katharine Hepburn's type when they made *Summertime* together, but he was definitely my kind of man, although I would have preferred him in his prime."

"At least he revealed to me why women so eagerly pursue Italian men as lovers."

"When I made *The Barefoot Contessa* (1954) with Ava Gardner, she invited me to her bed many many times. Then, when I starred with Joan Crawford in *The Story of Esther Costello* (1957), I found her insatiable. I wasn't successful on the set of *South Pacific* (1958) with Mitzi Gaynor. But I didn't really try. I was a bit depressed, back then, I think. I did go after Olivia de Havilland in *Light in the Piazza* (1962), but I was so subtle I don't think she really caught on."

Then Linda turned her attention to the also-very-charming Vittorio Gassman. Born in Genoa to a mother who had been a (persecuted) Jewess from the Tuscan city of Pisa, he was known for having performed in Italian translations of Shakespeare, although he'd also played the brutish Stanley Kowalski in an Italian translation of Tennessee Williams' *Un tram che si chiama desiderio (A Streetcar Named Desire)*. "I think I was better in *Othello* and *Hamlet*," he told Linda. "Since I am not a brutish man like Kowalski."

Gassman possessed a natural charisma and was the most proficient of all the actors in English "When I was married to Shelley Winters, I learned

578

a lot of Anglo curse words."

"Unlike Rossano, I did not always seduce my leading ladies," Gassman said. "Shelley threatened to cut off my *cazzo* if I did. I did manage to slip away with Elizabeth Taylor during the filming of *Rhapsody* (1954), and that was my greatest achievement in the boudoir."

"I had an affair with the actress, Juliette Maynel, who gave me my son, Alessandro. I truly don't recall if I had an affair with Silvana Mangano in *Riso amaro [*aka *Bitter Rice; 1950]*. There have been so many women. A man forgets. Did I seduce Carroll Baker? I don't think so. I played a gypsy opposite her in *The Miracle* (1959). I also don't think I let Burt Reynolds fuck me when we made *Sharky's Machine* (1981). And although I am not homosexual, I vaguely remember crawling into bed with Marlon Brando that night. It happened that drunken night when Stanley Kowalski fucked Stanley Kowalski instead of Blanche DuBois. A man needs some variety, or else life would be hideously boring. I also wanted to make sure that gay guys weren't having more fun that I was, a bonafide heterosexual."

Of the trio of actors in De Sica's suite that evening, Mastroianni was the most self-deprecatory. He did not boast of his affairs, although she knew he'd been in a two-year relationship with Faye Dunaway. There were also rumors of an affair he was said to have had with Sophia Loren. She'd heard more recent rumors that he'd just emerged from an affair with Catherine Deneuve when they'd co-starred together in *It Only Happens to Others* (1972).

"To tell the truth, I'm not a great fucker," he said. "At this point in my life, I'm too old to be a Latin Lover. At my age, if I have sex, I have to go to bed and rest for three days. Actually, I find lovemaking a bit of a chore at times. I must love my co-star. Otherwise, how will the audience believe me?"

"Ah, Marcello, you are too unkind to yourself," Gassman said. "*[Federico]* Fellini told me, 'Marcello represents a kind of ideal man. He is the man every woman would want.'"

"That's very nice, but I warned all my lovers— Susan Strasberg, Jeanne Moreau, Ursula Andress— that I refuse to take off my socks while making love."

Years later, in reference to her encounter that night with the three Italian actors, Jay Garon's researchers pressed Linda for more details.

"All those uncut Italian salamis are a bit of a

Linda: "**Vittorio Gassman** *(photo above)* wasn't completely honest with me in describing his star seductions. There were just too many 'I don't remember' cop-outs."

"I bet he remembered that blow-job from Linda Lovelace. I virtually had to force him to admit that it was better than what Shelley Winters delivered, or Elizabeth Taylor."

579

blur," she recalled. "There was a bit of sameness to them. But I did fellate them. Because each of them treated me like a lady, I became their slut for the night."

***

[Linda couldn't wait to complete her contractual obligation to the Laure *production team so that she could begin working with Vittorio De Sica.*

"It will be the movie that puts me over the top," she claimed. "I just know it will."

Then tragedy struck. On November 13, 1974, a news bulletin came out of the Neuilly-sur-Seine hospital in Paris. The great De Sica had died in the aftermath of surgery.

She sent her condolences to the Spanish actress, Maria Mercader, De Sica's widow and the half-sister of Ramon Mercader, the notorious assassin of Leon Trotsky, the Soviet Marxist revolutionary and theorist, whose murder in Mexico had been ordered by Josef Stalin in 1940.

"I'm not only mourning the death of De Sica," Linda said, "but mourning the loss of my last hope for a legitimate film career."]

***

Linda: "I learned **Marcello Mastroianni**'s *(photo above)* secret. He always warned women that he was not all that great in bed. A total lie! He was fantastic in bed. He just didn't want to get a gal's hopes up before bed time."

"When I was in Rome, I heard some rumor about this gay pope who had the hots for Marcello-- not that I blamed him."

After the filming of *Laure* in Rome, its production crew gave Linda and Larry tickets to fly to Manila in The Philippines for filming of its scenes. Their flight from Rome required a transfer in New Delhi, India, but when it landed there, Linda and Larry had each swallowed too many Seconals and were in a stupor. In their drugged state, and unable to manage the logistics of the transfers on their own, they were roughly and unceremoniously escorted by Indian police officers, each carrying automatic weapons, to the departure gate of their ongoing flight to Manila.

Trapped in a hotel room in rain-soaked Manila, Linda and Larry came to loathe Filipino *[Tagalog-language]* television. "It consisted mostly of locals getting executed by the government," she said.

Waiting for the rains to stop, they grew bored, depressed, frustrated, and alienated from and by this poverty-stricken country.

580

When the sun finally emerged from behind its monsoon clouds, Linda faced trouble on the movie set. Once again, the director wanted her to perform a scene in the nude, and she balked.

Through Victor Yannacone, her attorney in the States, she sent the producers a letter, asserting that *Laure* had "no other purpose but to degrade me as a woman and a human being. It is nothing more than ill-disguised references to my past performances."

At this point, there were no more compromises. When Linda was told she'd been dismissed, she shouted back, "You can't fire me. I QUIT!"

The organizers of *Laure* complained to Winters, "She won't come out of her dressing room unless she's covered up to her neck. What in the fuck is going on?"

At this point, Winters had grown completely exasperated with Linda. In total disgust, he went to the producer, telling him, "Fire the bitch. I'm getting the next plane out of Manila."

Consequently, the production company notified the Filipino immigration authorities that Linda was no longer needed to work in the country. Shortly thereafter, she was ordered out of The Phillipines within twenty-four hours.

"Fleeing Manila, Larry and I had enough money to fly to Honolulu," she said. "We had only one-hundred dollars between us. To reach Los Angeles, we had to beg, borrow, and steal to get back to the U.S. mainland. People were asking for my autograph in the Honolulu airport. Me, bigtime movie star Linda Lovelace, multi-million dollar grosser. And we didn't have a pot to piss in."

***

Broke, unemployed, and desperate in Los Angeles, Linda commented, "I was a famous movie star who wondered where her next meal was coming from. On top of everything else, a doctor told me I was pregnant."

"If that wasn't enough, everyone in the U.S. and abroad wanted to sue me, including the production people at *Laure* "

In March of 1977, with her career in shambles, Linda, with Larry Marchiano, wanted to attend a Led Zeppelin concert at the Los Angeles Forum. She didn't have money to buy tickets, so she called Peter Grant, the band's tour manager. In exchange for two free tickets, she agreed to introduce the band at the debut of their performance.

After the show, she went backstage to greet the members of Led Zeppelin. They included guitarist Jimmy Page, singer Robert Plant, bassist John Paul Jones, and drummer John Bonham. One of the most famous of all rock groups, the Britishers were used to groupies spontaneously emerging from the woodwork backstage for sex.

Someone had mistakenly informed them that Linda was planning to fellate each of them.

As it happened, each of the band members was scheduled for a midnight engagement and didn't have a lot of time to waste with preliminaries. After she entered their dressing room, one of the band members locked the door. Then, after greeting her, each member of the band allegedly pulled out his dick for her to suck.

The "new" Linda was horrified at being treated "like a cheap, Saturday night whore," and quickly fled from the room. She felt humiliated and despondent.

Perhaps to cheer her up, Larry suggested that they get married.

The subsequent wedding was almost a "non-event." She didn't report any of the details of the marriage ceremony, nor did she reveal even the time and place it occurred. Additionally, she didn't even seem to have acquired or retained from the ceremony any semblance of a marriage license. Years later, her family suspected that she had never been officially married a second time. In her third memoir, *Ordeal,* she didn't even name her husband, perhaps not wanting to embarrass him.

In the midst of all this chaos, the IRS placed a lien on the Marchiano's pathetic bank account. Subsequently, they literally had nothing to live on.

Yet despite her fall from a-list grace, job offers and endorsement deals continued to trickle in. She claimed that on six different occasions, she had visited "the suits" within various business offices. "The story was always the same. It started out with a beautiful love story, but in the end, I was getting it in the end, so to speak, while I sucked off my husband or lover's best friend with three other guys waiting for their chance at me. I maintained my position—no nudity, no sex scenes. Sometimes, before I barged out of the room, the so-called producers would ask me to suck them off."

"With their rent three months overdue, Larry made the decision for them. With the help

Rolling Stone defined **Led Zeppelin** *(photo above)* as "the heaviest band of all time, the biggest band of the 70s, and unquestionably one of the most enduring bands in rock history."

Linda later recalled her meeting with them. "I must have had a feather up my ass. I ran away from a sexual encounter with them. Now, I wish I hadn't. At least I could have had a tale to relate to my grandchildren one day. I'm sure future generations will still be listening to their music."

of a lawyer friend, Victor Yannacone, they drove back across country to his native Long Island, to a lonely out-of-season beach cottage the attorney had found for them near Montauk Point.

Cold winds blew in through cracks in the wall, and she often had nothing but flour and College Inn chicken stock in the house. "Great meals if you like dumplings."

The days dragged on. Larry was gone most of the time, often not returning home until ten o'clock at night. Usually, he said he was hanging out with friends from long ago, or else looking for work.

Even though she knew it was bad for the baby growing inside her, she used what money came in to buy beer or wine. "I often drank a case of beer a day or a gallon of wine. I was also smoking too much weed. We got food packages from Victor to keep us alive."

With Larry gone, she stayed at home, not wanting to venture outside for fear that she'd be recognized. They needed medical treatment, more food, and better shelter.

Amazingly, at this time, two different producers in Hollywood offered her anywhere from $100,000 to one million dollars (to be deposited in a Swiss bank) if she would return to the screen as a participant in an "all out porn movie." At that time, she had exactly $1.86 in her purse, but nonetheless, she rejected these lucrative offers. "I WILL NOT DO PORN," she told Larry. "NEVER AGAIN!"

Desperate for cash, and with a baby on the way, she would not change her mind.

After a few weeks, she located a small house in the South Shore *[of Long Island, NY]* hamlet of Center Moriches. It had originally been part of a long-abandoned Army barracks. The rent was only $50 a month, so they moved in.

As 1977 neared its end, a son was born to her. She named him Dominic Paul Marchiano. In the first stages of her life with a baby, she doted on being a mother, finding that it brought her more satisfaction than anything else in her previous life.

But trouble soon began. Word leaked out that the notorious Linda Lovelace was living in Center Moriches. Cars filled with schoolboys began to drive by their modest home. Sometimes, the cars would stop, and two or three boys would emerge from the car and moon her house. In a few cases, some of these boys unzipped their jeans and flashed their cocks at her, often yelling, "Suck on this, Lovelace!"

She noticed that Larry was drinking more and more and obsessing about all the pain Chuck had inflicted on her. At times, he threatened to kill Chuck.

Yannacone became the first person to realize that Linda needed medical help. "She complained of her breasts hurting because of those silicone injections Chuck Traynor had forced on her. Also, she was ashamed to show her legs, because she'd been kicked and beaten so frequently that she'd developed varicose veins. At one point, her left leg became swollen to twice its size, and she had to be rushed to the hospital."

She later referred to Yannacone as "a modern-day Don Quixote, a man looking very much like an unmade bed—always on the run, always seeking justice for some cause. He even brought food to our house when he knew we were starving."

[Yannacone was a controversial, and pioneering environmental attorney. He led a successful campaign to ban the pesticide, DDT, in the United States. He also exposed the long term after-effects of the jungle defoliant, Agent Orange, on Vietnam veterans.

After getting to know Linda, he agreed to file suit on her behalf, hoping to recover a portion of some of the millions earned by Deep Throat. *He filed a lawsuit in Nassau County, New York, but it was eventually dismissed without a trial. Her contract was deemed by the court as a legitimate "work for hire" agreement which clearly stated that she would be paid $1,200, with no percentage points.*

Concluding that her argument was hopeless, Yannacone did not appeal.]

During the depths of her despair, a lucrative offer suddenly arrived from Vegas. "It wasn't porn. I was back in show biz again."

***

On site once again in Vegas, she entered rehearsals for her last theatrical appearance, a sex farce entitled *My Daughter's Rated X.*

"The script seemed harmless enough to me," she said, "and I was to be paid $2,500 a week. It was better than scrounging for cigarette butts on Long Island."

A luxurious suite, paid for by the producers, was waiting for them at the Aladdin, and Larry retrieved her "celebrity rags" from storage. A full-time babysitter was employed for Dominic.

"At long last, I went from a starvation diet to lobster, champagne, and shrimp, all I wanted. I was back on top of the world, celebrated again. After the Las Vegas run, the producers had booked me on a nine-month tour of America, where they predicted I'd play to packed houses."

The play had been written by Arthur Marx *[not to be confused with the producer, Arthur Marks, from Linda's earlier association with* Linda Lovelace for President.*]* Linda soon learned that both Bob Hope and Milton Berle had been invited to the show, although dates had not been nailed down for their arrivals.

584

Scheduled for an opening on January 21, 1977, the sex comedy revolved around a New York City actress who returns to her hometown with a child but no husband. Her conservative father had been a movie censor who, during the course of his career, had rigorously objected to the onscreen filming of even a man and a wife sleeping together in a double bed. During her absence, he'd learned that his daughter had appeared nude in a film and had performed sex acts on camera, obvious references to Linda and *Deep Throat.*

On opening night, the house was packed with revelers and porn fans who came expecting her to perform in the nude. In the lobby, there was wild speculation, summed up by a man who asked: "Is she actually going to give blowjobs...live, on stage?"

She hardly remembered opening night, knowing that her comic lines weren't going over with the audience. "I just wanted to get through it—that was all. The play was dumb and I was even dumber performing in it."

The first visitor backstage was the comedian, Bob Hope, who had made her the butt of many a joke on national TV. She knew that he was a friend of David Winters, and that they had previously worked together on a TV special. Hope had never been one of her favorites, and she'd heard that his best lines were the work of an army of scriptwriters.

When she was introduced to him, the round-faced, British-born comedian had already done his best work and was deep into a long, slow decline. He was in his 70s when he shook her hand.

"I don't want to say that he was old," she said, "Let's put it this way. He was rejected as an inductee into the Army in 1942 because he was thirty-nine years old. I hadn't even been born yet."

"When I first met him, Hope was an institution—not a man," she said. "He'd slowed down quite a bit, but in Vegas, he had a reputation for bedding a lot of showgirls, though he tried to keep low profile."

Emblematic of his health problems, he wore a black patch over his left eye. "What do you plan to do?" Linda asked him. "Impersonate Sammy Davis, Jr.?"

"Nothing like that, although I could do a better Sammy than Sammy," he said. "For years, my left eye has been prone to hemorrhaging."

"Hemorrhaging is the right word for this show I'm in," she said.

"Good luck with it," he said. "It does need work. If I had time, and I don't, I'd help you with your timing."

"I really didn't want to go, but I found myself accepting his invitation to meet him in an hour in his suite," she said. "There was a lot of espionage, because he had to keep up appearances by pretending he was still faithful to his wife."

[She was referring to the singer, Dolores Reade, who was Hope's second or third wife, depending on which biography you read.]

"Bob made arrangements for me to be ushered up to his suite by a bellhop, who directed me to the elevator in the rear. I don't know where Larry was, and didn't really care. Probably soaking up all that free liquor back at the Aladdin. On Long Island, accumulating money to buy booze was one of our real challenges."

"On the way to his suite, I remembered a lot of the rumors I'd heard about him," she said. "David knew a lot about his previous life. Here he was in his seventies—and still chasing after girls."

As regards his show business career, he'd once told a reporter, "I was lucky, you know. I always had a beautiful girl and the money was good."

His one-time partner and rival, Bing Crosby, said, "Hope is a fast man with the squaws, but a slow man with a buck."

Hope had been romantically linked to many stars, including his "Road" picture co-star Dorothy Lamour, as well as Marilyn Maxwell, Janis Paige, singer Frances Langford, Paulette Goddard, Rhonda Fleming, and Betty Hutton. His love affair with the former blonde starlet, Barbara Payton, who later evolved into a dope addict and hooker, had been exposed by *Confidential* magazine.

As his former lover, Payton, herself, had admitted, "My affair with Bob didn't happen because he was a great lover. For that, I had to turn to Tom Neal, Steve Cochran, Marlon Brando, or Franchot Tone. I did hear from gals that in the 1930s, Bob was a tiger in bed. But what I got in the 50s was one tired old hound dog."

In his suite, "Hope ordered drinks sent up by room service," she said. "He didn't like the waiter. After he'd gone, Hope said, 'I gave him only a quarter tip. After all, I've got to keep my reputation for being stingy. Jack Benny and I compete as to who can be the cheapest Shit.'"

He expressed another complaint about the waiter. "I can't believe all the Jew boys who work as waiters in Vegas. When I first hit this

BOB HOPE--THEN AND LATER

"I don't want to say anything bad about **Bob Hope** *(photos above)*," Linda said. "He was a national institution and beloved by many fans. But when the cameras were turned off, he was quite a different man--selfish and rather arrogant. "

"I hate to say this, but I found him a bit of a sleazeball. Imagine me, Linda Lovelace, calling any other entertainer a sleazeball. I've got some nerve."

Larry Gelbart, screen and TV writer, said, "Hope fooled around with anyone who was young and nubile and guest-starred on his show."

cowtown, Jew waiters were a no-no. Now they're popping up everywhere."

She found it almost impossible to believe that Hope was anti-Semitic. "I ran into Uncle Miltie *[Milton Berle]*, " Hope said. "That horny bastard is in town. You gotta watch him. I used to room with him when we were in vaudeville together. You can't trust him at night, or at least not back in those days. You might wake up in the wee hours and find him sucking you off. When he dresses in drag, it's no joke. He told me he's coming tomorrow night to catch your show."

"Did I fuck around with Bob Hope? I must confess I went down on him," she later told Jay Garon's researchers. "That momentous event took place in his living room, as I sat on the sofa, and he stood in front of me. He didn't even take off his suit, but unzipped his pants."

"It was a limp, withered cock that had seen the light of day in Edwardian London," she said. "I was blowing him not because I was attracted to him—not at all. I was turned on by the fact that he'd been on the cover of *Time* magazine and could pick up the phone and put through a call to the President of the United States, regardless of who sat in the Oval Office."

"I'd heard he used to give starlets mink coats when he was younger and freer with his dough," she said. "But with me, he lived up to his reputation as a tightwad."

As he showed her out the door to his suite, she said, sarcastically, "Thanks, Bob. It's been a belly full of laughs."

"YOU BITCH!" he said. "Just for that, I'll stop publicizing *Deep Throat* with my jokes."

***

The next morning, she faced the devastating reviews for *My Daughter's Rated X*. A critic for *The Los Angeles Times* wrote: "As a fully clothed actress, Ms. Lovelace continually smiles at the audience in total disregard of whatever else is happening on stage. She delivers her lines as if she were reading them for the first time. The dialogue was embarrassingly bad. She stole from Bob Hope the line, 'I thought *Deep Throat* was a Disney picture about a giraffe.' The audience expected nudity at the very least, and possibly more displays of her singular fellating talent. They left disappointed. As for nudity, she came out wearing enough clothes to get through the worst cold snap of the season."

The reviewer for *The Hollywood Reporter* wasn't any kinder, asserting that Linda and her fellow actors were "more victims than perpetrators of this hapless, unfunny, and altogether dreadful ninety-minute waste of time and talent."

***

587

After her performance three nights later, a sixty-six year old Milton Berle came backstage to greet her. She'd later define him as "a lusty old fart."

Berle's reputation had preceded him. Betty Grable, the most visible pinup girl of World War II, was quoted as saying, "They say the two best hung men in Hollywood are Forrest Tucker and Milton Berle. What a shame! It's never the handsome ones. The bigger they are, the homelier."

At a drunken party one night, Bob Hope, who had shared a bed with Berle in the 1920s in New York, called out: "Go ahead, Milton, just take out enough to win!" Berle had been willing to bet that he was the "most exceptionally endowed man" in the room.

A frequent visitor in the 1930s at Polly Adler's New York whorehouse, Berle began seducing showgirls at an early age, even bedding Theda Bara, the original vamp of the Silent Screen.

He had once bragged, "Chaplin called his penis 'The Eighth Wonder of the World,' but his wife, Lita Grey Chaplin, said I had him beat by two inches."

Berle, along with Ronald Reagan, had even bedded the controversial Christian evangelist and purported faith healer, Aimee Semple McPherson, the Billy Graham of her day. He had made it to the boudoirs of everyone from Lucille Ball to Marilyn Monroe. He had even seduced Nancy Davis before her marriage to Reagan.

In Linda's dressing room, after Berle had kissed her on both cheeks, he said, "Have I got a big surprise waiting for you! I ran into Hope. He told me he'd already visited you. Call me Johnny-*cum*-lately."

She understood the implications of his *double entendre,* as she'd long ago become accustomed to being addressed that way.

En route to his hotel room, he amused her with stories of his decades of interaction with show biz people. "In 1960, when I made *Let's Make Love* with Marilyn Monroe, she told me that every time she went to the home of her husband's *[playwright Arthur Miller's]* parents, his mother served matzo ball soup. Marilyn asked me, 'I wonder if she knows how to cook any other part of the matzo.'"

"I was chatting with Stephen Boyd *[the evil Messala in the 1959* Ben-Hur*]* and the handsome devil dropped dead in my arms outside the Beverly Hills Hotel."

"For me, dressing in drag is just another way to get laughs. My drag is too gay to be gay. I once arrived at Grand Central Station dressed as Greta Garbo, and had photographers following me until they discovered who I really was."

"Everybody was always talking about how hung Frank Sinatra was," Berle said. "One night backstage at one of his concerts, I whipped it out and told him, 'Now, Frankie boy, that's what a real man's dick looks like.'"

"Liberace virtually stalked me. He once told me, 'Before I die, my greatest ambition is to get fucked by the cock of Milton Berle. I've had Elvis, and I hear you have six times as much as he does.'"

Linda later recalled the hour she spent in Uncle Miltie's suite. "He did not exaggerate, even though he was a bit of a braggart. He had a foot-long *schlong* of circumcised dick with a big vermilion head. Unlike clothes horse Bob Hope, Milton removed all his clothes, even his black knee-high socks. He wanted the works. I shocked him by taking every inch down my throat. That amazed him. 'There are very few bitches who can do that,' he told me. As an older man, it took him a rather long time to blast off, but he *came* through for me. At the end of our shack-up, he slipped me a hundred-dollar bill. 'Buy yourself some lingerie,' he advised me."

"Before I left his suite, he told me what I really wanted to hear,"

"Up to now, I always thought Nancy Davis *[Reagan]* was the Fellatio Queen of Hollywood," he said. "After you, baby, I can now pronounce that Nancy, that darling girl, has been dethroned."

***

When word-of-mouth circulated about Linda's play, the audiences dwindled to nothing. One night only thirty men, all older, showed up. In the wake of that, the producers handed her a check for two week's work, which amounted to $5,000, hardly enough to cover expenses. Linda, with Larry, had barely enough for gas and food money after paying off their expenses in Las Vegas.

"After my flop in Vegas, my last real show business gig, Larry and I returned to our life on Long Island. It was all too much."

"But before we left, Larry

Milton Berle in drag *(upper photo)*, in his prime *(lower photo, left)*, and during his dooling *(right)*.

Linda: "At least I found a lover who could compare my fellatio skills to those of starlet Nancy Davis (later Reagan). He'd had both of us in our prime and in his prime."

He told me I was the best. He also said that he wished he'd had a nickel for "every Jew Nancy was under--I'd be rich."

Biographer Anne Edwards echoed some of Berle's sentiments: "Nancy was one of those girls whose phone number got passed around a lot."

went out of control. He started shouting and waving his arms. He threw me against a wall. I feared another beating like that jerk, Chuck Traynor, used to give me. But this time, I fought back. I became a screaming, clawing wildcat. I wasn't going to get beaten up by another man. I defended myself...and how. I kicked, I bit, I hit."

"When Larry backed off from me, he attacked the furniture, breaking lamps and picking up pieces of furniture and throwing them. He shattered mirrors and broke whatever he could."

"A security guard, who looked like a giant, more than seven feet tall, barged in and put Larry in handcuffs. At a hospital, a doctor shot something in his arm to tranquilize him."

"We tested him," the doctor told Linda. "Instead of blood, alcohol flows through his veins. That's not all. He's got an ulcer and a spastic colon."

Larry was given prescription tranquilizers for the cross-country trip they eventually made in a broken-down Volkswagen sold to them at a cut-rate price by a crooked Las Vegas used car dealer.

"When we returned from the hospital, the hotel manager presented me with a bill for the damage to our suite," she said. "There would go the rest of our money. I had to raise money...and fast."

She still had some jewelry left from her glory days in Hollywood and Las Vegas. All of it had been gifts from celebrities she'd fellated.

She couldn't even remember the name of a woman friend she'd had at the time. She had volunteered to have the jewelry cleaned for Linda.

When Linda took the gems to a pawn shop in Las Vegas, she was shocked to hear that the stones within the settings had been replaced with paste. "The bitch sure cleaned the jewelry. Cleaned me out would be more like it."

With help from Larry's lawyer, Victor Yannacone, it was "back to Long Island, back to welfare, back to poverty." After they arrived there, Larry said, "Linda won't take off her clothes on camera and on stage, so there go all future bookings, especially after that failure in Vegas."

"The first day back, we went to Victor's office to tell him about our plight and to thank him for all his previous help," Linda said. "He looked across his desk at me, and said, "I've got an idea. Forget those two other so-called memoirs of yours, where you depicted yourself as a sex-crazed fiend. They sounded like they were written by Chuck Traynor or David Winters."

"They more or less dictated them," she said.

"Write an honest and true memoir," Yannacone advised her. "The real story of what happened to you, all the ordeals you went through."

"That's it," she said, jumping up. "I'll need some help, but I'll write that book. You just gave me the title. I'll call it *Ordeal.*"

CHAPTER FIFTEEN
Lovelace:
Feminist and Anti-Porn Crusader

"You went through all that sex, with all those guys, and didn't enjoy one minute of it?"

That was the first question that Mike McGrady, Linda's co-author on *Ordeal,* put to her.

"Not when it was happening," she claimed. "I had to do it. Otherwise, I'd get the shit beat out of me. How can you enjoy sex when you're forced into it, with a gun pointed at your head?"

In Linda's search for a co-author, Victor Yannacone had sent her to an attorney friend of his, Anthony Curto. He had become celebrated for assisting in the publication in 1970 of Aleksandr Solzhenitsyn's *The Gulag Archipelago,* whose manuscript had to be smuggled out of the Soviet Union for publication in the West. It had created a sensation in the United States and in Western Europe, much to the fury of the Kremlin.

Curto asked one of his clients, Mike McGrady, if he'd like to ghost write the autobiography of Linda Lovelace. A prize-winning reporter for *Newsday,* McGrady was known mainly for having perpetrated one of the major literary hoaxes in the history of American publishing. Entitled *Naked Came the Stranger,* the book, whose author was cited as "Penelope Ashe," became an ironic commentary on the public's appetite for Jacqueline Susann, her *The Valley of the Dolls,* and the literary genre she created.

Published by Lyle Stuart, *Naked Came the Stranger* was a tell-all chronicle of a suburban housewife's sexual liaisons, each chapter recounting a different sexual escapade, each written by a different journalist, with men who ranged from rabbis to mobsters. First published in 1969, it became an instant hit, spending thirteen weeks on *The New York Times* bestseller list. Some two dozen different journalists, including a few women, contributed a chapter. McGrady rejected chapters that were too well-written.

In spite of the subterfuges and ironies associated with that literary hoax, New York-based McGrady was actually a serious and committed writer. He had written many books, including *A Dove in Vietnam* (1968), based on a series of antiwar commentaries. Since he'd covered the march on Selma in Alabama and anti-police riots associated with the Democratic National Convention in Chicago in 1968, he didn't think anything Linda revealed would shock him very much.

Both McGrady and Linda had immediate reservations about each other. Although McGrady was a serious writer and reporter, his association with a literary hoax might render Linda's accusations, as they later appeared in *Ordeal,* unbelievable. Inversely, McGrady maintained a dim overview of Linda, and had never seen *Deep Throat.* He had previously written an unflattering article about her.

Yannacone urged the author to accept the assignment. "Here's this big-time porn star, featured in a picture that is grossing millions, and she's hiding out and eating dog food from a tin can."

McGrady found Linda personable and easy to work with, in distinct contrast to Larry. McGrady defined him as "the-foam-at-the-mouth-type." She finally won the writer over, and he became convinced she was telling the truth.

Often in tears, she relayed her whole story to McGrady, except for her most intimate encounters with such celebrities as William Holden or Robert Ryan. "Nearly all of these men were married, and I did not want to destroy their marriages. That would have been so wrong for me."

It was agreed, however, that she would include some of her experiences with Sammy Davis, Jr., or Hugh Hefner, because so many witnesses had seen her at one time or another with

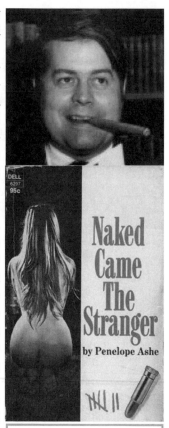

A cigar-smoking, hard-drinking newspaperman, **Mike Mc-Grady** *(top photo)*, rallied his colleagues at *Newsday* to collectively write a 1969 sexcapade, **Naked Came the Stranger**, under a pseudonym.

The book that emerged was a hoax, a mockery of trashy, sex-filled fiction then flooding the bookstores of America. "I had two dozen journalists bait my fellow Americans with all the sickness of their little minds."

McGrady was the author of the last two of Linda's memoirs-- *Ordeal* and *Out of Bondage*-- each of which dealt mostly with her sexual degradation and her later commitment to feminism.

each of these two celebrated icons.

In two cases, in an attempt to protect her celebrity clients, she denied that anything sexual had ever transpired between Elvis Presley or Warren Beatty and herself.

She later claimed that the process of articulating the horrors of her previous life to the sympathetic McGrady was like "going to the most expensive psychiatrist in the world. It was therapy for me. For Mike, it often sent him to a local bar after one of our sessions for that extra martini."

She was even able to describe "my worst nightmare," the 8mm fornication loop with the German shepherd.

At one point during her weeks of revelations, she experienced a nervous breakdown. "I hated Mike. I hated all men."

"It was almost worse for Larry," she said. "He was living every degrading moment of my life for the first time, and it was ripping his guts out. He began to feel that every time he walked out the door, he was being trailed by members of the Mafia, who still had a vested interest in *Deep Throat."* He became convinced that McGrady and Linda were conspiring "to write another dirty book."

"Larry was a puritan and would never read *Playboy,"* she claimed. "He went with me to see *Midnight Express* (1978), that saga of a young American arrested for trying to smuggle drugs out of Turkey. He walked out on a shower scene between two men getting ready to have sex. He won't even watch an R-rated movie with me."

In her previous two memoirs *[Inside Linda Lovelace* and *The Intimate Diary of Linda Lovelace],* she had not revealed the names of any of her sexual contacts. But in this new attempt at self-expression *[Ordeal]* with Mike McGrady, she opted to at least attempt to be more specific. Years after its completion, she reviewed the experience of her collaboration with McGrady in her fourth and final memoir *[Out of Bondage]:*

"We decided not to prettify any part of *Ordeal.* That meant the language would be as harsh as the scenes were describing. It also meant that we wouldn't change the names of anyone, not the Hollywood superstars or the mobsters."

But whereas that instinct might have represented her original intention, the lawyers associated with the project, each of whom specialized in publishing and libel laws, had a different take.

Attorney Leo Nugent told her: "If you start claiming you've had sex with Tony Curtis, Joe DiMaggio, Dean Martin, Frank Sinatra, Desi Arnaz, Richard Burton, *et al.,* you're liable to spend the rest of your life in court. Go on and record your complete story, but wait before publishing it until all these jerks are dead. If they outlive you, leave it in your will that your heirs should publish the full story, with names of celebrities and all of their sordid details, but only after everybody is gone. The dead can't sue, although you might piss off a lot of

Hollywood wives in their dotage."

After hearing that, Linda was forced to back down on her hopes of revealing "all the names" in both the McGrady project, *Ordeal*, and in her final memoir, *Out of Bondage.*

Yet despite her concealments and camouflage of many of the key points she'd wanted to make in *Ordeal*, she still kept hearing repeated the words "It's libelous," and "It's probably libelous," from insiders within the publishing industry.

When the draft of *Ordeal* was ready for presentation, McGrady's literary agent began shopping the memoir, with nearly all of the celebrity names removed, to publishers across New York. Even so, despite the fact that the names of Linda's clients had been removed, thirty-two publishers rejected it.

"The editors seemed to think I was a figure midway between Hitler and Lucretia Borgia," she said. "Others said I was *passé,* a word I didn't even know at the time, One editor wrote, 'Linda Lovelace is a sick product of the early seventies, an era that America would like to forget.'"

Another editor suggested, "We'd be interested if she'd pen a book called *How to Please a Man.* " Another editor wanted a book devoted entirely to the art of fellatio.

***

On McGrady's thirty-third submission, *Ordeal* was finally accepted for publication by maverick publisher Lyle Stuart. The author later said, "I should have gone to Lyle in the first place. After all, he published my *Naked Came the Stranger.* "

Stuart defined himself as "the last publisher in America with guts." His previous controversial books, among many others, had included biographies devoted to such figures as J. Edgar Hoover (*Inside the F.B.I.*), and Jacqueline Kennedy Onassis (Kitty Kelley's *Jackie Oh!*). His most provocative book was *The Anarchist Cookbook,* a 1970 guide to mak-

The publisher of Linda's last two memoirs, *Ordeal* and *Out of Bondage* was maverick **Lyle Stuart** *(photo above)*. He had helped to launch the trend in sex-related books in the late 1960s, releasing such titles as *The Sensuous Woman*.

"Partly because I developed a reputation as a madman, the controversial authors always called on me," he said.

As he once told *The Washington Post*, "I've always tested the limits of the First Amendment. I'm a great believer in letting anybody publish the most outrageous, unpopular things there are."

ing bombs, by William Powell (not the famous actor, of course). It told readers how to make Molotov cocktails for blowing up police stations.

Linda wanted people to believe the statements she'd made within *Ordeal,* and to that effect, she agreed to take the lie detector test which had been proposed and then arranged by Stuart. For the test, the publisher booked the nation's expert, Natale ("Nat") Laurendi. From 1961 to 1975, he'd been New York City's chief polygraphist. One of his most celebrated cases had involved him in the legal aftermath of Patricia Hearst's controversial 1976 bank robbery in San Francisco as an associate of the Symbionese Liberation Army.

Linda spent two days with Laurendi, defining the time she spent with him as "grueling." She grasped the irony associated with having what she called "my fate resting with a machine."

After the tests, Laurendi announced to Stuart, "This Lovelace woman is incapable of lying."

Ordeal would be published in 1980, setting off another firestorm in the life of Linda Lovelace and opening the door on a whole new career.

***

The first news about the publication of *Ordeal* appeared in *The New York Post:*

"Linda (Deep Throat) *Lovelace, perhaps the most famous (and uniquely talented) porn star ever, clearly reveled in the glory of it all when her first film came out in the early 70s. Now she has emerged from recent obscurity to tell a different story. Not totally emerged, of course; actually, she says she has gone into hiding to escape years of unspeakable sexual tortures—and the celebrities who made her undergo them. Naturally, said celebs will be named in the little book titled* Ordeal *Ms. Lovelace happens to be putting on paper with the help of a writer."*

The Post reporter had not read the book or any of its galleys when he wrote that. As mentioned, that large roster of celebrities would not be named. *[Linda's name-dropping had to wait until 2013, with the publication of this book.]*

Press reactions, especially from male reviewers, was largely negative, although a few women critics interpreted her tale as "horrifying but believable," in the words of one female reporter. She then added, "Women in societies around the world have been abused by men far too long."

"Why has Ms. Lovelace waited so long to unburden her soul?" asked London's *Daily Mail.* Why is she now talking with such remarkable earnestness? The answer is simple: Ms. Lovelace has a book to sell."

Long her supporter, *Playboy* struck back. Hugh Hefner denied the statements Linda made against him.

Perhaps in defense of Hefner, a reporter for *Playboy* wrote: "Linda Lovelace hops onto the bandwagon with *Ordeal,* in which she claims she was forced into *Deep Throat. "* The cynicism of the writer was all too evident. To accompany the article, *Playboy* ran an old nude photo of her.

The *Playboy* writer concluded: "What's interesting in *Ordeal* is that it is just as lurid and graphic as any of Lovelace's films. In fact, for a reformed woman, she seems to dwell inordinately on the seamier side of her life, making sure to mention all the famous people she claims to have had affairs with."

Had the *Playboy* reporter read the book? Except for Hefner and Sammy Davis, Jr., as mentioned before, the famous names were eliminated in the book's final version. Had she reported all the names and all of her affairs with famous men, fleeting though some of them were, *Ordeal* would have been at least 150 to 200 pages longer.

Al Goldstein of *Screw* also struck back against her. "It sounds like nothing more than another cheap attempt to cash in on the thriving memoir market. As we remember it, Linda didn't look one bit dissatisfied in that loop she did with a dog. We don't doubt Linda got fucked over. She was part of an era in which X-rated performers were routinely exploited. But what a shoddy way to attempt a comeback."

The *Boston Globe* expressed its editorial opinion: "Educational as this collaboration may be, it hardly inspires you to reach for your handkerchief. As has been said recently about a different subject altogether, what we need nowadays is a better class of victim."

People magazine, in its January, 1980, issue, wrote: "What happened to Linda Lovelace is told in her just-published autobiography *Ordeal,* a nightmarish portrayal of sexual perversion and enslavement. Between 1971 and 1973, she says she was transformed from the relatively innocent manager of a clothing boutique into a numb and brutalized sex machine who graduated from cheap street-corner tricks to celebrity bedrooms, among them Sammy Davis, Jr.. (Davis responds: 'The whole thing is ludicrous.')."

The Los Angeles *Herald-Examiner* provocatively asked: "Is this too much to swallow or what?"

Publishers Weekly asserted "Once again, Miss Lovelace is exposing herself, this time in print. We are not impressed with her allegations. Her melodrama would hardly put a sweet-savage heroine to the blush—although it might the celebrities named."

She found comments made by Chip Visci in the *Detroit Free Press* especially hard to take. Visci wrote: "Lie detector tests notwithstanding, believing her story is not easy. Many who have seen *Deep Throat* or another, even sleazier film in which her co-star was a dog, will argue that Linda Lovelace liked what she was doing—and liked it a lot."

Linda shot back: "How could any moron believe that I loved getting fucked by a dog?"

Visci concluded: "Ultimately, Mrs. Marchiano's story is believable, especially when you consider the many battered wives who refuse to leave their husbands. Believable, but not very readable. The language is crude and profane, the sexual descriptions not at all erotic. The book has a hard-edged, matter-of-fact tone."

Visci's comments really bothered her. She said, "Would some people read the diary of an Auschwitz survivor and wonder why it wasn't sexier, more amusing?"

Predictably, many women critics were kinder in their appraisal of *Ordeal.* Writing in *The Toronto Globe and Mail,* Judith Finlayson said: "There's a very dark side to our sexual culture which Linda Lovelace experienced firsthand. All women should be horrified by the thought that 'respectable' men—even rich and famous ones—paid for the privilege of abusing the *Deep Throat* girl. Lovelace was successful as a porn queen because she had the fresh-scrubbed good looks of the girl next door, and enough dramatic ability to convince the camera that she loved being degraded. What does that say about the mainstream men who flocked in droves to see the film?"

In London's *The Guardian,* Jill Tweedie wrote: "What no one questions or contemplates or gives any thought to at all, is simply this: Never mind that Linda Lovelace did what she did—why, why, a thousand times why did her husband, Chuck Traynor, do what he did? Why did other men, including celebrities, do what they did, with his contrivance?"

Beyond press critiques, the big question was what would be the reaction of the limited numbers of men whose names remained within the text of *Ordeal?* Not only did Sammy Davis, Jr. and Hugh Hefner deny the book's veracity, but Linda's former lover, David Winters, weighed in too: "She couldn't write another book about how great sex was. Who cares? No one is going to buy it anymore. So by going the reverse, I thought it was very clever."

Chuck vehemently denied Linda's allegations. He went on to telephone Mike McGrady, asking him to ghost write his own autobiography which he tentatively wanted to entitle *On Training Women.* In response, McGrady told Chuck to "go fuck yourself!"

Chuck also placed a call to Victor Yannacone, threatening a million dollar libel suit. The attorney responded with the threat of a counter lawsuit against Chuck, charging "civil kidnapping and bondage," seeking heavy punitive damages for Linda. Subsequently, Chuck withdrew his threat of a libel suit.

Sammy, who was in England at the time, contacted Chuck, wondering if they should jointly sue. Chuck advised against it. "If we sue, she'll just sell millions of copies, and we won't get a red cent."

Larry Marchiano allegedly promised not to read the book. "I didn't have to," he said. "I'd heard it firsthand." Eventually, however, he did read it and found much of it "disgusting." He phoned McGrady and complained that he had included "too many disturbing sexual parts."

It was to be expected that persons in the porn industry would hit back. People who had worked with Linda refuted many of her allegations. Her most outspoken critic was Gloria Leonard, a former porn actress who was publisher of *High Society* magazine from 1977 to 1991. It had pioneered such novelties as nude celebrity photographs, which brought lawsuits from Margot Kidder, Ann-Margret, and Barbra Streisand.

Leonard almost made a deal for Norman Mailer, one of the early devotees of Linda's talents, to write the script for a porn film.

Subsequently, Mailer told author Truman Capote that he'd like to bring Linda "out of retirement and put her back on the screen doing what she does so well—and I should know firsthand what that is. Has she ever sucked you off, Truman?"

"Hell, no!" Capote answered. "About the last place I'd put my dick is in the overused mouth of Linda Lovelace. I'd much prefer Warren Beatty to suck me off. He's hot! Just ask Tennessee!"

Leonard told Jennifer Osborne, co-author of *The Other Hollywood,* "Lovelace was a woman who never took responsibility for her own shitty choices, but instead blamed everything that happened to her in her life on porn. You know, 'The Devil made me do it.' She got beaten up, of course, but porn was not the real culprit. The reason was her choice of mate, Chuck Traynor. Lovelace was a wacko. I was in a green room once for a TV show in New York. She was on the show, too. She came in looking like hell, squints her eyes, looks at me—and goes, 'You're in porn—I can tell from your eyes.'"

Richard Cohen, writing in *The Washington Post,* said "Whether pornography plays a role in violence directed at women is a question that for now can't be answered. But it's clear that at the least, it's a raging insult to women. But so strong

No spokesperson for any cause, porn or otherwise, was quite as sexy looking as **Gloria Leonard**, a former porn actress who later emerged as the publisher of *High Society* magazine, known for printing nudes of celebrities who included Barbra Streisand.

Bronx-born Leonard, once a publicist for Johnny Carson (Linda's former conquest), established the first phone sex line in 1983.

Leonard became the most outspoken critic of Linda's new role--that of a victim of the porn industry and an anti-porn activist.

598

is the hold it has on the male imagination that when a book comes out by the star of *Deep Throat,* exposing it for the lie it is, the book fades from sight, while the movie plays on and on."

Linda had a comment about that critique. *"Ordeal* didn't fade. It squatted down on the best-seller lists—and stayed there for quite a while. My voice at long last was being heard."

***

Back home on Long Island, as the press digested *Ordeal,* Linda cared for her four-year-old son Dominic and awaited her next baby, due sometime around July of 1980.

She was home to receive Lyle Stuart's call, informing her that he'd set up some television interviews and wanted her to fly to twelve cities in just ten days, where she was slated to give between eight and nine interviews every twenty-four hours.

When informed of the tour, Larry expressed his main concern: "My fear is that you'll be raped in some of the more dangerous cities we're going to, especially Chicago, Detroit, and Los Angeles." That night, they drank ten bottles of Mumm Cordon Rouge, paid for by Stuart's advance money for *Ordeal.*

Her first promotional appearance, slated for January 10, 1980, was on *The Tomorrow Show,* hosted by the handsome, hard-driving interviewer, Tom Snyder. "If Chuck Traynor were still around," Linda told her co-author Mike McGrady, "he would suggest I give Tom a blow-job."

With cigarette in hand, Snyder was known for asking very personal questions. His provocative guests had previously included John Lennon, convicted serial killer Charles Manson (in handcuffs), and author/philosopher Ayn Rand.

As Linda recalled, "Tom turned out to be a pussycat. Mostly I had to recite the main themes from *Ordeal."*

"He treated me with great respect, and even wished me well with my pregnancy."

Later, Snyder told his crew, "I felt the gal had gone through enough abuse, and I didn't want to pile the shit onto her. Let's face it: She'd been a cocksucking two-bit whore, but that didn't mean I had to treat her like one."

At one point, he asked her if she thought the producers of *Deep Throat* should be behind bars, and she said they should.

During the tour, her other TV and radio interviews went reasonably well. In Detroit, Radio Host Gene Taylor, within the on-air context of his interview, gave Linda a hundred-dollar bill when he learned she was broke. Once, when Larry perceived that an interviewer was mocking Linda, he grabbed her and pulled her off the show, even though the interview had fifteen minutes more to

599

go.

In New York City, she'd been told to expect easy questions from radio host Stanley Siegel. "I went on with a false sense of security," she said. "The first question was, "What does it feel like to have sex with five men at the same time?"

Years later, she said, "I don't have a tape of the show. But if memory serves, Siegel asked me every filthy question in the book, stuff I wouldn't even talk over with my husband, and he wanted me to get that personal with millions of viewers. At the end of the show, Larry told him. 'You suck.'" Then Linda confronted Siegel: "You bastard! You pig! You look and sound like a dirty old man. Let's tape it again, and this time ask me decent questions."

"No way, baby," he said. Standing up and walking away. "I'm called one-take Siegel."

During the book tour, the interview that drew the biggest audience was on *The Phil Donahue Show.* Donahue often focused on issues, including abortion, that divided the nation. At the time Linda met him, he had just married actress Marlo Thomas.

What Linda didn't know was that the affable TV host was experimenting

TV host **Phil Donahue** was instrumental in the development of talk shows as a format for the on-air discussion of hot-button issues.

One of his most controversial guests was Linda Lovelace, in the wake of the publication of her third memoir, *Ordeal.*

On his show, Donahue searched for a reason she'd become trapped into such a degrading life, finally blaming her parents.

"It seemed to me that the blame belonged to my captor, Chuck Traynor," Linda said, "and to all the men who bought me, including all those celebrities, and rented me and used me and abused me."

with, and about to give birth to, something that later became known as "shock journalism."

During advance viewings of his show, Donahue had seemed like a liberal as regards most social issues. He'd told the press that he was a very good Roman Catholic, but that he opposed the "antisexual theology" of his church.

At first, his interview with Linda was fairly routine, similar to others she'd given. At its debut, he referred to *Ordeal* as "the grimmest book I've ever read in my life."

Then she reiterated her familiar refrain, blaming Chuck Traynor for how he'd made her "a prisoner of sexual abuse who was forced to make *Deep Throat."*

Halfway through the show, questions from the audience grew hostile. She was asked by one woman, "What in your childhood led you to become so promiscuous." She was accused of fabricating *Ordeal* for money, and yet another critic from the audience equated her memoir to porn.

One question particularly disturbed her, and it came from Donahue himself: "How could a nice girl like you get involved in something like this?" Before the end of his show, he accused her "of blaming other people and not taking responsibility on your own."

Donahue criticized her for referring to the celebrities who had seduced her as being "as bad as Chuck Traynor." On the show, she'd alleged that, "They participated for their own satisfaction and didn't do anything to try to help me."

Donahue told the audience that it "wasn't fair for Linda to have expected these famous men to understand entirely the slave-like kind of thing she was under."

On the air, before amplifying the interview's focus onto the studio audience for their (outraged) questions and comments, Donahue chastised her for not sparing the feelings of the families, including wives and children, of the celebrities who had seduced her in adulterous affairs.

The allegation shocked her because she had mentioned only a few celebrities in her book, notably Sammy Davis, Jr., and Hugh Hefner, and had not revealed the names of any of the others, including such family men as Dean Martin, Richard Widmark, and Vice President Spiro Agnew.

Both Larry and Linda agreed that her appearance on the Donahue show had been a disaster, catalyzing a maelstrom of explosive controversy and sparking a debate about sexuality and pornography in the United States.

Apparently, each of the subsequent interviewers scheduled for the remainder of her tour had seen the Donahue fiasco. From that moment onward, she came under fire, and her credibility became an issue.

She braved the attacks better than Larry, who always seemed "fighting mad."

One person watching *The Phil Donahue Show* who soon developed strong opinions of her own about the Lovelace phenomenon was a highly vocal feminist activist, Gloria Steinem, who would greatly influence Linda's future.

***

Next, Linda's publisher booked her on a promotional tour through England, Sweden, and Norway, as a means of boosting foreign sales of *Ordeal.* During the early stages of the tour, she sounded like a right-wing zealot, referring to porn—as manifested in the windows of London's sex shops—as "an epidemic and a sickness."

Seeing all the sex toys on display, including dildos and life-sized inflatable dolls, evoked a painful incident from her past "when a photographer squirted catsup on my back and handed another girl a whip."

One of her best-attended appearances was in London at the Café Royal, a former haunt of such literary lights as Oscar Wilde. "I thought his name was Wilde Oscar," Linda said, amusing London reporters. *[Her reference was to the award she'd won at Harvard, which had reversed the order of the Victorian author's name.]*

As she'd later recall, "I appeared before the London Literary Club. Members laughed as I tried to speak to them about pornography involving infants and children. That drunken crowd could just as easily laughed about Hitler and the concentration camps."

The worst moment of her entire tour occurred when William Hickey, a reporter for *The Daily Express* rose to his feet. In the press, he had been called a "rude and objectionable fellow" because of his aggression in pursuit of a story.

His question brought hysterical laughter: "Oh, please, could you tell us what happened to Rufus?"

Suddenly, Larry, dressed in a hunting jacket, confronted Hickey. "That's the worst shit she ever went through. Why don't we talk about the Jews in the ovens if that's the kind of conversations you really want. Anyone in this room who wants to humiliate my wife is invited to step outside with me."

At this point, Linda had had enough. "I feel sorry for all you people," she said, as she hurriedly exited from the room.

By the time the news about this incident reached the American press, the story was that Larry had flattened Hickey, knocking him out on the floor.

For some reason, Stuart had not booked Linda for any presentation in Copenhagen, the porn capital of Western Europe. Instead, she went off to Sweden.

Arriving there, she and Larry were not adequately dressed for the bitter Scandinavian winter. At first, she threatened her Swedish publishers, saying, "I'm getting on the next plane out." But they convinced her to stay and go through with the interviews. Starting slowly, the number of readers attending her book signings mushroomed, and soon she was signing 425 copies of *Ordeal* on an almost daily basis.

Her subsequent trip to Norway repeated her success in Sweden. "We didn't have enough books to meet the demand," she later claimed.

She had arrived in Norway wearing moccasins, but some thoughtful person brought her a pair of boots. Larry was managing to survive the cold wearing only a sweater. In Oslo, she was presented with a full-length down overcoat.

After concluding her two-week tour of Sweden and Norway, Linda proclaimed, "For the first time in my life, I feel my own power. I no longer need people to tell me what to do. I am my own woman."

***

Gloria Steinem, a forceful advocate of women's rights, had appeared on the Donahue Show on April 10, 1970, to discuss the Equal Rights Amendment, which the U.S. Senate was debating at the time.

Steinem was most sympathetic to Linda's later appearance on Donahue, claiming that both the host and his audience had attacked Linda's character and trivialized her point of view.

In a magazine (*Ms.,* which she had co-founded with a team of other feminists in 1971), Steinem had emphasized the difference between erotica and pornography, referring to the latter as "violence, dominance, and conquest."

In the introduction she wrote to *Out of Bondage,* feminist activist **Gloria Steinem** asked a question of the millions of viewers who had seen *Deep Throat:*

"Did viewers ask if the young woman was there of her own free will? They ignored the bruises visible on her body, the terror in her eyes, even the simple empathy that should cause each of us to wonder whether another human being really could enjoy humiliations and dangers that we ourselves would never tolerate."

She went on to say, "Whereas erotica suggested sexual love and mutual pleasure, pornography was a depiction and manifestation of female sexual slavery."

When Steinem finally met Linda, she did more to acquaint her with feminism than any other person. Linda was only vaguely aware of the ideologies associated with the movement. As she wrote, "It had barely dented my consciousness."

After Steinem and Linda came together in April of 1980, the writer defended Linda in her magazine, *Ms.* in an article entitled "Tell Me, Linda, What in Your Background Led You to a Concentration Camp?"

In May of 1980, both Steinem and Linda appeared on the late-night TV talk venue, *The Tomorrow Show,* because each of them perceived that Tom Snyder, the host, had "a compassionate ear."

Of all the women in the women's rights movement, Linda was most impressed with Steinem, calling her "clever, full of grace, full of conviction, and a gal who has got the smarts."

At one point, Linda confessed, "I'm not bright enough to talk to Gloria. When I first started out in the movement, I didn't know what promiscuous meant. I do now."

For a few years, Linda and Steinem became

603

close allies in the anti-porn crusade. Steinem even agreed to write the introduction to Linda's fourth and final memoir, the lackluster *Out of Bondage* (1986) that rambled on and on about her legal conflicts with a Miami attorney, Phil Mandina. Her attacks on Mandina held little interest to most of her dwindling number of fans.

In the prologue she wrote, Steinem claimed, "Those who have protested Linda's story, even threatened her because of it, have yet to deliver proof that counters any part of it. Six years of knowing her have strengthened my early conclusion as a reporter that she is telling the truth."

Steinem faced the charge that Linda had outed celebrities just for financial gain. She defended Linda's *Ordeal* for having left out "newsworthy incidents of sex and celebrity," that could possibly have involved sexual encounters with such figures as Yul Brynner, Tony Curtis, and Mick Jagger. In one memoir, she only mentioned the name of John Lennon, eliminating all other details about her somewhat bizarre sexual encounter with him.

Steinem lashed out at "Hefner and his Playboy mansion," maintaining that the key issue with pornography was "free will. Pornography is to women of all groups what Nazi literature is to Jews and Ku Klux Klan literature is to blacks."

The leader of the feminist movement finally concluded that, "The miracle is that Linda has survived to tell her story."

Steinem drew leading feminists to Linda's allegations and ultimately to her anti-porn crusade. However, those more intimately involved in the industry continued to challenge Linda's charges.

Chuck told *E!*, "I just thought *Ordeal* was funny. I didn't think anybody would believe it. I never forced her to have sex against her will, either on camera or off-camera. And I never beat her. I probably grabbed her and shook her a few times. She was a very hysterical person. Let her say what she wants to say: To me, she's just a raving woman who got scorned. I thought she thought I was a great guy until she left. I guess she didn't, or at least didn't after she started meeting other people who put ideas in her head."

After her association with the anti-porn crusaders became known, a new phrase, "The Linda Syndrome," entered the American vocabulary, suggesting a former porn performer who disavows not only the industry itself, but his or her own participation in it.

Gloria Leonard, head of the Free Speech Coalition, and a former porn star herself, denounced Linda as a "Benedict Arnold." Film producer Candida Royalle attacked the feminists themselves. "It infuriated me that Women Against Pornography (WAP) would take this deeply troubled, traumatized woman and just basically use her for the movement."

Georgina Spelvin, who had appeared in Gerard Damiano's *The Devil in Miss Jones*, met Linda in a talk show green room and extended her hand. "The bitch turned her back on me," she later claimed.

When Marilyn Chambers, who was married to Chuck Traynor at the time, was asked about Gloria Steinem's transfiguration of Linda into a feminist icon, she said, "Well, you can tell Steinem that I am a totally healthy human being and not a sex slave. Linda Lovelace is full of it. I am not scripted in anything to say. People like Steinem ought to use their vibrators a lot more, especially if they're so damn frustrated sexually."

Al Goldstein predictably echoed the torrent of attacks on Linda from the porn industry. Interpreting her as a traitor, he said, "Anti-porn crusaders are using her as their poster child…yes, the same woman who over the years was the jerk-off fantasy for millions of guys. In some bizarre way, 'Linda Lovelace, the masturbatory fantasy,' will be her epitaph rather than 'Linda Lovelace, the anti-porn crusader.'"

***

Deep Throat was still playing in theaters in Manhattan's Times Square district. Organized by Steinem, Linda agreed to join in a protest against the film, echoing her oft-repeated refrain, "*[In Deep Throat],* the public is watching me get raped."

That day, Linda met other feminists from WAP, each of whom believed her story and supported her.

Although the movement had existed for many months before Linda ever joined it, she became one of its most visible members in her role as a former porn star turned feminist activist. Some reporters arguably claimed that "Linda Lovelace is at the heart of the debate on feminism and sexuality in American life today."

By July of 1980, Linda had given birth to her daughter, naming her Lindsay Marchiano. "I was no longer Venus de Milo, assuming I ever was. Instead of the sex goddess of the 70s, I was more a housewife tending to my two kids, trying to be a wife to Larry, and waging a war against pornography in my spare time."

During each of her interviews, Linda never promoted a sleazy image. She wore conservative

Catherine MacKinnon, the scholar, lawyer, teacher, and activist, did more than any other woman in the feminist movement to protect and guide Linda through her many legal challenges.

MacKinnon accepted Linda's view that she had been forced to star in *Deep Throat.* The lawyer also asked viewers of other porn involving women to "look for the skinned knees, the bruises, the welts from the whippings, the scratches, the gashes. Many of them are not simulated."

clothes, unflattering and oversized glasses, and her hair was wild, untamed, and rather frizzy, as was often noted.

"After *Deep Throat,* the business simply passed Linda by," said porn star Eric Edwards. "She wasn't particularly attractive—nor could she act. If she'd told the truth about her life, her book may not have sold as well as making up a story that claims she was forced to do these disgusting things."

WAP members soon discovered they didn't like "some of the bedfellows" in the anti-porn crusade. A Catholic church located close to the Times Square headquarters of WAP told the feminists there, "The church does not want to become involved with you people."

Activist Susan Male said, "We were feminists, we were pro-abortion, we were pro-gay rights, and we were anti-pornography. But WAP members did not endorse the right-wing agenda."

In addition to Steinem, three of the leading feminists in American befriended Linda, believing her story and welcoming her as a symbol of the anti-porn crusade.

Scholar, attorney, and teacher, the Minnesota-born (in 1944) activist, Catharine MacKinnon was a graduate of Yale Law School. As a social revolutionary, she focused on pornography and sexual harassment as vehicles for changing anti-women laws in such countries as Mexico, Japan, Israel, and

As a co-founder of Women Against Pornography (WAP), attorney **Susan Brownmiller** had a great influence on Linda.

As she addressed students at college campuses across the nation, Linda often articulated anti-porn arguments, word for word, as composed by Brownmiller.

India.

Her book, *Sexual Harassment of Working Women,* is the eighth most frequently cited American legal text published since 1978.

Linda found sympathetic support from MacKinnon, who viewed pornography as a form of "forced sex." As a lawyer, MacKinnon represented Linda from 1980 until her death in 2002.

Another leader among feminists was Susan Brownmiller, one of the co-founders of WAP. She set out to convince the public that there were "good, sound, feminist, humanitarian reasons to be against pornography." Previously in her promotion of these tenets, she, too, had appeared on *The Phil Donahue Show,* telling women that pornography facilitated a climate whereby rape was more easily indulged and tolerated.

When Donahue asked Brownmiller, on TV, about Linda's appearance in *Deep Throat,* and about how she at least appeared to be having a good time, the feminist responded, "I can't believe she was having a good time. I can't believe it."

Brownmiller was born in 1935 in Brooklyn to middle-class Jewish parents. As she grew into adulthood, she remained single, attributing her celibacy to the fact that she was "not willing to compromise." One of her greatest achievements involved the 1975 publication of her book, *Against Our Will: Men, Women, and Rape*. In it, she stated that "men use rape as a means of perpetuating male dominance, keeping all women in a state of fear."

In 1995, the New York Public Library selected it as one of the 100 most important books of the 20th Century.

From 1980 to 1981, MacKinnon and Andrea Dworkin worked together on building a lawsuit against the men who had abused Linda. Since the statue of limitations had run out on a criminal case, the women opted instead to pursue a venue based on the violation of her civil rights. As their arguments evolved, Linda was advised by several dozen authorities that the grounds for such a lawsuit were weak. She finally decided not to pursue it out of fear of losing and humiliating herself.

Dworkin, born right after World War II in New Jersey, became a radical feminist who was best known for her criticism of pornography, arguing that it was linked to rape and other forms of violence against women. She held Linda up as a prime example of that theory. Her best-known book is *Pornography: Men Possessing Women* (1979).

She identified with Linda about having been abused. After her graduation from Bennington College in 1968, Dworkin had married the Dutch anarchist Cornelius Dirk de Bruin, who beat her severely, often burning her with cigarettes. Like Linda, she, too defined herself as a battered wife forced to work as a prostitute.

In New York, Dworkin had participated in demonstrations for lesbian rights, and it was rumored, but never proven, that she engaged in lesbian sex with Linda. Allegedly, Dworkin was the aggressor, with Linda reluctantly (since she found the

Perhaps the most radical of feminists, the anarchist and anti-porn crusader **Andrea Dworkin** wrote ten books on radical feminist theories and gained national fame as a spokeswoman for the anti-porn movement.

In later life, her enemies called her "a fat slob," but she must have been more attractive during her younger days when she worked as a prostitute on the sidewalks of Amsterdam.

Known for her appearances in public and on television wearing coveralls, Dworkin was nicknamed "Rolling Thunder" by Susan Brownmiller.

feminist "spectacularly unattractive") submitting to (or merely enduring) her overtures.

It was at one point during their intimacies that Linda shared with Dworkin access to what she called her "Book of Johns." In it, Linda had written details about all the men in Hollywood, Las Vegas, and New York she had serviced. It was comparable to her diary in some respects, although not as lush.

Dworkin shared information from those interchanges with some of her colleagues. "I couldn't believe some of the names on that list, some of the biggest names in Hollywood. With one exception, there was no record of physical violence, but even so, these celebrities were taking advantage of a relatively naïve girl."

Individuals within the porn industry responded to that, angrily accusing the feminists—but not the Hollywood celebrities—of using Linda to advance their own causes.

The anti-porn crusades would reach the highest levels of government during the 1980s administration of Ronald Reagan, who, at least publicly, believed in "good, clean movies."

But according to a report leaked from the White House, Reagan had watched *Deep Throat* three times.

During his controversial presidency, screen actor **Ronald Reagan** made a last-ditch effort to stop the spread of pornography across America.

"As usual," said author Gore Vidal, "Reagan stood on the wrong side of history." Reportedly, Reagan had seen *Deep Throat*, which was screened for him at the White House, three times.

"I never made movies like that," he told some of his staff members.

When Linda heard that, she said, "William Holden never set up that date between Reagan and me. So it was only through the movie that he got to compare my technique with that of his own in-house Fellatio Queen of yesteryear."

***

With the organizational help of MacKinnon and others, Linda was booked into a series of cross-country lectures on college campuses, where she attacked pornography, relating her own "nightmarish" experiences in the industry. For most of these engagements, she earned a speaking fee of $4,000, which became her only means of support. She'd foolishly signed away future royalties on her memoirs during her marriage to Chuck Traynor.

With no formal education, Linda found herself addressing students at such

Ivy League Universities as Harvard and Yale. Although she was occasionally heckled, in most cases she met with responsive and highly supportive audiences.

She found it amusing that many of the bodyguards who had volunteered, usually through WAP, to protect her during her tours were women dressed in military fatigues. "They looked very butch to me," Linda jokingly said. She always felt uncomfortable getting entangled in censorship debates, since she generally opposed it in any form. "Hitler believed in censorship. I do not."

On occasion, she also wandered into the pit of what constitutes the subtle differences between erotica and pornography. Across America, everybody seemingly had a different opinion. Some echoed Justice Stewart Potter's position: "I know it when I see it."

When Linda actively participated in city council meetings, debating whether to enact stringent anti-porn laws, she often faced derision. Many in the audience "considered me a mere whore and weren't interested in what I had to say."

Ironically, the feminist movement soon began to splinter on the issue of porn. By 1985, there arose a counter movement, FACT (Feminists' Anti-Censorship Taskforce). Its prominent members included Rita Mae Brown *[author of the lesbian-themed novel,* Rubyfruit Jungle *(1971)]*, Kate Millet *[author of the bestselling feminist treatist* Sexual Politics *(1970)].* and Betty Friedan *[Founder and first president of the National Organization for Women and author of* The Feminine Mystique *(1963)]*, who asserted "We're not being manipulated by dirty old men. Women can actually enjoy sex."

These feminists were ardent defenders of free speech. They attacked an ordinance, passed in Indianapolis, which they defined as contrary to the rights of women, vilifying it as "a throwback to the Victorian view of sexuality."

Caught up in the complexities of the issue, Linda was often

Edwin (Ed) Meese was one of the most controversial attorney generals in U.S. history, serving as Ronald Reagan's appointee from February of 1985 to August of 1988, when he resigned because of his embarrassing involvement in a financial scandal.

He lent his name to the last-ditch effort of the government to prevent the spread of pornography. Linda was summoned to testify before the Commission, whose recommendations were eventually quashed on grounds of their violation of the First Amendment.

perplexed, not having the education or intellectual abilities of these other feminists. Ultimately, the Seventh Circuit Court of Appeals threw out the Indianapolis ordinance on the ground that it violated the First Amendment guarantee of free speech.

Ultimately, MacKinnon and Dworkin failed in their efforts to outlaw porn, as did Linda. They were clever enough, however, to have pursued pornography as a violation of the rights of women, and not as a violation of community standards of decency.

***

In 1986, one of the milestones in Linda's life came when she was called to testify against pornography at the Attorney General's Commission on Pornography, a coven of right-wingers also known as the Meese Commission. It had been named for Edwin Meese III, whom President Ronald Reagan had named as his attorney general. Meese was Reagan's link to the right wing evangelistic movement. During his service to Reagan, he was viewed, contemptuously, as "almost an alter ego of Reagan himself." In 1988, Meese was connected with financial improprieties in the Iraq-Jordan Pipeline Scandal and resigned as a means of escaping prosecution.

Al Goldstein of *Screw* showed up at the Meese Commission waving copies —as was his habit— of *The Dog Fucker,* Linda's 1969 bestiality loop. "No doubt this endeared me even more to the angry, fat, anti-porn feminist, Andrea Dworkin," Goldstein said.

Goldstein contemptuously defined The Meese Commission "an eleven-member panel of retired vice cops, right-wing academics, 'porn victims,' a smut-busting D.A., and the soon-to-be exposed child-molesting Father Bruce Ritter."

Linda told the commission. "I am trying to teach my children God, and then they turn around and see that I was raped in *Deep Throat.* I was beaten, and this film is still being allowed to be shown, and people are still making money off it, and my family and my children and I are suffering because of it. It is not fair. It is inhumane."

As part of her anti-porn testimony before the Meese Commission, Andrea Dworkin had presented a copy of Linda's *Ordeal.* She said, "The only thing atypical about Linda is that she had the courage to make a public fight against what had happened to her. Whatever you come up with, it has to help her or it's not going to help anyone."

The Meese Commission successfully enforced their ruling that convenience store chains remove from their shelves men's magazine such as *Playboy.* Dworkin, before the commission, had charged that *Playboy* in both text and pictures "promotes both rape and child sexual abuse." She also attacked *Penthouse.* In the immediate aftermath, many retail stores stopped carrying those magazines.

Eventually, however, the Meese Commission's campaign was quashed with a First Amendment admonishment against prior restraint by a Washington, D.C. Federal Court in *Meese vs. Playboy.*

Despite the heat, sound, and fury it had generated, the commission did not stop the distribution of *Deep Throat,* nor did it inaugurate a Federal criminal statute which would have allowed Linda to seek recourse in the courts against Chuck Traynor or against anyone who had financed and profited from *Deep Throat [i.e., The Perainos].*

Eventually, although the Meese report had concluded that pornography was in "varying degrees harmful" to American society, it soon became obvious that it was on the wrong side of history in its attempt to stamp out pornography, as anyone who owns cable TV or an internet connection can testify today.

Linda's appearance before the Meese Commission, which involved mostly a recitation of her own familiar refrain of abuses, was her last major public appearance. After that, she became more reclusive, appearing rarely and to much smaller groups, if at all.

A truly self-destructive period of her life had begun.

***

A year after she delivered her testimony, Dworkin sent Linda a copy of her latest book, *Intercourse* (1987). After reading it, Linda began to re-evaluate many of Dworkin's radical positions. In her book, Dworkin loudly asserted that the act of sexual intercourse itself was ultimately demeaning to women. She argued: "All forms of heterosexual sex within our patriarchal society are coercive and degrading to women, and that sexual penetration may, by its very nature, doom women to inferiority and submission—and may be immune to reform."

At that point in her life, as she settled down on Long Island to be a good wife to her husband and a good mother to her children, Linda had no interest in defending such a position. Except for an occasional interruption, she had become a typical housewife, known for her cooking skills.

When her breasts started hurting her, she feared the silicone was leaking. Their examination at Manhattan's Sloan-Kettering Hospital proved that she was correct.

That initial diagnosis was later amplified into something even more serious. She came home to tell Larry, "I have to have a new liver. A transplant." She was believed to have been suffering from acute hepatitis, dating back to the blood transfusions she had received in New York State after her near-fatal auto acci-

611

dent in 1970.

Doctors informed her just how dangerous the transplant operation would be—that is, if she could even find a donor. In 1987, the majority of liver transplants resulted in the death of the recipient.

Another problem was also pressing. The Marchianos didn't have the $200,000 for such an expensive operation.

Around the country, Linda's fans and supporters contributed cash in both large and small amounts. In March of 1987, she checked into the Presbyterian Hospital in Pittsburgh, waiting for a donor. In a development that surprised even her doctors, a human liver became available in just one week. The process of inserting it into Linda lasted fourteen hours.

Larry was her constant companion, disguising himself as a member of the hospital's medical staff so he could remain with Linda for more than the regular visiting hours.

After two weeks, doctors cautiously, and with many warnings, determined that her body wasn't going to reject the foreign organ.

After six weeks, she was taken home. She told Larry about her favorite Susan Hayward movie, *I Want to Live* (1958). "I agree with Susan," she said. "I want to live. I will survive. Sounds like the name of a song."

***

The Hollywood director and producer, Ron Howard (of all people), optioned *Ordeal* for a big-screen version. After paying off the publisher, Linda made $3,000 off the deal. The film was originally planned for development by Imagine Entertainment in the 1990s, but the option lapsed in 1998. At one time, it was bruited around the entertainment industry that Tatum O'Neal was interested in interpreting the role of Linda onscreen.

Although usually fairly optimistic and upbeat, Linda entered a dark, depressing period of her life. She was often despondent. Her sister, Jean Boreman, Larry's first girlfriend, had died of breast cancer on April 27, 1988. That had been followed by the bankruptcy of Larry's faltering dry-wall installation business.

During a 1989 visit to his sister in Denver, Larry had discovered a different world. In Colorado, he got a job with a home developer that paid $30,000 a year. He called Linda and convinced her to relocate their family to Littleton, Colorado.

They moved into a small house with three bedrooms. At this time, Dominic was thirteen; and Linda's daughter, the very independent Lindsay Marchiano, was eight.

Linda often left her family whenever she received an invitation—and a paycheck—to speak at college campuses as part of her continuing anti-porn campaign.

Colorado turned out to be "not paradise at all." Larry started to drink more heavily than before. Linda's pot smoking increased and intensified.

Larry's alcohol consumption began to interfere with his work. She matched him drink for drink. Finally, he decided to join Alcoholics Anonymous. He invited her to go with him, but she refused to attend the meetings.

During a phone call to Andrea Dworkin, Linda claimed, "My marriage to Larry is over except for the burial."

Her drinking became so heavy that at one point she boasted, "I can drink any fucking man in Colorado under the table."

As money from his new job dwindled, Larry was able to get Linda a position working as a secretary for a Colorado-based construction company. There were two problems, however: Linda often showed up for work drunk, and many men on the construction staff harassed her sexually—or, in her words, "demanded that I suck them off."

It soon became clear that Linda was both a pill addict and a drunk.

***

"I thought I could escape my past," she said. "But it was so horrific I fear now that I'll always be Linda Lovelace, subjected to mockery or even rape."

When son Dominic learned of his mother's porn past, he took it in stride, as he collected porn magazines himself.

For Lindsay, it was more difficult. When she was twelve, some of the boys at her school unearthed an aging copy of *Playboy* featuring her mother in the nude.

As she matured into her teens, Lindsay became increasingly rebellious. One afternoon, she came home and informed Linda, "I'm pregnant." She also told her mother that she'd be moving in with the father of her child. A few months later, a son was born to Lindsay.

For the first time, Linda Lovelace, love goddess of the 70s, was a grandmother. She doted on her grandchild.

Reportedly, the end of Linda's marriage came when Larry arrived home one afternoon and found Lindsay and her school friends smoking pot and drinking beer in his kitchen while an intoxicated Linda was passed out drunk in an upstairs bedroom.

In April of 1996, after twenty-two years of marriage, he filed for divorce. She, too, wanted the divorce. She spoke to a reporter about it, vilifying Larry but not as severely as she had Chuck Traynor.

"He is an emotionally abusive alcoholic that I loved for only the first two years of my marriage. I prostituted myself to him so I could have my kids. They were the most important thing to me. They were all I ever wanted."

She moved out, finding a small studio apartment in Littleton. She had no real skills and was forced to accept a series of menial jobs, none of which she kept very long. Her father, John Boreman, lent her $89,000 to buy a condo. A very loving man, he continued to offer her financial support until the end.

Linda launched herself into the new millennium with a return to porn, posing for both the cover of *Leg Show* and for various inside features.

Whereas these included full frontal nudes of her from the early 1970s, the photos of her as a middle-aged woman were fully, albeit provocatively, clothed.

Despite this deviation from her previous refusals to return to porn, and despite her self-definition as an anti-porn activist, she said, "I needed money, and I decided to make a buck off it. After all, I had earned millions for the industry--but not for myself."

One of the big-letter headlines within the article that *Leg Show* devoted to Linda reminded viewers about how, "In a ten-minute film directed by Chuck Traynor, Linda...takes the entire foot in her vagina, her labia distending enormously."

When Linda learned that Larry had found another wife, she reportedly increased her consumption of crystal meth. Her excessive drug intake began to interfere with her dialysis, which had become a mandatory medical requirement in the aftermath of her liver transplant.

During her final years, she made infrequent appearances at feminist functions, giving an occasional speech on a college campus when she was sober enough to travel. But her speeches had grown tired as she repeated the same accusations over and over again.

"Thank God for freshmen who hadn't heard the story of her past before," Dworkin said. "Otherwise, Linda had nothing new to say, no new insights. She hadn't grown like some of us."

***

An unexpected offer came in from a porn magazine, *Leg Show*. The staff wanted her as the feature in a Linda Lovelace Collector's Edition, scheduled for release in January, 2001. She agreed to appear within its pages when she learned that her fee would be $5,000.

She flew to New York in the autumn of 2000 to pose for *Leg Show,* appearing for the photographer Warren Tang wearing a combination of low-cut corsets, lingerie, long black gloves, good jewelry, feather boas, and stiletto shoes. There was no nudity, although the magazine ran two full frontal topless photos of her from times gone by.

She posed for the cover wearing sparkly silver lamé leggings as a means of concealing her varicose veins. The magazine promoted that issue as containing "The Original Sex Star's First Photos in Twenty Years." In subheads, it disseminated three of her comments: "I guess I'm more disappointed in the Women's Movement than anything," and "I'm still a feminist, I still hate porn, but..." and "I don't want to be fifty trying to look sexy like I'm twenty. I want to be fifty, trying to look sexy like I'm fifty."

Eric Danville wrote the brief article that accompanied the photos.

As the years had gone by, her opinion of her radical feminist friends dimmed. She told Danville, "Oh, those people made a lot of money off me. I think the feminist movement got a good start on what they wanted to do because of me, but they haven't really helped me."

After the *Leg Show* spread, Linda, needing money, began to profit off her porn past. She appeared at various porn conventions around America and hawking Linda Lovelace collector items and signing autographs. She even signed her name on videotaped copies of *Deep Throat.* "I might as well make some money off that damn thing," she said. "If some sucker wants to give me ten or even twenty dollars for a signed copy of *Deep Throat*, I'm his baby."

Linda even agreed to endorse T-shirts that proclaimed, "I choked Linda Lovelace." At many of these appearances, she was drugged, as she was swallowing a lot of over-the-counter medication. In addition to that, she had to take medication "to keep my body from rejecting that liver that belonged to somebody."

In Florida during a visit to her family, her kidneys—not her liver—began to fail. She flew back to Denver for dialysis treatments.

Back in Denver and under treatment again, she told her newly minted friend, Ruth Nash, "I get frequent dizzy spells. I'm afraid I'm going to fall down the steps." Her doctors warned her not to drive a car, asserting that dialysis patients can experience sudden drops in blood pressure that can cause momentary blackness.

"They took everything else away from me," she said to Nash. "Damn it, I'll drive if I want to."

On the morning of April 3, 2002, she drove over to have breakfast with Nash. After that, she promised to meet with her later that afternoon after the completion at a hospital of her latest dialysis treatment.

Prior to that, after doctors had warned her that she was "rushing to the graveyard," Linda had embarked on a health regime as a means of restoring her body. During the final weeks of her life, she had given up liquor and drugs. By this time of her life, in the aftermath of her marriage to Larry, her interest in sexual love had faded away. She told anyone who was interested: "I don't want to have sex any more. I've sucked my last cock."

Linda left Nash's home at around ten that morning and drove along Route 470 on the outskirts of Denver, heading for the hospital. She was neither drunk nor drugged, and apparently there was no desire for suicide. The weather was clear and temperate.

Suddenly, without warning, for reasons not known, her car swerved off the road and hurled down a steep embankment, rolling over three times.

The door to the driver's seat had opened violently, and she was thrown fifty feet from the wreckage. She had always refused to wear a seat belt. Passing motorists saw the accident and immediately telephoned for an ambulance and the police.

Amazingly, she was still alive, but just barely when she arrived at the Denver Health Medical Center.

In another part of town, Linda's dialysis technicians noticed that she had not kept her appointment. Later, Nash was disturbed when Linda did not keep her three o'clock appointment for a late lunch. Repeated phone calls to Linda's home went unanswered. For two entire days, Linda Lovelace disappeared from all of her usual friends, schedules, and contacts.

Finally, she was discovered comatose at the Denver Health Medical Center, where she had been admitted as Linda Boreman, based on a letter from Linda's mother found in Linda's purse. Dorothy had always addressed her daughter as Linda Boreman, steadfastly refusing to acknowledge either Lovelace or any of her married names.

In Florida, the Boreman family was immediately notified of her condition. Linda was put on life support. In addition to brain damage, she'd suffered thirty-seven broken bones, and one of her lungs had collapsed.

John and Dorothy Boreman flew across country to find their daughter barely alive. She'd never regained consciousness after the accident. The Boremans met Larry at the hospital. Even though they'd already divorced, he was there every day. "We tried to comfort each other. Dominic and Lindsay knew her as mom, our grandson knew her as Gramma, and I knew her as Lin. She was still breathing, but we knew she'd already left us."

After two weeks with no chance of recovery, the Boremans agreed to take Linda off life support.

The machines keeping her alive were disconnected. Her pulse grew weaker by the second, and within minutes, her breathing stopped.

On April 22, 2002, the most famous throat in America drew its last breath. Linda was only fifty-three years old.

***

Although she'd made only one feature-length porn movie, the death of Linda Lovelace generated headlines around the world. Some television stations interrupted their regular programming to announce the news.

Many obituaries quoted her: "I'm not ashamed of my past or sad about it. And what people think of me…well, that's not real. I look in the mirror, and I know that I've survived."

Thousands of fans wrote in from many countries. Most of them contained the same theme. "We love you and we respect you, but we love you as Linda Lovelace, not Linda Boreman."

Her daughter, Lindsay Marchiano, told the press. "One day I'm going to tell my son, "Kid, your Gramma was a fighter. Linda Lovelace was a survivor."

***

Reactions to her death revealed the degree to which Linda had been a polarizing figure during her lifetime.

Andrea Dworkin said, "Linda was gang raped and then she was serially raped. There was at least one horrible incident of gang rape I heard about in Colorado, which she kept from her husband. She was safe in no town once word got out among the local pool hall jerks that cocksucker Linda was in town."

Catherine MacKinnon, writing in *Time,* said, "Linda Lovelace sought the dignity of an ordinary life. From forced sex freak of the 70s, she became a beacon of resistance and hope—and changed the debate on pornography forever. Brave, gentle, miraculous, resilient, and valiant beyond words, Linda never accepted that her violation was constitutionally protected, as was her violator's speech. She asked the question, 'Why do pimps' rights matter and mine do not?' Having survived so much and fought so hard, she died without an answer."

The Porn Industry delivered some of its harshest judgments after her death.

Gloria Leonard, an ex-porn star, the president of the Coalition for Free Speech, and the editor of the XXX magazine *High Society,* weighed in with an opinion that was worded in the present tense, as if Linda had still been alive:

"As I come from the same generation of performers as Linda Lovelace, and have been subjected endlessly to her tired old bullshit, I find it compelling that she continues to blame Chuck Traynor for her lot in life. If a woman doesn't like what's happening in any relationship, well then, there's the fucking door. Take a hike, call the police. Something!"

"But no, even thirty years later, she absolutely refuses to take responsibility for her crappy life choices and decisions. As we all know, Linda made some 8mm loops having sex with a fucking German shepherd, pre-Traynor—now, who made her do that? She claims not to be anti-pornography, but contradicts that position elsewhere. And if she feels exploited, she is in fact nicely exploiting herself by appearing at porn conventions, tattoo conventions, promoting her book, appearing in a porn magazine, *Leg Show,* doing interviews, *ad nauseum.*"

"She is a whiny hypocrite who is so easily influenced that, back in the 80s, she also became the child porn-pawn of the so-called feminist movement, joining their ranks and railing against adult entertainment. Bottom line—get a life and get over it, you famously talented cocksucker!"

Al Goldstein, on hearing of her death, delivered his own eulogy: "Good riddance to trash. She was a good cocksucker. She was a piece of shit. Her book, *Ordeal,* was a lying piece of crap. She was a hooker, a scumbag, a lying trollop. I'm glad Chuck Traynor taught her to suck cock. I dropped several ejaculations down her throat. I want to do a final load, so when she goes to Hell my sperm will go with her."

Linda's own final judgment of her legacy was more optimistic. "I made one movie that changed American culture, at least in the bedroom. My movie title became synonymous with oral sex, which I turned many women onto. Gay guys always knew of its pleasure, Many men have benefitted from my film, enjoying greater sex from their wives or girlfriends."

"I was also the launch pad for what is today a multi-billion dollar industry that supports thousands of people who entertain millions all over the world. Although hundreds will follow after me, I was the original porn queen. I legitimatized pornography for better or worse, even though I campaigned against it for years."

"But in the final years of my life, as I set out to capitalize off my porn past, I have become more tolerant as I talked to hundreds of Americans and came to see that in some cases, porn enriched their lives and even saved their marriages. It's got its bad points, God knows, but what doesn't?"

"Now, as I enter the final stage of my life, I've adopted a new policy—

Live and let live."

Darwin Porter

As an intense and precocious nine-year-old, **Darwin Porter** began meeting movie stars, TV personalities, politicians, and singers through his vivacious and attractive mother, Hazel, a somewhat eccentric Southern girl who had lost her husband in World War II. Migrating from the depression-ravaged valleys of western North Carolina to Miami Beach during its most ebullient heyday, Hazel became a stylist, wardrobe mistress, and personal assistant to the vaudeville comedienne Sophie Tucker, the bawdy and irrepressible "Last of the Red Hot Mamas."

Virtually every show-biz celebrity who visited Miami Beach paid a call on "Miss Sophie," and Darwin as a pre-teen loosely and indulgently supervised by his mother, was regularly dazzled by the likes of Judy Garland, Dinah Shore, Veronica Lake, Linda Darnell, Martha Raye, and Ronald Reagan, who arrived to pay his respects to Miss Sophie with a young blonde starlet on the rise— Marilyn Monroe.

Hazel's work for Sophie Tucker did not preclude an active dating life: Her *beaux* included Richard Widmark, Victor Mature, Frank Sinatra (who "tipped" teenaged Darwin the then-astronomical sum of ten dollars for getting out of the way), and that alltime "second lead," Wendell Corey, when he wasn't emoting with Barbara Stanwyck and Joan Crawford.

As a late teenager, Darwin edited *The Miami Hurricane* at the University of Miami, where he interviewed Eleanor Roosevelt, Tab Hunter, Lucille Ball, and Adlai Stevenson. He also worked for Florida's then-Senator George Smathers, one of John F. Kennedy's best friends, establishing an ongoing pattern of picking up "Jack and Jackie" lore while still a student.

After graduation, as a journalist, he was commissioned with the opening of a bureau of *The Miami Herald* in Key West (Florida), where he took frequent morning walks with retired U.S. president Harry S Truman during his vacations in what had functioned as his "Winter White House." He also got to know, sometimes very well, various celebrities "slumming" their way through off-the-record holidays in the orbit of then-resident Tennessee Williams. Celebrities hanging out in the permissive arts environment of Key West during those days included Tallulah Bankhead, Cary Grant, Tony Curtis, the stepfather of Richard Burton, a gaggle of show-biz and publishing moguls, and the once-notorious stripper, Bettie Page.

For about a decade in New York, Darwin worked in television journalism and advertising with his long-time partner, the journalist, art director, and distinguished arts-industry socialite Stanley Mills Haggart. Jointly, they produced TV commercials starring such high-powered stars as Joan Crawford (then feverishly promoting Pepsi-Cola), Ronald Reagan (General Electric), and Debbie Reynolds (selling Singer Sewing Machines), along with such other entertainers as Louis Armstrong, Lena Horne, Arlene Dahl, and countless other show-biz personalities hawking commercial products.

During his youth, Stanley had flourished as an insider in early Hollywood as a "leg man" and source of information for Hedda Hopper, the fabled gossip columnist. When Stanley wasn't dishing newsy revelations with Hedda, he had worked as a Powers model; a romantic lead opposite Silent-era film star Mae Murray; the intimate companion of superstar Randolph Scott before Scott became emotionally involved with Cary Grant; and a man-about-town who archived gossip from everybody who mattered back when the movie colony was small, accessible, and confident that details about their tribal rites would absolutely never be reported in the press. Over the years, Stanley's vast cornucopia of inside Hollywood information was passed on to Darwin, who amplified it with copious interviews and research of his own.

After Stanley's death in 1980, Darwin inherited a treasure trove of memoirs, notes, and interviews detailing Stanley's early adventures in Hollywood, including in-depth recitations of scandals that even Hopper during her heyday was afraid to publish. Most legal and journalistic standards back then interpreted those oral histories as "unprintable." Times, of course, changed.

Beginning in the early 1960s, Darwin joined forces with the then-fledgling Arthur Frommer organization, playing a key role in researching and writing more than 50 titles and defining the style and values that later emerged as the world's leading travel accessories, THE FROMMER GUIDES, with particular emphasis on Europe, California, and the Caribbean. Between the creation and updating of hundreds of editions of detailed travel guides to England, France, Italy, Spain, Portugal, Austria, Germany, California, and Switzerland, he continued to interview and discuss the triumphs, feuds, and frustrations of celebrities, many by then reclusive, whom he either sought out or encountered randomly as part of his extensive travels. Ava Gardner and Lana Turner were particularly insightful.

One day when Darwin lived in Tangier, he walked into an opium den to discover Marlene Dietrich sitting alone in the corner.

Darwin has also written several novels, including the best-selling cult classic *Butterflies in Heat* (which was later made into a film, *Tropic of Desire,* starring Eartha Kitt), *Venus* (inspired by the life of the fabled eroticist and diarist, Anaïs Nin), and *Midnight in Savannah,* a satirical overview of the sexual eccentricities of the Deep South inspired by Savannah's most notorious celebrity murder. He also transformed into literary format the details which he and Stanley Haggart had compiled about the relatively underpublicized scandals of the Silent Screen, releasing them in 2001 as *Hollywood's Silent Closet,* "an uncensored, underground history of Pre-Code Hollywood, loaded with facts and rumors from generations past." A few years later, he did the same for the country-western music industry when he issued *Rhinestone Country.*

Since then, Darwin has penned more than a dozen uncensored Hollywood biographies, many of them award-winners, on subjects who have included Marlon Brando, Merv Griffin, Katharine Hepburn, Howard Hughes, Humphrey Bogart, Michael Jackson, Paul Newman, Steve McQueen, Marilyn Monroe, Elizabeth Taylor, Frank Sinatra, John F. Kennedy, Vivien Leigh, and Laurence Olivier.

As a departure from his usual repertoire, Darwin also wrote the controversial *J. Edgar Hoover & Clyde Tolson: Investigating the Sexual Secrets of America's Most Famous Men and Women,* a book about celebrity, voyeurism, political and sexual repression, and blackmail within the highest circles of the U.S. government.

He has also co-authored, in league with Danforth Prince, four *Hollywood Babylon* anthologies, plus four separate volumes of film critiques, reviews, and commentary.

His biographies, over the years, have won more than 30 First Prize or runner-up awards at literary festivals in cities which include Boston, New York, Los

Angeles, San Francisco, and Paris.

Darwin can be heard at regular intervals as a radio commentator (and occasionally on television), "dissing" celebrities, pop culture, politics, and scandal.

A resident of New York City, Darwin is currently at work on his latest biography: *Those Glamorous Gabors, Bombshells from Budapest.*

*****

Danforth Prince

Danforth Prince has been described as one of the "Young Turks" of the post-millennium publishing industry. Today, he's president of Blood Moon Productions, a firm devoted to the research, compilation and marketing of "tell-all" celebrity biographies, most of whose subjects are associated with the Golden Years of Hollywood.

One of his famous predecessors, the late Lyle Stuart (self-described as "the last publisher in America with guts") once defined Prince as "one of my natural successors." In 1956, that then-novice maverick launched himself with $8,000 he'd won in a libel judgment against gossip columnist Walter Winchell. It was Stuart who published Linda Lovelace's two authentic memoirs—*Ordeal* and *Out of Bondage.*

"I like to see someone following in my footsteps in the 21st Century," Stuart told Prince. "You publish scandalous biographies. I did, too. My books on J. Edgar Hoover, Jacqueline Kennedy Onassis, and Barbara Hutton stirred up the natives. You do, too."

Prince launched his career in journalism in the 1970s at the Paris Bureau of *The New York Times.* In the early '80s, he resigned to join Darwin Porter in researching, developing and publishing various titles within *The Frommer Guides,* jointly reviewing the travel scenes of more than 50 nations for Simon & Schuster. Authoritative and comprehensive, they were perceived as best-selling "travel bibles" for millions of readers, with recommendations and travel advice about the major nations of Western Europe, the Caribbean, Bermuda, The Bahamas, Georgia and the Carolinas, and California.

Prince, along with Porter, is also the co-author of several award-winning celebrity biographies, each configured as a title within Blood Moon's Babylon series. These have included *Elizabeth Taylor, There Is Nothing Like a Dame; Hollywood Babylon—It's Back!; Hollywood Babylon Strikes Again; The Kennedys: All the Gossip Unfit to Print;* and *Frank Sinatra, The Boudoir Singer.* Prince, with Porter, have also co-authored four separate books of film criticism.

Prince is the president and founder (in 1996) of the Georgia Literary Association, and of the Porter and Prince Corporation, founded in 1983, which has produced dozens of titles for both Prentice Hall and John Wiley & Sons. In 2011, he was named "Publisher of the Year" by a consortium of literary critics and marketers spearheaded by the J.M. Northern Media Group.

According to Prince, "Indeed, there are drudge aspects associated with any attempt to create a body of published work. But Blood Moon provides the luxurious illusion that a reader is a perpetual guest at some gossippy dinner party populated with brilliant but occasionally self-delusional figures from bygone eras of The American Experience. Blood Moon's success at salvaging, documenting, and articulating the (till now) orally transmitted histories of the Entertainment Industry, in ways that have never been seen before, is one of the most distinctive aspects of our backlist."

Publishing in collaboration with the National Book Network (www.NBN-Books.com), he has electronically documented some of the controversies associated with his stewardship of Blood Moon in more than 40 videotaped documentaries, book trailers, public speeches, and TV or radio interviews. Any of these can be watched, without charge, by performing a search for "Danforth Prince" on YouTube.com, checking him out on Facebook, on Twitter (#BloodyandLunar) or by clicking on BloodMoonProductions.com.

During the rare moments when he isn't writing, editing, neurosing about, or promoting Blood Moon, he works out at a New York City gym, rescues stray animals, talks to strangers, and attends Episcopal Mass every Sunday.

INDEX

636

If you liked this book, check out these other titles from

BLOOD MOON PRODUCTIONS

Entertainment About How America Interprets Its Celebrities

Blood Moon Productions is a New York-based publishing enterprise dedicated to researching, salvaging, and indexing the oral histories of America's entertainment industry.

Reorganized with its present name in 2004, Blood Moon originated in 1997 as the Georgia Literary Association, a vehicle for the promotion of obscure writers from America's Deep South. For many years, Blood Moon was a key player in the writing, research, and editorial functions of THE FROMMER GUIDES, a respected name in travel publishing.

Blood Moon maintains a back list of 25 critically acclaimed biographies, film guides, and novels. Its titles are distributed within North America and Australia by the National Book Network (www.NBNBooks.com), within the U.K. by Turnaround (www.Turnaround-uk.com), and through secondary wholesalers and online retailers everywhere.

Since 2004, Blood Moon has been awarded dozens of nationally recognized literary prizes. They've included both silver and bronze medals from the IPPY (Independent Publishers Assn.) Awards; four nominations and two Honorable Mentions for BOOK OF THE YEAR from Foreword Reviews; nominations from The Ben Franklin Awards; two separate awards for Best Summer Reading from the "Beach Book Festival," and Awards and Honorable Mentions from the New England, the Los Angeles, the Paris, the New York, the San Francisco, and the Hollywood Book Festivals.

For more about us, including access to a growing number of videotaped book trailers and public addresses, each accessible via YouTube, click on **WWW.BLOODMOONPRODUCTIONS.COM,** visit our page on Facebook, subscribe to us on Twitter (#BloodyandLunar), or refer to the pages which immediately follow.

Thanks for your interest, best wishes, and happy reading.

Danforth Prince, President
Blood Moon Productions, Ltd.

At last, the story that Hollywood has been waiting for:
Lurid inside information about those "Man-Eating Magyars,"
those "Hungarian Hussies from Hell,"

THOSE GLAMOROUS GABORS

Those Glamorous **Gabors**

Bombshells from Budapest

Great Courtesans of the 20th Century

DARWIN PORTER

Born in Central Europe during the twilight of the Austro-Hungarian Empire, three *"vonderful vimmen"*—Zsa Zsa, Eva, and Magda Gabor—transferred their glittery dreams and gold-digging ambitions to Hollywood. They supplemented America's most Imperial Age with "guts, glamour, and goulash," and reigned there as the Hungarian equivalents of Helen of Troy, Madame du Barry, and Madame de Pompadour.

More effectively than any army, these Bombshells from Budapest conquered kings, dukes, and princes, always with a special passion for millionaires, as they amassed fortunes, broke hearts, and amused sophisticated voyeurs on two continents. With their wit, charm, and beauty, thanks to training inspired by the glittering traditions of the Imperial Habsburgs, they became famous for being famous.

"We sold the New World high-priced goods from the Old World that it didn't need, but bought anyway," Zsa Zsa said.

In time, they would collectively entrap some 20 husbands and seduce perhaps 500 other men as well, many plucked directly from the pages of Who's Who in the World.

At long last, Blood Moon lifts the "mink-and-diamond" curtain on this amazing trio of blood-related sisters, whose complicated intrigues have never been fully explored before.

Orson Welles asserted, "The world will never see the likes of the Gabor sisters again. From the villas of Cannes to the mansions of Bel Air, they were the centerpiece of countless boudoirs. They were also the most notorious mantraps since Eve. Ask me about it...I know."

THOSE GLAMOROUS GABORS, BOMBSHELLS FROM BUDAPEST

GREAT COURTESANS OF THE 20TH CENTURY

Darwin Porter

Softcover, 450 pages, with photos, ISBN 978-1-936003-35-8

COMING IN JUNE OF 2013. ALSO AVAILABLE FOR E-READERS

PINK TRIANGLE

The Feuds and Private Lives of Tennessee Williams, Gore Vidal, Truman Capote,
and Famous Members of their Entourages

Darwin Porter

Available in October of 2013
Softcover, 528 pages, with photos   ISBN 978-1-936003-37-2
Also available for e-readers

The *enfants terribles* of America at mid-20th century challenged the sexual censors of their day while indulging in "bitchfests" for love, glory, and boyfriends.

This book exposes their literary slugfests and offers an intimate look at their relationships with the glitterati—Jaqueline Onassis, MM, Brando, the Paleys, a gaggle of other movie stars and millionaires, and dozens of others.

This is for anyone who's interested in the formerly concealed scandals of Hollywood and Broadway, and the values and pretentions of both the literary world and the entertainment industry.

Within its pages, celebrity biographer Darwin Porter takes Myra Breckinridge on a rocky, Cold-Blooded ride on a Streetcar Named Desire.

ABOUT THE AUTHOR:

Darwin Porter, himself an unrepentant *enfant terrible*, moved through the entourages of this Pink Triangle with impunity for several decades of their heyday. In October of 2013, he'll release a book about it.

"Every literate person in America has strong ideas about The Pink Triangle. This exposé of its members' feuds, vanities, and idiosyncrasies will be required reading if you're interested in the literary climate of 'The American Century.'"
—Danforth Prince

J. EDGAR'S FBI VS. HOLLYWOOD

Darwin Porter's saga of power and corruption has a revelation on every page—cross dressing, gay parties, sexual indiscretions, hustlers for sale, alliances with the Mafia, and criminal activity by the nation's chief law enforcer.

It's all here, with chilling details about the abuse of power on the dark side of the American saga. But mostly it's the decades-long love story of America's two most powerful men who could tell presidents "how to skip rope." (Hoover's words.)

Winner of 2012 literary awards from both the **Los Angeles** and the **Hollywood Book Festivals**

"EVERYONE'S DREDGING UP J. EDGAR HOOVER. Leonardo DiCaprio just immortalized him, and now comes Darwin Porter's paperback, *J. Edgar Hoover & Clyde Tolson: Investigating the Sexual Secrets of America's Most Famous Men and Women.*

It shovels Hoover's darkest secrets dragged kicking and screaming from the closet. It's filth on every VIP who's safely dead and some who are still above ground."

—**Cindy Adams**
The New York Post

"This book is important, because it destroys what's left of Hoover's reputation. Did you know he had intel on the bombing of Pearl Harbor, but he sat on it, making him more or less responsible for thousands of deaths? Or that he had almost nothing to do with the arrests or killings of any of the 1930s gangsters that he took credit for catching?

"A lot of people are angry with its author, Darwin Porter. They say that his outing of celebrities is just cheap gossip about dead people who can't defend themselves. I suppose it's because Porter is destroying carefully constructed myths that are comforting to most people. As gay men, we benefit the most from Porter's work, because we know that except for AIDS, the closet was the most terrible thing about the 20th century. If the closet never existed, neither would Hoover. The fact that he got away with such duplicity under eight presidents makes you think that every one of them was a complete fool for tolerating it."

—**Paul Bellini**
FAB Magazine (Toronto)

J. EDGAR HOOVER AND CLYDE TOLSON
Investigating the Sexual Secrets of America's Most Famous Men and Women
Darwin Porter
Softcover, 564 pages, with photos   ISBN 978-1-936003-25-9. Also available for E-Readers

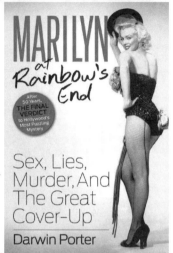

PAUL NEWMAN
THE MAN BEHIND THE BABY BLUES
HIS SECRET LIFE EXPOSED

Hardcover, 520 pages, with dozens of photos. **ISBN 978-0-9786465-1-6**

Also available for E-readers

Darwin Porter

COMPLETELY UNVARNISHED, THIS IS THE MOST COURAGEOUS AND COMPELLING BIOGRAPHY OF THE ICONIC ACTOR EVER PUBLISHED.

Drawn from firsthand interviews with insiders who knew Paul Newman intimately, and compiled over a period of nearly a half-century, this is the world's most honest and most revelatory biography about Hollywood's pre-eminent male sex symbol, with dozens of potentially shocking revelations.

Whereas the situations it exposes were widely known within Hollywood's inner circles, they've never before been revealed to the general public.

If you're a fan of Newman (and who do you know who isn't) you really should look at this book. It's a respectful but candid cornucopia of once-concealed information about the sexual and emotional adventures of a workaday actor as he evolved into a major star.

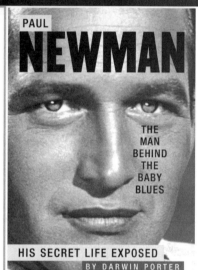

PAUL NEWMAN

THE MAN BEHIND THE BABY BLUES

HIS SECRET LIFE EXPOSED
BY DARWIN PORTER

"One wonders how he ever managed to avoid public scrutiny for so long."

THIS BOOK IS ABOUT A FAMOUS, FULL-TIME RESIDENT OF CONNECTICUT. SHORTLY AFTER NEWMAN'S DEATH IN 2009, IT WON AN HONORABLE MENTION FROM HIS NEIGHBORS AT THE NEW ENGLAND BOOK FESTIVAL

Paul Newman was a potent, desirable, and ambiguous sex symbol, a former sailor from Shaker Heights, Ohio, who parlayed his ambisexual charm and extraordinary good looks into one of the most successful careers in Hollywood.

It's all here, as recorded by celebrity chronicler Darwin Porter--the giddy heights and agonizing lows of a great American star, with revelations and insights never published in any other biography.

KATHARINE THE GREAT

HEPBURN,
A LIFETIME OF SECRETS REVEALED

DARWIN PORTER

Softcover, 569 pages, with dozens of photos, ISBN 978-0-9748118-0-2
Also Available for E-Readers

Katharine Hepburn was the world's greatest screen diva--the most famous actress in American history. But until the appearance of this biography, no one had ever published the intimate details of her complicated and ferociously secretive private life.

Thanks to the "deferential and obsequious whitewashes" which followed in the wake of her death, readers probably know WHAT KATE REMEMBERED. Here, however, is an unvarnished account of what Katharine Hepburn desperately wanted to forget.

"Darwin Porter's biography of Hepburn cannot be lightly dismissed or ignored. Connoisseurs of Hepburn's life would do well to seek it out as a forbidden supplement."
The Sunday Times (London)

"Behind the scenes of her movies, Katharine Hepburn played the temptress to as many women as she did men, ranted and raved with her co-stars and directors, and broke into her neighbors' homes for fun. And somehow, she managed to keep all of it out of the press. As they say, Katharine the Great is hard to put down."
The Dallas Voice

"The door to Hepburn's closet has finally been opened. This is the most honest and least apologetic biography of Hollywood's most ferociously private actress ever written."
Senior Life Magazine, Miami

The only book of Its kind, a fiercely unapologetic and long-overdue exposé of the most obsessively secretive actress in Hollywood

MERV GRIFFIN

A LIFE IN THE CLOSET

Darwin Porter

Hardcover, with photos. ISBN 978-0-9786465-0-9. Also available for E-Readers.

"Darwin Porter told me why he tore the door off Merv's closet.......*Heeeere's Merv!* is 560 pages, 100 photos, a truckload of gossip, and a bedful of unauthorized dish."

Cindy Adams, The NY Post

"Darwin Porter tears the door off Merv Griffin's closet with gusto in this sizzling, superlatively researched biography...It brims with insider gossip that's about Hollywood legends, writ large, smart, and with great style."

Richard LaBonté, BOOKMARKS

Merv Griffin, A Life in the Closet

Merv Griffin began his career as a Big Band singer, moved on to a failed career as a romantic hero in the movies, and eventually rewrote the rules of everything associated with the broadcasting industry. Along the way, he met and befriended virtually everyone who mattered, made billions operating casinos and developing jingles, contests, and word games. All of this while maintaining a male harem and a secret life as America's most famously closeted homosexual.

In this comprehensive biography—the first published since Merv's death in 2007—celebrity biographer Darwin Porter reveals the amazing details behind the richest, most successful, and in some ways, the most notorious mogul in the history of America's entertainment industry.

HOT, CONTROVERSIAL, & RIGOROUSLY RESEARCHED

HERE'S MERV!

JACKO
HIS RISE AND FALL

The History of Michael Jackson

Darwin Porter

This is the world's most comprehensive historical overview of a pop star's rise, fall, and to some extent, rebirth as an American Icon.

Read it for the real story of the circumstances and players who created the icon which the world will forever remember as "the gloved one," Michael Jackson.

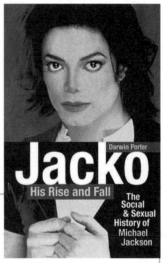

"This is the story of Peter Pan gone rotten. Don't stop till you get enough. Darwin Porter's biography of Michael Jackson is dangerously addictive."
The Sunday Observer

"I'd have thought that there wasn't one single gossipy rock yet to be overturned in the microscopically scrutinized life of Michael Jackson, but Darwin Porter has proven me wrong. Definitely a page-turner. But don't turn the pages too quickly. Almost every one holds a fascinating revelation."
Books to Watch Out For

"In this compelling glimpse of Jackson's life, Porter provides what many journalists have failed to produce in their writings about the pop star: A real person behind the headlines."
Foreword Magazine

He rewrote the rules of America's entertainment industry, and he led a life of notoriety. Even his death was the occasion for scandals which continue to this day.

This book, a winner of literary awards from both *Foreword Magazine* and the Hollywood Book Festival, was originally published during the lifetime of Michael Jackson. This, the revised, post-mortem edition, with extra analysis and commentary, was released after his death.

Hardcover 600 indexed pages with about a hundred photos ISBN 978-0-936003-10-5.
Also available for E-readers

HOLLYWOOD BABYLON
STRIKES AGAIN!

THE PROFOUNDLY OUTRAGEOUS VOLUME TWO OF
BLOOD MOON'S BABYLON SERIES

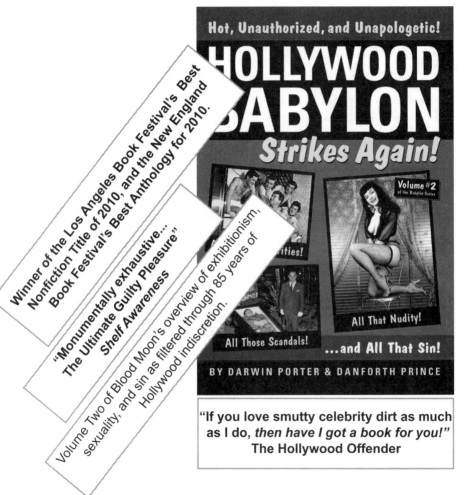

Hot, Unauthorized, and Unapologetic!

HOLLYWOOD BABYLON

Strikes Again!

Volume #2
of the Babylon Series

...ities!

All Those Scandals!

All That Nudity!

...and All That Sin!

BY DARWIN PORTER & DANFORTH PRINCE

Winner of the Los Angeles Book Festival's Best Nonfiction Title of 2010, and the New England Book Festival's Best Anthology for 2010.

"Monumentally exhaustive... The Ultimate Guilty Pleasure"
Shelf Awareness

Volume Two of Blood Moon's overview of exhibitionism, sexuality, and sin as filtered through 85 years of Hollywood indiscretion.

"If you love smutty celebrity dirt as much as I do, *then have I got a book for you!*"
The Hollywood Offender

"These books will set the graves of Hollywood's cemeteries spinning"   **Daily Express**

Hollywood Babylon Strikes Again!

Darwin Porter and Danforth Prince
Hardcover, 380 outrageous pages, with hundreds of photos

ISBN 978-1-936003-12-9 Also available for E-readers